Docker on Amazon Web Services

Build, deploy, and manage your container applications at scale

Justin Menga

Packt>

BIRMINGHAM - MUMBAI

Docker on Amazon Web Services

Commissioning Editor: Gebin George
Acquisition Editor: Rohit Rajkumar
Content Development Editor: Nithin George Varghese
Technical Editor: Mohit Hassija
Copy Editor: Safis Editing
Project Coordinator: Drashti Panchal
Proofreader: Safis Editing
Indexer: Pratik Shirodkar
Graphics: Tom Scaria
Production Coordinator: Shantanu Zagade

First published: August 2018

Production reference: 1280818

Published by Packt Publishing Ltd.
Livery Place
35 Livery Street
Birmingham
B3 2PB, UK.

ISBN 978-1-78862-650-7

www.packtpub.com

For Simba and Chandy

Mapt

Mapt is an online digital library that gives you full access to over 5,000 books and videos, as well as industry leading tools to help you plan your personal development and advance your career. For more information, please visit our website.

Why subscribe?

- Spend less time learning and more time coding with practical eBooks and Videos from over 4,000 industry professionals

- Improve your learning with Skill Plans built especially for you

- Get a free eBook or video every month

- Mapt is fully searchable

- Copy and paste, print, and bookmark content

PacktPub.com

Did you know that Packt offers eBook versions of every book published, with PDF and ePub files available? You can upgrade to the eBook version at www.PacktPub.com and as a print book customer, you are entitled to a discount on the eBook copy. Get in touch with us at service@packtpub.com for more details.

At www.PacktPub.com, you can also read a collection of free technical articles, sign up for a range of free newsletters, and receive exclusive discounts and offers on Packt books and eBooks.

Contributors

About the author

Justin Menga is a full-stack technologist with over 20 years experience of working with organizations to build large-scale applications and platforms, with a focus on end-to-end application architecture, the cloud, continuous delivery, and infrastructure automation. Justin started his career as an infrastructure and network engineer/architect, working with many large enterprise and service provider customers. In the past few years, Justin has switched his focus to building applications and full-service platforms, working with a wide array of technologies, yet still maintaining and applying his prior infrastructure and network expertise to containers and public clouds. He has programmed in Objective C, C#, ASP.NET, JavaScript, Scala, Python, Java, and Go, and has a keen interest in continuous delivery, Docker, and automation tools that speed the path from development to production.

I would like to thank my family: Tania, Chloe, Jayden, Fluffy, Minky, Simba (RIP), and Chandy (RIP) - who all have persevered through the countless hours and sleepless nights of burning the midnight oil to accumulate the knowledge and experience required to complete such a book.

About the reviewer

Rickard von Essen works as a continuous delivery and cloud consultant at Diabol. He helps companies deliver faster, improve continuously, and worry less. In his spare time, he helps maintain Packer and contributes to numerous other FOSS projects. He has been tinkering with Linux and BSD since the late 1990s, and has been hacking since the Amiga era. He lives with his wife and two children in Stockholm, Sweden, and he has a Master of Computer Science and Engineering from Linköping University.

Packt is searching for authors like you

If you're interested in becoming an author for Packt, please visit authors.packtpub.com and apply today. We have worked with thousands of developers and tech professionals, just like you, to help them share their insight with the global tech community. You can make a general application, apply for a specific hot topic that we are recruiting an author for, or submit your own idea.

Table of Contents

Preface

Welcome to *Docker on Amazon Web Services*! I'm very excited to have written this book and to share how to leverage the wonderful technologies that the Docker and **Amazon Web Services** (**AWS**) ecosystems provide to build truly world-class solutions for deploying and operating your applications in production.

Docker has become the modern standard for building, packaging, publishing, and operating applications, leveraging the power of containers to increase the speed of application delivery, increase security, and reduce costs. This book will show you how to supercharge your process of building Docker applications, using the best practices of continuous delivery to provide a fully automated, consistent, reliable, and portable workflow for testing, building, and publishing your Docker applications. In my view, this is a fundamental prerequisite before you even consider deploying your application to the cloud, and the first few chapters will focus on establishing a local Docker environment and creating a local continuous delivery workflow for a sample application that we will be using throughout the book.

AWS is the world's leading public cloud provider, and provides a rich set of solutions for managing and operating your Docker applications. This book will cover all of the major services that AWS provides to support Docker and containers, including the **Elastic Container Service** (**ECS**), Fargate, Elastic Beanstalk, and **Elastic Kubernetes Service** (**EKS**), and also will discuss how you can leverage the Docker for AWS solution provided by Docker Inc to deploy Docker Swarm clusters.

Running a complete application environment in AWS comprises much more than your container platform, and this book will also describe best practices for managing access to your AWS account and leveraging other AWS services to support the requirements of your applications. For example, you will learn how to set up AWS application load balancers to publish highly available, load-balanced endpoints for your application, create AWS **Relational Database Service** (**RDS**) instances to provide a managed application database, integrate your applications with the AWS Secrets Manager to provide a secure secrets management solution, and create a complete continuous delivery pipeline using the AWS CodePipeline, CodeBuild, and CloudFormation services that will automatically test, build, and publish Docker images for any new changes to your application, and then automatically deploy it into development and production environments.

You will build all of this supporting infrastructure using the AWS CloudFormation service, which provides powerful infrastructure-as-code templates that allow you define all of the AWS services and resources I have mentioned in a single manifest that you can deploy to AWS with a single click of a button.

I'm sure by now you are just as excited as I am to learn about all of these wonderful technologies, and I'm sure by the end of this book, you will have developed the expert knowledge and skills required to be able to deploy and manage your Docker applications, using the latest cutting-edge techniques and best practices.

Who this book is for

Docker on Amazon Web Services is for anybody who wants to build, deploy, and operate applications using the power of containers, Docker, and AWS.

Readers ideally should have a basic understanding of Docker and containers, and have worked with AWS or another cloud provider, although no previous experience with containers or AWS is required, as this book takes a step-by-step approach and explains key concepts as you progress. An understanding of how to use the Linux command line, Git, and basic Python scripting knowledge will be useful, but is not required.

See the *To get the most out of this book* section for a complete list of the recommended prerequisite skills.

What this book covers

Chapter 1, *Container and Docker Fundamentals*, will provide a brief introduction to Docker and containers, and provide an overview of the various services and options available in AWS to run your Docker applications. You will set up your local environment, installing Docker, Docker Compose, and various other tools that are required to complete the examples in each chapter. Finally, you will download the sample application and learn how to test, build, and run the application locally, so that you have a good understanding of how the application works and specific tasks you need to perform to get the application up and running.

Chapter 2, *Building Applications Using Docker*, will describe how to build a fully automated Docker-based workflow for testing, building, packaging, and publishing your applications as production-ready Docker release images, using Docker, Docker Compose, and other tools. This will establish the foundation of a portable continuous delivery workflow that you can consistently execute across multiple machines without having to install application-specific dependencies in each local environment.

Chapter 3, *Getting Started with AWS*, will describe how to create a free AWS account and start using a variety of free-tier services that allow you to get familiar with the wide array of AWS services on offer. You will learn how to establish best practice administrative and user access patterns to your account, configuring **multi-factor authentication** (**MFA**) for enhanced security and installing the AWS command-line interface, which can be used for a wide variety of operational and automation use cases. You will also be introduced to CloudFormation, which is a management tool and service provided free by AWS that you will use throughout this book that allows you to deploy complex environments with a single click of a button, using a powerful and expressive infrastructure as code template format.

Chapter 4, *Introduction to ECS*, will get you up and running with the **Elastic Container Service** (**ECS**), which is the flagship service for running your Docker applications in AWS. You will learn about the architecture of ECS, create your first ECS cluster, define your container configurations using ECS task definitions, and then deploy a Docker application as an ECS service. Finally, you will be briefly introduced to the ECS **command-line interface** (**CLI**), which allows you to interact with local Docker Compose files and automatically deploy Docker Compose resources to AWS using ECS.

Chapter 5, *Publishing Docker Images Using ECR*, will teach you how to establish a private Docker registry using the **Elastic Container Registry** (**ECR**), authenticate to your registry using IAM credentials, and then publish Docker images to private repositories within your registry. You will also learn how to share your Docker images with other accounts and AWS services, and how to configure life cycle policies to automatically clean up orphaned images, ensuring you only pay for active and current images.

Chapter 6, *Building Custom ECS Container Instances*, will show you how to use a popular open source tool called Packer to build and publish custom **Amazon Machine Images** (**AMIs**) for the EC2 instances (ECS container instances) that run your container workloads in ECS clusters. You will install a set of helper scripts that enable your instances to integrate with CloudFormation and download custom provisioning actions at instance creation time, allowing you to dynamically configure the ECS cluster your instances will join, configure the CloudWatch logs groups your instances should publish logging information to, and finally, signal back to CloudFormation that provisioning has succeeded or failed.

Chapter 7, *Creating ECS Clusters*, will teach you how to build ECS clusters based upon EC2 auto-scaling groups that leverage the features of the custom AMI you created in the previous chapter. You will define your EC2 auto-scaling group, ECS cluster, and other supporting resources using CloudFormation, and configure CloudFormation Init metadata to perform custom runtime configuration and provisioning of the ECS container instances that make up your ECS cluster.

Chapter 8, *Deploying Applications Using ECS*, will expand the environment created in the previous chapter, adding supporting resources such as **Relational Database Service** (**RDS**) instances and AWS **Application Load Balancers** (**ALBs**) to your CloudFormation template. You will then define an ECS task definition and ECS service for the sample application, and learn how ECS can perform automated rolling deployments and updates for your applications. To orchestrate required deployment tasks such as running database migrations, you will extend CloudFormation and write your own Lambda function to create an ECS task runner custom resource, providing the powerful capability to run any provisioning action that can be executed as an ECS task.

Chapter 9, *Managing Secrets*, will introduce the AWS Secrets Manager, which is a fully managed service that stores secret data in an encrypted format that can be easily and securely accessed by authorized parties such as your users, AWS resources, and applications. You will interact with Secrets Manager using the AWS CLI, creating secrets for sensitive credentials such as database passwords, and then learn how to use an entrypoint script for your containers that injects secret values as internal environment variables at container startup before handing off to the main application. Finally, you will create a CloudFormation custom resource that exposes secrets to other AWS services that do not support AWS Secrets Manager, such as providing an administrative password for Relational Database Service (RDS) instances.

Chapter 10, *Isolating Network Access*, describes how to use the awsvpc networking mode in your ECS task definitions to isolate network access and separate ECS control plane communications from your container and application communications. This will allow you to adopt best practice security patterns such as deploying your containers on private networks, and implement solutions for providing internet access, including the AWS VPC NAT Gateway service.

Chapter 11, *Managing the ECS Infrastructure Life Cycle*, will provide you with an understanding of operational challenges when running ECS clusters, which includes taking your ECS container instances out of service, whether it be to scale in your auto-scaling groups or to replace your ECS container instances with a new Amazon machine image. You will learn how to leverage EC2 auto-scaling life cycle hooks to invoke an AWS Lambda function whenever an ECS container instance is about to be terminated, which allows you to perform graceful shutdown operations such as draining active containers to other instances in the cluster, before signaling EC2 auto-scaling to proceed with instance termination.

Chapter 12, *ECS Auto Scaling*, will describe how ECS clusters manage resources such as CPU, memory, and network ports, and how this affects the capacity of your clusters. If you want to be able to dynamically auto-scale your clusters, you need to dynamically monitor ECS cluster capacity, and scale out or scale in the cluster at capacity thresholds that ensure you will meet the service level expectations of your organization or use case. You will be implement a solution that calculates ECS cluster capacity whenever an ECS container instance state change event is generated via the AWS CloudWatch Events service, publishes capacity metrics to CloudWatch, and dynamically scales your cluster up or down using CloudWatch alarms. With a dynamic cluster capacity solution in place, you will then be able to configure the AWS application auto-scaling service to dynamically adjust the number of instances of service based upon appropriate metrics, such as CPU utilization or active connections, without needing to concern yourself with the effect on underlying cluster capacity.

Chapter 13, *Continuously Delivering ECS Applications*, will establish a continuous delivery pipeline using the AWS CodePipeline service that integrates with GitHub to detect changes to your application source code and infrastructure deployment scripts, use the AWS CodeBuild service to run unit tests, build application artifacts and publish a Docker image using the sample application Docker workflow, and continuously deploy your application changes to AWS using the CloudFormation templates you have used so far in this book.

This will automatically deploy into an AWS development environment that you test, and then create a change set and manual approval action for deployment into production, providing you with a rapid and repeatable path to production for all of your applications new features and bug fixes.

Chapter 14, *Fargate and ECS Service Discovery*, will introduce AWS Fargate, which provides a solution that fully manages both the ECS service control plane and ECS clusters that you traditionally have to manage using the regular ECS service. You will deploy the AWS X-Ray daemon as an ECS service using Fargate, and configure ECS service discovery to dynamically publish your service endpoints using DNS and Route 53. This will allow you to add support for X-Ray tracing to your sample application, which can be used to trace incoming HTTP requests to your application and monitor AWS service calls, database calls, and other types of calls that are made to service each incoming request.

Chapter 15, *Elastic Beanstalk*, will provide an overview of the popular **Platform-as-a-Service** (**PaaS**) offering, which includes support for Docker applications. You will learn how to create an Elastic Beanstalk multi-container Docker application, establish an environment that consists of a managed EC2 instance, an RDS database instance, and an **Application Load Balancer** (**ALB**), and then extend the environment using various techniques to support the requirements of your Docker applications, such as volume mounts and running single-shot tasks per application deployment.

Chapter 16, *Docker Swarm in AWS*, will focus on how to run Docker Swarm clusters in AWS, using the Docker for AWS blueprint provided for Docker Swarm community edition. This blueprint provides you with a CloudFormation template that establishes a pre-configured Docker Swarm cluster in AWS within minutes, and features integrations with key AWS services such as the Elastic Load Balancing (ELB), Elastic File System (EFS) and Elastic Block Store (EBS) services. You will define a stack using Docker Compose, which configures a multi-service environment expressed in the familiar Docker Compose specification format, and learn how to configure key Docker Swarm resources such as services, volumes, and Docker secrets. You will learn how to create shared Docker volumes that are backed by EFS, relocatable Docker volumes backed by EBS that Docker Swarm will automatically reattach to new containers redeployed after a node failure, and publish an external service endpoint for your application using an ELB that is automatically created and managed for you by Docker Swarm.

`Chapter 17`, *Elastic Kubernetes Service*, introduces the newest container management platform offering from AWS, which is based on the popular open source Kubernetes platform. You will first set up Kubernetes in your local Docker Desktop environment, which includes native support for Kubernetes with the Docker 18.06 CE release, and learn how to create a complete environment for your Docker applications using a number of Kubernetes resources, including pods, deployments, services, secrets, persistent volumes, and jobs. You will then establish an EKS cluster in AWS, create an EC2 auto-scaling group that connects worker nodes to your cluster, and ensure your local Kubernetes client can authenticate and connect to the EKS control plane, after which you will deploy the Kubernetes dashboard to provide a comprehensive management interface for your cluster. Finally, you will define a default storage class that uses the Elastic Block Store (EBS) service for persistent volumes and then deploy your Docker applications to AWS, leveraging the same Kubernetes definitions you created earlier for your local environment, providing you with a powerful solution to quickly deploy Docker applications locally for development purposes, and then deploy straight to production using EKS.

To get the most out of this book

- **A basic, working knowledge of Docker** - if you haven't used Docker before, you should learn about the basic concepts of Docker at `https://docs.docker.com/engine/docker-overview/` and then step through Parts 1 (`https://docs.docker.com/get-started/`) and 2 (`https://docs.docker.com/get-started/part2`) of the Docker Get Started tutorial. For a more comprehensive understanding of Docker, check out the `Learn Docker – Fundamentals of Docker 18.x` book from Packt Publishing.
- **A basic, working knowledge of Git** - if you haven't used Git before, you should run through the Beginner and Getting Started tutorials at `https://www.atlassian.com/git/tutorials`. For a more comprehensive understanding of Git, check out the `Git Essentials` book from Packt Publishing.
- **Familiarity with AWS** - if you haven't used AWS before, running through the Launch a Linux Virtual Machine tutorial at `https://aws.amazon.com/getting-started/tutorials/launch-a-virtual-machine/` will provide a useful introduction.

- **Familiarity with the Linux/Unix command line** - if you haven't used the Linux/Unix command line before, I recommend running through a basic tutorial such as `https://maker.pro/linux/tutorial/basic-linux-commands-for-beginners`, using the Linux Virtual Machine you created when you went through the Launch a Linux Virtual Machine tutorial.
- **Basic understanding of Python** - the sample application for this book is written in Python, and some of the examples in later chapters include basic Python scripts. If you have not worked with Python before, you may want to read through the first few lessons at `https://docs.python.org/3/tutorial/`.

Download the example code files

You can download the example code files for this book from your account at `www.packtpub.com`. If you purchased this book elsewhere, you can visit `www.packtpub.com/support` and register to have the files emailed directly to you.

You can download the code files by following these steps:

1. Log in or register at `www.packtpub.com`.
2. Select the **SUPPORT** tab.
3. Click on **Code Downloads & Errata**.
4. Enter the name of the book in the **Search** box and follow the onscreen instructions.

Once the file is downloaded, please make sure that you unzip or extract the folder using the latest version of:

- WinRAR/7-Zip for Windows
- Zipeg/iZip/UnRarX for Mac
- 7-Zip/PeaZip for Linux

The code bundle for the book is also hosted on GitHub at `https://github.com/PacktPublishing/Book-Name`. In case there's an update to the code, it will be updated on the existing GitHub repository.

We also have other code bundles from our rich catalog of books and videos available at `https://github.com/PacktPublishing/`. Check them out!

Download the color images

We also provide a PDF file that has color images of the screenshots/diagrams used in this book. You can download it here: `https://www.packtpub.com/sites/default/files/downloads/DockeronAmazonWebServices_ColorImages.pdf`

Code in Action

Visit the following link to check out videos of the code being run: `http://bit.ly/2Noqdpn`

Conventions used

There are a number of text conventions used throughout this book.

`CodeInText`: Indicates code words in text, database table names, folder names, filenames, file extensions, pathnames, dummy URLs, user input, and Twitter handles. Here is an example: "Note that the gist includes a placeholder called `PASTE_ACCOUNT_NUMBER` within the policy document, so you will need to replace this with your actual AWS account ID."

A block of code is set as follows:

```
AWSTemplateFormatVersion: "2010-09-09"

Description: Cloud9 Management Station

Parameters:
  EC2InstanceType:
    Type: String
    Description: EC2 instance type
    Default: t2.micro
  SubnetId:
    Type: AWS::EC2::Subnet::Id
    Description: Target subnet for instance
```

Any command-line input or output is written as follows:

```
> aws configure
AWS Access Key ID [None]:
```

Bold: Indicates a new term, an important word, or words that you see onscreen. For example, words in menus or dialog boxes appear in the text like this. Here is an example: "To create the admin role, select **Services | IAM** from the AWS console, select **Roles** from the left-hand menu, and click on the **Create role** button."

Warnings or important notes appear like this.

Tips and tricks appear like this.

Get in touch

Feedback from our readers is always welcome.

General feedback: Email `feedback@packtpub.com` and mention the book title in the subject of your message. If you have questions about any aspect of this book, please email us at `questions@packtpub.com`.

Errata: Although we have taken every care to ensure the accuracy of our content, mistakes do happen. If you have found a mistake in this book, we would be grateful if you would report this to us. Please visit `www.packtpub.com/submit-errata`, selecting your book, clicking on the Errata Submission Form link, and entering the details.

Piracy: If you come across any illegal copies of our works in any form on the Internet, we would be grateful if you would provide us with the location address or website name. Please contact us at `copyright@packtpub.com` with a link to the material.

If you are interested in becoming an author: If there is a topic that you have expertise in and you are interested in either writing or contributing to a book, please visit `authors.packtpub.com`.

Reviews

Please leave a review. Once you have read and used this book, why not leave a review on the site that you purchased it from? Potential readers can then see and use your unbiased opinion to make purchase decisions, we at Packt can understand what you think about our products, and our authors can see your feedback on their book. Thank you!

For more information about Packt, please visit packtpub.com.

Container and Docker Fundamentals

1

Docker and Amazon Web Services are two of the hottest and most popular technologies available right now. Docker is the most popular container platform on the planet right now, while Amazon Web Services is the number 1 public cloud provider. Organizations both large and small are adopting containers en masse, and the public cloud is no longer the playground of start-ups, with large enterprises and organizations migrating to the cloud in droves. The good news is that this book will give you practical, real-world insights and knowledge of how to use both Docker and AWS together to help you test, build, publish, and deploy your applications faster and more efficiently than ever before.

In this chapter, we will briefly discuss the history of Docker, why Docker is so revolutionary, and the high level architecture of Docker. We will describe the various services that support running Docker in AWS, and discuss why you might choose one service over another based upon the requirements of your organization.

We will then focus on getting your local environment up-and-running with Docker, and install the various software prerequisites required to run the sample application for this book. The sample application is a simple web application written in Python that stores data in a MySQL database, and this book will use the sample application to help you solve real-world challenges such as testing, building, and publishing Docker images, as well as deploying and running Docker applications in a variety of container management platforms on AWS. Before you can package the sample application as a Docker image, you need to understand the application's external dependencies and the key tasks that are required to test, build, deploy, and run the application, and you will learn how to install application dependencies, run unit tests, start the application up locally, and orchestrate key operational tasks such as establishing the initial database schema and tables required for the sample application to run.

The following topics will be covered in this chapter:

- Introduction to containers and Docker
- Why containers are revolutionary
- Docker architecture
- Docker in AWS
- Setting up a local Docker environment
- Installing the sample application

Technical requirements

The following lists the technical requirements to complete this chapter:

- A computer environment that meets the minimum specifications as defined in the software and hardware list

The following GitHub URL contains the code samples used in this chapter: `https://github.com/docker-in-aws/docker-in-aws/tree/master/ch1`.

Check out the following video to see the Code in Action:
`http://bit.ly/2PEK1VQ`

Introduction to containers and Docker

In recent times, containers have become a common lingua franca in the technology world, and it's difficult to imagine a world where, just a mere few years ago, only a small portion of the technology community had even heard about containers.

To trace the origins of containers, you need to rewind way back to 1979, when Unix V7 introduced the chroot system call. The chroot system call provided the ability to change the root directory of a running process to a different location in the file system, and was the first mechanism available to provide some form of process isolation. chroot was added to the Berkeley Software Distribution (BSD) in 1982 (this is an ancestor of the modern macOS operating system), and not much more happened in terms of containerization and isolation for a number of years, until a feature called FreeBSD Jails was released in 2000, which provided separate environments called "jails" that could each be assigned their own IP address and communicate independently on the network.

Later, in 2004, Solaris launched the first public beta of Solaris Containers (which eventually became known as Solaris Zones), which provided system resource separation by creating zones. This was a technology I remember using back in 2007 to help overcome a lack of expensive physical Sun SPARC infrastructure and run multiple versions of an application on a single SPARC server.

In the mid 2000s, a lot more progress in the march toward containers occurred, with Open Virtuozzo (Open VZ) being released in 2005, which patched the Linux kernel to provide operating system level virtualization and isolation. In 2006, Google launched a feature called process containers (which was eventually renamed to control groups or cgroups) that provided the ability to restrict CPU, memory, network, and disk usage for a set of processes. In 2008, a feature called Linux namespaces, which provided the ability to isolate different types of resources from each other, was combined with cgroups to create Linux Containers (LXC), forming the initial foundation to modern containers as we know them today.

In 2010, as cloud computing was starting to gain popularity, a number of Platform-as-a-Service (PaaS) start-ups appeared, which provided fully managed runtime environments for specific application frameworks such as Java Tomcat or Ruby on Rails. One start-up called dotCloud was quite different, in that it was the first "polyglot" PaaS provider, meaning that you could run virtually any application environment you wanted using their service. The technology underpinning this was Linux Containers, and dotCloud added a number or proprietary features to provide a fully managed container platform for their customers. By 2013, the PaaS market had well and truly entered the Gartner hype cycle (`https://en.wikipedia.org/wiki/Hype_cycle`) trough of disillusionment, and dotCloud was on the brink of financial collapse. One of the co-founders of the company, Solomon Hykes, pitched an idea to the board to open source their container management technology, sensing that there was huge potential. The board disagreed, however Solomon and his technical team proceeded regardless, and the rest, as they say, is history.

After announcing Docker as a new open source container management platform to the world in 2013, Docker quickly rose in prominence, becoming the darling of the open source world and vendor community alike, and is likely one of the fastest growing technologies in history. By the end of 2014, during which time Docker 1.0 was released, over 100 million Docker containers had been downloaded – fast forward to March 2018, and that number sat at *37 billion* downloads. At the end of 2017, container usage amongst Fortune 100 companies sat at 71%, indicating that Docker and containers have become universally accepted for both start-ups and enterprises alike. Today, if you are building modern, distributed applications based upon microservice architectures, chances are that your technology stack will be underpinned by Docker and containers.

Why containers are revolutionary

The brief and successful history of containers speaks for itself, which leads to the question, *why are containers so popular*? The following provides some of the more important answers to this question:

- **Lightweight**: Containers are often compared to virtual machines, and in this context, containers are much more lightweight that virtual machines. A container can start up an isolated and secure runtime environment for your application in seconds, compared with the handful of minutes a typical virtual machine takes to start. Container images are also much smaller than their virtual machine counterparts.

- **Speed**: Containers are fast – they can be downloaded and started within seconds, and within a few minutes you can test, build, and publish your Docker image for immediate download. This allows organizations to innovate faster, which is critical in today's ever increasing competitive landscape.

- **Portable**: Docker makes it easier than ever to run your applications on your local machine, in your data center, and in the public cloud. Because Docker packages are complete runtime environments for your application complete with operating system dependencies and third-party packages, your container hosts don't required any special prior setup or configuration specific to each individual application – all of these specific dependencies and requirements are self-contained within the Docker image, making comments like "But it worked on my machine!" relics of the past.

- **Security**: There has been a lot of debate about the security of containers, but in my opinion, if implemented correctly, containers actually offer greater security than non-container alternative approaches. The main reason for this is that containers express security context very well – applying security controls at the container level typically represents the right level of context for those controls. A lot of these security controls are provided by "default" – for example, namespaces are inherently a security mechanism in that they provide isolation. A more explicit example is that they can apply SELinux or AppArmor profiles on a per container basis, making it very easy to define different profiles depending on specific security requirements of each container.

- **Automation**: Organizations are adopting software delivery practices such as continuous delivery, where automation is a fundamental requirement. Docker natively supports automation – at its core, a Dockerfile is an automation specification of sorts that allows the Docker client to automatically build your containers, and other Docker tools such as Docker Compose allow you express connected multi-container environments that you can automatically create and tear down in seconds.

Docker architecture

As discussed in the preface of this book, I assume that you have at least a basic working knowledge of Docker. If you are new to Docker, then I recommend that you supplement your learning in this chapter by reading the Docker overview at `https://docs.docker.com/engine/docker-overview/`, and running through some of the Docker tutorials at `https://docs.docker.com/get-started/`.

The Docker architecture includes several core components, as follows:

- **Docker Engine**: This provides several server code components for running your container workloads, including an API server for communications with Docker clients, and the Docker daemon that provides the core runtime of Docker. The daemon is responsible for the complete life cycle of your containers and other resources, and also ships with built-in clustering support to allow you to build clusters or swarms of your Docker Engines.
- **Docker client**: This provides a client for building Docker images, running Docker containers, and managing other resources such as Docker volumes and Docker networks. The Docker client is the primary tool you will work with when using Docker, and interacts with both the Docker Engine and Docker registry components.
- **Docker registry**: This is responsible for storing and distributing Docker images for your application. Docker supports both public and private registries, and the ability to package and distribute your applications via a Docker registry is one of the major reasons for Docker's success. In this book, you will download third-party images from Docker Hub, and you will store your own application images in the private AWS registry service called **Elastic Container Registry** (**ECR**).

- **Docker Swarm**: A swarm is a collection of Docker Engines that form a self-managing and self-healing cluster, allowing you to horizontally scale your container workloads and provide resiliency in the event of Docker Engine failures. A Docker Swarm cluster includes a number of master nodes that form the cluster control plane, and a number of worker nodes that actually run your container workloads.

When you work with the preceding components, you interact with a number of different types of objects in the Docker architecture:

- **Images**: An image is built using a Dockerfile, which includes a number of instructions on how to build the runtime environment for your containers. The result of executing each of these build instructions is stored as a set of layers and is distributed as a downloadable and installable image, and the Docker Engine reads the instructions in each layer to construct a runtime environment for all containers based on a given image.

- **Containers**: A container is the runtime manifestation of a Docker image. Under the hood, a container is comprised of a collection of Linux namespaces, control groups, and storage that collectively create an isolated runtime environment form which you can run a given application process.

- **Volumes**: By default, the underlying storage mechanism for containers is based upon the union file system, which allows a virtual file system to be constructed from the various layers in a Docker image. This approach is very efficient in that you can share layers and build up multiple containers from these shared layers, however this does have a performance penalty and does not support persistence. Docker volumes provide access to a dedicated pluggable storage medium, which your containers can use for IO intensive applications and to persist data.

- **Networks**: By default, Docker containers each operate in their own network namespace, which provides isolation between containers. However, they must still provide network connectivity to other containers and the outside world. Docker supports a variety of network plugins that support connectivity between containers, which can even extend across Docker Swarm clusters.

- **Services**: A service provides an abstraction that allows you to scale your applications by spinning up multiple containers or replicas of your service that can be load balanced across multiple Docker Engines in a Docker Swarm cluster.

Running Docker in AWS

Along with Docker, the other major technology platform we will target in this book is AWS.

AWS is the world's leading public cloud provider, and as such offers a variety of ways to run your Docker applications:

- **Elastic Container Service (ECS)**: In 2014, AWS launched ECS, which was the first dedicated public cloud offering that supported Docker. ECS provides a hybrid managed service of sorts, where ECS is responsible for orchestrating and deploying your container applications (such as the control plane of a container management platform), and you are responsible for providing the Docker Engines (referred to as ECS container instances) that your containers will actually run on. ECS is free to use (you only pay for the ECS container instances that run your containers), and removes much of the complexity of managing container orchestration and ensuring your applications are always up and running. However, this does require you to manage the EC2 infrastructure that runs your ECS container instances. ECS is considered Amazon's flagship Docker service and as such will be the primary service that we will focus on in this book.

- **Fargate**: Fargate was launched in late 2017 and provides a fully managed container platform that manages both the ECS control plane and ECS container instances for you. With Fargate, your container applications are deployed onto shared ECS container instance infrastructures that you have no visibility of which AWS manages, allowing you to focus on building, testing, and deploying your container applications without having to worry about any underlying infrastructure. Fargate is a fairly new service that, at the time of writing this book, has limited regional availability, and has some constraints that mean it is not suitable for all use cases. We will cover the Fargate service in Chapter 14, *Fargate and ECS Service Discovery*.

- **Elastic Kubernetes Service (EKS)**: EKS launched in June 2018 and supports the popular open source Kubernetes container management platform. EKS is similar to ECS in that it is a hybrid managed service where Amazon provides fully managed Kubernetes master nodes (the Kubernetes control plane), and you provide Kubernetes worker nodes in the form of EC2 autoscaling groups that run your container workloads. Unlike ECS, EKS is not free and at the time of writing this book costs 0.20c USD per hour, plus any EC2 infrastructure costs associated with your worker nodes. Given the ever growing popularity of Kubernetes as a cloud/infrastructure agnostic container management platform, along with its open source community, EKS is sure to become very popular, and we will provide an introduction to Kubernetes and EKS in `Chapter 17`, *Elastic Kubernetes Service*.

- **Elastic Beanstalk (EBS)**: Elastic Beanstalk is a popular Platform as a Service (PaaS) offering provided by AWS that provides a complete and fully managed environment that targets different types of popular programming languages and application frameworks such as Java, Python, Ruby, and Node.js. Elastic Beanstalk also supports Docker applications, allowing you to support a wide variety of applications written in the programming language of your choice. You will learn how to deploy a multi-container Docker application in Chapter 15, *Elastic Beanstalk*.

- **Docker Swarm in AWS**: Docker Swarm is the native container management and clustering platform built into Docker that leverages the native Docker and Docker Compose tool chain to manage and deploy your container applications. At the time of writing this book, AWS does not provide a managed offering for Docker Swarm, however Docker provides a CloudFormation template (CloudFormation is a free Infrastructure as Code automation and management service provided by AWS) that allows you to quickly deploy a Docker Swarm cluster in AWS that integrates with native AWS offerings include the Elastic Load Balancing (ELB) and Elastic Block Store (EBS) services. We will cover all of this and more in the chapter *Docker Swarm in AWS*.

- **CodeBuild**: AWS CodeBuild is a fully managed build service that supports continuous delivery use cases by providing a container-based build agent that you can use to test, build, and deploy your applications without having to manage any of the infrastructure traditionally associated with continuous delivery systems. CodeBuild uses Docker as its container platform for spinning up build agents on demand, and you will be introduced to CodeBuild along with other continuous delivery tools such as CodePipeline in the chapter *Continuously Delivering ECS Applications*.

- **Batch**: AWS Batch provides a fully managed service based upon ECS that allows you to run container-based batch workloads without needing to worry about managing or maintaining any supporting infrastructure. We will not be covering AWS Batch in this book, however you can learn more about this service at `https://aws.amazon.com/batch/`.

With such a wide variety of options to run your Docker applications on AWS, it is important to be able to choose the right solution based upon the requirements of your organization or specific use cases.

If you are a small to medium sized organization that wants to get up and running quickly with Docker on AWS, and you don't want to manage any supporting infrastructure, then Fargate or Elastic Beanstalk are options that you may prefer. Fargate supports native integration with key AWS services, and is a building block component that doesn't dictate how your build, deploy, or operate your applications. At the time of writing this book, Fargate is not available in all regions, is comparatively expensive when compared to other solutions, and has some limitations such as not being able to support persistent storage. Elastic Beanstalk provides a comprehensive end-to-end solution for managing your Docker applications, providing a variety of integrations out of the box, and includes operational tooling to manage the complete life cycle of your applications. Elastic Beanstalk does require you to buy into a very opinionated framework and methodology of how to build, deploy, and run your applications, and can be difficult to customize to meet your needs.

If you are a larger organization that has specific requirements around security and compliance, or just wants greater flexibility and control over the infrastructure that runs your container workloads, then you should consider ECS, EKS, and Docker Swarm. ECS is the native flagship container management platform of choice for AWS, and as such has a large customer base that has been running containers at scale for a number of years. As you will learn in this book, ECS is integrated with CloudFormation, which allows you to define all of your clusters, application services, and container definitions using an Infrastructure as Code approach that can be combined with other AWS resources to provide you with the ability to deploy complete, complex environments with the click of a button. That said, the main criticism of ECS is that it is a proprietary solution specific to AWS, meaning that you can't use it in other cloud environments or run it on your own infrastructure. Increasingly larger organizations are looking to infrastructure and cloud agnostic cloud management platforms, and this is where you should consider EKS or Docker Swarm if these are your goals. Kubernetes has taken the container orchestration world by storm, and is now one of the largest and most popular open source projects. AWS now offers a managed Kubernetes service in the form of EKS, which makes it very easy to get Kubernetes up and running in AWS, and leverage core integrations with CloudFormation, and the Elastic Load Balancing (ELB) and Elastic Block Store (EBS) services. Docker Swarm is a competitor to Kubernetes, and although it seems to have lost the battle for container orchestration supremacy to Kubernetes, it does have the advantage of being a native out-of-the-box feature integrated with Docker which is very easy to get up and running using familiar Docker tools. Docker does currently publish CloudFormation templates and support key integrations with AWS services that makes it very easy to get up and running in AWS. However, there are concerns around the longevity of such solutions given that Docker Inc. is a commercial entity and the ever growing popularity and dominance of Kubernetes may force Docker Inc. to focus solely on its paid Docker Enterprise Edition and other commercial offerings in the future.

As you can see, there are many considerations when it comes to choosing a solution that is right for you, and the great thing about this book is that you will learn how to use each of these approaches to deploy and run your Docker applications in AWS. Regardless of which solution you think might sounds more suited to you right now, I encourage you to read through and complete all of the chapters in this book, as much of the content you will learn for one specific solution can be applied to the other solutions, and you will be in a much better position to tailor and build a comprehensive container management solution based upon your desired outcomes.

Setting up a local Docker environment

With introductions out of the way, it is time to get started and set up a local Docker environment that you will use to test, build, and deploy a Docker image for the sample application used for this book. For now, we will focus on getting Docker up and running, however note that later on we will also use your local environment to interact with the various container management platforms discussed in this book, and to manage all of your AWS resources using the AWS console, AWS command-line interface, and AWS CloudFormation service.

Although this book is titled Docker on Amazon Web Services, it is important to note that Docker containers come in two flavors:

- Linux containers
- Windows containers

This book is exclusively focused on Linux containers, which are designed to run on a Linux-based kernel with the Docker Engine installed. When you want to use your local environment to build, test, and run Linux containers locally, this means you must have access to a local Linux-based Docker Engine. If you are operating on a Linux-based system such as Ubuntu, you can install a Docker Engine natively in your operating system. However, if you are using Windows or macOS, this requires you to set up a local virtual machine that runs the Docker Engine and install a Docker client for your operating system.

Luckily, Docker has great packaging and tooling for making this process very simple on Windows and macOS environments, and we will now discuss how to set up a local Docker environment for macOS, Windows 10, and Linux, along with other tools that will be used in this book such as Docker Compose and GNU Make. For Windows 10 environments, I will also cover how to set up the Windows 10 Linux subsystem to interact with your local Docker installation, which will provide you with access to an environment where you can run the other Linux-based tools that are used throughout this book.

Before we continue, it's also important to note that from a licensing perspective, Docker is currently available in two different editions, which you can learn more about at `https://docs.docker.com/install/overview/`:

- Community edition (CE)
- Enterprise edition (EE)

We will be working exclusively with the free community edition (Docker CE), which includes the core Docker Engine. Docker CE is suitable for use with all of the technologies and services we will cover in this book, including Elastic Container Service (ECS), Fargate, Docker Swarm, Elastic Kubernetes Service (EKS), and Elastic Beanstalk.

Along with Docker, we also need a few other tools to help automate a number of build, test, and deployment tasks that we will be performing throughout this book:

- **Docker Compose**: This allows you to orchestrate and run multi-container environments both locally and on Docker Swarm clusters
- **Git**: This is required to fork and clone the sample application from GitHub and create your own Git repositories for the various applications and environments you will create in this book
- **GNU Make 3.82 or higher**: This provides task automation, allowing you run simple commands (for example, `make test`) to execute a given task
- **jq**: A command-line utility for parsing JSON
- **curl**: A command-line HTTP client
- **tree**: A command-line client for displaying folder structures in the shell
- **Python interpreter**: This is required for Docker Compose and the AWS Command-Line Interface (CLI) tool that we will install in a later chapter
- **pip**: A Python package manager for installing Python applications such as the AWS CLI

Some of the tools used in this book are representative only, meaning that you can replace them with alternatives if you desire. For example, you could replace GNU Make with another tool to provide task automation.

One other important tool that you will need is a decent text editor – Visual Studio Code (`https://code.visualstudio.com/`) and Sublime Text (`https://www.sublimetext.com/`) are excellent choices which are available on Windows, macOS, and Linux.

Now, let's discuss how to install and configure your local Docker environment for the following operating systems:

- macOS
- Windows 10
- Linux

Setting up a macOS environment

If you are running macOS, the quickest way to get Docker up and running is to install Docker for Mac, which you can read more about at `https://docs.docker.com/docker-for-mac/install/` and download from `https://store.docker.com/editions/community/docker-ce-desktop-mac`. Under the hood, Docker for Mac leverages the native macOS hypervisor framework, creating a Linux virtual machine to run the Docker Engine and installing a Docker client in your local macOS environment.

You will first need to create a free Docker Hub account in order to proceed, and once you have completed registration and logged in, click the **Get Docker** button to download the latest version of Docker:

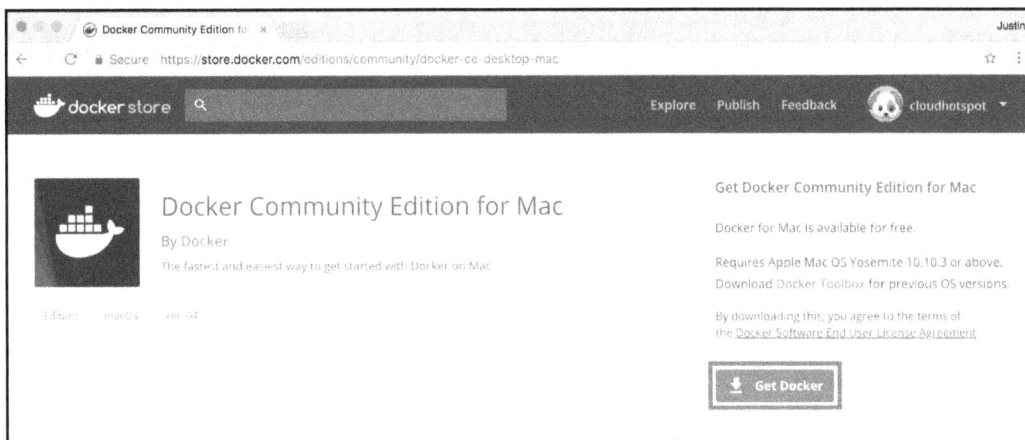

Downloading Docker for Mac

Once you have completed the download, open the download file, drag the Docker icon to the **Applications** folder, and then run Docker:

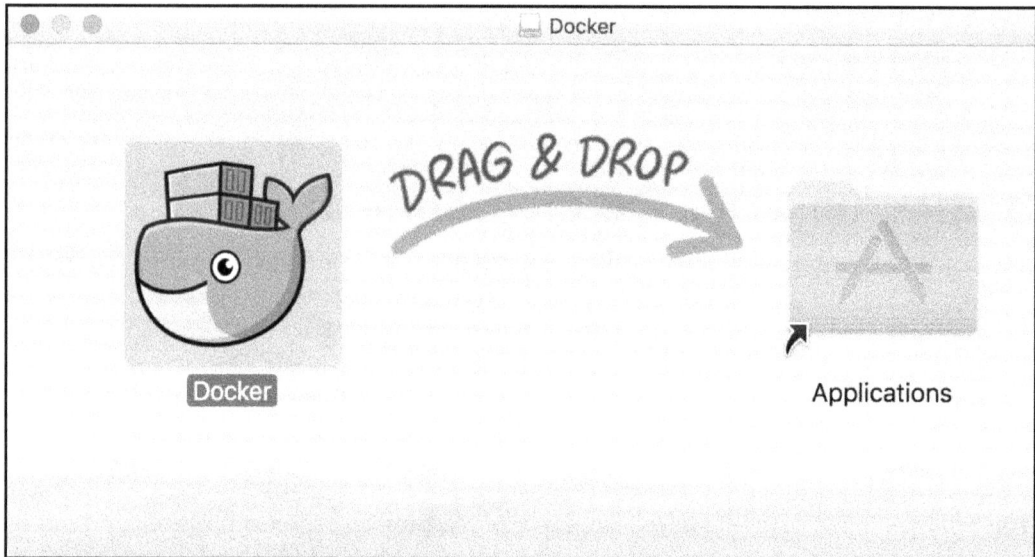

Installing Docker

Proceed through the Docker installation wizard and once complete, you should see a Docker icon on your macOS toolbar:

Docker icon on macOS toolbar

If you click on this icon and select **Preferences**, a Docker Preferences dialog will be displayed, which allows you to configure various Docker settings. One setting you may want to immediately change is the memory allocated to the Docker Engine, which in my case I have increased from the default of 2 GB to 8 GB:

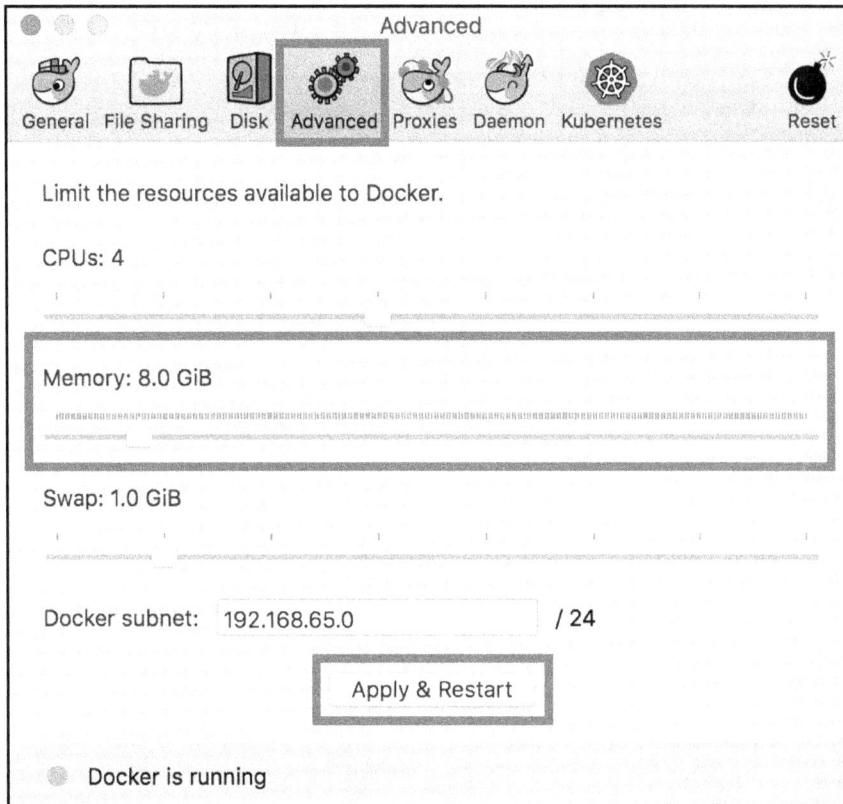

Increasing memory

At this point, you should be able to start up a Terminal and run the `docker info` command:

```
> docker info
Containers: 0
 Running: 0
 Paused: 0
 Stopped: 0
Images: 0
Server Version: 18.06.0-ce
Storage Driver: overlay2
 Backing Filesystem: extfs
 Supports d_type: true
 Native Overlay Diff: true
...
...
```

You can also start a new container using the `docker run` command:

```
> docker run -it alpine echo "Hello World"
Unable to find image 'alpine:latest' locally
latest: Pulling from library/alpine
ff3a5c916c92: Pull complete
Digest:
sha256:e1871801d30885a610511c867de0d6baca7ed4e6a2573d506bbec7fd3b03873
f
Status: Downloaded newer image for alpine:latest
Hello World
> docker ps -a
CONTAINER ID      IMAGE     COMMAND               CREATED         STATUS
a251bd2c53dd      alpine    "echo 'Hello World'"  3 seconds ago Exited
(0) 2 seconds ago
> docker rm a251bd2c53dd
a251bd2c53dd
```

In the preceding example, you must run the `alpine` image, which is based on the lightweight Alpine Linux distribution, and run the `echo "Hello World"` command. The `-it` flags specify that you need to run the container in an interactive terminal environment, which allows you to see standard output and also interact with the container via a console.

Once the container exits, you can use the `docker ps` command to show running containers, and append the `-a` flag to show both running and stopped containers. Finally, you can use the `docker rm` command to remove a stopped container.

Installing other tools

As discussed earlier in this section, we also require a number of other tools to help automate a number of build, test, and deployment tasks. On macOS, some of these tools are already included, and are outlined as follows:

- **Docker Compose**: This is already included when you install Docker for Mac.
- **Git**: When you install the Homebrew package manager (we will discuss Homebrew shortly), XCode command-line utilities are installed, which include Git. If you use another package manager, you may need to install Git using your package manager.

- **GNU Make 3.82 or higher**: macOS includes Make 3.81, which doesn't quite meet the requirements of version 3.82, therefore you need to install GNU Make using a third-party package manager such as Homebrew.
- **curl**: This is included by default with macOS, and therefore requires no installation.
- **jq and tree**: These are not included by default in macOS, and therefore they need to be installed via a third-party package manager such as Homebrew.
- **Python interpreter**: macOS includes a system installation of Python that you can use to run Python applications, however I recommend leaving the system Python installation alone and instead install Python using the Homebrew package manager (`https://docs.brew.sh/Homebrew-and-Python`).
- **pip**: The system install of Python does not include the popular PIP Python package manager, hence you must install this separately if using the system Python interpreter. If you choose to install Python using Homebrew, this will include PIP.

The easiest way to install the preceding tools on macOS is to first install a third-party package manager called Homebrew. You can install Homebrew by simply browsing to the Homebrew homepage at `https://brew.sh/`:

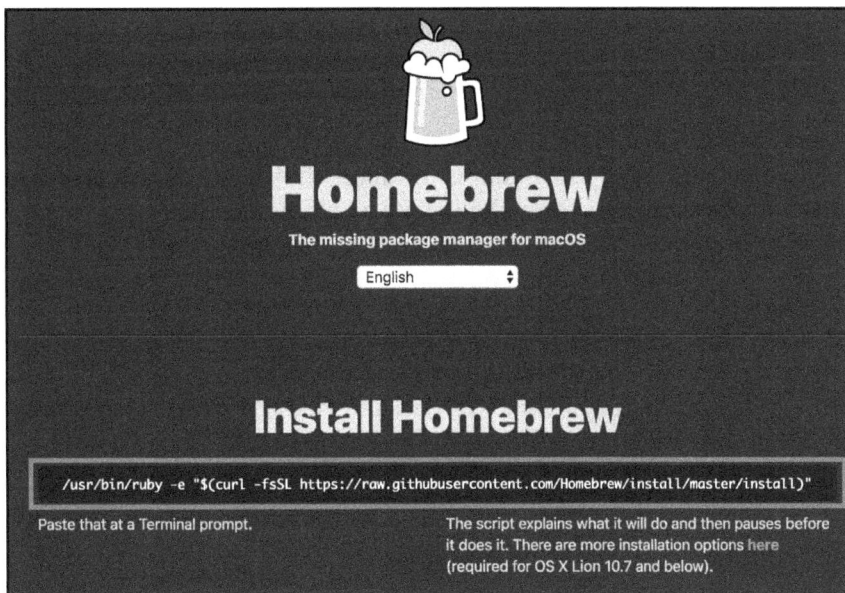

Installing Homebrew

Simply copy and paste the highlighted command into your terminal prompt, which will automatically install the Homebrew package manager. Once complete, you will be able to install each of the previously listed utilities using the `brew` command:

```
> brew install make --with-default-names
==> Downloading https://ftp.gnu.org/gnu/make/make-4.2.1.tar.bz2
Already downloaded:
/Users/jmenga/Library/Caches/Homebrew/make-4.2.1.tar.bz2
==> ./configure --prefix=/usr/local/Cellar/make/4.2.1_1
==> make install
/usr/local/Cellar/make/4.2.1_1: 13 files, 959.5KB, built in 29 seconds
> brew install jq tree
==> Downloading
https://homebrew.bintray.com/bottles/jq-1.5_3.high_sierra.bottle.tar.g
z
Already downloaded:
/Users/jmenga/Library/Caches/Homebrew/jq-1.5_3.high_sierra.bottle.tar.
gz
==> Downloading
https://homebrew.bintray.com/bottles/tree-1.7.0.high_sierra.bottle.1.t
ar.gz
Already downloaded:
/Users/jmenga/Library/Caches/Homebrew/tree-1.7.0.high_sierra.bottle.1.
tar.gz
==> Pouring jq-1.5_3.high_sierra.bottle.tar.gz
/usr/local/Cellar/jq/1.5_3: 19 files, 946.6KB
==> Pouring tree-1.7.0.high_sierra.bottle.1.tar.gz
/usr/local/Cellar/tree/1.7.0: 8 files, 114.3KB
```

You must first install GNU Make using the `--with-default-names` flag, which will replace the system version of Make that is installed on macOS. If you prefer to omit this flag, then the GNU version of make will be available via the `gmake` command, and the existing system version of make will not be affected.

Finally, to install Python using Homebrew, you can run the `brew install python` command, which will install Python 3 and also install the PIP package manager. Note that when you use `brew` to install Python 3, the Python interpreter is accessed via the `python3` command, while the PIP package manager is accessed via the `pip3` command rather than the `pip` command:

```
> brew install python
==> Installing dependencies for python: gdbm, openssl, readline,
sqlite, xz
...
...
==> Caveats
```

```
Python has been installed as
  /usr/local/bin/python3

Unversioned symlinks `python`, `python-config`, `pip` etc. pointing to
`python3`, `python3-config`, `pip3` etc., respectively, have been
installed into
  /usr/local/opt/python/libexec/bin

If you need Homebrew's Python 2.7 run
  brew install python@2

Pip, setuptools, and wheel have been installed. To update them run
  pip3 install --upgrade pip setuptools wheel

You can install Python packages with
  pip3 install <package>
They will install into the site-package directory
  /usr/local/lib/python3.7/site-packages

See: https://docs.brew.sh/Homebrew-and-Python
==> Summary
/usr/local/Cellar/python/3.7.0: 4,788 files, 102.2MB
```

On macOS, if you use Python which has been installed via brew or another package manager, you should also add the site module USER_BASE/bin folder to your local path, as this is where PIP will install any applications or libraries that you install with the --user flag (the AWS CLI is an example of such an application that you will install in this way later on in this book):

```
> python3 -m site --user-base
/Users/jmenga/Library/Python/3.7
> echo 'export PATH=/Users/jmenga/Library/Python/3.7/bin:$PATH' >>
~/.bash_profile
> source ~/.bash_profile
```

Ensure that you use single quotes in the preceding example, which ensures the reference to $PATH is not expanded in your shell session and is instead written as a literal value to the .bash_profile file.

In the preceding example, you call the site module with the `--user-base` flag, which tells you where user binaries will be installed. You can then add the `bin` subfolder of this path to your `PATH` variable and append this to the `.bash_profile` file in your home directory, which is executed whenever you spawn a new shell, ensuring that you will always be able to execute Python applications that have been installed with the `--user` flag. Note that you can use the `source` command to process the `.bash_profile` file immediately without having to log out and log back in.

Setting up a Windows 10 environment

Just like for macOS, if you are running Windows 10, the quickest way to get Docker up and running is to install Docker for Windows, which you can read more about at `https://docs.docker.com/docker-for-windows/` and download from `https://store.docker.com/editions/community/docker-ce-desktop-windows`. Under the hood, Docker for Windows leverages the native Windows hypervisor called Hyper-V, creating a virtual machine to run the Docker Engine and installing a Docker client for Windows.

You will first need to create a free Docker Hub account in order to proceed, and once you have completed registration and logged in, click the **Get Docker** button to download the latest version of Docker for Windows.

Once you have completed the download, start the installation and ensure that the **Use Windows containers** option is NOT selected:

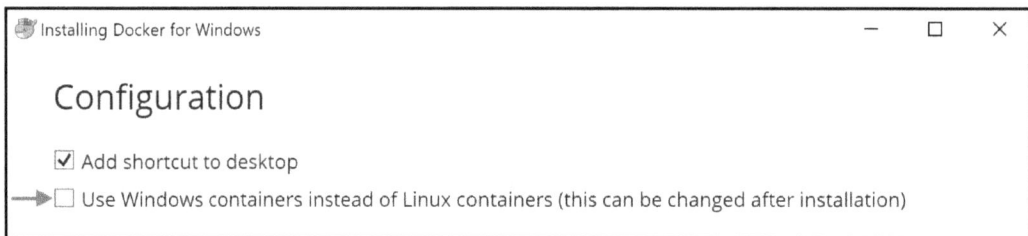

Using Linux containers

The installation will continue and you will be asked to log out of Windows to complete the installation. After logging back into Windows, you will be prompted to enable Windows Hyper-V and Containers features:

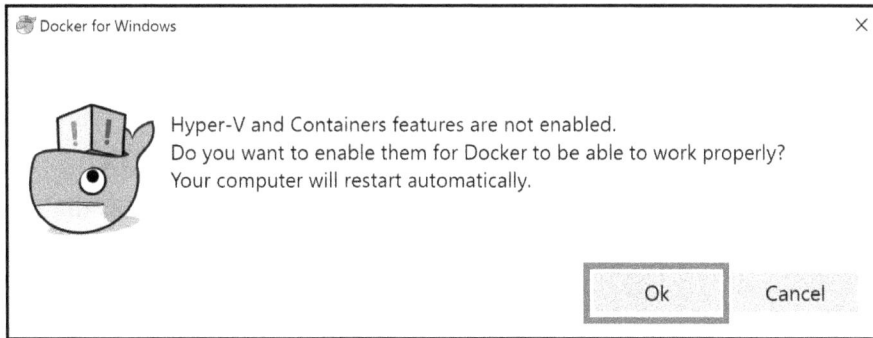

Enabling Hyper-V

Your computer will now enable the required Windows features and reboot. Once you have logged back in, open the Docker for Windows application and ensure that you select the **Expose daemon on tcp://localhost:2375 without TLS** option:

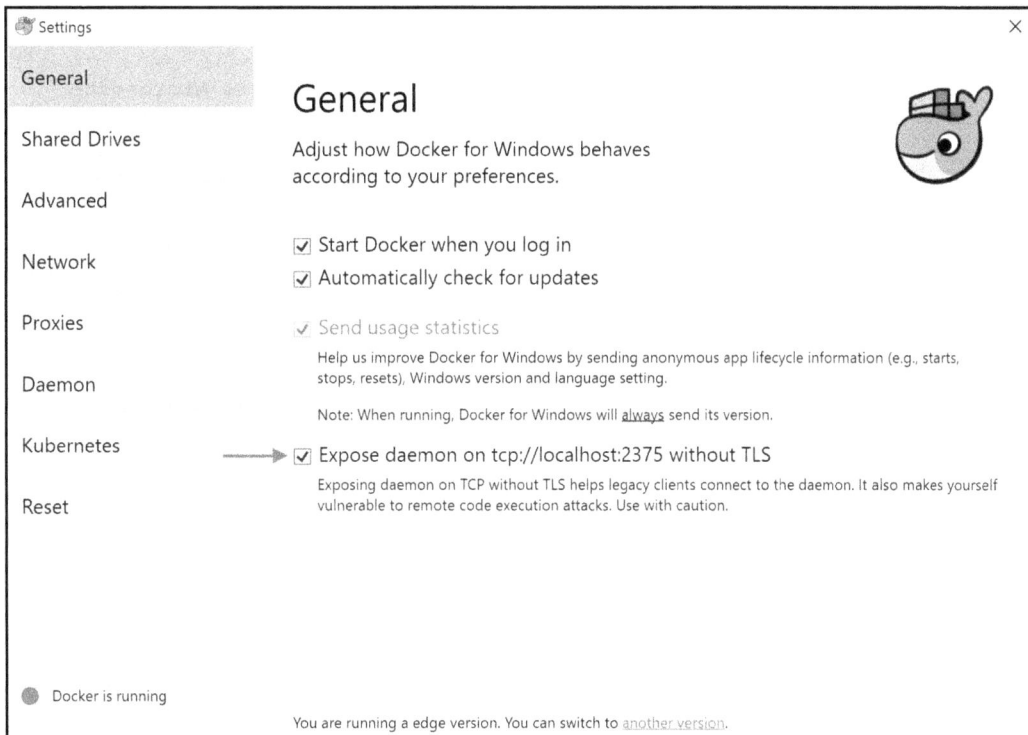

Enabling legacy client access to Docker

This setting must be enabled in order to allow the Windows subsystem for Linux to access the Docker Engine.

Installing the Windows subsystem for Linux

Now that you have installed Docker for Windows, you next need to install the Windows subsystem for Linux, which provides a Linux environment where you can install the Docker client, Docker Compose, and the other tools we will use throughout this book.

> If you are using Windows, then throughout this book I am assuming that you are using the Windows subsystem for Linux as your shell environment.

To enable the Windows subsystem for Linux, you need to run PowerShell as an Administrator (right-click the PowerShell program and select **Run as Administrator**) and then run the following command:

```
PS > Enable-WindowsOptionalFeature -Online -FeatureName Microsoft-
Windows-Subsystem-Linux
```

After enabling this feature, you will be prompted to reboot your machine. Once your machine has rebooted, you then need to install a Linux distribution. You can find links to the various distributions in the article `https://docs.microsoft.com/en-us/windows/wsl/install-win10` – see step 1 in `Install Your Linux Distribution of Choice`.

For example, the link for Ubuntu is `https://www.microsoft.com/p/ubuntu/9nblggh4msv6` and if you click on **Get the app**, you will be directed to the Microsoft Store app on your local machine and you can download the application for free:

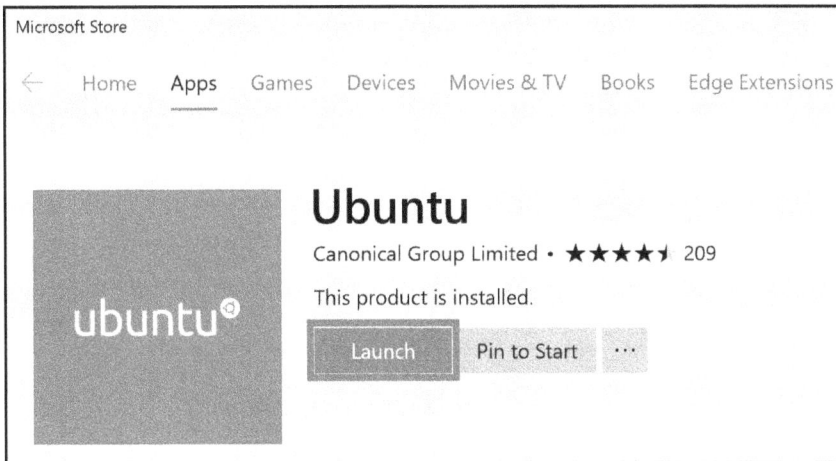

Ubuntu distribution for Windows

Once the download is complete, click on the **Launch** button, which will run the Ubuntu installer and install Ubuntu on the Windows subsystem for Linux. You will be prompted to enter a username and password, and assuming you are using the Ubuntu distribution, you can run the `lsb_release -a` command to show the specific version of Ubuntu that was installed:

Installing the Ubuntu distribution for Windows

> The information that has been provided is for recent versions of Windows 10. For older versions of Windows 10, you may need to follow the instructions at https://docs.microsoft.com/en-us/windows/wsl/install-win10#for-anniversary-update-and-creators-update-install-using-lxrun.

Note that the Windows file system is mounted into the Linux subsystem for Windows under /mnt/c (where c corresponds to the Windows C: drive), so in order to use a text editor installed on Windows to modify files that you can access in the Linux subsystem, you may want to change your home directory to your Windows home folders under /mnt/c/Users/<user name> as follows:

```
> exec sudo usermod -d /mnt/c/Users/jmenga jmenga
[sudo] password for jmenga:
```

Note that the Linux subsystem will exit immediately after entering the preceding command. If you open the Linux subsystem again (click on the **Start** button and type **Ubuntu**), your home directory should now be your Windows home directory:

```
> pwd
/mnt/c/Users/jmenga
> echo $HOME
/mnt/c/Users/jmenga
```

Installing Docker in the Windows subsystem for Linux

Now that you have the Windows subsystem for Linux installed, you need to install the Docker client, Docker Compose, and other supporting tools in your distribution. In this section, I will assume that you are using the Ubuntu Xenial (16.04) distribution.

To install Docker, follow the instructions at https://docs.docker.com/install/linux/docker-ce/ubuntu/#install-docker-ce to install Docker:

```
> sudo apt-get update
Get:1 http://security.ubuntu.com/ubuntu xenial-security InRelease [107 kB]
Hit:2 http://archive.ubuntu.com/ubuntu xenial InRelease
Get:3 http://archive.ubuntu.com/ubuntu xenial-updates InRelease [109 kB]
...
...
> sudo apt-get install \
    apt-transport-https \
```

```
    ca-certificates \
    curl \
    software-properties-common
...
...
> curl -fsSL https://download.docker.com/linux/ubuntu/gpg | sudo apt-
key add -
OK
> sudo add-apt-repository \
   "deb [arch=amd64] https://download.docker.com/linux/ubuntu \
   $(lsb_release -cs) stable"
> sudo apt-get update
...
...
> sudo apt-get install docker-ce
...
...
> docker --version
Docker version 18.06.0-ce, build 0ffa825
> docker info
Cannot connect to the Docker daemon at unix:///var/run/docker.sock. Is
the docker daemon running?
```

In the preceding example, you must follow the various instructions to add the Docker CE repository to Ubuntu. After installation is completed, you must execute the `docker --version` command to check the installed version, and then the `docker info` command to connect to the Docker Engine. Notice that this fails, as the Windows subsystem for Linux is a user space component that does not include the necessary kernel components required to run a Docker Engine.

> The Windows subsystem for Linux is not a virtual machine technology and instead relies on kernel emulation features provided by the Windows kernel that makes the underlying Windows kernel appear like a Linux kernel. This kernel emulation mode of operation does not support the various system calls that support containers, and hence cannot run the Docker Engine.

To enable the Windows subsystem for Linux to connect to the Docker Engine that was installed by Docker for Windows, you need to set the `DOCKER_HOST` environment variable to `localhost:2375`, which will configure the Docker client to connect to TCP port `2375` rather than attempt to connect to the default `/var/run/docker.sock` socket file:

```
> export DOCKER_HOST=localhost:2375
> docker info
Containers: 0
 Running: 0
 Paused: 0
 Stopped: 0
Images: 0
Server Version: 18.06.0-ce
Storage Driver: overlay2
 Backing Filesystem: extfs
 Supports d_type: true
 Native Overlay Diff: true
...
...
> echo "export DOCKER_HOST=localhost:2375" >> ~/.bash_profile
```

Because you enabled the **Expose daemon on tcp://localhost:2375 without TLS** option earlier when you installed Docker and Windows to expose local ports to the Windows subsystem for Linux, the Docker client can now communicate with the Docker Engine running in a separate Hyper-V virtual machine that was installed by Docker for Windows. You also add the `export DOCKER_HOST` command to the `.bash_profile` file in the home directory of your user, which is executed every time you spawn a new shell. This ensures that your Docker client will always attempt to connect to the correct Docker Engine.

Installing other tools in the Windows subsystem for Linux

At this point, you need to install the following supporting tools that we will be using throughout this book in the Windows Subsystem for Linux:

- Python
- pip package manager
- Docker Compose

- Git
- GNU Make
- jq
- Build essentials and Python development libraries (required to build dependencies of the sample application)

You just need to follow the normal Linux distribution procedures for installing each of the preceding components. The Ubuntu 16.04 Windows subsystem for Linux distribution already includes Python 3, so you can run the following commands to install the pip package manager, and also set up your environment to be able to locate Python packages that you can install as user packages with the --user flag:

```
> curl -O https://bootstrap.pypa.io/get-pip.py
> python3 get-pip.py --user
Collecting pip
...
...
Installing collected packages: pip, setuptools, wheel
Successfully installed pip-10.0.1 setuptools-39.2.0 wheel-0.31.1
> rm get-pip.py
> python3 -m site --user-base
/mnt/c/Users/jmenga/.local
> echo 'export PATH=/mnt/c/Users/jmenga/.local/bin:$PATH' >>
~/.bash_profile
> source ~/.bash_profile
```

Now, you can install Docker Compose by using the pip install docker-compose --user command:

```
> pip install docker-compose --user
Collecting docker-compose
...
...
Successfully installed cached-property-1.4.3 docker-3.4.1 docker-
compose-1.22.0 docker-pycreds-0.3.0 dockerpty-0.4.1 docopt-0.6.2
jsonschema-2.6.0 texttable-0.9.1 websocket-client-0.48.0
> docker-compose --version
docker-compose version 1.22.0, build f46880f
```

Finally, you can install Git, GNU Make, jq, tree, build essentials, and Python3 development libraries using the `apt-get install` command:

```
> sudo apt-get install git make jq tree build-essential python3-dev
Reading package lists... Done
Building dependency tree
...
...
Setting up jq (1.5+dfsg-1) ...
Setting up make (4.1-6) ...
Processing triggers for libc-bin (2.23-0ubuntu10) ...
> git --version
git version 2.7.4
> make --version
GNU Make 4.1
Built for x86_64-pc-linux-gnu
Copyright (C) 1988-2014 Free Software Foundation, Inc.
License GPLv3+: GNU GPL version 3 or later
<http://gnu.org/licenses/gpl.html>
This is free software: you are free to change and redistribute it.
There is NO WARRANTY, to the extent permitted by law.
> jq --version
jq-1.5-1-a5b5cbe
```

Setting up a Linux environment

Docker is natively supported on Linux, meaning that you can install and run the Docker Engine in your local operating system without needing to set up a virtual machine. Docker officially supports the following Linux distributions (`https://docs.docker.com/install/`) for installing and running Docker CE:

- CentOS: See `https://docs.docker.com/install/linux/docker-ce/centos/`
- Debian: See `https://docs.docker.com/install/linux/docker-ce/debian/`
- Fedora: See `https://docs.docker.com/install/linux/docker-ce/fedora/`
- Ubuntu: See `https://docs.docker.com/install/linux/docker-ce/ubuntu/`

Once you have installed Docker, you can install the various tools required to complete this book as follows:

- **Docker Compose**: See the Linux tab at `https://docs.docker.com/compose/install/`. Alternatively, as you require Python to install the AWS CLI tool, you can use the `pip` Python package manager to install Docker Compose, as demonstrated earlier for Mac and Windows, by running `pip install docker-compose`.
- **Python, pip, Git, GNU Make, jq, tree, build essentials, and Python3 development libraries**: Use your Linux distribution's package manager (for example, `yum` or `apt`) to install these tools. See the preceding example for a demonstration of this when using Ubuntu Xenial.

Installing the sample application

Now that you have set up your local environment to support Docker and the various tools required to complete this book, it's time to install the sample application for this course.

The sample application is a simple Todo items web service called **todobackend** that provides a REST API that allows you to create, read, update, and delete Todo items (for example, *Wash the car* or *Walk the dog*). This application is a Python application based on Django, which is a popular framework for creating web applications. You can read more about this at `https://www.djangoproject.com/`. Don't worry if you are not familiar with Python – the sample application is already created for you and all you need to do as you read through this book is build and test the application, package and publish the application as a Docker image, and then deploy your application using the various container management platforms discussed in this book.

Forking the sample application

To install the sample application, you will need to *fork* the application from GitHub (we will discuss what this means shortly), which requires you to have an active GitHub account. If you already have a GitHub account, you can skip this step, however if you don't have an account, you can sign up for a free account at `https://github.com`:

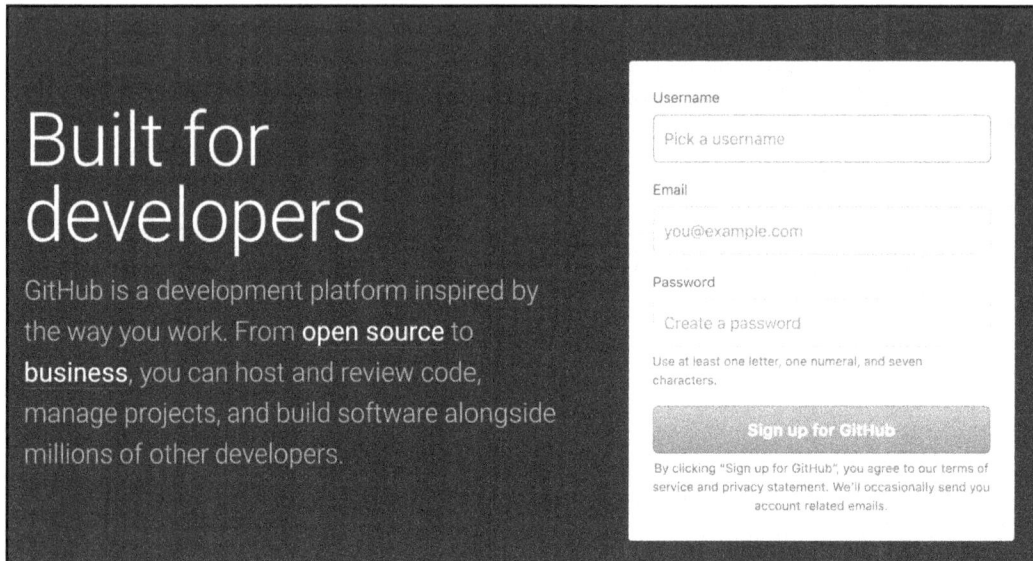

Signing up for GitHub

Once you have an active GitHub account, you can access the sample application repository at `https://github.com/docker-in-aws/todobackend`. Rather than clone the repository, a better approach is to *fork* the repository, which means that a new repository will be created in your own GitHub account that is linked to the original `todobackend` repository (hence the term *fork*). Forking is a popular pattern in the open source community, and allows you to make your own independent changes to the forked repository. This is particularly useful for this book, as you will be making your own changes to the `todobackend` repository, adding a local Docker workflow to build, test, and publish the sample application as a Docker image, and other changes as you progress throughout this book.

To fork the repository, click on the fork button that is located in the top right hand corner:

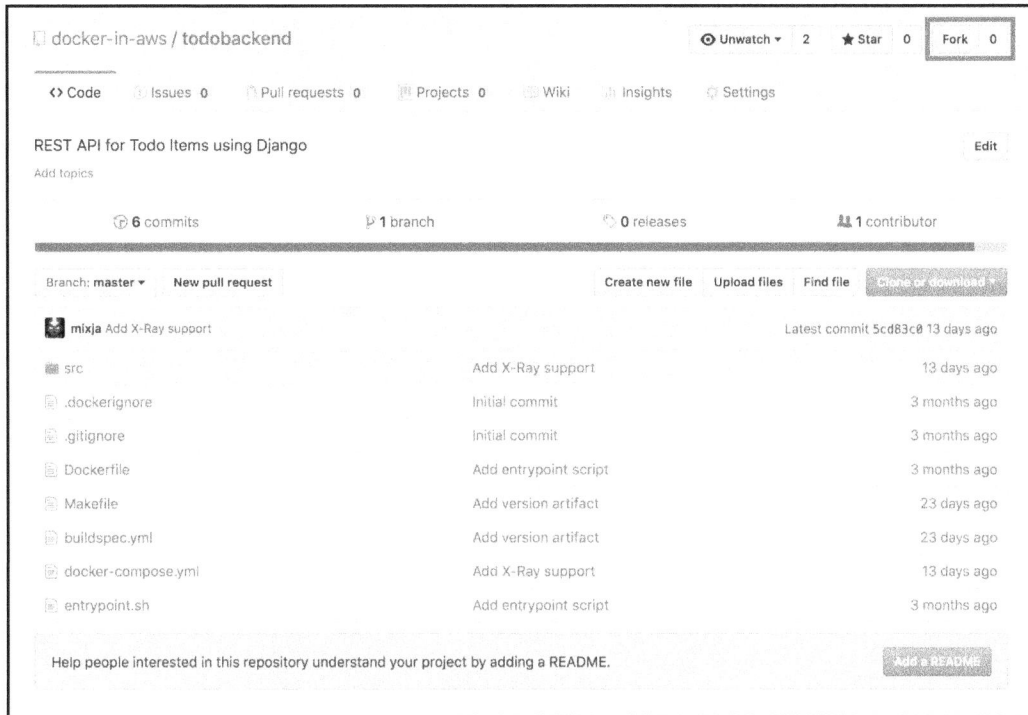

Forking the todobackend repository

A few seconds a after clicking the fork button, a new repository should be created with the name `<your-github-username>/todobackend`. At this point, you can now clone your fork of the repository by clicking on the **Clone or download** button. If you have just set up a new account, choose the **Clone with HTTPS** option and copy the URL that's presented:

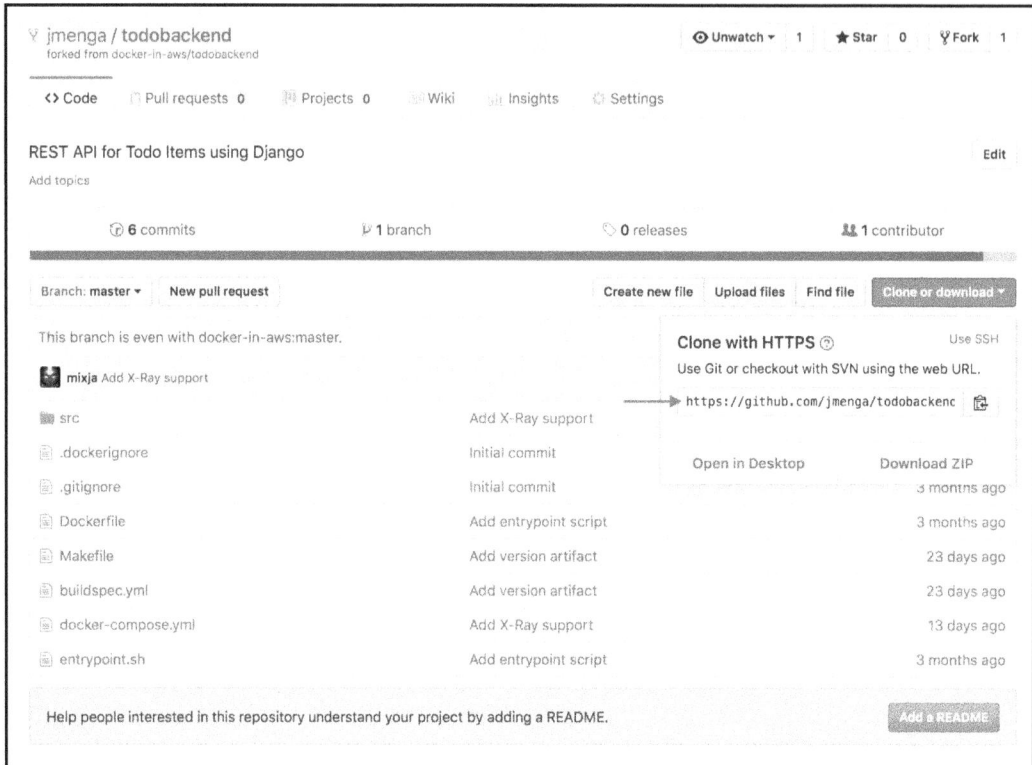

Getting the Git URL for the todobackend repository

Open a new terminal and run the `git clone <repository-url>` command, where `<repository-url>` is the URL you copied in the preceding example, and then go into the newly created `todobackend` folder:

```
> git clone https://github.com/<your-username>/todobackend.git
Cloning into 'todobackend'...
remote: Counting objects: 231, done.
remote: Total 231 (delta 0), reused 0 (delta 0), pack-reused 231
Receiving objects: 100% (231/231), 31.75 KiB | 184.00 KiB/s, done.
```

```
Resolving deltas: 100% (89/89), done.
> cd todobackend
todobackend>
```

As you work through this chapter, I encourage you to commit any changes you make frequently, along with descriptive messages that clearly identify the changes you make.

The sample repository includes a branch called `final`, which represents the final state of the repository after completing all chapters in this took. You can use this as a reference point if you run into any issues by running the command `git checkout final`. You can switch back to the master branch by running `git checkout master`.

If you are unfamiliar with Git, you can refer to any of the numerous tutorials online (for example, `https://www.atlassian.com/git/tutorials`), however in general you will need to perform the following commands when committing a change:

```
> git pull
Already up to date.
> git diff
diff --git a/Dockerfile b/Dockerfile
index e56b47f..4a73ce3 100644
--- a/Dockerfile
+++ b/Dockerfile
-COPY --from=build /build /build
-COPY --from=build /app /app
-WORKDIR /app
+# Create app user
+RUN addgroup -g 1000 app && \
+ adduser -u 1000 -G app -D app

+# Copy and install application source and pre-built dependencies
> git status
On branch master
Your branch is up to date with 'origin/master'.

Changes not staged for commit:
  (use "git add <file>..." to update what will be committed)
  (use "git checkout -- <file>..." to discard changes in working
directory)

  modified: src/todobackend/settings.py
  modified: src/todobackend/wsgi.py
```

```
Untracked files:
  (use "git add <file>..." to include in what will be committed)

  docker-compose.yml
  src/acceptance.bats
> git add -A
> git commit -a -m "Some commit message"
> git push -u origin master
> git push
```

You should always check frequently that you have the most up-to-date version of the repository by running the git pull command, as this avoids messy automatic merges and push failures, particularly when you are working with other people that may be collaborating on your project. Next, you can use the git diff command to show, at a content level, any changes you have made to existing files, while the git status command shows, at a file level, changes to existing files and also identifies any new files that you may have added to the repository. The git add -A command adds all new files to the repository, and the git commit -a -m "<message>" command commits all changes (including any files you have added with git add -A) with the specified message. Finally, you can push your changes using the git push command – the first time you push, you must specify the remote branch at the origin using the git push -u origin <branch> command – after which you can just use the shorter git push variant to push your changes.

> A common mistake is to forget to add new files to your Git repository, which may not be apparent until you clone the repository to a different machine. Always ensure that you run the git status command to identify any new files that are not currently being tracked before committing your changes.

Running the sample application locally

Now that you have downloaded the source code for the sample application locally, you can now build and run the application locally. When you are packaging an application into a Docker image, you need to understand at a detailed level how to build and run your application, so running the application locally is the first step in the journey of being able to build a container for your application.

Installing application dependencies

To run the application, you need to first install any dependencies that the application requires. The sample application includes a file called `requirements.txt` in the `src` folder, which lists all required Python packages that must be installed for the application to run:

```
Django==2.0
django-cors-headers==2.1.0
djangorestframework==3.7.3
mysql-connector-python==8.0.11
pytz==2017.3
uwsgi==2.0.17
```

To install these requirements, ensure you have changed to the `src` folder and configure the PIP package manager to read the requirements file using the `-r` flag. Note that the best practice for day to day development is to install your application dependencies in a virtual environment (see `https://packaging.python.org/guides/installing-using-pip-and-virtualenv/`) however given we are installing the application mainly for demonstration purposes, I won't be taking this approach here:

```
todobackend> cd src
src> pip3 install -r requirements.txt --user
Collecting Django==2.0 (from -r requirements.txt (line 1))
...
...
Successfully installed Django-2.0 django-cors-headers-2.1.0
djangorestframework-3.7.3 mysql-connector-python-8.0.11 pytz-2017.3
uwsgi-2.0.17
```

> Over time, the specific versions of each dependency may change to ensure that the sample application continues to work as expected.

Running database migrations

With the application dependencies installed, you can run the `python3 manage.py` command to perform various Django management functions, such as running tests, generating static web content, running database migrations, and running a local instance of your web application.

In a local development context, you first need to run database migrations, which means your local database will be initialized with an appropriate database schema, as configured by your application. By default, Django uses the lightweight *SQLite* database that's included with Python, which is suitable for development purposes and requires no setup to get up and running. Therefore, you simply run the `python3 manage.py migrate` command, which will run all database migrations that are configured in the application automatically for you:

```
src> python3 manage.py migrate
Operations to perform:
  Apply all migrations: admin, auth, contenttypes, sessions, todo
Running migrations:
  Applying contenttypes.0001_initial... OK
  Applying auth.0001_initial... OK
  Applying admin.0001_initial... OK
  Applying admin.0002_logentry_remove_auto_add... OK
  Applying contenttypes.0002_remove_content_type_name... OK
  Applying auth.0002_alter_permission_name_max_length... OK
  Applying auth.0003_alter_user_email_max_length... OK
  Applying auth.0004_alter_user_username_opts... OK
  Applying auth.0005_alter_user_last_login_null... OK
  Applying auth.0006_require_contenttypes_0002... OK
  Applying auth.0007_alter_validators_add_error_messages... OK
  Applying auth.0008_alter_user_username_max_length... OK
  Applying auth.0009_alter_user_last_name_max_length... OK
  Applying sessions.0001_initial... OK
  Applying todo.0001_initial... OK
```

When you run Django migrations, Django will automatically detect if an existing schema is in place, and create a new schema if one does not exist (this is the case in the preceding example). If you run the migrations again, notice that Django detects that an up-to-date schema is already in place, and therefore nothing is applied:

```
src> python3 manage.py migrate
Operations to perform:
  Apply all migrations: admin, auth, contenttypes, sessions, todo
Running migrations:
  No migrations to apply.
```

Running the local development web server

With the local SQLite database now in place, you can run your application by executing the `python3 manage.py runserver` command, which starts a local development web server on port 8000:

```
src> python3 manage.py runserver
Performing system checks...

System check identified no issues (0 silenced).
July 02, 2018 - 07:23:49
Django version 2.0, using settings 'todobackend.settings'
Starting development server at http://127.0.0.1:8000/
Quit the server with CONTROL-C.
```

If you open a browser to `http://localhost:8000/`, you should see a web page titled **Django REST framework**:

The todobackend application

This page is the root of the application, and you can see that the Django REST framework provides a graphical interface for navigating the API when you use a browser. If you use the `curl` command instead of a browser, notice that Django detects a simple HTTP client and just returns a JSON response:

```
src> curl localhost:8000
{"todos":"http://localhost:8000/todos"}
```

If you click on the hypermedia link for the todos item (`http://localhost:8000/todos`), you will be presented with a list of Todo items, which is currently empty:

Todo Item List

Notice that you can create a new Todo item with a title and order using the web interface, which will populate the list of Todo items once you click on the POST button:

```
Django REST framework

Api Root / Todo Item List

Todo Item List                    DELETE   OPTIONS   GET ▾

POST /todos


HTTP 201 Created
Allow: GET, POST, DELETE, HEAD, OPTIONS
Content-Type: application/json
Location: http://localhost:8000/todos/1
Vary: Accept
{
    "url": "http://localhost:8000/todos/1",
    "title": "Walk the dog",
    "completed": false,
    "order": 1
}
```

Creating a Todo Item

Of course, you also can use the command line and the `curl` command to create new Todo items, list all Todo items, and update Todo items:

```
> curl -X POST -H "Content-Type: application/json"
localhost:8000/todos \
        -d '{"title": "Wash the car", "order": 2}'
{"url":"http://localhost:8000/todos/2","title":"Wash the
car","completed":false,"order":2}

> curl -s localhost:8000/todos | jq
[
  {
  "url": "http://localhost:8000/todos/1",
  "title": "Walk the dog",
  "completed": false,
  "order": 1
  },
```

```
 {
"url": "http://localhost:8000/todos/2",
"title": "Wash the car",
"completed": false,
"order": 2
 }
]

> curl -X PATCH -H "Content-Type: application/json"
localhost:8000/todos/2 \
        -d '{"completed": true}'
{"url":"http://localhost:8000/todos/2","title":"Wash the
car","completed":true,"order":1}
```

In the preceding example, you first create a new Todo item using the HTTP POST
method, and then verify that the Todos list now contains two Todo items, piping the
output of the curl command to the jq utility you installed previously to format the
returned items. Finally, you use the HTTP PATCH method to make a partial update to
the Todo item, marking the item as completed.

All of the Todo items you created and modified will be persisted in the application
database, which in this case is a SQLite database running on your development
machine.

Testing the sample application locally

Now that you have had a walkthrough of the sample application, let's take a look at
how you can run tests locally to verify that the application is functioning as expected.
The todobackend application includes a small set of tests for Todo items that are
located in the src/todo/tests.py file. Understanding how these tests are written
is outside the scope of this book, however knowing how to run these tests is critical in
being able to test, build, and ultimately package the application into a Docker image.

When testing your application, it is very common to have additional dependencies
that are specific to application testing, and are not required if you are building your
application to run in production. This sample application defines test dependencies
in a file called src/requirements_test.txt, which imports all of the core
application dependencies in src/requirements.txt and adds additional test-
specific dependencies:

```
-r requirements.txt
colorama==0.3.9
coverage==4.4.2
```

```
django-nose==1.4.5
nose==1.3.7
pinocchio==0.4.2
```

To install these requirements, you need to the run the PIP package manager, referencing the `requirements_test.txt` file:

```
src> pip3 install -r requirements_test.txt --user
Requirement already satisfied: Django==2.0 in
/usr/local/lib/python3.7/site-packages (from -r requirements.txt (line
1)) (2.0)
Requirement already satisfied: django-cors-headers==2.1.0 in
/usr/local/lib/python3.7/site-packages (from -r requirements.txt (line
2)) (2.1.0)
...
...
Installing collected packages: django-coverage, nose, django-nose,
pinocchio
Successfully installed django-nose-1.4.5 pinocchio-0.4.2
```

You can now run tests for the sample application by running the `python3 manage.py test` command, passing in the `--settings` flag, which allows you specify a custom settings configuration. In the sample application, there are additional test settings which are defined in the `src/todobackend/settings_test.py` file that extend the default settings included in `src/todobackend/settings.py`, which add testing enhancements such as specs style formatting and code coverage statistics:

```
src> python3 manage.py test --settings todobackend.settings_test
Creating test database for alias 'default'...

Ensure we can create a new todo item
- item has correct title
- item was created
- received 201 created status code
- received location header hyperlink

Ensure we can delete all todo items
- all items were deleted
- received 204 no content status code

Ensure we can delete a todo item
- received 204 no content status code
- the item was deleted

Ensure we can update an existing todo item using PATCH
- item was updated
```

```
    - received 200 ok status code

    Ensure we can update an existing todo item using PUT
    - item was updated
    - received 200 created status code


    ----------------------------------------------------------------
    XML: /Users/jmenga/todobackend/src/unittests.xml
    Name                               Stmts   Miss  Cover
    ----------------------------------------------------------------
    todo/__init__.py                       0      0   100%
    todo/admin.py                          1      1     0%
    todo/migrations/0001_initial.py        5      0   100%
    todo/migrations/__init__.py            0      0   100%
    todo/models.py                         6      6     0%
    todo/serializers.py                    7      0   100%
    todo/urls.py                           6      0   100%
    todo/views.py                         17      0   100%
    ----------------------------------------------------------------
    TOTAL                                 42      7    83%
    ----------------------------------------------------------------
    Ran 12 tests in 0.281s

    OK

    Destroying test database for alias 'default'...
```

Notice that Django test runner scans the various folders in the repository for tests, creates a test database, and then runs each test. After all tests are complete, the test runner automatically destroys the test database, so you don't have to perform any manual setup or cleanup tasks.

Summary

In this chapter, you were introduced to Docker and containers, and learned about the history of containers and how Docker has risen to become one of most popular solutions for testing, building, deploying, and running your container workloads. You learned about the basic architecture of Docker, which includes the Docker client, Docker Engine, and Docker registry, and we introduced the various types of objects and resources that you will work with when using Docker, which include Docker images, volumes, networks, services, and, of course, Docker containers.

We also discussed the wide array of options you have to run your Docker applications in AWS, which include the Elastic Container Service, Fargate, Elastic Kubernetes Service, Elastic Beanstalk, and running your own Docker platforms, such as Docker Swarm.

You then installed Docker in your local environment, which is supported natively on Linux and requires a virtual machine on macOS and Windows platforms. Docker for Mac and Docker for Windows automatically installs and configures a virtual machine for you, making it easier than ever to get up and running with Docker on these platforms. You also learned how to integrate the Windows subsystem for Linux with Docker for Windows, which will allow you to support the *nix-based tooling that we will use throughout this book.

Finally, you set up a GitHub account, forked the sample application repository to your account, and cloned the repository to your local environment. You then learned how to install the sample application dependencies, how to run a local development server, how to run database migrations to ensure that the application database schema and tables are in place, and how to run unit tests to ensure that the application is functioning as expected. All of these tasks are important to understand before you can expect to be able to test, build, and publish your applications as Docker images, which will be the focus of the next chapter, where you will create a complete local Docker workflow to automate the process of creating production-ready Docker images for your application.

Questions

1. True/false: The Docker client communicates with the Docker Engine using named pipes.
2. True/false: The Docker Engine runs natively on macOS.
3. True/false: Docker images are published to the Docker store for download.
4. You install the Windows subsystem for Linux and install a Docker client. Your Docker client cannot communicate with your Docker for Windows installation. How can you resolve this?
5. True/false: Volumes, networks, containers, images, and services are all entities that you can work with using Docker.
6. You install Docker Compose by running the `pip install docker-compose --user` command flag, however you receive a message stating **docker-compose: not found** when attempting to run the program. How can you resolve this?

Further reading

You can check the following links for more information about the topics covered in this chapter:

- Docker Overview: `https://docs.docker.com/engine/docker-overview/`
- Docker Getting Started: `https://docs.docker.com/get-started/`
- Docker for Mac Install Instructions: `https://docs.docker.com/docker-for-mac/install/`
- Docker for Windows Install Instructions: `https://docs.docker.com/docker-for-windows/install/`
- Docker for Ubuntu Install Instructions: `https://docs.docker.com/install/linux/docker-ce/ubuntu/`
- Docker for Debian Install Instructions: `https://docs.docker.com/install/linux/docker-ce/debian/`
- Docker for Centos Install Instructions: `https://docs.docker.com/install/linux/docker-ce/centos/`
- Docker for Fedora Install Instructions: `https://docs.docker.com/install/linux/docker-ce/fedora/`
- Windows Subsystem for Linux Install Instructions: `https://docs.microsoft.com/en-us/windows/wsl/install-win10`
- Homebrew Package Manager for macOS: `https://brew.sh/`
- PIP Package Manager User Installs: `https://pip.pypa.io/en/stable/user_guide/#user-installs`
- Git User Manual: `https://git-scm.com/docs/user-manual.html`
- GitHub Guides: `https://guides.github.com/`
- Forking a GitHub Repository: `https://guides.github.com/activities/forking/`
- Django Web Framework: `https://www.djangoproject.com/`
- Django REST Framework: `http://www.django-rest-framework.org/`

Building Applications Using Docker

2

In the previous chapter, you were introduced to the sample application, and you were able to download and run the application locally. At present, your development environment is set up for local development; however, before you can get your application to production, you need to be able to package up your application and all of its dependencies, ensure the target production environment has the correct supporting operating system libraries and configuration, select an appropriate web server to host your application, and have a mechanism to be able to package this all together, ideally in a self-contained artifact that requires minimal external configuration. Traditionally, all of this has been very difficult to achieve reliably and consistently – but this is where Docker has changed the landscape dramatically. With Docker and supporting tools, you now have the ability to achieve all of this and more in a much faster, more reliable, more consistent, and more portable fashion than ever before.

In this chapter, you will learn how to create a comprehensive workflow that allows you to test, build, and publish your applications in a portable, repeatable, and consistent manner using Docker. The approach you will learn about has numerous benefits—for example, you will be able to perform all tasks by running a handful of simple, easy-to-remember commands, and you will be able to do so without needing to install any application-specific or operating-system-specific dependencies into your local development or build environment. This makes it very easy to move to another machine or configure a continuous-delivery service to perform the same workflow—as long as you have the core Docker-based environment you set up in the previous chapter, you will be able to run the workflow on any machine, regardless of the specifics of your application or programming language.

You will learn how to define test and runtime environments for your application using a Dockerfile, configuring support for multi-stage builds that allow you to build application artifacts in an image that has all development tools and libraries available, and then copy those artifacts to other stages of your Dockerfile. You will leverage Docker Compose as a tool to orchestrate complex Docker environments with multiple containers, which allows you to test integration scenarios, such as your application interacting with a database, and also mimic how you would run your application in production environments. An important concept that will be introduced is the concept of building a release image, which is a production-ready image that can be shipped to production, assuming any new application features and functionality work as expected. You will build and run this release image in your local Docker environment, connect your application to a database, and then create acceptance tests that verify the application works as expected, from the perspective of an external client connecting to your application.

Finally, you will bring all you have learned together using GNU Make to automate your workflow. Once finished, you will be able to run unit tests and build application artifacts by simply running `make test`, and then build your release image, start up a production-like environment, and run acceptance tests by running `make release`. This will make it very simple to test and publish new application changes with confidence as they are developed, using a portable and consistent workflow that can be easily run in a local development environment and in any continuous-delivery environment that supports Docker and Docker Compose.

The following topics will be covered:

- Testing and building applications using Docker
- Creating multi-stage builds
- Creating a test stage to build and test application artifacts
- Creating a release stage to build and test a release image
- Using Docker Compose to test and build applications
- Creating acceptance tests
- Automating the workflow

Technical requirements

The following lists the technical requirements to complete this chapter:

- Prerequisite software installed as per instructions in Chapter 1
- GitHub account created as per instructions in Chapter 1

The following GitHub URL contains the code samples used in this chapter: `https://github.com/docker-in-aws/docker-in-aws/tree/master/ch2`.

Check out the following video to see the Code in Action:
`http://bit.ly/2PJG2Zm`

Testing and building the application using Docker

In the previous chapter, you gained a good understanding of what the sample application is, and how to test and run the application in your local development environment. You are now ready to start creating a Docker workflow that will test, build, and package your application into a Docker image.

It is important to understand that whenever you are packaging an application into a Docker image, the best-practice approach is to reduce or eliminate all development and test dependencies from your final packaged application. By my own convention, I refer to this packaged application—free of test and development dependencies—as a *release image*, which supports the paradigm of continuous delivery, where every successful build should be a release candidate that is able to be published to production if required.

To achieve this goal of creating a release image, an approach that works well is to split the Docker build process into two stages:

- **Test stage**: This stage has all the test and development dependencies available to compile and build your application source into an application artifact, and run unit and integration tests.
- **Release stage**: This stage copies the tested and built application artifact(s) from the test stage into a minimalistic runtime environment configured appropriately for running the application in production.

Docker natively supports such an approach using a feature called multi-stage builds, and this is the approach we will adopt in this book. For now, we will focus on the test stage, and move on to the release stage in the next section.

Creating a test stage

We will get started by creating a `Dockerfile` at the root of
the `todobackend` repository, meaning your repository structure should look
something like this:

```
todobackend> tree -L 2
.
├── Dockerfile
├── README.md
└── src
    ├── coverage.xml
    ├── db.sqlite3
    ├── manage.py
    ├── requirements.txt
    ├── requirements_test.txt
    ├── todo
    ├── todobackend
    └── unittests.xml

3 directories, 8 files
```

Let's now define a couple of directives in the newly created Dockerfile:

```
# Test stage
FROM alpine AS test
LABEL application=todobackend
```

The `FROM` directive is the first directive you define in a Dockerfile, and note that we
are using the Alpine Linux distribution as the base image. Alpine Linux is a
minimalistic distribution that has a much smaller footprint than the more traditional
Linux distributions, such as Ubuntu and CentOS, and has become very popular in the
container world since Docker adopted Alpine as the distribution of choice for official
Docker images.

One keyword you may not have come across is the `AS` keyword, which is appended
to the `FROM` directive, which configures the Dockerfile as a `multi-stage build` and
names the current stage as `test`. When you have a multi-stage build, you can include
multiple `FROM` directives, with each stage defined as including the
current `FROM` directive and subsequent directives, up until the next `FROM` directive.

Next, we use the `LABEL` directive to attach a label called `application` with a value
of `todobackend`, which is useful for being able to identify Docker images that
support the todobackend application.

Installing system and build dependencies

We now need to install the various system and build operating system dependencies that will support testing and building the application:

```
# Test stage
FROM alpine AS test
LABEL application=todobackend

# Install basic utilities
RUN apk add --no-cache bash git

# Install build dependencies
RUN apk add --no-cache gcc python3-dev libffi-dev musl-dev linux-
headers mariadb-dev
RUN pip3 install wheel
```

In the preceding example, we install the following dependencies:

- **Basic utilities**: In Alpine Linux, the package manager is called apk, and a common pattern used in Docker images is apk add --no-cache, which installs the referenced packages and ensures the downloaded packages are not cached. We install bash, which is useful for troubleshooting, and git, which is required as we will use Git metadata later on to generate application-version tags for the Docker release image.
- **Build dependencies**: Here we install the various development libraries required to build the application. This includes gcc, python3-dev, libffi-dev, musl-dev, and linux-headers for compiling any Python C extensions and their supporting standard libraries, as well as the mariadb-dev package, which is required to build the MySQL client in the todobackend application. You also install a Python package called wheel that allows you to build Python *wheels*, which are a precompiled and pre-built packaging format that we will use later on.

Installing application dependencies

The next step is to install application dependencies, which, as you learned in the previous chapter, means installing packages defined in the src/requirements.txt and src/requirements_test.txt files:

```
# Test stage
FROM alpine AS test
LABEL application=todobackend
```

```
# Install basic utilities
RUN apk add --no-cache bash git

# Install build dependencies
RUN apk add --no-cache gcc python3-dev libffi-dev musl-dev linux-
headers mariadb-dev
RUN pip3 install wheel

# Copy requirements
COPY /src/requirements* /build/
WORKDIR /build

# Build and install requirements
RUN pip3 wheel -r requirements_test.txt --no-cache-dir --no-input
RUN pip3 install -r requirements_test.txt -f /build --no-index --no-
cache-dir
```

You first use the COPY directive to copy
the src/requirements.txt and src/requirements_test.txt files to a folder in
the /build container, which you then specify as the working directory via
the WORKDIR directive. Note that /src/requirements.txt is not a physical path
on your Docker client - it is a path within the Docker *build context,* which is a
configurable location on your Docker client file system that you specify whenever
you execute a build. To ensure all relevant application source code files are available
for the Docker build process, a common practice is to set the root of your application
repository as the build context, so in the example above /src/requirements.txt
refers to <path-to-repository>/src/requirements.txt on your Docker client.

Next, you use the pip3 wheel command to build Python wheels into
the /build working directory for all of the base application and test dependencies,
using the --no-cache-dir flag to avoid bloating our image and the --no-
input flag to disable prompting for user confirmations. Finally, you install the
previously built wheels into the container using the pip3 install command, using
the --no-index flag to instruct pip not to attempt to download any packages from
the internet, and instead install all packages from the /build folder as specified by
the -f flag.

This approach may seem a little strange, however, it is based upon the principle that
you should only build your application dependencies once as installable packages,
and then install the built dependencies as required. Later on, we will install the same
dependencies into the release image, ensuring that your release image accurately
reflects the exact set of dependences your application was tested and built against.

Copying application source and running tests

The final steps in the test stage are to copy the application source into the container and add support for running tests:

```
# Test stage
FROM alpine AS test
LABEL application=todobackend

# Install basic utilities
RUN apk add --no-cache bash git

# Install build dependencies
RUN apk add --no-cache gcc python3-dev libffi-dev musl-dev linux-
headers mariadb-dev
RUN pip3 install wheel

# Copy requirements
COPY /src/requirements* /build/
WORKDIR /build

# Build and install requirements
RUN pip3 wheel -r requirements_test.txt --no-cache-dir --no-input
RUN pip3 install -r requirements_test.txt -f /build --no-index --no-
cache-dir

# Copy source code
COPY /src /app
WORKDIR /app

# Test entrypoint
CMD ["python3", "manage.py", "test", "--noinput", "--
settings=todobackend.settings_test"]
```

In the preceding example, you first copy the entire /src folder to a folder called /app, and then change the working directory to /app. You might be wondering why we didn't just copy all of the application source earlier when we copied the requirements files. The answer here is that we are implementing a caching optimization, as your requirements files require the building of application dependencies, and by building them in a separate, earlier layer, if the requirements files remain the same (which they tend to do), Docker can leverage cached versions of the most recent layers that were built, rather than having to build and install application dependencies each time your image is built.

Finally, we add the CMD directive, which defines the default command that will be executed should a container based from this image be created and executed. Note that we specify the same python3 manage.py test command we used in the previous chapter to run our application tests locally.

> You might wonder why we didn't just run our tests in the image using the RUN directive. The answer here is that you may want to collect artifacts as part of the build process, such as test reports, which are much easier to copy from a container that you spawn from a Docker image, than during the actual image-build process.

At this point, we have defined the first stage of our Docker build process, which will create a ready-to-test self-contained environment complete with the required operating-system dependencies, application dependencies and application source code. To build the image, you can run the docker build command, tagging the image with a name of todobackend-test:

```
> docker build --target test -t todobackend-test .
Sending build context to Docker daemon 311.8kB
Step 1/12 : FROM alpine AS test
 ---> 3fd9065eaf02
Step 2/12 : LABEL application=todobackend
 ---> Using cache
 ---> afdd1dee07d7
Step 3/12 : RUN apk add --no-cache bash git
 ---> Using cache
 ---> d9cd912ffa68
Step 4/12 : RUN apk add --no-cache gcc python3-dev libffi-dev musl-dev
linux-headers mariadb-dev
 ---> Using cache
 ---> 89113207b0b8
Step 5/12 : RUN pip3 install wheel
 ---> Using cache
 ---> a866d3b1f3e0
Step 6/12 : COPY /src/requirements* /build/
 ---> Using cache
 ---> efc869447227
Step 7/12 : WORKDIR /build
 ---> Using cache
 ---> 53ced29de259
Step 8/12 : RUN pip3 wheel -r requirements_test.txt --no-cache-dir --
no-input
 ---> Using cache
 ---> ba6d114360b9
Step 9/12 : RUN pip3 install -r requirements_test.txt -f /build --no-
index --no-cache-dir
```

```
---> Using cache
---> ba0ebdace940
Step 10/12 : COPY /src /app
---> Using cache
---> 9ae5c85bc7cb
Step 11/12 : WORKDIR /app
---> Using cache
---> aedd8073c9e6
Step 12/12 : CMD ["python3", "manage.py", "test", "--noinput", "--
settings=todobackend.settings_test"]
---> Using cache
---> 3ed637e47056
Successfully built 3ed637e47056
Successfully tagged todobackend-test:latest
```

In the preceding example, the --target flag allows you to target a specific stage in a multi-stage Dockerfile. Although we only have a single stage at the moment, this flag allows us to build only the test stage in the event we have multiple stages in the Dockerfile. By convention, the docker build command looks for a Dockerfile file in the directory where you run the command, and the period at the end of the command specifies the current directory (i.e. the application repository root in this example) as the build context that should be copied to the Docker Engine when building the image.

With the image built and tagged with an image name of todobackend in your local Docker Engine, you can now start a container from the image, which by default will run the python3 manage.py test command as specified by the CMD directive:

```
todobackend> docker run -it --rm todobackend-test
Creating test database for alias 'default'...

Ensure we can create a new todo item
- item has correct title
- item was created
- received 201 created status code
- received location header hyperlink

Ensure we can delete all todo items
- all items were deleted
- received 204 no content status code

Ensure we can delete a todo item
- received 204 no content status code
- the item was deleted

Ensure we can update an existing todo item using PATCH
```

```
- item was updated
- received 200 ok status code

Ensure we can update an existing todo item using PUT
- item was updated
- received 200 created status code
-------------------------------------------------------------------
XML: /app/unittests.xml
Name                                    Stmts   Miss   Cover
-------------------------------------------------------------------
todo/__init__.py                            0      0    100%
todo/admin.py                               1      1      0%
todo/migrations/0001_initial.py             5      0    100%
todo/migrations/__init__.py                 0      0    100%
todo/models.py                              6      6      0%
todo/serializers.py                         7      0    100%
todo/urls.py                                6      0    100%
todo/views.py                              17      0    100%
-------------------------------------------------------------------
TOTAL                                      42      7     83%
-------------------------------------------------------------------
Ran 12 tests in 0.433s

OK

Destroying test database for alias 'default'...
```

The -it flag specifies to run the container with an interactive terminal, and the --rm flag will automatically delete the container once it exits. Note that the tests all pass successfully, so we know the application built in the image is in a good state, at least in terms of the current tests that have been defined for the application.

Configuring the release stage

With the test stage in place, we now have an image that includes all application dependencies packaged in a format that can be installed without compilation or development dependencies, along with our application source code in a state that we can easily verify passes all tests.

The next stage that we need to configure is the release stage, which copies the application source code and various application dependencies built during the test stage to a new production-ready release image. Because the application dependencies are now available in a precompiled format, the release image does not require development dependencies or source code compilation tools, allowing us to create a smaller, leaner release image with a reduced attack surface.

Installing system dependencies

To get started creating the release stage, we can add a new FROM directive at the bottom of the Dockerfile, which Docker will treat as the start of a new stage:

```
# Test stage
FROM alpine AS test
LABEL application=todobackend
...
...
...
...
# Test entrypoint
CMD ["python3", "manage.py", "test", "--noinput", "--settings=todobackend.settings_test"]

# Release stage
FROM alpine
LABEL application=todobackend

# Install operating system dependencies
RUN apk add --no-cache python3 mariadb-client bash
```

In the preceding example, you can see the release image is based, once again, on the Alpine Linux image, which is an excellent choice for a release image given its very small footprint. You can see that we install fewer operating-system dependencies, which includes the following:

- python3: The Python 3 interpreter and runtime is required given the sample application is a Python application
- mariadb-client: Includes system libraries required to communicate with the MySQL application database
- bash: Useful for troubleshooting and executing entry point scripts, which we will discuss in later chapters.

Note that instead of installing the `python3-dev` and `mariadb-dev` packages, we only need to install the non development versions of these packages, given we compiled and built all application dependences as precompiled wheels in the test stage.

Creating an application user

The next step is to create an application user that our application will run as. By default, Docker containers run as root, which is fine for test and development purposes, however, in production, even with the isolation mechanisms that containers provide, it is still considered best practice to run your containers as a non-root user:

```
# Test stage
...
...
# Release stage
FROM alpine
LABEL application=todobackend

# Install operating system dependencies
RUN apk add --no-cache python3 mariadb-client bash

# Create app user
RUN addgroup -g 1000 app && \
    adduser -u 1000 -G app -D app
```

In the preceding example, we first create a group named `app` with a group ID of `1000`, and then create a user called `app` with a user ID of `1000`, which belongs to the `app` group.

Copying and installing application source code and dependencies

The final step is to copy the application source code and dependencies that were previously built in the test stage, install the dependencies into the release image, and then remove any temporary files used during this process. We also need to set the working directory to `/app`, and configure the container to run as the `app` user we created in the previous section:

```
# Test stage
...
```

```
...
# Release stage
FROM alpine
LABEL application=todobackend

# Install operating system dependencies
RUN apk add --no-cache python3 mariadb-client bash

# Create app user
RUN addgroup -g 1000 app && \
    adduser -u 1000 -G app -D app

# Copy and install application source and pre-built dependencies
COPY --from=test --chown=app:app /build /build
COPY --from=test --chown=app:app /app /app
RUN pip3 install -r /build/requirements.txt -f /build --no-index --no-
cache-dir
RUN rm -rf /build

# Set working directory and application user
WORKDIR /app
USER app
```

You first use the COPY directive with the --from flag, which tells Docker to look in the stage specified in the --from flag for the files to copy. Here we copy the /build and /app folders from the test stage image to folders with the same names in the release stage, and also configure the --chown flag to change the ownership of these copied folders to the application user. We then use the pip3 command to install only the core requirements specified in the requirements.txt file (you don't need the dependencies specified in requirements_test.txt for running the application), using the --no-index flag to disable the PIP connecting to the internet to download packages, and instead use the /build folder, as referenced by the -f flag, to find the dependencies previously built during the test stage and copied to this folder. We also specify the --no-cache-dir flag to avoid unnecessarily caching packages in the local filesystem, and remove the /build folder once everything is installed.

Finally, you set the working directory as /app, and configure the container to run as the app user by specifying the USER directive.

Building and running the release image

Now that we have completed the configuration of the release stage of the Dockerfile, it's time to build our new released image and verify we can actually run our application successfully.

To build the image, we can use the `docker build` command, and because the release stage is the last stage of the Dockerfile, you don't need to target a specific stage, as we did previously for the test stage:

```
> docker build -t todobackend-release .
Sending build context to Docker daemon 312.8kB
Step 1/22 : FROM alpine AS test
 ---> 3fd9065eaf02
...
...
Step 13/22 : FROM alpine
 ---> 3fd9065eaf02
Step 14/22 : LABEL application=todobackend
 ---> Using cache
 ---> afdd1dee07d7
Step 15/22 : RUN apk add --no-cache python3 mariadb-client bash
 ---> Using cache
 ---> dfe0b6487459
Step 16/22 : RUN addgroup -g 1000 app && adduser -u 1000 -G app -D app
 ---> Running in d75df9cadb1c
Removing intermediate container d75df9cadb1c
 ---> ac26efcbfea0
Step 17/22 : COPY --from=test --chown=app:app /build /build
 ---> 1f177a92e2c9
Step 18/22 : COPY --from=test --chown=app:app /app /app
 ---> ba8998a31f1d
Step 19/22 : RUN pip3 install -r /build/requirements.txt -f /build --no-index --no-cache-dir
 ---> Running in afc44357fae2
Looking in links: /build
Collecting Django==2.0 (from -r /build/requirements.txt (line 1))
Collecting django-cors-headers==2.1.0 (from -r /build/requirements.txt (line 2))
Collecting djangorestframework==3.7.3 (from -r /build/requirements.txt (line 3))
Collecting mysql-connector-python==8.0.11 (from -r /build/requirements.txt (line 4))
Collecting pytz==2017.3 (from -r /build/requirements.txt (line 5))
Collecting uwsgi (from -r /build/requirements.txt (line 6))
Collecting protobuf>=3.0.0 (from mysql-connector-python==8.0.11->-r /build/requirements.txt (line 4))
```

```
Requirement already satisfied: setuptools in /usr/lib/python3.6/site-
packages (from protobuf>=3.0.0->mysql-connector-python==8.0.11->-r
/build/requirements.txt (line 4)) (28.8.0)
Collecting six>=1.9 (from protobuf>=3.0.0->mysql-connector-
python==8.0.11->-r /build/requirements.txt (line 4))
Installing collected packages: pytz, Django, django-cors-headers,
djangorestframework, six, protobuf, mysql-connector-python, uwsgi
Successfully installed Django-2.0 django-cors-headers-2.1.0
djangorestframework-3.7.3 mysql-connector-python-8.0.11 protobuf-3.6.0
pytz-2017.3 six-1.11.0 uwsgi-2.0.17
Removing intermediate container afc44357fae2
 ---> ab2bcf89fe13
Step 20/22 : RUN rm -rf /build
 ---> Running in 8b8006ea8636
Removing intermediate container 8b8006ea8636
 ---> ae7f157d29d1
Step 21/22 : WORKDIR /app
Removing intermediate container fbd49835ca49
 ---> 55856af393f0
Step 22/22 : USER app
 ---> Running in d57b2cb9bb69
Removing intermediate container d57b2cb9bb69
 ---> 8170e923b09a
Successfully built 8170e923b09a
Successfully tagged todobackend-release:latest
```

At this point, we can run the Django application that is located in the release image, but you might be wondering exactly how that works. When we ran the `python3 manage.py runserver` command earlier, it spun up a local development web server which is not recommended for production-user cases, so we require an alternative web server to run our application in production.

You may have noticed earlier in the `requirements.txt` file a package called `uwsgi`—this is a very popular web server that can be used in production, and, conveniently for our use case, can be installed via PIP. This means that `uwsgi` is already available as a web server in our release container and can be used to serve the sample application:

```
> docker run -it --rm -p 8000:8000 todobackend-release uwsgi \
    --http=0.0.0.0:8000 --module=todobackend.wsgi --master
*** Starting uWSGI 2.0.17 (64bit) on [Tue Jul 3 11:44:44 2018] ***
compiled with version: 6.4.0 on 02 July 2018 14:34:31
os: Linux-4.9.93-linuxkit-aufs #1 SMP Wed Jun 6 16:55:56 UTC 2018
nodename: 5be4dd1ddab0
machine: x86_64
clock source: unix
detected number of CPU cores: 1
```

```
current working directory: /app
detected binary path: /usr/bin/uwsgi
!!! no internal routing support, rebuild with pcre support !!!
your memory page size is 4096 bytes
detected max file descriptor number: 1048576
lock engine: pthread robust mutexes
thunder lock: disabled (you can enable it with --thunder-lock)
uWSGI http bound on 0.0.0.0:8000 fd 4
uwsgi socket 0 bound to TCP address 127.0.0.1:35765 (port auto-
assigned) fd 3
Python version: 3.6.3 (default, Nov 21 2017, 14:55:19) [GCC 6.4.0]
*** Python threads support is disabled. You can enable it with --
enable-threads ***
Python main interpreter initialized at 0x55e9f66ebc80
your server socket listen backlog is limited to 100 connections
your mercy for graceful operations on workers is 60 seconds
mapped 145840 bytes (142 KB) for 1 cores
*** Operational MODE: single process ***
WSGI app 0 (mountpoint='') ready in 0 seconds on interpreter
0x55e9f66ebc80 pid: 1 (default app)
*** uWSGI is running in multiple interpreter mode ***
spawned uWSGI master process (pid: 1)
spawned uWSGI worker 1 (pid: 7, cores: 1)
spawned uWSGI http 1 (pid: 8)
```

We use the -p flag to map port 8000 on the container to port 8000 on your host, and execute the uwsgi command passing in various configuration flags that run the application on port 8000 and specify the todobackend.wsgi module as the application served by uwsgi.

> The Web Server Gateway Interface (WSGI) is a standard interface used by Python applications to interact with web servers. Every Django application includes a WSGI module for communicating with a web server, which can be accessed via <application-name>.wsgi.

At this point, you can browse to http://localhost:8000 and although the application does return a response, you will find that the web server and application are missing a bunch of static content:

```
Django REST framework

   • Api Root

   GET

          • json
          • api

   OPTIONS

   Api Root

   The default basic root view for DefaultRouter

   GET /

   HTTP 200 OK
   Allow: GET, HEAD, OPTIONS
   Content-Type: application/json
   Vary: Accept

   {
       "todos": "http://localhost:8000/todos"
   }
```

The problem here is that Django automatically generates static content when you run the Django development web server, however, when you run the application in production along with an external web server, you are responsible for generating static content yourself. We will learn how to do this later on in this chapter, however for now, you can verify the API works by using `curl`:

```
> curl -s localhost:8000/todos | jq
[
 {
 "url": "http://localhost:8000/todos/1",
 "title": "Walk the dog",
 "completed": false,
 "order": 1
 },
 {
 "url": "http://localhost:8000/todos/2",
 "title": "Wash the car",
 "completed": true,
 "order": 2
 }
]
```

One thing to note here is that the todobackend data has the same data that we loaded back in Chapter 1, despite us having built a Docker image from scratch. The problem here is that the SQLite database that was created back in Chapter 1 resides in the `src` folder, in a file called `db.sqlite3`. Clearly, we don't want to copy this file into our Docker image during the build process, and one way to achieve this is to create a `.dockerignore` file at the root of the repository:

```
# Ignore SQLite database files
**/*.sqlite3

# Ignore test output and private code coverage files
**/*.xml
**/.coverage

# Ignore compiled Python source files
**/*.pyc
**/pycache

# Ignore macOS directory metadata files
**/.DS_Store
```

The `.dockerignore` file works similarly to `.gitignore` in a Git repository, and is used to exclude files from the Docker build context. Because the `db.sqlite3` file is located in a subfolder, we use a wildcard globing pattern of `**` (note this is different from `.gitignore` behavior, which globs by default), which means we recursively exclude any file matching the wildcard pattern. We also exclude any test output files that have a `.xml` extension, code coverage files, the __pycache__ folder, and any compiled Python files with `.pyc` extensions, which are intended to be generated on the fly at runtime.

If you now rebuild the Docker image and start-up the the `uwsgi` web server locally on port `8000`, when you browse to the application (`http://localhost:8000`), you will get a different error:

```
OperationalError at /todos

no such table: todo_todoitem

        Request Method:  GET
          Request URL:   http://localhost:8000/todos
        Django Version:  2.0
       Exception Type:   OperationalError
       Exception Value:  no such table: todo_todoitem
    Exception Location:  /usr/lib/python3.6/site-packages/django/db/backends/sqlite3/base.py in execute, line 303
    Python Executable:   /usr/bin/uwsgi
       Python Version:   3.6.3
          Python Path:   ['.',
                          '',
                          '/usr/lib/python36.zip',
                          '/usr/lib/python3.6',
                          '/usr/lib/python3.6/lib-dynload',
                          '/usr/lib/python3.6/site-packages']
           Server time:  Wed, 4 Jul 2018 10:52:59 +0000
```

The problem now is that no database exists for the todobackend application, so the application is failing as it cannot locate the table that stores Todo items. To resolve this problem, we are now at the point where we need to integrate with an external database engine, meaning we need a solution to work with multiple containers locally.

Testing and building the application using Docker Compose

In the previous section, you used Docker commands to perform the following tasks:

- Build a test image
- Run tests
- Build a release image
- Run the application

Each time we ran a Docker command, we had to supply quite a bit of configuration, and trying to remember the various commands that you need to run is already starting to become difficult. In addition to this, we also discovered that to start the release image for the application, we need to have an operational external database. For local testing use cases, running an external database in another container is an excellent approach, but having to orchestrate this by running a series of Docker commands with lots of different input parameters very quickly becomes difficult to manage.

Docker Compose is a tool that allows you to orchestrate multi-container environments using a declarative approach, making it much easier to orchestrate complex workflows that may require multiple containers. By convention, Docker Compose looks for a file called `docker-compose.yml` in the current directory, so let's create this file at the root of the `todobackend` repository, alongside our `Dockerfile`:

```
version: '2.4'

services:
  test:
    build:
      context: .
      dockerfile: Dockerfile
      target: test
  release:
    build:
      context: .
      dockerfile: Dockerfile
```

> Docker Compose files are defined in a YAML format, which requires proper indentation to infer the correct relationships between parent, siblings and child objects or properties. If you have not worked with YAML before, you can check out the `Ansible YAML Syntax guide`, which provides a brief introduction to YAML formatting. You can also use an online YAML linting tool such as http://www.yamllint.com/ to check your YAML, or install YAML support in your favourite text editor.

We first specify the `version` property, which is mandatory and references the version of the Compose file format syntax that we are using. If you are using Docker for local development and build tasks, I recommending using version 2.x of the Compose file format, as it includes some useful features, such as health checks on dependent services, that we will learn how to use shortly. If you are using Docker Swarm to run your containers, then you should use version 3.x of the Compose file format, as this version supports a number of features that relate to managing and orchestrating Docker Swarm.

> If you choose to use version 3.x, your applications will need to be more robust in terms of dealing with scenarios such as your database not being available at application startup (see `https://docs.docker.com/compose/startup-order/`), which is a problem we will encounter later on in this chapter.

We next specify the `services` property, which defines one or more services that run in our Docker Compose environment. In the preceding example, we create two services that correspond to the test and release stages of our workflow, and then add a single `build` property to each service, which defines how we want to build the Docker image for each service. Note that the `build` properties are based upon the various flags that we passed to the `docker build` command—for example, when we build the test stage image, we set the build context to the local folder, used the local Dockerfile as the build specification for the image, and targeted only the test stage for building the image. Rather than imperatively specifying these settings each time we run a Docker command, we are declaratively defining the desired configuration for the build process, which is an important distinction.

Of course we need to run a command to actually build these services, which you can do by running the `docker-compose build` command at the root of the `todobackend` repository:

```
> docker-compose build test
Building test
Step 1/12 : FROM alpine AS test
 ---> 3fd9065eaf02
Step 2/12 : LABEL application=todobackend
 ---> Using cache
 ---> 23e0c2657711
...
...
Step 12/12 : CMD ["python3", "manage.py", "test", "--noinput", "--
settings=todobackend.settings_test"]
 ---> Running in 1ac9bded79bf
Removing intermediate container 1ac9bded79bf
```

```
---> f42d0d774c23

Successfully built f42d0d774c23
Successfully tagged todobackend_test:latest
```

You can see that running the `docker-compose build test` command achieves the equivalent of the earlier `docker build` command we ran, however, we don't need to pass any build options or configuration to the `docker-compose` command, given all of our specific settings are captured in the `docker-compose.yml` file.

If you now want to run tests from the newly built image, you can execute the `docker-compose run` command:

```
> docker-compose run test
Creating network "todobackend_default" with the default driver
nosetests --verbosity=2 --nologcapture --with-coverage --cover-
package=todo --with-spec --spec-color --with-xunit --xunit-
file=./unittests.xml --cover-xml --cover-xml-file=./coverage.xml
Creating test database for alias 'default'...

Ensure we can create a new todo item
- item has correct title
- item was created
- received 201 created status code
- received location header hyperlink
...
...
...
...
Ran 12 tests in 0.316s

OK

Destroying test database for alias 'default'...
```

You can also extend the Docker Compose file to add port mapping and command configurations to services, as demonstrated in the following example:

```
version: '2.4'

services:
  test:
    build:
      context: .
      dockerfile: Dockerfile
      target: test
  release:
```

```
build:
  context: .
  dockerfile: Dockerfile
ports:
  - 8000:8000
command:
  - uwsgi
  - --http=0.0.0.0:8000
  - --module=todobackend.wsgi
  - --master
```

Here we specify that when the release service is run, it should create a static port mapping from port 8000 on the host to port 8000 on the container, and pass the uwsgi command we used earlier to the release container. If you now run the release stage using the docker-compose up command, note that Docker Compose will automatically build the image for a service if it does not yet exist, and then start the service:

```
> docker-compose up release
Building release
Step 1/22 : FROM alpine AS test
 ---> 3fd9065eaf02
Step 2/22 : LABEL application=todobackend
 ---> Using cache
 ---> 23e0c2657711
...
...

Successfully built 5b20207e3e9c
Successfully tagged todobackend_release:latest
WARNING: Image for service release was built because it did not
already exist. To rebuild this image you must use `docker-compose
build` or `docker-compose up --build`.
Creating todobackend_release_1 ... done
Attaching to todobackend_release_1
...
...
release_1 | *** uWSGI is running in multiple interpreter mode ***
release_1 | spawned uWSGI master process (pid: 1)
release_1 | spawned uWSGI worker 1 (pid: 6, cores: 1)
release_1 | spawned uWSGI http 1 (pid: 7)
```

You typically use the `docker-compose up` command for long-running services, and the `docker-compose run` command to run short-lived tasks. You also cannot override the command arguments passed to `docker-compose up`, whereas you can pass command overrides to the `docker-compose run` command.

Adding a database service using Docker Compose

To resolve the application error we currently have when running the release image, we need to run a database that the application can connect to, and ensure the application is configured to use the database.

We can achieve this using Docker Compose by adding a new service called db, which is based on the official MySQL server container:

```
version: '2.4'

services:
  test:
    build:
      context: .
      dockerfile: Dockerfile
      target: test
  release:
    build:
      context: .
      dockerfile: Dockerfile
    ports:
      - 8000:8000
    command:
      - uwsgi
      - --http=0.0.0.0:8000
      - --module=todobackend.wsgi
      - --master
  db:
    image: mysql:5.7
    environment:
      MYSQL_DATABASE: todobackend
      MYSQL_USER: todo
      MYSQL_PASSWORD: password
      MYSQL_ROOT_PASSWORD: password
```

Note that you can specify an external image using the `image` property, and the environment settings configure the MySQL container with a database called todobackend, a username, password, and a root password.

Now, you might be wondering how we configure our application to use MySQL and the new `db` service. The todobackend application includes a settings file called `src/todobackend/settings_release.py`, which configures support for MySQL as the database backend:

```
# Import base settings
from .settings import *
import os

# Disable debug
DEBUG = True

# Set secret key
SECRET_KEY = os.environ.get('SECRET_KEY', SECRET_KEY)

# Must be explicitly specified when Debug is disabled
ALLOWED_HOSTS = os.environ.get('ALLOWED_HOSTS', '*').split(',')

# Database settings
DATABASES = {
    'default': {
        'ENGINE': 'mysql.connector.django',
        'NAME': os.environ.get('MYSQL_DATABASE','todobackend'),
        'USER': os.environ.get('MYSQL_USER','todo'),
        'PASSWORD': os.environ.get('MYSQL_PASSWORD','password'),
        'HOST': os.environ.get('MYSQL_HOST','localhost'),
        'PORT': os.environ.get('MYSQL_PORT','3306'),
    },
    'OPTIONS': {
      'init_command': "SET sql_mode='STRICT_TRANS_TABLES'"
    }
}

STATIC_ROOT = os.environ.get('STATIC_ROOT', '/public/static')
MEDIA_ROOT = os.environ.get('MEDIA_ROOT', '/public/media')
```

The DATABASES setting includes a configuration that specifies an engine
of mysql.connector.django, which provides support for MySQL overriding the
default SQLite driver, and you can see that the database name, username, and
password can be obtained from the environment via the os.environ.get call. Also
note that the STATIC_ROOT setting – this is where Django looks for static content,
such as HTML, CSS, JavaScript, and images—and by default, Django will look
in /public/static if this environment variable is not defined. As we saw earlier,
currently our web application is missing this content, so keep this setting in mind for
later when we fix the missing content issue.

Now that you understand how the todobackend application can be configured to
support a MySQL database, let's modify the Docker Compose file to use
the db service:

```
version: '2.4'

services:
  test:
    build:
      context: .
      dockerfile: Dockerfile
      target: test
  release:
    build:
      context: .
      dockerfile: Dockerfile
    ports:
      - 8000:8000
    depends_on:
      db:
        condition: service_healthy
    environment:
      DJANGO_SETTINGS_MODULE: todobackend.settings_release
      MYSQL_HOST: db
      MYSQL_USER: todo
      MYSQL_PASSWORD: password
    command:
      - uwsgi
      - --http=0.0.0.0:8000
      - --module=todobackend.wsgi
      - --master
  db:
    image: mysql:5.7
    healthcheck:
      test: mysqlshow -u $$MYSQL_USER -p$$MYSQL_PASSWORD
      interval: 3s
```

```
    retries: 10
  environment:
    MYSQL_DATABASE: todobackend
    MYSQL_USER: todo
    MYSQL_PASSWORD: password
    MYSQL_ROOT_PASSWORD: password
```

We first configure the `environment` property on the `release` service, which configures environment variables that will be passed to the container. Note that for Django applications, you can configure the `DJANGO_SETTINGS_MODULE` environment variable to specify which settings should be used, and this allows you to use the `settings_release` configuration that adds MySQL support. This configuration also allows you to use environment variables to specify the MySQL database settings, which must match the configuration of the `db` service.

We next configure the `depends_on` property for the `release` service, which describes any dependencies the service may have. Because the application must have a working connection to the database before it can start, we specify a condition of `service_healthy`, which means the `db` service must have passed a Docker health check before Docker Compose will attempt to start the `release` service. To configure the Docker health check on the `db` service, we configure the `healthcheck` property, which will configure Docker to run the command specified by the `test` parameter inside the `db` service container to verify service health, and to retry this command every 3 seconds up to 10 times until the `db` service is healthy. For this scenario, we use the `mysqlshow` command, which will only return a successful zero exit code once the MySQL process is accepting connections. Because Docker Compose will interpret single dollar signs as environment variables it should evaluate and replace in the Docker Compose file, we escape the environment variables referenced in the `test` command with double dollar signs to ensure that the command will literally execute `mysqlshow -u $MYSQL_USER -p$MYSQL_PASSWORD`.

At this point, we can test the changes by tearing down the current environment by pressing *Ctrl + C* in the terminal running the `release` service and typing the `docker-compose down -v` command (the `-v` flag will also delete any volumes created by Docker Compose), and then executing the `docker-compose up release` command:

```
> docker-compose down -v
Removing todobackend_release_1 ... done
Removing todobackend_test_run_1 ... done
Removing network todobackend_default
> docker-compose up release
Creating network "todobackend_default" with the default driver
```

```
Pulling db (mysql:5.7)...
5.7: Pulling from library/mysql
683abbb4ea60: Pull complete
0550d17aeefa: Pull complete
7e26605ddd77: Pull complete
9882737bd15f: Pull complete
999c06ab75f6: Pull complete
c71d695f9937: Pull complete
c38f847c1491: Pull complete
74f9c61f40bf: Pull complete
30b252a90a12: Pull complete
9f92ebb7da55: Pull complete
90303981d276: Pull complete
Digest:
sha256:1203dfba2600f140b74e375a354b1b801fa1b32d6f80fdee5f155d1e9f38c84
1
Status: Downloaded newer image for mysql:5.7
Creating todobackend_db_1 ... done
Creating todobackend_release_1 ... done
Attaching to todobackend_release_1
release_1 | *** Starting uWSGI 2.0.17 (64bit) on [Thu Jul 5 07:45:38
2018] ***
release_1 | compiled with version: 6.4.0 on 04 July 2018 11:33:09
release_1 | os: Linux-4.9.93-linuxkit-aufs #1 SMP Wed Jun 6 16:55:56
UTC 2018
...
...
*** uWSGI is running in multiple interpreter mode ***
release_1 | spawned uWSGI master process (pid: 1)
release_1 | spawned uWSGI worker 1 (pid: 7, cores: 1)
release_1 | spawned uWSGI http 1 (pid: 8)
```

In the preceding example, note that Docker Compose automatically pulls the MySQL 5.7 image as configured via the `image` property, and then starts the `db` service. This will take between 15-30 seconds, and during this period, Docker Compose is waiting for Docker to report back that the `db` service is healthy. Every 3 seconds Docker runs the `mysqlshow` command as configured in the health check, repeating this continuously until the command returns a successful exit code (that is, an exit code of 0), at which point Docker will mark the container as healthy. Only at this point will Docker Compose start up the `release` service, which should start successfully given the `db` service is fully operational.

If you browse once again to `http://localhost:8000/todos`, you will find that even though we added a `db` service and configure the release service to use this database, you are still receiving the `no such table` error you saw previously in the previous screenshot.

Running database migrations

We are still receiving errors about missing tables, and the reason is because we have not run database migrations to establish the required database schema the application expects to be in place. Recall that we used the `python3 manage.py migrate` command locally to run these migrations, so we need to do the same in our Docker environment.

If you tear down the environment again by pressing *Ctrl + C* and running `docker-compose down -v`, one approach would be to use the `docker-compose run` command:

```
> docker-compose down -v
...
...
> docker-compose run release python3 manage.py migrate
Creating network "todobackend_default" with the default driver
Creating todobackend_db_1 ... done
Traceback (most recent call last):
  File "/usr/lib/python3.6/site-packages/mysql/connector/network.py",
line 515, in open_connection
    self.sock.connect(sockaddr)
ConnectionRefusedError: [Errno 111] Connection refused
...
...
```

In the preceding example, note that when you use the `docker-compose run` command, Docker Compose does NOT support the health check behavior we previously observed when we ran `docker-compose up`. This means you can take one of two approaches:

- Ensure you run `docker-compose up release` first, and then run `docker-compose run python3 manage.py migrate` - this will leave your application in a state where it will raise errors until the migrations complete.
- Define the migrations as a separate service, called `migrate`, with a dependency on the `db` service, bring up the `migrate` service, which will execute the migrations and exit, and then bring up the application.

Although as you will soon see, option 1 is simpler, option 2 is more robust as it ensures the database is in the correct state before starting the application. Option 2 also aligns with the approach we will take later on in this book when we have to orchestrate running database migrations in AWS, so we will implement option 2 now.

The following example demonstrates the changes we need to make to run the migrations as a separate service:

```
version: '2.4'

services:
  test:
    build:
      context: .
      dockerfile: Dockerfile
      target: test
  release:
    build:
      context: .
      dockerfile: Dockerfile
    environment:
      DJANGO_SETTINGS_MODULE: todobackend.settings_release
      MYSQL_HOST: db
      MYSQL_USER: todo
      MYSQL_PASSWORD: password
  app:
    extends:
      service: release
    depends_on:
      db:
        condition: service_healthy
    ports:
      - 8000:8000
    command:
      - uwsgi
      - --http=0.0.0.0:8000
      - --module=todobackend.wsgi
      - --master
  migrate:
    extends:
      service: release
    depends_on:
      db:
        condition: service_healthy
    command:
      - python3
      - manage.py
      - migrate
      - --no-input
  db:
    image: mysql:5.7
    healthcheck:
      test: mysqlshow -u $$MYSQL_USER -p$$MYSQL_PASSWORD
```

```
            interval: 3s
            retries: 10
        environment:
          MYSQL_DATABASE: todobackend
          MYSQL_USER: todo
          MYSQL_PASSWORD: password
          MYSQL_ROOT_PASSWORD: password
```

In the preceding example, note that in addition to the `migrate` service, we have added a new service, called `app`, as well. The reason is that we want to extend migrate from the `release` service (as defined by the `extends` parameter) so it will inherit the release image and release service settings, however, one limitation of extending another service is that you cannot extend a service that has a `depends_on` statement. This requires us to use the `release` service as more of a base configuration that other services inherit from, and shift the `depends_on`, `ports`, and `command` parameters from the release service to the new `app` service.

With this configuration in place, we can tear down the environment and stand up our new environment, as demonstrated in the following example:

```
> docker-compose down -v
...
...
> docker-compose up migrate
Creating network "todobackend_default" with the default driver
Building migrate
Step 1/24 : FROM alpine AS test
 ---> 3fd9065eaf02
...
...
Successfully built 5b20207e3e9c
Successfully tagged todobackend_migrate:latest
WARNING: Image for service migrate was built because it did not
already exist. To rebuild this image you must use `docker-compose
build` or `docker-compose up --build`.
Creating todobackend_db_1 ... done
Creating todobackend_migrate_1 ... done
Attaching to todobackend_migrate_1
migrate_1 | Operations to perform:
migrate_1 | Apply all migrations: admin, auth, contenttypes, sessions,
todo
migrate_1 | Running migrations:
migrate_1 | Applying contenttypes.0001_initial... OK
migrate_1 | Applying auth.0001_initial... OK
migrate_1 | Applying admin.0001_initial... OK
```

```
migrate_1 | Applying admin.0002_logentry_remove_auto_add... OK
migrate_1 | Applying contenttypes.0002_remove_content_type_name... OK
migrate_1 | Applying auth.0002_alter_permission_name_max_length... OK
migrate_1 | Applying auth.0003_alter_user_email_max_length... OK
migrate_1 | Applying auth.0004_alter_user_username_opts... OK
migrate_1 | Applying auth.0005_alter_user_last_login_null... OK
migrate_1 | Applying auth.0006_require_contenttypes_0002... OK
migrate_1 | Applying auth.0007_alter_validators_add_error_messages...
OK
migrate_1 | Applying auth.0008_alter_user_username_max_length... OK
migrate_1 | Applying auth.0009_alter_user_last_name_max_length... OK
migrate_1 | Applying sessions.0001_initial... OK
migrate_1 | Applying todo.0001_initial... OK
todobackend_migrate_1 exited with code 0
> docker-compose up app
Building app
Step 1/24 : FROM alpine AS test
 ---> 3fd9065eaf02
...
...
Successfully built 5b20207e3e9c
Successfully tagged todobackend_app:latest
WARNING: Image for service app was built because it did not already
exist. To rebuild this image you must use `docker-compose build` or
`docker-compose up --build`.
todobackend_db_1 is up-to-date
Creating todobackend_app_1 ... done
Attaching to todobackend_app_1
app_1 | *** Starting uWSGI 2.0.17 (64bit) on [Thu Jul 5 11:21:00 2018]
***
app_1 | compiled with version: 6.4.0 on 04 July 2018 11:33:09
app_1 | os: Linux-4.9.93-linuxkit-aufs #1 SMP Wed Jun 6 16:55:56 UTC
2018
...
...
```

In the preceding example, note that Docker Compose builds new images for each service, however these builds complete very quickly as they are identical to the release image, given each service extends the release service. You will observe a 15-30 second delay when you bring up the migrate service waiting for the db service health check to pass, after which the migrations are run, creating the appropriate schema and tables the todobackend application expects. After starting the app service, you should be able to interact with the todobackend API without receiving any errors:

```
> curl -s localhost:8000/todos | jq
[]
```

Generating static web content

If you browse to `http://localhost:8000/todos`, although the application is no longer returning an error, the formatting of the web page still is broken. The problem here is that Django requires you to run a separate `manage.py` management task called `collectstatic`, which generates static content and places it at the location defined by the `STATIC_ROOT` setting. The release settings for our application define the file location for this as `/public/static`, so we somehow need to run the `collectstatic` task before our application starts up. Note that Django serves all static content from the `/static` URL path, for example `http://localhost:8000/static`.

There are a couple of approaches that you can use to solve this:

- Create an entrypoint script that runs on startup and executes the `collectstatic` task before starting the application.
- Create an external volume and run a container that executes the `collectstatic` task, generating static files in the volume. Then start the application with the external volume mounted, ensuring it has access to static content.

Both of these approaches are valid, however, to introduce the concept of Docker volumes and how you can use them in Docker Compose, we will adopt the second approach.

To define a volume in Docker Compose, you use the top-level `volumes` parameter, which allows you to define one or more named volumes:

```
version: '2.4'

volumes:
  public:
    driver: local

services:
  test:
    ...
    ...
  release:
    ...
    ...
  app:
    extends:
      service: release
```

```
        depends_on:
          db:
            condition: service_healthy
        volumes:
          - public:/public
        ports:
          - 8000:8000
        command:
          - uwsgi
          - --http=0.0.0.0:8000
          - --module=todobackend.wsgi
          - --master
          - --check-static=/public
    migrate:
      ...
      ...
    db:
      ...
      ...
```

In the preceding example, you add a volume called public and specify the driver as local, meaning it is a standard Docker volume. You then use the volumes parameter in the app service to mount the public volume to the /public path in the container, and finally you configure uwsgi to serve requests for static content from the /public path, which avoids expensive application calls to the Python interpreter to serve static content.

After tearing down your current Docker Compose environment, all that is required to generate static content is the docker-compose run command:

```
> docker-compose down -v
...
...
> docker-compose up migrate
...
...
> docker-compose run app python3 manage.py collectstatic --no-input
Starting todobackend_db_1 ... done
Copying '/usr/lib/python3.6/site-
packages/django/contrib/admin/static/admin/js/prepopulate.js'
Traceback (most recent call last):
  File "manage.py", line 15, in <module>
    execute_from_command_line(sys.argv)
  File "/usr/lib/python3.6/site-
packages/django/core/management/__init__.py", line 371, in
execute_from_command_line
    utility.execute()
```

```
...
...
PermissionError: [Errno 13] Permission denied: '/public/static'
```

In the preceding example, the `collectstatic` task fails because, by default, volumes are created as root and the container runs as the app user. To resolve this, we need to pre-create the `/public` folder in `Dockerfile` and make the app user the owner of this folder:

```
# Test stage
...
...
# Release stage
FROM alpine
LABEL application=todobackend
...
...
# Copy and install application source and pre-built dependencies
COPY --from=test --chown=app:app /build /build
COPY --from=test --chown=app:app /app /app
RUN pip3 install -r /build/requirements.txt -f /build --no-index --no-cache-dir
RUN rm -rf /build

# Create public volume
RUN mkdir /public
RUN chown app:app /public
VOLUME /public

# Set working directory and application user
WORKDIR /app
USER app
```

Note that the approach shown above only works for volumes that are created using Docker volume mounts, which is what Docker Compose uses if you don't specify a host path on your Docker Engine. If you specify a host path, the volume is bind mounted, which causes the volume to have root ownership by default, unless you pre-create the path on the host with the correct permissions. We will encounter this issue later on when we use the Elastic Container Service, so keep this in mind.

Because you modified the Dockerfile, you need to tell Docker Compose to rebuild all images, which you can do by using the `docker-compose build` command:

```
> docker-compose down -v
...
...
> docker-compose build
```

```
Building test
Step 1/13 : FROM alpine AS test
...
...
Building release
...
...
Building app
...
...
Building migrate
...
...
> docker-compose up migrate
...
...
> docker-compose run app python3 manage.py collectstatic --no-input
Copying '/usr/lib/python3.6/site-
packages/django/contrib/admin/static/admin/js/prepopulate.js'
Copying '/usr/lib/python3.6/site-
packages/django/contrib/admin/static/admin/js/SelectFilter2.js'
Copying '/usr/lib/python3.6/site-
packages/django/contrib/admin/static/admin/js/change_form.js'
Copying '/usr/lib/python3.6/site-
packages/django/contrib/admin/static/admin/js/inlines.min.js'
...
...
> docker-compose up app
```

If you now browse to `http://localhost:8000`, the correct static content should be displayed.

> When you define a local volume in Docker Compose, the volume will be automatically be destroyed when you run the `docker-compose down -v` command. If you wish to persist storage independently of Docker Compose, you can define an external volume, which you are then responsible for creating and destroying. See `https://docs.docker.com/compose/compose-file/compose-file-v2/#external` for more details.

Creating acceptance tests

Now that the application is configured correctly, the final task to configure for the release stage is to define acceptance tests that verify the application is working as expected. Acceptance tests are all about ensuring the release image you have built works in an environment that is as close to production as possible, within the constraints of a local Docker environment. At a minimum, if your application is a web application or API service, such as the todobackend application, you might just verify the application returns a valid HTTP response, or you might run through key features, such as creating an item, updating an item, and deleting an item.

For the todobackend application, we will create a few basic tests to demonstrate the approach, using a tool called BATS (Bash automated test system). BATS is great for system administrators who are more comfortable using bash, and leverages out-of-the-box tools to execute tests.

To get started with BATS, we need to create a test script, called `acceptance.bats`, in the `src` folder of the **todobackend** repository using the BATS syntax, which you can read more about at `https://github.com/sstephenson/bats`:

```
setup() {
  url=${APP_URL:-localhost:8000}
  item='{"title": "Wash the car", "order": 1}'
  location='Location: ([^[:space:]]*)'
  curl -X DELETE $url/todos
}

@test "todobackend root" {
  run curl -oI -s -w "%{http_code}" $APP_URL
  [ $status = 0 ]
  [ $output = 200 ]
}

@test "todo items returns empty list" {
  run jq '. | length' <(curl -s $url/todos)
  [ $output = 0 ]
}

@test "create todo item" {
  run curl -i -X POST -H "Content-Type: application/json" $url/todos -d "$item"
  [ $status = 0 ]
  [[ $output =~ "201 Created" ]] || false
  [[ $output =~ $location ]] || false
  [ $(curl ${BASH_REMATCH[1]} | jq '.title') = $(echo "$item" | jq '.title') ]
}
```

```
}

@test "delete todo item" {
  run curl -i -X POST -H "Content-Type: application/json" $url/todos -
d "$item"
  [ $status = 0 ]
  [[ $output =~ $location ]] || false
  run curl -i -X DELETE ${BASH_REMATCH[1]}
  [ $status = 0 ]
  [[ $output =~ "204 No Content" ]] || false
  run jq '. | length' <(curl -s $APP_URL/todos)
  [ $output = 0 ]
}
```

The BATS file includes a `setup()` function and a number of test cases, which are each prefixed with the `@test` marker. The `setup()` function is a special function that will be run before each test case, and is useful for defining common variables and ensuring the application state is consistent before each test. You can see that we set a few variables that are used in the various test cases:

- `url`: Defines the URL of the application under test. This is defined by the `APP_URL` environment variable, defaulting to `localhost:8000` if `APP_URL` is not defined.
- `item`: Defines a test Todo item in JSON format that is created via the Todos API during the tests.
- `location`: Defines a regular expression intended to locate and capture the value of the Location header that is returned in the HTTP response whenever you create a Todo item. The `([^[:space:]]*)` portion of the regular expression captures zero or more characters until whitespace (as designated by the `[:space:]` indicator) is encountered. For example, if the location header was `Location: http://localhost:8000/todos/53`, the regular expression will capture `http://localhost:8000/todos/53`.
- The `curl` command: The final setup task is to delete all todo items in the database, which you can do by sending a DELETE request to the `/todos` URL. This ensures the todobackend database is clean on each test run, reducing the likelihood of different tests introducing side effects that break other tests.

The BATS file next defines several test cases:

- `todobackend root`: This includes the `run` function, which runs the specified command and captures the exit code of the command in a variable called status, and the output of the command in a variable called `output`. For this scenario, the test runs a special configuration of the `curl` command that captures only the HTTP status code that is returned, and then verifies the `curl` command completed successfully by calling [`$status = 0`], and that the returned HTTP status code was a 200 code by calling [`$output = 200`]. These tests are regular shell *test expressions*, and are the equivalent of the canonical `assert` statement found in many programming languages.

- `todo items returns empty list`: This test case uses the `jq` command to pass the output calling the `/todos` path. Note that because you can't use pipes in conjunction with the special `run` function, I have used the bash process substitution syntax, `<(...)`, to make the output of the `curl` command appear as a file that is being read by the `jq` command.

- `create todo item`: This first creates a todo item, checks whether the returned exit code is zero, and then uses a *bash conditional expression* (as indicated by the `[[...]]` syntax) to verify that the output of the `curl` command includes `201 Created` in the HTTP response, which is a standard response when creating an item. When using the bash conditional expressions, it is important to note that BATS will not detect an error if the conditional expression fails, hence we use the `|| false` special syntax, which is only evaluated in the event the conditional expression fails and returns a non-zero response of `false`, causing the test case to fail if the test expression fails. The conditional expressions use the `=~` regular expression operator (this operator is not available in conditional expressions, hence our use of bash test expressions), with the second conditional expression evaluating the `location` regular expression defined in the setup function. The final command uses the special `BASH_REMATCH` variable that includes the results of the most recent conditional expression evaluation, which in this case is the URL matched in the Location header. This allows us to capture the returned location when we create a Todo item, and verify that the created item matches the item that we posted.

- `delete todo item`: This creates a Todo item, captures the location returned for the item, deletes the item, and then verifies that the item was in fact deleted by verifying the number of Todo items in the database is zero after the deletion. Recall that the setup function runs before each test case, which clears all Todo items, hence at the beginning of this test case the Todo item count will always be zero, and the action of creating and then deleting an item should always return the count to zero. The various commands used in this test case are based upon the concepts introduced in the `create todo item` test case, hence I won't describe each command in detail.

Now that we have define a suite of acceptance tests, it's time to modify the Docker environment to support the execution of these tests once the application is started successfully.

We first need to add the `curl`, `bats`, and `jq` packages to the `Dockerfile` at the root of the todobackend repository:

```
# Test stage
FROM alpine AS test
LABEL application=todobackend
...
...
# Release stage
FROM alpine
LABEL application=todobackend

# Install dependencies
RUN apk add --no-cache python3 mariadb-client bash curl bats jq
...
...
```

Next we need to add a new service called `acceptance` to the `docker-compose.yml` file, which will wait until the `app` service is healthy and then run acceptance tests:

```
version: '2.4'

volumes:
  public:
    driver: local

services:
  test:
    ...
    ...
  release:
```

```
    ...
    ...
app:
  extends:
    service: release
  depends_on:
    db:
      condition: service_healthy
  volumes:
    - public:/public
  healthcheck:
    test: curl -fs localhost:8000
    interval: 3s
    retries: 10
  ports:
    - 8000:8000
  command:
    - uwsgi
    - --http=0.0.0.0:8000
    - --module=todobackend.wsgi
    - --master
    - --check-static=/public
acceptance:
  extends:
    service: release
  depends_on:
    app:
      condition: service_healthy
  environment:
    APP_URL: http://app:8000
  command:
    - bats
    - acceptance.bats
migrate:
  ...
  ...
db:
  ...
  ...
```

We first add a `healthcheck` property to the `app` service, which uses the `curl` utility
to check connectivity to the local web server endpoint. We then define the acceptance
service, which we extend from the `release` image and configure with
the `APP_URL` environment variable, which configures the correct URL the acceptance
tests should be executed against, whilst the `command` and `depends_on` properties are
used to run the acceptance tests once the `app` service is healthy.

With this configuration in place, you now need to tear down the current environment, rebuild all images, and perform the various steps to get the application up and running, except when you get to the point where you are about to run the docker-compose up app command, you should now run the docker-compose up acceptance command, as this will automatically start the app service in the background:

```
> docker-compose down -v
...
...
> docker-compose build
...
...
> docker-compose up migrate
...
...
> docker-compose run app python3 manage.py collectstatic --no-input
...
...
> docker-compose up acceptance
todobackend_db_1 is up-to-date
Creating todobackend_app_1 ... done
Creating todobackend_acceptance_1 ... done
Attaching to todobackend_acceptance_1
acceptance_1 | Processing secrets []...
acceptance_1 | 1..4
acceptance_1 | ok 1 todobackend root
acceptance_1 | ok 2 todo items returns empty list
acceptance_1 | ok 3 create todo item
acceptance_1 | ok 4 delete todo item
todobackend_acceptance_1 exited with code 0
```

As you can see, all tests pass successfully, as indicated by the ok status for each test.

Automating the workflow

At this point, you have managed to successfully configure Docker Compose to build, test, and create a working local environment for the sample application, complete with MySQL database integration and acceptance tests. You can now stand up this environment with a handful of commands, but even though using Docker Compose has significantly simplified the commands you need to run, it is still difficult to remember which commands to use and in which order. Ideally we want a single command to run the complete workflow, and this is where a tool such as GNU Make is very useful.

Make has been around a long time, and is still considered the build tool of choice for many C and C++ applications. Task automation is a key feature of Make, and the ability to define tasks or targets in a simple format that can be invoked with a single command has made Make a popular automation tool, particularly when dealing with Docker containers.

By convention make looks for a file, called Makefile, in the current working directory, and you can create a very simple Makefile, as demonstrated here:

```
hello:
    @ echo "Hello World"
    echo "How are you?"
```

In the preceding example, you create a *target* called `hello` with two shell commands, which you can execute by running `make <target>`, or `make hello` in this example. Each target can include one or more commands, which are executed in the sequence provided.

One important point to note is that make expects tabs (not spaces) to be used when you define the various commands for a given target, so if you receive a missing separator error, such as `Makefile:2: *** missing separator. Stop.`, check that you have used tabs to indent each command.

```
> make hello
Hello World
echo "How are you?"
How are you?
```

In the preceding example, you can see that the output of the each command is displayed on screen. Note that the special @ character on the first command suppresses echoing each command as it is run.

Any decent modern text editor, such as Sublime Text or Visual Studio Code, should automatically take care of tabs for you in Makefiles.

One important piece of housekeeping you should perform in your Makefiles when using them for task automation is to configure the somewhat amusingly-named special target called `.PHONY`, with the names of each target that you will be executing:

```
.PHONY: hello

hello:
    @ echo "Hello World"
    echo "How are you?"
```

Because `make` is really a build tool for compiling source code files, the `.PHONY` target tells make that if it sees a file named `hello`, it should still run the target. If you didn't specify `.PHONY` and there was a file called `hello` in the local directory, make would exit stating that the `hello` file has already been built. This clearly doesn't make much sense when you are using make to automate tasks, so you should always use the `.PHONY` target to avoid any strange surprises.

Automating the test stage

Now that you have been introduced to make, let's modify our Makefile to do something that is actually useful, and execute the various actions performed during the test stage. Recall that the test stage involves building the first stage of the Dockerfile as a service, called `test`, and then running the `test` service, which by default will run the `python3 manage.py test` command, executing application unit tests:

```
.PHONY: test

test:
    docker-compose build --pull release
    docker-compose build
    docker-compose run test
```

Note that rather than building the `test` service in the Docker Compose file, we actually build the release service and specify the `--pull` flag, which ensures that Docker will always check whether there are any newer releases of the Docker image referenced in the `FROM` directive. We build the `release` service this way because we only want to build the entire `Dockerfile` once, rather than rebuild the `Dockerfile` on each stage execution.

This guards against the unlikely, yet still possible, scenario where you could pull a newer base image if rebuilding during the release stage, which may result in a different runtime environment to what you tested in the test stage. We also run the docker-compose build command immediately afterwards, which ensures all services are built before we run tests. Because we built the entire `Dockerfile` in the previous command, this will ensure any cached images for other services are updated to the newest image build.

Automating the release stage

After completing the test stage, we next run the release stage, which requires us to perform the following actions:

- Run database migrations
- Collect static files
- Start the application
- Run acceptance tests

The following demonstrates creating a target, called `release`, in the Makefile:

```
.PHONY: test release

test:
    docker-compose build --pull release
    docker-compose build
    docker-compose run test

release:
    docker-compose up --abort-on-container-exit migrate
    docker-compose run app python3 manage.py collectstatic --no-input
    docker-compose up --abort-on-container-exit acceptance
```

Notice that we execute each of the required commands with one minor variation, which is to add the `--abort-on-container-exit` command to each of the `docker-compose up` commands. By default, the `docker-compose up` command will not return a non-zero exit code should any of the container(s) started by the command fail. This flag allows you to override this and specify should any service fail that was started by the `docker-compose up` command, then Docker Compose should exit with an error. Setting this flag is important if you want your make commands to fail whenever there is an error.

Refining the workflow

There's a few more minor enhancements we can make to the workflow that will ensure we have a robust, consistent, and portable mechanism for testing and building our application.

Cleaning up the Docker environment

Throughout this chapter, we have been cleaning up our environment by running the `docker-compose down` command, which stops and destroys any containers associated with the todobackend Docker Compose environment.

One other aspect of housekeeping that you need to be aware of when building Docker images is the concept of orphaned or dangling images, which are images that have been superseded by a newer build. You can get a sense of this by running the `docker images` command, and I have indicated which images are dangling in bold:

```
> docker images
REPOSITORY            TAG         IMAGE ID        CREATED
SIZE
todobackend_app       latest      ca3e62e168f2    13 minutes ago
137MB
todobackend_migrate   latest      ca3e62e168f2    13 minutes ago
137MB
todobackend_release   latest      ca3e62e168f2    13 minutes ago
137MB
<none>                <none>      03cc5d44bd7d    14 minutes ago
253MB
<none>                <none>      e88666a35577    22 minutes ago
137MB
<none>                <none>      8909f9001297    23 minutes ago
253MB
<none>                <none>      3d6f9a5c9322    2 hours ago
137MB
todobackend_test      latest      60b3a71946cc    2 hours ago
253MB
<none>                <none>      53d19a2de60d    9 hours ago
136MB
<none>                <none>      54f0fb70b9d0    15 hours ago
135MB
alpine                latest      11cd0b38bc3c    23 hours ago
4.41MB
```

Note that each highlighted image has no repository and no tag, hence why they are referred to as orphaned or dangling. These dangling images are of no use and take up resources and storage, so it is ideal that you clean up these images regularly, to ensure the performance of your Docker environment. Back in our Dockerfile, we added the LABEL directive to each stage, which allows for easy identification of images that relate to our todobackend application.

We can leverage these labels to target dangling images built for the todobackend application, so let's add a new target, called clean, to our Makefile, which brings down the Docker Compose environment and removes dangling images:

```
.PHONY: test release clean

test:
    docker-compose build --pull release
    docker-compose build
    docker-compose run test

release:
    docker-compose up --abort-on-container-exit migrate
    docker-compose run app python3 manage.py collectstatic --no-input
    docker-compose up --abort-on-container-exit acceptance

clean:
    docker-compose down -v
    docker images -q -f dangling=true -f label=application=todobackend
| xargs -I ARGS docker rmi -f --no-prune ARGS
```

We use the -q flag to only print out image IDs, and then use the -f flag to add filters that specify to only show dangling images that have a label of application=todobackend. We then pipe the output of this command to the xargs command, which captures the list of filtered images in the ARGS parameter and passes ARGS to the docker rmi -f --no-prune command, removing the images forcibly as specified by the -f flag with the --no-prune flag ensuring any untagged images that include layers from current tagged images are not removed. We use xargs here because it deals with the list of images intelligently – for example, if there are no images to delete, then xargs exits silently without an error.

The following demonstrates the output of running the make clean command:

```
> make test
. . .
. . .
> make release
. . .
```

```
...
> make clean
docker-compose down -v
Stopping todobackend_app_1 ... done
Stopping todobackend_db_1 ... done
Removing todobackend_app_run_2 ... done
Removing todobackend_app_1 ... done
Removing todobackend_app_run_1 ... done
Removing todobackend_migrate_1 ... done
Removing todobackend_db_1 ... done
Removing todobackend_test_run_1 ... done
Removing network todobackend_default
Removing volume todobackend_public
docker images -q -f dangling=true -f label=application=todobackend |
xargs -I ARGS docker rmi -f --no-prune ARGS
Deleted:
sha256:03cc5d44bd7dec8d535c083dd5a8e4c177f113bc49f6a97d09f7a1deb64b772
8
Deleted:
sha256:6448ea330f415f773fc4cd5fe35862678ac0e35a1bf24f3780393eb73637f76
5
Deleted:
sha256:baefcaca3929d6fc419eab06237abfb6d9ba9a1ba8d5623040ea4f49b2cc22d
4
Deleted:
sha256:b1dca5a87173bfa6a2c0c339cdeea6287e4207f34869a2da080dcef28cabcf6
f
...
...
```

One thing you may notice when running the `make clean` command is that stopping the todobackend app service takes some time, in fact, it takes around 10 seconds to stop. This is because Docker first sends a SIGTERM signal to the container when stopping a container, which signals to the container that it is about to be terminated. By default, if the container does not exit within 10 seconds, Docker sends a SIGKILL signal, which forcibly terminates the container.

The problem here is that the `uwsgi` process running in our app container ignores SIGTERM signals by default, so we need to add the `--die-on-term` flag in the Docker Compose file that configures `uwsgi` to shut down if it receives a SIGTERM signal, ensuring it will be able to shut down gracefully and in a timely fashion:

```yaml
version: '2.4'

volumes:
  public:
    driver: local

services:
  test:
    ...
    ...
  release:
    ...
    ...
  app:
    extends:
      service: release
    depends_on:
      db:
        condition: service_healthy
    volumes:
      - public:/public
    healthcheck:
      test: curl -fs localhost:8000
      interval: 3s
      retries: 10
    ports:
      - 8000:8000
    command:
      - uwsgi
      - --http=0.0.0.0:8000
      - --module=todobackend.wsgi
      - --master
      - --check-static=/public
      - --die-on-term
      - --processes=4
      - --threads=2
  acceptance:
    ...
    ...
  migrate:
    ...
    ...
```

```
db:
   ...
   ...
```

In the preceding example, I have also added the `--processes` and `--threads` flags, which enable concurrent processing. You can read about these and more configuration options at `https://uwsgi-docs.readthedocs.io/en/latest/WSGIquickstart.html#adding-concurrency-and-monitoring`.

Using dynamic port mapping

Currently, the release stage workflow runs the application using a static port-mapping, where port 8000 on the app service container is mapped to port `8000` on your Docker Engine. Although this will typically work fine when running locally (unless you have some other application that is using port 8000), this may cause problems when it comes to running the release-stage workflow on a remote continuous-delivery build service, which may be running multiple builds for many different applications.

A better approach is to use dynamic port-mapping, which maps the `app` service container port to a dynamic port on your Docker Engine that is currently not in use. The port is picked from what is referred to as the *ephemeral port range*, which is a port range reserved for dynamic use by applications.

To configure dynamic port-mapping, you need to change the port-mapping in the `docker-compose.yml` file for the `app` service:

```
version: '2.4'

volumes:
  public:
    driver: local

services:
  test:
    ...
    ...
  release:
    ...
    ...
  app:
    extends:
      service: release
    depends_on:
```

```
        db:
            condition: service_healthy
        volumes:
          - public:/public
        healthcheck:
            test: curl -fs localhost:8000
            interval: 3s
            retries: 10
        ports:
          - 8000
        command:
          - uwsgi
          - --http=0.0.0.0:8000
          - --module=todobackend.wsgi
          - --master
          - --check-static=/public
          - --die-on-term
          - --processes=4
          - --threads=2
    acceptance:
        ...
        ...
    migrate:
        ...
        ...
    db:
        ...
        ...
```

In the preceding example, we simply change the port-mapping from a static mapping of `8000:8000` to `8000`, which enables dynamic port-mapping. With this configuration in place, one problem is that you don't know in advance what port is going to be assigned, however, you can use the `docker-compose port <service> <container-port>` command to determine the current dynamic port-mapping for a given service on a given container port:

```
> docker-compose port app 8000
0.0.0.0:32768
```

Of course, rather than manually type this command each time, we can incorporate it into our automation workflow:

```
.PHONY: test release clean

test:
    docker-compose build --pull release
    docker-compose build
```

```
        docker-compose run test

release:
    docker-compose up --exit-code-from migrate migrate
    docker-compose run app python3 manage.py collectstatic --no-input
    docker-compose up --exit-code-from acceptance acceptance
    @ echo App running at http://$$(docker-compose port app 8000 | sed
s/0.0.0.0/localhost/g)

clean:
    docker-compose down -v
    docker images -q -f dangling=true -f label=application=todobackend
| xargs -I ARGS docker rmi -f --no-prune ARGS
```

In the preceding example, we use a command substitution to obtain the current port-mapping and pipe the output to a `sed` expression that replaces `0.0.0.0` with `localhost`. Note that because GNU Make interprets the dollar sign symbol as a Make variable reference, you are required to double-escape dollar signs (`$$`) if you want a single dollar sign evaluated by the shell command that will be executed.

With this in place, the output of the `make release` command will now complete with the following:

```
> make release
...
...
docker-compose run app bats acceptance.bats
Starting todobackend_db_1 ... done
1..4
ok 1 todobackend root
ok 2 todo items returns empty list
ok 3 create todo item
ok 4 delete todo item
App running at http://localhost:32771
```

Adding a version target

Versioning your applications is critical, particularly when building Docker images and you want to distinguish between various images. Later on, when we publish our Docker images, we will need to include a version tag on each published image, and a simple convention for versioning is to use the Git commit hash of the current commit in your application repository.

The following demonstrates how you can capture this in a Make variable and display the current version:

```
.PHONY: test release clean version

export APP_VERSION ?= $(shell git rev-parse --short HEAD)

version:
    @ echo '{"Version": "$(APP_VERSION)"}'

test:
    docker-compose build --pull release
    docker-compose build
    docker-compose run test

release:
    docker-compose up --abort-on-container-exit migrate
    docker-compose run app python3 manage.py collectstatic --no-input
    docker-compose up --abort-on-container-exit acceptance
    @ echo App running at http://$$(docker-compose port app 8000 | sed s/0.0.0.0/localhost/g)

clean:
    docker-compose down -v
    docker images -q -f dangling=true -f label=application=todobackend | xargs -I ARGS docker rmi -f --no-prune ARGS
```

We first declare a variable called APP_VERSION and prefix this with the export keyword, which means the variable will be available in the environment for each target. We then use a Make function called shell to execute the git rev-parse --short HEAD command, which returns the seven-character short hash of the current commit. Finally, we add a new target, called version, that simply prints the version in a JSON format to the terminal, which will be useful later in this book when we automate the continuous delivery of our application. Note that make uses the dollar sign to reference variables and also to execute Make functions, which you can read more about at https://www.gnu.org/software/make/manual/html_node/Functions.html.

> If you just run the make command without specifying a target, make will execute the first target in the Makefile. This means, for our scenario, just running make will output the current version.

The following demonstrates running the `make version` command:

```
> make version
{"Version": "5cd83c0"}
```

Testing the end-to-end workflow

At this point, all of the pieces of our local Docker workflow are in place, and now is a good time to review the workflow and verify everything is working.

The core workflow now consists of the following tasks:

- Run the test stage – `make test`
- Run the release stage – `make release`
- Clean up – `make clean`

I will leave this up to you to test, but I encourage you to get comfortable with the workflow and ensure everything completes without error. After running `make release`, verify you can navigate to the application, the application displays HTML content correctly, and that you can perform create, read, update, and delete operations.

Once you are satisfied everything is working as expected, ensure you have committed and pushed your changes to the GitHub repository you forked in the previous chapter.

Summary

In this chapter, you implemented a Docker workflow that tests, builds, and packages your application into a Docker image that is ready to publish and deploy to production. You learned how you can build your application in two stages using Docker multi-stage builds—the test stage uses a development environment complete with development libraries and source compilation tools that allows you to build and test your application and its dependencies in precompiled packages, while the release stage takes those built packages and installs them into a production-ready operating environment, free of development libraries and other tools, significantly reducing the attack surface of your application.

You learned how you to use Docker Compose to help simplify the various commands and actions you need to perform during the test and release stages, creating a `docker-compose.yml` file with a number of services, each defined in a declarative, easy-to-understand format. You learned how to replicate a number of deployment tasks required to get your application up and running, such as running database migrations, collecting static files, and ensuring the application database was healthy before you attempted to run your application. Being able to perform each of these tasks in a local environment provides you with the confidence and understanding of how these tasks will work in your actual production environments, and gives you early warning should any of your application or configuration changes break these processes locally. After starting your application in the correct state and connected to the application database, you learned how you can run acceptance tests from the point of view of an external client, which gives you great confidence that your image is working as expected, and early warning when these acceptance tests fail as part of the ongoing development of your application.

Finally, you learned how to bring all of this together in a fully automated workflow using GNU Make, which provides you with simple high-level commands that you can use to execute the workflow. You now have the ability to execute the test stage by simply running `make test`, run the release stage by running `make release`, and clean up your environment using `make clean`. This makes it very easy to run the workflow, and later in this book, will simplify the configuration of continuous-delivery build systems that we will be using to automatically test, build, and publish your Docker applications.

In coming chapters, you will learn how to actually publish the Docker release image you created in this chapter, but before you can do this, you need to establish an AWS account, configure access to your account, and install tools that support interacting with AWS, which will be the focus of the next chapter.

Questions

1. True/false: You use the `FROM` and `TO` directives to define a multi-stage Dockerfile.
2. True/false: The `docker` command `--rm` flag automatically deletes a container after it has exited.

3. True/false: When you run your workflow, you should only build application artifacts once.

4. True/false: When running the `docker-compose run` command with no additional flags, if the targeted services started fails with an error, docker-compose will exit with a non-zero code.

5. True/false: When running the `docker-compose up` command with no additional flags, if one of the services started fails with an error, docker-compose will exit with a non-zero code.

6. True/false: You should configure a Docker Compose version of 3.x if you want to use Docker Swarm.

7. You configure the service_healthy condition on a dependency of a service in your Docker file. Then you run the service using the `docker-compose run` command; the dependency is started, however, Docker Compose does not wait until the dependency is healthy and starts the service immediately, causing a failure. How could you resolve this?

8. You create a service in Docker Compose with a port-mapping of `8000:8000`. When you attempt to start this service, an error is raised indicating the port is in use. How could you resolve this and ensure it never happens again?

9. After creating a Makefile, you receive an error about a missing separator when attempting to run a target. What is the most likely cause of this error?

10. Which GNU Make function allows you to capture the output of a shell command?

11. You define a target called test in a Makefile, however when you run `make test`, you get a response saying there is nothing to do. How could you resolve this?

12. Which properties must be configured in a Docker Compose service definition to use the `docker-compose push` command?

Further reading

You can check the following links for more information about the topics covered in this chapter:

- Docker Command-Line Reference: `https://docs.docker.com/engine/reference/commandline/cli/`
- Docker multi-stage builds: `https://docs.docker.com/develop/develop-images/multistage-build/`
- Docker Compose Version 2 Specification: `https://docs.docker.com/compose/compose-file/compose-file-v2/`
- Docker Compose Command-Line Reference: `https://docs.docker.com/compose/reference/`
- Docker Compose start order: `https://docs.docker.com/compose/startup-order/`
- uWSGI Quickstart for Python Applications: `http://uwsgi-docs.readthedocs.io/en/latest/WSGIquickstart.html`
- Bash-Automated Test System: `https://github.com/sstephenson/bats`
- GNU Make Phony Targets: `https://www.gnu.org/software/make/manual/html_node/Phony-Targets.html`
- GNU Make Functions: `https://www.gnu.org/software/make/manual/html_node/Functions.html#Functions`

3
Getting Started with AWS

In the previous chapter, we discussed the various options you have for deploying your container applications to AWS, and it's now time to start implementing practical solutions using the Elastic Container Service (ECS), Fargate, Elastic Kubernetes Service (EKS), Elastic Beanstalk, and Docker Swarm. Before we can cover all of this exciting material, you need to establish an AWS account, understand how to set up access for your account, and ensure you have a solid grasp of the various tools we will use throughout this book to interact with AWS.

Getting started with AWS is very easy—AWS offers a free tier suite of services that enable you to test and try out a number of AWS services at no cost for 12 months, or, in some cases, indefinitely. Of course, there are limitations imposed that ensure you can't set up your own Bitcoin mining services for free, but for the most part, you can leverage these free tier services to test a wide number of scenarios, including almost all of the material we will work through in this book. So, this chapter will start off with establishing a new AWS account, which will require you to have a valid credit card, just in case you do follow through on that great new Bitcoin mining venture.

Once you have an account in place, the next step is to set up administrative access to your account. By default, all AWS accounts are created with a root user that has the highest level of account privileges, however AWS do not recommend using the root account for day-to-day administrative use. Therefore, we will configure the AWS Identity Access and Management (IAM) service, creating IAM users and groups, and learning how to implement enhanced security using multi-factor authentication (MFA).

With access to your AWS account established, we will then focus on the various tools that you can use to interact with AWS, including the AWS console that provides a web-based management interface that you access with your web browser, and the AWS CLI tool for interacting with AWS via the command line.

Finally, we will introduce a management service and toolset called AWS CloudFormation, which provides an infrastructure as code approach for defining your AWS infrastructure and services. CloudFormation allows you to define templates that enable you to build complete environments with the single click of a button, and do so in a repeatable and consistent fashion. We will be using CloudFormation extensively throughout this book, as in practice, most organizations that are deploying Docker-based applications are adopting infrastructure as code tooling such as CloudFormation, Ansible, or Terraform to automate the deployment of their Docker applications and supporting infrastructure. You will learn how to create a simple CloudFormation template and then deploy that template using both the AWS console and AWS CLI.

In this chapter, the following topics will be covered:

- Setting up an AWS account
- Logging in as the root account
- Creating IAM users, groups, and roles
- Creating an EC2 key pair
- Installing the AWS CLI
- Configuring credentials and profiles in the AWS CLI
- Interacting with AWS using the AWS CLI
- Introducing AWS CloudFormation
- Defining a simple AWS CloudFormation template
- Deploying an AWS CloudFormation stack
- Deleting an AWS CloudFormation stack

Technical requirements

The technical requirements for this chapter are as follows:

- Prerequisite software installed as per the instructions in Chapter 1, *Container and Docker Fundamentals*
- A valid credit card is required to create a free AWS account in this chapter

The following GitHub URL contains the code samples that are used in this chapter: `https://github.com/docker-in-aws/docker-in-aws/tree/master/ch3`.

Check out the following video to see the Code in Action:
`http://bit.ly/2N1nzJc`

Setting up an AWS account

The first step on your AWS journey is to establish an AWS account, which is a foundational building block of AWS that defines a security and administrative context for managing your AWS services and resources that you consume. To encourage adoption of AWS and ensure that first time users have an opportunity to try out AWS for free, AWS offers a free tier that grants you free access to some AWS services (with some limitations around usage). You can find out more about the free tier and what services are offered at `https://aws.amazon.com/free/`. Make sure you have a good understanding of what you can and can't use for free to avoid an unnecessary bill shock.

In this book, we will make use of a number of free tier services with the following monthly usage limits:

Service	Limit
EC2	750 hours of Linux t2.micro (Single vCPU, 1 GB Memory) instance
Elastic Block Storage	30 GB block-level storage (SSD or traditional spinning disk)
RDS	750 hours of db.t2.micro (Single vCPU, 1 GB Memory) MySQL instance
Elastic Container Registry	500 MB of storage
Elastic Load Balancing	750 hours of classic or application load balancers
S3	5 GB of S3 storage
Lambda	1,000,000 requests
CloudWatch	10 custom metrics
SNS	1,000,000 publications
CodeBuild	100 build minutes
CodePipeline	1 active pipeline
X-Ray	100,000 traces
Key Management Service	20,000 requests
Secrets Manager	30-day free trial period, then $0.40 per secret/month

As you can see, we will be covering a number of AWS services in this book and almost all of them are free, assuming you honor the usage limits described in the preceding table. In fact, the only service that we will use in this book that is not free is the AWS Fargate service, so bear this in mind when you read through the Fargate chapter and try to minimize your usage if you are worried about the cost of this.

To sign up for free tier access, click on the **Create a Free Account** button at `https://aws.amazon.com/free/`:

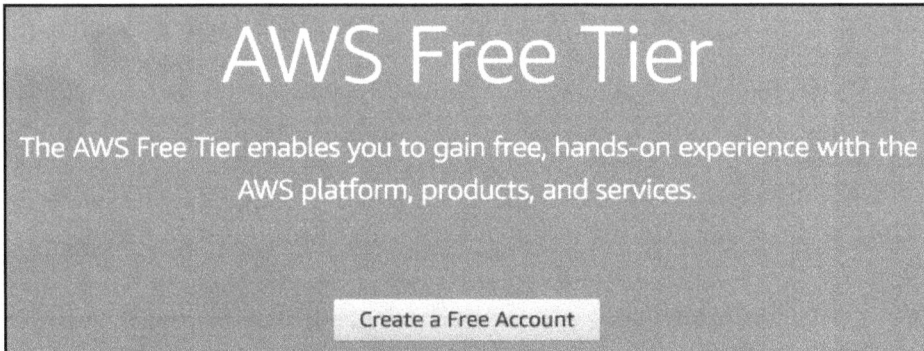

Creating a free account

You will be prompted to enter an email address, password, and AWS account name. It's important to understand that the email address and password you enter here is referred to as the root account for your AWS account, which has the highest level of access to your account. For the AWS account name, you can enter any name you like, however it must be unique across all of the other AWS accounts, so at the very least you won't be able to use the account name I chose, which is `docker-in-aws`. This account name is used when you sign in and is much easier to remember than your AWS account number, which is a 12-digit number.

The rest of the sign-up process is self-explanatory, so I won't bore you with the details here, but understand that you will be required to provide credit card details and will be responsible for any charges over and above the free tier usage limits. You will also be required to verify the phone number you specify during signup, which involves an automated phone call to your number, so ensure you enter a valid phone number during registration.

Installing Google Authenticator

The steps described in this section are completely optional, however, as a security best practice you should always enable multi-factor authentication (MFA) on your root account. In fact, you should enable this for all user-based access to your AWS accounts, regardless of the level of access required. Enabling MFA is increasingly becoming a mandatory requirement for many organizations using AWS, so getting used to working with AWS when MFA is involved is important. Consequently, we will actually use MFA throughout this book.

Before you can use MFA, you need to have an MFA device, which can be a hardware or virtual MFA device. A virtual MFA device is typically installed in the form of an application on your smart phone, completing the multi-factor paradigm of something you know (password) and something you have (your phone).

A popular MFA application available for both Android and iOS is the Google Authenticator app, which you can download from the Google Play or Apple App Stores. Once you have installed the application, you can proceed to logging into the root account and setting up MFA access.

Logging in as the root account

After setting up and activating your account, you should be able to log in to the AWS console, which you can access at `https://console.aws.amazon.com/console/home`.

After logging in with your root credentials, the first thing you should do is immediately enable MFA access. This provides an extra level of security, ensuring that if your username and password are compromised, an attacker cannot access your account without possession of your MFA device (in our example, that means the Google Authenticator application on your smart phone).

To enable MFA for your root account, select the drop-down that specifies your account name (in my case, this is **docker-in-aws**) and select **My Security Credentials**:

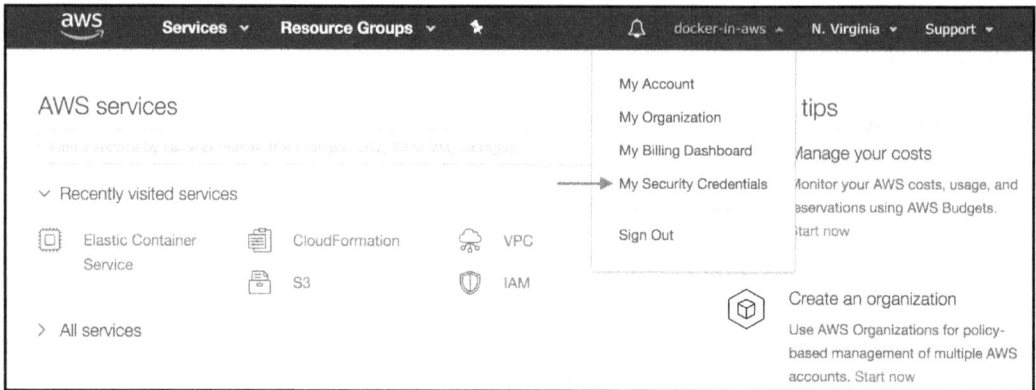

Accessing My Security Credentials

On the next prompt, click the **Continue to Security Credentials** button, expand the **Multi-factor authentication (MFA)** option on the **Your Security Credentials** page, and click the **Activate MFA** button:

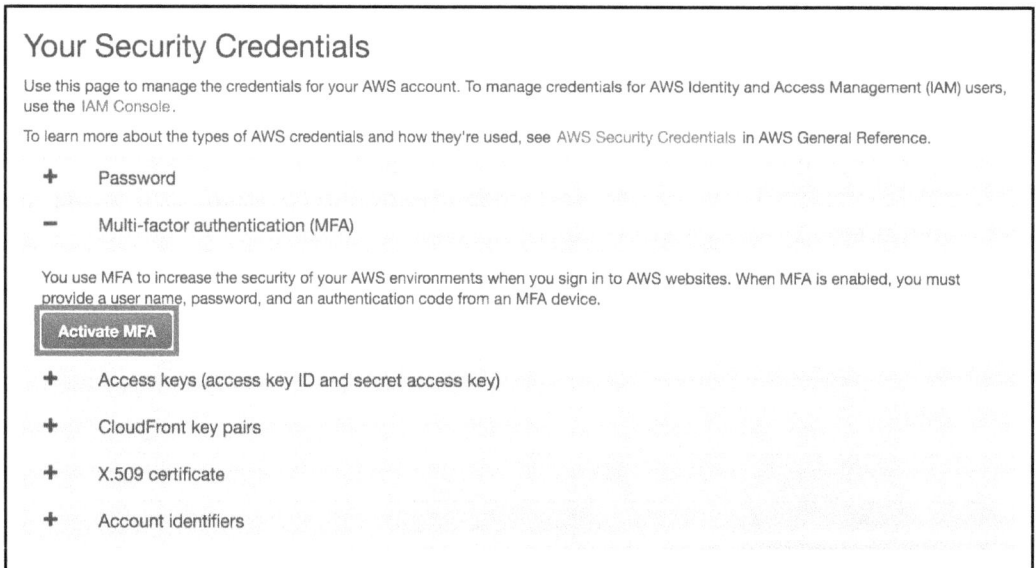

The Your Security Credentials screen

In the **Manage MFA device** screen, click on the **A virtual MFA device** option and click **Next Step** twice, at which point you will be presented with a QR code:

Obtaining a QR code

You can scan this code using the Google Authenticator application on your smart phone by clicking the add button, selecting **Scan barcode**, and scanning the QR code in the AWS console:

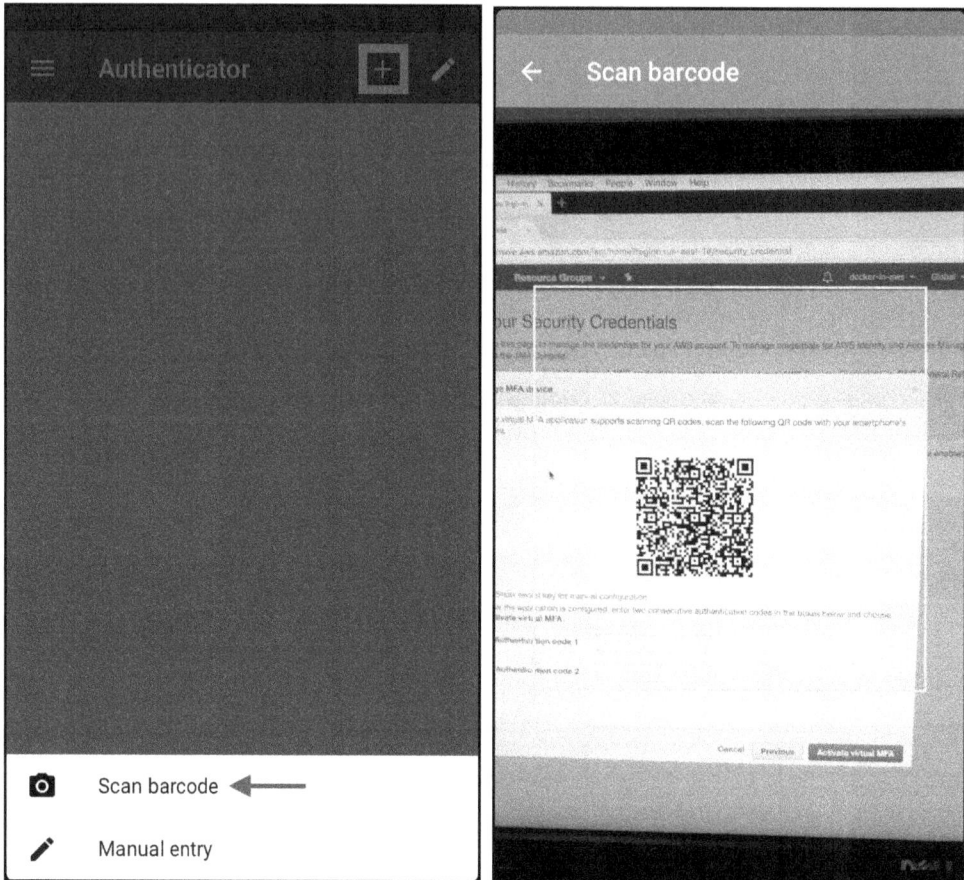

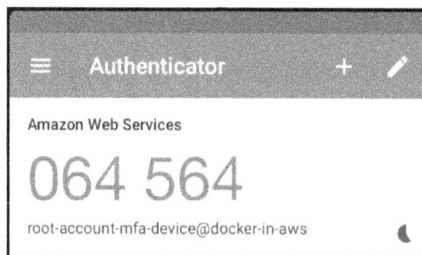

Registering an MFA device

Once scanned, you need to input the six-digit code presented in the **Authentication code 1** input in the **Manage MFA device** screen.

Once the code rotates, enter the next value of the code into the **Authentication code 2** input and click the **Activate virtual MFA** button to complete the registration of your MFA device:

Your Security Credentials

Use this page to manage the credentials for your AWS account. To manage credentials for AWS Identity and Access Management (IAM) users, use the IAM Console.

To learn more about the types of AWS credentials and how they're used, see AWS Security Credentials in AWS General Reference.

+   Password

—   Multi-factor authentication (MFA)

You use MFA to increase the security of your AWS environments when you sign in to AWS websites. When MFA is enabled, you must provide a user name, password, and an authentication code from an MFA device.

Device type	Serial number	Actions
Virtual MFA	arn:aws:iam::385605022855:mfa/root-account-mfa-device	Re-sync | Deactivate

————————This is your AWS Account ID

Your Security Credentials with the MFA device

Creating IAM users, groups, and roles

After securing your root account using MFA, you should next immediately create identity access and management (IAM) users, groups, and roles in your account for day-to-day access. IAM is the recommended approach for day-to-day administration and access to your AWS account and you should restrict root account access for billing or emergency purposes only. Before you can continue, you will need to know your AWS account ID, which you can see in the previous screenshot, in the serial number of your MFA device (note that this will be a different number than that which is shown). Write this account number down, as it will be required as you configure various IAM resources.

Creating IAM roles

The standard practice for creating IAM resources is to create *roles* that a given user can assume, which grants the user elevated privileges for a limited period of time (typically up to 1 hour). At a minimum, you need to create one IAM role by default:

- **admin**: This role grants full administrative control of the account, except for billing information

To create the admin role, select **Services** | **IAM** from the AWS console, select **Roles** from the left hand menu, and click on the **Create role** button. In the **Select type of trusted entity** screen, select the **Another AWS account** option and configure your account ID in the **Account ID** field:

Selecting a trusted entity for admin role

After clicking the **Next: Permissions** button, select the **AdministratorAccess** policy, which grants the role administrative access:

Attaching a policy to an IAM role

Finally, specify a role name of **admin** and then click **Create role** to complete the creation of the admin role:

Creating an IAM role

This creates the admin IAM role. If you click on the newly created role, take note of the Role ARN (Amazon Resource Name) of the role, as you will need this value later on:

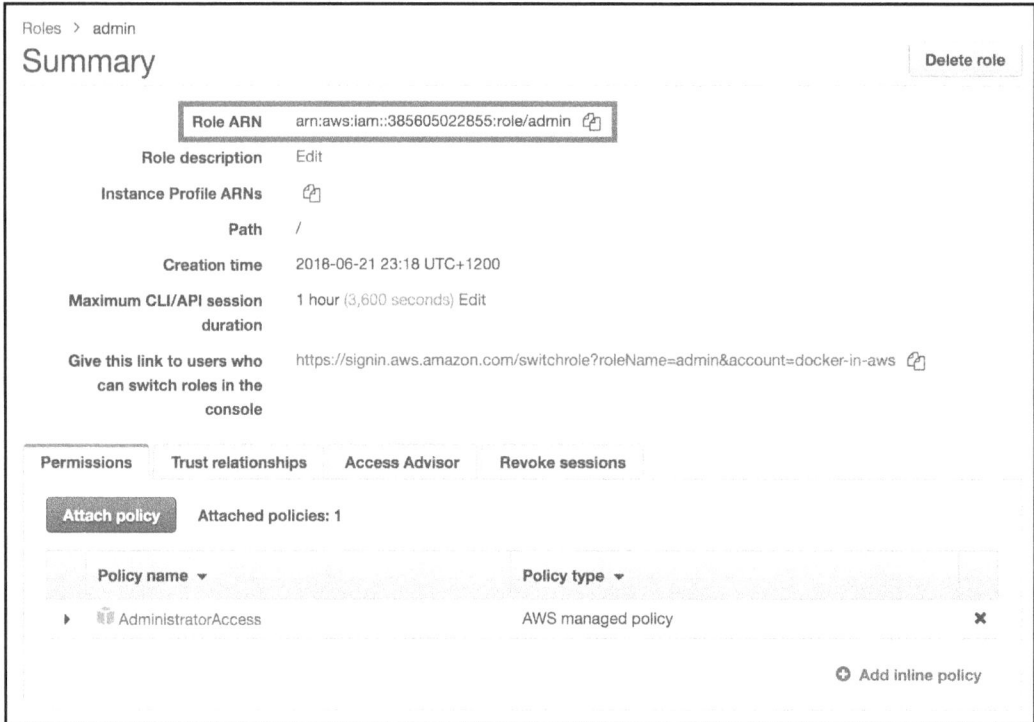

Roles > admin

Summary

Delete role

Role ARN	arn:aws:iam::385605022855:role/admin
Role description	Edit
Instance Profile ARNs	
Path	/
Creation time	2018-06-21 23:18 UTC+1200
Maximum CLI/API session duration	1 hour (3,600 seconds) Edit
Give this link to users who can switch roles in the console	https://signin.aws.amazon.com/switchrole?roleName=admin&account=docker-in-aws

Permissions   Trust relationships   Access Advisor   Revoke sessions

Attach policy   Attached policies: 1

Policy name ▼	Policy type ▼	
AdministratorAccess	AWS managed policy	✕

⊕ Add inline policy

The admin role

Creating an Administrators group

With an administrative role in place, the next step is to assign your role to a user or group. Instead of assigning privileges directly to a user, it is strongly recommended to instead assign them to groups, as this provides a much more scalable way of managing permissions. Given we have created a role with administrative privileges, it now makes sense to create a group called Administrators, which will be granted permission to *assume* the admin role you just created. Note that I refer to assuming a role, which is analogous to Linux and Unix systems, where you log in as a regular user and then use the `sudo` command to temporarily assume root privileges.

You will learn how to assume a role later on in this chapter, but for now you need to create the Administrators group by selecting **Groups** from the left hand menu in the IAM console and clicking the **Create New Group** button:

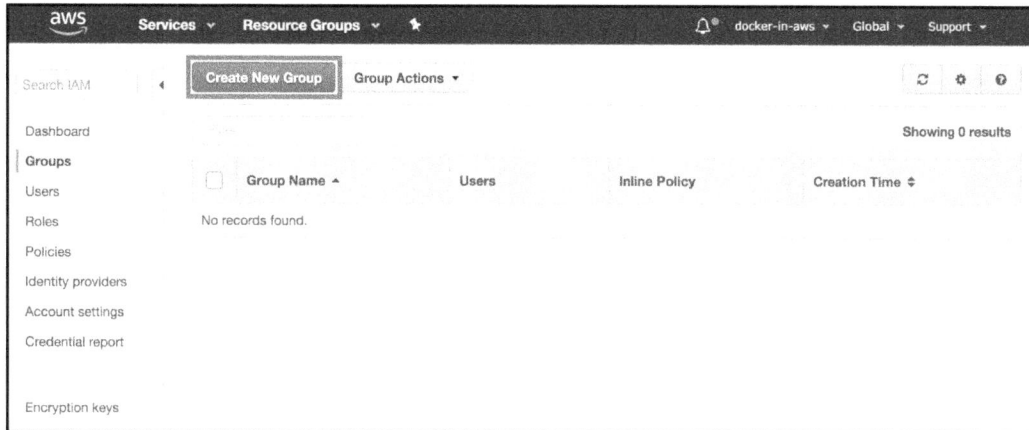

Creating an IAM group

You first need to specify a **Group Name** of Administrators and then click **Next Step** twice to skip the **Attach Policy** screen and finally click **Create Group** to complete creation of the group:

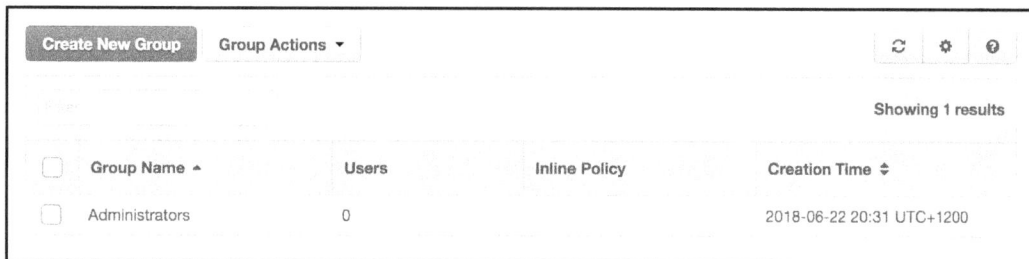

The Administrators group

This has created a group with no attached permissions, however if you click on the group and select **Permissions**, you now have the option to create an inline policy:

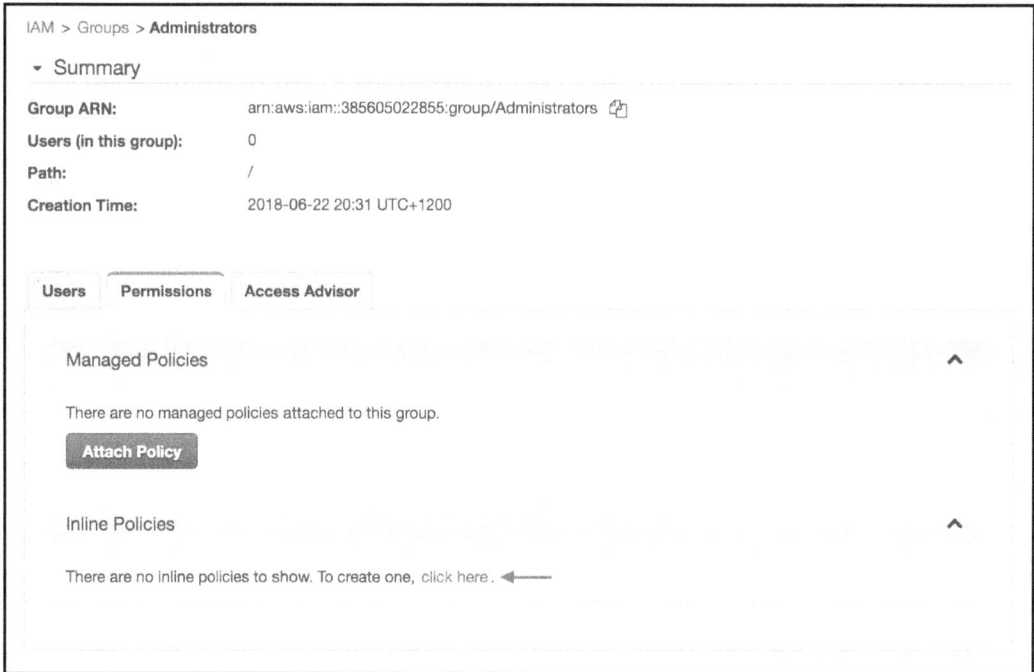

IAM > Groups > **Administrators**

▾ Summary

Group ARN:	arn:aws:iam::385605022855:group/Administrators
Users (in this group):	0
Path:	/
Creation Time:	2018-06-22 20:31 UTC+1200

| Users | **Permissions** | Access Advisor |

Managed Policies ⌃

There are no managed policies attached to this group.

Attach Policy

Inline Policies ⌃

There are no inline policies to show. To create one, click here. ◄——

Creating an inline policy

After selecting the **click here** link in the preceding screenshot, choose the **Custom Policy** option and click **Select**, which allows you to configure an IAM policy document that grants the ability to assume the admin role you created earlier:

Review Policy

Customize permissions by editing the following policy document. For more information about the access policy language, see Overview of Policies in the *Using IAM* guide. To test the effects of this policy before applying your changes, use the IAM Policy Simulator.

This policy is valid.

Policy Name

AssumeAdminRole

Policy Document

```
 1 - {
 2       "Version": "2012-10-17",
 3 -     "Statement": [
 4 -         {
 5               "Effect": "Allow",
 6               "Action": "sts:AssumeRole",
 7               "Resource": "arn:aws:iam::385605022855:role/admin"
 8          }
 9      ]
10 }
```

☑ Use autoformatting for policy editing   Cancel   **Validate Policy**   **Apply Policy**

Administrators group inline policy

The policy includes a single statement that allows the action `sts:AssumeRole` – `sts` here refers to the Security Token Service, which is the service you interact with whenever you assume a role (the action of assuming a role grants you temporary session credentials linked to the role you have assumed). Notice that the resource is the ARN of the IAM role you created, so this policy grants anybody that is a member of the **Administrators** group to assume the **admin** role. After clicking the **Apply Policy** button, you will have successfully created and configured the **Administrators** group.

Creating a Users group

The other group I typically recommend creating is a Users group, which every human user accessing your AWS account should belong to, including your administrators (who will also be members of the Administrators group). The core function of the Users group is to ensure that with the exception of a very small set of permissions, all actions performed by any member of the users group must be MFA authenticated, regardless of the permissions that may be granted to that user via other groups. This is essentially a force MFA policy, which you can read more about at `https://www.trek10.com/blog/improving-the-aws-force-mfa-policy-for-IAM-users/`, and implementing this approach adds to the overall security protections you put in place for access to your AWS accounts. Note that the policy does allow the user to perform a minimal set of operations without requiring MFA, which includes logging in, changing the user's password, and most importantly allowing the user to register an MFA device. This allows new users to log in with a temporary password, change their password, and self-enroll their MFA device, and once the user has logged out and logged back in with MFA, the policy does permit the user to create an AWS access key for API and CLI access.

To implement the Users group, we first need to create a managed IAM policy, which is a more scalable and reusable mechanism for assigning policies to groups and roles when compared with the inline approach we took in the preceding screenshot. To create a new managed policy, select **Policies** from the right hand menu and click on the **Create policy** button, which opens the **Create policy** screen. The policy you need to create is quite extensive and is published in a GitHub gist at `https://bit.ly/2KfNfAz`, which is based upon the policy discussed in the blog post referenced previously, adding a few additional security enhancements.

Note that the gist includes a placeholder called PASTE_ACCOUNT_NUMBER within the policy document, so you will need to replace this with your actual AWS account ID:

```
Create policy                                                    ①  2

A policy defines the AWS permissions that you can assign to a user, group, or role. You can create and edit a policy in the visual editor and using
JSON. Learn more

Visual editor   JSON                                                  Import managed policy

  1 · {
  2       "Version": "2012-10-17",
  3 ·     "Statement": [
  4 ·         {
  5               "Sid": "AllowAllUsersToListAccounts",
  6               "Effect": "Allow",
  7 ·             "Action": [
  8                   "iam:ListAccountAliases",
  9                   "iam:GetAccountPasswordPolicy",
 10                   "iam:ListUsers",
 11                   "iam:GetAccountSummary"
 12               ],
 13 ·             "Resource": [
 14                   "*"
 15               ]
 16           },
 17 ·         {
 18               "Sid": "AllowIndividualUserToSeeTheirAccountInformationAndCreateAccessKey"
                  ,
 19               "Effect": "Allow",
 20 ·             "Action": [
 21                   "iam:ChangePassword",
 22                   "iam:CreateLoginProfile",
 23                   "iam:DeleteLoginProfile"

                                                          Cancel    Review policy
```

Creating an IAM managed policy

After clicking the **Review policy** button, you need to configure a name for the policy, which we will call RequireMFAPolicy, and, after clicking **Create policy** to create the policy, you need to create a Users group using the same instructions you followed earlier in this chapter when you created the Administrators group.

When you get to the **Attach Policy** screen while you are creating the **Users** group, you can type in the first few letters of the **RequireMFAPolicy** managed policy you just created, which you need to attach to the group:

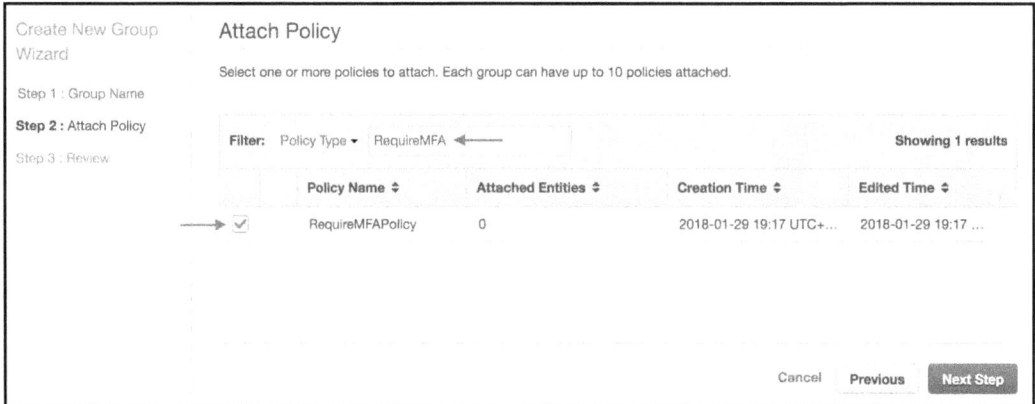

Attaching the RequireMFAPolicy to the Users group

After completing the wizard for creating the **Users** group, you should now have an **Administrators** group and **Users** group in your IAM console.

Creating an IAM user

The final IAM setup task you need to perform is to create an IAM user to administer your account. As discussed earlier in this chapter, you should never use your root credentials for day-to-day administrative tasks, and instead create an administrative IAM user.

To create a user, select **Users** from the right-hand menu in the IAM console and click on the **Add user** button. In the **Add user** screen, specify a **User name** and only select **AWS Management Console access** for **Access type**, ensuring that the **Console password** is set to **Autogenerated password** and the **Require password reset** option is set:

Add user   1   2   3   4

Set user details

You can add multiple users at once with the same access type and permissions. Learn more

User name*   justin.menga

⊕ Add another user

Select AWS access type

Select how these users will access AWS. Access keys and autogenerated passwords are provided in the last step. Learn more

Access type*   **Programmatic access**
                        Enables an **access key ID** and **secret access key** for the AWS API, CLI, SDK,
                        and other development tools.

                   ✓   **AWS Management Console access**
                        Enables a **password** that allows users to sign-in to the AWS Management
                        Console.

Console password*   ● Autogenerated password
                          Custom password

Require password reset ✓ User must create a new password at next sign-in

* Required   Cancel   Next: Permissions

Creating a new user

After clicking the **Next: Permissions** button, add the user to the **Administrators** and **Users** groups you created earlier:

Add user   1   2   3   4

Set permissions for justin.menga

| Add user to group | Copy permissions from existing user | Attach existing policies directly |

Add user to an existing group or create a new one. Using groups is a best-practice way to manage user's permissions by job functions. Learn more

Add user to group

Create group   Refresh

Q Search   Showing 2 results

Group ▾	Attached policies
✓ Administrators ◄———	AssumeAdminRole
✓ Users ◄———	RequireMFAPolicy

Adding users to groups

You can now click on the **Next: review** and **Create user** buttons to create the user. The user will be created and, because you chose to create an autogenerated password, you can click the **Show** link in the **Password** field to reveal the initial password for the user. Take note of this value, as you will need it to test logging in as the IAM user you just created:

Add user

1 2 3 4

Success

You successfully created the users shown below. You can view and download user security credentials. You can also email users instructions for signing in to the AWS Management Console. This is the last time these credentials will be available to download. However, you can create new credentials at any time.

Users with AWS Management Console access can sign-in at: https://docker-in-aws.signin.aws.amazon.com/console

⬇ Download .csv

User	Password
justin.menga	⟶ 1BeU&pVFG8() Hide

✓ Created user justin.menga
✓ Added user justin.menga to group Administrators
✓ Added user justin.menga to group Users
✓ Created login profile for user justin.menga

Close

Newly created user temporary password

Logging in as an IAM user

Now that you have created an IAM user, you can test the first time login experience for the user by clicking your account alias/ID in the menu and selecting **Sign Out**. If you now click on the **Sign In to the Console** button or browse to `https://console.aws.amazon.com/console/home`, select the **Sign in to a different account** option, enter your account alias or account ID, and click **Next**, and then enter the username and temporary password of the IAM user you just created:

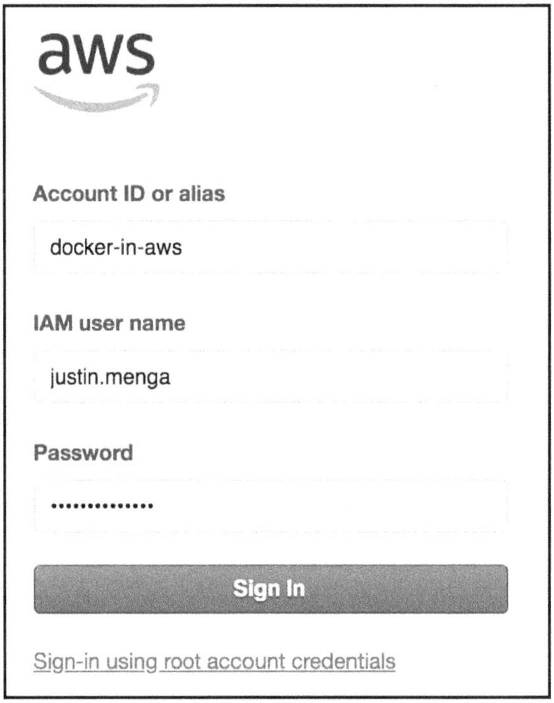

aws

Account ID or alias

docker-in-aws

IAM user name

justin.menga

Password

••••••••••••

Sign In

Sign-in using root account credentials

Logging in for the first time as an IAM user

You will then be prompted to enter a new password:

Entering a new password

After confirming the password change, you will have successfully logged in as the new user.

Enabling MFA for an IAM user

At this point, you have logged in with an IAM user for the first time, and the next step you need to perform is to enroll your MFA device for the new user. To do this, select **Services** | **IAM** to open the IAM console, select **Users** from the left hand menu, and click on your IAM user.

In the **Security credentials** tab, click on the pencil icon next to the **Assigned MFA device** field:

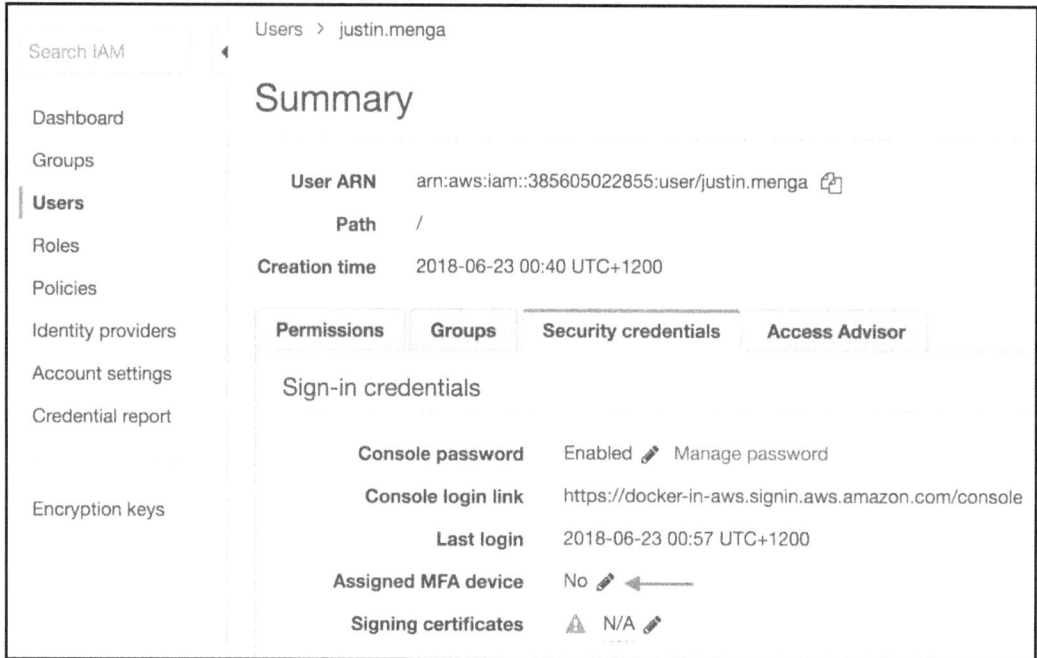

Users > justin.menga

Summary

User ARN	arn:aws:iam::385605022855:user/justin.menga
Path	/
Creation time	2018-06-23 00:40 UTC+1200

Permissions   **Groups**   **Security credentials**   **Access Advisor**

Sign-in credentials

Console password	Enabled Manage password
Console login link	https://docker-in-aws.signin.aws.amazon.com/console
Last login	2018-06-23 00:57 UTC+1200
Assigned MFA device	No
Signing certificates	⚠ N/A

Search IAM

Dashboard
Groups
Users
Roles
Policies
Identity providers
Account settings
Credential report

Encryption keys

IAM user security credentials

The Manage MFA Device dialog will pop up, which allows you to register a new MFA device. The process for this is identical to how you set up MFA for the root account earlier in this chapter, so I won't repeat the instructions for this, however once you have registered your MFA device, it is important for you to log out and log back in to the console to force MFA authentication.

If you have configured everything correctly, when you log back in to the console, you should be prompted for an MFA code:

MFA prompt

Assuming an IAM role

Once you have completed registering an MFA device and have logged out and back in to the AWS console using MFA, you now meet the requirements that cause the following statement in the `RequireMFAPolicy` you created back previously to not be applied:

```
{
    "Sid": "DenyEverythingExceptForBelowUnlessMFAd",
    "Effect": "Deny",
    "NotAction": [
        "iam:ListVirtualMFADevices",
        "iam:ListMFADevices",
        "iam:ListUsers",
        "iam:ListAccountAliases",
        "iam:CreateVirtualMFADevice",
        "iam:EnableMFADevice",
        "iam:ResyncMFADevice",
        "iam:ChangePassword",
        "iam:CreateLoginProfile",
        "iam:DeleteLoginProfile",
        "iam:GetAccountPasswordPolicy",
        "iam:GetAccountSummary",
        "iam:GetLoginProfile",
        "iam:UpdateLoginProfile"
```

```
    ],
    "Resource": "*",
    "Condition": {
        "Null": {
            "aws:MultiFactorAuthAge": "true"
        }
    }
}
```

In the preceding code, it's important to note that the IAM effect of `Deny` is absolute—as soon as IAM encounters a `Deny` for a given permission or set of permissions, there is no way for that permission to be permitted. The `Condition` property however makes this broad reaching `Deny` conditional—it will only be applied in the event that the special condition `aws:MultiFactorAuthAge` is false, which is the case if you have logged in without MFA.

Given that the IAM user has logged in via MFA and is attached to the **Administrators** group that has permission to assume the **admin** role, there is nothing in the `RequireMFAPolicy` that is denying this action, so you should be able to now assume the **admin** role.

To assume the admin role using the AWS console, click on the drop down that reads `<username> @ <account-name-or-id>` and select **Switch Role**:

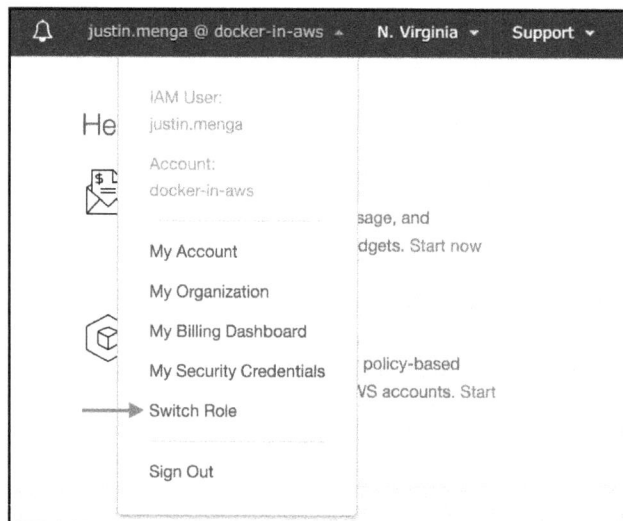

Switching roles

After clicking on the **Switch Role** button, you will be prompted to enter an account ID or name, and the role that you want to assume in the configure account:

Switching roles

You should now notice that the header in the AWS console indicates that you have to assume the admin role, and you now have full administrative access to your AWS account:

Assumed admin role

For the remainder of this book, whenever you need to perform administrative tasks in your account, I will be assuming you have assumed the admin role as demonstrated in the previous screenshot.

Creating an EC2 Key Pair

A key setup task that is required if you are going to running any EC2 instances in your AWS account is to establish one or more EC2 key pairs, which for Linux EC2 instances, can be used to define an SSH key pair that grants SSH access to your EC2 instances.

When you create an EC2 key pair, an SSH public/private key pair will be automatically generated, with the SSH public key being stored as a named EC2 key pair in AWS, and the corresponding SSH private key downloaded to your local client. If you subsequently create any EC2 instances and reference a named EC2 key pair at instance creation, you will be able to automatically use the associated SSH private key to access your EC2 instances.

SSH access to Linux EC2 instances requires you to use the SSH private key associated with the configured EC2 key pair for the instance, and also requires appropriate network configuration and security groups to permit access to the EC2 instance SSH port from wherever your SSH client is located.

To create an EC2 Key Pair, first navigate to **Services** | **EC2** in the AWS console, select **Key Pairs** from the **Network & Security** section within the left hand menu, and then click on the Create Key Pair button:

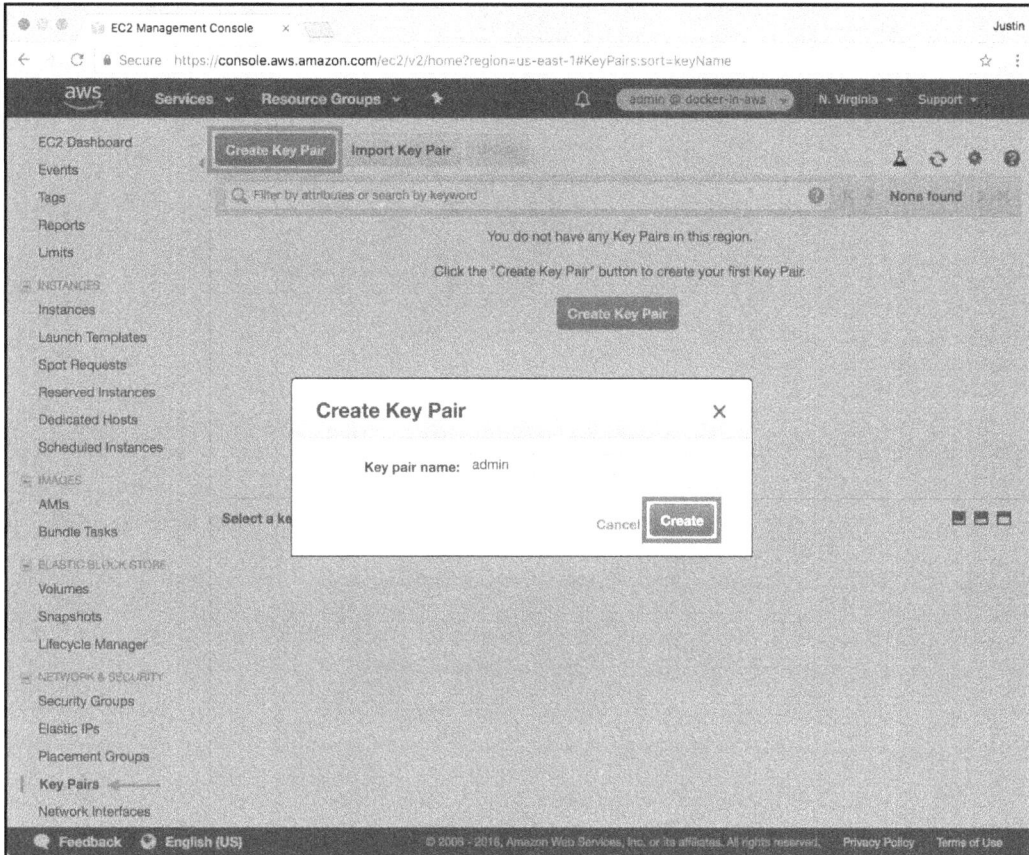

Here you have configured an EC2 key pair name admin, and after clicking on the Create button, a new EC2 key pair will be created, with the SSH private key downloaded to your computer:

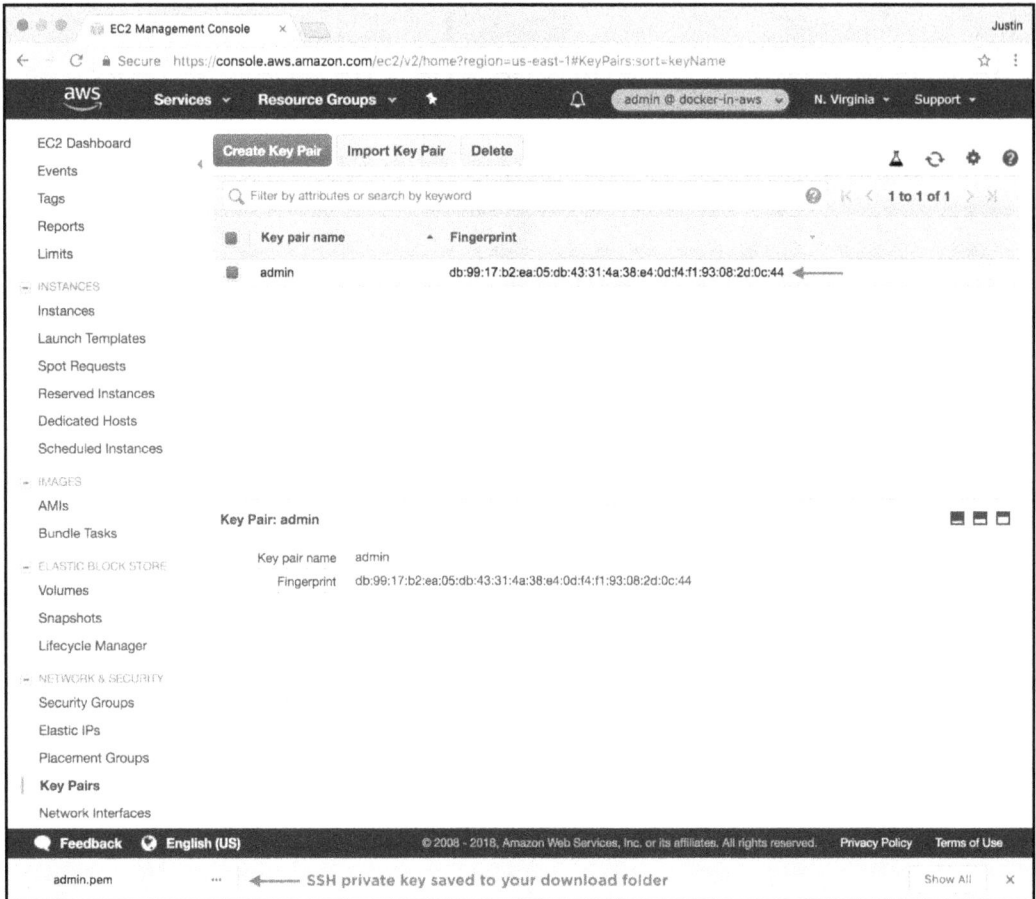

At this point you need to move the SSH private key to an appropriate location on your computer, and modify the default permissions on the private key file as demonstrated below:

```
> mv ~/Downloads/admin.pem ~/.ssh/admin.pem
> chmod 600 ~/.ssh/admin.pem
```

Note that if you don't modify the permissions using the chmod command, when you attempt to use the SSH key you will be presented with the following error:

```
> ssh -i ~/.ssh/admin.pem 192.0.2.1
@@@@@@@@@@@@@@@@@@@@@@@@@@@@@@@@@@@@@@@@@@@@@@@@@@@@@@@@@@@@
@ WARNING: UNPROTECTED PRIVATE KEY FILE! @
@@@@@@@@@@@@@@@@@@@@@@@@@@@@@@@@@@@@@@@@@@@@@@@@@@@@@@@@@@@@
Permissions 0644 for '/Users/jmenga/.ssh/admin.pem' are too open.
It is required that your private key files are NOT accessible by
others.
This private key will be ignored.
Load key "/Users/jmenga/.ssh/admin.pem": bad permissions
```

Using the AWS CLI

So far in this chapter, you have only interacted with the AWS console, which is accessed from your web browser. Although having AWS console access is very useful, there are many situations where you may prefer to use command-line tools, especially where you need to automate key operational and deployment tasks.

Installing the AWS CLI

The AWS CLI is written in Python, and therefore you must have either Python 2 or Python 3 installed, along with the PIP Python package manager.

> The instructions and examples used throughout this book assume a MacOS or Linux environment.
> For instructions on how to set up the AWS CLI using Windows, refer to https://docs.aws.amazon.com/cli/latest/userguide/awscli-install-windows.html.

Assuming you have met these prerequisites, you can install the AWS CLI in a terminal using the `pip` command, along with the `--upgrade` flag to upgrade to the latest AWS CLI version if already installed, and the `--user` flag to avoid modifying your system libraries:

```
> pip install awscli --upgrade --user
Collecting awscli
  Downloading
https://files.pythonhosted.org/packages/69/18/d0c904221d14c45098da04de
5e5b74a6effffb90c2b002bc2051fd59222e/awscli-1.15.45-py2.py3-none-
any.whl (1.3MB)
    100% |████████████████████████████████| 1.3MB 1.2MB/s
...
...
Successfully installed awscli-1.15.45 botocore-1.10.45 colorama-0.3.9
pyasn1-0.4.3 python-dateutil-2.7.3
```

> Depending on your environment, if you are using Python 3, you may need to replace the `pip install` command with `pip3 install`.

If you now attempt to run an AWS CLI command, the command will fail, indicating that you must configure your environment:

```
> aws ec2 describe-vpcs
You must specify a region. You can also configure your region by
running "aws configure".
```

Creating an AWS access key

If you run the `aws configure` command as suggested in the preceding code, you will be prompted to enter an AWS Access Key ID:

```
> aws configure
AWS Access Key ID [None]:
```

To use the AWS CLI and AWS SDKs, you must create an AWS access key, which is a credential that consists of an access key ID and secret access key value. To create an access key, open the IAM dashboard in the AWS console, select **Users** from the left hand menu, and then click on your username. In the **Security credentials** tab, under the **Access keys** section, click on the **Create access key** button, which will open a dialog box that allows you to view both the access key ID and secret access key value:

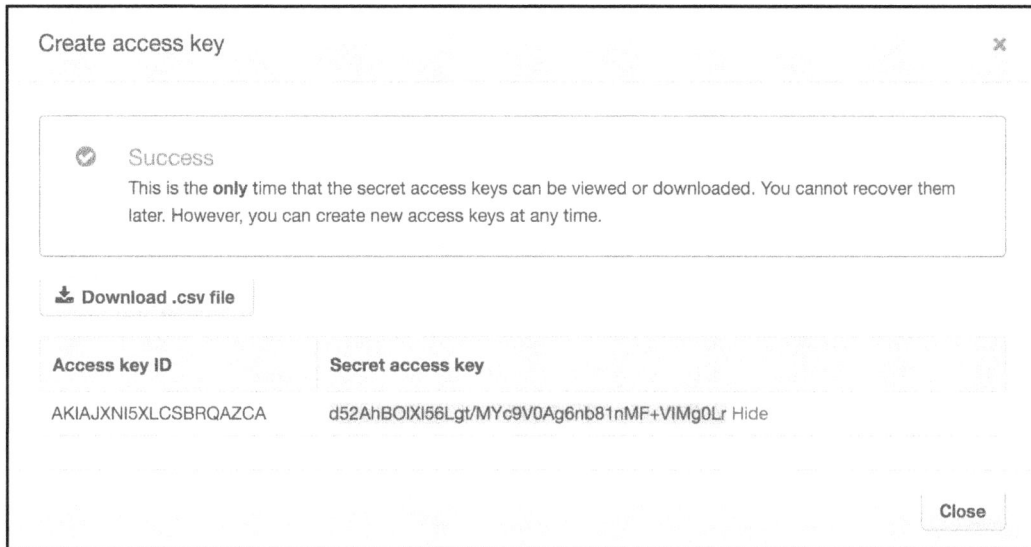

Create access key ⨯

⊘ Success
This is the **only** time that the secret access keys can be viewed or downloaded. You cannot recover them later. However, you can create new access keys at any time.

⬇ Download .csv file

Access key ID	Secret access key
AKIAJXNI5XLCSBRQAZCA	d52AhBOIXI56Lgt/MYc9V0Ag6nb81nMF+VIMg0Lr Hide

Close

Access key credentials

Take a note of both the access key ID and secret access key values, as you will need these values to configure your local environment.

Configuring the AWS CLI

Back in your terminal, you can now complete the `aws configure` setup process:

```
> aws configure
AWS Access Key ID [None]: AKIAJXNI5XLCSBRQAZCA
AWS Secret Access Key [None]: d52AhBOlX156Lgt/MYc9V0Ag6nb81nMF+VIMg0Lr
Default region name [None]: us-east-1
Default output format [None]:
```

If you now attempt to run the `aws ec2 describe-vpcs` command attempted earlier, the command still fails; however, the error is different:

```
> aws ec2 describe-vpcs

An error occurred (UnauthorizedOperation) when calling the
DescribeVpcs operation: You are not authorized to perform this
operation.
```

The problem now is that you are not authorized to execute this command, given the access key you just created is linked to your user account, and you must assume the admin role to obtain administrative privileges.

Configuring the AWS CLI to assume a role

At this point, the AWS CLI is running in the context of your user account and you need to configure the CLI to assume the admin role to be able to do anything useful.

When you run the `aws configure` command, the AWS CLI creates two important files in a folder called `.aws` within your home directory:

```
> ls -l ~/.aws

total 16
-rw------- 1 jmenga staff 29  23 Jun 19:31 config
-rw------- 1 jmenga staff 116 23 Jun 19:31 credentials
```

The `credentials` file holds your AWS credentials in one or more named profiles:

```
> cat ~/.aws/credentials
[default]
aws_access_key_id = AKIAJXNI5XLCSBRQAZCA
aws_secret_access_key = d52AhBOlX156Lgt/MYc9V0Ag6nb81nMF+VIMg0Lr
```

In the preceding code, notice that the `aws configure` command created a profile called `default` and stored the access key ID and secret access key values in this file. As a best practice, particularly if you are working with multiple AWS accounts, I recommend avoiding the use of the default profile, as the AWS CLI will use this profile by default if you enter an AWS CLI command. You will soon learn how to work with multiple AWS accounts by using named profiles, and if you have a default profile, it is very easy to accidentally forget to specify the profile you want to work with and accidentally perform an unexpected operation in the account reference by your default profile. I prefer to name each profile based upon the name of the account you are working with—for example, here, I have renamed the default profile in the credentials file to `docker-in-aws`, given I named my AWS account `docker-in-aws`:

```
[docker-in-aws]
aws_access_key_id = AKIAJXNI5XLCSBRQAZCA
aws_secret_access_key = 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
```

The other file that is created by the AWS CLI is the `~/.aws/config` file, which is demonstrated as follows:

```
[default]
region = us-east-1
```

This file includes named configuration profiles, and because you specified a default region when you ran the `aws configure` command, a `region` variable has been added to the `default` profile. Configuration profiles support a number of variables that allow you to perform more advanced tasks like automatically assuming a role, so this is where we need to configure the CLI to assume the `admin` role we created earlier in this chapter. Given that we renamed the `default` profile in the `credentials` file, the following code demonstrates renaming the `default` profile to `docker-in-aws` and adding support for assuming the `admin` role:

```
[profile docker-in-aws]
source_profile = docker-in-aws
role_arn = arn:aws:iam::385605022855:role/admin
role_session_name=justin.menga
mfa_serial = arn:aws:iam::385605022855:mfa/justin.menga
region = us-east-1
```

Notice that we add the `profile` keyword in front of the profile name, which is required when configuring named configuration profiles. We also configure a number of variables in the profile:

- `source_profile`: This is the credential profile that should be used to obtain credentials. We specify `docker-in-aws`, given that we renamed the profile in the `credentials` file earlier to `docker-in-aws`.
- `role_arn`: This is the ARN of the IAM role to assume. Here, you specify the ARN of the `admin` role you created in the previous screenshot.
- `role_session_name`: This is the name of the temporary session that is created when you assume the configured role. As a best practice, you should specify your IAM username, as this helps with auditing any actions that you perform using the role. When you use an assumed role to perform an action in AWS, your identity is actually `arn:aws:sts::<account-id>:assumed-role/<role-name>/<role-session-name>`, so setting a username as the role session name ensures the user that performed the operation can be easily determined.
- `mfa_serial`: This is the ARN of the MFA device that should be used to assume the role. Given your IAM user belongs to the Users group, MFA is required for all actions, including any API calls made via the AWS CLI or SDK. By configuring this variable, the AWS CLI will automatically prompt you for an MFA code before attempting to assume the configured role. You can obtain the ARN of your MFA device in the Security credentials tab of your IAM user account (see the **Assigned MFA device** field, however it will always follow a naming convention of `arn:aws:iam::<account-id>:mfa/<user-id>`.

> See `https://docs.aws.amazon.com/cli/latest/topic/config-vars.html` for a complete description of all variables supported in both credentials and configuration profiles.

Configuring the AWS CLI to use a named profile

With the configuration in place, you no longer have a default profile in place, so running the AWS CLI will return the same output. To use a named profile, you have two options available:

- Specify the profile name using the `--profile` flag in the AWS CLI command.
- Specify the profile name in an environment variable called `AWS_PROFILE`. This is my preferred mechanism and I will assume that you are taking this approach throughout this book.

The preceding code demonstrates using both of these approaches:

```
> aws ec2 describe-vpcs --profile docker-in-aws
Enter MFA code for arn:aws:iam::385605022855:mfa/justin.menga: ******
{
    "Vpcs": [
        {
            "VpcId": "vpc-f8233a80",
            "InstanceTenancy": "default",
            "CidrBlockAssociationSet": [
                {
                    "AssociationId": "vpc-cidr-assoc-32524958",
                    "CidrBlock": "172.31.0.0/16",
                    "CidrBlockState": {
                        "State": "associated"
                    }
                }
            ],
            "State": "available",
            "DhcpOptionsId": "dopt-a037f9d8",
            "CidrBlock": "172.31.0.0/16",
            "IsDefault": true
        }
    ]
}
> export AWS_PROFILE=docker-in-aws
> aws ec2 describe-vpcs --query Vpcs[].VpcId
[
    "vpc-f8233a80"
]
```

In the preceding example, notice that when you run first run the `aws` command, you are prompted for your MFA token, however when you next run the command, you are not prompted. This is because, by default, the temporary session credentials obtained from assuming a role are valid for one hour, and the AWS CLI caches the credentials so that you reuse them without having to refresh the credentials on each command execution. Of course, after one hour, you will be prompted once again for your MFA token, given that the temporary session credentials will have expired.

One other interesting point to note in the preceding code is the use of the `--query` flag in the last command example. This allows you to specify a JMESPath query, which is a query language that can be used to query JSON data structures. The AWS CLI outputs JSON by default, so you can use queries to extract specific information from the AWS CLI output. Throughout this book, I will frequently use examples of these queries, and you can read more about the JMESPath query language at `http://jmespath.org/tutorial.html`.

Introduction to AWS CloudFormation

AWS CloudFormation is a managed AWS service that allows you to define AWS services and resources using infrastructure as code, and is an alternative to using the AWS console, CLI, or various SDKs for deploying your AWS infrastructure. Although there is bit of a learning curve to master CloudFormation, once you have the basics of using CloudFormation under your belt, it represents an extremely powerful approach to deploying your AWS infrastructure, particularly once you start deploying complex environments.

When using CloudFormation, you define one or more resources in a CloudFormation template, which is a convenient mechanism to group related resources in a single place. When you deploy your template, CloudFormation will create a *stack* that comprises the physical resources defined in your template. CloudFormation will deploy each resource, automatically determining any dependencies between each resource, and optimise the deployment so that resources can be deployed in parallel where applicable, or in the correct sequence when there are dependencies between resources. The best news is that all of this powerful capability comes for free – you only pay for the resources you consume when you deploy your stacks via CloudFormation.

It's also important to note that there are many third-party alternatives to CloudFormation – for example, Terraform is very popular, and traditional configuration management tools such as Ansible and Puppet also include support for deploying AWS resources. My personal favorite is CloudFormation given it is natively supported by AWS, has good support for a wide variety of AWS services and resources, and natively integrates with the AWS CLI and services such as CodePipeline (we will leverage this integration later on in this book in Chapter 13 - *Continuous Delivering ECS Applications*).

Defining a CloudFormation template

The easiest way to get started with CloudFormation is to create a CloudFormation template. This template is defined in either a JSON or YAML format, with the latter being the format I recommend given YAML is much easier for humans to work with than JSON.

The `CloudFormation user guide` describes the `template structure in great detail,` however for the purposes of this book, we only need to worry about a basic template structure which is best demonstrated with a real example, which you can save in a file called `stack.yml` in a convenient location on your computer:

```
AWSTemplateFormatVersion: "2010-09-09"

Description: Cloud9 Management Station

Parameters:
  EC2InstanceType:
    Type: String
    Description: EC2 instance type
    Default: t2.micro
  SubnetId:
    Type: AWS::EC2::Subnet::Id
    Description: Target subnet for instance

Resources:
  ManagementStation:
    Type: AWS::Cloud9::EnvironmentEC2
    Properties:
      Name: !Sub ${AWS::StackName}-station
      Description:
        Fn::Sub: ${AWS::StackName} Station
      AutomaticStopTimeMinutes: 15
```

```
InstanceType: !Ref EC2InstanceType
SubnetId:
  Ref: SubnetId
```

In the preceding code, the CloudFormation defines a Cloud9 management station – Cloud9 provides a cloud-based IDE and terminal, which under the hood runs on an EC2 instance in AWS. Let's walk through this example to discuss the structure and features of the template.

The `AWSTemplateFormatVersion` property is required, which specifies the CloudFormation template format version that is always expressed in date terms. The `Parameters` property defines a set of input parameters that you can supply to your template, which is a good way to deal with multiple environments where you may have different input values between each environment. For example, the `EC2InstanceType` parameter specifies the EC2 instance type for the management station, while the `SubnetId` parameter specifies the subnet the EC2 instance should be attached to. Both of these values could be different between a non-production environment and production environment, so having them as input parameters makes it easier to change depending on the target environment. Notice that the `SubnetId` parameter specifies a type of `AWS::EC2::Subnet::Id`, which means CloudFormation can use this to lookup or validate the input value. For a list of supported parameter types, see `https://docs.aws.amazon.com/AWSCloudFormation/latest/UserGuide/parameters-section-structure.html`. You can also see that the `EC2InstanceType` parameter defines a default value for the parameter, which will be used if no input is provided for this parameter.

The `Resources` property defines all of the resources in your stack – this truly is the meat or body of the template, and may contain up to two hundred resources. In the preceding code, we only define a single resource which we call `ManagementStation`, and this creates Cloud9 EC2 Environment, as expressed via a `Type` value of `AWS::Cloud9::EnvironmentEC2`. All resources must specify a `Type` property, which defines the type of resource and determines the various configuration properties available for each type. The CloudFormation user guide includes a section that defines all supported resource types, and at last count there were 300 different types of resources.

Every resource also includes a **Properties** property, which holds all of the various configuration properties available for the resource. In the preceding code, you can see that we have defined five different properties—the properties available will vary depending on the resource type and are fully documented in the CloudFormation user guide:

- `Name`: This specifies the name of the Cloud9 EC2 environment. The value of properties can be simple scalar values like a string or number, however the value can also reference other parameters or resources in the template. Notice that the value of the `Name` property includes what is referred to as an `intrinsic function` called `Sub`, and can be identified by the preceding exclamation mark (`!Sub`). The `!Sub` syntax is actually a shorthand for `Fn::Sub`, an example of which you can see with the `Description` property. The `Fn::Sub` intrinsic function allows you to define an expression that includes interpolated references to other resources or parameters in your stack. For example, the value of the `Name` property is `${AWS::StackName}-station`, where the `${AWS::StackName}` is an interpolated reference known as a `pseudo parameter` that will be replaced with the name of the CloudFormation stack you deploy from the template. If the name of your stack is `cloud9-management`, then the value of `${AWS::StackName}-station` will be expanded to `cloud9-management-station` when your stack is deployed.
- `Description`: This provides a description for the Cloud9 EC2 environment. This includes an example of the long hand version of the `Fn::Sub` intrinsic function, which requires you to indent a new line, whereas the shorthand `!Sub` format allows you to specify the value on the same line as the property.
- `AutomaticStopTime`: This defines the amount of idle time in minutes to wait before stopping the Cloud9 EC2 instance. This saves on costs, but only when running the EC2 instance when you are using it (Cloud9 will automatically start your instance and resume your session from where you previously were). In the preceding code, the value is a simple scalar value of 15.
- `InstanceType`: This is the type of EC2 instance. This references the `EC2InstanceType` parameter using the Ref intrinsic function (`!Ref` is the shorthand form), which allows you to reference other parameters or resources in the stack. This means that whatever value is provided for this parameter when you deploy the stack will be applied for the `InstanceType` property.

- `SubnetId`: This is the target subnet ID where the EC2 instance will be deployed. This property references the SubnetID parameter using the long hand version of the `Ref` intrinsic function, which requires to you express this reference on an indented new line.

Deploying a CloudFormation stack

Now that you have defined a CloudFormation template, you can deploy the resources in your template in the form of a CloudFormation stack.

You can deploy a stack using the AWS console by choosing **Services** | **CloudFormation**, which will open the CloudFormation dashboard. Before you continue, ensure that you have assumed the admin role in your account and have also selected US East N. Virginia (**us-east-1**) as the region:

> For all examples in this book, we will be using the us-east-1 (N. Virginia) region.

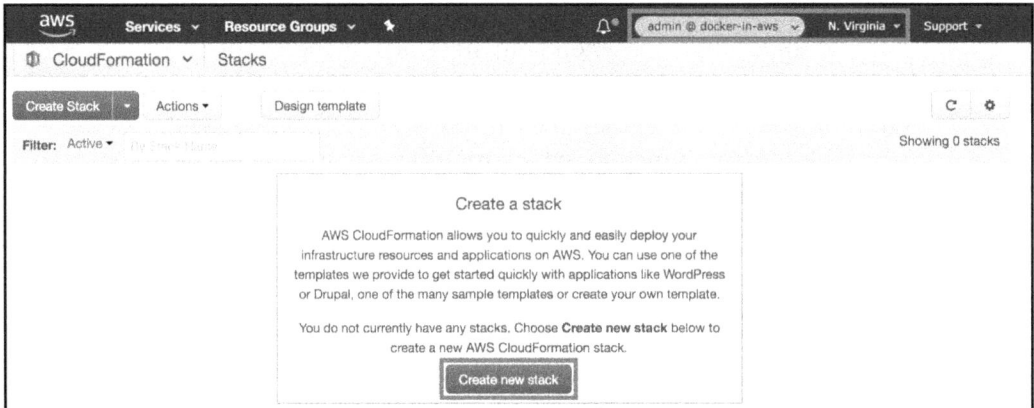

CloudFormation dashboard

If you click on the **Create new stack** button, you will be prompted to select a template, where you can either select a sample template, upload a template, or specify an S3 template URL. Because we defined our stack in a file called `stack.yml`, select the option to upload a template and click the **Choose file** button to select the file on your computer:

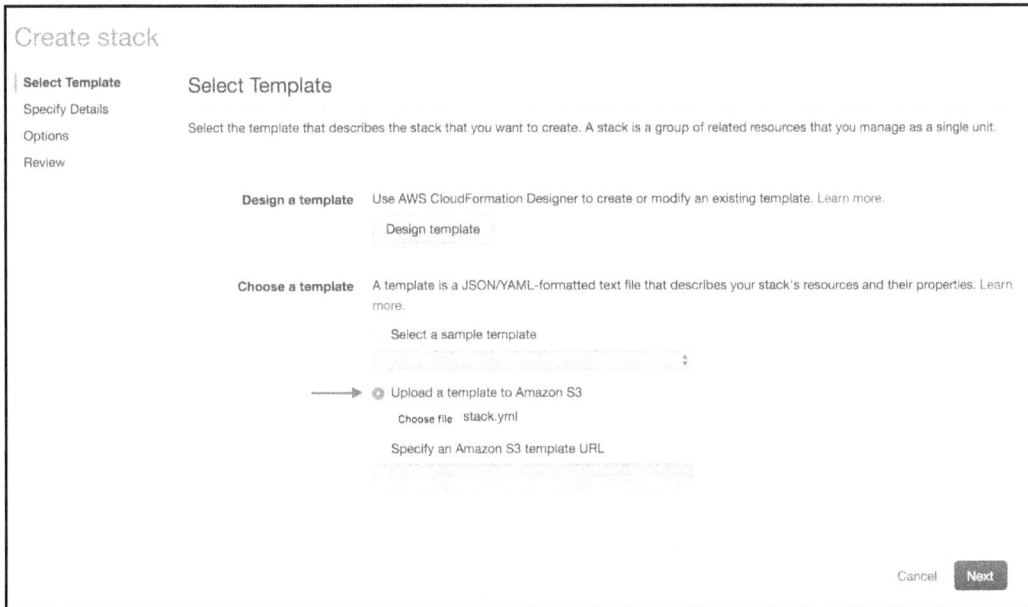

Create stack

Select Template
Specify Details
Options
Review

Select Template

Select the template that describes the stack that you want to create. A stack is a group of related resources that you manage as a single unit.

Design a template   Use AWS CloudFormation Designer to create or modify an existing template. Learn more.

Design template

Choose a template   A template is a JSON/YAML-formatted text file that describes your stack's resources and their properties. Learn more.

Select a sample template

Upload a template to Amazon S3

Choose file   stack.yml

Specify an Amazon S3 template URL

Cancel   Next

Selecting a CloudFormation template

After uploading the template, the CloudFormation service will parse the template and ask you to specify a name for the stack and also provide values for any parameters in the stack:

Specifying template details

In the preceding screenshot, the value `t2.micro` is set by default for the `EC2InstanceType` parameter, given you set this as a default value in your template. Because you specified `AWS::EC2::Subnet::Id` as the type of the `SubnetId` parameter, the **Create stack** wizard automatically finds all of the subnets in your account and region and presents them in a dropdown. Here, I have selected the subnet from the default VPC that is created with every new AWS account that is located in the **us-east-1a** availability zone.

You can determine which availability zone each of the subnets belongs to by either selecting **Services** | **VPC** | **Subnets** in the AWS console, or by running the `aws ec2 describe-subnets` AWS CLI command with a JMESPath query:

```
> aws ec2 describe-subnets --query
'Subnets[].[SubnetId,AvailabilityZone,CidrBlock]' \
   --output table
------------------------------------------------------
|  DescribeSubnets                                    |
+-----------------+---------------+-------------------+
|  subnet-a5d3ecee |  us-east-1a  |  172.31.16.0/20   |
|  subnet-c2abdded |  us-east-1d  |  172.31.80.0/20   |
```

```
| subnet-aae11aa5 | us-east-1f  | 172.31.48.0/20  |
| subnet-fd3a43c2 | us-east-1e  | 172.31.64.0/20  |
| subnet-324e246f | us-east-1b  | 172.31.32.0/20  |
| subnet-d281a2b6 | us-east-1c  | 172.31.0.0/20   |
+-----------------+-------------+-----------------+
```

At this point, you can click **Next** and then **Create** in the **Create stack** wizard to commence deployment of your new stack. In the CloudFormation dashboard, you will see that a new stack called **cloud9-management** is created, which initially has a status of CREATE_IN_PROGRESS. An interesting behavior associated with deploying Cloud9 environments via CloudFormation is that a separate child CloudFormation stack is automatically created via the AWS::Cloud9::Environment resource—this is somewhat unusual as for every other type of CloudFormation resource you will create, you will not see this type of behavior. Once deployment is complete, the status of the stack will change to CREATE_COMPLETE:

Deploying a CloudFormation stack

In the preceding screenshot, you can click on the **Events** tab to display events associated with stack deployment. This will show you the progress of each resource as it is deployed, and will indicate if there are any failures.

Now that you have successfully deployed your first CloudFormation stack, you should have a brand new Cloud9 IDE environment available for you to use. If you select **Services | Cloud9** from the AWS console menu bar, you should see a single environment called `cloud9-management-station`:

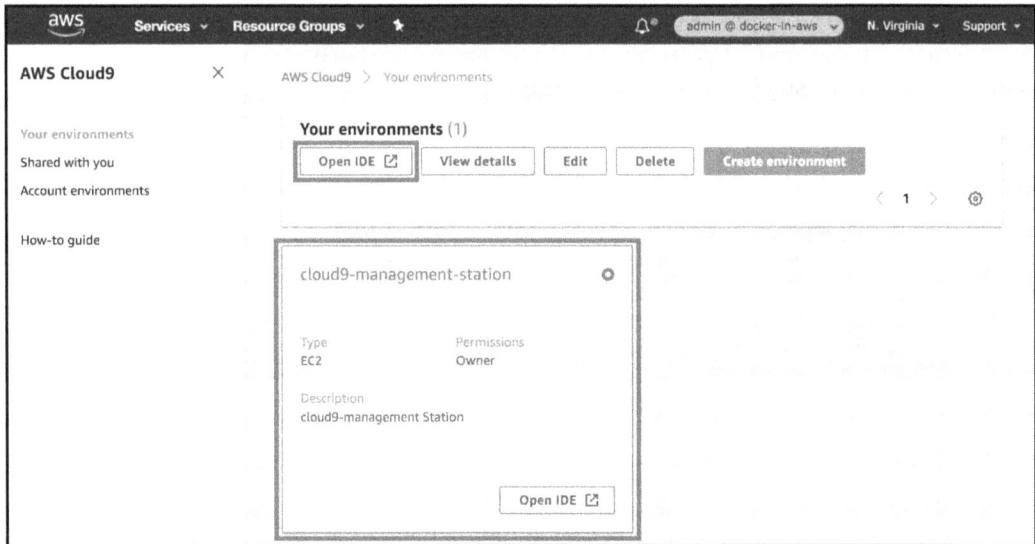

Cloud9 environments

If you click on the **Open IDE** button, this will open a new IDE session which includes an integrated terminal with AWS CLI installed. Note that the session has all of the permissions associated with the user that created the Cloud9 environment—in this case, this is the assumed **admin** role, hence you can perform any administrative task from the terminal. The Cloud9 environment is also running within your VPC, so if you deploy other resources such as EC2 instances, you can manage them locally from this environment, even if your other resources are deployed in private subnets without internet connectivity:

Make sure you understand the implications of creating a Cloud9 environment that has full administrative privileges. Although this is very convenient, it does represent a potential security backdoor that could be used to compromise your environment and account. Cloud9 also allows you to share your IDE with other users, which could allow other users to masquerade as you and perform any action that you are allowed to perform.

Cloud9 IDE

Updating a CloudFormation Stack

After you have created a CloudFormation stack, you may want to make changes to the stack, such as adding additional resources, or changing the configuration of existing resources. CloudFormation defines three key life cycle events related to stacks – CREATE, UPDATE, and DELETE – and these can apply to individual resources within the stack, or to the stack as a whole.

To update a stack, you simply make any required changes to your CloudFormation template and submit the modified template—the CloudFormation service will calculate the required changes for each resource, which may result in the creation of new resources, updating or replacement of existing resources, or deletion of existing resources. CloudFormation will also make any new changes first, and only if these changes are successful will it then clean up any resources that should be removed. This provides a higher chance of recovery in the event that a CloudFormation stack update fails, in which case CloudFormation will attempt to roll back the changes to restore the stack to its original state.

To test updating your CloudFormation stack, let's make a small change to the `stack.yml` template:

```
AWSTemplateFormatVersion: "2010-09-09"

Description: Cloud9 Management Station

Parameters:
  EC2InstanceType:
    Type: String
    Description: EC2 instance type
    Default: t2.micro
  SubnetId:
    Type: AWS::EC2::Subnet::Id
    Description: Target subnet for instance
```

```
Resources:
  ManagementStation:
    Type: AWS::Cloud9::EnvironmentEC2
    Properties:
      Name: !Sub ${AWS::StackName}-station
      Description:
        Fn::Sub: ${AWS::StackName} Station
      AutomaticStopTimeMinutes: 20
      InstanceType: !Ref EC2InstanceType
      SubnetId:
        Ref: SubnetId
```

To apply this change, instead of using the AWS console, we will use the AWS CLI, which supports deploying your CloudFormation templates via the `aws cloudformation deploy` command. We will be using this command extensively throughout the remainder of this book, so now is a good time to introduce the command:

```
> export AWS_PROFILE=docker-in-aws
> aws cloudformation deploy --stack-name cloud9-management --template-file stack.yml \
--parameter-overrides SubnetId=subnet-a5d3ecee
Enter MFA code for arn:aws:iam::385605022855:mfa/justin.menga: ******

Waiting for changeset to be created..
Waiting for stack create/update to complete

Failed to create/update the stack. Run the following command
to fetch the list of events leading up to the failure
aws cloudformation describe-stack-events --stack-name cloud9-management
```

In the preceding code, we first ensure that the correct profile is configured, and then run the `aws cloudformation deploy` command, specifying the stack name using the `--stack-name` flag and template file with the `--template-file` flag. The `--parameter-overrides` flag allows you to supply input parameter values in the format `<parameter>=<value>` – note that in an update scenario like this one, if you don't specify any parameter overrides, the previous parameter values provided (when you created the stack, in this case) will be used.

Notice that the update actually fails, and if you view the stack events via the CloudFormation console, you can find out why the stack update failed:

	Overview	Outputs	Resources	Events	Template	Parameters	Tags	Stack Policy	Change Sets	Rollback Triggers	

Filter by: Status ▾

2018-06-24	Status	Type	Logical ID	Status Reason
▶ 21:31:44 UTC+1200	UPDATE_ROLLBACK_COMPLETE	AWS::CloudFormation::Stack	cloud9-management	
21:31:43 UTC+1200	DELETE_COMPLETE	AWS::CloudFormation::ManagedCustomResource	ManagementStation	
▶ 21:31:41 UTC+1200	UPDATE_ROLLBACK_COMPLETE_CLEANUP_IN_PROGRESS	AWS::CloudFormation::Stack	cloud9-management	
▶ 21:31:40 UTC+1200	UPDATE_COMPLETE	AWS::Cloud9::EnvironmentEC2	ManagementStation	
▶ 21:31:25 UTC+1200	UPDATE_ROLLBACK_IN_PROGRESS	AWS::CloudFormation::Stack	cloud9-management	The following resource(s) failed to update: [ManagementStation].
▶ 21:31:24 UTC+1200	UPDATE_FAILED	AWS::Cloud9::EnvironmentEC2	ManagementStation	There is already an environment with this name for the user. Environment name needs to be unique per user. Retry with a different name.
▶ 21:31:17 UTC+1200	UPDATE_IN_PROGRESS	AWS::Cloud9::EnvironmentEC2	ManagementStation	Requested update requires the creation of a new physical resource; hence creating one.
▶ 21:31:09 UTC+1200	UPDATE_IN_PROGRESS	AWS::CloudFormation::Stack	cloud9-management	User Initiated
▶ 20:51:15 UTC+1200	CREATE_COMPLETE	AWS::CloudFormation::Stack	cloud9-management	
▶ 20:51:14 UTC+1200	CREATE_COMPLETE	AWS::Cloud9::EnvironmentEC2	ManagementStation	
▶ 20:50:27 UTC+1200	CREATE_IN_PROGRESS	AWS::Cloud9::EnvironmentEC2	ManagementStation	Resource creation Initiated
▶ 20:50:11 UTC+1200	CREATE_IN_PROGRESS	AWS::Cloud9::EnvironmentEC2	ManagementStation	
▶ 20:50:08 UTC+1200	CREATE_IN_PROGRESS	AWS::CloudFormation::Stack	cloud9-management	User Initiated

CloudFormation stack update failure

In the preceding screenshot, you can see that the stack update failed because the change required CloudFormation to create and replace the existing resource (in this case, the Cloud9 environment) with a new resource. As CloudFormation always attempts to create new resources before destroying any old resources that have been replaced, because the resource is configured with a name, CloudFormation cannot create a new resource with the same name, causing a failure. This highlights one of the important gotchas of CloudFormation—be very careful when defining your resources with static names—if CloudFormation ever needs to replace the resource in an update scenario like this one, the update will fail as generally, resource names must be unique.

> **TIP**
>
> For guidance on when CloudFormation will choose to replace a resource if you are updating the resource, refer to the resource properties defined for each resource type in the `AWS Resource Types Reference` document.

You can see that CloudFormation automatically rolls back the change after the failure, reversing any changes that were made leading up to the failure. The status of the stack eventually changes to `UPDATE_ROLLBACK_COMPLETE`, indicating that a failure and rollback took place.

One fix for resolving the stack failure would be to remove the `Name` property on the `ManagementStation` resource in your stack – in this instance, CloudFormation will ensure it generates a unique name (typically based from the CloudFormation stack name with some random alphanumeric characters appended), meaning any time you update the resource so that it requires a replacement, CloudFormation will simply generate a new unique name and avoid the failure scenario we encountered.

Deleting a CloudFormation stack

Now that you understand how to create and update a stack, let's discuss how to delete a stack. You can delete a stack very easily using the CloudFormation dashboard by simply selecting the stack, selecting **Actions**, and then clicking **Delete Stack**:

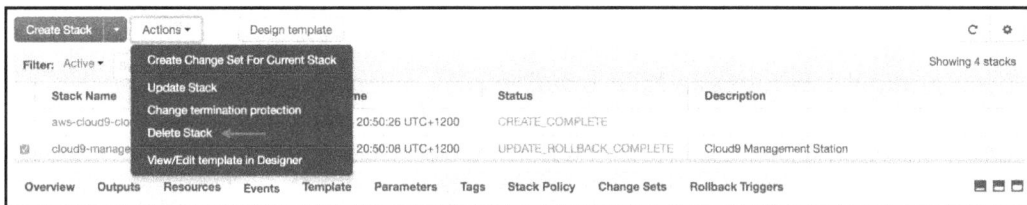

Deleting a CloudFormation stack

After clicking **Yes, Delete** to confirm deletion of your stack, CloudFormation will proceed to delete each resource defined in your stack. Once complete, the stack will disappear from the CloudFormation dashboard, although you change the **Filter** dropdown that is located below the **Create Stack** button to click **Deleted** to view any previously deleted stacks.

> Some might argue it is a little *too* easy to delete your stacks. If you are worried about accidental deletion of your stacks, you can select the **Change termination protection** option in the preceding screenshot to enable termination protection, which will prevent your stacks from being accidentally deleted.

Summary

In this chapter, you learned how to get started with AWS by creating a free account and establishing a root user for your account. You learned how to secure root access using multi-factor authentication, and then created a number of IAM resources that are required to administer your account. You first created an administrative IAM role called **admin**, and then created an Administrators group which you assigned the single permission of being permitted to assume your administrative IAM role. This approach of assuming roles is the recommend and best practice method of administering AWS, and supports more complex multi-account topologies where you can host all of your IAM users in one account and assume administrative roles in other accounts.

You then created a Users group and assigned a managed policy that forces a requirement for multi-factor authentication (MFA) for any user belonging to that group. MFA should be considered a mandatory security requirement these days for any organization that uses AWS, and the approach of simply assigning your users to a Users group that enforces an MFA requirement is a very simple and scalable mechanism to achieve this. After creating a user and assigning it to both the Administrators and Users group, you learned what is required for a first time user to set up their access, which involves logging in with a one-time password, establishing a new password, and then setting up an MFA device. Once a user has logged in using MFA, the user is then able to perform whatever permissions have been assigned to them – for example, the user you created in this chapter was assigned to the Administrators group, and so was able to assume the administrative IAM role, which you were able to perform in the AWS console by using the Switch Role functionality that is built into the console.

With your IAM setup complete and the ability to assume the admin role via the console, we next turned our attention to the command line, installing the AWS CLI, generating an access key via the console, and then configuring your access key credentials in the local `~/.aws` folder that is used by the AWS CLI to store credentials and configuration profiles. You learned how to configure a named configuration profile in the `~/.aws/configuration` file, which automatically assumes the admin role and prompts for an MFA code whenever the CLI detects that new temporary session credentials are required. You also created an EC2 key pair so that you will be able to access EC2 instances using SSH.

Finally, you were introduced to AWS CloudFormation, and learned how to define a CloudFormation template and deploy a CloudFormation stack, which is a collection of resources based upon your CloudFormation template definition. You learned about the basic structure of a CloudFormation template, how to create a stack using the AWS console, and how to deploy a stack using the AWS CLI.

In the next chapter, you will be introduced to the Elastic Container Service, where you will put your new AWS account to good use and learn how to create ECS clusters and deploy Docker applications to ECS.

Questions

1. True/false: A valid credit card is required to establish a free AWS account.
2. True/false: You should always perform administrative actions using the root account.
3. True/false: You should allocate IAM permissions directly to your IAM users and/or groups.
4. Which IAM managed policy would you use to assign administrative permissions?
5. What command do you run to install the AWS CLI?
6. True/false: When you configure the AWS CLI, you must store your IAM username and password locally.
7. Where do you store credentials for the AWS CLI?
8. You set up an IAM user that requires MFA to perform administrative actions. The IAM user sets up their AWS CLI but complains about unauthorized errors when attempt to run AWS CLI commands. The named profile includes the `source_profile`, `role_arn`, and `role_session_name` parameters, and you confirm that these are configured correctly. How would you fix this issue?
9. True/false: CloudFormation templates can be written using JSON or YAML.
10. True/false: You can use the `!Ref` keyword to refer to another resource or parameter in a CloudFormation template.

11. You define a resource in a CloudFormation template that includes an optional `Name` property that you configure as `my-resource`. You create a new stack from the template successfully, and then make a change to the resource that the documentation states will require replacement of the entire resource. Will you be able to deploy this change successfully?

Further reading

You can check the following links for more information about the topics covered in this chapter:

- Setting up a Free Tier account: `https://aws.amazon.com/free`
- IAM best practices: `https://docs.aws.amazon.com/IAM/latest/UserGuide/best-practices.html`
- Your AWS Account ID and alias: `https://docs.aws.amazon.com/IAM/latest/UserGuide/console_account-alias.html`
- Improving the AWS Force MFA policy: `https://www.trek10.com/blog/improving-the-aws-force-mfa-policy-for-IAM-users/`
- Installing the AWS CLI: `https://docs.aws.amazon.com/cli/latest/userguide/installing.html`
- AWS CLI reference: `https://docs.aws.amazon.com/cli/latest/reference/`
- AWS CLI configuration variables: `https://docs.aws.amazon.com/cli/latest/topic/config-vars.html`
- AWS shell: `https://github.com/awslabs/aws-shell`
- AWS CloudFormation user guide: `https://docs.aws.amazon.com/AWSCloudFormation/latest/UserGuide/Welcome.html`
- AWS CloudFormation template anatomy: `https://docs.aws.amazon.com/AWSCloudFormation/latest/UserGuide/template-anatomy.html`
- AWS CloudFormation resource types reference: `https://docs.aws.amazon.com/AWSCloudFormation/latest/UserGuide/aws-template-resource-type-ref.html`
- AWS CloudFormation intrinsic functions: `https://docs.aws.amazon.com/AWSCloudFormation/latest/UserGuide/intrinsic-function-reference.html`
- AWS CloudFormation pseudo parameters: `https://docs.aws.amazon.com/AWSCloudFormation/latest/UserGuide/pseudo-parameter-reference.html`

Introduction to ECS

4

Elastic Container Service (**ECS**) is a popular AWS-managed service that provides container orchestration for your applications and integrates with a wide variety of AWS services and tools.

In this chapter, you will learn key concepts of ECS; how ECS is architected, and understand the various components of ECS, which include the **Elastic Container Registry** (**ECR**), ECS clusters, ECS container instances, ECS task definitions, ECS tasks, and ECS services. The primary focus of this chapter will be using the AWS console to create your first ECS cluster, define an ECS task definition, and configure an ECS service to deploy your first container application to ECS. You will take a closer look at how ECS clusters are formed from ECS container instances, and inspect an ECS container instance under the hood to understand further how ECS is connected to your infrastructure and how containers are deployed and managed. Finally, you will be introduced to the ECS command-line interface (CLI), which is a useful tool for quickly standing up ECS clusters, task definitions, and services that uses the popular Docker Compose format to define your containers and services.

The following topics will be covered:

- ECS architecture
- Creating an ECS cluster
- Understanding ECS container instances
- Creating ECS task definitions
- Creating ECS services
- Deploying ECS services
- Running an ECS task
- Using the ECS CLI

Technical requirements

The following are the technical requirements to complete this chapter:

- Docker Engine 18.06 or higher
- Docker Compose 1.22 or higher
- jq
- Administrator access to an AWS account
- Local AWS profile configured, as per instructions in Chapter 3
- Working Docker workflow for the sample application, as configured in Chapter 2 (see `https://github.com/docker-in-aws/docker-in-aws/tree/master/ch2`).

The following GitHub URL contains the code samples used in this chapter: `https://github.com/docker-in-aws/docker-in-aws/tree/master/ch4`.

Check out the following video to see the Code in Action:
`http://bit.ly/2MTG1n3`

ECS architecture

ECS is an AWS-managed service that provides you with core building blocks to construct how you want to deploy and operate container applications in AWS.

> Prior to December 2017, the Elastic Container Service was known as the EC2 Container Service.

ECS allows you to:

- Build and publish your Docker images in private repositories
- Create definitions that describe the container images, configuration, and resources required to run your applications
- Launch and run your containers using your own EC2 infrastructure or using an AWS-managed infrastructure
- Manage and monitor your containers
- Orchestrate rolling deployments of new versions or revisions of your container applications

To provide these capabilities, ECS includes a number of components illustrated in the following diagram and described in the following table:

Component	Description
Elastic Container Registry (ECR)	Provides secure private Docker image repositories where you can publish and pull your Docker images. We will examine ECR in depth in `Chapter 5`, *Publishing Docker Images using ECR*.
ECS cluster	A collection of ECS Container Instances that run your container applications.
ECS container instance	An EC2 instance that runs the Docker Engine and ECS agent, which communicates with the AWS ECS service and allows ECS to manage the lifecycle of your container applications. Each ECS container instance is joined to a single ECS cluster.
ECS agent	A software component that runs in the form of a Docker container and communicates with the AWS ECS service. The agent is responsible for managing the Docker Engine on behalf of ECS, pulling Docker images from registries, starting and stopping ECS tasks, and publishing metrics to ECS.
ECS task definition	Defines one or more containers and associated resources that comprise your application. Each container definition includes information specifying the container image, how much CPU and memory should be allocated to the container, runtime environment variables, and many more configuration options.
ECS Task	An ECS task is the runtime manifestation of an ECS task definition, and represents the containers defined in your task definitions running on a given ECS cluster. ECS tasks can be run as short-lived, adhoc tasks, or run as long-lived tasks, which form the building blocks of ECS services.
ECS service	An ECS service defines zero or more instances of a long-lived ECS task running on a given ECS cluster and represent what you would commonly think of as your application or microservice instances. ECS services define an ECS task definition, target an ECS cluster, and also include a desired count, which defines how many instances or ECS tasks based from the ECS task definition are associated with the service. Your ECS services can be integrated with the AWS Elastic Load Balancing service, which allows you to provide a highly available, load-balanced service endpoint for your ECS service, and also supports rolling deployments of new versions of your application.
AWS ECS	Manages all components in the ECS architecture. Provides service endpoints that manage ECS agents, integrate with other AWS services, and allow customers to manage their ECR repositories, ECS task definitions, and ECS clusters.

As we progress through this chapter, refer to the following diagram to obtain a visual overview of how the various ECS components relate to each other.

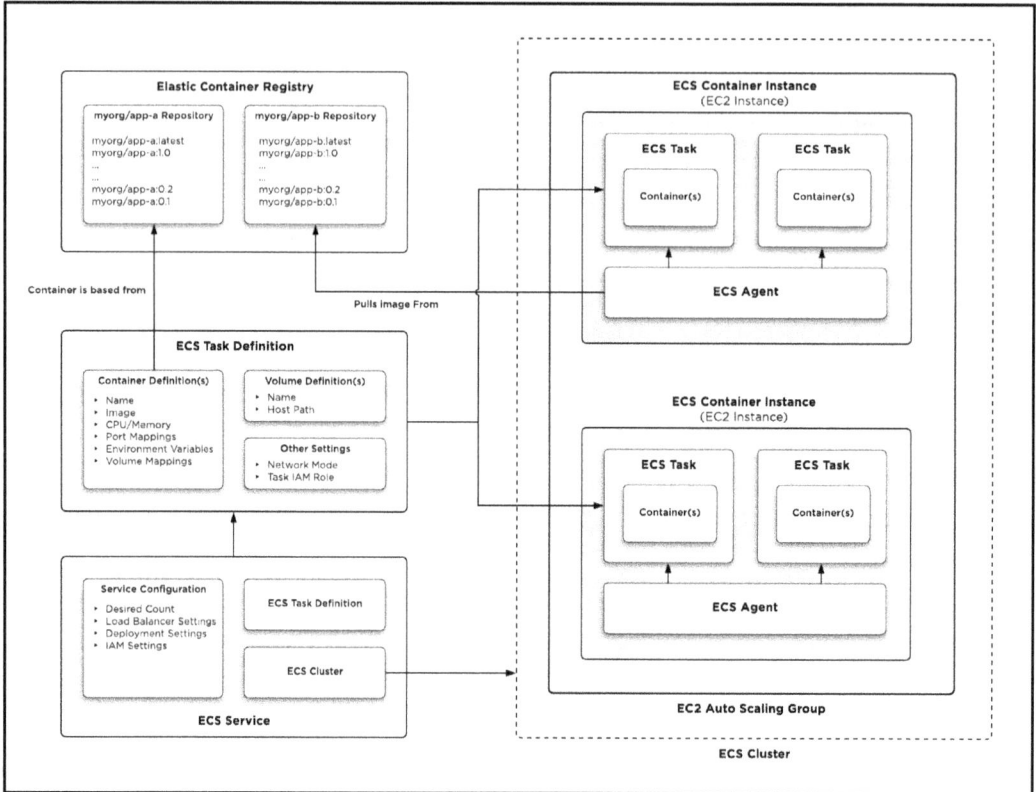

ECS architecture

Creating an ECS cluster

To help you understand the basics of ECS, we will now step through a series of configuration tasks using the AWS console.

We will first create an ECS cluster, which is a collection of ECS container instances that will run your container applications, and often are closely related to EC2 Auto Scaling groups, as shown in the following figure.

Creating an ECS cluster can be performed using the following steps:

> All AWS console configuration examples in this chapter are based on you having logged in to the AWS console and assumed an appropriate administrative role, as described in the earlier Chapter 3, *Getting Started with AWS*. At the time of writing this chapter, the tasks described in this section are specific to the us-east-1 (North Virginia) region so before proceeding, ensure you have selected this region in the AWS console.

1. From the main AWS console, select **Services** | **Elastic Container Service** within the **Compute** section.
2. If you haven't used or configured ECS before in your AWS account and region, you will be presented with a Welcome screen, and you can invoke a getting started configuration wizard by clicking the **Get started** button.
3. At at the time of writing, the getting started wizard only allows you to get started using the Fargate deployment type. We will learn about Fargate in later chapters, so scroll to the bottom of the screen and click on **Cancel**.
4. You will be returned to the ECS console and we can now get started creating an ECS cluster by clicking on the **Create Cluster** button.
5. On the **Select cluster template** screen, select the **EC2 Linux + Networking** template, which will set up network resources and an EC2 autoscaling group with support for Docker for Linux by launching EC2 instances based upon a special ECS-optimized Amazon Machine Image (AMI) that we'll learn more about later on. Once complete, click on **Next step** to continue.

6. On the **Configure cluster** screen, configure a cluster name of **test-cluster**, ensure the **EC2 instance type** is set to **t2.micro** to qualify for free tier access, and set the **Key pair** to the EC2 key pair you created in earlier chapters. Notice that a new VPC and subnets will be created, along with a security group that permits inbound web access (TCP port 80) from the internet (0.0.0.0/0). Once complete, click on **Create** to commence creation of the cluster:

Create Cluster

Step 1: Select cluster template

Step 2: Configure cluster

Configure cluster

Cluster name*   test-cluster

Create an empty cluster

Instance configuration

Provisioning Model   ● On-Demand Instance

With On-Demand Instances, you pay for compute capacity by the hour, with no long-term commitments or upfront payments.

Spot

Amazon EC2 Spot Instances allow you to bid on spare Amazon EC2 computing capacity for up to 90% off the On-Demand price. Learn more

EC2 instance type*   t2.micro

Number of instances*   1

EC2 Ami Id*   amzn-ami-2017.09.g-amazon-ecs-optimized [ami-28456852]

EBS storage (GiB)*   22

Key pair   admin

You will not be able to SSH into your EC2 instances without a key pair. You can create a new key pair in the EC2 console

Configuring the ECS cluster

7. At this point, the **Launch** status screen will be displayed and a number of resources will be created that are required to support your ECS cluster. Once the cluster creation is complete, click on the **View Cluster** button to continue.

You will now be taken to the details screen for the `test-cluster` that was just created. Congratulations—you have successfully deployed your first ECS cluster!

The cluster details screen provides you with configuration and operational data about your ECS cluster—for example, if you click on the **ECS Instances** tab, you are presented with a list of each of the ECS container instances in the cluster:

ECS cluster details

You can see that the wizard created a single container instance, which is running from an EC2 instance that is deployed to the displayed availability zone. Note you can also see other information about the ECS container instance, such as ECS agent version and status, running tasks, CPU/memory usage, along with the version of the Docker Engine.

There's not much more than this to an ECS cluster—it is essentially a collection of ECS container instances, which in turn are EC2 instances running the Docker Engine along with an ECS agent that provide CPU, memory, and networking resources for running your containers.

Understanding ECS container instances

Creating an ECS cluster was very easy using the wizard provided by the AWS console, however it should be obvious that a lot of things were happening under the hood to get your ECS cluster up and running. A full discussion of all of the resources that were created is outside the scope of this introductory chapter, however at this stage, it is useful to focus on ECS container instances and examine them in further detail, given they collectively form the heart of ECS clusters.

Joining an ECS cluster

As the ECS create cluster wizard launched instances and created our ECS cluster, you may have wondered how exactly an ECS container instance joins an ECS cluster. The answer to this is very simple and can be understood easily by clicking on the EC2 instance ID link of the ECS container instance in your newly created cluster.

This link will take you to the EC2 Dashboard with the EC2 instance associated with the container instance selected, as shown in the following screenshot. Note that I have highlighted a number of elements that I will refer back to as we discuss ECS container instances:

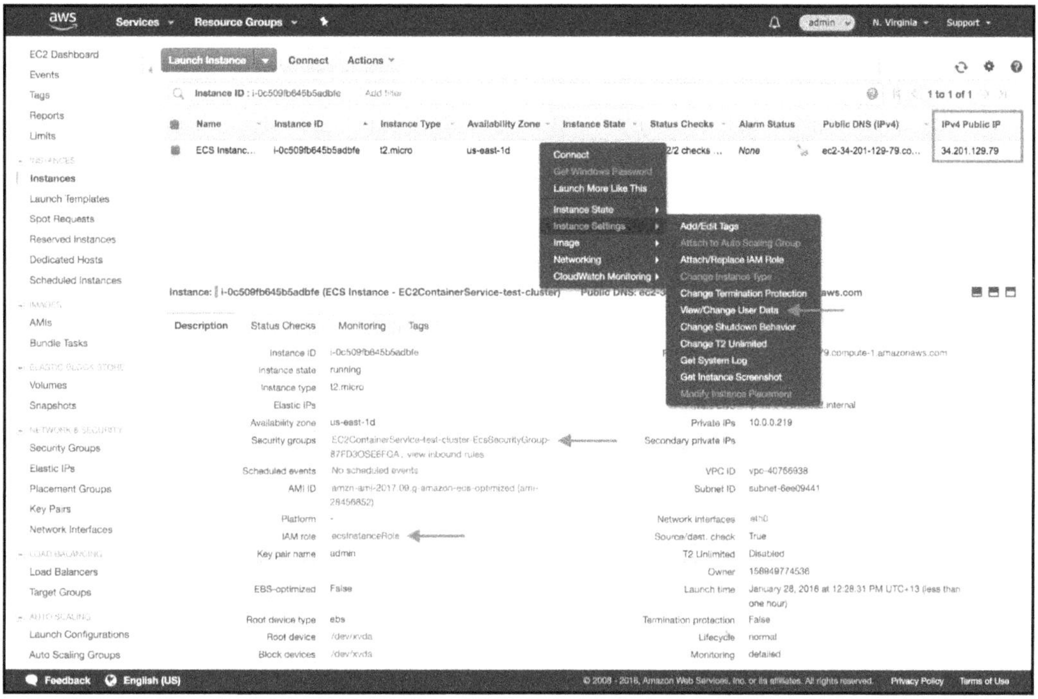

EC2 Instance details

If you right-click the instance and select **Instance Settings** | **View/Change User Data** (see the previous screenshot), you will be presented with the user data for the instance, which is a script that is run on instance creation and can be used to help initialize your EC2 instances:

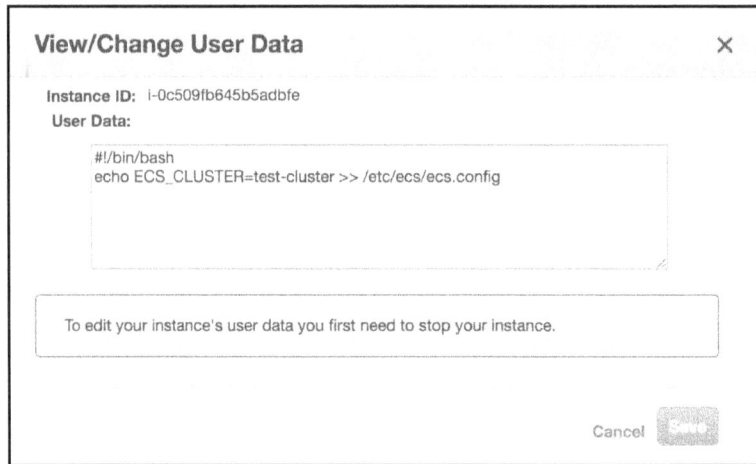

```
View/Change User Data                                    ×

Instance ID:   i-0c509fb645b5adbfe
User Data:

    #!/bin/bash
    echo ECS_CLUSTER=test-cluster >> /etc/ecs/ecs.config




    To edit your instance's user data you first need to stop your instance.




                                              Cancel
```

EC2 Instance User Data Script for Joining an ECS Cluster

The user data script that was configured by the getting started wizard is shown in the previous screenshot, which, as you can see, is a very simple bash script that writes the `ECS_CLUSTER=test-cluster` text to a file called `/etc/ecs/ecs.config`. In this example, recall that `test-cluster` is the name you configured for your ECS cluster, so this single configuration line in the referenced ECS agent configuration file simply tells the agent running on the ECS container instance to attempt to register with an ECS cluster called `test-cluster`.

> The `/etc/ecs/ecs.config` file includes many other configuration options, which we will examine in further detail in `Chapter 6`, *Building Custom ECS Container Instances*.

Granting access to join an ECS cluster

In the previous screenshot, notice that there are no credentials required to connect to the ECS cluster—you could be forgiven for thinking that ECS simply allows any EC2 instance to join an ECS cluster, but of course that would not be very secure.

EC2 instances include a feature called IAM instance profiles, which attaches an IAM role to the EC2 instance that defines various AWS service operations the instance can perform. In the EC2 dashboard for your EC2 instance, you can see that a role called **ecsInstanceRole** has been assigned to your instance, and if you click on this role, you will be taken to the IAM dashboard showing the **Summary** page for the role.

In the **Permissions** tab you can see that an AWS-managed policy called `AmazonEC2ContainerServiceforEC2Role` is attached to the role, and if you expand the policy, you can see the various IAM permissions associated with this policy as shown in the following screenshot:

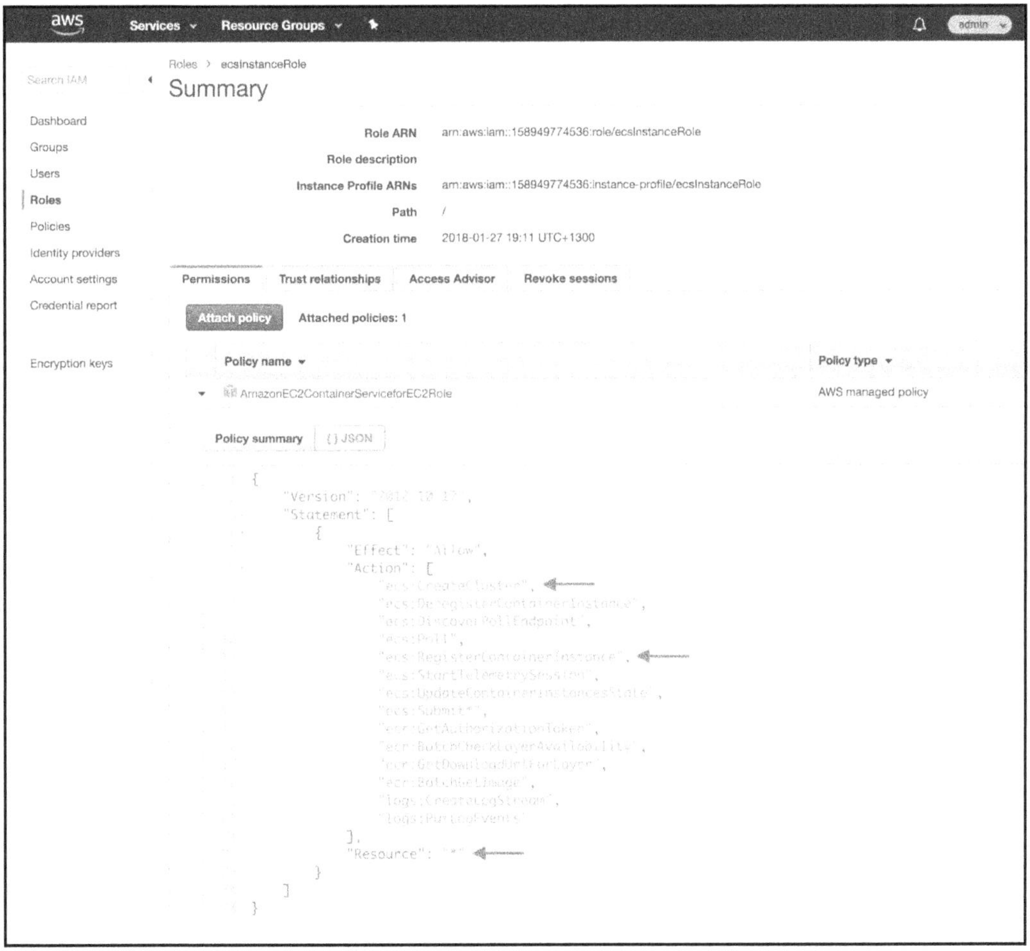

EC2 Instance Role IAM Policy

Notice that the policy permits the `ecs:RegisterContainerInstance` action, which is the ECS permission required for an ECS container instance to join an ECS cluster, and that the policy also grants the `ecs:CreateCluster` permission, which means an ECS container instance attempting to register to an ECS cluster that does not currently exist will automatically create a new cluster.

One further thing to note is that the policy applies to all resources as designated by the `"Resource"`: `"*"` property, meaning any EC2 instance that is assigned a role with this policy will be able to join any ECS cluster in your account and region. Again, this may not seem very secure, but bear in mind this is a policy intended to simplify granting the necessary permissions for your ECS container instances, and in later chapters we will discuss how to create your own custom IAM roles and policies to restrict which ECS clusters a given ECS container instance can join.

Managing ECS container instances

In general, ECS container instances should be self-managing and require very little direct management, but nevertheless there will be times you need to troubleshoot your ECS container instances, hence it is useful to learn how you can connect to your ECS container instances and understand what happens under the hood of an ECS container instance.

Connecting to ECS container instances

ECS container instances are regular Linux hosts, so as you might expect, connecting to your instances simply means being able to establish a secure shell (SSH) session to the instance:

1. If you navigate back to your instance in the EC2 dashboard, we first need to configure the security group attached to your instance to permit inbound SSH access. You can do this by clicking on the security group, selecting the Inbound tab and clicking the **Edit button** to modify the inbound rules of the security group.
2. In the **Edit inbound rules** dialog, click on the **Add Rule** button and add a new rule with the following settings:
   - **Protocol**: TCP
   - **Port Range**: 22
   - **Source**: My IP

Add a Security Group Rule for SSH Access

3. After clicking **Save**, you will have enabled inbound SSH access from your public IP address to the ECS container instance. If you click back in your browser to return to your EC2 instance, you can now copy the public IP address and SSH to your instance.

The following example demonstrates how to establish an SSH connection to the instance, using the `-i` flag to reference the private key of the EC2 key pair you associated with the instance. You also need to log in with a username of `ec2-user`, which is the default non-root user included in Amazon Linux:

```
> ssh -i ~/.ssh/admin.pem ec2-user@34.201.120.79
The authenticity of host '34.201.120.79 (34.201.120.79)' can't be
established.
ECDSA key fingerprint is
SHA256:c/MniTAq931tJj8bCVtRUP9gixM/ZXZSqDuMENqpod0.
Are you sure you want to continue connecting (yes/no)? yes
Warning: Permanently added '34.201.120.79' (ECDSA) to the list of
known hosts.

   __|  __|  __|
   _|  (  \__ \  Amazon ECS-Optimized Amazon Linux AMI 2017.09.g
  ____|\___|____/

For documentation visit, http://aws.amazon.com/documentation/ecs
5 package(s) needed for security, out of 7 available
Run "sudo yum update" to apply all updates.
```

The first thing to notice is that the login banner indicates this instance is based on the the Amazon ECS-Optimized Amazon Linux AMI, which is the default and recommended Amazon Machine Image (AMI) to work with when creating ECS container instances. AWS maintains this AMI and updates it periodically with versions of Docker and ECS agent recommended for use with ECS, so this is by far the simplest platform to use for your ECS container instances and I strongly recommend using this AMI as the foundation for your ECS container instances.

You can learn more about this AMI here: `https://docs.aws.amazon.com/AmazonECS/latest/developerguide/ecs-optimized_AMI.html`. It includes a list of current AMI image IDs for each of the regions supported by ECS.

> In `Chapter 6`, *Building Custom ECS Container Instances* you will learn how to customize and enhance the Amazon ECS-Optimized Amazon Linux AMI.

Inspecting the local Docker environment

As you might expect, your ECS container instance will have an active Docker Engine running, which you can gather information about by running the `docker info` command:

```
> docker info
Containers: 1
 Running: 1
 Paused: 0
 Stopped: 0
Images: 2
Server Version: 17.09.1-ce
Storage Driver: devicemapper
 Pool Name: docker-docker--pool
 Pool Blocksize: 524.3kB
 Base Device Size: 10.74GB
 Backing Filesystem: ext4
...
...
```

Here you can see the instance is running Docker version 17.09.1-ce, using the device mapper storage driver, and currently has a single container running.

Let's now take a look at the running container by executing the `docker container ps` command:

```
> docker ps
CONTAINER ID    IMAGE                          COMMAND     CREATED
STATUS          NAMES
a1b1a89b5e9e    amazon/amazon-ecs-agent:latest  "/agent"   36 minutes
ago    Up 36 minutes    ecs-agent
```

You can see that the ECS agent actually runs as a container called `ecs-agent`, which should always be running on your ECS container instances in order for your ECS container instance to be managed by ECS.

Inspecting the ECS agent

As shown previously, the ECS agent runs as a Docker container, and we can use the `docker container inspect` command to gather some insight about how this container works. In the previous example, we reference the name of the ECS agent container, and then use a Go template expression along with the `--format` flag to filter the command output, displaying the various bind mounts or volume mappings from the ECS agent container to the ECS container instance host.

> In many of the command examples, I am piping output to the `jq` utility, which is a useful utility used for parsing JSON output at the command line. `jq` is not included by default in the Amazon Linux AMI, so you will need to install `jq` by running the `sudo yum install jq` command.

```
> docker container inspect ecs-agent --format '{{json
.HostConfig.Binds}}' | jq
[
  "/var/run:/var/run",
  "/var/log/ecs:/log",
  "/var/lib/ecs/data:/data",
  "/etc/ecs:/etc/ecs",
  "/var/cache/ecs:/var/cache/ecs",
  "/cgroup:/sys/fs/cgroup",
  "/proc:/host/proc:ro",
  "/var/lib/ecs/dhclient:/var/lib/dhclient",
  "/lib64:/lib64:ro",
  "/sbin:/sbin:ro"
]
```

Running the docker container inspect command

Notice that the `/var/run` folder is mapped from the host to the agent, which provides access to the Docker Engine socket located at `/var/run/docker.sock`, allowing the ECS agent to manage the Docker Engine. You can also see that ECS agent logs will be written to `/var/log/ecs` on the Docker Engine host file system.

Verifying the ECS agent

The ECS agent includes a local web server that can be used to introspect current ECS agent status.

The following example demonstrates introspecting the ECS agent using the `curl` command:

```
> curl -s localhost:51678 | jq
{
  "AvailableCommands": [
    "/v1/metadata",
    "/v1/tasks",
    "/license"
  ]
}
> curl -s localhost:51678/v1/metadata | jq
{
  "Cluster": "test-cluster",
  "ContainerInstanceArn": "arn:aws:ecs:us-
east-1:385605022855:container-instance/f67cbfbd-1497-47c0-b56c-
a910c923ba70",
  "Version": "Amazon ECS Agent - v1.16.2 (998c9b5)"
}
```

Introspecting the ECS Agent

Notice that the ECS agent listens on port 51678 and provides three endpoints you can query:

- `/v1/metadata`: Describes the cluster the container instance is joined to, the container instance **Amazon Resource Name (ARN)**, and the ECS agent version
- `/v1/tasks`: Returns a list of currently-running tasks. At the moment we haven't deployed any ECS services or tasks to our cluster, hence this list is empty
- `/license`: Provides the various software licenses that apply for the ECS agent software

The `/v1/metadata` endpoint is particularly useful, as you can use this endpoint to determine whether or not the ECS agent has successfully joined a given ECS cluster. We will use this later on in `Chapter 6`, *Building Custom ECS Container Instances* to perform a health check on instance creation to ensure our instances have successfully joined the correct ECS cluster.

ECS container instance logs

Each ECS container instance includes log files that can help troubleshoot your instance.

The primary logs you will work with include the following:

- Docker Engine logs: Located at `/var/log/docker`
- ECS Agent logs: Located at `/var/log/ecs`

Note that there are two types of ECS agent logs:

- Init logs: Located at `/var/log/ecs/ecs-init.log`, these logs provide output related to the `ecs-init` service, which is an Upstart service that ensures the ECS agent is running on container instance startup.
- Agent logs: Located at `/var/log/ecs/ecs-agent.log.*`, these logs provide output related to ECS agent operation. These logs are the most common logs you will inspect for any ECS agent related issues.

Creating an ECS task definition

Now that you have set up your ECS cluster and understand how ECS container instances register with the cluster, it's time to configure an ECS task definition, which defines the configuration of the containers you want to deploy for your application. ECS task definitions can define one or more containers, along with other elements, such as volumes, that your containers may need to read or write to.

To keep things simple, we are going to create a very basic task definition that will run the official Nginx Docker image, which is published at `https://hub.docker.com/_/nginx/`. Nginx is a popular web server, which by default will serve a Welcome to Nginx page, and for now this will suffice to represent a simple web application.

Let's now create an ECS task definition for our simple web application by performing the following steps:

1. Navigate to the ECS console at **Services** | **Elastic Container Service**. You can create a new task definition by selecting **Task Definitions** from the left-hand menu and clicking the **Create new Task Definition** button.

2. In the **Select launch type compatibility** screen, select the **EC2 launch type**, which will configure the task definition to be launched on ECS clusters based upon the infrastructure that you own and manage.

3. In the **Configure task and container definitions** screen, configure a **Task Definition Name** of **simple-web** and then scroll down and click **Add container** to add a new container definition.

4. In the **Add container** screen, configure the following settings and once complete click the **Add button** to create the container definition. This container definition will map port 80 on ECS container hosts to port 80 in the container, allowing access to the Nginx web server from the outside world:

   - **Container name**: nginx
   - **Image**: nginx
   - **Memory Limits**: 250 MB Hard limit
   - **Port mappings**: Host port 80, Container port 80, Protocol tcp:

Add container   ✕

▾ Standard

Container name*   nginx   ❶ ⟵

Image*   nginx   ❶ ⟵

Custom image format: [registry-url]/[namespace]/[image]:[tag]

Memory Limits (MiB)*   Hard limit ▾   250   ❶ ⟵

⊕ Add Soft limit

Define hard and/or soft memory limits in MiB for your
container. Hard and soft limits correspond to the 'memory'
and 'memoryReservation' parameters, respectively, in task
definitions.
ECS recommends 300-500 MiB as a starting point for web
applications.

Port mappings   Host port   Container port   Protocol   ❶

⟶   80   80   tcp ▾   ⊗

⊕ Add port mapping

▾ Advanced container configuration

ENVIRONMENT

CPU units   ❶

* Required   Cancel   **Add**

Creating a Container Definition

5. Complete creation of the task definition by clicking the **Create** button at the bottom of the **Configure task and container definitions** page.

Creating an ECS service

We have created an ECS cluster and configured an ECS task definition that includes a single container running Nginx with an appropriate port mapping configuration to expose the Nginx web server to the outside world.

We now need to define an ECS service, which will configure ECS to deploy one or more instances of our ECS task definition to our ECS cluster. ECS services deploy a given ECS task definition to a given ECS cluster, allowing you to configure how many instances (ECS tasks) of the referenced ECS task definition you would like to run, and controlling more advanced features, such as load balancer integration and rolling updates of your application.

To create a new ECS service, complete the following steps:

1. In the ECS console, select **Clusters** from the left and click on the **test-cluster** you created earlier in this chapter:

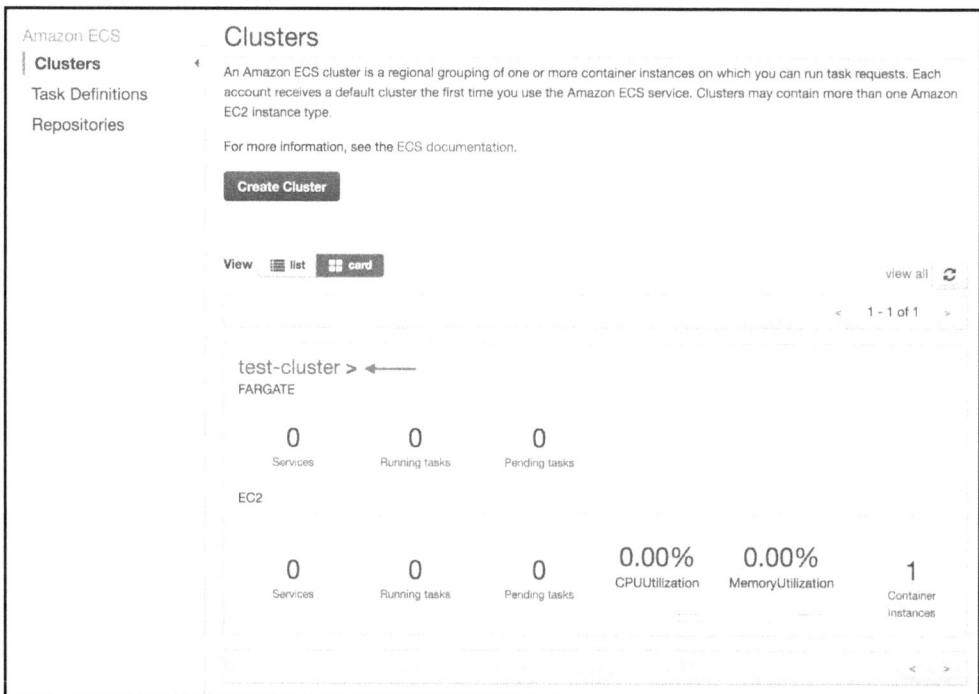

Selecting an ECS Cluster to Create an ECS Service

2. In the **Cluster** details page, select the **Services** tab and click on **Create** to create a new service.

3. On the **Configure service** screen, configure the following settings and once complete click the **Next step** button. Notice that we reference both the task definition and ECS cluster we created earlier in this chapter:
   - **Launch type**: EC2
   - **Task Definition**: simple-web:1
   - **Cluster**: test-cluster
   - **Service name**: simple-web
   - **Number of tasks**: 1

4. The remainder of the ECS service configuration settings are optional. Keep on clicking **Next step** until you reach the **Review** screen, where you can review your settings and click **Create Service** to complete creation of the ECS service.

5. The **Launch Status** screen will now appear and once your service has been created, click on the **View Service** button.

6. The **Service details** screen will now appear for your new ECS service, and you should see a single ECS task in a **RUNNING** state, meaning the Nginx container associated with the simple-web ECS task definition was successfully launched:

Completing Creation of a New ECS Service

At this stage, you should now be able to browse to your newly deployed Nginx web server, which you can verify by browsing to the public IP address of the ECS container instance you created earlier as part of your ECS cluster. If everything is working as expected, you should be presented with the default **Welcome to nginx** page, as shown in the following screenshot:

Browsing to the Nginx Web Server

Deploying ECS services

Now that you have successfully created an ECS service, let's examine how ECS manages new deployments of container applications. It is important to understand that ECS task definitions are immutable—that is, you cannot modify a task definition once it has been created, and instead you need to either create a completely new task definition or create a *revision* of your current task definition, which you can think of as a new version of a given task definition.

ECS defines the logical name of an ECS task definition as the *family*, and a given revision of an ECS task definition is expressed in the form *family:revision*—for example, `my-task-definition:3` refers to revision 3 from the *my-task-definition* family.

This means that in order to deploy a new version of a container application, you need to perform a couple of steps:

1. Create a new revision of your ECS task definition with configuration settings that have been changed for the new version of your application. This often will just be the image tag associated with the Docker images you build for your applications, however any configuration change, such as a change in allocated memory or CPU resource, will result in a new revision of your ECS task definition being created.
2. Update your ECS service to use the new revision of the ECS task definition. Whenever you update an ECS service in this manner, ECS will automatically perform a rolling update of your application, attempting to gracefully replace each running container that comprises your ECS service with new containers based on the new ECS task definition revision.

To demonstrate this behavior, let's now modify the ECS task definition you created earlier in this chapter and update the ECS service by performing the following steps:

1. In the ECS console, select **Task Definitions** from the left and click on the **simple-web** task definition you created earlier.
2. Notice that a single revision of the task definition currently exists—the revision number is denoted after the colon following the task definition name. For example, **simple-web:1** refers to revision 1 of a simple-web task definition. Select the current task definition revision, and then click **Create new revision** to create a new revision based on the existing task definition revision.
3. The **Create new revision of Task Definition** screen is displayed, which is very similar to the **Create new Task Definition** screen you configured earlier. Scroll down to the **Container Definitions** section and click on the Nginx container to modify the Nginx container definition.

4. The change we will make to the task definition is to modify the port mapping from the current static host mapping of port 80 to a dynamic port mapping on the host. This can be achieved by simply leaving the host port setting empty, in which case the Docker Engine will assign a dynamic port from the ephemeral port range on underlying ECS container instances. For the Amazon Linux AMI we are using, this port range is between 32768 and 60999. The benefit of dynamic port mapping is that we can run multiple instances of our container on the same host—if the static port mapping was in place, only one container could be launched, as subsequent containers would attempt to bind to the already-in-use port 80. Once you have completed the configuration change, click on the **Update** button to continue.

5. Click the **Create** button at the bottom of the **Create new revision of Task Definition** screen to complete creation of the new revision.

> To obtain the ephemeral port range used by Docker, you can inspect the contents of the `/proc/sys/net/ipv4/ip_local_port_range` file. If this file is not available on your operating system, Docker will use the port range of `49153` through `65535`.

At this point, a new revision (revision 2) has been created from your ECS task definition. Now you need to update your ECS service to use the new task definition revision by completing the following steps:

1. In the ECS console, select **Clusters** from the left and select your test-cluster. On the **Services** tab, select the checkbox next to your ECS service and click the **Update** button.

2. In the **Task Definition** drop-down on the **Configure service** screen, you should be able to select the new revision (**simple-web:2**) of the task definition you just created. Once complete, keep on clicking the **Next step** button until you reach the **Review** screen, at which point you can click the **Update Service** button to complete your configuration changes:

Update Service

Step 1: Configure service	
Step 2. Configure network	
Step 3: Set Auto Scaling (optional)	
Step 4: Review	

Configure service

A service lets you specify how many copies of your task definition to run and maintain in a cluster. You can optionally use an Elastic Load Balancing load balancer to distribute incoming traffic to containers in your service. Amazon ECS maintains that number of tasks and coordinates task scheduling with the load balancer. You can also optionally use Service Auto Scaling to adjust the number of tasks in your service.

Task Definition	simple-web:2
Force new deployment	
Cluster	test-cluster
Service name	simple-web
Number of tasks	1
Minimum healthy percent	50
Maximum percent	200

*Required   Cancel Next step

Modifying ECS Service Task Definition

3. Similar to what you saw previously when you created your ECS service, the **Launch Status** screen will be displayed. If you click on the **View Service** button, you will be taken to the ECS service details screen, and if you select the **Deployments** tab, you should see the new version of your task definition being deployed:

ECS Service Deployment

Notice that there are two deployments—the **ACTIVE** deployment shows the existing ECS service deployment, and indicates there is currently a single running container. The **PRIMARY** deployment shows the new ECS service deployment based on the new revision, and indicates a desired count of 1 but notice the running count is not yet 1.

If you periodically refresh the deploy status, you will be able to observe the various state changes as the new task definition revision is deployed:

> **TIP** The deployment changes will be performed reasonably quickly, so if you don't see any of these changes, you can always update the ECS service to use the first revision of the ECS task definition to force a new deployment.

1. The **PRIMARY** deployment should indicate a pending count of **1**, meaning the new version of the container is about to start.

Deploymen...	Status	Desired co...	Pending co...	Running co...	Created ti...	Updated ti...
ecs-svc/922...	PRIMARY	1	1	0	2018-01-28 ...	2018-01-28 ...
ecs-svc/922...	ACTIVE	1	0	1	2018-01-28 ...	2018-01-28 ...

New Deployment Pending Transition

2. The **PRIMARY** deployment will next transition to a running count of 1, meaning the new version of the container is running alongside the existing container:

Deploymen...	Status	Desired co...	Pending co...	Running co...	Created ti...	Updated ti...
ecs-svc/922...	PRIMARY	1	0	1	2018-01-28 ...	2018-01-28 ...
ecs-svc/922...	ACTIVE	1	0	1	2018-01-28 ...	2018-01-28 ...

New Deployment Running Transition

3. At this point, the existing container can now be stopped, so you should see the **ACTIVE** deployment running count drop to zero:

Deploymen...	Status	Desired co...	Pending co...	Running co...	Created ti...	Updated ti...
ecs-svc/922...	PRIMARY	1	0	1	2018-01-28 ...	2018-01-28 ...
ecs-svc/922...	ACTIVE	1	0	0	2018-01-28 ...	2018-01-28 ...

Filter in this page ‹ **1-2** ›

Old Deployment Stopping Transition

4. The **ACTIVE** deployment disappears from the **Deployments** tab and the rolling deployment is complete:

Deploymen...	Status	Desired co...	Pending co...	Running co...	Created ti...	Updated ti...
ecs-svc/922...	PRIMARY	1	0	1	2018-01-28 ...	2018-01-28 ...

Filter in this page ‹ **1-1** ›

Notice that the previous ACTIVE deployment has now been removed

Rolling Deployment Completion

At this point, we have successfully performed a rolling update of an ECS service, and it is worthwhile to point out that the new dynamic port-mapping configuration means that your Nginx web server is no longer listening on port 80 to the outside world, and instead is listening on a port dynamically chosen by the ECS container instance.

You can verify this by attempting to browse to your Nginx web server public IP address—this should result in a connection failure as the web server is no longer operational on port 80. If you select the **Tasks** tab for the **simple-web** ECS service, you can click on the task to find out which port our web server is now listening on.

After expanding the Nginx container which is shown as follows, you can see that in this case port 32775 on the ECS container instance host is mapped to port 80 on the Nginx container, which you won't be able to reach from the Internet, given the security group assigned to the ECS container instance only permits inbound access on port 80.

For dynamic port mapping to be useful, you need to associate your ECS services with an application load balancer, which will automatically detect the dynamic port mapping of each ECS service instance and load balance incoming requests to a static port defined on the load balancer to each ECS service instance. You will learn more about this in later chapters.

Amazon ECS		
Clusters	Clusters > test-cluster > Task: bda7cb38-da39-4542-92d7-210091cc8400	
Task Definitions	**Task : bda7cb38-da39-4542-92d7-210091cc8400**	Run more like this · Stop
Repositories	**Details**	

Details

Cluster	test-cluster
Container instance	d1e98eff-adfe-49bf-b8a1-1b3dcfcf3337
EC2 instance id	i-0c509fb645b5adbfe
Launch type	EC2
Task definition	simple-web:2
Group	service:simple-web
Task role	None
Last status	RUNNING
Desired status	RUNNING
Created at	2018-01-29 02:09:15 +1300

Network

Network mode	bridge

Containers

Last updated on January 29, 2018 2:40:13 AM (0m ago)

Name	Container Id	S...	I...	C...	H...	E...
▾ nginx	22553515-97a9-4675-8bd0-bd39a88545de	R...	ng...	0	25...	true

Details

Network bindings

Host Port	Container Port	Protocol	External Link
32775	80	tcp	34.201.129.79:32775

ECS Service Dynamic Port Mapping

Running ECS tasks

We've seen how we can deploy long-running applications as ECS services, but how do we run ad-hoc tasks or short-lived containers using ECS? The answer of course is to create an ECS task, which typically are used to run ad-hoc tasks, such as running a deployment script, performing database migrations, or perhaps performing scheduled batch processing.

Although ECS services are essentially long-running ECS tasks, ECS does treat ECS tasks that you create yourself quite differently from ECS services, as described in the following table:

Scenario/feature	ECS service behavior	ECS task behavior
Container is stopped or fails	ECS will always attempt to maintain the desired count of a given ECS service, and will attempt to restart a container if the active count falls below the desired count due to a container being stopped or failing.	ECS tasks are one-shot executions that are either success or fail. ECS will never attempt to re-run a failed ECS task.
Task definition configuration	You cannot override any of the ECS task definition configuration for a given ECS service.	ECS tasks allow you to override environment variables and command-line settings, allow you to leverage a single ECS task definition for a variety of different types of ECS tasks.
Load balancer integration	ECS services feature full integration with the AWS Elastic Load Balancing service.	ECS tasks offer no integration with any load balancing services.

ECS Services vs ECS Tasks

Let's now see how you run ECS tasks using the AWS console. You will create a very simple ECS task that runs the `sleep 300` command from the Nginx image defined in your ECS tasks definition.

This will cause the task to sleep for five minutes before executing, simulating a short-lived ad-hoc task:

1. In the ECS console, select **Clusters** on the left and click on your cluster named **test-cluster**.

2. Select the **Tasks** tab and click on the **Run new Task** button to create a new ECS task:

Running an ECS Task

3. In the **Run Task** screen, first select **EC2** as the **Launch type** and ensure that the **Task Definition** and **Cluster** settings are configured correctly. If you expand the **Advanced Options** section, notice that you can specify container overrides for the **nginx** container. Note that to configure a command override, you must supply the command you want to run along with any arguments in a comma separated format—for example, to execute the `sleep 300` command, you must configure a command override of **sleep,300**. Once configuration is complete, click on **Run Task** to execute your new ECS task:

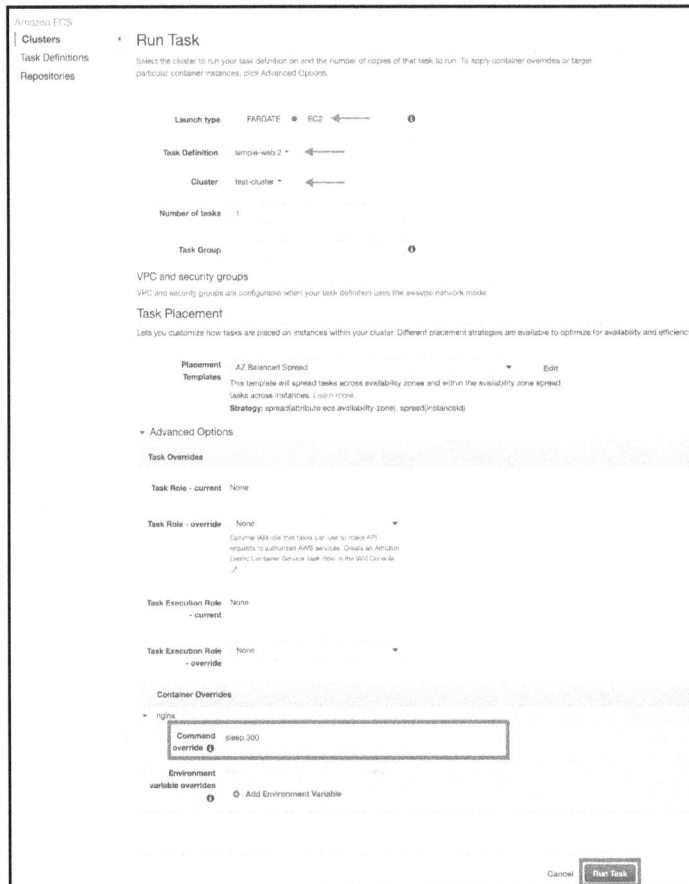

Configuring an ECS Task

At this point, you will be returned to the **Tasks** tab for the ECS cluster and you should see a new task with a state of **PENDING**:

Services	Tasks	ECS Instances	Metrics	Scheduled Tasks

| Run new Task | Stop | Stop All | | | | Last updated on January 29, 2018 2:08:01 AM (0m ago) | | |

Desired task status: (Running) Stopped

▼ Filter in this page		Launch type	ALL	▼			‹ 1-2 › Page size 50 ▼
	Task	Task de...	Contain...	Last sta...	Desired...	Started ...	Group	Launch ...	Platfor...
	4b379d7...	simple-...	d1e98eff...	PENDING	RUNNING		family:simple-web	EC2	--
	abd76e2...	simple-...	d1e98eff...	RUNNING	RUNNING	ecs-svc/...	service:simple-web	EC2	--

ECS Task in a Pending State

The new task should quickly transition to a status of **RUNNING**, and if we left the task to run it would eventually exit after five minutes.

Let's now take this opportunity to observe the behavior of ECS tasks when they are stopped. If you select all tasks and click the **Stop** button, you will be prompted to confirm you want to stop each task. After confirming you want to stop each task, the **Tasks** pane should immediately display no active tasks, and after clicking the refresh button a few times, you should see a single task start back up. This task was automatically started by ECS, in order to maintain a desired count of 1 for the simple-web service.

Using the ECS CLI

In this chapter, we have focused solely on using the AWS console to get started with ECS. Another tool that is written and maintained by AWS is called the ECS CLI, which allows you to create ECS clusters and deploy ECS tasks and services from the command line.

The ECS CLI is different from the AWS CLI in a variety of ways, but the main differences include:

- The ECS CLI is focused on interacting with ECS and only supports interacting with other AWS services that provide supporting resources for ECS, such as the AWS CloudFormation and EC2 service.
- ECS CLI operations are more coarse-grained than AWS CLI operations. For example, the ECS CLI will orchestrate creating an ECS cluster and all of its supporting resources, much like the behavior of the ECS cluster wizard you used earlier in this chapter, whereas the AWS CLI is focused on more fine-grained operations that perform a single specific task.
- The ECS CLI is written in Golang, whereas the AWS CLI is written in Python. This does introduce some behavioral differences—for example, the ECS CLI does not support the use of AWS profiles with MFA (multi-factor authentication) enabled, meaning you need to use AWS credentials and roles that do not mandate MFA.

A particularly useful feature of the ECS CLI is that it supports version 1 and version 2 of Docker Compose files, meaning you can use Docker Compose to provide a generic description of your multi-container environments. The ECS CLI also allows you to define your infrastructure using a YAML-based configuration file, and as such can be considered a simple and functional infrastructure-as-code tool.

In general, the ECS CLI is useful for quickly standing up sandbox/development environments for rapid prototyping or testing. For deploying your formal non-production and production environments, you should use tools and services such as Ansible, AWS CloudFormation, or Terraform, which provide much broader support for all of the AWS resources you will need to run production-grade environments.

> The ECS CLI includes complete documentation, which you can find at `https://docs.aws.amazon.com/AmazonECS/latest/developerguide/ECS_CLI.html`. You can also view the ECS CLI source code and raise issues at `https://github.com/aws/amazon-ecs-cli`.

Deleting the Test Cluster

At this point, you should delete the test cluster you created in this chapter by following these steps in the ECS dashboard:

1. Select the test-cluster from Clusters
2. Select and update the simple-web ECS service to have a desired count of 0
3. Wait until the simple-web ECS task count falls to 0
4. Select the test-cluster and then click the Delete Cluster button

Summary

In this chapter, you were introduced to the ECS architecture and learned about the core components that make up ECS. You learned how ECS clusters are a collection of ECS container instances, which run the Docker Engine atop EC2 autoscaling group instances. AWS provide you with a pre-built ECS-optimized AMI, making it very easy to get up and running quickly with ECS. Each ECS container instance includes an ECS agent, which runs as a system container and communicates with ECS, providing the management and control plane required to start, stop, and deploy your containers.

You next created an ECS task definition, which defines a collection of one or more container and volume definitions, including information such as container image, environment variables, and CPU/memory resource allocations. With your ECS cluster and ECS task definition in place, you were then able to create and configure an ECS service, referencing the ECS task definition to define the container configuration for the ECS service, and targeting one or more instances of your ECS service to your ECS cluster.

ECS supports rolling deployments for updates to your container applications, and you were able to successfully deploy a new application change by simply creating a new revision of your ECS task definition and then associating the definition with your ECS service.

Finally, you learned how to use the ECS CLI to simplify the creation of ECS clusters and services, using Docker Compose as a generic mechanism to define task definitions and ECS services.

In the next chapter, you will take a closer look at the Elastic Container Registry (ECR) service, where you will learn how to create your own private ECR repositories and publish your Docker images to these repositories.

Questions

1. Name three ECS components required to run a long running Docker container using ECS
2. True/false: The ECS agent runs as an upstart service
3. What configuration file format do you use to define infrastructure when using the ECS CLI?
4. True/false: You can deploy two instances of an ECS task with a static port mapping to a single instance ECS cluster
5. True/false: The ECS CLI is considered the best tool for deploying Docker environments to production
6. What would you configure when using ECS to run a batch job that runs for 15 minutes every night?
7. True/false: ECS task definitions are mutable and can be modified
8. True/false: You can inspect the current status of an agent on a given Docker Engine by running the `curl localhost:51678` command

Further information

You can check the following links for more information about the topics covered in this chapter:

- ECS Developer Guide: `https://docs.aws.amazon.com/AmazonECS/latest/developerguide/Welcome.html`
- Amazon ECS-Optimized AMI: `https://docs.aws.amazon.com/AmazonECS/latest/developerguide/ecs-optimized_AMI.html`
- Permissions required for ECS container instances: `https://docs.aws.amazon.com/AmazonECS/latest/developerguide/instance_IAM_role.html`
- ECS agent documentation: `https://docs.aws.amazon.com/AmazonECS/latest/developerguide/ECS_agent.html`
- Using the ECS CLI: `https://docs.aws.amazon.com/AmazonECS/latest/developerguide/ECS_CLI.html`
- ECS agent GitHub repository: `https://github.com/aws/amazon-ecs-agent`
- ECS init GitHub repository: `https://github.com/aws/amazon-ecs-init`
- ECS CLI GitHub repository: `https://github.com/aws/amazon-ecs-cli`

5
Publishing Docker Images Using ECR

Docker registries are a critical component of the Docker and container ecosystem, providing a universal mechanism to publish and distribute your container applications, both publicly and privately.

The ECR provides a fully-managed private Docker registry that features tight integration with the ECS components introduced in the previous chapter and other AWS services. ECR is highly scalable, secure, and offers tooling to integrate with the native Docker client that is used to build and publish Docker images.

In this chapter, you will learn how to create ECR repositories to store your Docker images, using a variety of mechanisms, including the AWS console, AWS CLI, and CloudFormation. Once you have established your first ECR repository, you will learn how to authenticate with ECR, pull Docker images stored in your repositories, and build and publish Docker images to ECR using the Docker client. To close out this chapter, you will learn how to deal with more advanced scenarios of using and managing ECR, including configuring cross-account access to allow Docker clients running in other AWS accounts access to your ECR repositories, and configuring lifecycle policies, which ensure orphaned Docker images are periodically cleaned up, reducing administrating effort and cost.

The following topics will be covered:

- Understanding ECR
- Creating ECR repositories
- Logging into ECR

- Publishing Docker images to ECR
- Pulling Docker images from ECR
- Configuring lifecycle policies

Technical requirements

The following lists the technical requirements to complete this chapter:

- Docker 18.06 or higher
- Docker Compose 1.22 or higher
- GNU Make 3.82 or higher
- jq
- AWS CLI 1.15.71 or higher
- Administrator access to an AWS account
- Local AWS profile configured as per instructions in Chapter 3
- Working Docker workflow for the sample application as configured in Chapter 2 (see `https://github.com/docker-in-aws/docker-in-aws/tree/master/ch2`).

This GitHub URL contains the code samples used in this chapter: `https://github.com/docker-in-aws/docker-in-aws/tree/master/ch5`.

Check out the following video to see the Code in Action:
`http://bit.ly/2PKMLSP`

Understanding ECR

Before we get started creating and configuring ECR repositories, it is important to provide a brief introduction to the core concepts of ECR.

ECR is a fully-managed private Docker registry provided by AWS and offers tight integration with ECS and other AWS services. ECR consists of a number of components, as shown in the following diagram:

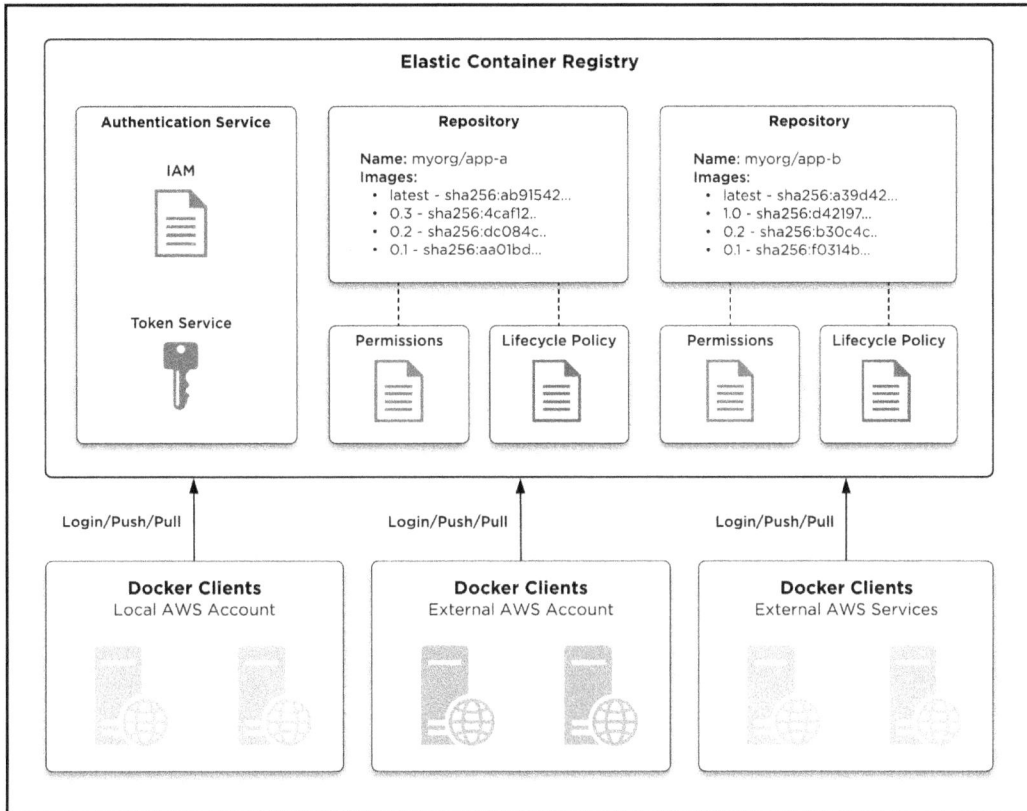

Elastic Container Registry

Authentication Service

IAM

Token Service

Repository

Name: myorg/app-a
Images:
• latest - sha256:ab91542...
• 0.3 - sha256:4caf12..
• 0.2 - sha256:dc084c..
• 0.1 - sha256:aa01bd...

Repository

Name: myorg/app-b
Images:
• latest - sha256:a39d42...
• 1.0 - sha256:d42197...
• 0.2 - sha256:b30c4c..
• 0.1 - sha256:f0314b...

Permissions

Lifecycle Policy

Permissions

Lifecycle Policy

Login/Push/Pull

Login/Push/Pull

Login/Push/Pull

Docker Clients
Local AWS Account

Docker Clients
External AWS Account

Docker Clients
External AWS Services

ECR architecture

The core components of ECR include:

- **Repositories**: A repository stores all versions of images for a given Docker image. Each repository is configured with a name and URI, which is unique to your AWS account and region.

- **Permissions**: Each repository includes permissions that allow you to grant access for various ECR operations, such as pushing or pulling Docker images.

- **Lifecycle policy**: Each repository can be configured with an optional lifecycle policy, which can be used to clean up orphaned Docker images that have been superseded by newer versions, or remove older Docker images that you may no longer use.

- **Authentication service**: ECR includes an authentication service that includes a token service that can be used to authenticate your IAM credentials in exchange for a temporary authentication token compatible with the Docker client authentication process.

It's also important to consider the consumers of ECR. As shown in the previous diagram, these include:

- **Docker clients in the same local AWS account as your repositories**: This would most commonly include ECS container instances running in ECS clusters.
- **Docker clients in a different AWS account from your repositories**: This is a common scenario for larger organizations, and again would typically include ECS container instances running in ECS clusters in remote accounts.
- **Docker clients used by AWS services**: Some AWS services can utilize your own Docker images published in ECR, such as the AWS CodeBuild service.

> At the time of writing this book, ECR is only offered as a private registry - meaning if you want to publish public your Docker images publicly, then ECR is not the correct solution for you, at least in terms of publishing your public Docker images.

Creating ECR repositories

Now that you have a basic overview of ECR, let's get started creating your first ECR repository. Recall in earlier chapters, you were introduced to the sample **todobackend** application for this book, and you built a Docker image in your local environment. To be able to run containers on your ECS clusters based from this image, you need to publish this image to a Docker registry that your ECS container instances can access, and ECR is the perfect solution for this.

To create an ECR repository for the **todobackend** application, we will focus on the three popular methods to create and configure your repositories:

- Creating ECR repositories using the AWS Console
- Creating ECR repositories using the AWS CLI
- Creating ECR repositories using the AWS CloudFormation

Creating ECR repositories using the AWS Console

Creating an ECR repository can be performed using the AWS Console by performing the following steps:

1. From the main AWS console, select **Services** | **Elastic Container Service** within the **Compute** section, select **Repositories** from the left menu, and then click on the **Get Started** button.
2. You will be prompted to configure a name for your repository. A standard convention is to name your repositories in the `<organization>/<application>` format, which will result in a fully-qualified repository URI of `<registry>/<organization>/<application>`. In the following example, I am calling the repository `docker-in-aws/todobackend`, but you can name your image whatever you like. Once complete, click on **Next step** to continue:

Configuring a Repository name

3. Your ECR repository will now be created and instructions on how to log in to ECR and publish your Docker image will be provided.

Creating ECR repositories using the AWS CLI

Creating an ECR repository can be performed using the AWS CLI by running the `aws ecr create-repository` command, however given you have already created your repository via the AWS console, let's see how you can check whether an ECR repository already exists and how to delete a repository using the AWS CLI.

To view a list of ECR repositories in your AWS account and local region, you can use the `aws ecr list-repositories` command, while to delete an ECR repository, you can use the `aws ecr delete-repository` command, as demonstrated here:

```
> aws ecr list-repositories
{
    "repositories": [
        {
            "repositoryArn": "arn:aws:ecr:us-
east-1:385605022855:repository/docker-in-aws/todobackend",
            "registryId": "385605022855",
            "repositoryName": "docker-in-aws/todobackend",
            "repositoryUri": "385605022855.dkr.ecr.us-
east-1.amazonaws.com/docker-in-aws/todobackend",
            "createdAt": 1517692382.0
        }
    ]
}
> aws ecr delete-repository --repository-name docker-in-
aws/todobackend
{
    "repository": {
        "repositoryArn": "arn:aws:ecr:us-
east-1:385605022855:repository/docker-in-aws/todobackend",
        "registryId": "385605022855",
        "repositoryName": "docker-in-aws/todobackend",
        "repositoryUri": "385605022855.dkr.ecr.us-
east-1.amazonaws.com/docker-in-aws/todobackend",
        "createdAt": 1517692382.0
    }
}
```

Describing and deleting an ECR Repository using the AWS CLI

Now that you have deleted the repository you created earlier using the AWS console, you can re-create it, as demonstrated here:

```
> aws ecr create-repository --repository-name docker-in-
aws/todobackend
{
    "repository": {
        "repositoryArn": "arn:aws:ecr:us-
east-1:385605022855:repository/docker-in-aws/todobackend",
        "registryId": "385605022855",
        "repositoryName": "docker-in-aws/todobackend",
        "repositoryUri": "385605022855.dkr.ecr.us-
east-1.amazonaws.com/docker-in-aws/todobackend",
        "createdAt": 1517693074.0
    }
}
```

Creating an ECR Repository using the AWS CLI

Creating ECR repositories using AWS CloudFormation

AWS CloudFormation supports the creation of ECR repositories via the `AWS::ECR::Repository` resource type, and at the time of writing, this allows you to manage ECR resource policies and lifecycle policies, which we will cover later in this chapter.

As a general rule of thumb, given the critical nature of ECR repositories as a distribution mechanism for your Docker images, I typically recommend the various ECR repositories for your account and region are defined in a single, shared CloudFormation stack dedicated solely to the creation and management of ECR repositories.

In keeping with this recommendation and for future chapters, let's create a repository called **todobackend-aws** that you can use to store the various infrastructure configurations you will create and manage throughout this book. I will leave you to create the corresponding repository on GitHub, after which you can configure your GitHub repository as a remote:

```
> mkdir todobackend-aws
> touch todobackend-aws/ecr.yml
> cd todobackend-aws
> git init
Initialized empty Git repository in /Users/jmenga/Source/docker-in-
aws/todobackend-aws/.git/
> git remote add origin https://github.com/jmenga/todobackend-aws.git
> tree .
.
└── ecr.yml
```

You can now configure a CloudFormation template file called `ecr.yml` that defines a single ECR repository for the `todobackend` Docker image:

```
AWSTemplateFormatVersion: "2010-09-09"

Description: ECR Repositories

Resources:
  TodobackendRepository:
    Type: AWS::ECR::Repository
    Properties:
      RepositoryName: docker-in-aws/todobackend
```

Defining an ECR Repository using the AWS CloudFormation

As you can see in the previous example, defining an ECR repository is very simple using CloudFormation and only requires the `RepositoryName` property to be defined, which, as you might expect, defines the name of the repository.

Assuming you have deleted the current todobackend ECR repository, as demonstrated earlier, you can now use the `aws cloudformation deploy` command to create the todobackend repository using CloudFormation:

```
> aws cloudformation deploy --template-file ecr.yml --stack-name ecr-repositories
Waiting for changeset to be created..
Waiting for stack create/update to complete
Successfully created/updated stack - ecr-repositories
```

Creating an ECR Repository using the AWS CloudFormation

Once the stack deploys successfully, you can view the stack in the CloudFormation console, as shown in the following screenshot:

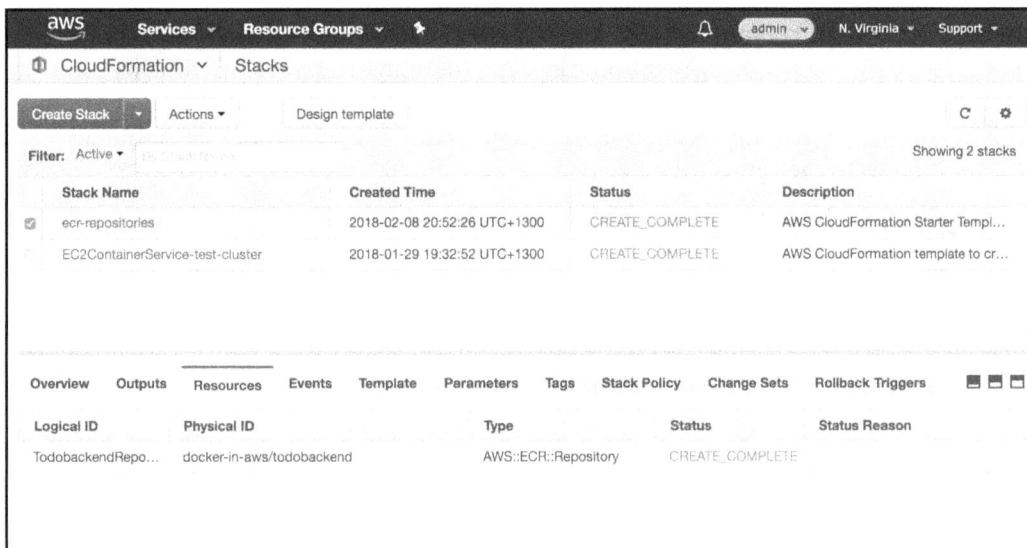

ECR Repository CloudFormation stack

If you now navigate back to the ECS console and select **Resources** from the left menu, you should see a single ECR repository called `docker-in-aws/todobackend`, as defined in your CloudFormation stack. If you click on the repository, you will be taken to the repository detail page, which provides you with the repository URI, a list of images published in the repository, ECR permissions, and lifecycle policy settings.

Logging into ECR

Once you have created a repository for your Docker image, the next step is to build and publish your images to ECR. Before you can do this, you must authenticate with ECR, given at the time of writing ECR is a private service that does not support public access.

The instructions and commands for logging into ECR were displayed as part of the ECR repository wizard, however you can view these instructions any time by selecting an appropriate repository and clicking the **View Push Commands** button, which will display the various commands required to log in, build, and publish Docker images to the repository.

The first command displayed is the `aws ecr get-login` command, which will generate a `docker login` expression that includes temporary authentication token valid for logging into ECR for 12 hours (note the command output has been truncated in the interests of saving space):

```
> aws ecr get-login --no-include-email
docker login -u AWS -p
eyJwYXl2ovSUVQUkJkbGJ5cjQ1YXJkcnNLV29ubVV6TTIxNTk3N1RYNklKdllvanZ1SFJa
eUNBYk84NTJ2V2RaVzJUYlk9Iiw
idmVyc2lvbiI6IjIiLCJ0eXBlIjoiREFUQV9LRVkiLCJleHBpcmF0aW9uIjoxNTE4MTIyN
TI5fQ== https://385605022855.dkr.ecr.us-east-1.amazonaws.com
```

Generating login commands for ECR

The `--no-include-email` flag is required for Docker versions 17.06 and higher, as the `-e` Docker CLI email flag was deprecated from this release.

Although you can copy and paste the generated command output in the preceding example, a faster method is to automatically execute the output of the `aws ecr get-login` command using a bash command substitution by surrounding the command with `$(...)`:

```
> $(aws ecr get-login --no-include-email)
Login Succeeded
```

Logging into ECR

Publishing Docker images to ECR

In earlier chapters, you learned how to build and tag Docker images locally, using the todobackend sample application as an example.

You can now extend this workflow to publish Docker images to ECR, which requires you to perform the following tasks:

- Ensure you are logged into ECR
- Build and tag your Docker image with the URI of your ECR repository
- Push your Docker image to ECR

Publishing Docker images using the Docker CLI

You've already seen how to log into ECR, and building and tagging your Docker image is much the same as the local use case, except you need to specify the URI of your ECR repository when tagging the image.

The following example demonstrates building the `todobackend` image, tagging the image with the URI of your new ECR repository (for the actual URI of your repository), and verifying the image name using the `docker images` command:

```
> cd ../todobackend
> docker build -t 385605022855.dkr.ecr.us-east-1.amazonaws.com/docker-in-aws/todobackend .
Sending build context to Docker daemon 129.5kB
Step 1/25 : FROM alpine AS build
 ---> 3fd9065eaf02
Step 2/25 : LABEL application=todobackend
```

```
 ---> Using cache
 ---> f955808a07fd
...
...
...
Step 25/25 : USER app
 ---> Running in 4cf3fcab97c9
Removing intermediate container 4cf3fcab97c9
---> 2b2d8d17367c
Successfully built 2b2d8d17367c
Successfully tagged 385605022855.dkr.ecr.us-
east-1.amazonaws.com/docker-in-aws/todobackend:latest
> docker images
REPOSITORY
TAG    IMAGE ID    SIZE
385605022855.dkr.ecr.us-east-1.amazonaws.com/docker-in-aws/todobackend
latest 2b2d8d17367c 99.4MB
```

Tagging an Image for ECR

Once you have built and tagged your image, you can push your image to ECR.

Note that to publish an image to ECR, you require various ECR permissions. Because you are using the admin role in your account, you automatically have all the required permissions. We will discuss ECR permissions in more detail later on in this chapter.

Because you have already logged into ECR, this is as simple as using the docker push command and referencing the name of your Docker image:

```
> docker push 385605022855.dkr.ecr.us-east-1.amazonaws.com/docker-in-
aws/todobackend
The push refers to repository [385605022855.dkr.ecr.us-
east-1.amazonaws.com/docker-in-aws/todobackend]
1cdf73b07ed7: Pushed
0dfffc4aa16e: Pushed
baaced0ec8f8: Pushed
e3b27097ac3f: Pushed
3a29354c4bcc: Pushed
a031167f960b: Pushed
cd7100a72410: Pushed
latest: digest:
sha256:322c8b378dd90b3a1a6dc8553baf03b4eb13ebafcc926d9d87c010f08e0339f
a size: 1787
```

Pushing an image to ECR

If you now navigate to the todobackend repository in the ECS console, you should see your newly published image appear with the default `latest` tag, as shown in the following figure. Notice that when you compare the built size of the image (99 MB in my example) with the size of the image stored in ECR (34 MB in my example), you can see that ECR stores the image in a compressed format, which reduces storage costs.

> In terms of charges for using ECR, AWS charges for both data storage and data transfer out (that is, pulling a Docker image). See `https://aws.amazon.com/ecr/pricing/` for more details.

Viewing ECR images

Publishing Docker images using Docker Compose

In earlier chapters, you learned how to use Docker Compose to help simplify the number of CLI commands required to test and build your Docker images. At the moment, Docker Compose is only building Docker images locally, but of course you now want to be able to publish your Docker images and leverage your Docker Compose workflow.

Docker Compose includes a service configuration property called `image`, which is commonly used to specify the image of a container that you would like to run:

```
version: '2.4'

services:
  web:
    image: nginx
```

Example Docker Compose file

Although this is a very common usage pattern for Docker Compose, another configuration and set of behaviors exist if you combine both the `build` and `image` properties, as demonstrated here, for the `docker-compose.yml` file in the todobackend repository:

```
version: '2.4'

volumes:
  public:
    driver: local

services:
  test:
    build:
      context: .
      dockerfile: Dockerfile
      target: test
  release:
    image: 385605022855.dkr.ecr.us-east-1.amazonaws.com/docker-in-aws/todobackend:latest
    build:
      context: .
      dockerfile: Dockerfile
    environment:
      DJANGO_SETTINGS_MODULE: todobackend.settings_release
      MYSQL_HOST: db
      MYSQL_USER: todo
      MYSQL_PASSWORD: password
  app:
    image: 385605022855.dkr.ecr.us-east-1.amazonaws.com/docker-in-aws/todobackend:${APP_VERSION}
    extends:
    ...
    ...
```

Todobackend Docker Compose file

In the preceding example, the `image` and `build` properties are both specified for the `release` and `app` services. When these two properties are used together, Docker will still build the image from the referenced Dockerfile, but will tag the image with the value to specify for the `image` property.

> You can apply multiple tags by creating new services that simply extend your release image and define a image property that includes the additional tag.

Notice that for the `app` service we reference the environment variable `APP_VERSION`, which is intended to tag the image with the current application version that is defined within the Makefile at the root of the todobackend repository:

```
.PHONY: test release clean version

export APP_VERSION ?= $(shell git rev-parse --short HEAD)

version:
  @ echo '{"Version": "$(APP_VERSION)"}'
```

> Replace the repository URI in the preceding examples with the appropriate URI generated for your own AWS account.

To demonstrate the tagging behavior when you combine the `image` and `build` properties, first delete the Docker image you created earlier in this chapter, as follows:

```
> docker rmi 385605022855.dkr.ecr.us-east-1.amazonaws.com/docker-in-aws/todobackend
Untagged: 385605022855.dkr.ecr.us-east-1.amazonaws.com/docker-in-aws/todobackend:latest
Untagged: 385605022855.dkr.ecr.us-east-1.amazonaws.com/docker-in-aws/todobackend@sha256:322c8b378dd90b3a1a6dc8553baf03b4eb13ebafcc926d9d87c010f08e0339fa
Deleted: sha256:2b2d8d17367c32993b0aa68f407e89bf4a3496a1da9aeb7c00a8e49f89bf5134
Deleted: sha256:523126379df325e1bcdccdf633aa10bc45e43bdb5ce4412aec282e98dbe076fb
Deleted: sha256:54521ab8917e466fbf9e12a5e15ac5e8715da5332f3655e8cc51f5ad3987a034
Deleted:
```

```
sha256:03d95618180182e7ae08c16b4687a7d191f3f56d909b868db9e889f0653add4
6
Deleted:
sha256:eb56d3747a17d5b7d738c879412e39ac2739403bbf992267385f86fce2f5ed0
d
Deleted:
sha256:9908bfa1f773905e0540d70e65d6a0991fa1f89a5729fa83e92c2a8b45f7bd2
9
Deleted:
sha256:d9268f192cb01d0e05a1f78ad6c41bc702b11559d547c0865b4293908d99a31
1
Deleted:
sha256:c6e4f60120cdf713253b24bba97a0c2a80d41a0126eb18f4ea5269034dbdc7e
1
Deleted:
sha256:0b780adf8501c8a0dbf33f49425385506885f9e8d4295f9bc63c3f895faed6d
1
```

Deleting a Docker image

If you now run the `docker-compose build release` command, once the command completes, Docker Compose will have built a new image tagged with your ECR repository URI:

```
> docker-compose build release
WARNING: The APP_VERSION variable is not set. Defaulting to a blank
string.
Building release
Step 1/25 : FROM alpine AS build
 ---> 3fd9065eaf02
Step 2/25 : LABEL application=todobackend
 ---> Using cache
 ---> f955808a07fd
...
...
Step 25/25 : USER app
 ---> Using cache
 ---> f507b981227f

Successfully built f507b981227f
Successfully tagged 385605022855.dkr.ecr.us-
east-1.amazonaws.com/docker-in-aws/todobackend:latest
> docker images
```

```
REPOSITORY
TAG                 IMAGE ID           CREATED          SIZE
385605022855.dkr.ecr.us-east-1.amazonaws.com/docker-in-aws/todobackend
latest              f507b981227f       4 days ago       99.4MB
```

Building a tagged image using Docker Compose

With your image built and tagged correctly, you can now execute the `docker-compose push` command, which can be used to push services defined in the Docker Compose file that include a `build` and `image` property:

```
> docker-compose push release
Pushing release (385605022855.dkr.ecr.us-east-1.amazonaws.com/docker-in-aws/todobackend:latest)...
The push refers to repository [385605022855.dkr.ecr.us-east-1.amazonaws.com/docker-in-aws/todobackend]
9ae8d6169643: Layer already exists
cdbc5d8be7d1: Pushed
08a1fb32c580: Layer already exists
2e3946df4029: Pushed
3a29354c4bcc: Layer already exists
a031167f960b: Layer already exists
cd7100a72410: Layer already exists
latest: digest:
sha256:a1b029d347a2fabd3f58d177dcbbcd88066dc54ccdc15adad46c12ceac450378 size: 1787
```

Publishing images using Docker Compose

In the preceding example, the image associated with the service called `release` is pushed, given this is the service that you configured with the Docker image URI.

Automating the publish workflow

In previous chapters, you learned how to automate testing and building a Docker image for the todobackend application, using a combination of Docker, Docker Compose, and Make.

You can now enhance this workflow to perform the following additional actions:

- Log in and log out of ECR
- Publish to ECR

To achieve this, you will create new tasks in the Makefile of the todobackend repository.

Automating login and logout

The following example demonstrates adding a couple of new tasks called `login` and `logout`, which will perform these actions using the Docker client:

```
.PHONY: test release clean version login logout

export APP_VERSION ?= $(shell git rev-parse --short HEAD)

version:
  @ echo '{"Version": "$(APP_VERSION)"}'

login:
    $$(aws ecr get-login --no-include-email)

logout:
    docker logout https://385605022855.dkr.ecr.us-east-1.amazonaws.com

test:
    docker-compose build --pull release
    docker-compose build
    docker-compose run test

release:
    docker-compose up --abort-on-container-exit migrate
    docker-compose run app python3 manage.py collectstatic --no-input
    docker-compose up --abort-on-container-exit acceptance
    @ echo App running at http://$$(docker-compose port app 8000 | sed s/0.0.0.0/localhost/g)

clean:
    docker-compose down -v
    docker images -q -f dangling=true -f label=application=todobackend | xargs -I ARGS docker rmi -f ARGS
```

Logging in and logging out of ECR

Notice that the `login` task uses a double dollar sign ($$), which is required as Make uses single dollar signs to define Make variables. When you specify a double dollar sign, Make will pass a single dollar sign to the shell, which in this case will ensure a bash command substitution is executed.

When logging out with the `logout` task, notice that you need to specify the Docker registry, otherwise the Docker client assumes the default public Docker Hub registry.

With these tasks in place, you can now easily log out and log in of ECR using the `make logout` and `make login` commands:

```
> make logout
docker logout https://385605022855.dkr.ecr.us-east-1.amazonaws.com
Removing login credentials for 385605022855.dkr.ecr.us-
east-1.amazonaws.com

> make login
$(aws ecr get-login --no-include-email)
WARNING! Using --password via the CLI is insecure. Use --password-
stdin.
Login Succeeded
```

Running make logout and make login

Automating the publishing of Docker images

To automate the publishing workflow, you can add a new task called `publish` to the Makefile, which simply calls the `docker-compose push` command for the tagged `release` and `app` services:

```
.PHONY: test release clean login logout publish

export APP_VERSION ?= $(shell git rev-parse --short HEAD)

version:
  @ echo '{"Version": "$(APP_VERSION)"}'

...
...

release:
    docker-compose up --abort-on-container-exit migrate
    docker-compose run app python3 manage.py collectstatic --no-input
    docker-compose up --abort-on-container-exit acceptance
    @ echo App running at http://$$(docker-compose port app 8000 | sed
```

```
s/0.0.0.0/localhost/g)

publish:
    docker-compose push release app
clean:
    docker-compose down -v
    docker images -q -f dangling=true -f label=application=todobackend
| xargs -I ARGS docker rmi -f ARGS
```

Automating publishing to ECR

With this configuration in place, your Docker image will now be tagged with both the commit hash and latest tags, which you can then publish to ECR by simply running the `make publish` command.

Let's now commit your changes and run the full Make workflow to test, build, and publish your Docker images, as demonstrated in the following example. Notice that an image tagged with the commit hash of `97e4abf` is published to ECR:

```
> git commit -a -m "Add publish tasks"
[master 97e4abf] Add publish tasks
 2 files changed, 12 insertions(+), 1 deletion(-)

> make login
$(aws ecr get-login --no-include-email)
Login Succeeded

> make test && make release
docker-compose build --pull release
Building release
...
...
todobackend_db_1 is up-to-date
Creating todobackend_app_1 ... done
App running at http://localhost:32774
$ make publish
docker-compose push release app
Pushing release (385605022855.dkr.ecr.us-east-1.amazonaws.com/docker-
in-aws/todobackend:latest)...
The push refers to repository [385605022855.dkr.ecr.us-
east-1.amazonaws.com/docker-in-aws/todobackend]
53ca7006d9e4: Layer already exists
ca208f4ebc53: Layer already exists
1702a4329d94: Layer already exists
e2aca0d7f367: Layer already exists
c3e0af9081a5: Layer already exists
20ae2e176794: Layer already exists
```

```
cd7100a72410: Layer already exists
latest: digest:
sha256:d64e1771440208bde0cabe454f213d682a6ad31e38f14f9ad792fabc5100888
8 size: 1787
Pushing app (385605022855.dkr.ecr.us-east-1.amazonaws.com/docker-in-
aws/todobackend:97e4abf)...
The push refers to repository [385605022855.dkr.ecr.us-
east-1.amazonaws.com/docker-in-aws/todobackend]
53ca7006d9e4: Layer already exists
ca208f4ebc53: Layer already exists
1702a4329d94: Layer already exists
e2aca0d7f367: Layer already exists
c3e0af9081a5: Layer already exists
20ae2e176794: Layer already exists
cd7100a72410: Layer already exists
97e4abf: digest:
sha256:d64e1771440208bde0cabe454f213d682a6ad31e38f14f9ad792fabc5100888
8 size: 1787

> make clean
docker-compose down -v
Stopping todobackend_app_1 ... done
Stopping todobackend_db_1 ... done
...
...

> make logout
docker logout https://385605022855.dkr.ecr.us-east-1.amazonaws.com
Removing login credentials for 385605022855.dkr.ecr.us-
east-1.amazonaws.com
```

Running the updated Make workflow

Pulling Docker images from ECR

Now that you have learned how to publish Docker images to ECR, let's focus on how Docker clients running under a variety of scenarios can pull your Docker images from ECR. Recall from the introduction to ECR at the beginning of this chapter that a variety of scenarios exist for client access to ECR, and we will now focus on these scenarios in the context of ECS container instances as your Docker clients:

- ECS container instances running in the same account as your ECR repositories

- ECS container instances running in different accounts to your ECR repositories
- AWS services that require access to your ECR repositories

ECS container instance access to ECR from the same account

When your ECS container instances are running in the same account as your ECR repositories, the recommended method to enable the ECS agents running inside your ECS container instances to pull Docker images from ECR is to use IAM policies associated with the IAM instance role applied to EC2 instance that runs as an ECS container instance. You already saw this method in action in the previous chapter, where the ECS cluster wizard provided by AWS attached a managed policy, called `AmazonEC2ContainerServiceforEC2Role`, to the IAM instance role for ECS container instances in the cluster, and notice the following ECR permissions that are included in this policy:

```
{
  "Version": "2012-10-17",
  "Statement": [
    {
      "Effect": "Allow",
      "Action": [
        "ecs:CreateCluster",
        "ecs:DeregisterContainerInstance",
        "ecs:DiscoverPollEndpoint",
        "ecs:Poll",
        "ecs:RegisterContainerInstance",
        "ecs:StartTelemetrySession",
        "ecs:Submit*",
        "ecr:GetAuthorizationToken",
        "ecr:BatchCheckLayerAvailability",
        "ecr:GetDownloadUrlForLayer",
        "ecr:BatchGetImage",
        "logs:CreateLogStream",
        "logs:PutLogEvents"
      ],
      "Resource": "*"
    }
  ]
}
```

AmazonEC2ContainerServiceforEC2Role policy

In the preceding example, you can see four ECR permissions are granted, which collectively permit the ECS agent to login to ECR and pull Docker images:

- `ecr:GetAuthorizationToken`: Permits retrieval of an authentication token that is valid for 12 hours and can be used to log in to ECR using the Docker CLI.
- `ecr:BatchCheckLayerAvailability`: Checks the availability of multiple image layers in a given repository.
- `ecr:GetDownloadUrlForLayer`: Retrieves a pre-signed S3 download URL for a given layer in a Docker image.
- `ecr:BatchGetImage`: Retries detailed information for Docker images in a given repository.

These permissions are sufficient to log into ECR and pull images, but notice that the `Resource` property in the previous example allows access to all repositories in your account.

Depending on the security requirements of your organization, this broad access to all repositories may or may not be acceptable - if not, then you need to create custom IAM policies that restrict access to specific repositories, as demonstrated here:

```
{
  "Version": "2012-10-17",
  "Statement": [
    {
      "Effect": "Allow",
      "Action": "ecr:GetAuthorizationToken",
      "Resource": "*"
    },
    {
      "Effect": "Allow",
      "Action": [
        "ecr:BatchCheckLayerAvailability",
        "ecr:GetDownloadUrlForLayer",
        "ecr:BatchGetImage"
      ],
      "Resource": [
        "arn:aws:ecr:us-east-1:385605022855:repository/docker-in-aws/todobackend"
      ]
    }
  ]
}
```

Granting ECR login and pull permissions to specific repositories

In the preceding example, notice that the `ecr:GetAuthorizationToken` permission is still scoped to all resources, as you don't log into a specific ECR repository, rather you log into the ECR registry for your account in a given region. The other permissions required to pull Docker images however can be applied to individual repositories, and you can see that these permissions are only permitted to the ARN of your ECR repository.

Note that if you also wanted to grant push access to the ECR repository in the preceding example, additional ECR permissions would be required:

```
{
  "Version": "2012-10-17",
  "Statement": [
    {
      "Effect": "Allow",
      "Action": "ecr:GetAuthorizationToken",
      "Resource": "*"
    },
    {
      "Effect": "Allow",
      "Action": [
        "ecr:BatchCheckLayerAvailability",
        "ecr:GetDownloadUrlForLayer",
        "ecr:BatchGetImage",
        "ecr:PutImage",
        "ecr:InitiateLayerUpload",
        "ecr:UploadLayerPart",
        "ecr:CompleteLayerUpload"
      ],
      "Resource": [
        "arn:aws:ecr:us-east-1:385605022855:repository/docker-in-aws/todobackend"
      ]
    }
  ]
}
```

Granting ECR push permissions to specific repositories

ECS container instance access to ECR from a different account

In larger organizations, it is very common for resources and users to be split across multiple accounts, and a common pattern is to have a central build account, where application artifacts, such as Docker images, are centrally stored.

The following diagram illustrates this scenario, where you may have several accounts running ECS container instances that need to pull Docker images that store in your central repositories:

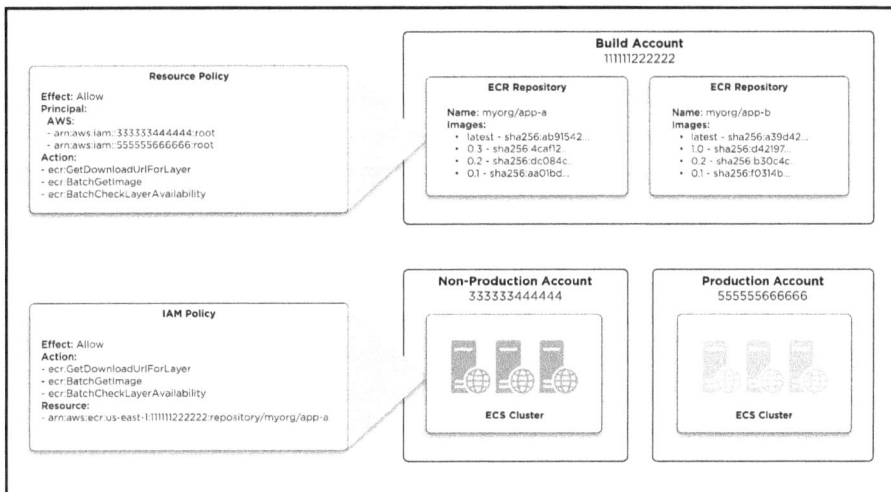

Multiple accounts requiring access to central ECR repositories

When you need to grant other accounts access to your ECR repositories, there are two configuration tasks that need to be performed:

1. Configure ECR *resource policies* in the account that hosts the repositories, which allow you to define policies that are scoped and applied to an individual ECR repository (this is the *resource*) and define *who* can access the repository (for example, AWS accounts) and *what* actions they can perform (for example, log in, push and/or pull images). This ability to define *who* can access a given repository is what allows for cross-account access to be enabled and controlled via resource policies. For example, in the preceding diagram, the repository is configured to permit access from accounts 333333444444 and 555555666666.

2. Administrators in the remote account need to assign permissions in the form of IAM policies to pull images from your ECR repositories. This is a form of delegated access, where the account hosting the ECR repositories trusts access from the remote account as long as access has been explicitly granted via an IAM policy. For example, in the preceding diagram, ECS container instances have an IAM policy assigned that permits them access to the myorg/app-a repository in account `111111222222`.

Configuring ECR resource policies using the AWS Console

You can configure ECR resource policies via the ECS Console by opening the appropriate ECR repository, selecting the **Permissions** tab, and clicking **Add** to add a new set of permissions:

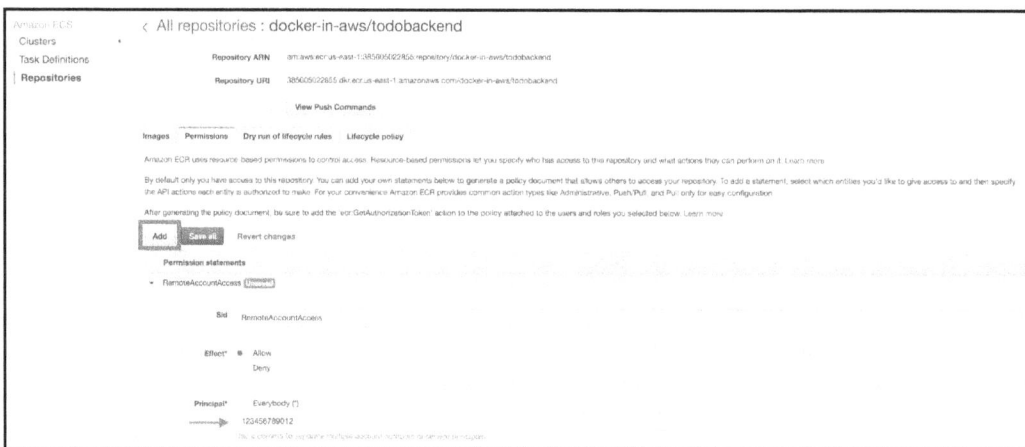

Configuring ECR resource policies

In the preceding figure, notice that you can configure AWS account IDs as principals via the Principal setting, and then easily permit pull access by selecting the **Pull only actions** option. With this configuration, you are permitting potentially any entity associated with the remote account the ability to pull Docker images from this repository.

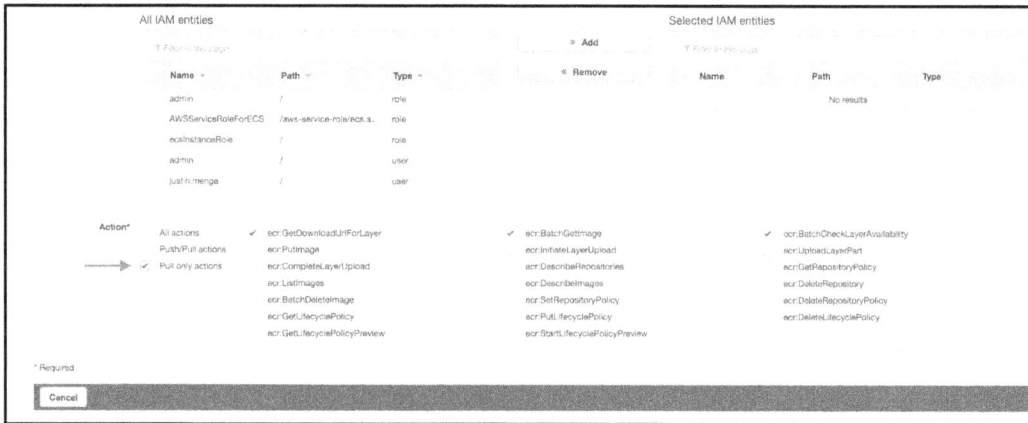

Configuring ECR resource policies

Note that if you attempt to save the configuration shown in the previous figure and the preceding figure, you will receive an error because I have used an invalid account. Assuming you did use a valid account ID and you saved the policy, the following policy document would be generated for the configuration:

```
{
    "Version": "2008-10-17",
    "Statement": [
        {
            "Sid": "RemoteAccountAccess",
            "Effect": "Allow",
            "Principal": {
                "AWS": "arn:aws:iam::<remote-account-id>:root"
            },
            "Action": [
                "ecr:GetDownloadUrlForLayer",
                "ecr:BatchGetImage",
                "ecr:BatchCheckLayerAvailability"
            ]
        }
    ]
}
```

Example ECR repository policy document

Configuring ECR resource policies using the AWS CLI

You can configure ECR resource policies via the AWS CLI by using the `aws ecr set-repository-policy` command, as demonstrated here:

```
> aws ecr set-repository-policy --repository-name docker-in-
aws/todobackend --policy-text '{
    "Version": "2008-10-17",
    "Statement": [
        {
            "Sid": "RemoteAccountAccess",
            "Effect": "Allow",
            "Principal": {
                "AWS": "arn:aws:iam::<remote-account-id>:root"
            },
            "Action": [
                "ecr:GetDownloadUrlForLayer",
                "ecr:BatchGetImage",
                "ecr:BatchCheckLayerAvailability"
            ]
        }
    ]
}'
```

Configuring ECR resource Policies via the AWS CLI

As demonstrated in the preceding example, you must specify the repository name using the `--repository-name` flag, and configure the repository policy as a JSON-formatted document using the `--policy-text` flag.

Configuring ECR resource policies using AWS CloudFormation

When using AWS CloudFormation to define your ECR repositories, you can configure the `RepositoryPolicyText` property of the `AWS::ECR::Repository` resource you created in earlier example to define an ECR resource policy:

```
AWSTemplateFormatVersion: "2010-09-09"

Description: ECR Repositories

Resources:
  TodobackendRepository:
```

```
Type: AWS::ECR::Repository
Properties:
  RepositoryName: docker-in-aws/todobackend
  RepositoryPolicyText:
    Version: "2008-10-17"
    Statement:
      - Sid: RemoteAccountAccess
        Effect: Allow
        Principal:
          AWS: arn:aws:iam::<remote-account-id>:root
        Action:
          - ecr:GetDownloadUrlForLayer
          - ecr:BatchGetImage
          - ecr:BatchCheckLayerAvailability
```

Configuring ECR resource policies using AWS CloudFormation

The policy text in the preceding example expresses the JSON policy you configured in earlier examples in a YAML format, and you can deploy the changes to your stack by running the `aws cloudformation deploy` command.

Configuring IAM policies in remote accounts

With the ECR resource policies in place configured either by the console, CLI, or CloudFormation, you can proceed to create IAM policies in the remote account(s) specified in your ECR resource policies. These policies are configured exactly how you would configure an IAM policy for local access in your account, and if required, you can refer to the ARN of the remote ECR repository if you wish to only grant access to this repository.

AWS service access to ECR

One final scenario we will discuss is the ability for AWS services to access your ECR images. An example of this is the AWS CodeBuild service, which performs automated continuous integration tasks using a container-based build agent. CodeBuild allows you to define your own custom build agents, and a common practice is to publish the image for these build agents in ECR. This means that the AWS CodeBuild service now requires access to ECR, and you can use ECR resource policies to achieve this.

The following example expands on the preceding example, adding the AWS CodeBuild service to the resource policy:

```
AWSTemplateFormatVersion: "2010-09-09"

Description: ECR Repositories

Resources:
  TodobackendRepository:
    Type: AWS::ECR::Repository
    Properties:
      RepositoryName: docker-in-aws/todobackend
      RepositoryPolicyText:
        Version: "2008-10-17"
        Statement:
          - Sid: RemoteAccountAccess
            Effect: Allow
            Principal:
              AWS: arn:aws:iam::<remote-account-id>:root
              Service: codebuild.amazonaws.com
            Action:
              - ecr:GetDownloadUrlForLayer
              - ecr:BatchGetImage
              - ecr:BatchCheckLayerAvailability
```

Configuring AWS service access to ECR repositories

In the preceding example, notice that you can use the `Service` property within the `Principal` property to identify AWS services that that policy statement will be applied to. In later chapters, you will see an example of this in action when you create your own custom CodeBuild image that is published to ECR.

Configuring lifecycle policies

If you have followed along in this chapter, you will have published the todobackend image to your ECR repository several times, and chances are, you will have created what are known as *orphan images* in your ECR repository. In earlier chapters, we discussed orphaned images that were being created in your local Docker Engine, and defined these an image whose tag has been superseded by a newer image, effectively leaving the older images nameless and hence "orphaned."

If you browse to your ECR repository and select the Images tab in the ECS console, you may notice that you have a few images that no longer have a tag, which will be because you pushed several images with the `latest` tag, that have superseded the now-orphaned images:

Orphaned ECR images

In the preceding figure, notice that your storage usage in ECR has now tripled, even though you only have one current `latest` image, which means you may also be paying triple the storage costs. Of course you can manually delete these images yourself, however this is prone to error and often will become a forgotten and neglected task.

Thankfully, ECR supports a feature called *lifecycle policies*, which allows you to define a set of rules contained within a policy that manages the lifecycle of your Docker images. A standard use case for lifecycle policies that you should always apply to every repository you create is the periodic removal of orphaned images, so let's now see how you can create and apply such a policy.

Configuring lifecycle policies using the AWS Console

When configuring lifecycle policies, because these policies may actually delete your Docker images, it is a good idea to always use the AWS console to initially test your policies, as the ECS console includes a feature that allows you to simulate what would happen if you were to apply a lifecycle policy.

To configure lifecycle policies using the AWS console, select the **Dry run of lifecycle rules** tab within your ECR repository and then click the **Add** button to create a new **Dry run rules**. This allows you to test your lifecycle policy rules without actually deleting any images in your ECR repository. Once you are satisfied your rules are behaving safely and as expected, you can convert them into actual lifecycle policies that will be applied to your repository:

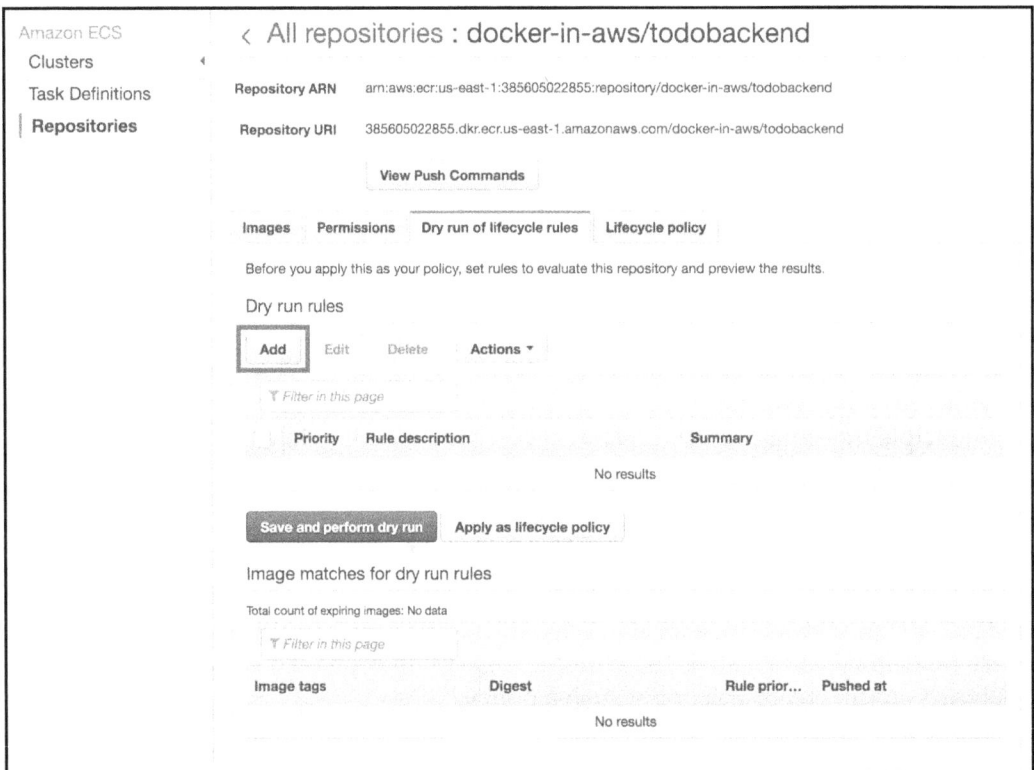

ECR dry run rules

You can now define a rule in the Add rule screen with the following parameters:

- **Rule priority**: Determines the rule evaluation order when multiple rules are defined in a policy.
- **Rule description**: A human-readable description of the rule.
- **Image status**: Defines which type of images the rule applies to. Note that you can only have a single rule that specifies **Untagged** images.
- **Match criteria**: Defines the criteria as to when the rule should be applied. For example, you might configure the criteria to match untagged images that were pushed more than seven days since the last push to the ECR repository.
- **Rule action**: Defines the action that should be performed to images that match the rule. At the time of writing, only the **expire** action is supported, which will delete matching images.

After clicking on the **Save** button, the new rule will be added to the **Dry run of lifecycle rules** tab. If you now click the **Save and perform dry run** button, any images that match your rule criteria will be displayed, which should include the orphaned images that were displayed earlier.

Now, depending on whether or not you have untagged images and how old they are in comparison to your last push to the repository, you may or may not see images that match your dry run rules. Regardless of the actual outcome, the key here is to ensure that whatever images were matched is what you expect, and that you are comfortable the dry run rules will not accidentally delete valid images that expect to be published and available.

If you are happy with the dry run rules, you can next click the **Apply as lifecycle policy** button, which will first display a dialog confirming the new rules, and once applied, if you navigate to the **Lifecycle policy** tab, you should see your lifecycle policy:

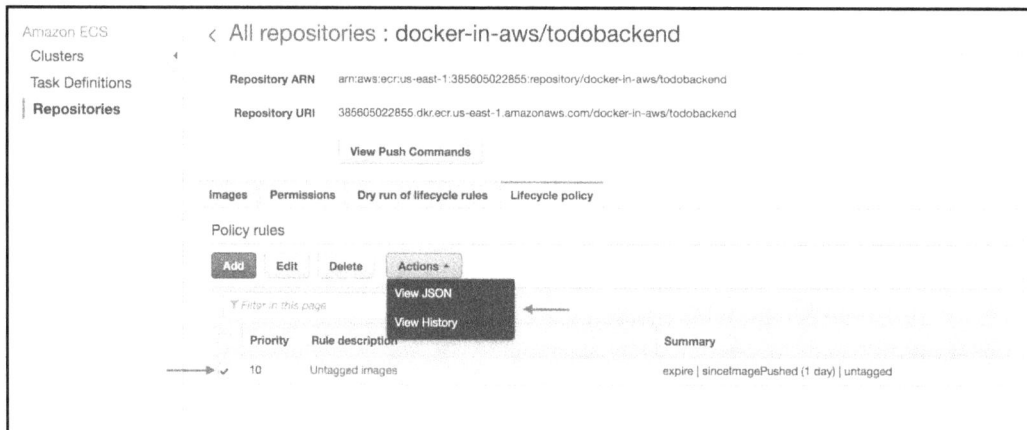

ECR lifecycle policies

To confirm your lifecycle policy is working, you can click on any policy rule and select **View History** from the **Actions** dropdown, which will display any actions that have been performed by ECR in relation to the policy rule.

Configuring lifecycle policies using the AWS CLI

The AWS CLI supports a similar workflow to configuring ECR lifecycle policies via the AWS console, which is outlined here:

- `aws ecr start-lifecycle-policy-preview --repository-name <name> --lifecycle-policy-text <json>`: Starts a dry run of the lifecycle policy against the repository
- `aws ecr get-lifecycle-policy-preview --repository-name <name>`: Obtains the status of the dry run
- `aws ecr put-lifecycle-policy --repository-name <name> --lifecycle-policy-text <json>`: Applies the lifecycle policy to the repository

- `aws ecr get-lifecycle-policy --repository-name <name>`: Displays the current lifecycle policy applied to the repository
- `aws ecr delete-lifecycle-policy --repository-name <name>`: Deletes the current lifecycle policy applied to the repository

When working with the CLI, you need to specify lifecycle policies in a JSON format, which you can see an example of by clicking the View JSON action in the preceding screenshot.

Configuring lifecycle policies using AWS CloudFormation

When using AWS CloudFormation to define your ECR repositories, you can configure the `LifecyclePolicy` property of the `AWS::ECR::Repository` resource you created earlier, to define an ECR lifecycle policy:

```
AWSTemplateFormatVersion: "2010-09-09"

Description: ECR Repositories

Resources:
  TodobackendRepository:
    Type: AWS::ECR::Repository
    Properties:
      RepositoryName: docker-in-aws/todobackend
      LifecyclePolicy:
        LifecyclePolicyText: |
          {
            "rules": [
              {
                "rulePriority": 10,
                "description": "Untagged images",
                "selection": {
                  "tagStatus": "untagged",
                  "countType": "sinceImagePushed",
                  "countUnit": "days",
                  "countNumber": 7
                },
                "action": {
```

```
            "type": "expire"
          }
        }
      ]
    }
```

Configuring ECR lifecycle policies using AWS CloudFormation

The policy text in the preceding example, expresses the JSON policy you configured in earlier examples as a JSON string - note the use of the pipe (|) YAML operator, which allows you to enter multiline text for improved readability.

With this configuration in place, you can apply the changes to your stack by running the `aws cloudformation deploy` command.

Summary

In this chapter, you learned how to create and manage ECR repositories that you can use to store your Docker images securely and privately. After creating your first ECR repository, you learned how to authenticate to ECR using the AWS CLI and Docker client, and then successfully tagged and published your Docker image to ECR.

With your Docker image published, you then learned about the various scenarios for which Docker clients may need to access your repository, which included ECS container instance access from the same account as your ECR repository, ECS container instance from a different account as your ECR repository (that is, cross-account access), and finally granting access to AWS services such as CodeBuild. You created ECR resource policies, which are required when configuring cross-account access and when granting access to AWS services, and you learned that despite the creation of ECR resource policies in a central account that define remote accounts as trusted, you still need to create IAM policies in each remote account that explicitly grant access to your central account repositories.

Finally, you created ECR lifecycle policy rules that allow you to automatically and periodically remove untagged (orphaned) Docker images, which helps to reduce your storage costs. In the next chapter, you will learn how to build and publish your own custom ECS container instance Amazon Machine Images (AMIs), using a popular open source tool called Packer.

Questions

1. What command do you execute to obtain an authentication token for ECR?
2. True/False: ECR allows you to publish and distribute Docker images publicly
3. Which ECR feature should you configure if you notice you have a lot of untagged images in your repository?
4. True/False: ECR stores Docker images in a compressed format
5. True/False: ECR resource policies are required for configuring access to ECR from ECS container instances in the same account
6. True/False: ECR resource policies are required for configuring access to ECR from ECS container instances in a remote account
7. True/False: ECR resource policies are required for configuring access to ECR from AWS CodeBuild
8. True/False: IAM policies are required for configuring access to ECR from ECS container instances in the same account
9. True/False: IAM policies are required for configuring access to ECR from ECS container instances in a remote account

Further reading

You can check the following links for more information about the topics covered in this chapter:

- **ECR user guide:** `https://docs.aws.amazon.com/AmazonECR/latest/userguide/what-is-ecr.html`
- **ECR repository CloudFormation resource:** `https://docs.aws.amazon.com/AWSCloudFormation/latest/UserGuide/aws-resource-ecr-repository.html`
- **Identity-based vs resource-based policies:** `https://docs.aws.amazon.com/IAM/latest/UserGuide/access_policies_identity-vs-resource.html`

- Resource-level permissions for ECR repositories : `https://docs.aws.amazon.com/AmazonECR/latest/userguide/ecr-supported-iam-actions-resources.html`
- Lifecycle policies for ECR: `https://docs.aws.amazon.com/AmazonECR/latest/userguide/LifecyclePolicies.html`
- AWS ECR CLI reference: `https://docs.aws.amazon.com/cli/latest/reference/ecr/index.html#cli-aws-ecr`

6
Building Custom ECS Container Instances

In earlier chapters, you learned how you use the Amazon ECS-Optimized Amazon Machine Image (AMI) to create ECS container instances and join them to an ECS cluster in a few simple steps. Although the ECS-Optimized AMI is great for getting up and running quickly, you may want to add additional features to your ECS container instances for your production environments, such as adding logging agents or including support for HTTP proxies so you can place your ECS clusters in private subnets.

In this chapter, you will learn how you can build your own custom ECS container instances, using the ECS-Optimized AMI as a base machine image and applying your own customizations using a popular open source tool called Packer. You will extend the base image to include the AWS CloudWatch logs agent, which enables centralized logging from your ECS container instances using the CloudWatch logs service, and install a useful set of CloudFormation helper scripts, called cfn-bootstrap, which will allow you to run powerful initialization scripts at instance-creation time and also provide powerful integration features with CloudFormation.

Finally, you will create a first-run script that will allow you to adapt your instances to the specifics of your target environment without needing to build a new AMI for every application and environment. This script will enable you to conditionally enable HTTP proxy support, allowing you to install your ECS container instances in more secure private subnets, and will also include a healthcheck that will wait until your ECS container instances have registered with their configured ECS cluster, before signalling CloudFormation that your instances have been successfully initialized.

The following topics will be covered:

- Designing a custom AMI
- Building a custom AMI using Packer
- Creating custom storage configurations
- Installing CloudFormation helper scripts
- Installing the CloudWatch logs agent
- Creating a first-run script
- Testing your custom ECS container instance

Technical requirements

The following lists the technical requirements to complete this chapter:

- Packer 1.0 or higher (instructions will be provided on how to install Packer)
- Administrator access to an AWS account
- Local AWS profile configured as per the instructions in Chapter 3
- GNU Make version 3.82 or higher (note that macOS does not ship with this version by default)
- AWS CLI 1.15.71 or higher

This GitHub URL contains the code samples used in this chapter: `https://github.com/docker-in-aws/docker-in-aws/tree/master/ch6`.

Check out the following video to see the Code in Action: `http://bit.ly/2LzoxaO`

Designing a custom Amazon Machine Image

Before you learn how to build a custom Amazon Machine Image, it is important to understand *why* you would want or need to build your own custom image.

The reasons for this vary depending on your use case or organizational requirements, however in general there are a number of reasons why you might want to build a custom image:

- **Custom storage configuration**: The default ECS-optimized AMI ships with a 30 GB volume that includes 8 GB for the operating system partition and a 22 GB volume for storing Docker images and container filesystems. One aspect of your configuration that I typically recommend to change is that, by default, Docker volumes, which do not use layered filesystems, are stored on the 8 GB operating system partition. This approach generally should be avoided for production use cases, and instead you should mount a dedicated volume for storing Docker volumes.

- **Installation of additional packages and tools**: In keeping with the minimalist philosophy of Docker, the ECS-optimized AMI ships with a minimal installation of Amazon Linux that only includes the core components required to run a Docker Engine and the supporting ECS agent. For real-world use cases, at a minimum, you will typically want to add the CloudWatch logs agent, which supports logging at a system level (for example, Operating system, Docker Engine, and ECS agent logs) to the AWS CloudWatch logs service. Another important set of tools you should consider installing are the cfn-bootstrap tools, which provide a set of CloudFormation helper scripts that you can use to define custom provisioning actions for your instances in CloudFormation templates, and also allow your EC2 instances to signal CloudFormation once provisioning and instance initialization is complete.

- **Adding first-run scripts**: When deploying ECS container instances to AWS, you may use them in a variety of use cases that require different configurations depending on the nature of the application. For example, a common security best practice is to deploy your ECS container instances into private subnets that have no default route attached. This means that your ECS container instance must be configured with an HTTP proxy in order to communicate with AWS services such as ECS and CloudWatch logs, or any other internet services the ECS container instance may rely on. However in some scenarios, using an HTTP proxy may not be feasible (for example, consider the ECS container instances that run ECS containers that provide the HTTP proxy service for your environment), and rather than build separate machine images (one with HTTP proxy enabled and one without an HTTP proxy), you can created provisioning scripts that will only run once on instance creation, that conditionally enable/disable a desired configuration, such as HTTP proxy settings, depending on the target use case.

Of course there are a whole bunch of other use cases that may drive you to build your own custom image, however in this chapter we will focus on examples of the use cases defined here, which will provide you with a solid foundation and understanding of how to apply any additional customizations that you may want to use.

Building a custom AMI using Packer

Now that you understand the rationale for building a custom ECS container instance image, let's introduce a tool called Packer, which allows you to build machine images for a wide variety of platforms, including AWS.

Packer is an open source tool created by HashiCorp, which you can find out more about at `https://www.packer.io/`. Packer can build machine images for a wide variety of target platforms, however in this chapter we will only focus on building Amazon Machine Images.

Installing Packer

Before you can get started using Packer, you need to install it on your local environment. Packer is supported for Linux, mac OS, and Windows platforms, and to install Packer for your target platform, follow the instructions located at `https://www.packer.io/intro/getting-started/install.html`.

Note that Packer is widely supported in operating systems and third-party package management tools—for example, on mac OS you can install Packer using the Brew package manager by running `brew install packer`.

Creating a Packer template

With Packer installed, you can now get started creating a Packer template that will define how to build your custom machine image. Before you do this though, I do recommend creating a separate repository for your Packer template, which should always be placed under version control, just like application source code and other infrastructure, as code repositories.

For this chapter, I will assume that you have created a repository called `packer-ecs`, and you can refer to the `ch6` folder at `https://github.com/docker-in-aws/docker-in-aws`, which provides an example repository based upon the content in this chapter.

Packer template structure

Packer templates are JSON documents that provide a declarative description that tells Packer how to build a machine image.

Packer templates are organized around four common top-level parameters, as demonstrated in the following example and described here:

- **variables**: An object that provides input variables for the build.
- **builders**: A list of Packer builders, which define the target machine image platform(s). In this chapter, you will be targeting a builder referred to as the `EBS-backed AMI builder`, which is the simplest and most popular builder for creating custom Amazon Machine Images. Builders are responsible for ensuring the correct image format and publishing the final image in a format suitable for deployment to the target machine platform.
- **provisioners**: A list or array of Packer provisioners, which perform various provisioning tasks as part of the image building process. The simplest provisioners include file and shell provisioners, which copy files into the image and perform shell tasks, such as installing packages.
- **post-processors**: A list or array of Packer post-processors, which perform post-processing tasks once the machine image has been built and published:

```
{
    "variables": {},
    "builders": [],
    "provisioners": [],
    "post-processors": []
}
```

Packer template structure

Configuring a builder

Let's get started configuring our Packer template by first creating a file called
`packer.json` at the root of the packer-ecs repository, and then defining the builders
section, as demonstrated in the following example:

```
{
  "variables": {},
  "builders": [
    {
      "type": "amazon-ebs",
      "access_key": "{{user `aws_access_key_id`}}",
      "secret_key": "{{user `aws_secret_access_key`}}",
      "token": "{{user `aws_session_token`}}",
      "region": "us-east-1",
      "source_ami": "ami-5e414e24",
      "instance_type": "t2.micro",
      "ssh_username": "ec2-user",
      "associate_public_ip_address": "true",
      "ami_name": "docker-in-aws-ecs {{timestamp}}",
      "tags": {
        "Name": "Docker in AWS ECS Base Image 2017.09.h",
        "SourceAMI": "{{ .SourceAMI }}",
        "DockerVersion": "17.09.1-ce",
        "ECSAgentVersion": "1.17.0-2"
      }
    }
  ],
  "provisioners": [],
  "post-processors": []
}
```

Defining an EBS-backed AMI builder

In the preceding example, a single object representing our builder is added to the
builders array. The `type` parameter defines the builder as an EBS-based AMI builder,
and the settings that follow are specific to this type of builder:

- `access_key`: Defines the AWS access key ID used to authenticate access to
  AWS when building and publishing the AMI.
- `secret_key`: Defines the AWS secret access key used to authenticate
  access to AWS when building and publishing the AMI.
- `token`: Optionally defines the AWS session token used when
  authenticating with temporary session credentials.

- `region`: The target AWS region.
- `source_ami`: The source AMI to build from. In this example, the source AMI of the latest ECS-Optimized AMI for the us-east-1 region at the time of writing is specified, for which you obtain an up-to-date list from `https://docs.aws.amazon.com/AmazonECS/latest/developerguide/ecs-optimized_AMI.html`.
- `instance_type`: The instance type used to build the AMI.
- `ssh_username`: The SSH username that Packer should use when attempting to connect to the temporary EC2 instance created as part of the Packer build process. For Amazon Linux-based AMIs, such as the ECS-Optimized AMI, this must be specified as the `ec2-user` user.
- `associate_public_ip_address`: When set to true associates a public IP address with the instance. This is required if you are using Packer over the internet and don't have private network access to the temporary EC2 instance created as part of the Packer build process.
- `ami_name`: A name for the AMI that will be created. This name must be unique and a common approach to ensure uniqueness is by using the `{{timestamp}}` Go template function, which will be automatically replaced with the current timestamp by Packer.
- `tags`: A list of tags to add to the created AMI. This allows you to attach metadata, such as the source AMI of the image, the ECS agent version, Docker version, or any other information that you might find useful. Notice that you can reference a special template variable called `SourceAMI`, which is added by the Amazon EBS builder and is based on the value of the `source_ami` variable.

One point to note in the is that rather than hardcode your AWS credentials into the template fail, you reference a Go template function called `{{user `<variable-name>`}}`, and this will inject user variables defined in the top-level variables parameter that we will configure shortly.

Packer templates are processed using Go's templating language, which you can read more about at `https://golang.org/pkg/text/template/`. Go templates allow you to define your own template functions and Packer includes a number of useful functions that are defined at `https://www.packer.io/docs/templates/engine.html`. Template functions are invoked through template expressions, which are expressed in the handlebars style format: `{{<function> <parameters>}}`.

Configuring variables

Variables are used to inject user-specific or environment-specific settings into your templates at build time, which is useful for making your machine image templates more generic and avoids the hardcoding of credentials in your templates.

Back in the previous example, you referenced user variables when defining AWS credential settings, and these must be defined in the variables section of your Packer template, as demonstrated in the previous example:

```
{
  "variables": {
    "aws_access_key_id": "{{env `AWS_ACCESS_KEY_ID`}}",
    "aws_secret_access_key": "{{env `AWS_SECRET_ACCESS_KEY`}}",
    "aws_session_token": "{{env `AWS_SESSION_TOKEN`}}",
    "timezone": "US/Eastern"
  },
  "builders": [
    {
      "type": "amazon-ebs",
      "access_key": "{{user `aws_access_key_id`}}",
      "secret_key": "{{user `aws_secret_access_key`}}",
      "token": "{{user `aws_session_token`}}",
      "region": "us-east-1",
      "source_ami": "ami-5e414e24",
      "instance_type": "t2.micro",
      "ssh_username": "ec2-user",
      "associate_public_ip_address": "true",
      "ami_name": "docker-in-aws-ecs {{timestamp}}",
      "tags": {
        "Name": "Docker in AWS ECS Base Image 2017.09.h",
        "SourceAMI": "{{ .SourceAMI }}",
        "DockerVersion": "17.09.1-ce",
        "ECSAgentVersion": "1.17.0-2"
      }
    }
  }
```

```
  ],
  "provisioners": [],
  "post-processors": []
}
```

Defining variables

In the preceding example, notice that you define each of the variables referenced in the user functions for the AWS credential settings in the builders section. For example, the builders section defines the `access_key` setting as `{{user `aws_access_key_id`}}`, which in turn references the `aws_access_key_id` variable defined in the variables section.

Each variable in turn references the `env` template function, which looks up the value of the environment variable passed to this function. This means you can control the value of each of the variables as follows:

- `aws_access_key_id`: Configured using the `AWS_ACCESS_KEY_ID` environment variable
- `aws_secret_access_key`: Configured using the `AWS_SECRET_ACCESS_KEY` environment variable
- `aws_session_token`: Configured using the `AWS_SESSION_TOKEN` environment variable
- `timezone`: Configured with a default value of **US/Eastern**. You can override the default variable when running the `packer build` command by setting the `-var '<variable>=<value>'` flag (for example, `-var 'timezone=US/Pacific'`)

Notice that we haven't defined the `timezone` variable yet in our Packer template, as you will use this variable later on in this chapter.

Configuring provisioners

Provisioners are the core of Packer templates, forming the various internal provisioning actions that are performed when customizing and building your machine images.

Packer supports a number of different types of provisioners, including popular configuration management tools such as Ansible and Puppet, and you can read more about the different types of provisioners at `https://www.packer.io/docs/provisioners/index.html`.

For our machine image, we are only going use two of the most basic and fundamental provisioners available:

- `Shell provisioner`: Performs provisioning of machine images using shell commands and scripts
- `File provisioner`: Copies files into the machine image

As an introduction to provisioners, let's define a simple shell provisioner that updates the installed operating system packages, as demonstrated in the following example:

```
{
  "variables": {
    "aws_access_key_id": "{{env `AWS_ACCESS_KEY_ID`}}",
    "aws_secret_access_key": "{{env `AWS_SECRET_ACCESS_KEY`}}",
    "aws_session_token": "{{env `AWS_SESSION_TOKEN`}}",
    "timezone": "US/Eastern"
  },
  "builders": [
    {
      "type": "amazon-ebs",
      "access_key": "{{user `aws_access_key_id`}}",
      "secret_key": "{{user `aws_secret_access_key`}}",
      "token": "{{user `aws_session_token`}}",
      "region": "us-east-1",
      "source_ami": "ami-5e414e24",
      "instance_type": "t2.micro",
      "ssh_username": "ec2-user",
      "associate_public_ip_address": "true",
      "ami_name": "docker-in-aws-ecs {{timestamp}}",
      "tags": {
        "Name": "Docker in AWS ECS Base Image 2017.09.h",
        "SourceAMI": "ami-5e414e24",
        "DockerVersion": "17.09.1-ce",
        "ECSAgentVersion": "1.17.0-2"
      }
    }
  ],
  "provisioners": [
    {
      "type": "shell",
      "inline": [
```

```
            "sudo yum -y -x docker\\* -x ecs\\* update"
        ]
    }
],
"post-processors": []
}
```

Defining an inline shell provisioner

The provisioner defined in the preceding example, uses the `inline` parameter to define a list of commands that will be executed during the provisioning stage. In this case, you are running the `yum update` command, which is the default package manager on Amazon Linux systems and updates all installed operation system packages. To ensure you use the recommended and tested versions of Docker and ECS agent packages included in the base ECS-Optimized AMI, you use the `-x` flag to exclude packages that start with `docker` and `ecs`.

> In the preceding example, the yum command will be executed as
> `sudo yum -y -x docker\* -x ecs\* update`. Because the back
> slash character (\) is used to as an escape character in JSON, in the
> preceding example, a double backslash (for example, `\\*`) is used to
> generate a literal back slash.

Finally, notice that you must run all shell provisioning commands with the `sudo` command, as Packer is provisioning the EC2 instance as the `ec2_user` user, as defined in the builders section.

Configuring post-processors

The final structural component of Packer templates we will introduce are `post-processors`, which allow you to perform actions once your machine image has been provisioned and built.

Post-processors can be used for a variety of different use cases that are outside the scope of this book, however one simple example of a post-processor that I like to use is the `Manifest post-processor`, which outputs a JSON file listing all artifacts that Packer produces. This output can be very useful when you create continuous delivery pipelines that first build your Packer images, and then need to test and deploy your images.

In this scenario, a manifest file can be used as an output artifact of your Packer build, describing the regions and AMI identifiers associated with your new machine image, and as an example used as an input into a CloudFormation template that deploys your new machine image into a test environment.

The following example demonstrates adding a manifest post-processor to your Packer template:

```
{
  "variables": {
    "aws_access_key_id": "{{env `AWS_ACCESS_KEY_ID`}}",
    "aws_secret_access_key": "{{env `AWS_SECRET_ACCESS_KEY`}}",
    "aws_session_token": "{{env `AWS_SESSION_TOKEN`}}",
    "timezone": "US/Eastern"
  },
  "builders": [
    {
      "type": "amazon-ebs",
      "access_key": "{{user `aws_access_key_id`}}",
      "secret_key": "{{user `aws_secret_access_key`}}",
      "token": "{{user `aws_session_token`}}",
      "region": "us-east-1",
      "source_ami": "ami-5e414e24",
      "instance_type": "t2.micro",
      "ssh_username": "ec2-user",
      "associate_public_ip_address": "true",
      "ami_name": "docker-in-aws-ecs {{timestamp}}",
      "tags": {
        "Name": "Docker in AWS ECS Base Image 2017.09.h",
        "SourceAMI": "ami-5e414e24",
        "DockerVersion": "17.09.1-ce",
        "ECSAgentVersion": "1.17.0-2"
      }
    }
  ],
  "provisioners": [
    {
      "type": "shell",
      "inline": [
        "sudo yum -y -x docker\\* -x ecs\\* update"
```

```
      ]
    }
  ],
  "post-processors": [
    {
      "type": "manifest",
      "output": "manifest.json",
      "strip_path": true
    }
  ]
}
```

Defining a manifest post-processor

As you can see in the preceding example, the manifest post-processor if very simple - the `output` parameter specifies the name of the file that the manifest will be written to locally, while the `strip_path` parameter strips any local filesystem path information for any built artifacts.

Building a machine image

At this point, you have created a simple Packer image that performs not too much in the way of customization, but nevertheless is a complete template that is ready to build.

Before you can actually run the build, you need to ensure your local environment is configured correctly for the build to complete successfully. Recall in the previous example, you defined variables for your template that reference environment variables that configure your AWS credentials, and a common approach here would be to set your local AWS access key ID and secret access key as environment variables.

In our use case however, I have assumed you are working with the best practice approach of using the multi-factor authentication introduced in earlier chapters, and hence your template is configured to use temporary session credentials as evidenced by the `aws_session_token` input variable that need to be dynamically generated and injected into your local environment before running your Packer build.

Generating dynamic session credentials

To generate temporary session credentials, assuming you have configured an appropriate profile using the AWS_PROFILE environment variable, you can run the aws sts assume-role command to generate credentials:

```
> export AWS_PROFILE=docker-in-aws
> aws sts assume-role --role-arn=$(aws configure get role_arn) --role-
session-name=$(aws configure get role_session_name)
Enter MFA code for arn:aws:iam::385605022855:mfa/justin.menga: ******
{
    "Credentials": {
        "AccessKeyId": "ASIAIIEUKCAR3NMIYM5Q",
        "SecretAccessKey": "JY7HmPMf/tPDXsgQXHt5zFZObgrQJRvNz7kb4KDM",
        "SessionToken":
"FQoDYXdzEM7//////////wEaDP0PBiSeZvJ9GjTP5yLwAVjkJ9ZCMbSY5w1EClNDK2lS3
nkhRg34/9xVgf9RmKiZnYVywrI9/tpMP8LaU/xH6nQvCsZaVTxGXNFyPz1BcsEGM6Z2ebI
FX5rArT9FWu3v7WVs3QQvXeDTasgdvq71eFs2+qX7zbjK0YHXaWuu7GA/LGtNj4i+yi6EZ
3OIq3hnz3+QY2dXL7O1pieMLjfZRf98KHucUhiokaq61cXSo+RJa3yuixaJMSxJVD1myx/
XNritkawUfI8Xwp6g6KWYQAzDYz3MIWbA5LyX9Q0jk3yXTRAQOjLwvL8ZK/InJCDoPBFWF
Jwrz+Wxgep+I8iYoijOhqTUBQ==",
        "Expiration": "2018-02-18T05:38:38Z"
    },
    "AssumedRoleUser": {
        "AssumedRoleId": "AROAJASB32NFHLLQHZ54S:justin.menga",
        "Arn": "arn:aws:sts::385605022855:assumed-
role/admin/justin.menga"
    }
}
> export AWS_ACCESS_KEY_ID="ASIAIIEUKCAR3NMIYM5Q"
> export
AWS_SECRET_ACCESS_KEY="JY7HmPMf/tPDXsgQXHt5zFZObgrQJRvNz7kb4KDM"
> export
AWS_SESSION_TOKEN="FQoDYXdzEM7//////////wEaDP0PBiSeZvJ9GjTP5yLwAVjkJ9Z
CMbSY5w1EClNDK2lS3nkhRg34/9xVgf9RmKiZnYVywrI9/tpMP8LaU/xH6nQvCsZaVTxGX
NFyPz1BcsEGM6Z2ebIFX5rArT9FWu3v7WVs3QQvXeDTasgdvq71eFs2+qX7zbjK0YHXaWu
u7GA/LGtNj4i+yi6EZ3OIq3hnz3+QY2dXL7O1pieMLjfZRf98KHucUhiokaq61cXSo+RJa
3yuixaJMSxJVD1myx/XNritkawUfI8Xwp6g6KWYQAzDYz3MIWbA5LyX9Q0jk3yXTRAQOjL
wvL8ZK/InJCDoPBFWFJwrz+Wxgep+I8iYoijOhqTUBQ=="
```

Generating temporary session credentials

In the preceding example, notice that you can use bash substitutions to dynamically obtain the `role_arn` and `role_session_name` parameters from your AWS CLI profile using the `aws configure get <parameter>` command, which are required inputs when generating temporary session credentials.

The output from the preceding example includes a credentials object that includes the following values that are mapped to the environment variables referenced in your Packer template:

- **AccessKeyId**: This value is exported as the `AWS_ACCESS_KEY_ID` environment variable
- **SecretAccessKey**: This value is exported as the `AWS_SECRET_ACCESS_KEY` environment variable
- **SessionToken**: This value is exported as the `AWS_SESSION_TOKEN` environment variable

Automating generation of dynamic session credentials

Although you can use the approach demonstrated in the preceding example to generate temporary session credentials as required, this approach will become tiresome very quickly. There are many ways you can automate the injection of the generated temporary session credentials into your environment, but given this book uses Make as an automation tool, The following example demonstrates how you can do this using a reasonably simple Makefile:

```
.PHONY: build
.ONESHELL:

build:
  @ $(if $(AWS_PROFILE),$(call assume_role))
  packer build packer.json

# Dynamically assumes role and injects credentials into environment
define assume_role
  export AWS_DEFAULT_REGION=$$(aws configure get region)
  eval $$(aws sts assume-role --role-arn=$$(aws configure get
role_arn) \
    --role-session-name=$$(aws configure get role_session_name) \
    --query "Credentials.[ \
      [join('=',['export AWS_ACCESS_KEY_ID',AccessKeyId])], \
      [join('=',['export AWS_SECRET_ACCESS_KEY',SecretAccessKey])],
\
```

```
        [join('=',['export AWS_SESSION_TOKEN',SessionToken])] \
    ]" \
  --output text)
endef
```

Generating temporary session credentials automatically using Make

> Ensure all indentation in your Makefile is performed using tabs rather than spaces.

In the preceding example, notice the introduction of a directive called `.ONESHELL`. This directive configures Make to spawn a single shell for all commands defined in a given Make recipe, meaning bash variable assignments and environment settings can be reused across multiple lines.

The `build` task conditionally calls a function named `assume_role` if the current environment is configured with `AWS_PROFILE`, and this approach is useful as it means if you were running this Makefile on a build agent that was configured to obtain AWS credentials in a different manner, the dynamic generation of temporary session credentials would not take place.

> When a command is prefixed with the @ symbol in a Makefile, the executed command will not output to stdout, and instead only the output of the command will be displayed.

The `assume_role` function uses an advanced JMESPath query expression (as specified by the `--query` flag) to generate a set of `export` statements that reference the various properties on the **Credentials** dictionary output of the command you ran in the previous example and assign the values to the relevant environment variables using the JMESPath join function (`http://jmespath.readthedocs.io/en/latest/specification.html#join`). This is wrapped in a command substitution, with the `eval` command used to execute each output `export` statement. Don't worry too much if you don't understand this query, but recognise that the AWS CLI does include a powerful query syntax that can create some quite sophisticated one liners.

> ### TIP
> Note in the preceding example that you can use back ticks (`` ` ``) as an alternative syntax for bash command substitutions. In other words, `$(command)` and `` `command` `` both represent command substitutions that will execute the command and return the output.

Building the image

Now that we have a mechanism of automating the generation of temporary session credentials, assuming that your `packer.json` file and Makefile are in the root of your packer-ecs repository, let's test out building your Packer image by running `make build`:

```
> export AWS_PROFILE=docker-in-aws
> make build
Enter MFA code for arn:aws:iam::385605022855:mfa/justin.menga: ******
packer build packer.json
amazon-ebs output will be in this color.

==> amazon-ebs: Prevalidating AMI Name: docker-in-aws-ecs 1518934269
    amazon-ebs: Found Image ID: ami-5e414e24
==> amazon-ebs: Creating temporary keypair:
packer_5a8918fd-018d-964f-4ab3-58bff320ead5
==> amazon-ebs: Creating temporary security group for this instance:
packer_5a891904-2c84-aca1-d368-8309f215597d
==> amazon-ebs: Authorizing access to port 22 from 0.0.0.0/0 in the
temporary security group...
==> amazon-ebs: Launching a source AWS instance...
==> amazon-ebs: Adding tags to source instance
    amazon-ebs: Adding tag: "Name": "Packer Builder"
    amazon-ebs: Instance ID: i-04c150456ac0748aa
==> amazon-ebs: Waiting for instance (i-04c150456ac0748aa) to become
ready...
==> amazon-ebs: Waiting for SSH to become available...
==> amazon-ebs: Connected to SSH!
==> amazon-ebs: Provisioning with shell script:
/var/folders/s4/1mblw7cd29s8xc74vr3jdmfr0000gn/T/packer-shell190211980
    amazon-ebs: Loaded plugins: priorities, update-motd, upgrade-
helper
    amazon-ebs: Resolving Dependencies
    amazon-ebs: --> Running transaction check
    amazon-ebs: ---> Package elfutils-libelf.x86_64 0:0.163-3.18.amzn1
will be updated
    amazon-ebs: ---> Package elfutils-libelf.x86_64 0:0.168-8.19.amzn1
will be an update
```

```
    amazon-ebs: ---> Package python27.x86_64 0:2.7.12-2.121.amzn1 will
be updated
    amazon-ebs: ---> Package python27.x86_64 0:2.7.13-2.122.amzn1 will
be an update
    amazon-ebs: ---> Package python27-libs.x86_64 0:2.7.12-2.121.amzn1
will be updated
    amazon-ebs: ---> Package python27-libs.x86_64 0:2.7.13-2.122.amzn1
will be an update
    amazon-ebs: --> Finished Dependency Resolution
    amazon-ebs:
    amazon-ebs: Dependencies Resolved
    amazon-ebs:
    amazon-ebs:
================================================================================
==========
    amazon-ebs: Package Arch Version Repository Size
    amazon-ebs:
================================================================================
==========
    amazon-ebs: Updating:
    amazon-ebs: elfutils-libelf x86_64 0.168-8.19.amzn1 amzn-updates
313 k
    amazon-ebs: python27 x86_64 2.7.13-2.122.amzn1 amzn-updates 103 k
    amazon-ebs: python27-libs x86_64 2.7.13-2.122.amzn1 amzn-updates
6.8 M
    amazon-ebs:
    amazon-ebs: Transaction Summary
    amazon-ebs:
================================================================================
==========
    amazon-ebs: Upgrade 3 Packages
    amazon-ebs:
    amazon-ebs: Total download size: 7.2 M
    amazon-ebs: Downloading packages:
    amazon-ebs: -----------------------------------------------------
---------------------------
    amazon-ebs: Total 5.3 MB/s | 7.2 MB 00:01
    amazon-ebs: Running transaction check
    amazon-ebs: Running transaction test
    amazon-ebs: Transaction test succeeded
    amazon-ebs: Running transaction
    amazon-ebs: Updating : python27-2.7.13-2.122.amzn1.x86_64 1/6
    amazon-ebs: Updating : python27-libs-2.7.13-2.122.amzn1.x86_64 2/6
    amazon-ebs: Updating : elfutils-libelf-0.168-8.19.amzn1.x86_64 3/6
    amazon-ebs: Cleanup : python27-2.7.12-2.121.amzn1.x86_64 4/6
    amazon-ebs: Cleanup : python27-libs-2.7.12-2.121.amzn1.x86_64 5/6
    amazon-ebs: Cleanup : elfutils-libelf-0.163-3.18.amzn1.x86_64 6/6
    amazon-ebs: Verifying : python27-libs-2.7.13-2.122.amzn1.x86_64
```

```
1/6
    amazon-ebs: Verifying : elfutils-libelf-0.168-8.19.amzn1.x86_64
2/6
    amazon-ebs: Verifying : python27-2.7.13-2.122.amzn1.x86_64 3/6
    amazon-ebs: Verifying : python27-libs-2.7.12-2.121.amzn1.x86_64
4/6
    amazon-ebs: Verifying : elfutils-libelf-0.163-3.18.amzn1.x86_64
5/6
    amazon-ebs: Verifying : python27-2.7.12-2.121.amzn1.x86_64 6/6
    amazon-ebs:
    amazon-ebs: Updated:
    amazon-ebs: elfutils-libelf.x86_64 0:0.168-8.19.amzn1
    amazon-ebs: python27.x86_64 0:2.7.13-2.122.amzn1
    amazon-ebs: python27-libs.x86_64 0:2.7.13-2.122.amzn1
    amazon-ebs:
    amazon-ebs: Complete!
==> amazon-ebs: Stopping the source instance...
    amazon-ebs: Stopping instance, attempt 1
==> amazon-ebs: Waiting for the instance to stop...
==> amazon-ebs: Creating the AMI: docker-in-aws-ecs 1518934269
    amazon-ebs: AMI: ami-57415b2d
==> amazon-ebs: Waiting for AMI to become ready...
==> amazon-ebs: Adding tags to AMI (ami-57415b2d)...
==> amazon-ebs: Tagging snapshot: snap-0bc767fd982333bf8
==> amazon-ebs: Tagging snapshot: snap-0104c1a352695c1e9
==> amazon-ebs: Creating AMI tags
    amazon-ebs: Adding tag: "SourceAMI": "ami-5e414e24"
    amazon-ebs: Adding tag: "DockerVersion": "17.09.1-ce"
    amazon-ebs: Adding tag: "ECSAgentVersion": "1.17.0-2"
    amazon-ebs: Adding tag: "Name": "Docker in AWS ECS Base Image
2017.09.h"
==> amazon-ebs: Creating snapshot tags
==> amazon-ebs: Terminating the source AWS instance...
==> amazon-ebs: Cleaning up any extra volumes...
==> amazon-ebs: No volumes to clean up, skipping
==> amazon-ebs: Deleting temporary security group...
==> amazon-ebs: Deleting temporary keypair...
==> amazon-ebs: Running post-processor: manifest
Build 'amazon-ebs' finished.

==> Builds finished. The artifacts of successful builds are:
--> amazon-ebs: AMIs were created:
us-east-1: ami-57415b2d
```

Running a Packer build

Referring back to the previous example and the output of the preceding one, notice in the `build` task that the command to build a Packer image is simply `packer build <template-file>`, which in this case is `packer build packer.json`.

If you review the output of the preceding example, you can see the following steps are performed by Packer:

- Packer initially validates the source AMI and then generates a temporary SSH key pair and security group so that it is able to access the temporary EC2 instance.
- Packer launches a temporary EC2 instance from the source AMI and then waits until it is able to establish SSH access.
- Packer executes the provisioning actions as defined in the provisioners section of the template. In this case, you can see the output of the yum `update` command, which is our current single provisioning action.
- Once complete, Packer stops the instance and creates a snapshot of the EBS volume instance, which produces an AMI with an appropriate name and ID.
- With the AMI created, Packer terminates the instance, deletes the temporary SSH key pair and security group, and outputs the new AMI ID.

Recall in the earlier example, that you added a manifest post-processor to your template, and you should find a file called `manifest.json` has been output at the root of your repository, which you typically would not want to commit to your **packer-ecs** repository:

```
> cat manifest.json
{
  "builds": [
    {
      "name": "amazon-ebs",
      "builder_type": "amazon-ebs",
      "build_time": 1518934504,
      "files": null,
      "artifact_id": "us-east-1:ami-57415b2d",
      "packer_run_uuid": "db07ccb3-4100-1cc8-f0be-354b9f9b021d"
    }
  ],
  "last_run_uuid": "db07ccb3-4100-1cc8-f0be-354b9f9b021d"
}
> echo manifest.json >> .gitignore
```

Viewing the Packer build manifest

Building custom ECS container instance images using Packer

In the previous section, you established a base template for building a custom AMI using Packer, and proceed to build and publish your first custom AMI. At this point, you have not performed any customization that is specific to the use case of provisioning ECS container instances, so this section will focus on enhancing your Packer template to include such customizations.

The customizations you will learn about now include the following:

- Defining a custom storage configuration
- Installing additional packages and configuring operating system settings
- Configuring a cleanup script
- Creating a first-run script

With these customizations in place, we will complete the chapter by building your final custom ECS Container Instance AMI and launching an instance to verify the various customizations.

Defining a custom storage configuration

The AWS ECS-Optimized AMI includes a default storage configuration that uses a 30 GB EBS volume, which is partitioned as follows:

- `/dev/xvda`: An 8 GB volume that is mounted as the root filesystem and serves as the operating system partition.
- `dev/xvdcz`: A 22 GB volume that is configured as a logical volume management (LVM) device and is used for Docker image and metadata storage.

> The ECS-Optimized AMI uses the devicemapper storage driver for Docker image and metadata storage, which you can learn more about at `https://docs.docker.com/v17.09/engine/userguide/storagedriver/device-mapper-driver/`.

For most use cases, this storage configuration should be sufficient, however there are a couple of scenarios in which you may want to modify the default configuration:

- **You need more Docker image and metadata storage**: This is easily addressed by simply configuring your ECS container instances with a larger volume size. The default storage configuration will always reserve 8GB for the operating system and root filesystem, with the remainder of the storage allocated for Docker image and metadata storage.
- **You need to support Docker volumes that have large storage requirements**: By default, the ECS-Optimized AMI stores Docker volumes at /var/lib/docker/volumes, which is part of the root filesystem on the 8GB /dev/xvda partition. If you have larger volume requirements, this can cause your operating system partition to quickly become full, so in this scenario you should separate out the volume storage to a separate EBS volume.

Let's now see how you can modify your Packer template to add a new dedicated volume for Docker volume storage and ensure this volume is mounted correctly on instance creation.

Adding EBS volumes

To add an EBS volume to your custom AMIs, you can configure the launch_block_device_mappings parameter within the Amazon EBS builder:

```
{
  "variables": {...},
  "builders": [
    {
      "type": "amazon-ebs",
      "access_key": "{{user `aws_access_key_id`}}",
      "secret_key": "{{user `aws_secret_access_key`}}",
      "token": "{{user `aws_session_token`}}",
      "region": "us-east-1",
      "source_ami": "ami-5e414e24",
      "instance_type": "t2.micro",
      "ssh_username": "ec2-user",
      "associate_public_ip_address": "true",
      "ami_name": "docker-in-aws-ecs {{timestamp}}",
      "launch_block_device_mappings": [
        {
          "device_name": "/dev/xvdcy",
          "volume_size": 20,
          "volume_type": "gp2",
```

```
          "delete_on_termination": true
        }
      ],
      "tags": {
        "Name": "Docker in AWS ECS Base Image 2017.09.h",
        "SourceAMI": "ami-5e414e24",
        "DockerVersion": "17.09.1-ce",
        "ECSAgentVersion": "1.17.0-2"
      }
    }
  ],
  "provisioners": [...],
  "post-processors": [...]
}
```

Adding a launch block device mapping

In the preceding example, I have truncated other portions of the Packer template for brevity, and you can see that we have added a single 20 GB volume called /dev/xvdcy, which is configured to be destroyed on instance termination. Notice that the volume_type parameter is set to gp2, which is the general-purpose SSD storage type that typically offers the best overall price/performance in AWS.

Formatting and mounting volumes

With the configuration of the preceding example in place, we next need to format and mount that new volume. Because we used the launch_block_device_mappings parameter (as opposed to the ami_block_device_mappings parameter), the block device is actually attached at image build time (the latter parameter is attached upon image creation only) and we can perform all formatting and mount configuration settings at build time.

To perform this configuration, we will add a shell provisioner that references a file called scripts/storage.sh to your Packer template:

```
{
  "variables": {...},
  "builders": [...],
  "provisioners": [
    {
      "type": "shell",
      "script": "scripts/storage.sh"
    },
    {
      "type": "shell",
```

```
      "inline": [
        "sudo yum -y -x docker\\* -x ecs\\* update"
      ]
    }
  ],
  "post-processors": [...]
}
```

Adding a shell provisioner for configuring storage

The referenced script is expressed as a path relative to the the Packer template, so you now need to create this script:

```
> mkdir -p scripts
> touch scripts/storage.sh
> tree
.
├── Makefile
├── manifest.json
├── packer.json
└── scripts
    └── storage.sh

1 directory, 4 files
```

Creating a scripts folder

With the script file in place, you can now define the various shell provisioning actions in this script as demonstrated in the following example:

```
#!/usr/bin/env bash
set -e

echo "### Configuring Docker Volume Storage ###"
sudo mkdir -p /data
sudo mkfs.ext4 -L docker /dev/xvdcy
echo -e "LABEL=docker\t/data\t\text4\tdefaults,noatime\t0\t0" | sudo
tee -a /etc/fstab
sudo mount -a
```

Storage provisioning script

As you can see in the preceding example, the script is a regular bash script, and it's important to always set the error flag for all of your Packer shell scripts (set -e), which ensures the script will exit with an error code should any command fail within the script.

You first create a folder called `/data`, which you will use to store Docker volumes, and then format the `/dev/xvdcy` device you attached earlier in the earlier example with the `.ext4` filesystem, and attach a label called `docker`, which makes mount operations simpler to perform. The next `echo` command adds an entry to the `/etc/fstab` file, which defines all filesystem mounts that will be applied at boot, and notice that you must pipe the `echo` command through to `sudo tee -a` `/etc/fstab`, which appends the `echo` output to the `/etc/fstab` file with the correct sudo privileges.

Finally, you auto-mount the new entry in the `/etc/fstab` file by running the `mount -a` command, which although not required at image build time, is a simple way to verify that the mount is actually configured correctly (if not, this command will fail and the resulting build will fail).

Installing additional packages and configuring system settings

The next customizations you will perform are to install additional packages and configuring system settings.

Installing additional packages

There are a few additional packages that we need to install into our custom ECS container instance, which include the following:

- **CloudFormation helper scripts**: When you use CloudFormation to deploy your infrastructure, AWS provide a set of CloudFormation helper scripts, collectively referred to as **cfn-bootstrap**, that work with CloudFormation to obtain initialization metadata that allows you to perform custom initialization tasks at instance-creation time, and also signal CloudFormation when the instance has successfully completed initialization. We will explore the benefits of this approach in later chapters, however, for now you need to ensure these helper scripts are present in your custom ECS container-instance image.

- **CloudWatch logs agent**: The AWS CloudWatch logs service offers central storage of logs from various sources, including EC2 instances, ECS containers, and other AWS services. To ship your ECS container instance (EC2 instance) logs to CloudWatch logs, you must install the CloudWatch logs agent locally, which you can then use to forward various system logs, including operating system, Docker, and ECS agent logs.
- `jq` **utility**: The `jq` utility (`https://stedolan.github.io/jq/manual/`) is handy for parsing JSON output, and you will need this utility later on in this chapter when you define a simple health check that verifies the ECS container instance has joined to the configured ECS cluster.

Installing these additional packages is very straightforward, and can be achieved by modifying the inline shell provisioner you created earlier:

```
{
  "variables": {...},
  "builders": [...],
  "provisioners": [
    {
      "type": "shell",
      "script": "scripts/storage.sh"
    },
    {
      "type": "shell",
      "inline": [
        "sudo yum -y -x docker\\* -x ecs\\* update",
        "sudo yum -y install aws-cfn-bootstrap awslogs jq"
      ]
    }
  ],
  "post-processors": [...]
}
```

Installing additional operating system packages

As you can see in the preceding example, each of the required packages can be easily installed using the `yum` package manager.

Configuring system settings

There are a few minor system settings that you need to make to your custom ECS container instance:

- Configure time-zone settings
- Modify default cloud-init behavior

Configuring timezone settings

Earlier, you defined a variable called `timezone`, which so far you have not referenced in your template. You can use this variable to configure the timezone of your custom ECS container instance image.

To do this, you first need to add a new shell provisioner into your Packer template:

```
{
  "variables": {...},
  "builders": [...],
  "provisioners": [
    {
      "type": "shell",
      "script": "scripts/storage.sh"
    },
    {
      "type": "shell",
      "script": "scripts/time.sh",
      "environment_vars": [
        "TIMEZONE={{user `timezone`}}"
      ]
    },
    {
      "type": "shell",
      "inline": [
        "sudo yum -y -x docker\\* -x ecs\\* update",
        "sudo yum -y install aws-cfn-bootstrap awslogs jq"
      ]
    }
  ],
  "post-processors": [...]
}
```

Adding a provisioner to configure time settings

In the preceding example, we reference a script called `scripts/time.sh`, which you will create shortly, but notice that we also include a parameter called `environment_vars`, which allows you to inject your Packer variables (`timezone` in this example) as environment variables into your shell provisioning scripts.

The following example shows the required `scripts/time.sh` script that is referenced in the new Packer template provisioning task:

```
#!/usr/bin/env bash
set -e

# Configure host to use timezone
# http://docs.aws.amazon.com/AWSEC2/latest/UserGuide/set-time.html
echo "### Setting timezone to $TIMEZONE ###"
sudo tee /etc/sysconfig/clock << EOF > /dev/null
ZONE="$TIMEZONE"
UTC=true
EOF

sudo ln -sf /usr/share/zoneinfo/"$TIMEZONE" /etc/localtime

# Use AWS NTP Sync service
echo "server 169.254.169.123 prefer iburst" | sudo tee -a
/etc/ntp.conf

# Enable NTP
sudo chkconfig ntpd on
```

Time settings provisioning script

In the preceding example, you first configure the `AWS recommended settings for configuring time`, configuring the `/etc/sysconfig/clock` file with the configured `TIMEZONE` environment variable, creating the symbolic `/etc/localtime` link, and finally ensuring the `ntpd` service is configured to use the `AWS NTP sync` service and start at instance boot.

> The AWS NTP sync service is a free AWS service that provides an NTP server endpoint at the `169.254.169.123` local address, ensuring your EC2 instances can obtain accurate time without having to traverse the network or internet.

Modifying default cloud-init behavior

cloud-init is a standard set of utilities for performing initialization of cloud images and associated instances. The most popular feature of cloud-init is the user-data mechanism, which is a simple means of running your own custom initialization commands at instance creation.

cloud-init is also used in the ECS-Optimized AMI to perform automatic security patching at instance creation, and although this sounds like a useful feature, it can cause problems, particularly in environments where your instances are located in private subnets and require an HTTP proxy to communicate with the internet.

The issue with the cloud-init security mechanism is that although it can be configured to work with an HTTP proxy by setting proxy environment variables, it is invoked prior to when userdata is executed, leading to a chicken-and-egg scenario where you have no option but to disable automated security patching if you are using a proxy.

To disable this mechanism, you first need to configure a new shell provisioner in your Packer template:

```
{
  "variables": {...},
  "builders": [...],
  "provisioners": [
    {
      "type": "shell",
      "script": "scripts/storage.sh"
    },
    {
      "type": "shell",
      "script": "scripts/time.sh",
      "environment_vars": [
        "TIMEZONE={{user `timezone`}}"
      ]
    },
    {
      "type": "shell",
      "script": "scripts/cloudinit.sh"
    },
    {
      "type": "shell",
      "inline": [
        "sudo yum -y -x docker\\* -x ecs\\* update",
        "sudo yum -y install aws-cfn-bootstrap awslogs jq"
      ]
    }
  ],
```

```
    "post-processors": [...]
}
```

Adding a provisioner to configure cloud-init settings

The referenced `scripts/cloudinit.sh` script can now be created as follows:

```
#!/usr/bin/env bash
set -e

# Disable cloud-init repo updates or upgrades
sudo sed -i -e '/^repo_update: /{h;s/: .*/:
false/};${x;/^$/{s//repo_update: false/;H};x}' /etc/cloud/cloud.cfg
sudo sed -i -e '/^repo_upgrade: /{h;s/: .*/:
none/};${x;/^$/{s//repo_upgrade: none/;H};x}' /etc/cloud/cloud.cfg
```

Disabling security updates for cloud-init

In the following example, the rather scary-looking `sed` expressions will either add or replace lines beginning with `repo_update` and `repo_upgrade` in the `/etc/cloud/cloud.cfg` cloud-init configuration file and ensure they are set to `false` and `none`, respectively.

Configuring a cleanup script

At this point, we have performed all required installation and configuration shell provisioning tasks. We will create one final shell provisioner, a cleanup script, which will remove any log files created while the instance used to build the custom image was running and to ensure the machine image is in a state ready to be launched.

You first need to add a shell provisioner to your Packer template that references the `scripts/cleanup.sh` script:

```
{
  "variables": {...},
  "builders": [...],
  "provisioners": [
    {
      "type": "shell",
      "script": "scripts/storage.sh"
    },
    {
      "type": "shell",
      "script": "scripts/time.sh",
      "environment_vars": [
        "TIMEZONE={{user `timezone`}}"
```

```
        ]
      },
      {
        "type": "shell",
        "script": "scripts/cloudinit.sh"
      },
      {
        "type": "shell",
        "inline": [
          "sudo yum -y -x docker\\* -x ecs\\* update",
          "sudo yum -y install aws-cfn-bootstrap awslogs jq"
        ]
      },
      {
        "type": "shell",
        "script": "scripts/cleanup.sh"
      }
    ],
    "post-processors": [...]
}
```

Adding a provisioner to clean up the Image

With the provisioner defined in the Packer template, you next need to create the cleanup script, as defined here:

```
#!/usr/bin/env bash
echo "### Performing final clean-up tasks ###"
sudo stop ecs
sudo docker system prune -f -a
sudo service docker stop
sudo chkconfig docker off
sudo rm -rf /var/log/docker /var/log/ecs/*
```

Cleanup script

In the following example, notice you don't execute the command `set -e`, given this is a cleanup script that you are not too worried about if there is an error and you don't want your build to fail should a service already be stopped. The ECS agent is first stopped, with the `docker system prune` command used to clear any ECS container state that may be present, and next the Docker service is stopped and then disabled using the `chkconfig` command. The reason for this is that on instance creation, we will always invoke a first-run script that will perform initial configuration of the instance and requires the Docker service to be stopped. Of course this means that once the first-run script has completed its initial configuration, it will be responsible for ensuring the Docker service is both started and enabled to start on boot.

Finally, the cleanup script removes any Docker and ECS agent log files that may have been created during the short period the instance was up during the custom machine-image build process.

Creating a first-run script

The final set of customizations we will apply to your custom ECS container instance image is to create a first-run script, which will be responsible for performing runtime configuration of your ECS container instance at instance creation, by performing the following tasks:

- Configuring ECS cluster membership
- Configuring HTTP proxy support
- Configuring the CloudWatch logs agent
- Starting required services
- Performing health checks

To provision the first-run script, you need to define a file provisioner task in your Packer template, as demonstrated here:

```
{
  "variables": {...},
  "builders": [...],
  "provisioners": [
    {
      "type": "shell",
      "script": "scripts/storage.sh"
    },
    {
      "type": "shell",
```

```
      "script": "scripts/time.sh",
      "environment_vars": [
        "TIMEZONE={{user `timezone`}}"
      ]
    },
    {
      "type": "shell",
      "script": "scripts/cloudinit.sh"
    },
    {
      "type": "shell",
      "inline": [
        "sudo yum -y -x docker\\* -x ecs\\* update",
        "sudo yum -y install aws-cfn-bootstrap awslogs jq"
      ]
    },
    {
      "type": "shell",
      "script": "scripts/cleanup.sh"
    },
    {
      "type": "file",
      "source": "files/firstrun.sh",
      "destination": "/home/ec2-user/firstrun.sh"
    }
  ],
  "post-processors": [...]
}
```

Adding a file provisioner

Notice that the provisioner type is configured as `file`, and specifies a local source file that needs to be located in `files/firstrun.sh`. The `destination` parameter defines the location within the AMI where the first-run script will be located. Note that the file provisioner task copies files as the `ec2-user` user, hence it has limited permissions as to where this script can be copied.

Configuring ECS cluster membership

You can now create the first-run script at the files/firstrun.sh location referenced by your Packer template. Before you get started configuring this file, it is important to bear in mind that the first-run script is designed to be run at initial boot of an instance created from your custom machine image, so you must consider this when configuring the various commands that will be executed.

We will first create configure the ECS agent to join the ECS cluster that the ECS container instance is intended to join, as demonstrated in the following example:

```
#!/usr/bin/env bash
set -e

# Configure ECS Agent
echo "ECS_CLUSTER=${ECS_CLUSTER}" > /etc/ecs/ecs.config
```

Configuring ECS cluster membership

Back in `Chapter 5`, *Publishing Docker Images using ECR*, you saw how the ECS cluster wizard configured ECS container instances using this same approach, although one difference is that the script is expecting an environment variable called `ECS_CLUSTER` to be configured in the environment, as designated by the `${ECS_CLUSTER}` expression. Rather than hardcode the ECS cluster name, which would make the first-run script very inflexible, the idea here is that the configuration being applied to a given instance defines the `ECS_CLUSTER` environment variable with the correct cluster name, meaning the script is reusable and can be configured with any given ECS cluster.

Configuring HTTP proxy support

A common security best practice is to place your ECS container instances in private subnets, meaning they are located in subnets that possess no default route to the internet. This approach makes it more difficult for attackers to compromise your systems, and even if they do, provides a means to restrict what information they can transmit back to the internet.

Depending on the nature of your application, you typically will require your ECS container instances to be able to connect to the internet, and using an HTTP proxy provides an effective mechanism to provide such access in a controlled manner with Layer 7 application-layer inspection capabilities.

Regardless of the nature of your application, it is important to understand that ECS container instances require internet connectivity for the following purposes:

- ECS agent control-plane and management-plane communications with ECS
- Docker Engine communication with ECR and other repositories for downloading Docker images

- CloudWatch logs agent communication with the CloudWatch logs service
- CloudFormation helper-script communication with the CloudFormation service

Although configuring a complete end-to-end proxy solution is outside the scope of this book, it is useful to understand how you can customize your ECS container instances to use an HTTP proxy, as demonstrated in the following example:

```
#!/usr/bin/env bash
set -e

# Configure ECS Agent
echo "ECS_CLUSTER=${ECS_CLUSTER}" > /etc/ecs/ecs.config

# Set HTTP Proxy URL if provided
if [ -n $PROXY_URL ]
then
  echo export HTTPS_PROXY=$PROXY_URL >> /etc/sysconfig/docker
  echo HTTPS_PROXY=$PROXY_URL >> /etc/ecs/ecs.config
  echo NO_PROXY=169.254.169.254,169.254.170.2,/var/run/docker.sock >>
/etc/ecs/ecs.config
  echo HTTP_PROXY=$PROXY_URL >> /etc/awslogs/proxy.conf
  echo HTTPS_PROXY=$PROXY_URL >> /etc/awslogs/proxy.conf
  echo NO_PROXY=169.254.169.254 >> /etc/awslogs/proxy.conf
fi
```

Configuring HTTP proxy support

In the preceding example, the script checks for the existence of a non-empty environment variable called PROXY_URL, and if present proceeds to configure proxy settings for various components of the ECS container instance:

- Docker Engine: Configured via /etc/sysconfig/docker
- ECS agent: Configured via /etc/ecs/ecs.config
- CloudWatch logs agent: Configured via /etc/awslogs/proxy.conf

Notice that in some cases you need to configure the NO_PROXY setting, which disables proxy communications for the following IP addresses:

- 169.254.169.254: This is a special local address that is used to communicate with the EC2 metadata service to obtain instance metadata, such as EC2 instance role credentials.
- 169.254.170.2: This is a special local address that is used to obtained ECS task credentials.

Configuring the CloudWatch logs agent

The next configuration task that you will perform in the first-run script is to configure the CloudWatch logs agent. On an ECS container instance, the CloudWatch logs agent is responsible for collecting system logs, such as operating system, Docker, and ECS agent logs.

> **TIP**
>
> Note that this agent is NOT required to implement CloudWatch logs support for your Docker containers - this is already implemented within the Docker Engine via the `awslogs` logging driver.

Configuring the CloudWatch logs agent requires you to perform the following configuration tasks:

- **Configure the correct AWS region**: For this task, you will inject the value of an environment variable called `AWS_DEFAULT_REGION` and write this to the `/etc/awslogs/awscli.conf` file.
- **Define the various log group and log stream settings that the CloudWatch logs agent will log to**: For this task, you will define the recommended set of log groups for ECS container instances, which is described at `https://docs.aws.amazon.com/AmazonECS/latest/developerguide/using_cloudwatch_logs.html#configure_cwl_agent`

The following example demonstrates the required configuration:

```
#!/usr/bin/env bash
set -e

# Configure ECS Agent
echo "ECS_CLUSTER=${ECS_CLUSTER}" > /etc/ecs/ecs.config

# Set HTTP Proxy URL if provided
if [ -n $PROXY_URL ]
then
  echo export HTTPS_PROXY=$PROXY_URL >> /etc/sysconfig/docker
  echo HTTPS_PROXY=$PROXY_URL >> /etc/ecs/ecs.config
  echo NO_PROXY=169.254.169.254,169.254.170.2,/var/run/docker.sock >>
/etc/ecs/ecs.config
  echo HTTP_PROXY=$PROXY_URL >> /etc/awslogs/proxy.conf
  echo HTTPS_PROXY=$PROXY_URL >> /etc/awslogs/proxy.conf
  echo NO_PROXY=169.254.169.254 >> /etc/awslogs/proxy.conf
fi

# Write AWS Logs region
```

```
sudo tee /etc/awslogs/awscli.conf << EOF > /dev/null
[plugins]
cwlogs = cwlogs
[default]
region = ${AWS_DEFAULT_REGION}
EOF

# Write AWS Logs config
sudo tee /etc/awslogs/awslogs.conf << EOF > /dev/null
[general]
state_file = /var/lib/awslogs/agent-state

[/var/log/dmesg]
file = /var/log/dmesg
log_group_name = /${STACK_NAME}/ec2/${AUTOSCALING_GROUP}/var/log/dmesg
log_stream_name = {instance_id}

[/var/log/messages]
file = /var/log/messages
log_group_name =
/${STACK_NAME}/ec2/${AUTOSCALING_GROUP}/var/log/messages
log_stream_name = {instance_id}
datetime_format = %b %d %H:%M:%S

[/var/log/docker]
file = /var/log/docker
log_group_name =
/${STACK_NAME}/ec2/${AUTOSCALING_GROUP}/var/log/docker
log_stream_name = {instance_id}
datetime_format = %Y-%m-%dT%H:%M:%S.%f

[/var/log/ecs/ecs-init.log]
file = /var/log/ecs/ecs-init.log*
log_group_name =
/${STACK_NAME}/ec2/${AUTOSCALING_GROUP}/var/log/ecs/ecs-init
log_stream_name = {instance_id}
datetime_format = %Y-%m-%dT%H:%M:%SZ
time_zone = UTC

[/var/log/ecs/ecs-agent.log]
file = /var/log/ecs/ecs-agent.log*
log_group_name =
/${STACK_NAME}/ec2/${AUTOSCALING_GROUP}/var/log/ecs/ecs-agent
log_stream_name = {instance_id}
datetime_format = %Y-%m-%dT%H:%M:%SZ
time_zone = UTC

[/var/log/ecs/audit.log]
```

```
file = /var/log/ecs/audit.log*
log_group_name =
/${STACK_NAME}/ec2/${AUTOSCALING_GROUP}/var/log/ecs/audit.log
log_stream_name = {instance_id}
datetime_format = %Y-%m-%dT%H:%M:%SZ
time_zone = UTC
EOF
```

Configuring the CloudWatch logs agent

You can see that the first-run script includes references to environment variables in the `log_group_name` parameter for each defined log group, which helps ensure unique log group naming in your AWS account:

- `STACK_NAME`: The name of the CloudFormation stack
- `AUTOSCALING_GROUP`: The name of the Autoscaling Group

Again, these environment variables must be injected at instance creation to the first-run script, so bear this in mind for future chapters when we will learn how to do this.

One other point to note in the preceding example is the value of each `log_stream_name` parameter - this is set to a special variable called `{instance_id}`, which the CloudWatch logs agent will automatically configure with the EC2 instance ID of the instance.

The end result is that you will get several log groups for each type of log, which are scoped to the context of a given CloudFormation stack and EC2 auto scaling group, and within each log group, a log stream for each ECS container instance will be created, as illustrated in the following diagram:

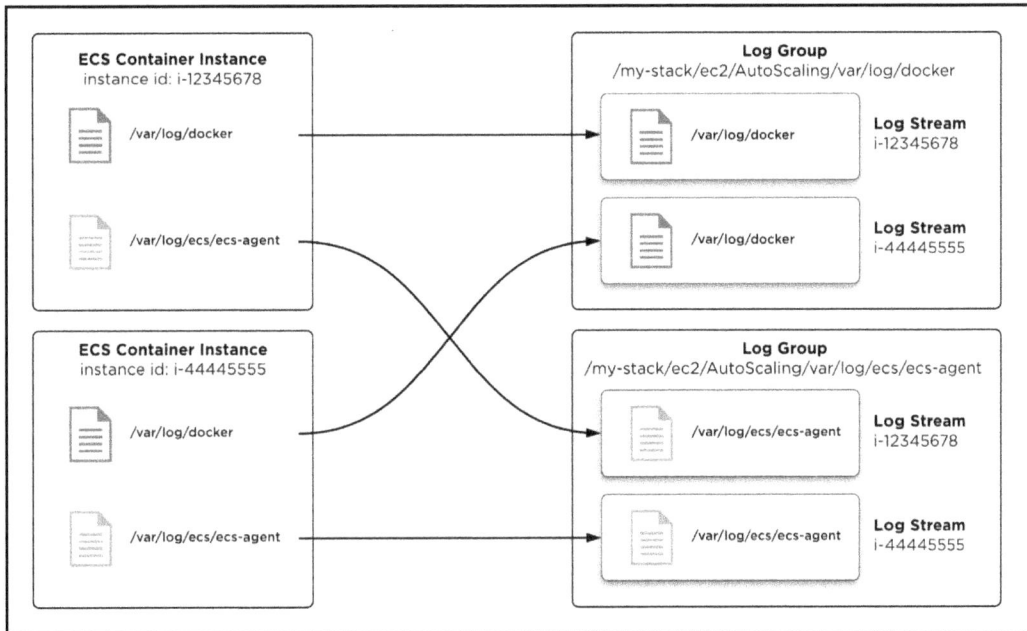

CloudWatch logs group configuration for ECS container instances

Starting required services

Recall in the previous examples, that you added a cleanup script as part of the image-build process, which disables the Docker Engine service from starting on boot. This approach allows you to perform required initialization tasks prior to starting the Docker Engine, and at this point in the first-run script we are ready to start the Docker Engine and other important system services:

```
#!/usr/bin/env bash
set -e

# Configure ECS Agent
echo "ECS_CLUSTER=${ECS_CLUSTER}" > /etc/ecs/ecs.config

# Set HTTP Proxy URL if provided
...
...

# Write AWS Logs region
...
...
```

```
# Write AWS Logs config
...
...

# Start services
sudo service awslogs start
sudo chkconfig docker on
sudo service docker start
sudo start ecs
```

Starting services

In the preceding example, note that I have omitted the earlier parts of the first-run script for brevity. Notice that you first start the awslogs service, which ensures the CloudWatch logs agent will pick up all Docker Engine logs, and then proceed to enable Docker to start on boot, start Docker, and finally start the ECS agent.

Performing required health checks

The final task we need to perform in the first-run script is a health check, which ensures the ECS container instance has initialized and successfully registered to the configured ECS cluster. This is a reasonable health check for your ECS container instances, given the ECS agent can only run if the Docker Engine is operational, and the ECS agent must be registered with the ECS cluster in order to deploy your applications.

Recall in the previous chapter, when you examined the internals of an ECS container instance that the ECS agent exposes a local HTTP endpoint that can be queried for current ECS agent status. You can use this endpoint to create a very simple health check, as demonstrated here:

```
#!/usr/bin/env bash
set -e

# Configure ECS Agent
echo "ECS_CLUSTER=${ECS_CLUSTER}" > /etc/ecs/ecs.config

# Set HTTP Proxy URL if provided
...
...

# Write AWS Logs region
...
...
```

```
# Write AWS Logs config
...
...

# Start services
...
...

# Health check
# Loop until ECS agent has registered to ECS cluster
echo "Checking ECS agent is joined to ${ECS_CLUSTER}"
until [[ "$(curl --fail --silent http://localhost:51678/v1/metadata |
jq '.Cluster // empty' -r -e)" == ${ECS_CLUSTER} ]]
 do printf '.'
 sleep 5
done
echo "ECS agent successfully joined to ${ECS_CLUSTER}"
```

Performing a health check

In the preceding example, a bash `until` loop is configured, which uses curl to query the `http://localhost:51678/v1/metadata` endpoint every five seconds. The output of this command is piped through to `jq`, which will either return the Cluster property or an empty value if this property is not present. Once the ECS agent registers to the correct ECS cluster and returns this property in the JSON response, the loop will complete and the first-run script will complete.

Testing your custom ECS container instance image

You have now completed all customizations and it is time to rebuild your image using the `packer build` command. Before you do this, now is a good time to verify you have the correct Packer template in place, and also have created the associated supporting files. The following example shows the folder and file structure you should now have in your packer-ecs repository:

```
> tree
.
├── Makefile
├── files
│   └── firstrun.sh
├── manifest.json
├── packer.json
```

```
└── scripts
    ├── cleanup.sh
    ├── cloudinit.sh
    ├── storage.sh
    └── time.sh


2 directories, 8 files
```

Verifying the Packer repository

Assuming everything is in place, you can now run your Packer build once again by running the `make build` command.

Once everything is complete and your AMI has been successfully created, you can now view your AMI in the AWS console by navigating to **Services** | **EC2** and selecting AMIs from the menu on the left:

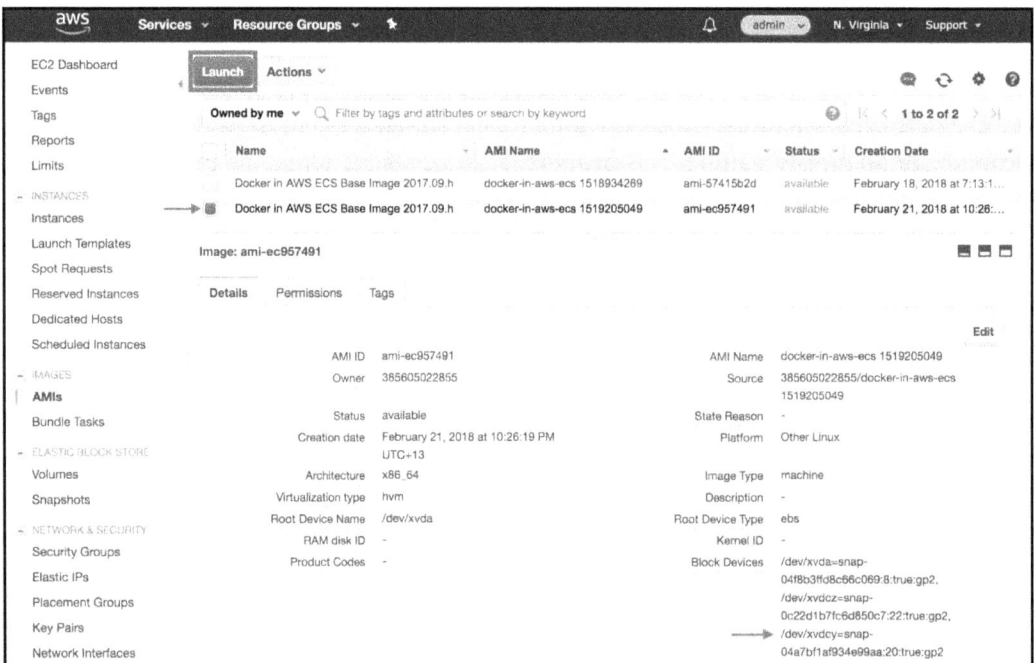

EC2 dashboard AMIs

In the preceding screenshot, you can see the two AMIs you built earlier in this chapter and just now. Notice that the most recent AMI now includes three block devices, with /dev/xvdcy representing the additional 20 GB gp2 volume you added earlier in this chapter.

At this point, you can actually test out your AMI by clicking on the **Launch** button, which will start the EC2 Instance Wizard. After clicking the **Review and Launch** button, click on the **Edit security groups** link to grant your IP address access via SSH to the instance, as shown in the following screenshot:

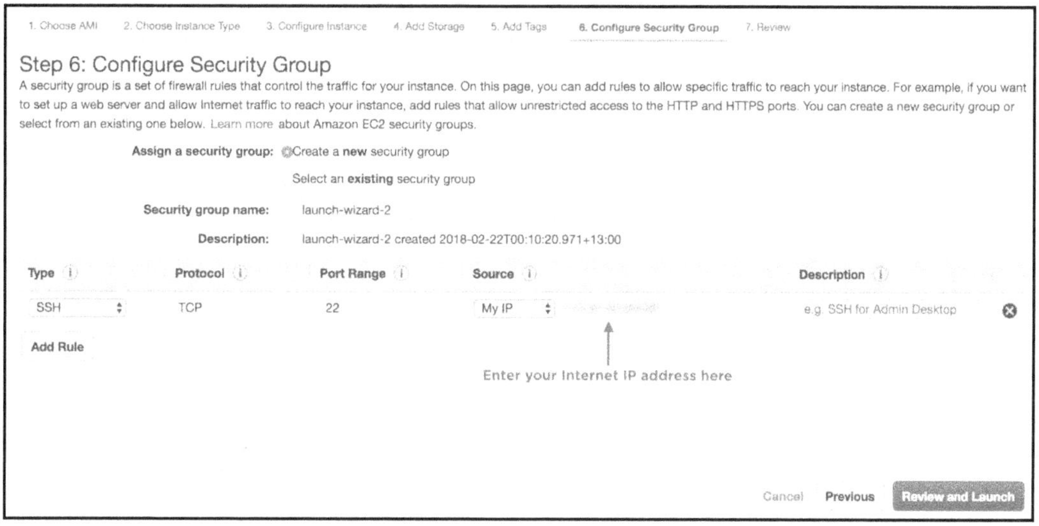

Launching a new EC2 instance

Once complete, click on **Review and Launch**, then click the **Launch** button, and finally configure an appropriate SSH key pair that you have access to.

On the launching instance screen, you can now click the link to your new EC2 instance, and copy the public IP address so that you can SSH to the instance, as shown in the following screenshot:

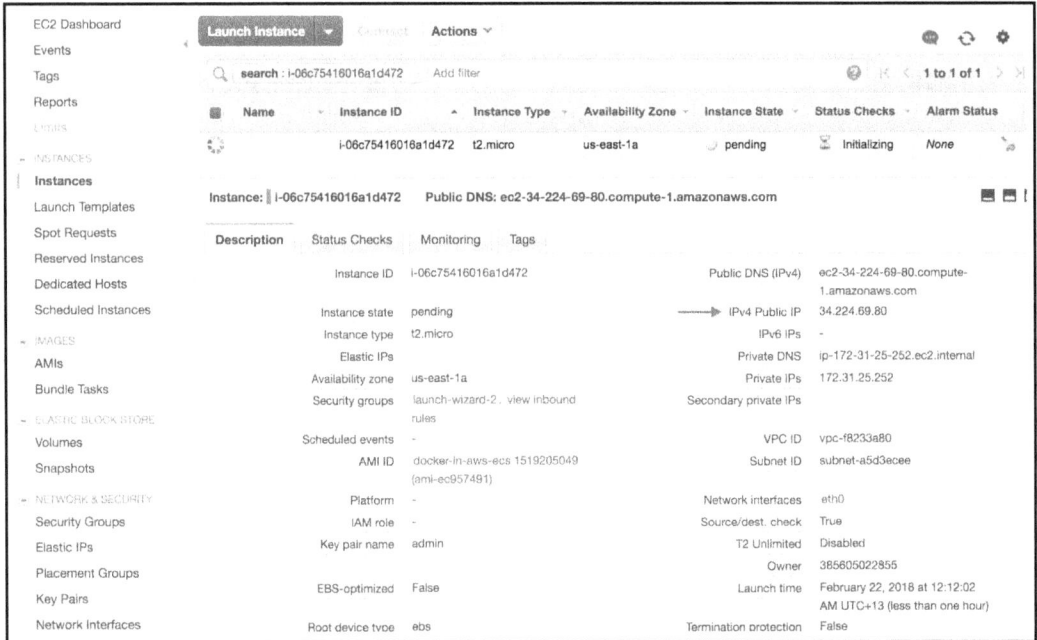

Connecting to a new EC2 instance

Once you have connected to the instance, you can verify that the additional 20 GB volume you configured for Docker volume storage has been successfully mounted:

```
> sudo mount
proc on /proc type proc (rw,relatime)
sysfs on /sys type sysfs (rw,relatime)
/dev/xvda1 on / type ext4 (rw,noatime,data=ordered)
devtmpfs on /dev type devtmpfs
(rw,relatime,size=500292k,nr_inodes=125073,mode=755)
devpts on /dev/pts type devpts
(rw,relatime,gid=5,mode=620,ptmxmode=000)
tmpfs on /dev/shm type tmpfs (rw,relatime)
/dev/xvdcy on /data type ext4 (rw,noatime,data=ordered)
none on /proc/sys/fs/binfmt_misc type binfmt_misc (rw,relatime)
```

Verifying storage mounts

You can check the timezone is configured correctly by running the `date` command, which should display the correct timezone (US/Eastern), and also verify the `ntpd` service is running:

```
> date
Wed Feb 21 06:45:40 EST 2018
> sudo service ntpd status
ntpd is running
```

Verifying time settings

Next, you can verify the cloud-init configuration has been configured to disable security updates, by viewing the `/etc/cloud/cloud.cfg` file:

```
> cat /etc/cloud/cloud.cfg
# WARNING: Modifications to this file may be overridden by files in
# /etc/cloud/cloud.cfg.d

# If this is set, 'root' will not be able to ssh in and they
# will get a message to login instead as the default user (ec2-user)
disable_root: true

# This will cause the set+update hostname module to not operate (if
true)
preserve_hostname: true

datasource_list: [ Ec2, None ]

repo_upgrade: none
repo_upgrade_exclude:
 - kernel
 - nvidia*
 - cudatoolkit

mounts:
 - [ ephemeral0, /media/ephemeral0 ]
 - [ swap, none, swap, sw, "0", "0" ]
# vim:syntax=yaml
repo_update: false
```

Verifying cloud-init settings

You should also verify that the Docker service is stopped and was disabled on boot, as per the cleanup script you configured:

```
> sudo service docker status
docker is stopped
> sudo chkconfig --list docker
docker 0:off 1:off 2:off 3:off 4:off 5:off 6:off
```

Verifying disabled services

Finally, you can verify that the first-run script is present in the `ec2-user` home directory:

```
> pwd
/home/ec2-user
> ls
firstrun.sh
```

Verifying first-run script

At this point, you have successfully verified that your ECS container instance has been built as per your customizations, and you should now terminate the instance from the EC2 console. You will notice that it is in an unconfigured state, your ECS container instance actually can't do much given the Docker service is disabled, and in the next chapter, you will learn how to use CloudFormation to leverage the CloudFormation helper scripts you installed into your custom machine image to configure your ECS container instances at instance creation and leverage the customizations you have created.

Summary

In this chapter, you learned how to build your custom ECS container instance machine image, using the popular open source tool called Packer. You learned how to create a Packer template, and learned about the various sections that make up a template including variables, builders, provisioners, and post-processors. You were able to inject temporary session credentials required to authenticate access to AWS as part of the image build process, using a combination of Packer variables, environment variables, and a dash of Make automation.

You successfully introduced a number of build-time customizations into your ECS container instance image, including installing CloudFormation helper scripts and the CloudWatch logs agent, and ensured the system was configured to run the NTP service on startup with the correct time zone. You disabled automatic security updates in the cloud-init configuration, which can cause problems if you are using an HTTP proxy.

Finally, you created a first-run script designed to configure your ECS container instances at instance creation and first boot. This script configures ECS cluster membership, enables optional HTTP proxy support, configures the CloudWatch logs agent for Docker and ECS agent system logs, and performs a health check to ensure your instance has initialized successfully.

In the next chapter, you will learn how to use your custom AMI to build an ECS cluster and an associated underlying EC2 autoscaling group, which will help you understand the rationale for the various customizations you performed to your custom machine image.

Questions

1. Which section of a Packer template defines the EC2 instance type of the temporary instance used during the Packer build process?
2. True/False: Packer requires SSH access to a temporary instance during the Packer build process.
3. What configuration file format do you use to define a Packer template?
4. True/False: You must hardcode your AWS credentials into your Packer template.
5. True/False: To capture the AMI ID created by Packer, you must parse the log output of the Packer build process.
6. What is the default storage configuration of the ECS-Optimized AMI?
7. What type of Packer provisioner would you use to write a file to the /etc directory?
8. You create an EC2 instance from a custom AMI that takes a long time to boot. The AMI is installed in a private subnet with no additional infrastructure configured in the environment. What is a likely cause of the slow boot time?

Further reading

You can check the following links for more information about the topics covered in this chapter:

- Packer Amazon EBS Builder documentation: `https://www.packer.io/docs/builders/amazon-ebs.html`, `https://docs.aws.amazon.com/AmazonECS/latest/developerguide/Welcome.html`
- Amazon ECS-Optimized AMI: `https://docs.aws.amazon.com/AmazonECS/latest/developerguide/ecs-optimized_AMI.html`
- Getting Started with CloudWatch logs: `https://docs.aws.amazon.com/AmazonCloudWatch/latest/logs/CWL_GettingStarted.html`
- CloudFormation Helper Scripts Reference: `https://docs.aws.amazon.com/AWSCloudFormation/latest/UserGuide/cfn-helper-scripts-reference.html`
- Using the ECS CLI: `https://docs.aws.amazon.com/AmazonECS/latest/developerguide/ECS_CLI.html`

7
Creating ECS Clusters

In the last chapter, you learned how to build a custom ECS container-instance Amazon Machine Image (AMI), which introduced features you will typically want in your production real-world use cases, including custom storage configurations, CloudWatch logs support, and integration with CloudFormation.

In this chapter, you will put your custom machine image to work, building an ECS cluster composed of ECS container instances based on your custom machine image. Rather than take the approach of previous chapters, of discussing each of the various methods of configuring AWS resources, in this chapter, we will focus on using an infrastructure-as-code approach, and define your ECS cluster and supporting resources using CloudFormation.

The standard model for deploying ECS clusters is based upon EC2 Auto Scaling groups, which consist of a group of EC2 instances that can automatically scale up or down based upon a variety of factors. In the use case of an ECS cluster, the EC2 Auto Scaling group is a collection of ECS container instances that collectively form an ECS cluster to which you can deploy your ECS services and ECS tasks. You will learn how to define EC2 auto-scaling groups, define launch configurations that control how your EC2 instances are deployed, and configure CloudFormation Init metadata, which allows you to trigger custom initialization logic at instance creation and wait for each of your instances to signal they have initialized successfully. Finally, you will configure supporting resources, such as IAM instance profiles and EC2 security groups, proceed to create your CloudFormation stack, and deploy your ECS cluster and underlying EC2 Auto Scaling group.

The following topics will be covered:

- Deployment overview
- Defining an ECS cluster
- Configuring EC2 Auto Scaling groups
- Defining EC2 Auto Scaling launch configurations
- Configuring CloudFormation Init Metadata
- Configuring Auto Scaling group creation policies
- Configuring EC2 Instance Profiles
- Configuring EC2 Security Groups
- Deploying and testing an ECS cluster

Technical requirements

The following lists the technical requirements to complete this chapter:

- Administrator access to an AWS account
- Local AWS profile configured as per instructions in Chapter 3
- AWS CLI

This GitHub URL contains the code samples used in this chapter: `https://github.com/docker-in-aws/docker-in-aws/tree/master/ch7`.

Check out the following video to see the Code in Action:
`http://bit.ly/2PaK6AM`

Deployment overview

The goal of the next two chapters is to establish the supporting infrastructure and resources to deploy Docker applications using AWS. In the spirit of the best practice of defining your infrastructure as code, you will be defining a CloudFormation template that will include all AWS resources required to support your Docker applications running in ECS. As you progress through each chapter, you will build on this template, slowly but surely adding more and more resources until you have a complete solution for deploying your Docker applications in AWS using ECS.

With this in mind, the focus of this chapter is to learn how to build ECS clusters using CloudFormation, and as you have already learned in previous chapters, an ECS cluster is a collection of ECS container instances that you can target when you run an ECS service or ECS task.

ECS clusters themselves are very simple constructs - they simply define a collection of ECS container instances and a cluster name. How these clusters are formed, however, is much more involved and requires several supporting resources, including the following:

- **EC2 Auto Scaling group**: Defines a collection of EC2 instances with identical configurations.
- **EC2 Auto Scaling Launch Configuration**: Defines the launch configuration of newly created instances in the Auto Scaling group. A launch configuration often includes user data scripts, which are executed by instances on first run and can be used to trigger the CloudFormation helper scripts you installed in your custom machine image in the previous chapter to interact with CloudFormation Init Metadata.
- **CloudFormation Init Metadata**: Defines initialization logic that each EC2 instance in the Auto Scaling group should run on initial creation, such as running provisioning commands, enabling services, and creating users and groups. CloudFormation Init Metadata is more powerful that the provisioning capabilities offered by user data, and most importantly, provides a mechanism for each instance to signal to CloudFormation that the instance has successfully provisioned itself.
- **CloudFormation Creation Policy**: Defines criteria that determines when CloudFormation can consider an EC2 Auto Scaling group as having been created successfully and to continue provisioning other dependencies in the CloudFormation stack. This is based upon CloudFormation receiving a configurable number of success messages from each EC2 instance that is part of the EC2 Auto Scaling group.

> There are other ways you can form ECS clusters, but for large-scale production environments, you generally want to use EC2 Auto Scaling groups and use CloudFormation and associated CloudFormation Init Metadata and Creation Policies to deploy your clusters in a robust, repeatable, infrastructure-as-code manner.

How each of these components work together is perhaps best described with a diagram, followed by a short description of how ECS clusters are formed from these components, after which you will proceed to learn how to perform each of the related configuration tasks required to create your own ECS clusters.

The following diagram illustrates the deployment process for creating an ECS cluster, assuming you are using EC2 Auto Scaling groups and CloudFormation:

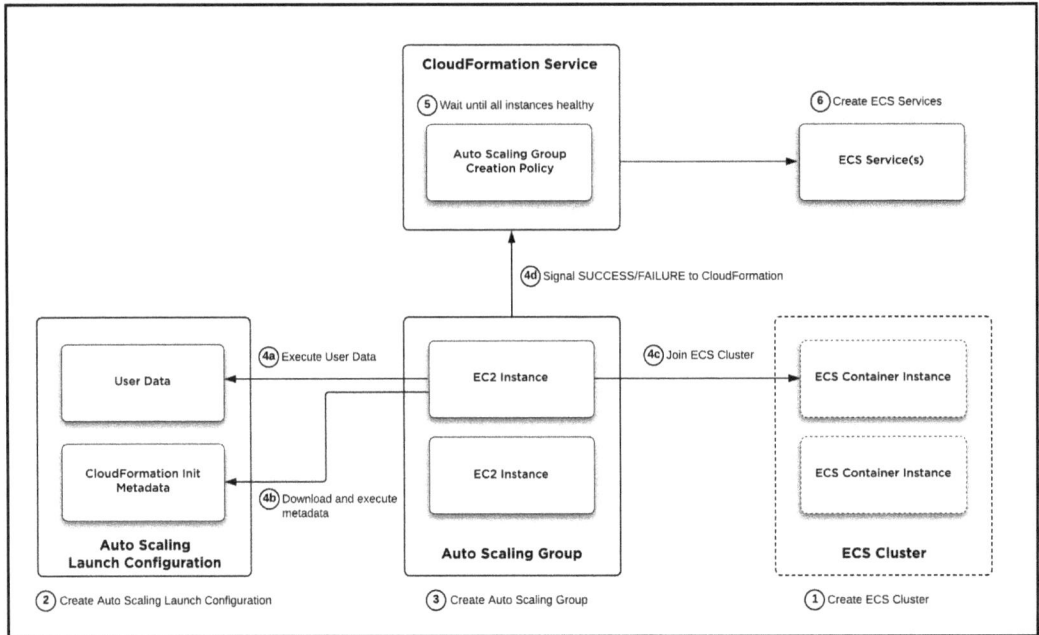

ECS cluster deployment overview using EC2 Auto Scaling Groups and CloudFormation

In the preceding diagram, the general approach is as follows:

1. As part of your CloudFormation deployment, CloudFormation determines it is ready to start creating the configured ECS cluster resource. The ECS cluster resource will be referenced in CloudFormation Init Metadata that is part of the EC2 Auto Scaling Launch Configuration resource, hence this ECS cluster resource must be created first. Note that at this point, the ECS cluster is empty and is awaiting ECS container instances to join the cluster.

2. CloudFormation creates an EC2 Auto Scaling Launch Configuration resource, which defines the launch configuration that each EC2 instance in the EC2 Auto Scaling group will apply on instance creation. The launch configuration includes a user data script that invokes CloudFormation helper scripts installed on the EC2 instance, which in turn downloads CloudFormation Init Metadata that defines a series of commands and other initialization actions each instance should perform on creation.

3. Once the launch configuration resource has been created, CloudFormation creates the EC2 Auto Scaling group resource. The creation of the Auto Scaling group will trigger the EC2 Auto Scaling service to create a configurable desired number of EC2 instances in the group.

4. As each EC2 instance launches, it applies the launch configuration, executes the user data script, and downloads and executes the provisioning tasks defined in CloudFormation Init Metadata. This will include various initialization tasks, and in our specific use case, the instance will execute the first run script you added to your custom machine image in the previous chapter, to join the configured ECS cluster, ensure the CloudWatch logs agent is configured to log to the correct CloudWatch log groups, start and enable Docker and the ECS agent, and finally, verify the EC2 instance successfully joined the ECS cluster and signal to CloudFormation that the EC2 instance was launched successfully.

5. The Auto Scaling group is configured with a Creation Policy, which is a special feature of CloudFormation that causes CloudFormation to wait until a configurable number of success signals is received from EC2 instances in the Auto Scaling group. Typically, you will configure this to be all instances in your EC2 autoscaling group, ensuring all instances have successfully joined the ECS cluster and are healthy before continuing other provisioning tasks.

6. With the ECS cluster in place with the correct number of ECS container instances derived from the EC2 Auto Scaling group, CloudFormation can safely provision other ECS resources that require a healthy ECS cluster to be in place. For example, you might create an ECS service, which will deploy your container applications to your ECS cluster.

Defining an ECS cluster

Now that you have an overview of the ECS cluster provisioning process, let's step through the configuration required to get an ECS cluster up and running.

As indicated in the deployment overview, you will be using CloudFormation to create your resources in an infrastructure-as-code manner, and because you are right at the start of this journey, you first need to create this CloudFormation template, which I will assume you are defining in a file called `stack.yml` at the root of the **todobackend-aws** repository you created earlier in Chapter 5 - *Publishing Docker Images Using ECR*, as demonstrated in the following example:

```
> touch stack.yml
> tree .
.
├── ecr.yml
└── stack.yml

0 directories, 2 files
```

Establishing the todobackend-aws repository

You can now establish a skeleton CloudFormation template in the `stack.yml` file and create your ECS cluster resource:

```
AWSTemplateFormatVersion: "2010-09-09"

Description: Todobackend Application

Resources:
  ApplicationCluster:
    Type: AWS::ECS::Cluster
    Properties:
      ClusterName: todobackend-cluster
```

Defining a CloudFormation template

As you can see in the preceding example, defining an ECS cluster is very simple, with the `AWS::ECS::Cluster` resource type only having a single optional property called `ClusterName`. After ensuring your environment is configured with the correct AWS profile, you can now create and deploy the stack using the `aws cloudformation deploy` command, and verify your cluster has been created by using the `aws ecs list-clusters` command, as demonstrated in the following example:

```
> export AWS_PROFILE=docker-in-aws
> aws cloudformation deploy --template-file stack.yml --stack-name todobackend
Enter MFA code for arn:aws:iam::385605022855:mfa/justin.menga:

Waiting for changeset to be created..
Waiting for stack create/update to complete
```

```
Successfully created/updated stack - todobackend
> aws ecs list-clusters
{
    "clusterArns": [
        "arn:aws:ecs:us-east-1:385605022855:cluster/todobackend-
cluster"
    ]
}
```

Creating an ECS cluster using CloudFormation

Configuring an EC2 Auto Scaling group

You have established an ECS cluster, but without ECS container instances to provide a container runtime and compute resources, the cluster is not of much use. At this point, you could create individual ECS container instances and join them to the cluster, however, such an approach is not feasible if you have the requirement to run production workloads that need to support tens or hundreds of containers, dynamically adding and removing ECS container instances to the cluster depending on the current resource requirements of the cluster.

The AWS mechanism to deliver such behavior for your ECS container instances is the EC2 Auto Scaling group, which operates as a collection of EC2 instances that share identical configurations referred to as launch configurations. The EC2 Auto Scaling service is a managed service provided by AWS, and takes care of managing the lifecycle your EC2 Auto Scaling groups and the EC2 instances that make up the group. This mechanism provides one of the core tenets of the cloud - elasticity - and allows you to dynamically scale up or scale down the number of EC2 instances that are servicing your applications.

In the context of ECS, you can generally think of an ECS cluster as having a close correlation to EC2 Auto Scaling groups, and ECS container instances as the EC2 instances within the EC2 Auto Scaling groups where the ECS agent and Docker Engine are the applications running on each EC2 instance. This is not strictly true, in that you can have ECS clusters that span multiple EC2 Auto Scaling groups, but it is typical to structure a one-to-one relationship between your ECS clusters and EC2 Auto Scaling groups, with a corresponding direct linkage of ECS container instances to EC2 instances.

Now that you understand the basic background of EC2 Auto Scaling groups and how are they related specifically to ECS, it's important to outline the various configuration constructs that you need to interact with when creating EC2 Auto Scaling groups:

- **Auto Scaling group**: Defines a collection of EC2 instances and specifies minimum, maximum, and desirable capacities for the group.
- **Launch configuration**: A launch configuration defines a generic configuration that is applied to each EC2 instance at instance creation.
- **CloudFormation Init metadata**: Defines custom initialization logic that can be applied at instance creation.
- **IAM instance profile and role**: Grants permissions to each EC2 instance to interact with the ECS service and publish to CloudWatch logs.
- **EC2 security groups**: Define ingress and egress network policy rules. At a minimum, these rules must allow the ECS agent running on each EC2 instance to communicate with the ECS API.

> Note that I am presenting a top-down approach of defining the requirements for an EC2 Auto Scaling group, which is possible when using a declarative infrastructure-as-code approach, such as CloudFormation. When it comes to the actual implementation of these resources, they will be applied in a bottom-up manner, where dependencies, such as security groups and IAM roles, are first created, after which the launch configuration, and finally the Auto Scaling group will be created. This, of course, is handled by CloudFormation, so we can focus on the desired state configuration and let CloudFormation deal with the specific imperative execution requirements of meeting the desired state.

Creating an EC2 Auto Scaling group

The first resource you need to define when creating EC2 Auto Scaling groups is the EC2 Auto Scaling group itself, which in CloudFormation terms is defined as a resource of the `AWS::AutoScaling::AutoScalingGroup` type:

```
AWSTemplateFormatVersion: "2010-09-09"

Description: Todobackend Application

Parameters:
  ApplicationDesiredCount:
    Type: Number
```

```
      Description: Desired EC2 instance count
    ApplicationSubnets:
      Type: List<AWS::EC2::Subnet::Id>
      Description: Target subnets for EC2 instances

  Resources:
    ApplicationCluster:
      Type: AWS::ECS::Cluster
      Properties:
        ClusterName: todobackend-cluster
    ApplicationAutoscaling:
      Type: AWS::AutoScaling::AutoScalingGroup
      Properties:
        LaunchConfigurationName: !Ref
  ApplicationAutoscalingLaunchConfiguration
        MinSize: 0
        MaxSize: 4
        DesiredCapacity: !Ref ApplicationDesiredCount
        VPCZoneIdentifier: !Ref ApplicationSubnets
        Tags:
          - Key: Name
            Value: !Sub ${AWS::StackName}-ApplicationAutoscaling-
  instance
            PropagateAtLaunch: "true"
```

Defining an EC2 Auto Scaling group

The configuration in the preceding example is a basic configuration that meets the minimum requirements for defining an EC2 Auto Scaling group as follows:

- `LaunchConfigurationName`: The name of the launch configuration that should be applied to each instance in the group. In the preceding example, we use the shorthand syntax of the `Ref` intrinsic function combined with the name of a resource called `ApplicationAutoscalingLaunchConfiguration`, which is a resource we will define shortly.

- `MinSize`, `MaxSize`, and `DesiredCapacity`: The absolute minimum, absolute maximum, and desired number of instances in the Auto Scaling group. The EC2 Auto Scaling group will always try to maintain the desired number of instances, although it may temporarily scale up or scale down the number of instances based upon your own criteria within the bounds of the `MinSize` and `MaxSize` properties. In the preceding example, you reference a parameter, called `ApplicationDesiredCount`, to define the desired number of instances, with the ability to scale down to zero instances or scale up to a maximum of four instances.

- `VPCZoneIdentifier`: A list of the target subnets that EC2 instances within the Auto Scaling group should be deployed to. In the previous example, you reference an input parameter, called `ApplicationSubnets`, which is defined as a parameter of the `List<AWS::EC2::Subnet::Id>` type. This can be supplied as simply a comma-separated list, and you will shortly see an example of defining such a list.

- `Tags`: Defines one or more tags to attach to the Auto Scaling group. At a minimum, it is useful to define the `Name` tag so that you can clearly identify your EC2 instances, and in the preceding example, you use the short form of the `Fn::Sub` intrinsic function to dynamically inject the name of the stack as defined by the `AWS::StackName` pseudo-parameter. The `PropagateAtLaunch` tag configures the tag to be attached to each EC2 instance at launch, ensuring the configured name will be visible for each instance.

> **TIP**
>
> Refer to the AWS CloudFormation documentation (`https://docs.aws.amazon.com/AWSCloudFormation/latest/UserGuide/aws-properties-as-group.html`) for more information on how to configure Auto Scaling group resources.

Configuring CloudFormation Input Parameters

In the preceding example, you added parameters to your CloudFormation template called `ApplicationDesiredCount` and `ApplicationSubnets`, which you will need to supply the values for when you deploy the template.

The `ApplicationDesiredCount` parameter simply needs to be a number between the configure MinSize and MaxSize properties (that is, between 0 and 4), however, to determine the value of the subnet IDs in your account, you can use the `aws ec2 describe-subnets` command, as demonstrated here:

```
> aws ec2 describe-subnets --query
"Subnets[].[SubnetId,AvailabilityZone]" --output table
---------------------------------
| DescribeSubnets               |
+-----------------+-------------+
| subnet-a5d3ecee | us-east-1a  |
| subnet-c2abdded | us-east-1d  |
| subnet-aae11aa5 | us-east-1f  |
| subnet-fd3a43c2 | us-east-1e  |
| subnet-324e246f | us-east-1b  |
| subnet-d281a2b6 | us-east-1c  |
+-----------------+-------------+
```

Querying subnets using the AWS CLI

In the preceding example, you use a JMESPath query expression to select the `SubnetId` and `AvailabilityZone` properties for each subnet, and display the output in a table format. Here we are just leveraging the default subnets that are created in the default VPC for your account, but you could use any subnets that may be defined in your account, depending on the nature of your network topology.

For this example, we will use two subnets in the `us-east-1a` and `us-east-1b` availability zones, and your next question might be, how do we pass these values to the CloudFormation stack? The AWS CLI only currently offers the ability to provide input parameters as key value pairs using a command-line flag in conjunction with the `aws cloudformation deploy` command, however, this approach quickly becomes tedious and unwieldy when you have a large number of stack input and want to persist them.

One very simple approach we will adopt is to define the various input parameters within a configuration file called `dev.cfg` at the root of the `todobackend-aws` repository:

```
ApplicationDesiredCount=1
ApplicationSubnets=subnet-a5d3ecee,subnet-324e246f
```

Defining a configuration file for stack parameters in dev.cfg

The approach with the configuration file is to add each parameter in the `<key>=<value>` format on a new line, and later on in this chapter, you will see how we can use this file in conjunction with the `aws cloudformation deploy` command. In the preceding example, notice that we configure the `ApplicationSubnets` parameter value as a comma-delimited list, which is the standard format for any List types when configuring CloudFormation parameters.

> Stack parameters are typically environment-specific, hence it makes sense to name your configuration files according to your environments. For example, if you had a development and production environment, you might call your configuration files `dev.cfg` and `prod.cfg`, respectively.

Defining an EC2 Auto Scaling launch configuration

Although you have defined an EC2 Auto Scaling group resource, you cannot yet deploy your CloudFormation template as the Auto Scaling group references a resource called `ApplicationAutoscalingLaunchConfiguration`, which is yet to be defined.

An EC2 Auto Scaling launch configuration defines the configuration that is applied to each instance at launch time, and provides a common approach to ensuring each instance in your Auto Scaling group is consistent.

The following example demonstrates configuring an Auto Scaling launch configuration within your CloudFormation template:

```
...
...
Parameters:
  ApplicationDesiredCount:
    Type: Number
    Description: Desired EC2 instance count
  ApplicationImageId:
    Type: String
    Description: ECS Amazon Machine Image (AMI) ID
  ApplicationSubnets:
    Type: List<AWS::EC2::Subnet::Id>
    Description: Target subnets for EC2 instances

Resources:
```

```
ApplicationAutoscalingLaunchConfiguration:
  Type: AWS::AutoScaling::LaunchConfiguration
  Properties:
    ImageId: !Ref ApplicationImageId
    InstanceType: t2.micro
    KeyName: admin
    IamInstanceProfile: !Ref ApplicationAutoscalingInstanceProfile
    SecurityGroups:
      - !Ref ApplicationAutoscalingSecurityGroup
    UserData:
      Fn::Base64:
        Fn::Sub: |
          #!/bin/bash
          /opt/aws/bin/cfn-init -v --stack ${AWS::StackName} \
            --resource ApplicationAutoscalingLaunchConfiguration \
            --region ${AWS::Region}
          /opt/aws/bin/cfn-signal -e $? --stack ${AWS::StackName} \
            --resource ApplicationAutoscaling \
            --region ${AWS::Region}
ApplicationCluster:
  Type: AWS::ECS::Cluster
  Properties:
    ClusterName: todobackend-cluster
ApplicationAutoscaling:
  Type: AWS::AutoScaling::AutoScalingGroup
  Properties:
    LaunchConfigurationName: !Ref
ApplicationAutoscalingLaunchConfiguration
    MinSize: 0
    MaxSize: 4
    DesiredCapacity: !Ref ApplicationDesiredCount
    VPCZoneIdentifier: !Ref ApplicationSubnets
    Tags:
      - Key: Name
        Value: !Sub ${AWS::StackName}-ApplicationAutoscaling-
instance
        PropagateAtLaunch: "true"
```

Defining an EC2 Auto Scaling Launch Configuration

Notice that you specify a `AWS::AutoScaling::LaunchConfiguration` resource type and configure the following properties for your launch configuration:

- `ImageId`: The AMI of the image that the EC2 instance will be launched from. For our use case, you will use the AMI that you created in the previous chapter. This property references a new parameter called `ApplicationImageId`, so you need to add this parameter with the AMI ID of your custom machine image to the `dev.cfg` file.
- `InstanceType`: The instance family and type of the EC2 instance.
- `KeyName`: The EC2 key pair that will be permitted SSH access to each EC2 instance.
- `IamInstanceProfile`: The IAM instance profile to attach to the EC2 instance. As you learned in earlier chapters, in order to support operation as an ECS container instance, the IAM instance profile must grant permissions for the EC2 instance to interact with the ECS service. In the previous example, you reference a resource called `ApplicationAutoscalingInstanceProfile`, which you will create later in this chapter.
- `SecurityGroups`: The EC2 security groups to attach to each instance. These define the ingress and egress security rules that are applied to network traffic, and, at a minimum, must permit communications to the ECS service, CloudWatch logs service, and other associated AWS services. Again, you reference a resource called `ApplicationAutoscalingSecurityGroup`, which you will create later in this chapter.
- `UserData`: Defines the user data script that is run upon instance creation. This must be supplied as a Base64-encoded string, and you can use the `Fn::Base64` intrinsic function to have CloudFormation automatically perform this conversion. You define a bash script that first runs the `cfn-init` command, which will download and execute CloudFormation Init metadata associated with the `ApplicationAutoscalingLaunchConfiguration` reference resource, and then runs the `cfn-signal` command to signal to CloudFormation whether or not `cfn-init` ran successfully (note that `cfn-signal` references the `AutoscalingGroup` resource, rather than the `ApplicationAutoscalingLaunchConfiguration` resource).

Notice the use of the `Fn::Sub` function followed by the pipe operator (`|`), which enables you to enter free-form text that will honour all line breaks and allows you to reference the correct stack name and AWS region using the `AWS::StackName` and `AWS::Region` pseudo-parameters.

> You may notice that the `set -e` flag is not set in the UserData bash script, and this is deliberate as we want the `cfn-signal` script to report the exit code of the `cfn-init` script to CloudFormation (as defined by `-e $?` option, where `$?` outputs the exit code of the last process). If you were to include `set -e`, the script would exit immediately if `cfn-init` returned an error, and `cfn-signal` would not be able to signal CloudFormation of the failure.

```
ApplicationDesiredCount=1
ApplicationImageId=ami-ec957491
ApplicationSubnets=subnet-a5d3ecee,subnet-324e246f
```

Adding the ApplicationImageId parameter to the dev.cfg file

Configuring CloudFormation Init Metadata

The most complex piece of configuration you have performed so far in our stack is the `UserData` property, defined as part of the Auto Scaling launch configuration.

Recall in the previous chapter when you created a custom machine image, you installed the `cfn-bootstrap` CloudFormation helper scripts, which include the `cfn-init` and `cfn-signal` scripts that are referenced in the previous example. These scripts are designed to work with a feature known as CloudFormation Init metadata, which we will configure now, as demonstrated in the following example:

```
...
...
Resources:
  ...
  ...
  ApplicationAutoscalingLaunchConfiguration:
    Type: AWS::AutoScaling::LaunchConfiguration
    Metadata:
      AWS::CloudFormation::Init:
        config:
          commands:
```

```
                    05_public_volume:
                      command: mkdir -p /data/public
                    06_public_volume_permissions:
                      command: chown -R 1000:1000 /data/public
                    10_first_run:
                      command: sh firstrun.sh
                      cwd: /home/ec2-user
                      env:
                        ECS_CLUSTER: !Ref ApplicationCluster
                        STACK_NAME: !Ref AWS::StackName
                        AUTOSCALING_GROUP: ApplicationAutoscaling
                        AWS_DEFAULT_REGION: !Ref AWS::Region
      Properties:
        ImageId: !Ref ApplicationImageId
        InstanceType: t2.micro
        KeyName: admin
        IamInstanceProfile: !Ref ApplicationAutoscalingInstanceProfile
        SecurityGroups:
          - !Ref ApplicationAutoscalingSecurityGroup
        UserData:
          Fn::Base64:
            Fn::Sub: |
              #!/bin/bash
              /opt/aws/bin/cfn-init -v --stack ${AWS::StackName} \
                --resource ApplicationAutoscalingLaunchConfiguration \
                --region ${AWS::Region}
              /opt/aws/bin/cfn-signal -e $? --stack ${AWS::StackName} \
                --resource ApplicationAutoscaling \
                --region ${AWS::Region}
...
...
```

Configuring CloudFormation Init Metadata

In the preceding example, you can see the CloudFormation Init metadata defines a configuration set that includes a `commands` directive, which defines a several command objects:

- `05_public_volume` - creates a folder called `public` under the `/data` mount that is configured in our custom ECS AMI. We require this path as recall our application needs a public volume where static files will be located, and our application runs as a non-root user. Later on we will create a Docker volume that references this path, and note that because ECS currently only supports bind mounts, this approach of pre-creating a folder on the underly Docker host is required (see `https://github.com/aws/amazon-ecs-agent/issues/1123#issuecomment-405063273` for more details).

- `06_public_volume_permissions` - this changes the ownership on the `/data/public` folder created in the previous command to be owned by the user and group with an ID of 1000. This is the same user ID/group ID that the todobackend application runs as, so will allow the application to read and write to the `/data/public` folder.

- `10_first_run` - runs the `sh firstrun.sh` command in the working directory of `/home/ec2-user`, which recall from the previous chapter refer to the first run script you included in your custom machine image to perform custom initialization tasks at instance creation. This first run script includes references to a number of environment variables, which are defined in the CloudFormation Init metadata under the `env` property and supply the appropriate values to the first run script.

To illustrate further how the `10_first_run` script works, the following snippet configures the ECS container instance to join an ECS cluster as defined by the `ECS_CLUSTER` environment variable:

```
#!/usr/bin/env bash
set -e

# Configure ECS Agent
echo "ECS_CLUSTER=${ECS_CLUSTER}" > /etc/ecs/ecs.config
...
...
```

First run script snippet

Similarly, the `STACK_NAME`, `AUTOSCALING_GROUP`, and `AWS_DEFAULT_REGION` variables are all used to configure the CloudWatch logs agent:

```
...
...
# Write AWS Logs region
sudo tee /etc/awslogs/awscli.conf << EOF > /dev/null
[plugins]
cwlogs = cwlogs
[default]
region = ${AWS_DEFAULT_REGION}
EOF

# Write AWS Logs config
sudo tee /etc/awslogs/awslogs.conf << EOF > /dev/null
[general]
state_file = /var/lib/awslogs/agent-state

[/var/log/dmesg]
file = /var/log/dmesg
log_group_name = /${STACK_NAME}/ec2/${AUTOSCALING_GROUP}/var/log/dmesg
log_stream_name = {instance_id}
...
...
```

First run script snippet

Configuring Auto Scaling group creation policies

In the previous section, you configured a user data script and CloudFormation Init metadata so that your ECS container instances can perform first time initialization and configuration appropriate to the given target environment. Although each instance will signal CloudFormation of success or failure of the CloudFormation Init process, you need to configure CloudFormation explicitly to wait for each instance in the Auto Scaling group to signal success, which is important if you want to ensure you don't attempt to try and deploy ECS services to your ECS clusters before they have registered with the ECS cluster or if they fail for some reason.

CloudFormation includes a feature referred to as creation policies, which allow you to specify optional creation success criteria when creating EC2 Auto Scaling groups and EC2 instances. When a creation policy is attached to an EC2 Auto Scaling group, CloudFormation will wait for a configurable number of instances in the Auto Scaling group to signal success before proceeding, which provides us with a powerful capability to ensure your ECS Auto Scaling groups and corresponding ECS clusters are in a healthy state, before proceeding to create other resources in your CloudFormation stack. Recall in the previous chapter that the final step of the first run script in your custom machine image is to query the local ECS agent metadata to verify the instance has joined to the configured ECS cluster, so if the first run script completes successfully and cfn-signal signals success to CloudFormation, we know that the instance has been successfully registered to the ECS cluster.

The following example demonstrates configuring a creation policy on your existing EC2 Auto Scaling group resource:

```
Resources:
  ...
  ...
  ApplicationAutoscaling:
    Type: AWS::AutoScaling::AutoScalingGroup
    CreationPolicy:
      ResourceSignal:
        Count: !Ref ApplicationDesiredCount
        Timeout: PT15M
    Properties:
      LaunchConfigurationName: !Ref
ApplicationAutoscalingLaunchConfiguration
      MinSize: 0
      MaxSize: 4
      DesiredCapacity: !Ref ApplicationDesiredCount
      VPCZoneIdentifier: !Split [",", !Ref ApplicationSubnets]
      Tags:
        - Key: Name
          Value: !Sub ${AWS::StackName}-ApplicationAutoscaling-
instance
          PropagateAtLaunch: "true"
```

Configuring a Creation Policy in CloudFormation

As you can see in the preceding example, creation policies are configured using the `CreationPolicy` attribute, and at the time of writing, these policies can only be configured for EC2 Auto Scaling group resources, EC2 instance resources and another special type of CloudFormation resource call wait conditions.

The `ResourceSignal` object includes a `Count` property that defines the minimum number of success signals required to determine whether the Auto Scaling group has been created successfully, and you reference the `ApplicationDesiredCount` parameter, meaning you expect all instances in the Auto Scaling group to be created successfully. The `Timeout` property defines the maximum amount to time to wait for all success signals - if the configured count is not met within this time frame, then the Auto Scaling group will be considered to not have created successfully and stack deployment will fail and roll back. This property is configured using a special format called **ISO8601 duration format**, and the value of `PT15M` means CloudFormation will wait up to 15 minutes for all success signals.

Configuring EC2 instance profiles

In the EC2 Auto Scaling launch configuration you defined in the previous example, you referenced an IAM instance profile, which we need to create as a separate resource in our stack. EC2 instance profiles allow you to attach an IAM role, which your EC2 instances can use to gain access to AWS resources and services, and in the ECS container instance use case. Recall from Chapter 4, when you created your first ECS cluster, that an IAM instance profile and associated IAM role that granted various ECS permissions was automatically attached to your ECS container instance.

Because we are configuring our ECS cluster and Auto Scaling group from scratch, we need to explicitly define an appropriate IAM instance profile and linked IAM role, as demonstrated in the following example:

```
Resources:
  ...
  ...
  ApplicationAutoscalingInstanceProfile:
    Type: AWS::IAM::InstanceProfile
    Properties:
      Roles:
        - Ref: ApplicationAutoscalingInstanceRole
  ApplicationAutoscalingInstanceRole:
    Type: AWS::IAM::Role
    Properties:
      AssumeRolePolicyDocument:
        Version: "2012-10-17"
        Statement:
          - Effect: Allow
            Principal:
              Service:
                - ec2.amazonaws.com
```

```
            Action:
              - sts:AssumeRole
        Policies:
          - PolicyName: ECSContainerInstancePermissions
            PolicyDocument:
              Version: "2012-10-17"
              Statement:
                - Effect: Allow
                  Action:
                    - ecs:RegisterContainerInstance
                    - ecs:DeregisterContainerInstance
                    - ecs:UpdateContainerInstancesState
                  Resource: !Sub ${ApplicationCluster.Arn}
                - Effect: Allow
                  Action:
                    - ecs:DiscoverPollEndpoint
                    - ecs:Submit*
                    - ecs:Poll
                    - ecs:StartTelemetrySession
                  Resource: "*"
                - Effect: Allow
                  Action:
                    - ecr:BatchCheckLayerAvailability
                    - ecr:BatchGetImage
                    - ecr:GetDownloadUrlForLayer
                    - ecr:GetAuthorizationToken
                  Resource: "*"
                - Effect: Allow
                  Action:
                    - logs:CreateLogGroup
                    - logs:CreateLogStream
                    - logs:PutLogEvents
                    - logs:DescribeLogStreams
                  Resource: !Sub
arn:aws:logs:${AWS::Region}:${AWS::AccountId}:log-
group:/${AWS::StackName}*
...
...
```

Defining an IAM instance profile and IAM role

In the preceding example, rather than attach the
`AmazonEC2ContainerServiceforEC2Role` managed policy, you attach a custom
policy that defines a similar set of permission, noting the following differences:

- The permission to create a cluster is not granted, as you are already
  creating the ECS cluster yourself within the stack.
- The permissions to register, deregister, and update container instance states
  are limited to the ECS cluster defined in your stack. In contrast, the
  `AmazonEC2ContainerServiceforEC2Role` role grants this permission to
  all clusters in your account, so your custom configuration is considered
  more secure.
- The custom policy grants the `logs:CreateLogGroup` permission - this is
  required as the CloudWatch logs agent expects this permission, even if the
  log group has already been created. In the preceding example, we constrain
  this permission to log groups that are prefixed with the current stack name,
  limiting the scope of these permissions.

Configuring EC2 security groups

You have almost completed the required configuration to be able to deploy your ECS
cluster and EC2 Auto Scaling group, however one final resource we need to create is
the `ApplicationAutoscalingSecurityGroup` resource, which you referenced
earlier in the `ApplicationAutoscalingLaunchConfiguration` resource
configuration:

```
Parameters:
  ApplicationDesiredCount:
    Type: Number
    Description: Desired EC2 instance count
  ApplicationImageId:
    Type: String
    Description: ECS Amazon Machine Image (AMI) ID
  ApplicationSubnets:
    Type: List<AWS::EC2::Subnet::Id>
    Description: Target subnets for EC2 instances
  VpcId:
    Type: AWS::EC2::VPC::Id
    Description: Target VPC

Resources:
  ApplicationAutoscalingSecurityGroup:
    Type: AWS::EC2::SecurityGroup
```

```
    Properties:
      GroupDescription: !Sub ${AWS::StackName} Application Autoscaling
Security Group
      VpcId: !Ref VpcId
      SecurityGroupIngress:
        - IpProtocol: tcp
          FromPort: 22
          ToPort: 22
          CidrIp: 0.0.0.0/0
      SecurityGroupEgress:
        - IpProtocol: udp
          FromPort: 53
          ToPort: 53
          CidrIp: 0.0.0.0/0
        - IpProtocol: tcp
          FromPort: 80
          ToPort: 80
          CidrIp: 0.0.0.0/0
        - IpProtocol: tcp
          FromPort: 443
          ToPort: 443
          CidrIp: 0.0.0.0/0
  ...
  ...
```

Defining an EC2 Security Group

In the preceding example, you permit inbound SSH access to your instances, and allow your instances to access DNS, HTTP, and HTTPS resources on the internet. This is not the most secure security group configuration, and in a production use case, at a minimum, you would limit SSH access to internal management addresses, but for the purposes of keeping things simple and accessible for demonstration purposes, you configure a reasonably lax set of security rules.

Notice that you also define a new parameter, called VPC ID, which specifies the ID of the VPC that the security group will be created in, and you can use the `aws ec2 describe-vpcs` command to obtain the ID of the default VPC that is created by default in your AWS account:

```
> aws ec2 describe-vpcs
{
    "Vpcs": [
        {
            "CidrBlock": "172.31.0.0/16",
            "DhcpOptionsId": "dopt-a037f9d8",
            "State": "available",
            "VpcId": "vpc-f8233a80",
```

```
        "InstanceTenancy": "default",
        "CidrBlockAssociationSet": [
            {
                "AssociationId": "vpc-cidr-assoc-32524958",
                "CidrBlock": "172.31.0.0/16",
                "CidrBlockState": {
                    "State": "associated"
                }
            }

        ],
        "IsDefault": true
    }
  ]
}
```

Determining your VPC ID

Once you have the correct VPC ID value, you need to update your `dev.cfg` file to include the `VpcId` parameter and value:

```
ApplicationDesiredCount=1
ApplicationImageId=ami-ec957491
ApplicationSubnets=subnet-a5d3ecee,subnet-324e246f
VpcId=vpc-f8233a80
```

Configuring the VpcId parameter in dev.cfg

> A more scalable approach to looking up the physical identifiers of external resources that your stack has dependencies on is to use a feature referred to as CloudFormation exports, which allow you to export data about a resource to other stacks. For example, you might define all of your networking resources in a stack called network-resources, and then configure a CloudFormation export that exports the VPC ID of VPC resources created by that stack. These exports can then be referenced in other CloudFormation stacks by using the `Fn::ImportValue` intrinsic function. See `https://docs.aws.amazon.com/AWSCloudFormation/latest/UserGuide/using-cfn-stack-exports.html` for more details on this approach.

Deploying and testing an ECS cluster

You have now completed the configuration of your CloudFormation template, and it's time to deploy the changes you made in the previous section. Recall that you created a separate configuration file, called `dev.cfg`, to store values for each stack parameter. The following example demonstrates how you can now use the `aws cloudformation deploy` command to deploy your updated stack and reference your input parameter values:

```
> aws cloudformation deploy --template-file stack.yml \
    --stack-name todobackend --parameter-overrides $(cat dev.cfg) \
    --capabilities CAPABILITY_NAMED_IAM

Waiting for changeset to be created..
Waiting for stack create/update to complete
Successfully created/updated stack - todobackend
```

Deploying a CloudFormation Stack with parameter overrides

In the preceding example, you use the `--parameter-overrides` flag to specify values for each of the parameters your template expects. Rather than type these out manually each time, you simply use a bash substitution and list the contents of the local `dev.cfg` file, which expresses each parameter name and value in the correct format.

Notice also that because your CloudFormation stack now includes IAM resources, you must specify the `--capabilities` flag with a value of either `CAPABILITY_IAM` or `CAPABILITY_NAMED_IAM`. When you do this, you are acknowledging that CloudFormation will be creating IAM resources on your behalf and that you grant permission. Although you only need to specify the `CAPABILITY_NAMED_IAM` value if you are creating named IAM resources (which we are not), I find it is just more universal and less error-prone to always reference this value.

Assuming your template has no configuration errors, your stack should deploy successfully and if you browse to the CloudFormation in the AWS console selecting the todobackend stack, you can review the various events that took place during stack deployment:

Viewing CloudFormation deployment status

In the preceding screenshot, you can see that CloudFormation starts creating an Auto Scaling group at 20:18:56, and then just over a minute and a half later, at 20:20:39, receives a **SUCCESS** signal from the single EC2 instance in the Auto Scaling group. This meets the creation policy criteria of receiving the desired count of instances, and the stack update completes successfully.

At this point, your ECS cluster should have a single ECS container instance registered and active, and you can use the aws ecs describe-cluster command to verify this:

```
> aws ecs describe-clusters --cluster todobackend-cluster
{
    "clusters": [
        {
            "clusterArn": "arn:aws:ecs:us-
east-1:385605022855:cluster/todobackend-cluster",
            "clusterName": "todobackend-cluster",
            "status": "ACTIVE",
            "registeredContainerInstancesCount": 1,
            "runningTasksCount": 0,
            "pendingTasksCount": 0,
            "activeServicesCount": 0,
            "statistics": []
        }
    ],
    "failures": []
}
```

Verifying an ECS cluster

In the previous example, you can see that the ECS cluster had a single registered ECS container instance and the status of the cluster is ACTIVE, meaning your ECS cluster is ready to run your ECS tasks and services.

You can also verify that your EC2 Auto Scaling group was created correctly by navigating to the EC2 console, and selecting Auto Scaling Groups from the left-hand menu:

Verifying EC2 Auto Scaling Groups

In the previous screenshot, notice that the name of your Auto Scaling group includes the stack name (`todobackend`), logical resource name (`ApplicationAutoscaling`), and a random string value (`XFSR1DDVFG9J`). This illustrates an important concept of CloudFormation - if you don't name your resources explicitly (assuming the resource has a `Name` or equivalent property), then CloudFormation will append a random string to ensure resources are named uniquely.

> If you have followed along and configured your stack without any errors, then your CloudFormation stack should deploy successfully, as demonstrated in previous screenshots. Chances are that, with a CloudFormation template with ~150 lines of configuration, there is a possibility you will make an error and your CloudFormation deployment will fail. If you do get stuck and can't resolve a deployment issue, refer to the this GitHub URL as a reference: `https://github.com/docker-in-aws/docker-in-aws/blob/master/ch7/todobackend-aws`

Summary

In this chapter, you learned how to create an ECS cluster, complete with an EC2 Auto Scaling group and ECS container instances based on a custom Amazon machine image, using an infrastructure-as-code approach to define all resources using CloudFormation.

You learned how an ECS cluster is simply a logical grouping of ECS container instances, and is composed of EC2 Auto Scaling groups that manage a collection of EC2 instances. EC2 Auto Scaling groups can dynamically scale up and down, and you attached an EC2 Auto Scaling launch configuration to your Auto Scaling group, which provides a common collection of settings applied to each new EC2 instance that is added to the group.

CloudFormation provides powerful features for ensuring instances in your Auto Scaling groups are initialized correctly, and you learned how you to configure user data to invoke the CloudFormation helper scripts you installed in your custom machine image, which then download configurable initialization logic defined in CloudFormation Init metadata that is attached to your launch configuration resources. Once the CloudFormation Init process is complete, the helper scripts signal success or failure of the initialization process to CloudFormation, and you configured a creation policy for your Auto Scaling group that defined the required number of instances that must report success for the overall Auto Scaling group resource to be considered healthy.

You next attached an IAM instance profile and security group to your launch configuration, ensuring your ECS container instances have necessary permissions to interact with the ECS service, download images from ECR, publish logs to CloudWatch logs, and communicate with the relevant AWS API endpoints.

With the core Auto Scaling group, launch configuration, and other supporting resources in place, you successfully deployed your cluster using CloudFormation, establishing the necessary infrastructure foundations required to run your ECS tasks and services. In the next chapter, you will build on this foundation, extending your CloudFormation template to define ECS task definitions, ECS services, and other supporting resources required to deploy a complete end-to-end application environment.

Questions

1. True/false: An EC2 Auto Scaling group allows you to define a fixed IP address for each instance.
2. What type of encoding needs to be applied to EC2 user data?
3. How can you refer to the current AWS region in your CloudFormation templates?
4. True/false: The `Ref` intrinsic function can only refer to resources in a CloudFormation template.
5. When using CloudFormation Init metadata, which two helper scripts do you need to run on your EC2 instances?
6. You are attempting to create an EC2 Auto Scaling group and ECS cluster using the standard ECS-optimized AMI published by Amazon, however you receive errors indicating no instances are registered to a target ECS cluster even though CloudFormation reports the Auto Scaling group has been created. How might you fix this problem?
7. True/false: The `aws cloudformation create` command is used for deploying and updating CloudFormation stacks.
8. You are attempting to deploy an ECS cluster in a private subnet with no default internet route, however the ECS container instances within the cluster fail to register to ECS. What is the most likely explanation for this?

Further reading

You can check the following links for more information about the topics covered in this chapter:

- CloudFormation EC2 Auto Scaling group Resource Reference: `https://docs.aws.amazon.com/AWSCloudFormation/latest/UserGuide/aws-properties-as-group.html`

- CloudFormation EC2 Auto Scaling Launch Configuration Resource Reference: `https://docs.aws.amazon.com/AWSCloudFormation/latest/UserGuide/aws-properties-as-launchconfig.html`

- CloudFormation IAM Instance Profile Resource Reference: `https://docs.aws.amazon.com/AWSCloudFormation/latest/UserGuide/aws-resource-iam-instanceprofile.html`

- CloudFormation IAM Role Resource Reference: `https://docs.aws.amazon.com/AWSCloudFormation/latest/UserGuide/aws-resource-iam-role.html`

- CloudFormation EC2 Security Group Resource Reference: `https://docs.aws.amazon.com/AWSCloudFormation/latest/UserGuide/aws-properties-ec2-security-group.html`

- Supported Resource-Level Permissions for Amazon ECS API Actions: `https://docs.aws.amazon.com/AmazonECS/latest/developerguide/ecs-supported-iam-actions-resources.html`

- CloudFormation Helper Scripts: `https://docs.aws.amazon.com/AWSCloudFormation/latest/UserGuide/cfn-helper-scripts-reference.html`

- CloudFormation Init Metadata Reference: `https://docs.aws.amazon.com/AWSCloudFormation/latest/UserGuide/aws-resource-init.html`

- CloudFormation Creation Policy Attribute: `https://docs.aws.amazon.com/AWSCloudFormation/latest/UserGuide/aws-attribute-creationpolicy.html`

Deploying Applications Using ECS

8

In the previous chapter, you learned how to configure and deploy ECS clusters in AWS using EC2 Auto Scaling groups, and the goal of this chapter is to deploy ECS applications to your newly built ECS cluster using CloudFormation.

You will first get started learning how to define and deploy the various supporting resources that are typically required for ECS applications in a production-grade environment. These resources include creating an application database to store data for your application, deploying application load balancers to service and load balance requests to your application, and configuring other resources, such as IAM roles and security groups, that control access to and from your application.

With these supporting resources in place, you will proceed to create ECS task definitions that define the run-time configuration of your containers and then configure ECS services that deploy your ECS task definitions to your ECS clusters, and also integrate with your application load balancers to manage features, such as rolling deployments. Finally, you will learn how to create CloudFormation custom resources to perform custom provisioning tasks, such as running database migrations, providing you with a complete application deployment framework based upon AWS CloudFormation.

The following topics will be covered:

- Creating an application database using RDS
- Configuring Application Load Balancers
- Creating ECS task definitions
- Deploying ECS services
- ECS rolling deployments
- Creating a CloudFormation custom resource

Technical requirements

The following lists the technical requirements to complete this chapter:

- Administrator access to an AWS account
- Local AWS profile configured as per instructions in Chapter 3
- AWS CLI
- This chapter continues on from Chapter 7 so requires you have successfully completed all configuration tasks defined there

The following GitHub URL contains the code samples used in this chapter: `https://github.com/docker-in-aws/docker-in-aws/tree/master/ch8`.

Check out the following video to see the Code in Action:
`http://bit.ly/2Mx8wHX`

Creating an application database using RDS

The sample todobackend application includes a MySQL database that is used to persist todo items that are created through the application API. When you first set up and ran the sample application back in Chapter 1, you used a Docker container to provide the application database, however, in production-grade environments, it is generally considered best practice to run databases, and other services that provide persistent storage, on dedicated machines optimized specifically for database and data access operations. One such service in AWS is the relational database services (RDS), which provides dedicated managed instances optimized for providing popular relational database engines, including MySQL, Postgres, SQL Server, and Oracle. RDS is a very mature and robust service, and is very commonly used to support database requirements for both ECS and other applications that are run in AWS.

RDS instances can be configured using CloudFormation. To get started, let's define a new resource in your todobackend CloudFormation template called `ApplicationDatabase`, with an `AWS::RDS::DBInstance` resource type, as demonstrated in the following example:

```
AWSTemplateFormatVersion: "2010-09-09"

Description: Todobackend Application
```

```
Parameters:
  ApplicationDesiredCount:
    Type: Number
    Description: Desired EC2 instance count
  ApplicationImageId:
    Type: String
    Description: ECS Amazon Machine Image (AMI) ID
  ApplicationSubnets:
    Type: List<AWS::EC2::Subnet::Id>
    Description: Target subnets for EC2 instances
  DatabasePassword:
    Type: String
    Description: Database password
    NoEcho: "true"
  VpcId:
    Type: AWS::EC2::VPC::Id
    Description: Target VPC

Resources:
  ApplicationDatabase:
    Type: AWS::RDS::DBInstance
    Properties:
      Engine: MySQL
      EngineVersion: 5.7
      DBInstanceClass: db.t2.micro
      AllocatedStorage: 10
      StorageType: gp2
      MasterUsername: todobackend
      MasterUserPassword: !Ref DatabasePassword
      DBName: todobackend
      VPCSecurityGroups:
        - !Ref ApplicationDatabaseSecurityGroup
      DBSubnetGroupName: !Ref ApplicationDatabaseSubnetGroup
      MultiAZ: "false"
      AvailabilityZone: !Sub ${AWS::Region}a
      Tags:
        - Key: Name
          Value: !Sub ${AWS::StackName}-db
  ApplicationAutoscalingSecurityGroup:
    Type: AWS::EC2::SecurityGroup
...
...
```

Creating RDS resources

The configuration in the preceding example is considered a minimal configuration for defining RDS instances, as described here:

- `Engine` and `EngineVersion`: The database engine, which in this case is MySQL, along with the major or minor version to deploy.
- `DBInstanceClass`: The RDS instance type to run the database on. To ensure you qualify for free-tier access, you hardcode this to `db.t2.micro`, although you would typically parameterize this property to use larger instance sizes for your production environments.
- `AllocatedStorage` and `StorageType`: Defines the amount of storage in GB and the storage type. In the first example, the storage type is set to 10 GB of SSD-based gp2 (general purpose 2) storage.
- `MasterUsername` and `MasterUserPassword`: Specifies the master username and password configured for the RDS instance. The `MasterUserPassword` property references an input parameter called `DatabasePassword`, which includes a property called `NoEcho` that ensures CloudFormation will not print the value of this parameter in any logs.
- `DBName`: Specifies the name of the database.
- `VPCSecurityGroups`: List of security groups to apply to network communications ingress and egress from the RDS instance.
- `DBSubnetGroupName`: References a resource of the `AWS::RDS::DBSubnetGroup` type, which defines the subnets that the RDS instance can be deployed to. Note that even if you only configure a single-availability-zone RDS instance, you still need to reference a least two subnets in the database subnet group resource you create. In the preceding example, you reference a resource called `ApplicationDatabaseSubnetGroup`, which you'll create shortly.
- `MultiAZ`: Defines whether or not to deploy the RDS instance in a highly available multi-availability-zone configuration. For the purposes of the demonstration application, this setting can be configured as `false`, however in a real-world application, you would typically configure this setting as `true`, at least for your production environments.
- `AvailabilityZone`: Defines the availability zone that the RDS instance will be deployed to. This setting is only applicable for single-availability-zone instances (that is, an instance with `MultiAZ` set to false). In the preceding example, you use the `AWS::Region` pseudo-parameter to reference availability zone `a` in your local region.

Configuring supporting RDS resources

Referring back to the preceding example, it is clear that you need to configure at least two additional supporting resources for the RDS instance:

- `ApplicationDatabaseSecurityGroup`: A security group resource that defines the ingress and egress security rules applied to the RDS instance.
- `ApplicationDatabaseSubnetGroup`: A list of subnets that the RDS instance can be deployed to.

In addition to these resources, the following example demonstrates we also need to add a few more:

```
...

Resources:
  ApplicationDatabase:
    Type: AWS::RDS::DBInstance
    Properties:
      Engine: MySQL
      EngineVersion: 5.7
      DBInstanceClass: db.t2.micro
      AllocatedStorage: 10
      StorageType: gp2
      MasterUsername: todobackend
      MasterUserPassword:
        Ref: DatabasePassword
      DBName: todobackend
      VPCSecurityGroups:
        - !Ref ApplicationDatabaseSecurityGroup
      DBSubnetGroupName: !Ref ApplicationDatabaseSubnetGroup
      MultiAZ: "false"
      AvailabilityZone: !Sub ${AWS::Region}a
      Tags:
        - Key: Name
          Value: !Sub ${AWS::StackName}-db
  ApplicationDatabaseSubnetGroup:
    Type: AWS::RDS::DBSubnetGroup
    Properties:
      DBSubnetGroupDescription: Application Database Subnet Group
      SubnetIds: !Ref ApplicationSubnets
      Tags:
        - Key: Name
          Value: !Sub ${AWS::StackName}-db-subnet-group
  ApplicationDatabaseSecurityGroup:
    Type: AWS::EC2::SecurityGroup
    Properties:
```

```
        GroupDescription: !Sub ${AWS::StackName} Application Database
  Security Group
      VpcId: !Ref VpcId
      SecurityGroupEgress:
        - IpProtocol: icmp
          FromPort: -1
          ToPort: -1
          CidrIp: 192.0.2.0/32
      Tags:
        - Key: Name
          Value: !Sub ${AWS::StackName}-db-sg
  ApplicationToApplicationDatabaseIngress:
    Type: AWS::EC2::SecurityGroupIngress
    Properties:
      IpProtocol: tcp
      FromPort: 3306
      ToPort: 3306
      GroupId: !Ref ApplicationDatabaseSecurityGroup
      SourceSecurityGroupId: !Ref ApplicationAutoscalingSecurityGroup
  ApplicationToApplicationDatabaseEgress:
    Type: AWS::EC2::SecurityGroupEgress
    Properties:
      IpProtocol: tcp
      FromPort: 3306
      ToPort: 3306
      GroupId: !Ref ApplicationAutoscalingSecurityGroup
      DestinationSecurityGroupId: !Ref
  ApplicationDatabaseSecurityGroup
  ...
  ...
```

Creating supporting RDS resources

In the preceding example, you first create the database subnet group resource, with the SubnetIds property referencing the same `ApplicationSubnets` list parameter you created in Chapter 7, meaning your database instance will be installed in the same subnets as your application ECS cluster and EC2 Auto Scaling group instances. In a production application, you would typically run your RDS instances on a separate dedicated subnet, ideally with no route to the internet for security purposes, however in the interests of keeping our example simple, we will just leverage the same subnet as the application ECS cluster.

You next create a security group resource called
`ApplicationDatabaseSecurityGroup`, and notice that this only contains a single
egress rule, which somewhat curiously permits ICMP access to the IP
address `192.0.2.0/32`. This IP address is a special address that is part of the "TEST-
NET" IP address range, which is an invalid IP address on the internet and is intended
for use in example code and documentation. The reason for including this as an
egress rule is that, by default, AWS automatically applys an allow any rule on egress
unless you explicitly override these rules, so by adding a single rule that permits
access to an unroutable IP address, you are effectively blocking any outbound
communications from being initiated by the RDS instance.

Finally, notice that you create two security-group-related
resources, `ApplicationToApplicationDatabaseIngress`
and `ApplicationToApplicationDatabaseEgress`, that respectively have resource
types of `AWS::EC2::SecurityGroupIngress`
and `AWS::EC2::SecurityGroupEgress`. These special resources avoid an issue
known as circular dependencies in CloudFormation, where you create a circular
dependency between two resources that need to reference each other for some reason.
In our specific scenario, we want to allow members of the
`ApplicationAutoscalingSecurityGroup` access to members of the
`ApplicationDatabaseSecurityGroup`, with appropriate security rules applied
ingress to the application database, and also applied egress from application
instances. If you try to configure these rules as demonstrated in the following
diagram, CloudFormation will throw an error and detect a circular dependency:

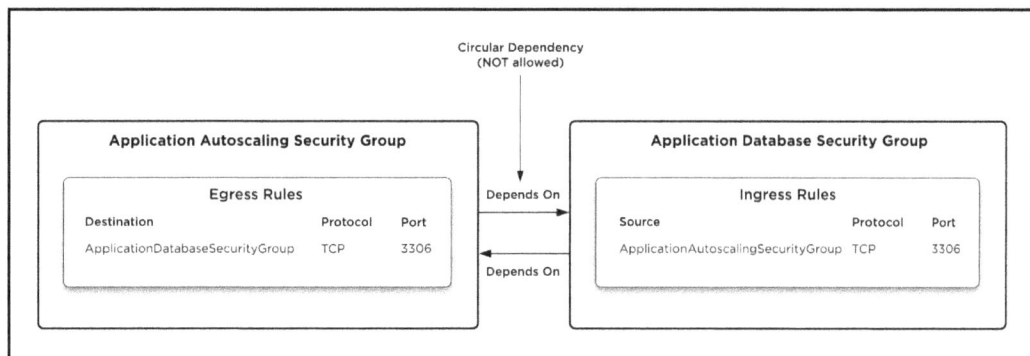

CloudFormation circular dependencies

To address this, the following diagram demonstrates an alternative approach using the resources you created in the previous example.

The `ApplicationToApplicationDatabaseIngress` resource will dynamically create an ingress rule in `ApplicationDatabaseSecurityGroup` (as specified by the `GroupId` property), which permits access to the MySQL port (TCP/3306) from `ApplicationAutoscalingSecurityGroup` (as specified by the `SourceSecurityGroupId` property). Similarly, the `ApplicationToApplicationDatabaseEgress` resource will dynamically create an egress rule in `ApplicationAutoscalingSecurityGroup` (as specified by the `GroupId` property), which permits access to the MySQL port (TCP/3306) associated with instances that belong to `ApplicationDatabaseSecurityGroup` (as specified by the `DestinationSecurityGroupId` property). This ultimately achieves the intention of the configuration illustrated in the preceding diagram, but without causing any circular dependency errors in CloudFormation:

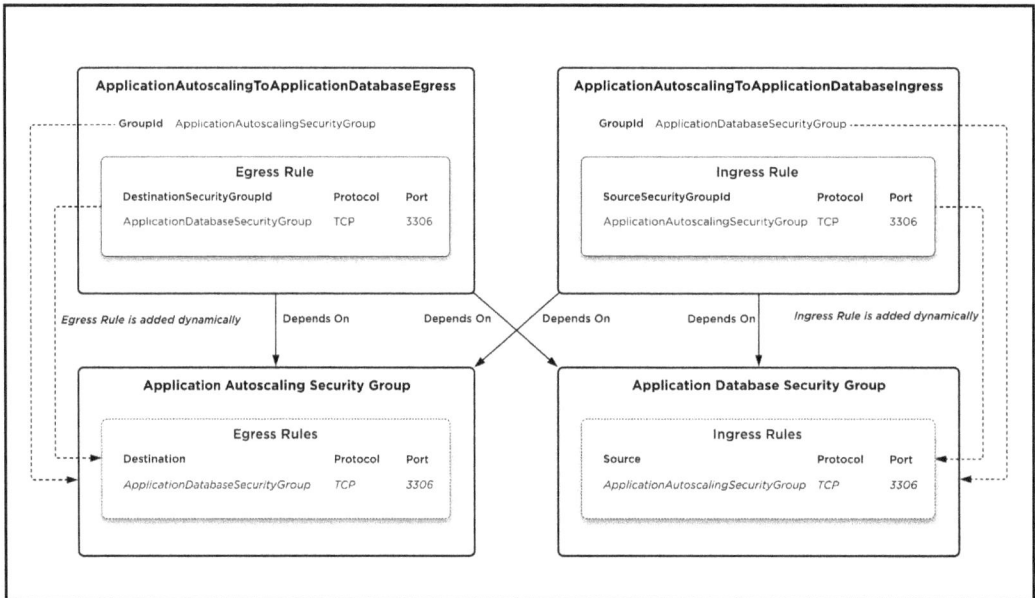

Solving CloudFormation circular dependencies

Deploying RDS resources using CloudFormation

With the configuration of the previous examples in place, you can now actually update your CloudFormation stack, which will add in the RDS instance and other supporting resources. Before you can do this, you need to update the `dev.cfg` file you created in Chapter 7, which provides environment specific values for the input parameters you need to provide to your CloudFormation stack. Specifically, you need to specify a value for the `MasterPassword` parameter, as demonstrated in the following example:

```
ApplicationDesiredCount=1
ApplicationImageId=ami-ec957491
ApplicationSubnets=subnet-a5d3ecee,subnet-324e246f
DatabasePassword=my-super-secret-password
VpcId=vpc-f8233a80
```

Adding a database password to the dev.cfg file

Now at this point, if you are alarmed that you are providing a password in clear text that will eventually be committed to source code, then well done, you are absolutely 100% correct to be very concerned about this approach. In the next chapter, we will deal specifically with managing credentials securely, but for now we won't address this, so bear in mind the approach demonstrated in the preceding example is not considered best practice and we will only leave this in place temporarily to get your application database instance up and running.

With the configuration of the preceding example in place, you can now proceed to deploy your updated stack using the `aws cloudformation deploy` command you previously used in Chapter 7:

```
> export AWS_PROFILE=docker-in-aws
> aws cloudformation deploy --template-file stack.yml \
    --stack-name todobackend --parameter-overrides $(cat dev.cfg) \
    --capabilities CAPABILITY_NAMED_IAM
Enter MFA code for arn:aws:iam::385605022855:mfa/justin.menga:
```

```
Waiting for changeset to be created..
Waiting for stack create/update to complete
Successfully created/updated stack - todobackend
> aws cloudformation describe-stack-resource --stack-name todobackend \
    --logical-resource-id ApplicationDatabase
{
    "StackResourceDetail": {
        "StackName": "todobackend",
        "StackId": "arn:aws:cloudformation:us-east-1:385605022855:stack/todobackend/297933f0-37fe-11e8-82e0-503f23fb55fe",
        "LogicalResourceId": "ApplicationDatabase",
        "PhysicalResourceId": "ta10udhxgd7s4gf",
        "ResourceType": "AWS::RDS::DBInstance",
        "LastUpdatedTimestamp": "2018-04-04T12:12:13.265Z",
        "ResourceStatus": "CREATE_COMPLETE",
        "Metadata": "{}"
    }
}
> aws rds describe-db-instances --db-instance-identifier ta10udhxgd7s4gf
{
    "DBInstances": [
        {
            "DBInstanceIdentifier": "ta10udhxgd7s4gf",
            "DBInstanceClass": "db.t2.micro",
            "Engine": "mysql",
            "DBInstanceStatus": "available",
            "MasterUsername": "todobackend",
            "DBName": "todobackend",
            "Endpoint": {
                "Address": "ta10udhxgd7s4gf.cz8cu8hmqtu1.us-east-1.rds.amazonaws.com",
                "Port": 3306,
                "HostedZoneId": "Z2R2ITUGPM61AM"
            }
...
...
```

Updating a CloudFormation stack with RDS resources

The deployment will take some time (typically 15-20 minutes) to complete, and once the deployment has completed, notice that you can use the `aws cloudformation describe-stack-resource` command to obtain further information about the `ApplicationDatabase` resource, including the `PhysicalResourceId` property, which specifies the RDS instance identifier.

Configuring Application Load Balancers

We have established an ECS cluster and created an application database to store application data, and we next need to create the frontend infrastructure that will service connections from the outside world to our Docker applications.

A popular approach within AWS to provide such infrastructure is to leverage the Elastic Load Balancing service, which provides a number of different options for load balancing connections to your applications:

- **Classic Elastic Load Balancers**: The original AWS load balancer that supports Layer 4 (TCP) load balancing. In general, you should use either the newer Application Load Balancer or the network load balancer, which collectively provide all of the existing functionality of classic load balancers and much more.
- **Application Load Balancers**: An HTTP-aware load balancer that specifically targets web-based applications and APIs.
- **Network Load Balancers**: A high performance Layer 4 (TCP) load-balancing service, typically used for non-HTTP TCP-based applications, or applications that require very high performance.

For our purposes, we will leverage the Application Load Balancer (ALB), which is a modern Layer 7 load balancer that can perform advanced actions based upon HTTP protocol information, such as host-header and path-based routing. For example, an ALB can route requests for a given HTTP host header to a given set of targets, and can also route requests for the some.domain/foo path to one group of targets, and requests for the some.domain/bar path to a different set of targets.

The AWS ALB integrates with the Elastic Container Service, supporting a number of key integration features:

- **Rolling updates**: ECS services can be deployed in a rolling fashion, with ECS leveraging the load balancer connection draining to take old versions of your applications out of service gracefully, terminate and replace each application container with a new version, and then add your new containers to the load balancer, ensuring updates are performed with no end user outages or impact.
- **Dynamic port mapping**: This feature allows you to map your container port to a dynamic port on the ECS container instance, with ECS taking care of ensuring the dynamic port mapping is correctly registered with the Application Load Balancer. The primary benefit of dynamic port mapping is that it allows multiple instances of the same application container to run on a single ECS container instance, providing much greater flexibility around dimensioning and scaling your ECS clusters.
- **Health checks**: ECS using Application Load Balancer health checks to determine the health of your Docker applications, automatically terminating and replacing any containers that may become unhealthy and fail load balancer health checks.

Application Load Balancer architecture

If you are familiar with the older classic Elastic Load Balancers, you will find that the architecture of the newer Application Load Balancers is more complex, given the nature of the advanced Layer 7/HTTP capabilities the ALBs support.

The following diagram shows the various components that comprise an Application Load Balancer:

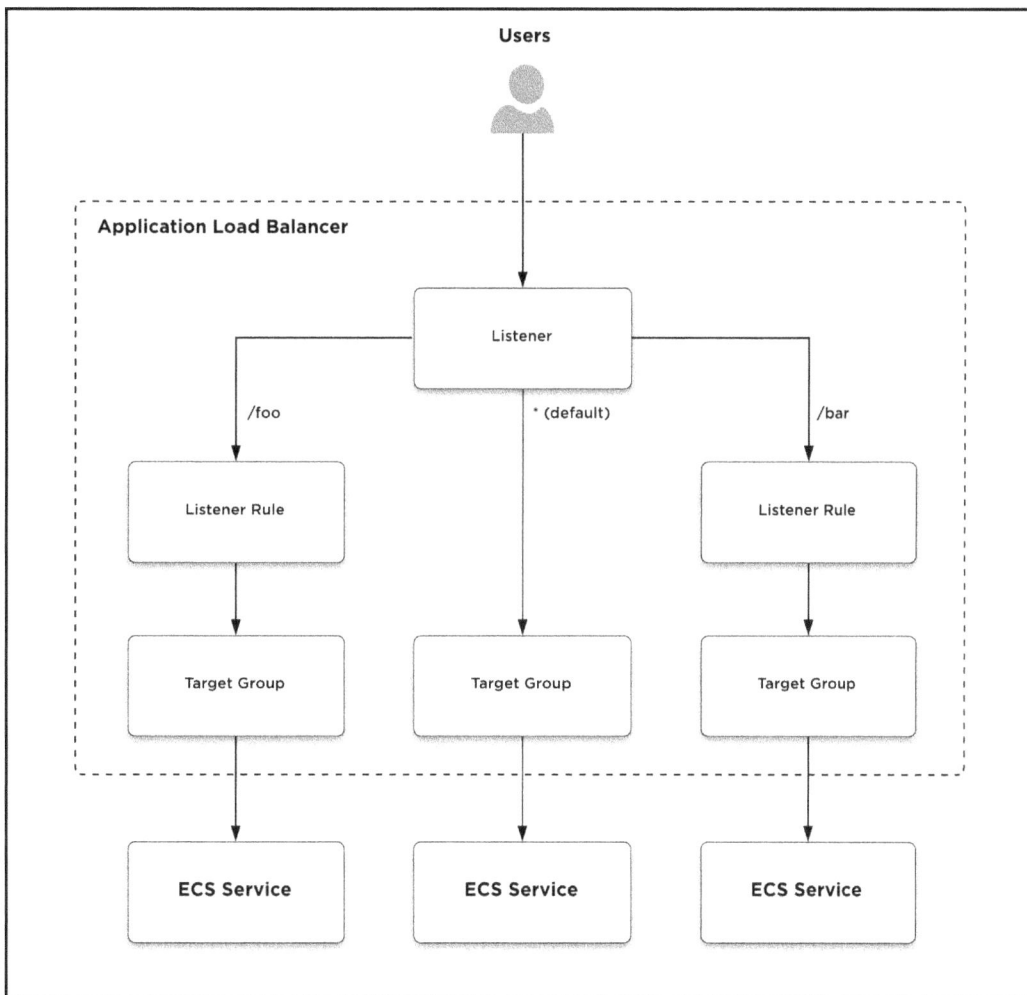

Application Load Balancer components

The following describes each of the components illustrated in the preceding diagram:

- **Application Load Balancer**: The Application Load Balancer is a physical resource that defines physical characteristics of the load balancer, such as the subnets the load balancer should run in and security groups that permit or deny network traffic to or from the load balancer.
- **Listener**: A listener defines a network port that end users and devices attach to. You can think of the listener as the frontend component of the load balancer, servicing incoming connections that ultimately will be routed to target groups that host your applications. Each Application Load Balancer can include multiple listeners—a common example of this might be a listener configuration that services both port 80 and port 443 network traffic.
- **Listener rule**: A listener rule optionally routes HTTP traffic received by a listener to different target groups, based upon the value of the received host header and/or request path. For example, as demonstrated in the preceding diagram, you might route all traffic sent to the /foo/* request path to one target group, whilst all traffic sent to /bar/* might be routed to the another target group. Note that every listener must define a default target group, where all traffic that does not route a listener rule will be routed to.
- **Target group**: A target group defines one or more targets that incoming connections should be routed to. You can think of the target group as the backend component of the load balancer, responsible for load-balancing-received connections to members within the target group. When integrating application load balancers with ECS, the target group is linked to an ECS service, with each instance of the ECS service (that is, container) considered a single target.

Configuring an Application Load Balancer

Now that you understand the basic architecture of application load balancers, let's define the various Application Load Balancer components in your CloudFormation template and proceed to deploy the new resources to your CloudFormation stack.

Creating an Application Load Balancer

The following example demonstrates adding a resource called
`ApplicationLoadBalancer`, which, as the name suggests, configures the base
Application Load Balancer resource:

```
...
...
Resources:
  ApplicationLoadBalancer:
    Type: AWS::ElasticLoadBalancingV2::LoadBalancer
    Properties:
      Scheme: internet-facing
      Subnets: !Ref ApplicationSubnets
      SecurityGroups:
        - !Ref ApplicationLoadBalancerSecurityGroup
      LoadBalancerAttributes:
        - Key: idle_timeout.timeout_seconds
          Value : 30
      Tags:
        - Key: Name
          Value: !Sub ${AWS::StackName}-alb
  ApplicationDatabase:
    Type: AWS::RDS::DBInstance
...
...
```

Creating an Application Load Balancer

In the preceding example, the following properties are configured for the
Application Load Balancer resource:

- `Scheme`: Defines whether the load balancer has public IP addressing (as
  specified by a value of `internet-facing`) or only has private IP
  addressing (as specified by a value of `internal`)
- `Subnets`: Defines the subnets that the Application Load Balancer
  endpoints will be deployed to. In the preceding example, you reference the
  `ApplicationSubnets` input parameter, which you have previously used
  for the EC2 Auto Scaling group and RDS database instance resources.
- `SecurityGroups`: Specifies a list of security groups to apply to the load
  balancer, which restricts ingress and egress network traffic. You reference a
  single security group called `ApplicationLoadBalancerSecurityGroup`,
  which you will create shortly.

- `LoadBalancerAttributes`: Configures various attributes of the Application Load Balancer in a key/value format. You can find a list of supported attributes at `https://docs.aws.amazon.com/elasticloadbalancing/latest/application/application-load-balancers.html#load-balancer-attributes`, and in the preceding example, you configure a single attribute that reduces the idle connection timeout from the default value of `60` seconds to `30` seconds.

A feature of CloudFormation is the ability to define your own *outputs*, which can be used to provide information about resources in your stack. One useful output that you can configure for your stack is the value of the public DNS name of the application load balancer endpoint, as this is where any applications served by the load balancer will be published:

```
...
...
Resources:
  ...
  ...
Outputs:
  PublicURL:
    Description: Public DNS name of Application Load Balancer
    Value: !Sub ${ApplicationLoadBalancer.DNSName}
```

Configuring a CloudFormation Output

In the preceding example, notice that the `ApplicationLoadBalancer` resource outputs a property called `DNSName`, which returns the public DNS name of the `ApplicationLoadBalancer` resource.

Configuring Application Load Balancer security groups

In the preceding example, you referenced a resource called `ApplicationLoadBalancerSecurityGroup`, which defines ingress and egress network access to and from your Application Load Balancer.

In addition to this resource, you also need to create
`AWS::EC2::SecurityGroupIngress`
and `AWS::EC2::SecurityGroupEgress` resources in a similar manner earlier
example, which ensure the Application Load Balancer can communicate with your
ECS service application instances:

```
...
...
Resources:
  ApplicationLoadBalancer:
    Type: AWS::ElasticLoadBalancingV2::LoadBalancer
    Properties:
      Scheme: internet-facing
      Subnets: !Ref ApplicationSubnets
      SecurityGroups:
        - !Ref ApplicationLoadBalancerSecurityGroup
      LoadBalancerAttributes:
        - Key: idle_timeout.timeout_seconds
          Value : 30
      Tags:
        - Key: Name
          Value: !Sub ${AWS::StackName}-alb
  ApplicationLoadBalancerSecurityGroup:
    Type: AWS::EC2::SecurityGroup
    Properties:
      GroupDescription: Application Load Balancer Security Group
      VpcId: !Ref VpcId
      SecurityGroupIngress:
        - IpProtocol: tcp
          FromPort: 80
          ToPort: 80
          CidrIp: 0.0.0.0/0
      Tags:
        - Key: Name
          Value:
            Fn::Sub: ${AWS::StackName}-alb-sg
  ApplicationLoadBalancerToApplicationIngress:
    Type: AWS::EC2::SecurityGroupIngress
    Properties:
      IpProtocol: tcp
      FromPort: 32768
      ToPort: 60999
      GroupId: !Ref ApplicationAutoscalingSecurityGroup
      SourceSecurityGroupId: !Ref ApplicationLoadBalancerSecurityGroup
  ApplicationLoadBalancerToApplicationEgress:
    Type: AWS::EC2::SecurityGroupEgress
    Properties:
```

```
        IpProtocol: tcp
        FromPort: 32768
        ToPort: 60999
        GroupId: !Ref ApplicationLoadBalancerSecurityGroup
        DestinationSecurityGroupId: !Ref
  ApplicationAutoscalingSecurityGroup
    ApplicationDatabase:
      Type: AWS::RDS::DBInstance
  ...
  ...
```

Configuring Application Load Balancer security group resources

In the preceding example, you first create the
`ApplicationLoadBalancerSecurityGroup` resource, permitting ingress access to
port 80 from the Internet. The `ApplicationLoadBalancerToApplicationIngress`
and `ApplicationLoadBalancerToApplicationEgress` resources add security
rules to the `ApplicationLoadBalancerSecurityGroup` and
`ApplicationAutoscalingSecurityGroup` resources without creating
circular dependencies (refer back to the previous diagram and the associated
description), and notice that these rules reference the ephemeral port range of `32768`
to `60999` on the application Auto Scaling group, given we will be configuring
dynamic port mapping for your ECS services.

Creating a listener

Now that you have established the base Application Load Balancer and related
security group resources, you can configure a listener for the Application Load
Balancer. For the purposes of this book, you only need to configure a single listener
that will service HTTP connections, however in any real-world production use case,
you would typically configure an HTTPS listener with associated certificates,
especially for any internet-facing service.

The following example demonstrates configuring a single listener that supports
access to the Application Load Balancer using port `80` (HTTP):

```
  ...
  ...
  Resources:
    ApplicationLoadBalancerHttpListener:
      Type: AWS::ElasticLoadBalancingV2::Listener
      Properties:
        LoadBalancerArn: !Ref ApplicationLoadBalancer
        Protocol: HTTP
```

```
        Port: 80
        DefaultActions:
          - TargetGroupArn: !Ref ApplicationServiceTargetGroup
            Type: forward
  ApplicationLoadBalancer:
    Type: AWS::ElasticLoadBalancingV2::LoadBalancer
    Properties:
      Scheme: internet-facing
      Subnets: !Ref ApplicationSubnets
      SecurityGroups:
        - !Ref ApplicationLoadBalancerSecurityGroup
      LoadBalancerAttributes:
        - Key: idle_timeout.timeout_seconds
          Value : 30
      Tags:
        - Key: Name
          Value: !Sub ${AWS::StackName}-alb
  ...
  ...
```

Creating an Application Load Balancer listener

In the preceding example, the listener is bound to the ApplicationLoadBalancer resource via the LoadBalancerArn property, with the Protocol and Port properties configuring the listener to expect incoming HTTP connections on port 80. Notice that you must define the DefaultActions property, which defines the default target group that incoming connections will be forwarded to.

Creating a target group

The final configuration task related to configuring an Application Load Balancer is to configure a target group, which will be used to forward incoming requests received by the listener resource to your application instances.

The following example demonstrates configuring a target group resource:

```
  ...
  ...
  Resources:
    ApplicationServiceTargetGroup:
      Type: AWS::ElasticLoadBalancingV2::TargetGroup
      Properties:
        Protocol: HTTP
        Port: 8000
        VpcId: !Ref VpcId
```

```
      TargetGroupAttributes:
        - Key: deregistration_delay.timeout_seconds
          Value: 30
  ApplicationLoadBalancerHttpListener:
    Type: AWS::ElasticLoadBalancingV2::Listener
    Properties:
      LoadBalancerArn: !Ref ApplicationLoadBalancer
      Protocol: HTTP
      Port: 80
      DefaultActions:
        - TargetGroupArn: !Ref ApplicationServiceTargetGroup
          Type: forward
  ApplicationLoadBalancer:
    Type: AWS::ElasticLoadBalancingV2::LoadBalancer
...
...
```

Creating a target group

In the preceding example, the following configuration is defined for the target group:

- `Protocol`: Defines the protocol of connections that will be forwarded to the target group.
- `Port`: Specifies the container port your application will run on. By default, the todobackend sample application runs on port `8000`, so you can configure this value for the port. Note that ECS will dynamically reconfigure this port when dynamic port mapping is configured.
- `VpcId`: Configures the VPC ID where your targets are located.
- `TargetGroupAttributes`: Defines the configuration attributes (`https://docs.aws.amazon.com/elasticloadbalancing/latest/application/load-balancer-target-groups.html#target-group-attributes`) for the target group. In the preceding example, the `deregistration_delay.timeout_seconds` attribute configures the time to wait before deregistering a target, which takes place when draining connections during a rolling deployment of your application.

Deploying an Application Load Balancer using CloudFormation

Now that all of your Application Load Balancer components have been defined in your CloudFormation template, you can deploy these components to AWS using the `aws cloudformation deploy` command.

Once your stack deployment is complete, if you open the AWS console and navigate to the EC2 dashboard, under the **Load Balancing** section you should be able to see your new Application Load Balancer resources.

The following screenshot demonstrates viewing the Application Load Balancer resource that was created as part of your deployment:

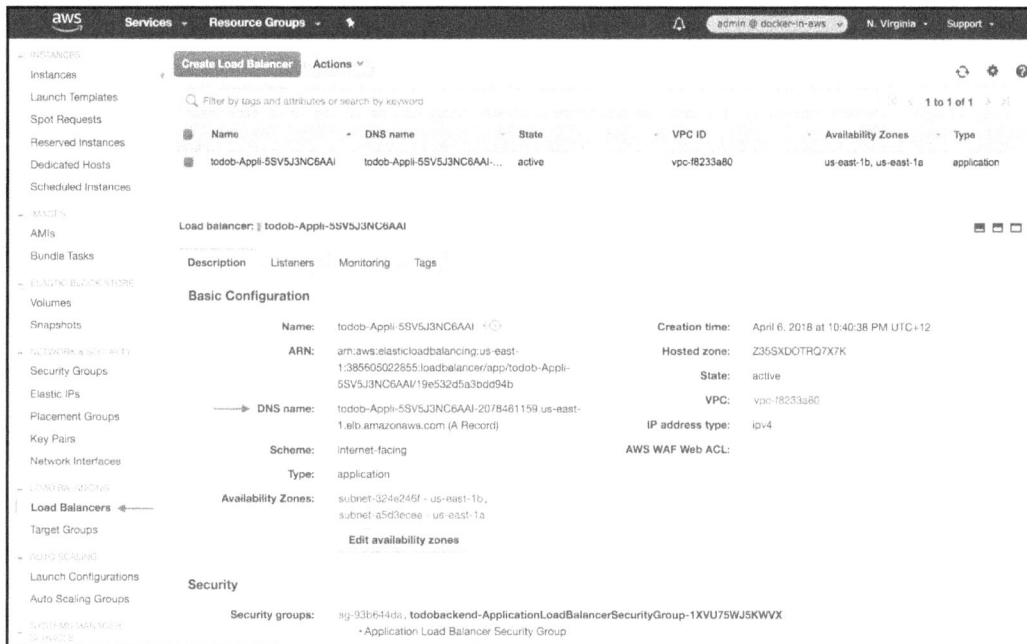

Viewing an Application Load Balancer

In the preceding screenshot, you can see the Application Load Balancer resource has a DNS name, which is the name of the endpoint your end users and devices need to connect to when accessing the applications behind the load balancer. You will use this name later on, once you have fully deployed all resources in your stack, but for now because your target group is empty, this URL will just return a 503 error, as demonstrated in the following example. Note that you can view your listener resources by clicking on the **Listeners** tab in the preceding screenshot, and your associated target group resources can be viewed by clicking the **Target Groups** link on the left-hand menu.

> You will notice that the DNS name of the Application Load Balancer is not a particularly friendly name that your end users will be able to recognize or remember. In a real-world application, you would typically create a CNAME or ALIAS DNS record, which configures a friendly canonical name, such as example.com, that points to your load balancer DNS name. See `https://docs.aws.amazon.com/Route53/latest/DeveloperGuide/routing-to-elb-load-balancer.html` for more details on how to do this, and note that you can and should create CNAME and ALIAS records using CloudFormation (`https://docs.aws.amazon.com/AWSCloudFormation/latest/UserGuide/quickref-route53.html#scenario-recordsetgroup-zoneapex`).

```
> aws cloudformation describe-stacks --stack-name todobackend --query
Stacks[].Outputs[]
[
    {
        "OutputKey": "PublicURL",
        "OutputValue": "todob-Appli-5SV5J3NC6AAI-2078461159.us-
east-1.elb.amazonaws.com",
        "Description": "Public DNS name of Application Load Balancer"
    }
]
> curl todob-Appli-5SV5J3NC6AAI-2078461159.us-east-1.elb.amazonaws.com
<html>
<head><title>503 Service Temporarily Unavailable</title></head>
<body bgcolor="white">
<center><h1>503 Service Temporarily Unavailable</h1></center>
</body>
</html>
```

Testing an Application Load Balancer endpoint

Notice in the preceding example that you can use the AWS CLI to query the outputs of your CloudFormation stack and obtain the public DNS name of your application load balancer. You can also view the outputs of your stack by clicking on the Outputs tab after selecting your stack in the CloudFormation dashboard.

Creating ECS task definitions

You have now reached the point where you have defined an ECS cluster using CloudFormation and created a number of supporting resources, including an RDS instance for your application database and an Application Load Balancer to service connections to your application.

At this stage, you are ready to create the ECS resources that will represent your application, which include ECS task definitions and ECS services.

We will get started by defining an ECS task definition in your CloudFormation template, as demonstrated in the following example:

```
Parameters:
  ...
  ...
  ApplicationImageId:
    Type: String
    Description: ECS Amazon Machine Image (AMI) ID
  ApplicationImageTag:
    Type: String
    Description: Application Docker Image Tag
    Default: latest
  ApplicationSubnets:
    Type: List<AWS::EC2::Subnet::Id>
    Description: Target subnets for EC2 instances
  ...
  ...

Resources:
  ApplicationTaskDefinition:
    Type: AWS::ECS::TaskDefinition
    Properties:
      Family: todobackend
      Volumes:
        - Name: public
          Host:
            SourcePath: /data/public
      ContainerDefinitions:
        - Name: todobackend
```

```
            Image: !Sub
${AWS::AccountId}.dkr.ecr.${AWS::Region}.amazonaws.com/docker-in-
aws/todobackend:${ApplicationImageTag}
            MemoryReservation: 395
            Cpu: 245
            MountPoints:
              - SourceVolume: public
                ContainerPath: /public
            Environment:
              - Name: DJANGO_SETTINGS_MODULE
                Value: todobackend.settings_release
              - Name: MYSQL_HOST
                Value: !Sub ${ApplicationDatabase.Endpoint.Address}
              - Name: MYSQL_USER
                Value: todobackend
              - Name: MYSQL_PASSWORD
                Value: !Ref DatabasePassword
              - Name: MYSQL_DATABASE
                Value: todobackend
              - Name: SECRET_KEY
                Value: some-random-secret-should-be-here
            Command:
              - uwsgi
              - --http=0.0.0.0:8000
              - --module=todobackend.wsgi
              - --master
              - --die-on-term
              - --processes=4
              - --threads=2
              - --check-static=/public
            PortMappings:
              - ContainerPort: 8000
                HostPort: 0
            LogConfiguration:
              LogDriver: awslogs
              Options:
                awslogs-group: !Sub /${AWS::StackName}/ecs/todobackend
                awslogs-region: !Ref AWS::Region
                awslogs-stream-prefix: docker
          - Name: collectstatic
            Essential: false
            Image: !Sub
${AWS::AccountId}.dkr.ecr.${AWS::Region}.amazonaws.com/docker-in-
aws/todobackend:${ApplicationImageTag}
            MemoryReservation: 5
            Cpu: 5
            MountPoints:
              - SourceVolume: public
```

```
                ContainerPath: /public
            Environment:
              - Name: DJANGO_SETTINGS_MODULE
                Value: todobackend.settings_release
            Command:
              - python3
              - manage.py
              - collectstatic
              - --no-input
            LogConfiguration:
              LogDriver: awslogs
              Options:
                awslogs-group: !Sub /${AWS::StackName}/ecs/todobackend
                awslogs-region: !Ref AWS::Region
                awslogs-stream-prefix: docker
  ApplicationLogGroup:
    Type: AWS::Logs::LogGroup
    Properties:
      LogGroupName: !Sub /${AWS::StackName}/ecs/todobackend
      RetentionInDays: 7
  ApplicationServiceTargetGroup:
    Type: AWS::ElasticLoadBalancingV2::TargetGroup
...
...
```

Defining an ECS task definition using CloudFormation

As you can see in the preceding example, configuring a task definition requires a reasonable amount of configuration, and requires a detailed understanding of the runtime configuration of the container application your task definition represents.

Back in Chapter 1, when you created the sample application and ran it locally, you had to perform a similar exercise using Docker Compose. The following example shows the relevant snippet from the Docker Compose file in the todobackend repository:

```
version: '2.3'

volumes:
  public:
    driver: local

services:
  ...
  ...
  app:
    image: 385605022855.dkr.ecr.us-east-1.amazonaws.com/docker-in-
```

```
aws/todobackend:${APP_VERSION}
    extends:
      service: release
    depends_on:
      db:
        condition: service_healthy
    volumes:
      - public:/public
    healthcheck:
      test: curl -fs localhost:8000
    ports:
      - 8000
    command:
      - uwsgi
      - --http=0.0.0.0:8000
      - --module=todobackend.wsgi
      - --master
      - --die-on-term
      - --processes=4
      - --threads=2
      - --check-static=/public
  acceptance:
    extends:
      service: release
    depends_on:
      app:
        condition: service_healthy
    environment:
      APP_URL: http://app:8000
    command:
      - bats
      - acceptance.bats
  migrate:
    extends:
      service: release
    depends_on:
      db:
        condition: service_healthy
    command:
      - python3
      - manage.py
      - migrate
      - --no-input
  ...
  ...
```

Todobackend application Docker Compose configuration

If you compare the configurations of both of the previous examples, you can see that you can use your local Docker Compose configuration to determine the configuration required for your ECS task definition.

Let's now examine each of the various ECS task definition configuration properties in greater detail.

Configuring ECS task definition families

The first property you define in the task definition is the **Family** property, which establishes the ECS task definition family name, and affects the way CloudFormation will create new instances of your task definition resources whenever you make changes to your task definition.

Recall in Chapter 4, that ECS task definitions support the concept of revisions, which you can think of as a specific version or configuration of your ECS task definition, and whenever you need to modify your task definition (for example, to modify the image tag), you can create a new revision of your ECS task definition.

So if your ECS task definition family name is **todobackend**, the first revision of your task definition will be **todobackend:1**, and any subsequent changes to the task definition will result in the creation of a new revision—for example, **todobackend:2**, **todobackend:3**, and so on. Configuring the **Family** property in your ECS task definition resource ensures CloudFormation will adopt this behavior of creating new revisions, whenever your ECS task definition resource is modified.

Note that if you did not configure the **Family** property as per the previous example, CloudFormation would generate a random name for the family with a revision of 1, and any subsequent changes to the task definition would result in a *new* family being created with a random name, again with a revision of 1.

Configuring ECS task definition volumes

Referring back to the `ApplicationTaskDefinition` resource in earlier example, the `Volumes` property defines local Docker volumes that will be created whenever an instance of the ECS task definition is deployed to an ECS container instance. Referring to the local Docker Compose configuration in the previous example, you can see that a volume called **public** is configured, which is then referenced as a mount point in the **app** service definition.

This volume is used to store static web files, which are generated by running the `python3 manage.py collectstatic --no-input` command in the local Makefile workflow, and must be available to the main application container, hence a volume is required to ensure the files generated by running this command are available to the application container:

```
...
...
release:
  docker-compose up --abort-on-container-exit migrate
  docker-compose run app python3 manage.py collectstatic --no-input
  docker-compose up --abort-on-container-exit acceptance
  @ echo App running at http://$$(docker-compose port app 8000 | sed
s/0.0.0.0/localhost/g)
...
...
```

Todobackend Makefile

Notice that in our ECS task definition, we are also required to specify a host source path of `/data/public`, which we created in the previous chapter as part of our ECS cluster auto scaling group CloudFormation init configuration. This folder has the correct permissions on the underlying ECS container instance, which ensures our application will be able to read and write to the public volume.

Configuring ECS task definition containers

The ECS task definition configured earlier includes a `ContainerDefinitions` property, which defines a list of one or more containers associated with the task definition. You can see that there are two containers defined:

- `todobackend` container: This is the main application container definition.
- `collectstatic` container: This container is a short lived container that runs the `python3 manage.py collectstatic` command to generate local static web files. An important configuration parameter associated with this container is the `Essential` property, which defines whether or not ECS should attempt to restart the container if it should fail or exit (in fact, ECS will attempt to restart all containers in the task definition, causing the main application container to be unnecessarily stopped and restarted). Given the `collectstatic` container is only intended to run as a short-lived task, you must set this property to false to ensure ECS does not attempt to restart your ECS task definition containers.

> There are many ways you could tackle the requirement to run the collect static process to generate static web files. For example, you could define a startup script that first runs collect static and then starts the application container, or you may wish to publish your static files to an S3 bucket, meaning you would run the collect static process quite differently.

Aside from the Essential property, the configuration properties of the `todobackend` and `collectstatic` container definitions are very similar, so we will just discuss the properties of the main `todobackend` container definition here and discuss any differences to the `collectstatic` container definition where appropriate:

- `Image`: This property defines the URI of the Docker image the container is based from. Notice that we publish the URI of the ECR repository you created in Chapter 5, for the todobackend application, and reference a stack parameter called `ApplicationImageTag`, which allows you to provide an appropriate version of your Docker Image when deploying the stack.

- `Cpu` and `MemoryReservation`: These properties allocate CPU and memory resources to your containers. We will discuss these resources in more detail in the coming chapters, but for now understand that these values reserve the configured amount of CPU shares and memory, yet allow your containers to use more CPU and memory (that is,"burst") if it is available. Notice that you allocate a minimal amount of CPU and memory to the `collectstatic` container, given it only needs to run for a short period of time and in all likelihood the ECS container instance will have spare CPU and memory capacity available to service the actual resource requirements of the container. This avoids reserving large amounts of CPU and memory for a container that only is active a fraction of the time.

- `MountPoints`: Defines the Docker volumes that will be mounted to the container. Each container has a single mount point that mounts the **public** volume to the `/public` container path for hosting static web files.

- `Environment`: Defines the environment variables that will be available to the container. Referring to the local Docker Compose configuration in the preceding example, you can see that the release service, which is a base service definition that the app service inherits from, indicates the container requires the `DJANGO_SETTINGS_MODULE` variable to be set to `todobackend.settings_release`, and requires a number of database-related environment variables to be defined that define connectivity to the application database. One other environment variable that is required is the `SECRET_KEY` variable, which is used for various cryptographic functions in the Django framework that powers the todobackend application, and should be configured with a secret, random value. As you can see, for now we have set a somewhat non-random plaintext value, in the next chapter, you will learn how you can inject this value as an encrypted secret

- `Command`: Defines the command that should be executed when starting the container. You can see the `todobackend` container definition uses the same `uwsgi` command that the local Docker Compose workflow uses to start the `uwsgi` application server, whilst the collectstatic container uses the `python3 manage.py collectstatic` command to generate static web files to be served from the main application.

- `PortMappings`: Specifies port mappings that should be exposed from the container. The todobackend container definition has a single port mapping, which specifies the default application port of `8000` for the container port, and specifies a host port value of `0`, meaning dynamic port mapping will be used (note that you can also omit the HostPort parameter when using dynamic port mapping).

- `LogConfiguration`: Configures the logging configuration for the container. In the previous example, you configure CloudWatch logs as the log driver by using the awslogs driver, and then configure options specific to this driver. The awslogs-group option specifies the log group that logs will be output to, and this references the name of a log group that is defined in the `ApplicationLogGroup` resource, just below the `ApplicationTaskDefinition` resource. The awslogs-stream-prefix is quite important, as it modifies the default log stream naming convention of container ID to the `<prefix-name>/<container-name>/<ecs-task-id>` format, with the key piece of information here being the ECS task ID, which is the primary task identifier you work with when using ECS rather than container IDs.

In Chapter 7, you granted your ECS container instances the ability to publish to any log group prefixed with the name of your CloudFormation stack. As long as your ECS task definitions and associated log groups follow this naming convention, the Docker Engine will be able to publish logs for your ECS tasks and containers to CloudWatch logs.

Deploying ECS task definitions using CloudFormation

Now that you have defined your ECS task definition, you can deploy it using the now-familiar `aws cloudformation deploy` command. Once your stack has been updated, a new task definition with a family name to todobackend should be created, which you can view using the AWS CLI, as demonstrated in the following example:

```
> aws ecs describe-task-definition --task-definition todobackend
{
    "taskDefinition": {
        "taskDefinitionArn": "arn:aws:ecs:us-east-1:385605022855:task-definition/todobackend:1",
        "family": "todobackend",
        "revision": 1,
        "volumes": [
            {
                "name": "public",
                "host": {
                    "sourcePath": "/data/public"
                }
            }
        ],
        "containerDefinitions": [
            {
                "name": "todobackend",
                "image": "385605022855.dkr.ecr.us-east-1.amazonaws.com/docker-in-aws/todobackend:latest",
                "cpu": 245,
                "memoryReservation": 395,
...
...
```

Verifying the todobackend task definition

Deploying ECS services

With your ECS cluster, ECS task definition, and various supporting resources in place, you can now define an ECS service that will deploy your container application as defined in the ECS task definition to your ECS cluster.

The following example demonstrates adding an ECS service resource to your CloudFormation template, which has a resource type of AWS::ECS::Service:

```
...
...
Resources:
  ApplicationService:
    Type: AWS::ECS::Service
    DependsOn:
      - ApplicationAutoscaling
      - ApplicationLogGroup
      - ApplicationLoadBalancerHttpListener
    Properties:
      TaskDefinition: !Ref ApplicationTaskDefinition
      Cluster: !Ref ApplicationCluster
      DesiredCount: !Ref ApplicationDesiredCount
      LoadBalancers:
        - ContainerName: todobackend
          ContainerPort: 8000
          TargetGroupArn: !Ref ApplicationServiceTargetGroup
      Role: !Sub arn:aws:iam::${AWS::AccountId}:role/aws-service-
role/ecs.amazonaws.com/AWSServiceRoleForECS

      DeploymentConfiguration:
  MaximumPercent: 200
  MinimumHealthyPercent: 100
    ApplicationTaskDefinition:
      Type: AWS::ECS::TaskDefinition
...
...
```

Creating an ECS service

One interesting aspect of the configuration in the preceding example is the `DependsOn` parameter, which defines other resources in the stack that must be created or updated before the ECS service resource can be created or updated. Although CloudFormation automatically creates dependencies when a resource directly references another resource, a resource may have dependencies on other resources that don't have a direct relationship to that resource. The ECS service resource is a good example of this—the service can't operate without a functional ECS cluster and associated ECS container instances (this is represented by the `ApplicationAutoscaling` resource) and can't write logs without the `ApplicationLogGroup` resource. A more subtle dependency is the `ApplicationLoadBalancerHttpListener` resource, which must be functional before the target group associated with the ECS service will register targets.

The various properties that are configured for the ECS service are described here:

- `TaskDefinition`, `DesiredCount`, and `Cluster`: Defines the ECS task definition, number of ECS tasks, and the target ECS cluster that the service will deploy to.
- `LoadBalancers`: Configures a load balancer resource that the ECS service should be integrated with. You must specify the container name, container port, and target group ARN that the ECS service will be registered with. Notice that you reference the `ApplicationServiceTargetGroup` resource you created earlier in this chapter.
- `Role`: This property is only required if you are integrating your ECS service with a load balancer and specifies an IAM role that grants permissions for the ECS service to manage the configured load balancer. In the preceding example, you reference the ARN of a special IAM role known as a service role (`https://docs.aws.amazon.com/IAM/latest/UserGuide/using-service-linked-roles.html`), which is automatically created by AWS whenever you create ECS resources. The `AWSServiceRoleForECS` service role grants a number of permissions typically required for ECS, including managing and integrating with application load balancers.

- `DeploymentConfiguration`: Configures settings related to rolling deployments of new versions of your ECS task definitions. During a deployment, ECS will stop existing containers and deploy new containers based on the new version of your ECS task definition, and the `MinimumHealthyPercent` setting defines minimum allowable percentage of containers in relation to the `DesiredCount` property that must be in service during a deployment. Similarly, the `MaximumPercent` setting defines the maximum allowable percentage of containers that can be deployed in relation to the `DesiredCount` property during a deployment.

Deploying an ECS service using CloudFormation

With your ECS service configuration in place, it's time to deploy the changes to your stack using the `aws cloudformation deploy` command. Once deployment is complete, you ECS service should register with the target group you created earlier in this chapter, and if you browse to the URL of your Application Load Balancer, you should see that the root URL of the sample application is loading correctly:

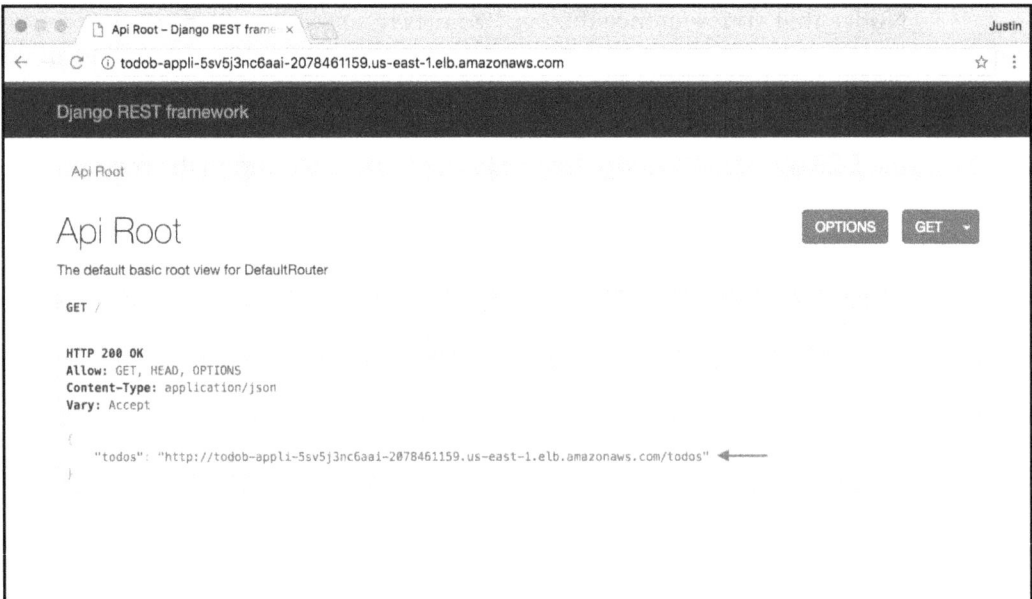

Testing the todobackend application

If, however, you click on the **todos** link shown in the preceding screenshot, you will receive an error, as demonstrated in the following screenshot:

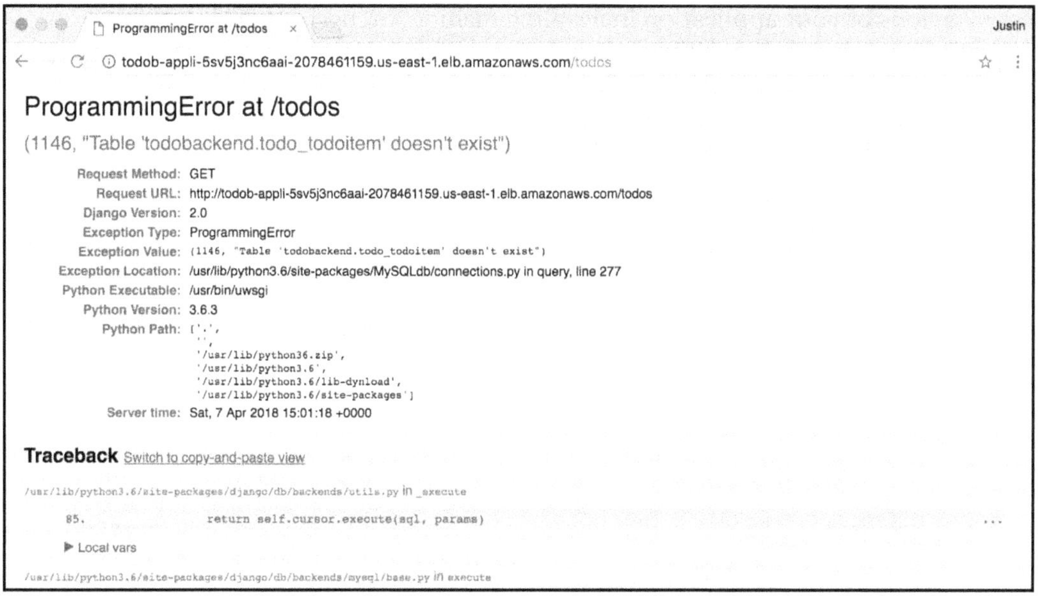

todobackend application error

The problem in the preceding screenshot is that the database tables expected in the application database have not been created, as we have not yet run database migrations against the application database. We will learn how to address this issue shortly, but before we do this, we have one more topic to discuss related to deploying ECS services: rolling deployments.

ECS rolling deployments

A key feature of ECS is rolling deployments, where ECS will automatically deploy new versions of your application in a rolling fashion, orchestrating the various operations in conjunction with your configured load balancers to ensure your application is successfully deployed with no down time and no impact to end users. The process of how ECS manages rolling deployments is actually quite detailed, and following diagram attempts to describe the process at a high level in a single diagram:

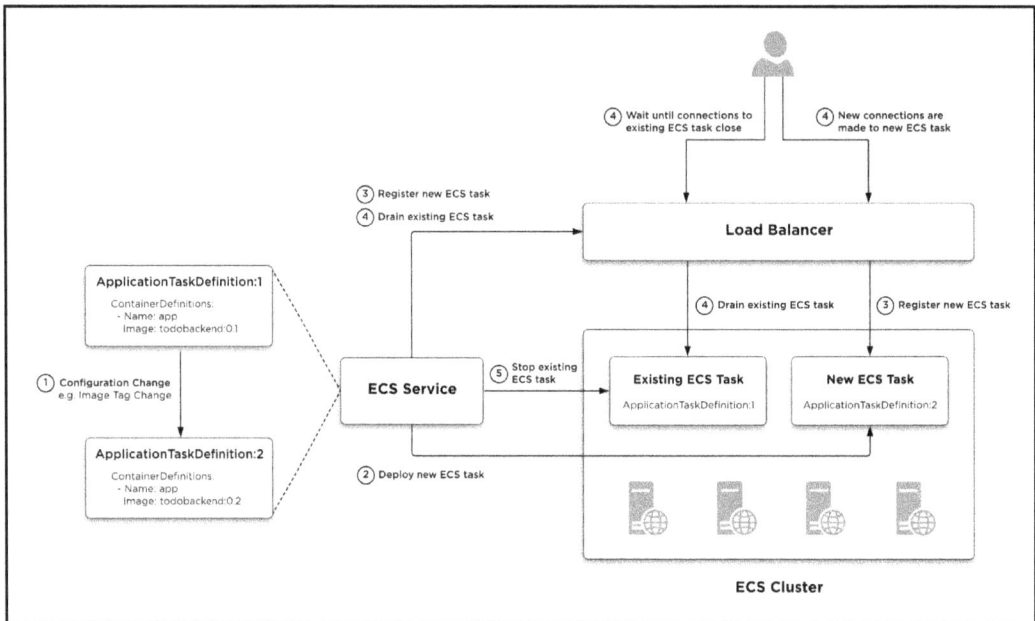

ECS rolling deployments

In the preceding diagram, the following events take place during a rolling deployment:

1. A configuration change is made to the `ApplicationTaskDefinition` ECS task definition linked to the ECS service, which generally will be a change in the image tag for new versions of an application, but could be any change made to the task definition. This results in a new revision of the task definition being created (revision 2 in this example).

2. The ECS service is configured to use the new task definition revision, which happens automatically when using CloudFormation to manage your ECS resources. The deployment configuration of the ECS service determines how ECS manages the rolling deployment - in the preceding diagram, ECS must ensure that a minimum of 100% of the configured desired task count is maintained during the deployment, and can temporarily increase the task count up to 200% during a deployment. Assuming the desired task count is one, this means ECS can deploy a new ECS task based on the new task definition revision and satisfy the deployment configuration. Note that your ECS cluster must have enough resources available to accommodate these deployments and you are responsible for managing ECS cluster capacity (that is, ECS will not increase ECS cluster capacity temporarily to accommodate deployments). You will learn how to dynamically manage ECS cluster capacity in later chapters.

3. Once the new ECS task starts successfully, ECS registers the new task with the configure load balancer (in the case of an Application Load Balancer, the task will be registered with a target group resource). The load balancer will perform health checks to determine the health of the new task, and once confirmed healthy, the new ECS task will be registered in the load balancer and able to accept incoming connections.

4. ECS now instructs the load balancer to drain the existing ECS task. The load balancer will take the existing ECS task out of service (that is, it won't forward any new connections to the task), however will wait for a configurable period of time for existing connections to "drain" or close. During this time, any new connections to the load balancer will be forwarded to the new ECS task that was registered with the load balancer in Step 3.

5. Once the draining process is complete, the load balancer removes the old ECS task completely from the target group, and ECS can now terminate the existing ECS task. Once this is complete, the deployment of the new application task definition is complete.

As you can see from this description, the deployment process is quite involved. The great news is that all of this comes out of the box with ECS - all that you need to understand is that any changes to your task definitions will trigger a new deployment, and that your deployment configuration, as determined by the `DeploymentConfiguration` property, gives you some control over the rolling deployment.

Executing a rolling deployment

Now that you understand how rolling deployments work, let's see the process in action by making a change to your ECS task definitions and deploying the change via CloudFormation, which will trigger a rolling deployment of your ECS service.

At the moment, your CloudFormation configuration is not specifying the `ApplicationImageTag` parameter, meaning your ECS task definitions are using the default value of `latest`. Back in Chapter 5, when you published your Docker image to ECR, you actually pushed two tags—the `latest` tag and also the commit hash of the todobackend repository. This provides us with a good opportunity to further improve our CloudFormation template—by referencing the commit hash, rather than the `latest` tag, we will always be able to trigger a configuration change to your ECS task definitions whenever you have a new version of your application to deploy.

The following example demonstrates adding the `ApplicationImageTag` parameter to the `dev.cfg` file in the todobackend-aws repository, referencing the commit hash of the currently published image in ECR:

```
ApplicationDesiredCount=1
ApplicationImageId=ami-ec957491
ApplicationImageTag=97e4abf
ApplicationSubnets=subnet-a5d3ecee,subnet-324e246f
VpcId=vpc-f8233a80
```

Adding ApplicationImageTag to the dev.cfg file

If you now deploy your changes using the `aws cloudformation deploy` command, although the image you have now referenced is identical to the current latest tagged image, CloudFormation will detect this as a configuration change, create a new revision of your ECS task definitions, and update the `ApplicationService` ECS service resource, triggering a rolling deployment.

While the deployment is running, if you browse to your ECS service in the ECS dashboard and select the Deployments tab, as demonstrated in the following screenshot, you will see two deployments—the **ACTIVE** deployment refers to the existing ECS tasks, while the **PRIMARY** deployment refers to the new ECS tasks that are being deployed:

Clusters > todobackend-cluster > Service: todobackend-ApplicationService-19WTUY4NO3YB2

Service : todobackend-ApplicationService-19WTUY4NO3YB2   Update   Delete

Cluster	todobackend-cluster	Desired count	1
Status	ACTIVE	Pending count	1
Task definition	todobackend:9	Running count	1
Launch type	EC2		
Service role	aws-service-role/ecs.amazonaws.com/AWSServiceRoleForECS		

Details   Tasks   Events   Auto Scaling   **Deployments**   Metrics   Logs

Task Placement

Strategy	No strategies
Constraint	No constraints

Service Deployment Options

Minimum healthy percent	100 🛈
Maximum percent	200 🛈

create pipeline ↗ | view pipelines ↗

Last updated on April 17, 2018 1:40:43 AM (0m ago) ⟳ ❓

🔽 *Filter in this page*   ‹ 1-2 ›

Deployment Id	Status	Desired count	Pending count	Running count	Created time	Updated time
ecs-svc/922337...	PRIMARY	1	1	0	2018-04-17 01:4...	2018-04-17 01:4...
ecs-svc/922337...	ACTIVE	1	0	1	2018-04-16 22:3...	2018-04-17 01:4...

ECS service rolling deployment

Eventually, the **ACTIVE** deployment will disappear once the rolling deployment process is complete, and if you click on the **Events** tab, you will see the various events that took place during the deployment, which correspond to the earlier description:

ECS service rolling deployment events

Creating a CloudFormation custom resource

Although our application has been deployed and is running, we clearly have a problem in that we haven't run database migrations, which is a required deployment task. We already have dealt with running another deployment task, which is to collect static files, however database migrations should only be run as a *single* deployment task per deployment. For example, if you are deploying multiple instances of your service, you don't want to run migrations for each instance you deploy, you just want to run migrations once per deployment, regardless of the number of instances that are in service.

One obvious solution is to manually run migrations after each deployment, however ideally you want to fully automate your deployments and ensure you have a mechanism to automatically run migrations. CloudFormation does not provide a resource that allows you run one-off ECS tasks, however an extremely powerful feature of CloudFormation is the ability to create your own custom resources, which allow you to perform custom provisioning tasks. A benefit of creating custom resources is that you can incorporate custom provisioning tasks into the workflow of deploying various AWS services and resources, using the CloudFormation framework to manage this for you.

Let's now learn how you can create a simple ECS task runner custom resource that will run the migrate task as part of creating and updating your application environment via CloudFormation.

Understanding CloudFormation custom resources

Before you get started configuring CloudFormation custom resources, it is worthwhile to discuss how they actually work and describe the key components that compose a custom resource.

The following diagram illustrates how CloudFormation custom resources work:

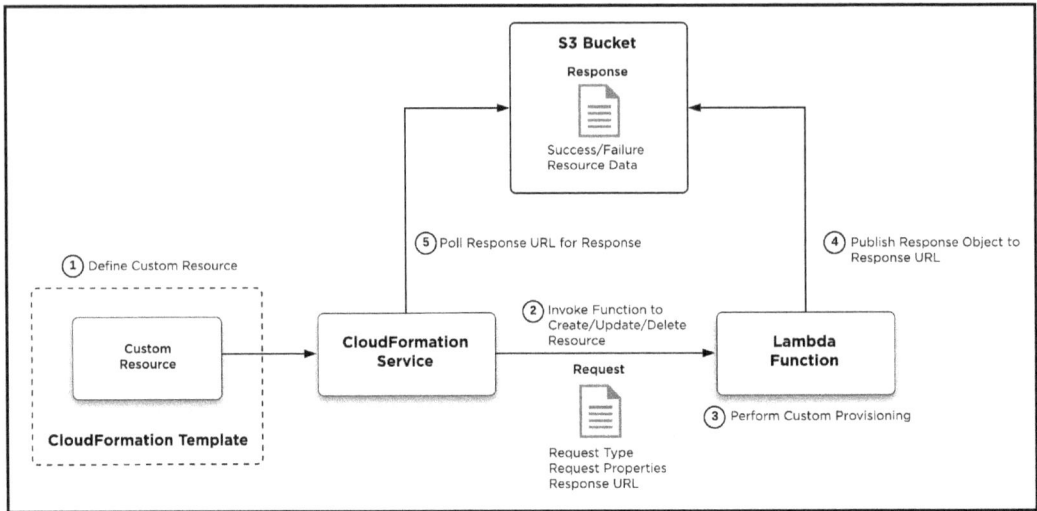

CloudFormation custom resources

In the preceding diagram, the following steps take place when you use custom resources in your CloudFormation templates:

1. You need to define custom resources in your CloudFormation templates. A custom resource has the `AWS::CloudFormation::CustomResource` resource type, or alternatively `Custom::<resource-name>`. When CloudFormation encounters a custom resource, it looks for a specific property called `ServiceToken`, which provides the ARN of a Lambda function that should provision the custom resource.

2. CloudFormation invokes the Lambda function, and passes a custom resource request to the function in the form of a JSON object. The event has a request type, which defines whether the request is to either create, update, or delete the resource, and includes request properties, which are custom properties you can define in your custom resource definition that will be passed to the Lambda function. Another important property of the request is the response URL, which provides a pre-signed S3 URL where the Lambda function should post a response once provisioning is complete.

3. The Lambda function processes the custom resource request and performs appropriate provisioning of the resource, based upon the request type and request properties. Once provisioning is complete, the function posts a success or failure response to the response URL received in the custom resource request, and includes a resource identifier in the event a resource has been created or updated. Assuming the response signals success, the response may include a `Data` property, which can include useful information about the provisioned custom resource that can be referenced elsewhere in the CloudFormation stack using the standard `!Sub` `${<resource-name>.<data-property>}` syntax, where `<data-property>` is a property included in the `Data` property of the response.

4. The CloudFormation service polls the response URL for a response. Once a response is received, CloudFormation parses the response and continues stack provisioning (or rolls back the stack in the event the response indicates a failure).

Creating a custom resource Lambda function

As discussed in the previous section, a custom resource requires you to create a Lambda function that processes an incoming event sent by CloudFormation, performs custom provisioning actions, and then responds to CloudFormation using a pre-signed S3 URL.

This sounds reasonably complicated, however there are a number of tools available that make this possible to achieve in a relatively straightforward manner for simple use cases, as demonstrated in the following example:

```
...
...
Resources:
  EcsTaskRunner:
    Type: AWS::Lambda::Function
    DependsOn:
    - EcsTaskRunnerLogGroup
    Properties:
      FunctionName: !Sub ${AWS::StackName}-ecsTasks
      Description: !Sub ${AWS::StackName} ECS Task Runner
      Handler: index.handler
      MemorySize: 128
      Runtime: python3.6
      Timeout: 300
      Role: !Sub ${EcsTaskRunnerRole.Arn}
      Code:
```

```
            ZipFile: |
              import cfnresponse
              import boto3
              client = boto3.client('ecs')

              def handler(event, context):
                try:
                  print("Received event %s" % event)
                  if event['RequestType'] == 'Delete':
                    cfnresponse.send(event, context, cfnresponse.SUCCESS,
{}, event['PhysicalResourceId'])
                    return
                  tasks = client.run_task(
                    cluster=event['ResourceProperties']['Cluster'],
taskDefinition=event['ResourceProperties']['TaskDefinition'],
overrides=event['ResourceProperties'].get('Overrides',{}),
                    count=1,
                    startedBy=event['RequestId']
                  )
                  task = tasks['tasks'][0]['taskArn']
                  print("Started ECS task %s" % task)
                  waiter = client.get_waiter('tasks_stopped')
                  waiter.wait(
                    cluster=event['ResourceProperties']['Cluster'],
                    tasks=[task],
                  )
                  result = client.describe_tasks(
                    cluster=event['ResourceProperties']['Cluster'],
                    tasks=[task]
                  )
                  exitCode =
result['tasks'][0]['containers'][0]['exitCode']
                  if exitCode > 0:
                    print("ECS task %s failed with exit code %s" % (task,
exitCode))
                    cfnresponse.send(event, context, cfnresponse.FAILED,
{}, task)
                  else:
                    print("ECS task %s completed successfully" % task)
                    cfnresponse.send(event, context, cfnresponse.SUCCESS,
{}, task)
                except Exception as e:
                  print("A failure occurred with exception %s" % e)
                  cfnresponse.send(event, context, cfnresponse.FAILED, {})
  EcsTaskRunnerRole:
    Type: AWS::IAM::Role
    Properties:
      AssumeRolePolicyDocument:
```

```
        Version: "2012-10-17"
        Statement:
        - Effect: Allow
          Principal:
            Service: lambda.amazonaws.com
          Action:
            - sts:AssumeRole
      Policies:
        - PolicyName: EcsTaskRunnerPermissions
          PolicyDocument:
            Version: "2012-10-17"
            Statement:
            - Sid: EcsTasks
              Effect: Allow
              Action:
              - ecs:DescribeTasks
              - ecs:ListTasks
              - ecs:RunTask
              Resource: "*"
              Condition:
                ArnEquals:
                  ecs:cluster: !Sub ${ApplicationCluster.Arn}
            - Sid: ManageLambdaLogs
              Effect: Allow
              Action:
              - logs:CreateLogStream
              - logs:PutLogEvents
              Resource: !Sub ${EcsTaskRunnerLogGroup.Arn}
  EcsTaskRunnerLogGroup:
    Type: AWS::Logs::LogGroup
    Properties:
      LogGroupName: !Sub /aws/lambda/${AWS::StackName}-ecsTasks
      RetentionInDays: 7
  ApplicationService:
    Type: AWS::ECS::Service
...
...
```

Creating an inline Lambda function using CloudFormation

The most important aspect of the preceding example to initially focus on is the `Code.ZipFile` property within the `EcsTaskRunner` resource, which defines an inline Python script that performs the custom provisioning actions of your custom resource. Note this approach of defining code inline is generally not recommended for real world use cases, and in later chapters we will create a more complex custom resource complete with its own source code repository for the Lambda function code, but for the purposes of keeping this example simple and introducing the core concepts of custom resources, I am using an inline approach for now.

Understanding the custom resource function code

Let's focus on discussing the custom resource function code, which I have isolated in the earlier example and added comments to describe what various statements are doing.

```python
# Generates an appropriate CloudFormation response and posts to the
pre-signed S3 URL
import cfnresponse
# Imports the AWS Python SDK (boto3) for interacting with the ECS
service
import boto3

# Create a client for interacting with the ECS service
client = boto3.client('ecs')

# Lambda functions require a handler function that is passed an event
and context object
# The event object contains the CloudFormation custom resource event
# The context object contains runtime information about the Lambda
function
def handler(event, context):
  # Wrap the code in a try/catch block to ensure any exceptions
generate a failure
  try:
    print("Received event %s" % event)
    # If the request is to Delete the resource, simply return success
    if event['RequestType'] == 'Delete':
      cfnresponse.send(event, context, cfnresponse.SUCCESS, {},
event.get('PhysicalResourceId'))
      return
    # Run the ECS task
    #
http://boto3.readthedocs.io/en/latest/reference/services/ecs.html#ECS.
Client.run_task
    # Requires 'Cluster', 'TaskDefinition' and optional 'Overrides'
```

```
custom resource properties
    tasks = client.run_task(
      cluster=event['ResourceProperties']['Cluster'],
      taskDefinition=event['ResourceProperties']['TaskDefinition'],
      overrides=event['ResourceProperties'].get('Overrides',{}),
      count=1,
      startedBy=event['RequestId']
    )
    # Extract the ECS task ARN from the return value from the run_task
call
    task = tasks['tasks'][0]['taskArn']
    print("Started ECS task %s" % task)

    # Creates a waiter object that polls and waits for ECS tasks to
reached a stopped state
    #
http://boto3.readthedocs.io/en/latest/reference/services/ecs.html#wait
ers
    waiter = client.get_waiter('tasks_stopped')
    # Wait for the task ARN that was run earlier to stop
    waiter.wait(
      cluster=event['ResourceProperties']['Cluster'],
      tasks=[task],
    )
    # After the task has stopped, get the status of the task
    #
http://boto3.readthedocs.io/en/latest/reference/services/ecs.html#ECS.
Client.describe_tasks
    result = client.describe_tasks(
      cluster=event['ResourceProperties']['Cluster'],
      tasks=[task]
    )
    # Get the exit code of the container that ran
    exitCode = result['tasks'][0]['containers'][0]['exitCode']
    # Return failure for non-zero exit code, otherwise return success
    # See
https://docs.aws.amazon.com/AWSCloudFormation/latest/UserGuide/aws-pro
perties-lambda-function-code.html for more details on cfnresponse
module
    if exitCode > 0:
      print("ECS task %s failed with exit code %s" % (task, exitCode))
      cfnresponse.send(event, context, cfnresponse.FAILED, {}, task)
```

```
    else:
        print("ECS task %s completed successfully" % task)
        cfnresponse.send(event, context, cfnresponse.SUCCESS, {}, task)
  except Exception as e:
    print("A failure occurred with exception %s" % e)
    cfnresponse.send(event, context, cfnresponse.FAILED, {})
```

Creating an inline Lambda function using CloudFormation

At a high level, the custom resource function receives CloudFormation custom resource event and calls the `run_task` method for the ECS service from the AWS Python SDK, passing in the ECS cluster, ECS task definition, and optional overrides to execute. The function then waits for the task to complete, inspects the result of the ECS task to determine whether the associated container completed successfully and then responds with either success or failure to CloudFormation.

Notice that the function imports a module called `cfnresponse`, which is a module included in the AWS Lambda Python runtime environment that provides a simple high-level mechanism for responding to CloudFormation custom resource requests. The function also imports a module called `boto3`, which provides the AWS Python SDK and is used to create a `client` object that interacts specifically with the ECS service. The Lambda function then defines a single function called `handler`, which is the entry point for new events passed to the Lambda function, and notice that the `handler` function must accept both an `event` object that contains the CloudFormation custom resource event, and a `context` object that provides runtime information about the Lambda environment. Note that the function should only attempt to run a task for CloudFormation create and update requests, and can simply return success when a request to delete the custom resource is received, given tasks are short-lived resources.

The code in the preceding example is by no means production-level code and has been simplified for demonstration purposes to only handle two primary scenarios related to success and failure.

Understanding the custom resource Lambda function resources

Now that you understand how the Lambda function code actually works, let's focus on the remainder of the configuration you added in earlier example.

The `EcsTaskRunner` resource defines the Lambda function, with key configuration properties described here:

- `FunctionName`: The name of the function. An important aspect to understand with function naming is that the associated CloudWatch logs group that is used to store function logs must follow a naming convention of `/aws/lambda/<function-name>`, and you see that the `FunctionName` property matches the `LogGroupName` property of the `EcsTaskRunnerLogGroup` resource. Notice that the `EcsTaskRunner` must also declare a dependency on the `EcsTaskRunnerLogGroup` resource, as per the configuration of the `DependsOn` setting.

- `Handler`: Specifies the entry point for the Lambda function in the `<module>.<function>` format. Note that when using the inline code mechanism of the module created for your Lambda function will always be called `index`.

- `Timeout`: It is important to understand that, at the time of writing, Lambda has a maximum five-minute (300 seconds) timeout, meaning your functions must complete within five minutes or they will be terminated. The default timeout for a Lambda function is 3 seconds, and because it does take time to deploy a new ECS task, run the ECS task and wait for the task to complete, this timeout has been increased to maximum timeout of 300 seconds.

- `Role`: Defines the IAM role to assign to the Lambda function. Note that the referenced `EcsTaskRunnerRole` resource must trust the lambda.amazonaws.com and at a minimum, every Lambda function must have permissions to write to the associated CloudWatch logs group if you want to capture any logs. The ECS task runner function requires permissions to run and describe ECS tasks, and the use of conditions is configured to only grant these permissions to the ECS cluster defined in the stack.

Creating custom resources

Now that your custom resource Lambda function and associated supporting resources are in place, you can define the actual custom resource object. For our use case, we need to define a custom resource that will run the `python3 manage.py migrate` command inside our application container, and given the migrate task interacts with the application database, the task must be configured with the various database environment variables that define connectivity to the application database resource.

One approach would be to leverage the `ApplicationTaskDefinition` resource you created earlier and specify a command override, however one issue is that the `ApplicationTaskDefinition` includes the `collectstatic` container, which we don't really want to run whenever you run migrations. To overcome this, you need to create a separate task definition called `MigrateTaskDefinition`, which only includes a single container definition that specifically runs database migrations:

```
...
...
Resources:
  MigrateTaskDefinition:
    Type: AWS::ECS::TaskDefinition
    Properties:
      Family: todobackend-migrate
      ContainerDefinitions:
        - Name: migrate
          Image: !Sub
${AWS::AccountId}.dkr.ecr.${AWS::Region}.amazonaws.com/docker-in-
aws/todobackend:${ApplicationImageTag}
          MemoryReservation: 5
          Cpu: 5
          Environment:
            - Name: DJANGO_SETTINGS_MODULE
              Value: todobackend.settings_release
            - Name: MYSQL_HOST
              Value: !Sub ${ApplicationDatabase.Endpoint.Address}
            - Name: MYSQL_USER
              Value: todobackend
            - Name: MYSQL_PASSWORD
              Value: !Ref DatabasePassword
            - Name: MYSQL_DATABASE
              Value: todobackend

  Command:
            - python3
            - manage.py
```

```
                - migrate
                - --no-input
            LogConfiguration:
              LogDriver: awslogs
              Options:
                awslogs-group: !Sub /${AWS::StackName}/ecs/todobackend
                awslogs-region: !Ref AWS::Region
                awslogs-stream-prefix: docker
    EcsTaskRunner:
      Type: AWS::Lambda::Function
  ...
  ...
```

Creating a migrate task definition

In the preceding example, notice that the `MigrateTaskDefinition` resource requires database-related environment variables to be configured, however does not require the volume mappings or port mappings you configured previously in the `ApplicationTaskDefinition` resource.

With this task definition in place, you can now create your custom resource, as demonstrated in the following example:

```
  ...
  ...
Resources:
  MigrateTask:
    Type: AWS::CloudFormation::CustomResource
    DependsOn:
        - ApplicationAutoscaling
        - ApplicationDatabase
    Properties:
      ServiceToken: !Sub ${EcsTaskRunner.Arn}
      Cluster: !Ref ApplicationCluster
      TaskDefinition: !Ref MigrateTaskDefinition
  MigrateTaskDefinition:
    Type: AWS::ECS::TaskDefinition
    ...
    ...
  ApplicationService:
    Type: AWS::ECS::Service
    DependsOn:
        - ApplicationAutoscaling
        - ApplicationLogGroup
        - ApplicationLoadBalancerHttpListener
        - MigrateTask
```

```
Properties:
  ...
  ...
```

Creating a migrate task custom resource

In the preceding example, notice that your custom resource is created with the `AWS::CloudFormation::CustomResource` type, and every custom resource you create must include the `ServiceToken` property, which references the ARN of the associated custom resource Lambda function. The remainder of the properties are specific to your custom resource function, which in our case must specify, at a minimum, the target ECS cluster and ECS task definition of the task that needs to be executed. Notice that the custom resource includes dependencies to ensure it is only run once the `ApplicationAutoscaling` and `ApplicationDatabase` resources have been created, and you also need to add a dependency on the `ApplicationService` resource you created earlier in this chapter, so that this resource is not created or updated until the `MigrateTask` custom resource has completed successfully.

Deploying custom resources

You are now ready to deploy your changes using the `aws cloudformation deploy` command. While the CloudFormation stack changes are deploying, once CloudFormation initiates creation of the custom resource and invokes your Lambda function, you can navigate to AWS Lambda console to view your Lambda function and also check function logs.

> CloudFormation custom resources can be time-consuming to initially get working, particularly if your code throws exceptions and you don't have appropriate code to catch these exceptions and send failure responses. It is possible for you to end up waiting several hours for a custom resource action to timeout, because your custom resource threw an exception and did not return an appropriate failure response to CloudFormation.

The following screenshot demonstrates viewing the `todobackend-ecsTasks` Lambda function that is created from your CloudFormation stack in the AWS Lambda console:

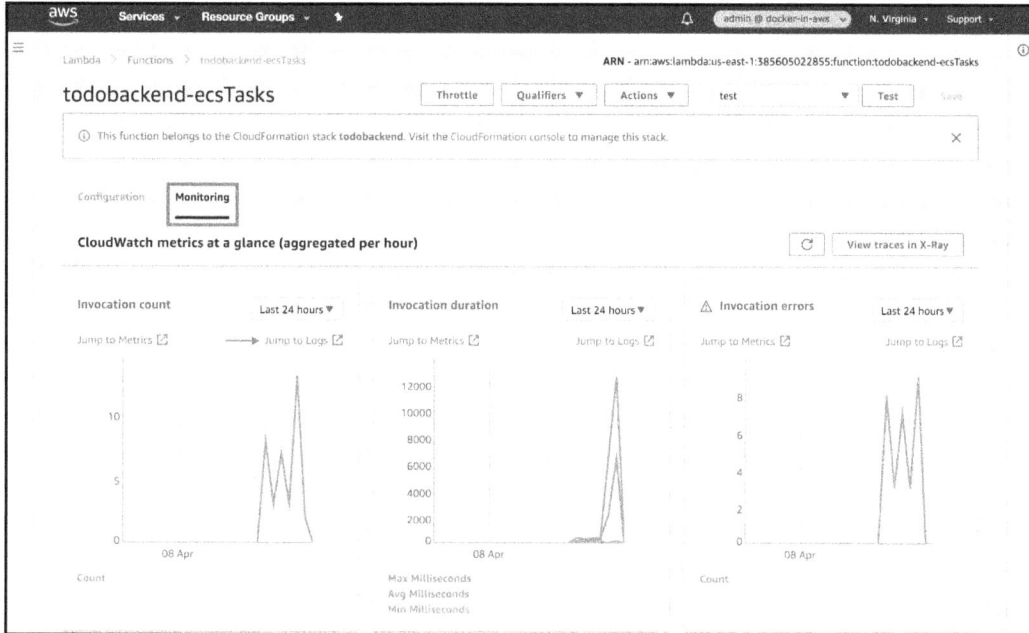

Viewing Lambda functions in the AWS console

In the preceding screenshot, the **Configuration** tab provides configuration details about your function, and even includes an inline code editor where you can review, test, and debug your code. The **Monitoring** tab provides access to various metrics for your function, and includes a useful **Jump to Logs** link that takes you straight to the logs for your function in CloudWatch logs:

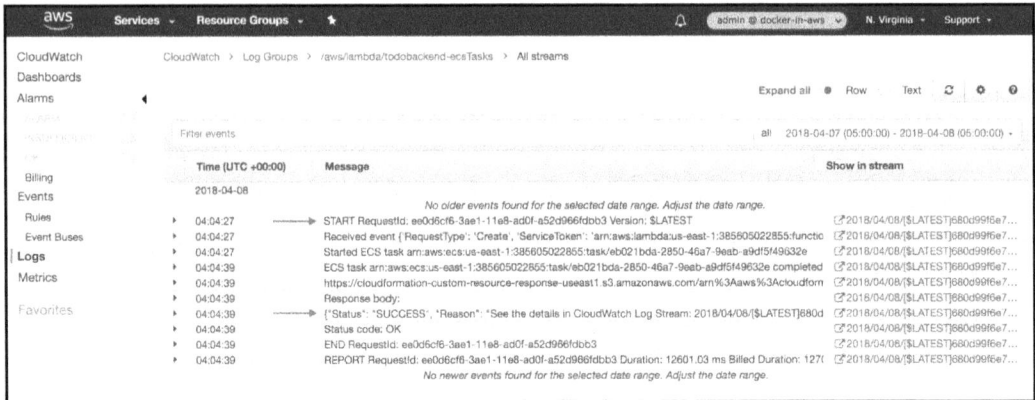

Viewing Lambda function logs in the AWS console

In the preceding screenshot, the **START** message indicates when the function was invoked, and you can see a response body with a status of **SUCCESS** was generated, which is published to the CloudFormation custom resource response URL.

Now is also a good time to review the CloudWatch logs for your ECS tasks—shows the **/todobackend/ecs/todobackend** log group, which is the log group configured in your CloudFormation stack that collects all ECS task logs for the application. Notice that there are several log streams - one for the **collectstatic** container that generated static tasks, one for the **migrate** container that ran migrations, and a log stream for the main todobackend application. Notice that each log stream includes the ECS task ID at the end of the log stream name - these correlate directly to the ECS task IDs that you interact with using the ECS console or AWS CLI:

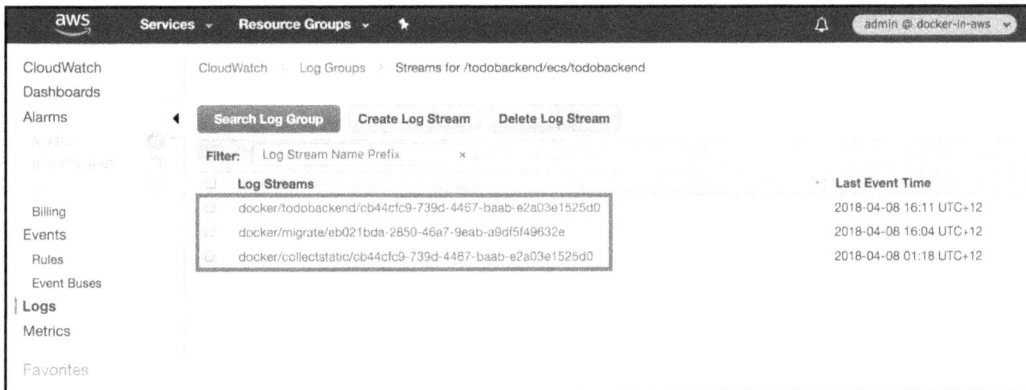

ECS log groups in CloudWatch logs

Verifying the application

As a final check, the sample application should now be fully functional - for example, the todos link that failed earlier in should now work, as demonstrated in the following screenshot.

You can interact with the API to add or remove todo items, and all of your todo items will now be persisted in the application database defined in your stack:

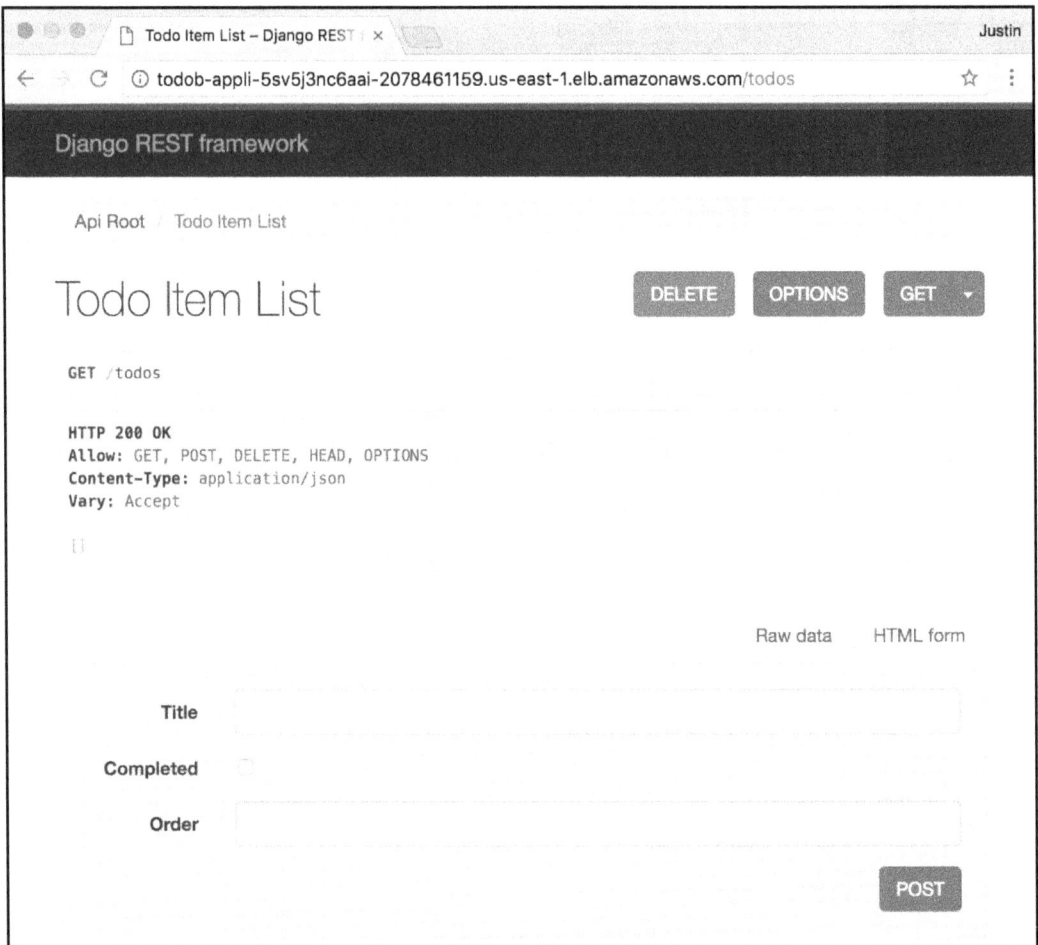

Working todobackend application

Summary

In this chapter, you successfully deployed the sample Docker application to AWS using ECS. You learned how to define key supporting application and infrastructure resources, including how to create an application database using the AWS RDS service, and how to integrate your ECS applications with application load balancers provided by the AWS Elastic Load Balancing service.

With these supporting resources in place, you learned how to create ECS task definitions that control the runtime configuration of your containers, and then deployed instances of your ECS task definitions to your ECS cluster by creating an ECS service for the sample application. You learned how an ECS task definition can define volumes and multiple container definitions, and you used this capability to create a separate non-essential container definition that always runs whenever your ECS task definition is deployed and generates static web files for the sample application. You also integrated the ECS service for the sample application with the various Application Load Balancer resources in your stack, ensuring connections to your application can be load balanced across multiple instances of your ECS service in a highly available manner.

Although you were able to successfully deploy your application as an ECS service, you discovered that your application was not fully functional, because the database migrations that establish the schema and tables for your application database had not been run. You addressed this issue by creating an ECS task runner CloudFormation custom resource, which allowed you to run migrations as a single-shot task per application deployment. The custom resource is defined as a simple Lambda function written in Python, which first runs a task for a given ECS task definition on a given ECS cluster, waits for the task to complete, and then reports the success or failure of the task based upon the exit code of the container associated with the task.

With this custom resource in place, your sample application is now fully functional, although it still has some deficiencies. In the next chapter, we will address one of those deficiencies—secrets management and ensuring passwords remain confidential—which is critical in secure, production-grade Docker applications.

Questions

1. True/False: An RDS instance requires you to create a DB subnet group with at least two subnets.
2. When configuring an Application Load Balancer, which component services frontend connections from end users?
3. True/False: A target group can accept registrations from targets before the Application Load Balancer listener is created.
4. When configuring security group rules permitting access between an application database and ECS container instances, you receive a CloudFormation error about circular dependencies. What type of resources can you use to overcome this issue?
5. You configure an ECS task definition that includes two container definitions. One of the container definition performs a short provisioning task and then exits. You discover that ECS is continuously restarting ECS services based on this task definition. How can you resolve this issue?
6. Which CloudFormation parameter can you configure to define explicit dependencies on other resources?
7. True/False: CloudFormation custom resources use AWS Lambda functions to perform custom provisioning tasks.
8. What are the three types of events you need to handle when receiving CloudFormation custom resource events?
9. You create a Lambda function with an inline Python function that performs custom provisioning tasks, however when attempting to view logs for this function nothing is being written to CloudWatch logs. You confirm that the log group name is configured correctly for the function. What is the most likely reason for the issue?

Further reading

You can check the following links for more information about the topics covered in this chapter:

- CloudFormation RDS Instance Resource Reference: `https://docs.aws.amazon.com/AWSCloudFormation/latest/UserGuide/aws-properties-rds-database-instance.html`
- CloudFormation Application Load Balancer Resource Reference: `https://docs.aws.amazon.com/AWSCloudFormation/latest/UserGuide/aws-resource-elasticloadbalancingv2-loadbalancer.html`
- CloudFormation Application Load Balancer Listener Resource Reference: `https://docs.aws.amazon.com/AWSCloudFormation/latest/UserGuide/aws-resource-elasticloadbalancingv2-listener.html`
- CloudFormation Application Load Balancer Target Group Resource Reference: `https://docs.aws.amazon.com/AWSCloudFormation/latest/UserGuide/aws-resource-elasticloadbalancingv2-targetgroup.html`
- CloudFormation ECS Task Definition Resource Reference: `https://docs.aws.amazon.com/AWSCloudFormation/latest/UserGuide/aws-resource-ecs-taskdefinition.html`
- CloudFormation ECS Service Resource Reference: `https://docs.aws.amazon.com/AWSCloudFormation/latest/UserGuide/aws-resource-ecs-service.html`
- CloudFormation Lambda Function Resource Reference: `https://docs.aws.amazon.com/AWSCloudFormation/latest/UserGuide/aws-resource-lambda-function.html`
- CloudFormation Lambda Function Code: `https://docs.aws.amazon.com/AWSCloudFormation/latest/UserGuide/aws-properties-lambda-function-code.html`
- CloudFormation Custom Resource Documentation: `https://docs.aws.amazon.com/AWSCloudFormation/latest/UserGuide/template-custom-resources.html`
- CloudFormation Custom Resource Reference: `https://docs.aws.amazon.com/AWSCloudFormation/latest/UserGuide/crpg-ref.html`

Managing Secrets

9

Secrets management is a critical security and operational requirement for modern applications and systems. Credentials such as usernames and passwords are commonly used to authenticate access to resources that may contain private and sensitive data, and it is very important that you can implement a secrets management solution that is able to provide these credentials to your applications in a secure manner that does not expose them to unauthorized parties.

Secrets management for container-based applications is challenging, in part due to the ephemeral nature of containers and the fundamental requirement to run your containers on disposable and repeatable infrastructure. Gone are the days of long-lived servers where you could store secrets in a local file – now your servers are ECS container instances that can come and go, and you need to have some mechanism to be able to dynamically inject secrets into your application at runtime. A naive solution that we have used to date in this book is to use environment variables to inject your secrets directly into your application; however, this approach is considered insecure as it often exposes your secrets in plain text via various operational data sources. A more robust solution is to implement a secure credential store where your applications can dynamically retrieve their secrets in a secure manner – however, setting up your own credential store can be costly, time consuming, and introduce significant operational overheads.

In this chapter, you will implement a simple yet effective secrets management solution powered by two key AWS services—the AWS Secrets Manager, and the Key Management Service or KMS. These services will provide you with a cloud-based secure credential store that is easy to manage, cost effective and is fully integrated with standard AWS security controls such as IAM policies and roles. You will learn how to integrate any application that supports configuration via environment variables with your secrets management solution, by creating an entry point script in your Docker images that uses the AWS CLI to dynamically retrieve and inject secrets securely into your internal container environments, and also learn how you can expose secrets to other resources in your CloudFormation stacks, when you are using CloudFormation to deploy your environments.

The following topics will be covered:

- Creating KMS keys
- Creating secrets using the AWS Secrets Manager
- Injecting secrets at container startup
- Provisioning secrets using CloudFormation
- Deploying secrets to AWS

Technical requirements

The following lists technical requirements to complete this chapter:

- Administrator access to an AWS account
- Local AWS profile configured as per instructions in Chapter 3
- AWS CLI version 1.15.71 or higher
- Chapter 8 needs to be completed along with a successfully deployed sample application to AWS

The following GitHub URL contains the code samples used in this chapter – `https://github.com/docker-in-aws/docker-in-aws/tree/master/ch9`.

Check out the following video to see the Code in Action:
`http://bit.ly/2LzpEY2`

Creating KMS keys

A key building block of any secrets management solution is the ability to encrypt your credentials using encryption keys, which ensures the privacy and confidentiality of your credentials. The AWS Key Management Service (KMS) is a managed service that allows you to create and control encryption keys, and provides a simple, low-cost solution that takes away many of the operational challenges of managing your encryption keys. Key features of KMS include centralized key management, compliance with a number of industry standards, built-in auditing and integration with other AWS services.

When building a secrets management solution that uses AWS Secrets Manager, you should create, at a minimum, at least one KMS key in your local AWS account and region that is used to encrypt your secrets. AWS does provide a default KMS key that you can use with AWS Secrets Manager, so this is not a strict requirement, however, in general, you should be comfortable with creating your own KMS keys based upon your security requirements.

You can easily create KMS keys using the AWS console and CLI, however in keeping with the general theme of adopting infrastructure as code, we will create a new KMS key using CloudFormation.

The following example demonstrates creating a KMS key and KMS alias in a new CloudFormation template file that you can place at the root of the todobackend-aws repository, which we will call `kms.yml`:

```
AWSTemplateFormatVersion: "2010-09-09"

Description: KMS Keys

Resources:
  KmsKey:
    Type: AWS::KMS::Key
    Properties:
      Description: Custom key for Secrets
      Enabled: true
      KeyPolicy:
        Version: "2012-10-17"
        Id: key-policy
        Statement:
          - Sid: Allow root account access to key
            Effect: Allow
            Principal:
              AWS: !Sub arn:aws:iam::${AWS::AccountId}:root
            Action:
              - kms:*
            Resource: "*"
  KmsKeyAlias:
    Type: AWS::KMS::Alias
    Properties:
      AliasName: alias/secrets-key
      TargetKeyId: !Ref KmsKey
```

```
Outputs:
  KmsKey:
    Description: Secrets Key KMS Key ARN
    Value: !Sub ${KmsKey.Arn}
    Export:
      Name: secrets-key
```

Creating KMS resources using CloudFormation

In the preceding example, you create two resources—an `AWS::KMS::Key` resource called `KmsKey` that creates a new KMS key, and an `AWS::KMS::Alias` resource called `KmsKeyAlias`, which creates an alias or friendly name for the key.

The `KmsKey` resource includes a `KeyPolicy` property, which defines a resource policy that grants root account access to the key. This is a requirement for any KMS key that you create, in order to ensure you always have at least some means to access the key, which you may have used to encrypt valuable data that would cause considerable cost to the business if the key was inaccessible.

> If you create a KMS key via the AWS console or CLI, the root account access policy will be automatically created for you.

One interesting feature of the CloudFormation template in the preceding example is the creation of a CloudFormation export, which is created whenever you add the `Export` property to a CloudFormation output. In the preceding example, the `KmsKey` output exports the ARN of the `KmsKey` resource as specified by the `Value` property, and the `Export` property creates a CloudFormation export that you can reference in other CloudFormation stacks to inject the value of the export, rather than having to explicitly specify the value of the export. You will see how to leverage this CloudFormation export later on in this chapter, so don't worry if this doesn't quite make sense right now.

With the configuration of the preceding example in place, assuming you have placed this template in a file called `kms.yml`, you can now deploy the new stack, which will result in the creation of a new KMS key and KMS resource:

```
> export AWS_PROFILE=docker-in-aws
> aws cloudformation deploy --template-file kms.yml --stack-name kms
Enter MFA code for arn:aws:iam::385605022855:mfa/justin.menga:

Waiting for changeset to be created..
Waiting for stack create/update to complete
```

```
Successfully created/updated stack - kms
> aws cloudformation list-exports
{
    "Exports": [
        {
            "ExportingStackId": "arn:aws:cloudformation:us-
east-1:385605022855:stack/kms/be0a6d20-3bd4-11e8-bf63-50faeaabf0d1",
            "Name": "secrets-key",
            "Value": "arn:aws:kms:us-
east-1:385605022855:key/ee08c380-153c-4f31-bf72-9133b41472ad"
        }
    ]
}
```

Deploying KMS Keys using CloudFormation

In the preceding example, after the CloudFormation stack is created, notice that the `aws cloudformation list-exports` command now lists a single export with a name of `secrets-key`. The value of this export is the ARN of the KMS Key resource in your stack, and you can now use the `Fn::ImportValue` intrinsic function in other CloudFormation stacks to import this value by simply referencing the export name of `secrets-key` (for example, `Fn::ImportValue: secrets-key`).

> Be careful with your use of CloudFormation exports. These exports are intended for referencing resources that are static in nature whose value that you are exporting will never change in the future. Once a CloudFormation export is referenced by another stack you cannot change the value of that export, nor delete the resource or stack that the export belongs to. CloudFormation exports are useful for resources such as IAM roles, KMS keys and network infrastructure (for example, VPCs and subnets), which often are very static in nature and do not change once implemented.

Encrypting and decrypting data using KMS

Now that you have created a KMS key, you can use this key to encrypt and decrypt data.

The following example demonstrates encrypting a simple plain text value using the AWS CLI:

```
> aws kms encrypt --key-id alias/secrets-key --plaintext "Hello World"
{
    "CiphertextBlob":
"AQICAHifCoHWAYb859mOk+pmJ7WgRbhk58UL9mhuMIcVAKJ18gHN1/SRRhwQVoVJvDS6i
7MoAAAAaTBnBgkqhkiG9w0BBwagWjBYAgEAMFMGCSqGSIb3DQEHATAeBglghkgBZQMEAS4
wEQQMYm4au5zNZG9wa5ceAgEQgCZdADZyWKTcwDfTpw60kUI8aIAtrECRyW+/tu58bYrMa
ZFlwVYmdA==",
    "KeyId": "arn:aws:kms:us-
east-1:385605022855:key/ee08c380-153c-4f31-bf72-9133b41472ad"
}
```

Encrypting Data Using a KMS Key

In the preceding example, note that you must specify the KMS key ID or alias using the `--key-id` flag, and whenever you use a KMS key alias, you always prefix the alias with `alias/<alias-name>`. The encrypted data is returned as a Base64-encoded binary blob in the `CiphertextBlob` property, which conveniently also encodes the key ID of the encrypted KMS key into the encrypted data, meaning the KMS service can decrypt the ciphertext blob without requiring you to explicitly specific the encrypting KMS key ID:

```
> ciphertext=$(aws kms encrypt --key-id alias/secrets-key --plaintext
"Hello World" --query CiphertextBlob --output text)
> aws kms decrypt --ciphertext-blob fileb://<(echo $ciphertext |
base64 --decode)
{
    "KeyId": "arn:aws:kms:us-
east-1:385605022855:key/ee08c380-153c-4f31-bf72-9133b41472ad",
    "Plaintext": "SGVsbG8gV29ybGQ="
}
```

Decrypting Data Using a KMS Key

In the preceding example, you encrypt some data, this time using the AWS CLI query and text output options to capture the `CiphertextBlob` property value in a bash variable called `ciphertext`. You then use the `aws kms decrypt` command to pass in the cipher text as a blob file using bash process substitution to feed the Base64 decoded value of the cipher text into the binary file URI indicator (`fileb://`). Notice that the returned `Plaintext` value is not the `Hello World` value that you originally encrypted—this is because the `Plaintext` value is in a Base64 encoded format, and the following example takes the `aws kms decrypt` command a step further to return the original plaintext value:

```
> aws kms decrypt --ciphertext-blob fileb://<(echo $ciphertext |
base64 --decode) \
    --query Plaintext --output text | base64 --decode
Hello World
```

Decrypting Data Using a KMS Key and Returning the Plaintext Value

> The `base64 --decode` command in the previous two examples are used to decode Base64 values on MacOS and most Linux platforms. On some Linux platforms such as Alpine Linux, the `--decode` flag is not recognized and you instead must use the `base64 -d` command.

Creating secrets using the AWS Secrets Manager

You have established a KMS key that can be used to encrypt and decrypt data, and you can now integrate this key with the AWS Secrets Manager service, which is a managed service launched in March 2018 that enables you to easily and cost effectively incorporate secrets management into your applications.

Creating secrets using the AWS console

Although we have focused on creating AWS resources via CloudFormation in the past few chapters, unfortunately at the time of writing, CloudFormation does not support AWS Secrets Manager resources, so if you are using AWS tools you need to provision your secrets via the AWS console or AWS CLI.

To create a new secret via the AWS console, select **AWS Secrets Manager** from the services list and click on the **Store a new secret** button. Select a secret type of **Other type of secrets**, specify a secret key and value, and select the `secrets-key` KMS key you created earlier in this chapter as demonstrated in the following screenshot:

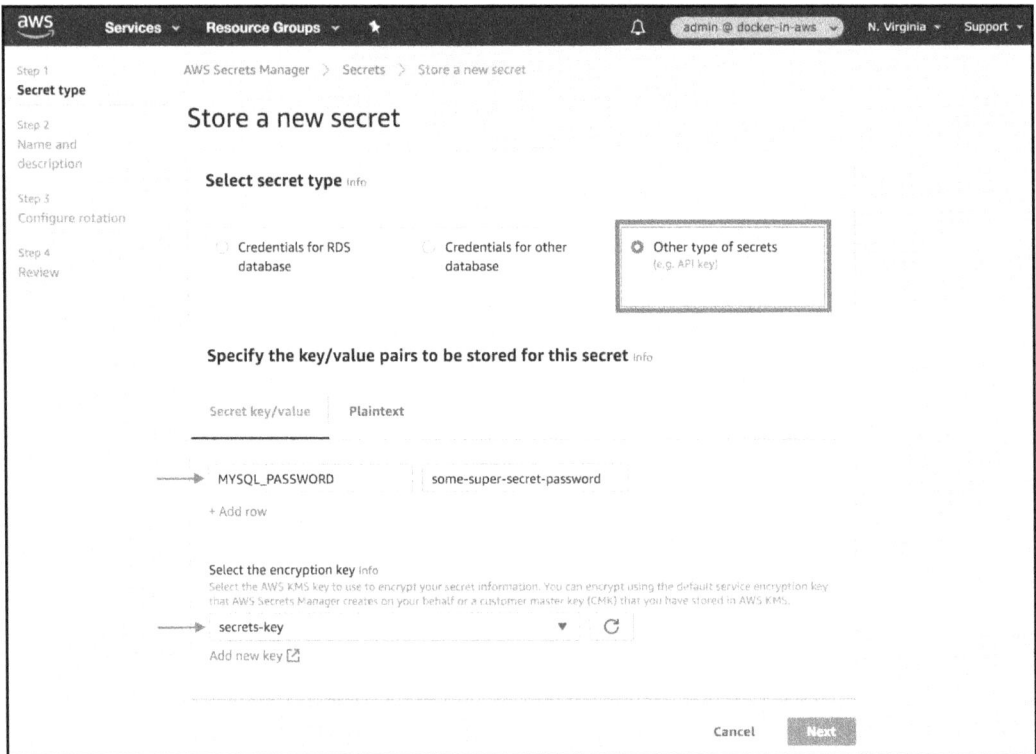

Creating a New Secret using AWS Secrets Manager

In the earlier example, notice that AWS Secrets Manager allows you to store multiple key/value pairs in a single secret. This is important as you often want to inject secrets as environment variables, so storing secrets in a key/value format allows you to specify the environment variable name as the key, and secret as the value.

After clicking **Next**, you can configure a secret name and optional description:

Configuring Secret Name and Description

In the preceding screenshot, you configure the secret to be called `todobackend/credentials`, which we will use later on in this chapter for the todobackend application. Once you have configured a secret name and description, you can click **Next**, skip the **Configure automatic rotation** section and finally click the **Store** button to complete creation of the secret.

Creating secrets using the AWS CLI

You can also create secrets via the AWS CLI by using the `aws secretsmanager create-secret` command:

```
> aws secretsmanager create-secret --name test/credentials --kms-key-
id alias/secrets-key \
    --secret-string '{"MYSQL_PASSWORD":"some-super-secret-password"}'
{
    "ARN": "arn:aws:secretsmanager:us-
east-1:385605022855:secret:test/credentials-l3JdTI",
    "Name": "test/credentials",
    "VersionId": "beab75bd-e9bc-4ac8-913e-aca26f6e3940"
}
```

Creating a Secret Using the AWS CLI

In the preceding example, notice that you specify the secret string as a JSON object, which provides the key/value format you saw earlier.

Retrieving secrets using the AWS CLI

You can retrieve secrets via the AWS CLI by using the `aws secretsmanager get-secret-value` command:

```
> aws secretsmanager get-secret-value --secret-id test/credentials
{
    "ARN": "arn:aws:secretsmanager:us-
east-1:385605022855:secret:test/credentials-l3JdTI",
    "Name": "test/credentials",
    "VersionId": "beab75bd-e9bc-4ac8-913e-aca26f6e3940",
    "SecretString": "{\"MYSQL_PASSWORD\":\"some-super-password\"}",
    "VersionStages": [
        "AWSCURRENT"
    ],
    "CreatedDate": 1523605423.133
}
```

Obtain a Secret Value Using the AWS CLI

Later on in this chapter, you will create a custom entrypoint script for the sample application container, which will use the command in the preceding example to inject secrets into the application container environment on startup.

Updating secrets using the AWS CLI

Recall from Chapter 8, that the Django framework that powers the todobackend application requires an environment variable called `SECRET_KEY` to be configured, which is used for various cryptographic operations. Earlier in this chapter, when you created the **todobackend/credentials** secret, you only created a single key/value pair for the `MYSQL_PASSWORD` variable that is used for the database password.

Let's see how we can now update the **todobackend/credentials** secret to add in a value for the SECRET_KEY variable. You can update secrets by running the aws secretsmanager update-secret command, referencing the ID of the secret and specifying the new secret value:

```
> aws secretsmanager get-random-password --password-length 50 --
exclude-characters "'\""
{
    "RandomPassword": "E2]eTfO~8Z5)&amp;OSlR-
&amp;XQf=yA:B(`,p.B#R6d]a~X-vf?%%/wY"
}
> aws secretsmanager update-secret --secret-id todobackend/credentials
\
    --kms-key-id alias/secrets-key \
    --secret-string '{
      "MYSQL_PASSWORD":"some-super-secret-password",
      "SECRET_KEY": "E2]eTfO~8Z5)&amp;OSlR-
&amp;XQf=yA:B(`,p.B#R6d]a~X-vf?%%/wY"
    }'
{
    "ARN": "arn:aws:secretsmanager:us-
east-1:385605022855:secret:todobackend/credentials-f7AQlO",
    "Name": "todobackend/credentials",
    "VersionId": "cd258b90-d108-4a06-b0f2-849be15f9c33"
}
```

Updating a Secret Value Using the AWS CLI

In the preceding example, notice that you can use the aws secretsmanager get-random-password command to generate a random password for you, which is ideal for the SECRET_KEY variable. It is important that you exclude quote and quotation characters using the --exclude-characters from this secret, as these characters will generally cause problems with bash scripts that process these values.

You then run the aws secretsmanager update-secret command, specifying the correct KMS key ID and providing an updated JSON object that includes both the MYSQL_PASSWORD and SECRET_KEY key/value pairs.

Deleting and restoring secrets using the AWS CLI

Deleting secrets can be achieved by running the `aws secretsmanager delete-secret` command, as demonstrated in the following example:

```
> aws secretsmanager delete-secret --secret-id test/credentials
{
    "ARN": "arn:aws:secretsmanager:us-
east-1:385605022855:secret:test/credentials-13JdTI",
    "Name": "test/credentials",
    "DeletionDate": 1526198116.323
}
```

Deleting a Secret Value Using the AWS CLI

Note that AWS Secrets Manager does not immediately delete your secret, and instead schedules the secret for deletion in 30 days. During this time the secret is inaccessible, however it can be restored before the schedule deletion date as demonstrated in the following example:

```
> aws secretsmanager delete-secret --secret-id todobackend/credentials
{
    "ARN": "arn:aws:secretsmanager:us-
east-1:385605022855:secret:todobackend/credentials-f7AQlO",
    "Name": "todobackend/credentials",
    "DeletionDate": 1526285256.951
}
> aws secretsmanager get-secret-value --secret-id
todobackend/credentials
An error occurred (InvalidRequestException) when calling the
GetSecretValue operation: You can't perform this operation on the
secret because it was deleted.

> aws secretsmanager restore-secret --secret-id
todobackend/credentials
{
    "ARN": "arn:aws:secretsmanager:us-
east-1:385605022855:secret:todobackend/credentials-f7AQlO",
    "Name": "todobackend/credentials"
}

> aws secretsmanager get-secret-value --secret-id
todobackend/credentials \
    --query SecretString --output text
```

```
{
  "MYSQL_PASSWORD":"some-super-secret-password",
  "SECRET_KEY": "E2]eTfO~8Z5)&amp;OSlR-&amp;XQf=yA:B(`,p.B#R6d]a~X-
vf?%%/wY"
}
```

Restoring a Secret Value Using the AWS CLI

You can see that after deleting the secret you are unable to access the secret, however once you restore the secret using the `aws secretsmanager restore-secret` command, you are once again able to access your secret.

Injecting secrets at container startup

One challenge with secrets management in Docker is passing secrets to your containers in a secure fashion.

The following diagram illustrates a somewhat naive but understandable approach that uses environment variables to inject your secrets directly as plaintext values, which is the approach we took in Chapter 8:

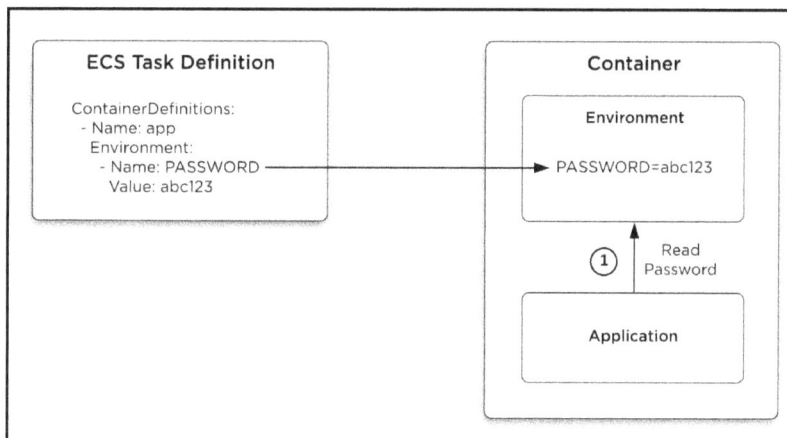

Injecting passwords via environment variables

This approach is simple to configure and understand, however it is not considered best practice from a security perspective. When you take such an approach, you can view your credentials in plaintext by inspecting the ECS task definition, and if you run `docker inspect` commands on your ECS container instances, you can also view your credentials in plaintext. You may also inadvertently end up logging your secrets using this approach, which could be shared inadvertently with unauthorized third parties, so clearly this approach is not considered good practice.

An alternative approach that is considered much more secure is to store your secrets in a secure credential store, and have your application retrieve the secret when it starts up or whenever it requires the secret. AWS Secrets Manager is an example of a secure credential store that provides such a capability, and obviously this is the solution we will focus on in this chapter.

When you store your secrets in a secure credential store such as AWS Secrets Manager, you have two general approaches to obtain your secrets as illustrated in the following diagram:

- **Application injects secrets:** With this approach, your applications include support for directly interfacing with your credential store. Here, your application may look for a secret with a static name, or may have the secret name injecting via an environment variable. In the example of AWS Secrets Manager, this means your application code would use the AWS SDK to make the appropriate API calls to the AWS Secrets Manager to retrieve secret values.
- **Entrypoint script injects secrets:** With this approach, you configure the name of the secret(s) that your application requires as a standard environment variable, with an entrypoint script that runs before your application, retrieving the secret(s) from AWS Secrets Manager and injecting them into the internal container environment as environment variables. Although this might sound like a similar approach to configuring environment variables at an ECS task definition level, the difference is that this happens inside the container after externally configured environment variables are applied, meaning they are not exposed to the ECS console or `docker inspect` commands:

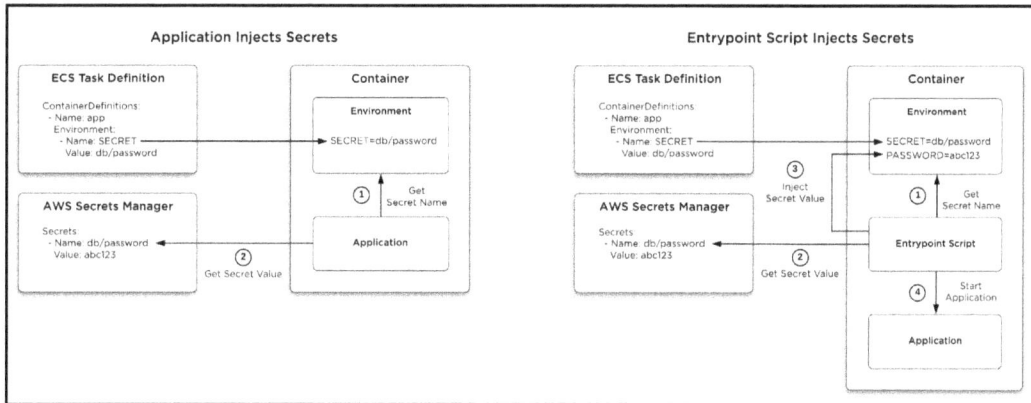

Using a Credential Store to Store and Retrieve Passwords

The approach where your application injects secrets is generally considered the best approach from a security perspective, however it does require the application to explicitly support interacting with the credential store that you use, meaning additional development and cost is required to support such an approach.

The entrypoint script approach is considered less secure because you are exposing a secret outside the application, however the visibility of the secret is only within the container itself and is not visible externally. Using an entrypoint script does provide the benefit of not requiring applications to specifically support interacting with a credential store, making it a much more universal solution for providing secrets at runtime in a manner that is secure enough for most organizations, and this is the approach we will now focus on.

Creating an entrypoint script

The Docker `ENTRYPOINT` directive configures the very first command or script that is executed by the container. When configured in conjunction with the `CMD` directive, the `ENTRYPOINT` command or script is executed, with the `CMD` commands passed as arguments to the entrypoint script. This establishes a very common pattern of an entrypoint performing initialization tasks such as injecting secrets into the environment, which then invokes the application based on the command arguments passed to the script.

The following example demonstrates creating an entrypoint script for the todobackend sample application, that you should place in the root of the todobackend repository:

```
> pwd
/Users/jmenga/Source/docker-in-aws/todobackend
> touch entrypoint.sh
> tree -L 1
.
├── Dockerfile
├── Makefile
├── docker-compose.yml
├── entrypoint.sh
└── src

1 directory, 4 files
```

Creating an Entrypoint Script in the Todobackend Repository

The following example shows the content of the entrypoint script, which injects secrets from AWS Secrets Manager into the environment:

```
#!/bin/bash
set -e -o pipefail

# Inject AWS Secrets Manager Secrets
# Read space delimited list of secret names from SECRETS environment
variable
echo "Processing secrets [${SECRETS}]..."
read -r -a secrets <<< "$SECRETS"
for secret in "${secrets[@]}"
do
  vars=$(aws secretsmanager get-secret-value --secret-id $secret \
    --query SecretString --output text \
    | jq -r 'to_entries[] | "export \(.key)='\''\(.value)'\''"')
  eval "$vars"
done

# Run application
exec "$@"
```

Defining an Entrypoint Script that Injects Secrets into the Environment

In the preceding example, an array called `secrets` is created from the `SECRETS` environment variable, which is expected to include the names of one or more secrets in a space delimited format that should be processed. For example, you could process two secrets called `db/credentials` and `app/credentials` by setting the `SECRETS` environment variable as demonstrated in the example:

```
> export SECRETS="db/credentials app/credentials"
```

Defining Multiple Secrets

Referring back to the preceding example, the script then loops through each secret in the array, using the `aws secretsmanager get-secret-value` command to obtain the `SecretString` value of each secret, and then passes each value to the `jq` utility to parse the `SecretString` value as a JSON object and generate a shell expression that will export each secret key and value as an environment variable. Note that the `jq` expression has a lot of escaping involved to ensure special characters are interpreted literally, but the essence of this expression is to output `export key='value'` for each key/value pair in the credential.

To understand this further, you can run the same command at the command line using the `todobackend/credentials` secret you created earlier:

```
> aws secretsmanager get-secret-value --secret-id
todobackend/credentials \
    --query SecretString --output text \
    | jq -r 'to_entries[] | "export \(.key)='\''\(.value)'\''"'
export MYSQL_PASSWORD='some-super-secret-password'
export SECRET_KEY='E2]eTfO~8Z5)&amp;0SlR-&amp;XQf=yA:B(`,p.B#R6d]a~X-
vf?%%/wY'
```

Generating a Shell Expression to Export Secrets into the Environment

In the preceding example, notice that the output is the individual `export` commands you would execute to inject the secret key/value pairs into the environment. Each environment variable value is also single quoted, to ensure bash treats all special characters as literal values.

Referring back to the previous example, the `eval $vars` statement in the for loop simply evaluates the generated export statements as shell commands, which results in each key/value pair being injected into the local environment.

> **TIP**
>
> Capturing the output of the `aws secretsmanager ...` command substitution in a separate variable ensures any errors that occur in this command substitution will be relayed back to your entrypoint script. You might be tempted to just run a single `eval $(aws secretsmanager ..)` statement in the for loop, however taking such an approach would mean if the `aws secretsmanager ...` command substitution exits with an error, your entrypoint script will not be aware of this error and will continue executing, which may lead to strange behavior for your application.

Once the loop is complete, the final `exec "$@"` statement hands off control to the arguments passed to the entrypoint script—these arguments are represented by the special `$@` shell variable. For example, if your entrypoint script was invoked as `entrypoint python3 manage.py migrate --noinput`, then the `$@` shell variable would hold the arguments `python3 manage.py migrate --noinput` and the final `exec` command would launch and hand off control to the `python3 manage.py migrate --noinput` command.

> **TIP**
>
> It is very important to use the `exec "$@"` approach in your container entrypoint scripts, as `exec` ensures that the parent process of your container becomes whatever the command arguments that were passed to the entrypoint. If you didn't use `exec` and just ran the commands, the parent bash process that is running the script would remain the parent process of your container, and the bash process (rather than your application) would received subsequent signals to terminate the container when the container is stopped. You typically want your application to receive these signals, so that your application can gracefully clean up before terminating.

Adding an entrypoint script to a Dockerfile

Now that you have established an entrypoint script in your todobackend repository, you need to add this script to the existing Dockerfile and ensure the script is specified as the entrypoint using the `ENTRYPOINT` directive:

```
...
...
# Release stage
FROM alpine
LABEL=todobackend
```

```
# Install operating system dependencies
RUN apk add --no-cache python3 mariadb-client bash curl bats jq && \
    pip3 --no-cache-dir install awscli

# Create app user
RUN addgroup -g 1000 app && \
    adduser -u 1000 -G app -D app

# Copy and install application source and pre-built dependencies
COPY --from=test --chown=app:app /build /build
COPY --from=test --chown=app:app /app /app
RUN pip3 install -r /build/requirements.txt -f /build --no-index --no-cache-dir
RUN rm -rf /build

# Create public volume
RUN mkdir /public
RUN chown app:app /public
VOLUME /public

# Entrypoint script
COPY entrypoint.sh /usr/bin/entrypoint
RUN chmod +x /usr/bin/entrypoint
ENTRYPOINT ["/usr/bin/entrypoint"]

# Set working directory and application user
WORKDIR /app
USER app
```

Add an Entrypoint Script to a Dockerfile

In the preceding example, notice that you modify the first RUN directive to ensure the AWS CLI is installed, by adding the highlighted pip3 --no-cache install awscli command.

Finally, you copy the entrypoint script to /usr/bin/entrypoint, ensure the script has the executable flag set, and specify the script as the entrypoint for the image. Note that you must configure the ENTRYPOINT directive in the exec style format, to ensure the command that you run in your container is passed as arguments to the entrypoint script (see first note at https://docs.docker.com/engine/reference/builder/#cmd).

With your Dockerfile now updated, you need to commit your changes, rebuild and publish your Docker image changes as demonstrated in the following example:

```
> git add -A
> git commit -a -m "Add entrypoint script"
[master 5fdbe62] Add entrypoint script
 4 files changed, 31 insertions(+), 7 deletions(-)
 create mode 100644 entrypoint.sh
> export AWS_PROFILE=docker-in-aws
> make login
$(aws ecr get-login --no-include-email)
Login Succeeded
> make test && make release
docker-compose build --pull release
Building release
Step 1/28 : FROM alpine AS test
latest: Pulling from library/alpine
...
...
docker-compose run app bats acceptance.bats
Starting todobackend_db_1 ... done
Processing secrets []...
1..4
ok 1 todobackend root
ok 2 todo items returns empty list
ok 3 create todo item
ok 4 delete todo item
App running at http://localhost:32784
> make publish
docker-compose push release
Pushing release (385605022855.dkr.ecr.us-east-1.amazonaws.com/docker-
in-aws/todobackend:latest)...
The push refers to repository [385605022855.dkr.ecr.us-
east-1.amazonaws.com/docker-in-aws/todobackend]
fdc98d6948f6: Pushed
9f33f154b3fa: Pushed
d8aedb2407c9: Pushed
f778da37eed6: Pushed
05e5971d2995: Pushed
4932bb9f39a5: Pushed
fa63544c9f7e: Pushed
fd3b38ee8bd6: Pushed
cd7100a72410: Layer already exists
latest: digest:
sha256:5d456c61dd23728ec79c281fe5a3c700370382812e75931b45f0f5dd1a8fc15
0 size: 2201
Pushing app (385605022855.dkr.ecr.us-east-1.amazonaws.com/docker-in-
aws/todobackend:5fdbe62)...
```

```
The push refers to repository [385605022855.dkr.ecr.us-
east-1.amazonaws.com/docker-in-aws/todobackend]
fdc98d6948f6: Layer already exists
9f33f154b3fa: Layer already exists
d8aedb2407c9: Layer already exists
f778da37eed6: Layer already exists
05e5971d2995: Layer already exists
4932bb9f39a5: Layer already exists
fa63544c9f7e: Layer already exists
fd3b38ee8bd6: Layer already exists
cd7100a72410: Layer already exists
34d86eb: digest:
sha256:5d456c61dd23728ec79c281fe5a3c700370382812e75931b45f0f5dd1a8fc15
0 size: 2201
```

Publishing the Updated Docker Image

In the preceding example, when the Docker image is published, take note of the Docker tag for the app service (this is `5fdbe62` in my example, the actual hash will vary for you), which you recall from Chapter 1, specifies the Git commit hash of your source code repository. You will need this tag later on in this chapter to ensure you can deploy your changes to your todobackend application running in AWS.

Provisioning secrets using CloudFormation

You have created a secret in AWS Secrets Manager and have added support for injecting secrets securely into your containers using an entrypoint script. Recall that the entrypoint script looks for an environment variable called `SECRETS`, and the `ApplicationTaskDefinition` and `MigrateTaskDefinition` resources in your CloudFormation template for the todobackend stack are currently injecting the application database directly. In order to support using secrets in your stack, you need to configure your ECS task definitions to include the `SECRETS` environment variable, configured with the name(s) of your secrets, and you also need to ensure your container have appropriate IAM permissions to retrieve and decrypt your secrets.

Another consideration is how the password for your `ApplicationDatabase` resource is configured—this is currently configured to use a password input via stack parameters; however, your database now needs to be able to somehow obtain its password from your newly created secret.

Configuring ECS task definitions to use secrets

Let's first deal with reconfiguring the ECS task definitions to use your newly created secret. Your containers now include an entrypoint script that will retrieve secrets from AWS Secrets Manager, and before you update the various ECS task definitions to import the names of your secrets as an environment variable, you need to ensure your containers have the correct permissions to do this. Although you could add such permissions to the ECS container instance role that is applied at an EC2 instance level, a more secure approach is to create specific IAM roles that you can assign to your containers, given you might be sharing your ECS clusters with multiple applications and don't want to grant access to your secrets from any container that runs on the cluster.

ECS includes a feature called IAM roles for tasks (`https://docs.aws.amazon.com/ AmazonECS/latest/developerguide/task-iam-roles.html`), which allows you to grant IAM permissions at an ECS task definition level, and is useful in our scenario of wanting to only grant access to the todobackend secret to the todobackend application. The following example demonstrates creating an IAM role that grants these privileges:

```
...
...
Resources:
  ...
  ...
  ApplicationTaskRole:
    Type: AWS::IAM::Role
    Properties:
      AssumeRolePolicyDocument:
        Version: "2012-10-17"
        Statement:
        - Effect: Allow
          Principal:
            Service: ecs-tasks.amazonaws.com
          Action:
            - sts:AssumeRole
      Policies:
        - PolicyName: SecretsManagerPermissions
          PolicyDocument:
            Version: "2012-10-17"
            Statement:
            - Sid: GetSecrets
              Effect: Allow
```

```
                Action:
                - secretsmanager:GetSecretValue
                Resource: !Sub
arn:aws:secretsmanager:${AWS::Region}:${AWS::AccountId}:secret:todobac
kend/*
              - Sid: DecryptSecrets
                Effect: Allow
                Action:
                - kms:Decrypt
                Resource: !ImportValue secrets-key
      ApplicationTaskDefinition:
        Type: AWS::ECS::TaskDefinition
...
...
```

Creating an IAM Task Role

In the preceding example, you create a new resource called `ApplicationTaskRole`, which includes an `AssumeRolePolicyDocument` property that defines the trusted entities that can assume the role. Notice that the principal here is the `ecs-tasks.amazonaws.com` service, which is the service context that your containers assume when they attempt to access AWS resources using permissions granted by the IAM role. The role includes a policy that grants the permission `secretsmanager:GetSecretValue`, which as you might expect allows you to retrieve secret values, and this permission is constrained to the ARN of all secrets that are named with a prefix of `todobackend/`. If you refer back to the previous example when you created a test secret via the AWS CLI, you can see that the ARN of the secret includes a random value at the end of the ARN, hence you need to use wildcards in your ARN to ensure you have permissions regardless of this random suffix. Note that the role also includes the `Decrypt` permission on the `secrets-key` KMS key, and you use the `!ImportValue` or `Fn::ImportValue` intrinsic function to import the ARN of the KMS key you exported back in the very first example.

With the `ApplicationTaskRole` resource in place, the following example demonstrates reconfiguring the `ApplicationTaskDefinition` and `MigrateTaskDefinition` resources in the `stack.yml` file located in the todobackend-aws repository:

```
Parameters:
  ...
  ...
  ApplicationSubnets:
    Type: List<AWS::EC2::Subnet::Id>
    Description: Target subnets for EC2 instances
```

```
    # The DatabasePassword parameter has been removed
    VpcId:
      Type: AWS::EC2::VPC::Id
      Description: Target VPC
    ...
    ...

Resources:
  ...
  ...
  MigrateTaskDefinition:
    Type: AWS::ECS::TaskDefinition
    Properties:
      Family: todobackend-migrate
      TaskRoleArn: !Sub ${ApplicationTaskRole.Arn}
      ContainerDefinitions:
        - Name: migrate
          Image: !Sub
${AWS::AccountId}.dkr.ecr.${AWS::Region}.amazonaws.com/docker-in-
aws/todobackend:${ApplicationImageTag}
          MemoryReservation: 5
          Cpu: 5
          Environment:
            - Name: DJANGO_SETTINGS_MODULE
              Value: todobackend.settings_release
            - Name: MYSQL_HOST
              Value: !Sub ${ApplicationDatabase.Endpoint.Address}
            - Name: MYSQL_USER
              Value: todobackend
            - Name: MYSQL_DATABASE
              Value: todobackend
            # The MYSQL_PASSWORD variable has been removed
            - Name: SECRETS
              Value: todobackend/credentials
            - Name: AWS_DEFAULT_REGION
              Value: !Ref AWS::Region
  ...
  ...
  ApplicationTaskDefinition:
    Type: AWS::ECS::TaskDefinition
    Properties:
      Family: todobackend
      TaskRoleArn: !Sub ${ApplicationTaskRole.Arn}
      Volumes:
        - Name: public
      ContainerDefinitions:
        - Name: todobackend
          Image: !Sub
```

```
${AWS::AccountId}.dkr.ecr.${AWS::Region}.amazonaws.com/docker-in-
aws/todobackend:${ApplicationImageTag}
          MemoryReservation: 395
          Cpu: 245
          MountPoints:
            - SourceVolume: public
              ContainerPath: /public
          Environment:
            - Name: DJANGO_SETTINGS_MODULE
              Value: todobackend.settings_release
            - Name: MYSQL_HOST
              Value: !Sub ${ApplicationDatabase.Endpoint.Address}
            - Name: MYSQL_USER
              Value: todobackend
            - Name: MYSQL_DATABASE
              Value: todobackend
          # The MYSQL_PASSWORD and SECRET_KEY variables have been
removed
            - Name: SECRETS
              Value: todobackend/credentials
            - Name: AWS_DEFAULT_REGION
              Value: !Ref AWS::Region
  . . .
  . . .
```

Configuring ECS Task Definitions to use Secrets

In the preceding example, you configure each task definition to use an IAM task role via the `TaskRoleArn` property, which references the `ApplicationTaskRole` resource you created in the previous example. You next add the `SECRETS` environment variable that the new entrypoint script in your Docker image expects, and remove the previous `MYSQL_PASSWORD` and `SECRET_KEY` variables that are now retrieved from the AWS Secrets Manager service. Notice that you need to include an environment variable called `AWS_DEFAULT_REGION`, as this is required by the AWS CLI to determine which region you are located in.

Because you are no longer injecting a database password into your stack as a parameter, you need to also update the `dev.cfg` file in the todobackend-aws repository, and also specify the updated Docker image tag that you published back in the earlier example:

```
ApplicationDesiredCount=1
ApplicationImageId=ami-ec957491
ApplicationImageTag=5fdbe62
ApplicationSubnets=subnet-a5d3ecee,subnet-324e246f
VpcId=vpc-f8233a80
```

Updating input parameters

In the preceding example, the `DatabasePassword=my-super-secret-password` line has been removed, and the value of the `ApplicationImageTag` parameter has been updated, referencing the commit hash that is tagged on your newly updated Docker image.

Exposing secrets to other resources

You have updated your ECS task definitions such that your application containers will now pull secrets from AWS Secrets Manager and inject them as environment variables. This works fine for your Docker images, as you have full control over how your images behave and can add features such as entrypoint scripts to inject secrets appropriately. For other resources that depend on these secrets, you don't have such a capability—for example, the `ApplicationDatabase` resource in your stack defines an RDS instance that as of the time of writing, does not include native support for AWS Secrets Manager.

One solution to this problem is to create a CloudFormation custom resource, whose job is to query the AWS Secrets Manager service and return the secret value associated with a given secret. Because custom resources can have data properties attached to them, you can then reference these properties in other resources, providing a simple mechanism to inject your secrets into any CloudFormation resource that does not natively support AWS Secrets Manager. If you are wondering about the security of such an approach, the CloudFormation custom resource response specification (`https://docs.aws.amazon.com/AWSCloudFormation/latest/UserGuide/crpg-ref-responses.html`) includes a property called `NoEcho`, which instructs CloudFormation to not expose data properties via the console or in logging information. By setting this property, you can therefore ensure you secrets are not inadvertently exposed by querying the CloudFormation API or by reviewing CloudFormation logs.

Creating a Secrets Manager Lambda function

The following example demonstrates adding a Lambda function resource to your CloudFormation stack that queries the AWS Secrets Manager service and returns a secret value given a target secret name and target key within the key/value pairs within the secret value:

```
...
...
Resources:
  SecretsManager:
    Type: AWS::Lambda::Function
    DependsOn:
    - SecretsManagerLogGroup
    Properties:
      FunctionName: !Sub ${AWS::StackName}-secretsManager
      Description: !Sub ${AWS::StackName} Secrets Manager
      Handler: index.handler
      MemorySize: 128
      Runtime: python3.6
      Timeout: 300
      Role: !Sub ${SecretsManagerRole.Arn}
      Code:
        ZipFile: |
          import cfnresponse, json, sys, os
          import boto3

          client = boto3.client('secretsmanager')

          def handler(event, context):
            sys.stdout = sys.__stdout__
            try:
              print("Received event %s" % event)
              if event['RequestType'] == 'Delete':
                cfnresponse.send(event, context, cfnresponse.SUCCESS,
{}, event['PhysicalResourceId'])
                return
              secret = client.get_secret_value(
                SecretId=event['ResourceProperties']['SecretId'],
              )
              credentials = json.loads(secret['SecretString'])
              # Suppress logging output to ensure credential values
are kept secure
              with open(os.devnull, "w") as devnull:
                sys.stdout = devnull
                cfnresponse.send(
                  event,
                  context,
```

```
                        cfnresponse.SUCCESS,
                        credentials, # This dictionary will be exposed to
CloudFormation resources
                        secret['VersionId'], # Physical ID of the custom
resource
                        noEcho=True
                    )
                except Exception as e:
                    print("A failure occurred with exception %s" % e)
                    cfnresponse.send(event, context, cfnresponse.FAILED, {})
  SecretsManagerRole:
    Type: AWS::IAM::Role
    Properties:
      AssumeRolePolicyDocument:
        Version: "2012-10-17"
        Statement:
        - Effect: Allow
          Principal:
            Service: lambda.amazonaws.com
          Action:
            - sts:AssumeRole
      Policies:
        - PolicyName: SecretsManagerPermissions
          PolicyDocument:
            Version: "2012-10-17"
            Statement:
            - Sid: GetSecrets
              Effect: Allow
              Action:
              - secretsmanager:GetSecretValue
              Resource: !Sub
arn:aws:secretsmanager:${AWS::Region}:${AWS::AccountId}:secret:todobac
kend/*
            - Sid: DecryptSecrets
              Effect: Allow
              Action:
              - kms:Decrypt
              Resource: !ImportValue secrets-key
            - Sid: ManageLambdaLogs
              Effect: Allow
              Action:
              - logs:CreateLogStream
              - logs:PutLogEvents
              Resource: !Sub ${SecretsManagerLogGroup.Arn}
```

```
SecretsManagerLogGroup:
 Type: AWS::Logs::LogGroup
 Properties:
 LogGroupName: !Sub /aws/lambda/${AWS::StackName}-secretsManager
 RetentionInDays: 7
  . . .
  . . .
```

Adding a Secrets Manager CloudFormation Custom Resource Function

The configuring of the preceding example is very similar to the configuration you performed back in Chapter 8, when you created the `EcsTaskRunner` custom resource function. Here, you create a `SecretsManager` Lambda function with an associated `SecretsManagerRole` IAM role that grants the ability to retrieve and decrypt secrets from AWS Secrets Manager in a similar fashion to the `ApplicationTaskRole` created earlier, along with a `SecretsManagerLogGroup` resource to collect logs from the Lambda function.

The function code is simpler than the ECS task runner code, and expects a single property called `SecretId` to be passed to the custom resource, which specifies the ID or name of the secret. The function obtains the secret from the AWS Secrets Manager, and then loads the secret key/value pairs as a JSON object into a variable called `credentials` using the `json.loads` method. The function then returns the `credentials` variable to CloudFormation, which means each credential can be access by other resources in your stack. Notice that you use a `with` statement to ensure the response data that is printed by the `cfnresponse.send` method is suppressed by setting the `sys.stdout` property to `/dev/null`, given the response data includes secret values that you don't want to expose in plaintext. This approach does require some care, and you need to restore the `sys.stdout` property to its default state (as represented by the `sys.__stdout__` property) at the beginning of the `handler` method, as your Lambda function runtime may be cached across multiple invocations.

The custom resource function code could be extended to also provision secrets into AWS Secrets Manager. For example, you could take as an input the KMS encrypted value of a intended secret value or even generate a random secret value, and then provision and expose this credential to other resources.

Creating a secrets custom resource

Now that you have a Lambda function in place for your custom resource, you can create the actual custom resource that will provide access to secrets stored in AWS Secrets Manager. The following example demonstrates adding a custom resource for the **todobackend/credentials** secret that you created earlier in this chapter, which is then accessed from your `ApplicationDatabase` resource:

```
...
...
Resources:
  Secrets:
    Type: AWS::CloudFormation::CustomResource
    Properties:
      ServiceToken: !Sub ${SecretsManager.Arn}
      SecretId: todobackend/credentials
  SecretsManager:
    Type: AWS::Lambda::FunctionResources:
  ...
  ...
  ApplicationDatabase:
    Type: AWS::RDS::DBInstance
    Properties:
      Engine: MySQL
      EngineVersion: 5.7
      DBInstanceClass: db.t2.micro
      AllocatedStorage: 10
      StorageType: gp2
      MasterUsername: todobackend
      MasterUserPassword: !Sub ${Secrets.MYSQL_PASSWORD}
  ...
  ...
```

Adding a Secrets Manager Custom Resource

In the preceding example, you create a custom resource called `Secrets` which references the `SecretsManager` function via the `ServiceToken` property, and then passes the name of the credential to retrieve via the `SecretId` property. The `MasterUserPassword` property on the existing `ApplicationDatabase` resource is then updated to reference the `MYSQL_PASSWORD` key that is accessible via the `Secrets` resource, which returns the correct password value stored in the **todobackend/credentials** secret.

Deploying secrets to AWS

At this point, you are ready to deploy your changes to your CloudFormation stack, which you can do using the `aws cloudformation deploy` command we have used throughout the past few chapters:

```
> aws cloudformation deploy --template-file stack.yml \
    --stack-name todobackend --parameter-overrides $(cat dev.cfg) \
    --capabilities CAPABILITY_NAMED_IAM

Waiting for changeset to be created..
Waiting for stack create/update to complete
Successfully created/updated stack - todobackend
```

Deploying CloudFormation stack changes

The deployment will affect a number of resources as follows:

- The resources supporting the custom resource will first be created, along with changes to the ECS task definitions being applied.
- The custom resource called `Secrets` will be created, which once created will expose the key/value pairs of the **todobackend/credentials** secret to other CloudFormation resources.
- The `ApplicationDatabase` resource will be updated, with the `MasterPassword` property updated based upon the value of the `MYSQL_PASSWORD` variable in the **todobackend/credentials** secret.
- The `MigrateTask` custom resource will be updated given the changes to the associated `MigrateTaskDefinition`, and run a new task that uses the entrypoint script in the updated todobackend image to export each of the key/value pairs in the **todobackend/credentials** secret into the environment, which includes the `MYSQL_PASSWORD` variable required for accessing the application database.
- The `ApplicationService` resource will be updated given the changes to the associated `ApplicationTaskDefinition`, and similar to the `MigrateTask` each application instance will now inject the environment variables associated with the **todobackend/credentials** secret upon startup. The update will trigger your a rolling deployment of the `ApplicationService`, which will bring the new version of your application into service, and then drain and remove the old version of your application without causing any outages.

Assuming the deployment is successful, you should be able to verify your application is still working successfully, and that you can list, add and remove todo items.

You should also verify that your `SecretsManagerFunction` resource is not logging the plaintext values of your secrets—the following screenshot shows the log output from this function, and you can see does suppress logging of the success response that is sent back to CloudFormation:

Viewing Log Output from the Secrets Manager Function

Summary

Secrets management is a challenge for the ephemeral nature of Docker applications, where the notion of preconfigured long-running servers with credentials stored in a configuration file is no longer an option, and injecting passwords directly as externally configured environment variables is considered a bad security practice. This requires a secrets management solution where your applications can dynamically fetch secrets from a secure credential store, and in this chapter you successfully implemented such a solution using the AWS Secrets Manager and KMS services.

You learned how to create a KMS key, which encrypts and decrypts confidential information, and is used by AWS Secrets Manager to ensure the privacy and confidentiality of secrets it stores. You next were introduced to the AWS Secrets Manager and learned how to create secrets using both the AWS console and AWS CLI. You learned how you can store multiple key/value pairs in your secrets, and were introduced to features such as deletion protection, where AWS Secrets Manager allows you to restore a previously deleted secret for up to 30 days.

With a credential store in place for your sample application, you learned how you can use entrypoint scripts in your containers to dynamically fetch and inject secret values at container startup, using a simple bash script in conjunction with the AWS CLI to inject one or more secret values as variables into your internal container environment. Although this approach is considered less secure than your applications fetching secrets directly, it does have the advantage that it can be applied to any application that supports environment variables for configuration, making it a much more universal solution.

After publishing updated Docker images for your application, you updated your ECS task definitions to inject the names of the secrets each of your containers should retrieve, and then created a simple custom resource that is able to expose your secrets to other types of AWS resources that don't support AWS Secrets Manager natively, and don't have mechanisms such as container entrypoint scripts to retrieve secrets. You ensured this custom resource was configured such that it does not disclose your credentials via logs or other forms of operational events, and updated your application database resource to retrieve the database password for the application via this custom resource.

With a secrets management solution in place, you have addressed a core security concern from previous chapters, and in the next chapter, you will learn how you can address another security concern for your applications, which is to be able to independently isolate network access and apply network access rules on a per container or ECS task definition basis.

Questions

1. True/False: The KMS service requires you to supply your own private key information.
2. What feature of KMS allows you to specify a logical name for your key, rather than the UUID-based identifier of the key?
3. You want to avoid manually configuring the ARN of a KMS key that you use in multiple CloudFormation stacks. Assuming you defined the KMS key in a separate CloudFormation stack, what CloudFormation feature can you use to solve this problem?
4. True/False: When you delete a secret from AWS Secrets Manager you can never recover the secret.
5. Which tools would you typically use in an entrypoint script to retrieve a secret from AWS Secrets Manager and transform the key/value pairs in the secret to be suitable for exporting to the container environment?
6. You receive an error in a container entrypoint script indicating you do not have sufficient permissions to access a secret. You check the IAM role and confirm it has a single permission `secretsmanager:GetSecretValue` allowed for the secret. What other permission do you need to grant to resolve this issue?
7. Which CloudFormation custom resource property should you set when dealing with sensitive data that should not be exposed as plaintext values?
8. You receive an error "**You must configure a region**" in a container entrypoint script that accesses AWS resources. What environment variable should you add to your container?

Further reading

You can check the following links for more information about what the topics covered in this chapter:

- CloudFormation KMS Key Resource Reference: `https://docs.aws.amazon.com/AWSCloudFormation/latest/UserGuide/aws-resource-kms-key.html`
- CloudFormation KMS Alias Resource Reference: `https://docs.aws.amazon.com/AWSCloudFormation/latest/UserGuide/aws-resource-kms-alias.html`
- AWS KMS Developer Guide: `https://docs.aws.amazon.com/kms/latest/developerguide/overview.html`
- AWS CLI KMS Reference: `https://docs.aws.amazon.com/cli/latest/reference/kms/index.html`
- AWS Secrets Manager User Guide: `https://docs.aws.amazon.com/secretsmanager/latest/userguide/intro.html`
- AWS CLI Secrets Manager Reference: `https://docs.aws.amazon.com/cli/latest/reference/secretsmanager/index.html`
- AWS Python SDK Secrets Manager Reference: `http://boto3.readthedocs.io/en/latest/reference/services/secretsmanager.html`
- CloudFormation Exports: `https://docs.aws.amazon.com/AWSCloudFormation/latest/UserGuide/using-cfn-stack-exports.html`
- General Discussion on Docker Secrets Management: `https://github.com/moby/moby/issues/13490`

10
Isolating Network Access

A fundamental component of application security is the ability to control network access, both inbound to and outbound from your applications. AWS provides EC2 security groups that provide such a capability, which you can apply on a per-network-interface basis to your EC2 instances. This mechanism works well for traditional applications that are deployed to EC2 instances, but historically has not been as effective for container applications, which often operate on shared EC2 instances that communicate via a shared host interface on the EC2 instance. For ECS, the approach until recently has been that you have two applied security groups that accommodate the network security requirements of all the containers you need to support running on a given ECS container instance, which reduces the effectiveness of your security rules, and for applications with high security requirements is not acceptable. The only alternative to this approach up until recently was to build dedicated ECS clusters per application, ensuring application security requirements could be met but at the price of additional infrastructure and operational overhead.

AWS announced a feature referred to as ECS task networking in late 2017, which introduces the ability to dynamically allocate an elastic network interface (ENI) to your ECS container instances, which is reserved for use for a given ECS task. This allows you to create security groups that are specific to each of your container applications, and run these applications concurrently on the same ECS container instance without compromising security.

In this chapter, you will learn how to configure ECS task networking, which requires you to understand how ECS task networking works, configure ECS task definitions for task networking, and create and deploy ECS services that are linked to your task-networking-enabled ECS task definitions. When combined with the ECS task roles feature you configured in the previous chapter, this will enable you to build highly secure container application environments that enforce isolation and separation at both an IAM-permissions and network-security level.

The following topics will be covered:

- Understanding ECS task networking
- Configuring a NAT Gateway
- Configuring ECS task networking
- Deploying and testing ECS task networking

Technical requirements

The following lists the technical requirements to complete this chapter:

- Administrator access to an AWS account
- Local AWS profile configured as per instructions in Chapter 3
- AWS CLI 1.15.71 or higher
- Completed Chapter 9 and successfully deployed sample application to AWS

The following GitHub URL contains the code samples used in this chapter: `https://github.com/docker-in-aws/docker-in-aws/tree/master/ch10`.

Check out the following video to see the Code in Action:
`http://bit.ly/2MUBJfs`

Understanding ECS task networking

Under the hood, ECS task networking is actually quite a complex feature that relies on a number of Docker networking features and requires a detailed understanding of Docker networking. As someone who designs, builds, and deploys container environments in AWS using ECS, the good news is that you don't have to understand this level of detail, and really you just need a high-level understanding of how ECS task networking works. I will therefore provide a high-level overview of how ECS task networking works in this section, however, if you are interested in how ECS task networking works in greater detail, this blog post from AWS (`https://aws.amazon.com/blogs/compute/under-the-hood-task-networking-for-amazon-ecs/`) provides further information.

Docker bridge networking

To understand ECS task networking, it helps to have a picture of how Docker networking and the standard configuration of an ECS container works by default. By default, ECS task definitions are configured with the Docker bridge networking mode, which is illustrated in the following diagram:

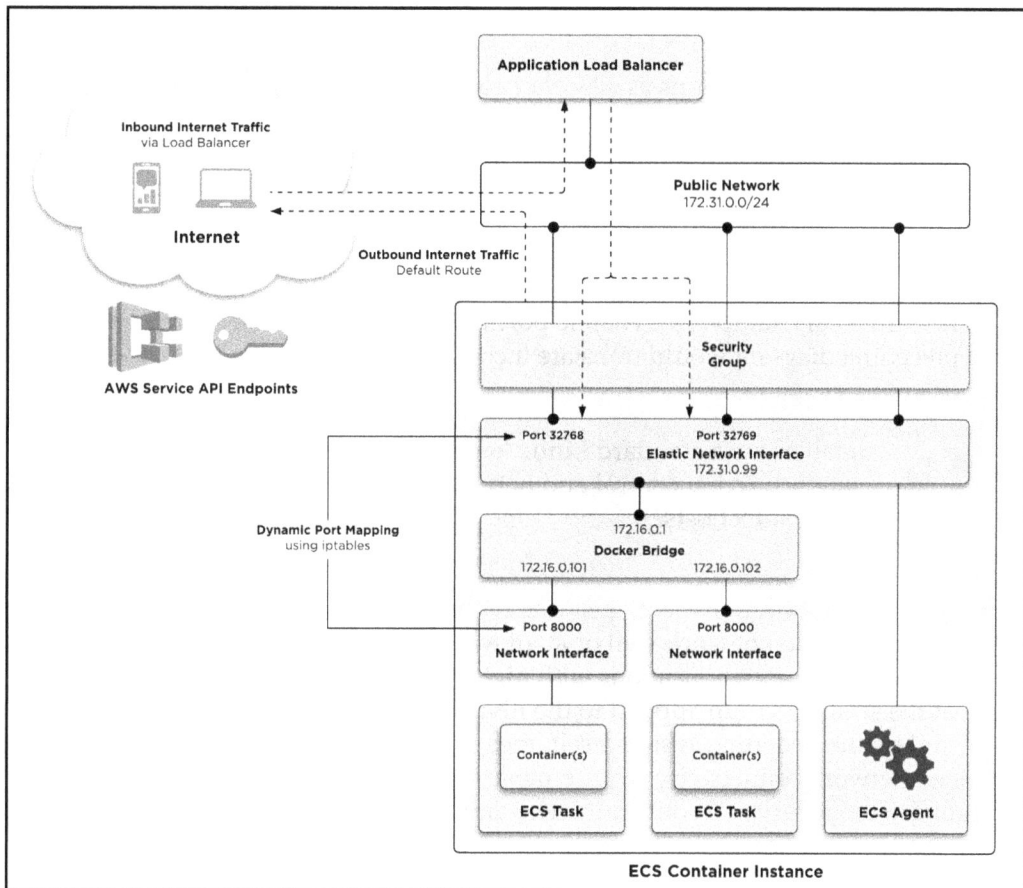

Docker bridge networking

In the preceding diagram, you can see that each ECS task has its own dedicated network interface, which is dynamically created by the Docker Engine when the ECS task container(s) are created. The Docker bridge interface is a Layer 2 networking component similar to an Ethernet switch that connects each of the Docker container network interfaces together within a network internal to the Docker Engine host.

Notice that each container has an IP address within the `172.16.0.x` subnet, whereas the external AWS public network and elastic network interface of the ECS container instance have IP addresses within the `172.31.0.x` subnet, and you can see that all container traffic routes through a single host network interface, which, in the case of an AWS EC2 instance, is the default elastic network interface allocated to the instance. An elastic network interface (ENI) is an EC2 resource that provides network connectivity to your VPC subnets, and is what you would consider the standard network interface that each of your EC2 instances uses.

The ECS agent, which also runs as a Docker container, is different from the other containers in that it operates in host-networking mode, meaning it uses the host operating system network interface (that is, the ENI) for its networking. Because the containers sit on a different IP network that is internal to the Docker Engine host, in order to provide network connectivity with the outside world, Docker configures iptables rules on the ENI, which translate all outbound network traffic to the elastic network interface IP address, and set up dynamic port-mapping rules for inbound network traffic. For example, a dynamic port-mapping rule for one of the containers in the preceding diagram would translate incoming traffic for `172.31.0.99:32768` to `172.16.0.101:8000`.

> iptables are a standard Linux kernel capability that provides network access control and network address translation features to your Linux hosts.

Although many applications work just fine with network address translation (NAT), some applications do not work well or at all with NAT, and using NAT can have a performance impact for applications with high volumes of network traffic. Notice also that the security group applied to the ENI is shared across all containers, the ECS agent, and by the operating system itself, meaning the security group must permit the combined network connectivity requirements of all of these components, which may compromise the security of your containers and ECS container instances.

It is possible to configure your ECS task definitions to operate in host-networking mode, meaning their network configuration would be similar to the ECS agent configuration, where no network address translation (NAT) is required. Host-networking mode has its own security implications and is generally not recommended for applications that want to avoid NAT or require network isolation—instead you should use ECS task networking for such requirements. Host networking should be used with care and only for ECS tasks that perform a system function, such as logging or monitoring a sidecar container.

ECS task networking

Now that you have a basic understanding of the default networking configuration for an ECS container instance and its associated containers, let's review how this picture changes when you configure ECS task networking. The following diagram illustrates how ECS task networking works at a high level:

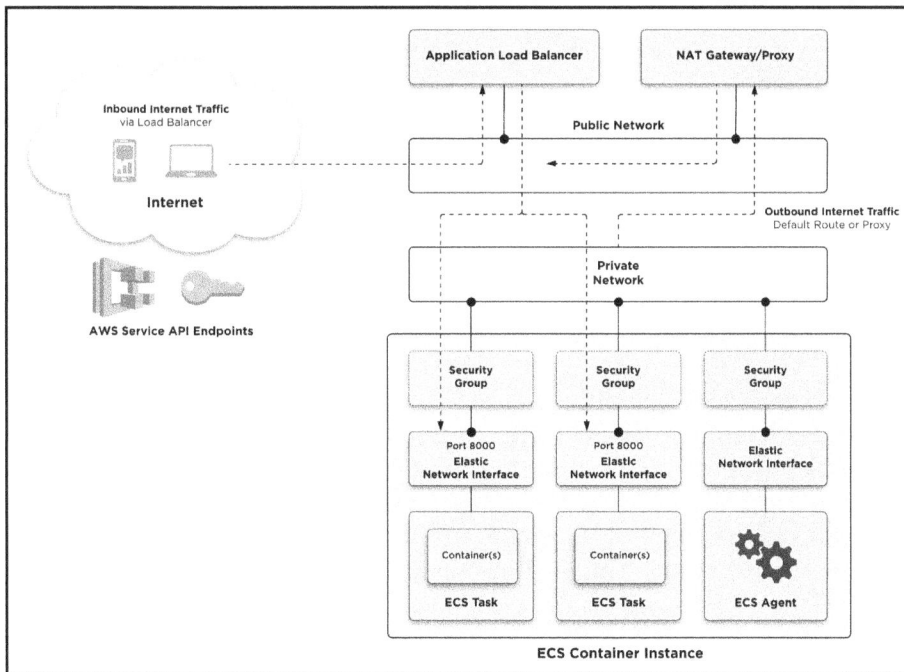

ECS task networking

In the preceding diagram, each ECS task is allocated and configured to use its own dedicated elastic network interface. This is quite different from the first diagram, where containers use an internal network interface that is dynamically created by Docker—instead, ECS is responsible for the dynamic creation of each ECS task elastic network interface. This is more complex for ECS, however comes with the advantage that your containers can be directly attached to your VPC subnets and can have their own independent security groups. This means your container network ports no longer require complicated features, such as dynamic port-mapping, that compromise both security and performance, with your container ports being exposed directly to the AWS networking environment and becoming directly accessible by your load balancers.

One point to note in the preceding diagram is the external networking configuration, which introduces the notion of a private subnet and public subnet. I have represented network connectivity in this manner because, at the time of writing, ECS task networking does not support allocation of public IP addresses to each dynamically created ENI, hence you do need an additional VPC network setup if your containers require internet connectivity. This setup involves creating either a NAT gateway or HTTP proxy on a public network, which your ECS tasks can then route internet traffic to. In the scenario of the current todobackend application, the entrypoint script introduced in Chapter 9 communicates with the AWS Secrets Manager API that is located on the internet, hence requires a network setup similar to that shown in the first diagram.

> The ECS agent does not have the limitation of being unable to assign a public IP address, given it uses the default EC2 instance ENI that is allocated to the instance on creation. So you could, for example in the preceding diagram, connect the default ENI used by the ECS agent to the public network or another network with internet connectivity.

As you can see by comparing both the previous diagrams, ECS task networking simplifies the internal networking configuration of your ECS container instances, making it look much like the traditional virtual machine networking model, if you imagine the ECS container instance is a bare-metal server and your containers are virtual machines. This comes with the benefit of greater performance and security, but at the expense of a more complicated network setup externally, where a NAT gateway or HTTP proxy configuration is required for outbound internet connectivity and ECS is responsible for dynamically attaching ENIs to your instances, which comes with its own limitations.

For example, the maximum number of ENIs that can be attached to a given EC2 instance varies depending on the EC2 instance type, and if you take a look at `https://docs.aws.amazon.com/AWSEC2/latest/UserGuide/using-eni.html#AvailableIpPerENI`, you can see that the free tier t2.micro instance type only supports a maximum of two ENIs, limiting the maximum number of ECS tasks you can run in the ECS task-networking mode to just one per instance (given one ENI will always be reserved for the host).

Configuring a NAT gateway

As you learned in the previous section, at the time of writing, ECS task networking does not support the assignment of public IP addresses, which means you must configure additional infrastructure to support any internet connectivity your application might require. Although the application can be accessed without outbound internet access via the application load balancers in your stack, the application container entrypoint script does need to communicate with the AWS Secrets Manager service on startup, which requires internet connectivity to communicate with the Secrets Manager API.

To provide this connectivity, there are two typical approaches you can adopt:

- **Configure a NAT Gateway**: This is an AWS-managed service that provides network address translation for outbound communications, enabling hosts and containers located on private subnets to access the internet.
- **Configure an HTTP Proxy**: This provides a forward proxy where applications configured with proxy support and forward HTTP, HTTPS, and FTP requests to your proxy.

I typically recommend the latter approach, because it provides you with the ability to restrict access to websites based upon DNS naming for both HTTP and HTTPS traffic (the latter depending on the capability of the HTTP proxy in use), whereas the NAT gateway only has the ability to restrict access based upon IP addresses. Setting up a proxy does however require more effort and incurs the operational overhead of managing an additional service, so in the interest of focusing on ECS task networking and keeping things simple, we will implement the NAT gateway approach in this chapter.

Configuring private subnets and route tables

In order to support NAT gateway with a typical routing configuration you would see in the real world, we need to first add a private subnet along with a private route table, which we will add as CloudFormation resources in your todobackend stack. The following example demonstrates performing this configuration in the `stack.yml` file located at the root of the todobackend-aws repository:

> In the interests of keeping this example simple, we are creating network resources in the todobackend application stack, however you typically would create network subnets and associated resources such as NAT gateways in a separate network-focused CloudFormation stack.

```
...
...
Resources:
  PrivateSubnet:
    Type: AWS::EC2::Subnet
    Properties:
      AvailabilityZone: !Sub ${AWS::Region}a
      CidrBlock: 172.31.96.0/20
      VpcId: !Ref VpcId
  PrivateRouteTable:
    Type: AWS::EC2::RouteTable
    Properties:
      VpcId: !Ref VpcId
  PrivateSubnetRouteTableAssociation:
    Type: AWS::EC2::SubnetRouteTableAssociation
    Properties:
      RouteTableId: !Ref PrivateRouteTable
      SubnetId: !Ref PrivateSubnet
...
...
```

Creating a private subnet and route table

In the preceding example, you create private subnet and route table resources, and then associate them via the `PrivateSubnetRouteTableAssociation` resource. This configuration means that all network traffic sent from the private subnet will be routed according to routes published in the private route table. Notice that you only specify a single subnet in availability zone A of your local AWS region—in a real-world scenario, you would typically configure at least two subnets in two availability zones for high availability. One other point to note is that you must ensure the `CidrBlock` configured for your subnets falls within the IP range configured for your VPC and is not allocated to any other subnets.

The following example demonstrates using the AWS CLI to determine the VPC IP range and to view existing subnet CIDR blocks:

```
> export AWS_PROFILE=docker-in-aws
> aws ec2 describe-vpcs --query Vpcs[].CidrBlock
[
    "172.31.0.0/16"
]
> aws ec2 describe-subnets --query Subnets[].CidrBlock
[
    "172.31.16.0/20",
    "172.31.80.0/20",
    "172.31.48.0/20",
    "172.31.64.0/20",
    "172.31.32.0/20",
    "172.31.0.0/20"
]
```

Querying VPC and subnet CIDR blocks

In the preceding example, you can see that the default VPC has been configured with a CIDR block of `172.31.0.0/16`, and you can also see the existing CIDR blocks that have been allocated to the default subnets created in the default VPC. If you refer back to the first example, you can see that we have chosen the next `/20` subnet in this block (`172.31.96.0/20`) for the newly defined private subnet.

Configuring NAT gateways

With a private routing configuration in place, you can now configure a NAT gateway and other supporting resources.

A NAT gateway requires an elastic IP address, which is the fixed public IP address that outbound traffic traversing the NAT gateway will appear to be sourced from, and must be installed on a public subnet that has internet connectivity.

The following example demonstrates configuring a NAT gateway along with an associated elastic IP address:

```
...
...
Resources:
  NatGateway:
    Type: AWS::EC2::NatGateway
    Properties:
      AllocationId: !Sub ${ElasticIP.AllocationId}
      SubnetId:
        Fn::Select:
          - 0
          - !Ref ApplicationSubnets
  ElasticIP:
    Type: AWS::EC2::EIP
    Properties:
      Domain: vpc
...
...
```

Configuring a NAT gateway

In the preceding example, you create an elastic IP address that is allocated for use with VPCs, and then link the allocated IP address to the NAT gateway via the `AllocationId` property.

> Elastic IP addresses are somewhat interesting from a billing perspective, in that AWS does not charge you for them as long as you are actively using them. If you create Elastic IP addresses but don't associate them with an EC2 instance or a NAT gateway, then AWS will charge you for them. See https://aws.amazon.com/premiumsupport/knowledge-center/elastic-ip-charges/ for more details on how billing works for Elastic IP addresses.

Note the use of the `Fn::Select` intrinsic function when specifying `SubnetId`, and it is important to understand that the subnet must be in the same availability zone as the subnet and route table resources that will be linked to the NAT gateway. In our use cases, this is availability zone A and the `ApplicationSubnets` input includes two subnet IDs that reside in availability zones A and B, respectively, hence you select the first zero-indexed subnet ID. Note you can verify the availability zone of your subnets by using the `aws ec2 describe-subnets` command demonstrated in the following example:

```
> cat dev.cfg
ApplicationDesiredCount=1
ApplicationImageId=ami-ec957491
ApplicationImageTag=5fdbe62
ApplicationSubnets=subnet-a5d3ecee,subnet-324e246f
VpcId=vpc-f8233a80
> aws ec2 describe-subnets --query
Subnets[].[AvailabilityZone,SubnetId] --output table
---------------------------------
|          DescribeSubnets        |
+-------------+-------------------+
|  us-east-1a |  subnet-a5d3ecee  |
|  us-east-1d |  subnet-c2abdded  |
|  us-east-1f |  subnet-aae11aa5  |
|  us-east-1e |  subnet-fd3a43c2  |
|  us-east-1b |  subnet-324e246f  |
|  us-east-1c |  subnet-d281a2b6  |
+-------------+-------------------+
```

Querying subnet IDs by availability zone

In the preceding example, you can see that the first item in the `ApplicationSubnets` input within the `dev.cfg` file is the subnet ID for `us-east-1a`, ensuring that the NAT gateway will be installed into the correct availability zone.

Configuring routing for your private subnets

The final step in configuring your NAT gateway is to configure a default route for your private subnets that points to your NAT gateway resource. This configuration will ensure all outbound internet traffic will be routed to your NAT gateway, which will then perform address translation, enabling your private hosts and containers to communicate with the internet.

The following example demonstrates adding a default route for the private route table you created earlier:

```
...
...
Resources:
  PrivateRouteTableDefaultRoute:
    Type: AWS::EC2::Route
    Properties:
      DestinationCidrBlock: 0.0.0.0/0
      RouteTableId: !Ref PrivateRouteTable
      NatGatewayId: !Ref NatGateway
...
...
```

Configuring a default route

In the preceding example, you can see that you configure the `RouteTableId` and `NatGatewayId` properties to ensure the default route for the private route table you created in the very first example is set to the NAT gateway you created in the later example.

You are now ready to deploy your changes, but before you do this, let's create a separate branch in the todobackend-aws repository called **ecs-task-networking**, so that you can easily revert your changes at the end of this chapter:

```
> git checkout -b ecs-task-networking
M stack.yml
Switched to a new branch 'ecs-task-networking'
> git commit -a -m "Add NAT gateway resources"
[ecs-task-networking af06d37] Add NAT gateway resources
 1 file changed, 33 insertions(+)
```

Creating an ECS task networking branch

Now you can deploy your changes using the familiar `aws cloudformation deploy` command you have been using through out this book for stack deployments:

```
> export AWS_PROFILE=docker-in-aws
> aws cloudformation deploy --template-file stack.yml \
    --stack-name todobackend --parameter-overrides $(cat dev.cfg) \
    --capabilities CAPABILITY_NAMED_IAM
Enter MFA code for arn:aws:iam::385605022855:mfa/justin.menga:

Waiting for changeset to be created..
Waiting for stack create/update to complete
```

```
Successfully created/updated stack - todobackend
> aws ec2 describe-subnets --query
"Subnets[?CidrBlock=='172.31.96.0/20'].SubnetId"
[
    "subnet-3acd6370"
]
> aws ec2 describe-nat-gateways
{
    "NatGateways": [
        {
            "CreateTime": "2018-04-22T10:30:07.000Z",
            "NatGatewayAddresses": [
                {
                    "AllocationId": "eipalloc-838abd8a",
                    "NetworkInterfaceId": "eni-90d8f10c",
                    "PrivateIp": "172.31.21.144",
                    "PublicIp": "18.204.39.34"
                }
            ],
            "NatGatewayId": "nat-084089330e75d23b3",
            "State": "available",
            "SubnetId": "subnet-a5d3ecee",
            "VpcId": "vpc-f8233a80",
...
...
```

Deploying changes to the todobackend application

In the preceding example, after successful deployment of the CloudFormation changes, you use the `aws ec2 describe-subnets` command to query the subnet ID of the new subnet you created, as you will need this value later on in this chapter. You also run the `aws ec2 describe-nat-gateways` command to verify the NAT gateway was created successfully and to view the elastic IP address of the gateway, which is represented by the highlighted `PublicIP` property. Note you should also check the default routes were created correctly, as demonstrated in the following example:

```
> aws ec2 describe-route-tables \
    --query "RouteTables[].Routes[?DestinationCidrBlock=='0.0.0.0/0']"
[
    [
        {
            "DestinationCidrBlock": "0.0.0.0/0",
            "NatGatewayId": "nat-084089330e75d23b3",
            "Origin": "CreateRoute",
            "State": "active"
```

```
        }
    ],
    [
        {
            "DestinationCidrBlock": "0.0.0.0/0",
            "GatewayId": "igw-1668666f",
            "Origin": "CreateRoute",
            "State": "active"
        }
    ]
]
...
...
...
```

Checking default routes

In the preceding example, you can see that two default routes exist, with one default route associated with a NAT gateway and the other with an internet gateway, confirming one of the route tables in your account is routing internet traffic to your newly created NAT gateway.

Configuring ECS task networking

Now that you have established networking infrastructure that will support the private IP addressing requirement of ECS task networking, you can proceed to configure ECS task networking on your ECS resources. This requires the following configurations and considerations:

- You must configure your ECS task definitions and ECS services to support ECS task networking.
- The network mode of your task definition must be set to `awsvpc`.
- An elastic network interface used for ECS task networking can only have one ECS task associated with it. Depending on your ECS instance type, this will limit the maximum number of ECS tasks you can run in any given ECS container instance.
- Deployment of ECS tasks with ECS task-networking-configured takes longer than traditional ECS deployments, as an elastic network interface needs to be created and bound to your ECS container instance.

- Because your container applications have a dedicated network interface, dynamic port mapping is no longer available and your container ports are exposed directly on the network interface.
- When an ECS service that uses the `awsvpc` network mode is used in conjunction with an application load balancer target group, the target type must be set to `ip` (the default is `instance`).

The implication of the removal of dynamic port mapping means that, for example, the todobackend application (which runs on port 8000) will be accessed on port `8000` externally with task networking enabled, rather than via a dynamically mapped port. This results in better performance for applications that generate large amounts of network traffic, and also means your security rules can target the specific port(s) your application runs on, rather than permitting access to the ephemeral range of network ports that are used with dynamic port mapping.

Configuring ECS task definitions for task networking

The first step in configuring ECS task networking is to configure your ECS task definitions. The following example demonstrates modifying the `ApplicationTaskDefinition` resource to support ECS task networking:

```
...
...
  ApplicationTaskDefinition:
    Type: AWS::ECS::TaskDefinition
    Properties:
      Family: todobackend
      NetworkMode: awsvpc
      TaskRoleArn: !Sub ${ApplicationTaskRole.Arn}
      Volumes:
        - Name: public
      ContainerDefinitions:
        - Name: todobackend
          ...
          ...
          PortMappings:
            - ContainerPort: 8000
          LogConfiguration:
            LogDriver: awslogs
            Options:
              awslogs-group: !Sub /${AWS::StackName}/ecs/todobackend
              awslogs-region: !Ref AWS::Region
```

```
                awslogs-stream-prefix: docker
       - Name: collectstatic
         Essential: false     .
...
...
```

Configuring ECS task definitions to use task networking

In the preceding example, the `NetworkMode` property has been added and configured with a value of `awsvpc`. By default, this property is set to `bridge`, which implements the default Docker behavior, as illustrated in the very first diagram, of including a Docker bridge interface with the network address translation configured to enable dynamic port mapping. By setting the network mode to `awsvpc`, ECS will ensure any ECS tasks that are deployed from this task definition are allocated a dedicated elastic network interface (ENI), and configure containers in the task definition to use the network stack of the ENI. The other configuration change in this example is that the `HostPort: 0` configuration has been removed from the `PortMappings` section, given ECS task networking does not use or support dynamic port mapping.

Configuring ECS services for task networking

With your ECS task definitions configured to use the correct network mode for task networking, you next need to configure your ECS services. Your ECS service configuration defines the target subnets where ECS should create an ENI, and also defines the security groups that should be applied to the ENI. The following example demonstrates updating the `ApplicationService` resource in your todobackend stack:

```
...
...
Resources:
  ...
  ...
  ApplicationService:
    Type: AWS::ECS::Service
    DependsOn:
        - ApplicationAutoscaling
        - ApplicationLogGroup
        - ApplicationLoadBalancerHttpListener
        - MigrateTask
    Properties:
      TaskDefinition: !Ref ApplicationTaskDefinition
      Cluster: !Ref ApplicationCluster
      DesiredCount: !Ref ApplicationDesiredCount
```

```
NetworkConfiguration:
  AwsvpcConfiguration:
    SecurityGroups:
      - !Ref ApplicationSecurityGroup
    Subnets:
      - !Ref PrivateSubnet
LoadBalancers:
  - ContainerName: todobackend
    ContainerPort: 8000
    TargetGroupArn: !Ref ApplicationServiceTargetGroup
# The Role property has been removed
DeploymentConfiguration:
  MaximumPercent: 200
  MinimumHealthyPercent: 100
...
...
```

Configuring ECS services to use task networking

In the preceding example, a new property called `NetworkConfiguration` is added to the ECS service definition. This property is required whenever you enable task networking, and you can see that you need to configure the subnets and security groups associated with the ENI that will be created by ECS. Notice that you reference the `PrivateSubnet` resource you created earlier in this chapter, which ensures your container network interface will not be reachable directly from the Internet. One change that is not immediately obvious is that the `Role` property has been removed - whenever you use have an ECS service that uses ECS task networking, AWS automatically configures the ECS role, and will raise an error if you attempt to set this role.

Configuring supporting resources for task networking

If you take a look back at the previous example, you will notice that you reference a new security group called `ApplicationSecurityGroup`, which needs to be added to your template, as demonstrated in the following example:

```
...
...
ApplicationSecurityGroup:
  Type: AWS::EC2::SecurityGroup
Properties:
```

```
GroupDescription: !Sub ${AWS::StackName} Application Security Group
VpcId: !Ref VpcId
SecurityGroupEgress:
- IpProtocol: udp
FromPort: 53
ToPort: 53
CidrIp: 0.0.0.0/0
- IpProtocol: tcp
FromPort: 443
ToPort: 443
CidrIp: 0.0.0.0/0
 ...
 ...
 ApplicationLoadBalancerToApplicationIngress:
   Type: AWS::EC2::SecurityGroupIngress
   Properties:
     IpProtocol: tcp
     FromPort: 8000
     ToPort: 8000
     GroupId: !Ref ApplicationSecurityGroup
     SourceSecurityGroupId: !Ref ApplicationLoadBalancerSecurityGroup
ApplicationLoadBalancerToApplicationEgress:
   Type: AWS::EC2::SecurityGroupEgress
   Properties:
     IpProtocol: tcp
     FromPort: 8000
     ToPort: 8000
     GroupId: !Ref ApplicationLoadBalancerSecurityGroup
     DestinationSecurityGroupId: !Ref ApplicationSecurityGroup
 ...
 ...
 ApplicationToApplicationDatabaseIngress:
   Type: AWS::EC2::SecurityGroupIngress
   Properties:
     IpProtocol: tcp
     FromPort: 3306
     ToPort: 3306
     GroupId: !Ref ApplicationDatabaseSecurityGroup
     SourceSecurityGroupId: !Ref ApplicationSecurityGroup
ApplicationToApplicationDatabaseEgress:
   Type: AWS::EC2::SecurityGroupEgress
   Properties:
     IpProtocol: tcp
     FromPort: 3306
     ToPort: 3306
```

```
GroupId: !Ref ApplicationSecurityGroup
      DestinationSecurityGroupId: !Ref
ApplicationDatabaseSecurityGroup
...
...
```

Configuring security groups for task networking

In the preceding example, you first create a security group that includes an egress rule set that permits outbound DNS and HTTPS traffic, which is required to allow the entrypoint script in your containers to communicate with the AWS Secrets Manager API. Notice that you need to modify the existing `AWS::EC2::SecurityGroupIngress` and `AWS::EC2::SecurityGroupEgress` resources, which previously permitted access between the application load balancer/application database and the application autoscaling group instances. You can see that for the `ApplicationLoadBalancerToApplicationEgress` and `ApplicationLoadBalancerToApplicationEgress` resources, the port range has been reduced from the ephemeral port range of `32768` to `60999` to just port `8000`, which results in a much more secure configuration. Also, the ECS container instance control plane (which is associated with the `ApplicationAutoscalingSecurityGroup` resource) can now no longer access your application database (only your application can do this now), which again is more secure.

There's one problem with the current modifications to the todobackend stack, which is that you have not updated your `MigrateTaskDefinition` to use task networking. The main reason I am not doing this is because it would require your ECS container instances to support more elastic network interfaces than what the free tier t2.micros supports, and also would require the ECS Task Runner custom resource to be updated to support running ad-hoc ECS tasks. Of course if you want to use ECS task networking in a production environment, you would need to address such concerns, however for the purposes of providing a basic understanding of ECS task networking, I have chosen not to do this. This does mean if you make any change that requires the migrate task to be run, it will fail with the configuration changes of the previous example, however, once this chapter is complete, you will revert your todobackend stack configuration to not use ECS task networking to ensure you can complete the remaining chapters.

Finally, there is one last change you need to make to your template, which is to modify the application-load-balancer target group associated with your ECS service. When your ECS services run tasks that operate in the `awsvpc` networking mode, you must change the target group type from the default of `instance` to a value of `ip`, as demonstrated in the following example, given your ECS tasks now have their own unique IP addresses:

```
Resources:
  ...
  ...
  ApplicationServiceTargetGroup:
      Type: AWS::ElasticLoadBalancingV2::TargetGroup
      Properties:
        Protocol: HTTP
        Port: 8000
        VpcId: !Ref VpcId
        TargetType: ip
        TargetGroupAttributes:
          - Key: deregistration_delay.timeout_seconds
            Value: 30
  ...
  ...
```

Updated application-load-balancer target group target type

Deploying and testing ECS task networking

You are now ready to deploy your changes and verify that ECS task networking is working correctly. If you run the `aws cloudformation deploy` command, the following should happen:

- A new revision of the application task definition will be created, which is configured for ECS task networking.
- The ECS service configuration will detect the changes and attempt to deploy the new revision, along with the ECS service configuration changes. ECS will dynamically attach a new ENI to the private subnet and allocate this ENI to a new ECS task for the `ApplicationService` resource.

Once deployment is complete, you should verify your application is still working and once you have done this, you can browse to the ECS console, click on your ECS service, and select the current task running for the service.

The following screenshot shows the ECS task screen:

Clusters > todobackend-cluster > Task: 414bb347-f4f2-4402-b7d2-2e170a12d266

Task : 414bb347-f4f2-4402-b7d2-2e170a12d266   Run more like this   Stop

Details   Logs

Cluster	todobackend-cluster
Container instance	3f1082b5-6e24-4434-9b4e-24020855b3ae
EC2 instance id	i-0281a29f4ffd30127
Launch type	EC2
Task definition	todobackend:18
Group	service:todobackend-ApplicationService-1KOV0OK7M8ZYF
Task role	todobackend-ApplicationTaskRole-1A4TSTP94C6EU
Last status	RUNNING
Desired status	RUNNING
Created at	2018-04-23 00:56:11 +1200

Network

Network mode	awsvpc
ENI Id	eni-a0446f3c
Subnet Id	subnet-3acd6370
Private IP	172.31.97.220
Public IP	--
Mac address	0a:39:eb:89:50:2e

Containers

Last updated on April 23, 2018 2:59:35 AM (29m ago)

ECS task in task networking mode

As you can see, the network mode of the task is now `awsvpc`, and an ENI has been dynamically allocated from the private subnet you created earlier in this chapter. If you click on the ENI ID link, you will be able to verify the security group(s) attached to the ENI, and also check that the ENI has been attached to one of your ECS container instances.

At this point, you should commit the final set of changes you made in this chapter to the ECS task networking branch, check out the master branch, and redeploy your CloudFormation stack. This will revert all of the changes made in this chapter, restoring your stack to the same state as it was at the end of the preceding chapter. This is required, given we don't want to have to upgrade to a larger instance type to accommodate the `MigrateTaskDefinition` resource and future auto scaling scenarios we will be testing in later chapters:

```
> git commit -a -m "Add ECS task networking resources"
 [ecs-task-networking 7e995cb] Add ECS task networking resources
 2 files changed, 37 insertions(+), 10 deletions(-)
> git checkout master
Switched to branch 'master'
> aws cloudformation deploy --template-file stack.yml --stack-name
todobackend \
    --parameter-overrides $(cat dev.cfg) --capabilities
CAPABILITY_NAMED_IAM

Waiting for changeset to be created..
Waiting for stack create/update to complete
Successfully created/updated stack - todobackend
```

Reverting the todobackend-aws repository

Summary

In this chapter, you learned how to increase the network isolation and security of your Docker applications using ECS task networking. ECS task networking changes the default out-of-the-box Docker bridge and NAT network configuration to a model where each ECS task receives its own dedicated elastic network interface or ENI. This means that your Docker applications are assigned their own dedicated security groups and can be accessed directly via their published ports, which avoids the need to implement features, such as dynamic port mapping, that can affect performance and require more permissive security rules to work. ECS task networking, however, does come with its own set of challenges and limitations, which include a more complex network topology to accommodate the current private IP address-only restrictions, and the ability to only run a single ECS task per ENI.

ECS task networking currently does not support public IP addresses, which means you must provide a NAT gateway or HTTP proxy if your tasks required outbound internet connectivity. NAT gateways are a managed service provided by AWS and you learned how to configure a private subnet used for your ECS tasks, and how to configure a private route table to route internet traffic to a NAT gateway you created in one of your pre-existing public subnets.

You learned that configuring ECS task networking requires you to specify the awsvpc network mode in your ECS task definitions, and that you need to add a network configuration to your ECS services that specifies the subnet(s) your ECS tasks will be connected to and the security group(s) that will be applied. If your application is serviced by an application load balancer, you also need to ensure the target type of the target group linked to your ECS service is configured as `ip`, rather than the default `instance` target type. If you are applying these changes to an existing environment, you may also need to update security groups attached to resources, such as load balancers and databases, given your ECS tasks are no longer associated with the security groups applied at an ECS container instance level and have their own dedicated security groups.

In the next two chapters, you will learn how to deal with some of the more challenging operational aspects of ECS, including managing the life cycle of your ECS container instances and autoscaling your ECS clusters.

Questions

1. True/false: The default Docker network configuration uses iptables to perform network address translation.
2. You have an application that forms application-level clusters and uses EC2 metadata to discover the IP addresses of other hosts running your application. When you run your application using ECS, you notice that your applications are using a `172.16.x.x/16` address but your EC2 instances are configured with an `172.31.x.x/16` address. Which Docker network modes could help resolve this problem?
3. True/false: The `host` value for `NetworkMode` in your ECS task definitions enables ECS task networking.

4. You enable ECS task networking for an ECS task definition, however your application load balancers can no longer reach your application. You check the rules on the security group attached to your ECS container instance and confirm that your load balancers are permitted access to your application. How can you resolve this issue?

5. You enable ECS task networking for an ECS task definition, however your containers fail on startup with an error unable to reach a location that is located on the internet. How can you resolve this issue?

6. What is the maximum number of ENIs you can run on a t2.micro instance?

7. What is the maximum number of ECS tasks that you can run in task-networking mode on a t2.micro instance?

8. What is the maximum number of containers that you can run in task-networking mode on a t2.micro instance?

9. After enabling the ECS task-networking mode, you receive a deployment error indicating a target group has a target type instance, which is incompatible with the awsvpc network mode. How can you resolve this?

10. After enabling the ECS task-networking mode, you receive a deployment error stating you cannot specify an IAM role for services that require a service-linked role. How can you resolve this?

Further reading

You can check out the following links for more information about the topics covered in this chapter:

- Docker networking overview: https://docs.docker.com/network/
- Task Networking with the awsvpc Network Mode: https://docs.aws.amazon.com/AmazonECS/latest/developerguide/task-networking.html
- Under the Hood: Task Networking for Amazon ECS: https://aws.amazon.com/blogs/compute/under-the-hood-task-networking-for-amazon-ecs/
- Maximum Network Interfaces for EC2 Instance Types: https://docs.aws.amazon.com/AWSEC2/latest/UserGuide/using-eni.html#AvailableIpPerENI
- NAT Gateways: https://docs.aws.amazon.com/AmazonVPC/latest/UserGuide/vpc-nat-gateway.html
- CloudFormation NAT Gateway Resource Reference: https://docs.aws.amazon.com/AWSCloudFormation/latest/UserGuide/aws-resource-ec2-natgateway.html

- CloudFormation EC2 Elastic IP Address Resource Reference: `https://docs.aws.amazon.com/AWSCloudFormation/latest/UserGuide/aws-properties-ec2-eip.html`
- CloudFormation EC2 Subnet Resource Reference: `https://docs.aws.amazon.com/AWSCloudFormation/latest/UserGuide/aws-resource-ec2-subnet.html`

- CloudFormation EC2 Subnet Route Table Association Resource Reference: `https://docs.aws.amazon.com/AWSCloudFormation/latest/UserGuide/aws-resource-ec2-subnet-route-table-assoc.html`
- CloudFormation EC2 Route Table Resource Reference: `https://docs.aws.amazon.com/AWSCloudFormation/latest/UserGuide/aws-resource-ec2-route-table.html`
- CloudFormation EC2 Route Resource Reference: `https://docs.aws.amazon.com/AWSCloudFormation/latest/UserGuide/aws-resource-ec2-route.html`
- Using Service-Linked Roles for Amazon ECS: `https://docs.aws.amazon.com/AmazonECS/latest/developerguide/using-service-linked-roles.html`

11
Managing ECS Infrastructure Life Cycle

A fundamental ongoing activity associated with operating ECS infrastructure is the requirement to manage the life cycle of your ECS container instances. In any production-grade scenario, you will be required to patch your ECS container instances, and ensure the core components of your ECS container instances such as the Docker Engine and ECS agent are updated frequently to ensure you have access to the latest features, and security and performance enhancements. In an immutable infrastructure world where your ECS container instances are considered "cattle", the standard approach is that you destroy and replace your ECS container instances by rolling in new Amazon Machine Images (AMIs), rather than taking the traditional approach of patching *pets* and keeping your ECS container instances around for a long period of time. Another common use case where you need to manage the life cycle is related to Auto Scaling—for example, if you scale your ECS clusters in after a period of heavy demand, you need to be able to remove ECS container instances from your cluster.

Taking an ECS container instance out of service probably sounds like quite a simple task, however consider what happens if you have running containers on your instance. If you take the instance out of service immediately, users connected to applications running on those containers will be disrupted, which might result in data loss and at the very least, unhappy users. What is required is a mechanism that enables your ECS container instances to be taken out of service gracefully, maintaining current user connections until they can be closed without any impact to the end user, and then actually terminate the instance once you can be sure the instance is completely out of service.

In this chapter, you will learn how to implement such a capability, by leveraging two key AWS features—EC2 Auto Scaling life cycle hooks and ECS container instance draining. EC2 Auto Scaling life cycle hooks let you be informed of a pending life cycle event related to an EC2 instance being started or being taken out of service, and provide you with an opportunity to perform any appropriate initialization or cleanup actions before signalling that the life cycle event can proceed. This is where you can leverage ECS container instance draining, which marks ECS tasks on the affected ECS container instance as draining or out of service, and proceeds to gracefully take the tasks out of service by starting new replacement ECS tasks on other ECS container instances in the cluster, and then draining connections to the affected ECS tasks until the tasks can be stopped and the ECS container instance is drained.

The following topics will be covered:

- Understanding ECS infrastructure life cycle management
- Building a new ECS container instance AMI
- Configuring EC2 Auto Scaling rolling updates
- Creating EC2 Auto Scaling life cycle hooks
- Creating a Lambda function for consuming life cycle hooks
- Deploying and testing Auto Scaling life cycle hooks

Technical requirements

The following lists the technical requirements to complete this chapter:

- Administrator access to an AWS account
- Local AWS profile configured as per instructions in Chapter 3
- AWS CLI version 1.15.71 or higher
- This chapter continues on from Chapter 9 (NOT Chapter 10) so it requires you to have successfully completed all configuration tasks defined in Chapter 9, and ensure you have reset the **todobackend-aws** repository to the master branch (which should be based upon completion of Chapter 9)

The following GitHub URL contains the code samples used in this chapter - `https://github.com/docker-in-aws/docker-in-aws/tree/master/ch11`.

Check out the following video to see the Code in Action:
`http://bit.ly/2BT7DVh`

Understanding ECS life cycle management

As described in the introduction to this chapter, ECS life cycle management refers to the process of taking existing ECS container instances out of service without impacting end users that may be connected to applications running on your affect instances.

This requires you to leverage two key features provided by AWS:

- EC2 Auto Scaling life cycle hooks
- ECS container instance draining

EC2 Auto Scaling life cycle hooks

EC2 Auto Scaling life cycle hooks allow you to receive notice of a pending life cycle event and perform some action before the event takes place. Currently, you can be notified of the following life cycle hook events:

- `EC2_INSTANCE_LAUNCHING`: Raised when an EC2 instance is about to be launched
- `EC2_INSTANCE_TERMINATING`: Raised when an EC2 instance is about to be terminated

In general, you don't need to worry about `EC2_INSTANCE_LAUNCHING` events, however anybody who runs a production-grade ECS cluster should be interested in `EC2_INSTANCE_TERMINATING` events, given an instance that is about to be terminated may be running containers with active end user connections. Once you have subscribed to a life cycle hook event, the EC2 Auto Scaling service will wait for you to signal that the life cycle action can proceed. This provides you with a mechanism that allows you to perform graceful tear down actions in the case of an `EC2_INSTANCE_TERMINATING` event, and this is where you can leverage ECS container instance draining.

ECS container instance draining

ECS container instance draining is a feature that allows you to gracefully *drain* your ECS container instances of running ECS tasks, with the end result being your ECS container instance has no running ECS tasks or containers, meaning it is safe to terminate the instance without impacting your container applications. ECS container instance draining first marks your ECS container instance in a **DRAINING** state, which will cause all ECS tasks running on the instance to be gracefully shut down and started on other container instances in the cluster. This draining activity uses the standard *rolling* behavior you have already seen with ECS services—for example, if you have an ECS task associated with an ECS service that has application load balancer integration, ECS will first attempt to register a new ECS task on another ECS container instance as a new target in the application load balancer target group, and then place the target associated with the ECS container instance that is being drained into a connection draining state.

Note that it is important that your ECS cluster has enough resources and ECS container instances to migrate each of the affected ECS tasks, which can be challenging given you are also reducing the ECS cluster capacity by an instance. This means, for example, if you are performing planned replacements of ECS container instances in your cluster (for example, you are updating to a new AMI), then you need to temporarily add extra capacity to your cluster so that you swap out instances in a rolling fashion without reducing overall cluster capacity. If you are using CloudFormation to deploy your EC2 Auto Scaling groups, a very useful feature is the ability to specify update policies that can temporarily add extra capacity to your Auto Scaling groups during a rolling update, and you will learn how to leverage this feature to always ensure you maintain ECS cluster capacity at all times when performing rolling updates.

ECS life cycle management solution

Now that you have some background of ECS life cycle management, let's discuss the solution that you will implement in this chapter, which will leverage EC2 life cycle hooks to trigger ECS container instance draining and signal the EC2 Auto Scaling service when it is safe to terminate your ECS container instances.

The following diagram illustrates a simple EC2 Auto Scaling group and an ECS cluster with two ECS container instances in service, supporting ECS **Service A** and ECS **Service B**, which both have two ECS tasks or instances of the ECS service running:

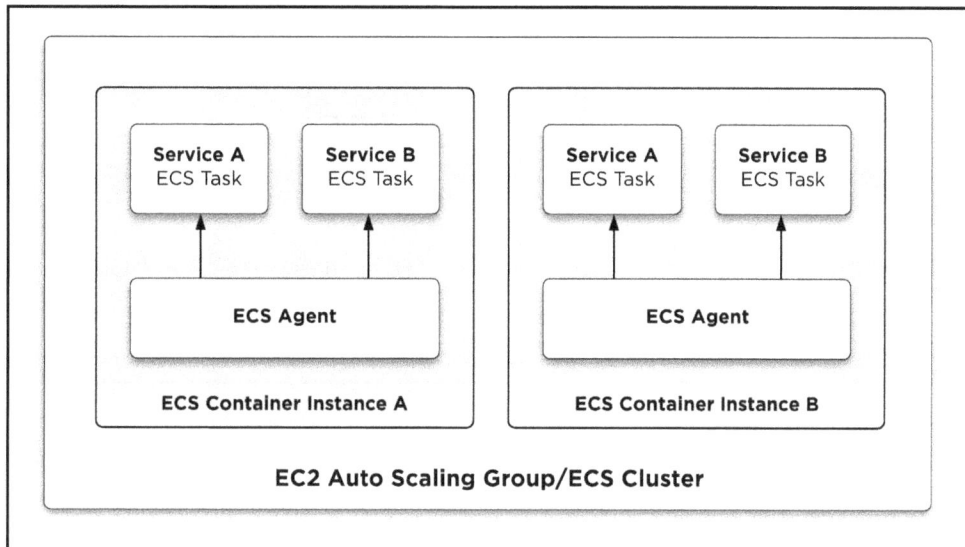

In Service EC2 Auto Scaling Group/ECS Cluster

Let's assume that you now want to update the ECS container instances in your EC2 Auto Scaling group with a new Amazon Machine Image, which requires the termination and replacement of each instance. The following diagram illustrates how our life cycle hook solution will deal with this requirement and ensure each of the instances in the Auto Scaling group can be replaced in a manner that does not disrupt end users that are connected to the applications serviced by each ECS service:

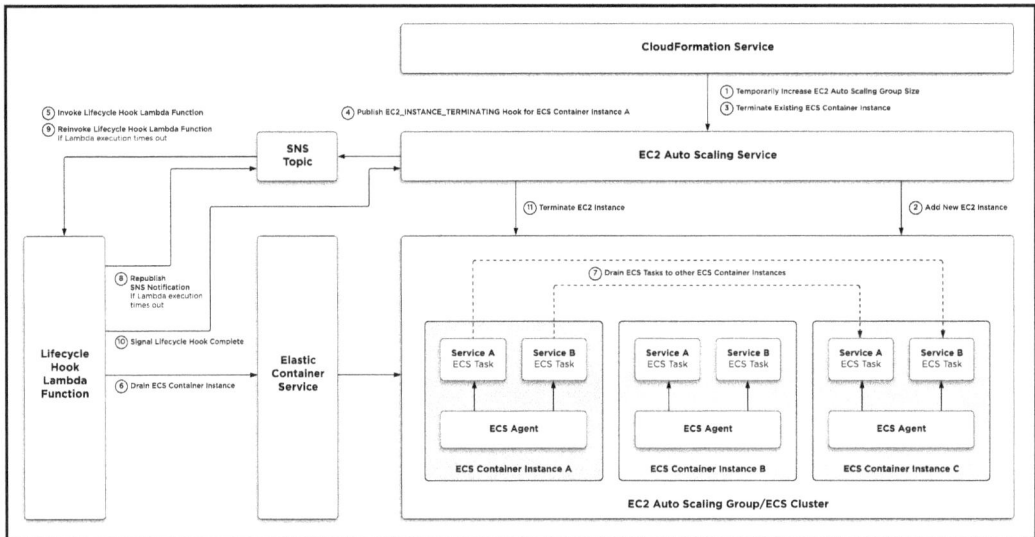

Performing Rolling Updates on an In-Service EC2 Auto Scaling Group/ECS Cluster

In the preceding diagram, the following steps take place:

1. CloudFormation rolling updates are configured for the EC2 Auto Scaling group, which causes the CloudFormation service to temporarily increase the size of the EC2 Auto Scaling group.
2. The EC2 Auto Scaling group adds a new EC2 instance (ECS container instance C) to the Auto Scaling group in response to the increase in group size from CloudFormation.

3. Once the new EC2 instance has started and signalled SUCCESS to CloudFormation, the CloudFormation service then instructs the EC2 Auto Scaling service to terminate ECS container instance A, given ECS container instance C is now joined to the EC2 Auto Scaling group and ECS cluster.

4. Before terminating the instance, the EC2 Auto Scaling service triggers a life cycle hook event, publishing this event to a configured Simple Notification Service (SNS) topic. SNS is a publish/subscribe style notification service that can be used for a variety of use cases, and in our solution we will subscribe a Lambda function to the SNS topic.

5. A Lambda function is invoked by the SNS topic in response to the life cycle hook event being published to the topic.

6. The Lambda function instructs ECS to drain the ECS container instance that is about to be terminated. The function then polls the running task count on the ECS container instance, waiting until the task count is zero before considering that the draining process is complete.

7. ECS drains the current tasks running on ECS container instance A to other container instances that have spare capacity. In the preceding diagram, because ECS container instance C was recently added to the cluster, the ECS tasks running on ECS container instance A can be drained to container instance C. Note that if container instance C had not been added to the cluster, there would be insufficient capacity in the cluster to drain container instance A, so ensuring your cluster has sufficient capacity for these types of events is very important.

8. In many cases, ECS container instance draining may take longer than the current five minute execution timeout limit for Lambda. In this scenario, you can simply republish the life cycle hook event notification to the SNS topic, which will automatically reinvoke the Lambda function.

9. The Lambda function once again instructs ECS to drain container instance A (which is already in progress), and continues to poll the running task count, waiting until the running task count is zero.

10. Assuming the container instance completes draining and the running task count reduces to zero, the Lambda function signals the EC2 Auto Scaling service that the life cycle hook is complete.

11. The EC2 Auto Scaling service terminates the ECS container instance now that the life cycle hook has completed.

At this point, the rolling update that was initiated way back in step 1 by CloudFormation is 50% complete, as the old ECS container instance A has been replaced by ECS container instance C. The process described in preceding diagram repeats once again, with a new ECS container instance introduced to the cluster and ECS container instance B marked for termination. Once draining of ECS container instance B has completed, all instances in the Auto Scaling group/cluster have been replaced, and the rolling update is complete.

Building a new ECS container instance AMI

To test our life cycle management solution, we need to have a mechanism to force your ECS container instances to be terminated. Although you could simply adjust the desired count of your Auto Scaling group (which actually is a common scenario when your Auto Scaling groups are scaling down), another common scenario where this can happen is when you need to update your ECS container instances by introducing a newly built Amazon Machine Image (AMI), complete with the latest operating system and security patches, and up-to-date versions of Docker Engine and the ECS agent. At the very least, if you are building a custom ECS container instance AMI using an approach similar to what you learned in Chapter 6, you should be rebuilding your AMI each time Amazon releases a new version of the base ECS-optimized AMI, and it is common practice to update your AMIs on a weekly or monthly basis.

To simulate introducing a new AMI into your ECS cluster, you can simply perform the same steps you executed in Chapter 6, which will output a new AMI that you can then use as an input into your stack and force your ECS cluster to upgrade each of its ECS container instances.

The following example demonstrates running the `make build` command from the root of the **packer-ecs** repository, which will output a new AMI ID for the newly created and published image. Ensure you note down this AMI ID as you will require it later on in this chapter:

```
> export AWS_PROFILE=docker-in-aws
> make build
packer build packer.json
amazon-ebs output will be in this color.

==> amazon-ebs: Prevalidating AMI Name: docker-in-aws-ecs 1518934269
...
...
Build 'amazon-ebs' finished.

==> Builds finished. The artifacts of successful builds are:
--> amazon-ebs: AMIs were created:
us-east-1: ami-77893508
```

Running a Packer build

Configuring EC2 Auto Scaling rolling updates

When you use CloudFormation to create and manage your EC2 Auto Scaling groups, a useful capability is the ability to manage rolling updates. Rolling updates refers to the ability to *roll* in new EC2 instances into your Auto Scaling group, in a controlled manner that ensures your update process can be completed without causing disruption. In Chapter 8, when you created an EC2 Auto Scaling group via CloudFormation, you learned how CloudFormation supports creation policies, that can help you ensure all instances in your EC2 Auto Scaling have initialized successfully. CloudFormation also supports update policies, which as you saw earlier in the previous diagram, help you manage and control how updates to your EC2 Auto Scaling group are managed.

If you open the todobackend-aws repository and browse to the CloudFormation template located in the `stack.yml` file, you can add an update policy to the `ApplicationAutoscaling` resource, as demonstrated in the following example:

```
...
...
Resources:
  ...
  ...
  ApplicationAutoscaling:
    Type: AWS::AutoScaling::AutoScalingGroup
    CreationPolicy:
      ResourceSignal:
        Count: !Ref ApplicationDesiredCount
        Timeout: PT15M
    UpdatePolicy:
      AutoScalingRollingUpdate:
        MinInstancesInService: !Ref ApplicationDesiredCount
        MinSuccessfulInstancesPercent: 100
        WaitOnResourceSignals: "true"
        PauseTime: PT15M
  ...
  ...
```

Configuring a CloudFormation Auto Scaling Group Update Policy

In the preceding example, the `UpdatePolicy` setting is applied to the `ApplicationAutoscaling` resource, which configures CloudFormation to orchestrate rolling updates according to the following `AutoScalingRollingUpdate` configuration parameters whenever instances within the Auto Scaling group need to be replaced (*updated*):

- `MinInstancesInService`: The minimum number of instances that must be in service during a rolling update. A standard approach here is to specify the desired count of the Auto Scaling group, which means the Auto Scaling will temporarily increase in size as new instances are added in order to maintain the minimum number of required instances.
- `MinSuccessfulInstancesPercent`: The minimum percentage of new instances that must be deployed successfully for the rolling update to be considered a success. If this percentage is not met, then CloudFormation will roll back the stack changes.

- `WaitOnResourceSignals`: When set to true, specifies that CloudFormation waits for a **SUCCESS** signal from each instance before it considers an instance successfully deployed. This requires your EC2 instances to have the `cfn-bootstrap` scripts that installed in Chapter 6 and configured in Chapter 7 to signal to CloudFormation once initialization of the instance has completed.
- `PauseTime`: When `WaitOnResourceSignals` is configured, specifies the maximum amount of time to wait for each instance to signal **SUCCESS**. This value is expressed in ISO8601 format and in the following example is configured to wait for up to 15 minutes.

Then, deploy your changes using the `aws cloudformation deploy` command as demonstrated in the following example, your Auto Scaling group will now have the update policy applied:

```
> export AWS_PROFILE=docker-in-aws
> aws cloudformation deploy --template-file stack.yml \
 --stack-name todobackend --parameter-overrides $(cat dev.cfg) \
 --capabilities CAPABILITY_NAMED_IAM
Enter MFA code for arn:aws:iam::385605022855:mfa/justin.menga:

Waiting for changeset to be created..
Waiting for stack create/update to complete
Successfully created/updated stack - todobackend
   ...
   ...
```

Configuring a CloudFormation Auto Scaling Group Update Policy

At this point, you can now update your stack to use the new AMI you created in the very first example. This requires you to first update the `dev.cfg` file at the root of the todobackend-aws repository:

```
ApplicationDesiredCount=1
ApplicationImageId=ami-77893508
ApplicationImageTag=5fdbe62
ApplicationSubnets=subnet-a5d3ecee,subnet-324e246f
VpcId=vpc-f8233a80
```

Updating the ECS AMI

Then, deploy the change using the same `aws cloudformation deploy` command.

While the deployment is running, if you open the AWS console, browse to the CloudFormation dashboard, and select the todobackend stack **Events** tab, you should be able to see how CloudFormation performs rolling updates:

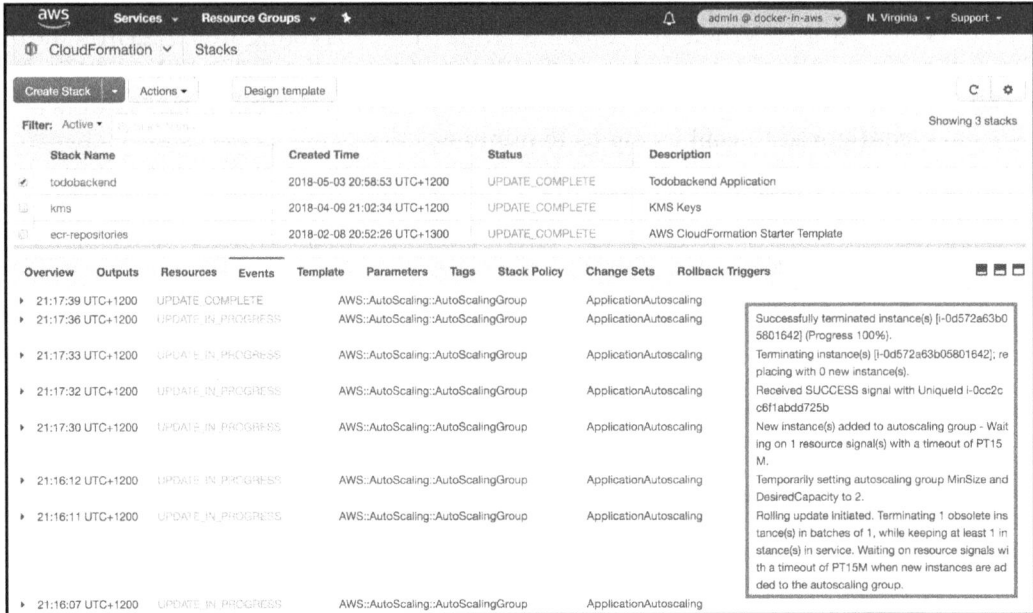

CloudFormation Rolling Updates

In the preceding screenshot, you can see that CloudFormation first temporarily increases the size of the Auto Scaling group, given it needs to keep at least one instance in service at all times. Once the new instance signals **SUCCESS** to CloudFormation, the old instance in the Auto Scaling group is terminated and the rolling update is complete.

At this point, you might be feeling pretty happy—with just a small change to your CloudFormation configuration, you have been able to add rolling updates to your stack. There is just one problem though, that being when the old EC2 instance was terminated, it was terminated *immediately*. This actually causes a disruption to the service, which you can see an indication of if you navigate to the CloudWatch console, select **Metrics**, in the **All metrics** tab select **ECS | ClusterName**, and then select the **MemoryReservation** metric for the cluster named **todobackend-cluster**.

The following screenshot shows this screen once you have clicked on the **Graphed metrics** tab and changed the **Statistic** column to **Minimum** and **Period** to **1 Minute**:

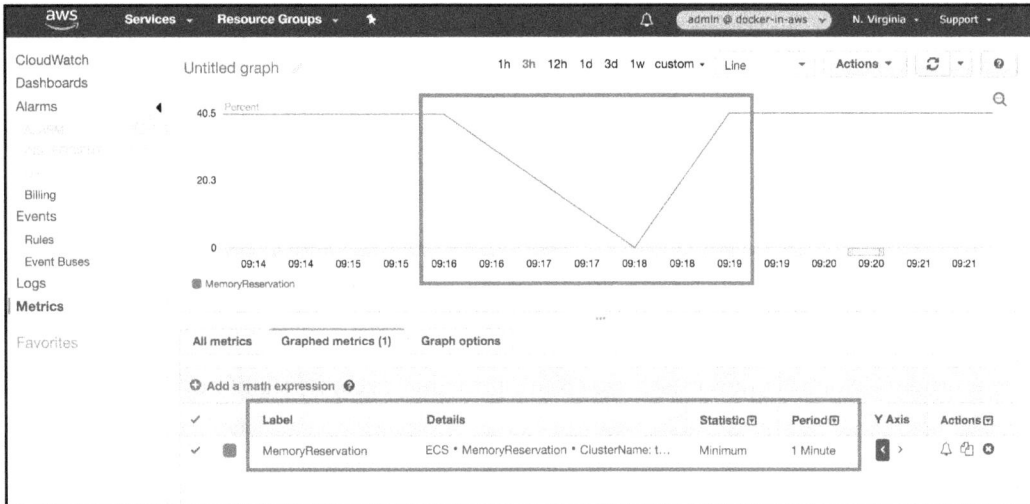

ECS Memory Reservation

If you look back at the timeline in the earlier screenshot, you can see that at 21:17:33 the old ECS container instance is terminated, and in the preceding screenshot, you can see a corresponding dip in the memory reservation of the cluster to 0% at 21:18 (09:18). This indicates that at this point in time, there were no actual containers running, given the percentage of cluster memory reserved was 0, illustrating there was a small, albeit brief, outage whilst ECS attempted to recover the todobackend service to the new ECS container instance after the old instance was abruptly terminated.

> Because the minimum CloudWatch metrics resolution is 1 minute, it is possible that you may not observe the dip to 0% in the previous figure if ECS is able to recover the ECS service within a minute, but rest assured there is an outage to your application.

Clearly this is not ideal and as we discussed earlier, we now need to introduce EC2 Auto Scaling life cycle hooks to resolve this situation.

Creating EC2 Auto Scaling life cycle hooks

To fix the problem of EC2 instance termination affecting our ECS services, we now need to create an EC2 Auto Scaling life cycle hook that will notify us that an EC2 instance is about to be terminated. Referring back to the first diagram, this requires several resources:

- The actual life cycle hook
- A life cycle hook role that grants the EC2 Auto Scaling group permission to publish life cycle hook notifications to an SNS topic
- An SNS topic where life cycle hooks can be published and subscribed to

The following example demonstrates creating the life cycle hook, life cycle hook role, and SNS topic:

```
...
...
Resources:
  ...
  ...
  LifecycleHook:
    Type: AWS::AutoScaling::LifecycleHook
    Properties:
      RoleARN: !Sub ${LifecycleHookRole.Arn}
      AutoScalingGroupName: !Ref ApplicationAutoscaling
      DefaultResult: CONTINUE
      HeartbeatTimeout: 900
      LifecycleTransition: autoscaling:EC2_INSTANCE_TERMINATING
      NotificationTargetARN: !Ref LifecycleHookTopic
  LifecycleHookRole:
    Type: AWS::IAM::Role
    Properties:
      AssumeRolePolicyDocument:
        Version: "2012-10-17"
        Statement:
          - Action:
              - sts:AssumeRole
            Effect: Allow
            Principal:
              Service: autoscaling.amazonaws.com
      Policies:
        - PolicyName: LifecycleHookPermissions
          PolicyDocument:
            Version: "2012-10-17"
```

```
      Statement:
        - Sid: PublishNotifications
          Action:
            - sns:Publish
          Effect: Allow
          Resource: !Ref LifecycleHookTopic
LifecycleHookTopic:
  Type: AWS::SNS::Topic
  Properties: {}
LifecycleHookSubscription:
  Type: AWS::SNS::Subscription
  Properties:
    Endpoint: !Sub ${LifecycleHookFunction.Arn}
    Protocol: lambda
    TopicArn: !Ref LifecycleHookTopic
  ...
  ...
```

Creating Life Cycle Hook Resources in CloudFormation

In the preceding example, the `LifecycleHook` resource creates a new hook, which is linked to the `ApplicationAutoscaling` resource using the `AutoScalingGroupName` property, and is triggered by EC2 instances within the Auto Scaling group that are about to be terminated, as specified by the value `autoscaling:EC2_INSTANCE_TERMINATING` configured for the `LifecycleTransition` property. The hook is configured to send a notification to a new SNS topic resource called `LifecycleHookTopic`, with the linked `LifecycleHookRole` IAM role granting the `autoscaling.amazonaws.com` service (as specified in the `AssumeRolePolicyDocument` section of the role) permissions to publish life cycle hook events to this topic. The `DefaultResult` property specifies the default result that should be created if the `HeartbeatTimeout` period is reached and no response has been received for the hook, which in this example is to send a `CONTINUE` message that instructs the Auto Scaling service to continue processing any other life cycle hooks that may be registered. The other option for the `DefaultResult` property is to send an `ABANDON` message, which still instructs the Auto Scaling service to continue with instance termination, but abandons processing any other life cycle hooks that may be configured.

The final `LifecycleHookSubscription` resource creates a subscription to the `LifecycleHookTopic` SNS topic resource, subscribing a Lambda function resource called `LifecycleHookFunction` that we will create soon, meaning this function will be invoked anytime a message is published to the SNS topic.

Creating a Lambda function for consuming life cycle hooks

With the various life cycle hook resources in place, the final piece of the puzzle is to create a Lambda function and associated resources that will subscribe to the life cycle hook SNS topic you defined in the previous section and will ultimately perform ECS container instance draining before signalling that the life cycle hook action can continue.

Let's first focus on the Lambda function itself and the associated source code that it will need to execute:

```
...
...
Resources:
  LifecycleHookFunction:
    Type: AWS::Lambda::Function
    DependsOn:
      - LifecycleHookFunctionLogGroup
    Properties:
      Role: !Sub ${LifecycleFunctionRole.Arn}
      FunctionName: !Sub ${AWS::StackName}-lifecycleHooks
      Description: !Sub ${AWS::StackName} Autoscaling Lifecycle Hook
      Environment:
        Variables:
          ECS_CLUSTER: !Ref ApplicationCluster
      Code:
        ZipFile: |
          import os, time
          import json
          import boto3
          cluster = os.environ['ECS_CLUSTER']
          # AWS clients
          ecs = boto3.client('ecs')
          sns = boto3.client('sns')
          autoscaling = boto3.client('autoscaling')

          def handler(event, context):
            print("Received event %s" % event)
            for r in event.get('Records'):
              # Parse SNS message
              message = json.loads(r['Sns']['Message'])
              transition, hook = message['LifecycleTransition'],
message['LifecycleHookName']
              group, ec2_instance = message['AutoScalingGroupName'],
message['EC2InstanceId']
```

```
            if transition != 'autoscaling:EC2_INSTANCE_TERMINATING':
              print("Ignoring lifecycle transition %s" % transition)
              return
            try:
              # Get ECS container instance ARN
              ecs_instance_arns = ecs.list_container_instances(
                cluster=cluster
              )['containerInstanceArns']
              ecs_instances = ecs.describe_container_instances(
                cluster=cluster,
                containerInstances=ecs_instance_arns
              )['containerInstances']
              # Find ECS container instance with same EC2 instance
ID in lifecycle hook message
              ecs_instance_arn = next((
                instance['containerInstanceArn'] for instance in
ecs_instances
                if instance['ec2InstanceId'] == ec2_instance
              ), None)
              if ecs_instance_arn is None:
                raise ValueError('Could not locate ECS instance')
              # Drain instance
              ecs.update_container_instances_state(
                cluster=cluster,
                containerInstances=[ecs_instance_arn],
                status='DRAINING'
              )
              # Check task count on instance every 5 seconds
              count = 1
              while count > 0 and
context.get_remaining_time_in_millis() > 10000:
                status = ecs.describe_container_instances(
                  cluster=cluster,
                  containerInstances=[ecs_instance_arn],
                )['containerInstances'][0]
                count = status['runningTasksCount']
                print("Sleeping...")
                time.sleep(5)
              if count == 0:
                print("All tasks drained - sending CONTINUE signal")
                autoscaling.complete_lifecycle_action(
                  LifecycleHookName=hook,
                  AutoScalingGroupName=group,
                  InstanceId=ec2_instance,
                  LifecycleActionResult='CONTINUE'
                )
              else:
                print("Function timed out - republishing SNS
```

```
message")
                    sns.publish(TopicArn=r['Sns']['TopicArn'],
Message=r['Sns']['Message'])
                except Exception as e:
                  print("A failure occurred with exception %s" % e)
                  autoscaling.complete_lifecycle_action(
                    LifecycleHookName=hook,
                    AutoScalingGroupName=group,
                    InstanceId=ec2_instance,
                    LifecycleActionResult='ABANDON'
                  )
      Runtime: python3.6
      MemorySize: 128
      Timeout: 300
      Handler: index.handler
  LifecycleHookFunctionLogGroup:
    Type: AWS::Logs::LogGroup
    DeletionPolicy: Delete
    Properties:
      LogGroupName: !Sub /aws/lambda/${AWS::StackName}-lifecycleHooks
      RetentionInDays: 7
  ...
  ...
```

Creating a Lambda Function to Process Life Cycle Hooks

The Lambda function is a little bit more involved than what we dealt with so far, but is still a relatively simple function that should be reasonably easy to follow if you have experience with Python.

The function first defines the required libraries and looks for an environment variable called ECS_CLUSTER, which is required so that the function knows which ECS cluster the life cycle hook relates to, and this environment variable value is passed in via the Environment property on the Lambda function resource.

Next, the function declares three AWS clients:

- ecs: Communicates with ECS to introspect ECS container instance information and drain the correct instance based upon the EC2 instance ID received in the life cycle hook.

- `autoscaling`: Signals the EC2 Auto Scaling service when the life cycle hook can continue.
- `sns`: Republishes the life cycle hook event if the Lambda function is about to reach the maximum five minute execution timeout and the ECS container instance has not drained yet. This will reinvoke the Lambda function again, until the ECS container instance has completely drained.

The `handler` method defines the entry point for the Lambda function, and first extracts out a number of variables that capture information from the received SNS message including the life cycle hook event type (`transition` variable), hook name (`hook` variable), Auto Scaling group name (`group` variable), and EC2 instance ID (`ec2_instance` variable). A check is then made immediately to verify the life cycle hook event type does relate to an EC2 instance terminating event, and if the event type (captured in the transition variable) does not equal the value `autoscaling:EC2_INSTANCE_TERMINATING`, then the function returns immediately, effectively ignoring the event.

Assuming the event does relate to an EC2 instance terminating, the handler next queries the ECS service via the `ecs` client, first describing all instances in the configured cluster and then attempting to locate the ECS container instance that matches the EC2 instance ID captured from the life cycle hook event. If the instance cannot be found, then a `ValueError` exception is raised, which will be caught by the catch statement, resulting in an error being logged and the function completing the life cycle hook with a result of `ABANDON`. If the instance is found, the handler proceeds to drain the instance by calling the `update_container_instances_state()` method on the `ecs` client, which sets the status of the instance to `DRAINING`, meaning ECS will no longer schedule any new tasks to the instance and attempt to migrate existing tasks to other instances in the cluster. At this point, the handler needs to wait for all current ECS tasks running on the instance to be drained, and this can be achieved by polling the ECS task count in a `while` loop every five seconds until the task count reduces to zero. You could attempt to do this indefinitely, however Lambda has a maximum five minute execution time limit at the time of writing, so the `while` loop uses the `context.get_remaining_time_in_millis()` method to check if the Lambda execution timeout is about to be reached.

> The `context` object is an object that is passed by the Lambda runtime environment to your handler method and includes information about the Lambda environment including memory, CPU, and remaining execution time.

In the event the task count reduces to zero, you can safely terminate the ECS container instance, and the autoscaling client completes the life cycle hook with a result of CONTINUE, meaning the EC2 Auto Scaling service will continue processing any other registered hooks and terminate the instance. If the task count does not reduce to zero before the function is about to exit, then the function simply republishes the original life cycle hook notification, which will reinvoke the function from the start again. Because all of the actions in the function are idempotent, that is updating the status of an ECS container instance that is already draining to DRAINING results in the same draining state, this approach is safe and a very simple and elegant approach to overcoming the execution timeout limits of Lambda.

Configuring permissions for the life cycle hook Lambda function

The Lambda function is now in place and the final configuration task is to add the required permissions for the various API calls and operations the Lambda function performs:

```
...
...
Resources:
  LifecycleHookPermission:
    Type: AWS::Lambda::Permission
    Properties:
      Action: lambda:InvokeFunction
      FunctionName: !Ref LifecycleHookFunction
      Principal: sns.amazonaws.com
      SourceArn: !Ref LifecycleHookTopic
  LifecycleFunctionRole:
    Type: AWS::IAM::Role
    Properties:
      AssumeRolePolicyDocument:
        Version: "2012-10-17"
        Statement:
          - Action:
              - sts:AssumeRole
            Effect: Allow
            Principal:
              Service: lambda.amazonaws.com
      Policies:
        - PolicyName: LifecycleHookPermissions
          PolicyDocument:
            Version: "2012-10-17"
```

```
      Statement:
        - Sid: ListContainerInstances
          Effect: Allow
          Action:
            - ecs:ListContainerInstances
          Resource: !Sub ${ApplicationCluster.Arn}
        - Sid: ManageContainerInstances
          Effect: Allow
          Action:
            - ecs:DescribeContainerInstances
            - ecs:UpdateContainerInstancesState
          Resource: "*"
          Condition:
            ArnEquals:
              ecs:cluster: !Sub ${ApplicationCluster.Arn}
        - Sid: Publish
          Effect: Allow
          Action:
            - sns:Publish
          Resource: !Ref LifecycleHookTopic
        - Sid: CompleteLifecycleAction
          Effect: Allow
          Action:
            - autoscaling:CompleteLifecycleAction
          Resource: !Sub
arn:aws:autoscaling:${AWS::Region}:${AWS::AccountId}:autoScalingGroup:
*:autoScalingGroupName/${ApplicationAutoscaling}
        - Sid: ManageLambdaLogs
          Effect: Allow
          Action:
          - logs:CreateLogStream
          - logs:PutLogEvents
          Resource: !Sub ${LifecycleHookFunctionLogGroup.Arn}
  LifecycleHookFunction:
    Type: AWS::Lambda::Function
  ...
  ...
```

Configuring Permissions for a Life Cycle Hook Lambda Function

In the preceding example, a resource called `LifecycleHookPermission` of type `AWS::Lambda::Permission` is required, which grants permission for the SNS service (as referenced by the `Principal` property) to invoke the Lambda function (as referenced by the `LambdaFunction` property) for notifications published to the SNS topic (as referenced by the `SourceArn` property). This approach to configuring permissions is typically required whenever you need to grant another AWS service the ability to invoke a Lambda function on your behalf, although there are exceptions to this rule (such as the CloudFormation custom resource use case, where CloudFormation implicitly has such a permission).

You also create an IAM role for the Lambda function called `LambdaFunctionRole`, which grants the function the ability to execute the various tasks and operations it needs to perform including:

- Listing, describing, and updating ECS container instances within the application cluster
- Republishing the life cycle hook event to SNS if the Lambda function is about to timeout
- Completing the life cycle action once the ECS container instance has drained
- Writing logs to CloudWatch logs

Deploying and testing Auto Scaling life cycle hooks

You can now deploy your complete Auto Scaling life cycle hooks solution using the `aws cloudformation deploy` command as demonstrated earlier in this chapter.

Once deployment is complete, to test life cycle management is working as expected, a simple change you can perform to force replacement of the current ECS container instance in your ECS cluster is to revert the AMI change you made earlier in this chapter:

```
ApplicationDesiredCount=1
ApplicationImageId=ami-ec957491
ApplicationImageTag=5fdbe62
ApplicationSubnets=subnet-a5d3ecee,subnet-324e246f
VpcId=vpc-f8233a80
```

Reverting the ECS AMI

Once you now deploy this change, again using the `aws cloudformation deploy` command as demonstrated in earlier example, next switch to the CloudFormation console and when the event to terminate the existing EC2 instance is raised, quickly navigate to the ECS dashboard and select your ECS cluster. On the container instances tab, you should see the status of one of your ECS container instances is draining as demonstrated in the following screenshot, and once all tasks have drained from this instance, the life cycle hook function will signal the EC2 Auto Scaling service to proceed with terminating the instance:

ECS Container Instance Draining

If you repeat the steps taken in the previous screenshots to view cluster memory reservation during the period the ECS container instances are drained and terminated, you should see a graph that looks something like as follows in the example:

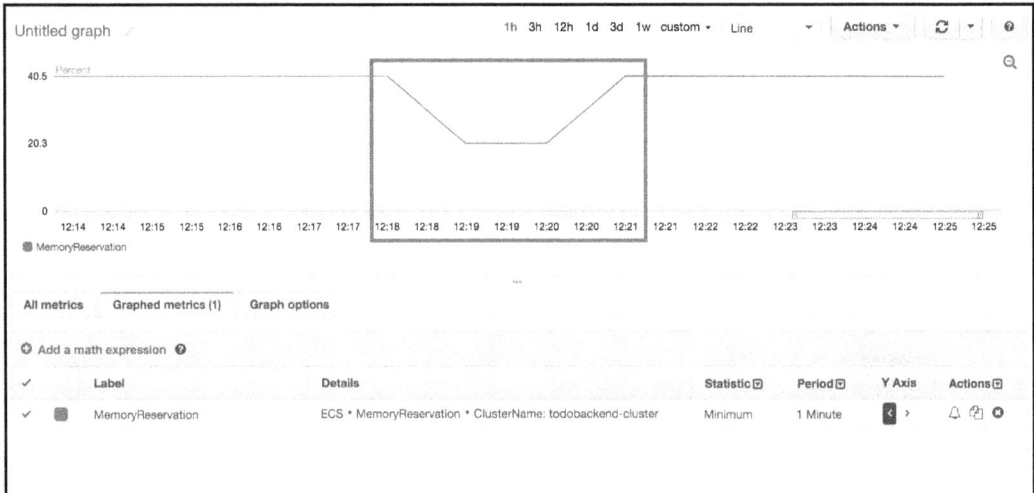

Cluster Memory Reservation during ECS Container Instance Draining

In the preceding screenshots, notice that the cluster memory reservation does not drop to 0% at any time during the rolling update. The memory utilization percentage does change due to their being two instances in the cluster during the rolling upgrade, but the ability for us to drain ECS container instances ensures uninterrupted service for your applications running on your clusters.

As a final check, you can also navigate to the CloudWatch logs group for the life cycle hooks function, which is shown in the following screenshot:

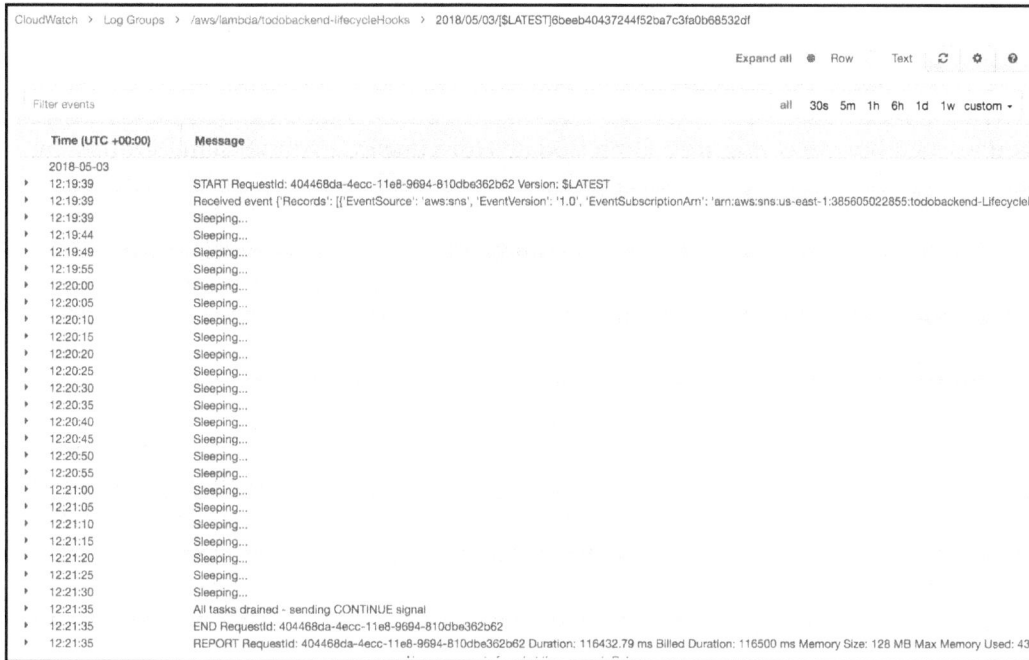

Life Cycle Hooks Function Logs

In the preceding screenshot, you can see that the function sleeps periodically whilst the container instance is draining, and after approximately two minutes in this case, all tasks drain and the function sends a `CONTINUE` signal for the hook to the Auto Scaling service.

Summary

In this chapter, you created a solution for managing the life cycle of your ECS container instances and ensuring the applications and services running on your ECS clusters are not impacted any time you need to terminate and replace an ECS container instance within your ECS cluster.

You learned how to configure rolling updates for your EC2 Auto Scaling groups, by leveraging CloudFormation update policies that enable you to control how new instances can be added to your Auto Scaling groups in a rolling fashion. You saw that this feature works well at an Auto Scaling and EC2 instance level, however you found that the abrupt termination of existing ECS container instances in your cluster causes outages for your applications.

To address this challenge, you created an EC2 life cycle hook registered for `EC2_INSTANCE_TERMINATING` events and configured this hook to publish notifications to an SNS topic, which in turn triggers a Lambda function. This function is responsible for locating the ECS container instance associated with the EC2 instance about to be terminated, draining the container instance, and then waiting until the ECS task count reaches 0, indicating all ECS tasks on the instance have been terminated and replaced. In the event the ECS container instance takes longer than the five minute maximum execution time of a Lambda function, you learned that you can simply republish the SNS event that contains the life cycle hook information, which in turn will trigger a new invocation of the function, and this process can continue indefinitely until the ECS task count on the instance reaches 0.

In the next chapter, you will learn how you can dynamically manage the capacity of your ECS clusters, which is critical to support the Auto Scaling requirements of your applications. This involves the ongoing adding and remove ECS container instances to your ECS cluster, so you can see that the ECS container instance life cycle mechanisms introduced in this chapter are critical for ensuring your applications are not affected by any Auto Scaling operations.

Questions

1. True/false: When you terminate an ECS container instance, the instance will automatically drain running ECS tasks to another instance in the cluster.
2. What are the types of EC2 Auto Scaling life cycle hooks you can receive?
3. What type of responses can you send once you have finished processing EC2 Auto Scaling life cycle hooks?
4. True/false: EC2 Auto Scaling life cycle hooks can publish events to AWS Kinesis.
5. You create a Lambda function that processes a life cycle hook and drains your ECS container instances. You have noticed that sometimes this takes around 4 – 5 minutes, but often takes 15 minutes. What can you do to resolve this issue?
6. What CloudFormation feature can you configure to enable rolling updates for Auto Scaling groups?
7. You want to perform rolling updates and ensure that you always have at least the current desired count of instances in service during the update. How would you achieve this?
8. When using CloudFormation to subscribe a Lambda function to an SNS topic, what type of resource do you need to create to ensure the SNS service has appropriate permissions to invoke the function?

Further reading

You can check the following links for more information about the topics covered in this chapter:

- CloudFormation UpdatePolicy attribute: `https://docs.aws.amazon.com/AWSCloudFormation/latest/UserGuide/aws-attribute-updatepolicy.html`
- Amazon EC2 Auto Scaling life cycle hooks: `https://docs.aws.amazon.com/autoscaling/ec2/userguide/lifecycle-hooks.html`
- CloudFormation life cycle hook resource reference: `https://docs.aws.amazon.com/AWSCloudFormation/latest/UserGuide/aws-resource-as-lifecyclehook.html`
- CloudFormation SNS topic resource reference: `https://docs.aws.amazon.com/AWSCloudFormation/latest/UserGuide/aws-properties-sns-topic.html`
- CloudFormation SNS subscription resource reference: `https://docs.aws.amazon.com/AWSCloudFormation/latest/UserGuide/aws-resource-sns-subscription.html`
- CloudFormation Lambda permission resource reference: `https://docs.aws.amazon.com/AWSCloudFormation/latest/UserGuide/aws-resource-lambda-permission.html`
- CloudFormation ECS task definition resource reference: `https://docs.aws.amazon.com/AWSCloudFormation/latest/UserGuide/aws-resource-ecs-taskdefinition.html`
- CloudFormation ECS service resource reference: `https://docs.aws.amazon.com/AWSCloudFormation/latest/UserGuide/aws-resource-ecs-service.html`
- CloudFormation Lambda function resource reference: `https://docs.aws.amazon.com/AWSCloudFormation/latest/UserGuide/aws-resource-lambda-function.html`
- CloudFormation Lambda function code: `https://docs.aws.amazon.com/AWSCloudFormation/latest/UserGuide/aws-properties-lambda-function-code.html`
- CloudFormation custom resource documentation: `https://docs.aws.amazon.com/AWSCloudFormation/latest/UserGuide/template-custom-resources.html`
- CloudFormation custom resource reference: `https://docs.aws.amazon.com/AWSCloudFormation/latest/UserGuide/crpg-ref.html`

12
ECS Auto Scaling

Elasticity is one of the fundamental tenets of cloud computing, and describes the ability to auto scale your applications on demand to ensure the best possible experience and responsiveness for your customers, while optimizing cost by only providing additional capacity for your application when it is actually required.

AWS supports scaling your Docker applications that are deployed using ECS via two key features:

- **Application Auto Scaling**: This uses the AWS application auto scaling service and supports Auto Scaling at an ECS service level, where the number of ECS tasks or containers running your ECS services can be scaled up or down.
- **EC2 Auto Scaling**: This uses the EC2 Auto Scaling service and supports Auto Scaling at an EC2 Auto Scaling group level, where the number of EC2 instances in your Auto Scaling group can be scaled up or down. In the context of ECS, your EC2 Auto Scaling groups typically correspond to ECS clusters, and the individual EC2 instances correspond to ECS container instances, so EC2 Auto Scaling is managing the overall capacity of your ECS cluster.

Because there are two paradigms at play here, the goal of Auto Scaling for your Docker applications can be a challenging technical concept to understand, let alone implement successfully in a predictable and reliable manner. This is further exacerbated by the fact that, as of the time of writing this book, application auto scaling and EC2 Auto Scaling are completely independent features that offer no integration with each other, hence, you are responsible for ensuring both features work together with one another.

When it comes to analyzing each of these features, the good news is that application auto scaling is very straightforward to understand and implement.

With application auto scaling, you simply need to define the key performance metrics for your applications, and scale up (increase) or scale down (decrease) the number of ECS tasks that run your application. The bad news is that EC2 auto scaling, when applied in the context of auto scaling ECS container instances in an ECS cluster, is definitely a much harder proposition to deal with. Here, you need to ensure your ECS clusters are providing enough compute, memory, and network resources across all ECS tasks running in your cluster, and you need to ensure that your cluster is able to add or remove capacity whenever application auto scaling scales individual ECS services up or down.

> Another challenge of scaling ECS clusters is ensuring you do not disrupt service and drain running tasks on an ECS container instance that is about to be removed from the cluster during a scale down/in event. The ECS life cycle hooks solution implemented in Chapter 11 - *Managing the ECS Infrastructure Life Cycle* takes care of this for you, ensuring the ECS container instances are drained of all running tasks before permitting the EC2 auto scaling service to take an instance out of service.

Dealing with the problem of scaling your ECS cluster resources is the primary focus of this chapter, as once solved, you will be able to arbitrarily scale each of your ECS services and be assured that your ECS cluster will dynamically add or remove ECS container instances to ensure there is always sufficient and optimal resources for your applications. In this chapter, we will first focus on solving the problem of ECS cluster-capacity management, and then discuss how to configure the AWS application auto scaling service to auto scale your ECS services and applications.

The following topics will be covered:

- Understanding the ECS cluster resources
- Calculating the ECS cluster capacity
- Implementing an ECS cluster-capacity management solution
- Configuring CloudWatch events to trigger capacity-management calculations
- Publishing custom CloudWatch metrics related to the ECS cluster capacity
- Configuring CloudWatch alarms and EC2 auto scaling policies to scale your ECS clusters
- Configuring ECS application auto scaling

Technical requirements

The following lists the technical requirements to complete this chapter:

- Administrator access to an AWS account
- Local AWS profile configured as per the instructions in Chapter 3
- AWS CLI
- This chapter continues on from Chapter 11, so it requires that you have successfully completed all the configuration tasks defined there.

The following GitHub URL contains the code samples used in this chapter: `https://github.com/docker-in-aws/docker-in-aws/tree/master/ch12`.

Check out the following video to see the Code in Action: `http://bit.ly/2PdgtPr`

Understanding ECS cluster resources

Before you can start to manage the capacity of your ECS clusters, you need to have a clear and solid understanding of the various resources that affect the capacity of your ECS clusters.

In general, there are three key resources that you need to consider:

- CPU
- Memory
- Network

CPU resources

CPU is a core resource that Docker supports and manages as a first-class citizen. ECS leverages the CPU resource management capabilities of Docker, and exposes the ability to manage these via your ECS task definitions. ECS defines CPU resources in terms of *CPU units*, where a single CPU core contains 1,024 CPU units. When you configure your ECS task definitions, you specify a CPU reservation, which defines how much CPU time will be allocated to the application whenever there is contention for CPU time.

Note that a CPU reservation is not a limit as to how much CPU the ECS task can use–each ECS task is free to burst and use all available CPU resources–the reservation is only applied when there is contention for CPU, and Docker attempts to allocate CPU time fairly based upon the configured reservation for each running ECS task.

It's important to understand that each CPU reservation deducts from the available CPU capacity of a given ECS container instance. For example, if your ECS container instance has 2 CPU cores, that equates to a total of 2,048 CPU units. If you run 3 ECS tasks that are configured with 500, 600, and 700 CPU units, this means that your ECS container instance has 2,048 - (500 + 600 + 700), or 248, CPU units available. Note that whenever the ECS scheduler needs to run a new ECS task, it will always ensure that a target ECS container instance has enough CPU capacity to run the task. Following on from the previous example, if a new ECS task needed to be started that reserves 400 CPU units, then the ECS container instance with 248 CPU units remaining would not be considered, given it does not have sufficient CPU resources currently available:

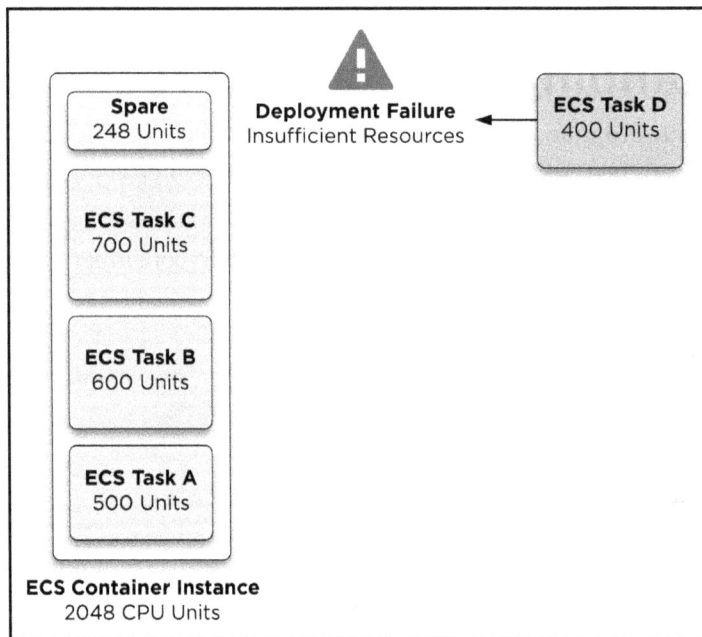

Allocating CPU resources

In terms of configuring CPU reservations, you have already learned how to do this via CloudFormation–see the *Defining an ECS task definition using CloudFormation* example in Chapter 8 - *Deploying applications using ECS*, where you assigned a value of 245 to the todobackend container definition, via a property called `Cpu`.

Memory resources

Memory is another fundamental resource that is managed via Docker, and works in a similar fashion to CPU, although you can both reserve and limit memory capacity for a given ECS task, whereas you can only reserve (not limit) CPU resources when it comes to managing CPU capacity. This additional ability to limit memory results in three scenarios when it comes to configuring memory for your ECS tasks:

- **Memory reservation only**: This scenario behaves identically to how CPU reservations work. Docker will deduct the configured reservation from the available memory of the ECS container instance, and attempt to allocate this amount of memory whenever there is contention for memory. ECS will allow the ECS task to use up to the maximum amount of memory supported by the ECS container instance. Memory reservations are configured using the `MemoryReservation` property within an ECS task container definition.
- **Memory reservation + limit**: In this scenario, the memory reservation works as the previous scenario, however, the maximum amount of memory that the ECS task can ever use is constrained by the configure memory limit. In general, configuring both a memory reservation and memory limit is considered the best option. Memory limits are configured using the `Memory` property within an ECS task container definition.
- **Memory limit only**: Here, ECS treats the memory reservation and memory limit values as one and the same, meaning ECS will deduct the configured memory limit from the available ECS container instance memory, and also limit memory usage to the same limit.

Configuring memory reservations and limits is straightforward–if you refer back to the *Defining an ECS task definition using CloudFormation* section of Chapter 8 - *Deploying Applications Using ECS*, you can see that you configure the `MemoryReservation` property to configure a reservation of 395 MB. If you wanted to configure a memory limit, you would also need to configure the `Memory` property with an appropriate maximum limit value.

Network resources

CPU and memory are typical and obvious resources that you would expect your ECS clusters to control and manage. One less obvious set of resources is *network resources*, which can be split into two categories:

- **Host network ports**: Whenever you configure static port mappings for your ECS services, host network ports is a resource that you will need to consider. The reason is that static port mappings use a common port exposed by the ECS container instance–for example, if you created an ECS task with a static port mapping that exposes port 80 for a given application, you won't be able to deploy another instance of the ECS task on the same ECS container instance host, given port 80 is still in use.
- **Host network interfaces**: If you are using ECS task networking, it is important to understand that this feature currently requires you to implement a single elastic network interface (ENI) per ECS task. Because EC2 instances have finite limits as to the number of ENIs each instance type can support, the number of ECS tasks configured with ECS task networking that can be supported will be restricted to the maximum number of ENIs the ECS container instance can support.

Calculating the ECS cluster capacity

Before you can calculate the ECS cluster capacity, you need to have a clear understanding of which resources affect capacity and how you can calculate the current capacity for each resource. Once you have defined this for each individual resource, you then need to apply an aggregate calculation across all resources, which will result in a final calculation of the current capacity.

Calculating capacity can appear to be quite a daunting task, especially when you consider the different types of resources and how they behave:

- **CPU**: This is the simplest resource you can work with, as each CPU reservation simply deducts from the available CPU capacity of the cluster.

- **Memory:** Calculating the current capacity of the cluster based upon memory is identical to CPU in that a memory reservation deducts from the available memory capacity of the cluster. As per our earlier discussion in this chapter, how the memory reservation is configured is complicated by the various permutations of memory limits and memory reservations, however fundamentally once you have determined the memory reservation, the calculation is the same as for CPU resources.

- **Static network ports**: If your ECS cluster needs to support *any* containers that are using static port mappings, then you need to consider your ECS container instance network ports as a resource. For example, if a container application always uses port 80 on the ECS container instance, then you can only ever deploy one container per instance, regardless of how much CPU, memory, or other resources that instance might possess.

- **Network interfaces**: If you are have any ECS services or tasks that are configured for ECS task networking, it is important to understand you can currently only run one ECS task per network interface. For example, if you are running a t2.micro instance, this means you can only run one ECS task with task networking enabled per instance, given a t2.micro can only support a single elastic network interface for ECS task networking.

> Given the sample application is not using ECS task networking and is being deployed using dynamic port mapping, we will only consider CPU and memory resources for the remainder of this chapter. If you are interested in an example solution that incorporates static network ports, check out the Auto Scaling ECS Applications module of my `Docker in Production Using Amazon Web Services` course.

The challenge here is how to consider all of your ECS services and tasks in terms of all of the preceding considerations, and then make a decision as to when you should scale up or scale down the number of instances in your cluster. A common and somewhat naive approach I have seen is to treat each resource independently and scale your instances accordingly. For example, you would add a new container instance as soon as your cluster runs out of memory capacity, and similarly if your cluster is about to run out of CPU capacity. This approach works fine if you consider purely the ability to scale out, however it does not work when you want to scale in your cluster. If you scale in your cluster solely based upon current memory capacity, you risk scaling in too soon in terms of CPU capacity, as your cluster may not have sufficient CPU capacity if you remove an instance from the cluster.

This will risk your cluster getting stuck in an auto scaling loop–that is, your cluster keeps on scaling out and then in, and this is because individual resource capacities are independently driving scale-in and scale-out decisions, without consideration of the impact to other resources.

The key to solving this challenge is that you need to make a *single* decision to scale out or in, and consider *all* applicable resources for your cluster. This might make the overall problem seem a whole lot harder to solve, however it is actually quite simple. The crux of the solution is that you always consider the *worst-case scenario*, and make a decision based upon that. For example, if you have plenty of CPU and memory capacity in your cluster, however all static port mappings for a given port are in use on all of your cluster instances, the worst-case scenario says if you scale in your cluster and remove an instance, you will no longer be able to support the current ECS tasks that are using the affected static port mapping. Therefore, the decision here is simple and is purely based upon the worst-case scenario–all other scenarios are ignored.

Calculating the container capacity

One key consideration when calculating the capacity of your cluster is that you need to normalize your resource capacity calculations, such that the capacity of each resource can be expressed in a common and equivalent format, independent of the specific units of measurement for each individual resource. This is critical in making a collective decision that considers all resources, and a natural way to do this is to express resource capacity in terms of the number of additional ECS tasks that can be supported using the currently available unallocated resources. In addition, keeping with the theme of worst-case scenarios, you don't need to consider all of the different ECS tasks that you need to support–you only need to consider the ECS task that is the worst case (the one requiring the most resources) for the resource you are currently calculating the capacity for.

For example, if you have two ECS tasks that require 200 CPU units and 400 CPU units, respectively, you only need to calculate the CPU capacity in terms of the ECS task with 400 CPU units:

$$maxTaskCpuCapacity = \max_{\forall taskCpu \in taskDefinitions}(taskCpu) = \max\{200, 400\} = 400$$

The expression with the somewhat strange upside down A in the formula means "for each taskCpu value in a given set of taskDefinitions".

Once you have determined the worst-case ECS task that needs to be supported, you can proceed to calculate the number of additional ECS tasks that the cluster can currently support. Given the worst-case ECS task requires 400 CPU units, if we now assume that you have two instances in your cluster that each have 600 CPU units of free capacity, this means you can currently support an additional 2 ECS tasks:

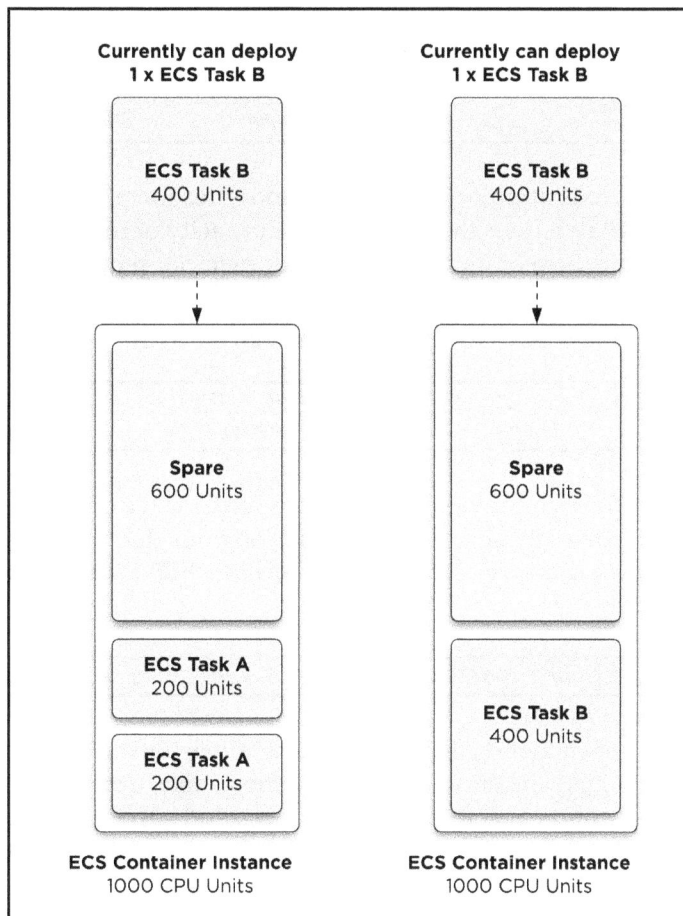

Calculating container capacity

It's important to note here that you need to make this calculation on a per-instance basis, rather than just making the calculation across the entire cluster. Using the previous example, if you consider the free CPU capacity across the entire cluster, you have 1,200 CPU units available and therefore you would calculate a free capacity of three ECS tasks, however the reality is that you can't *split* the ECS task across 2 instances, so if you consider the free capacity on a per-instance basis, it's obvious you can only support one additional ECS task on each instance for a correct total of 2 additional ECS tasks across the cluster.

This can be formalized as a mathematical equation, as follows, where $\lfloor x \rfloor$ the annotation on the right-hand side of the formula means to take *floor* or the lowest nearest integer value of the calculation, and represents an instance in the cluster:

$$cpuCapacity_{cluster} = \sum_{i \in cluster} \lfloor \frac{currentFreeCpuCapacity_i}{maxTaskCpuCapacity} \rfloor = \lfloor \frac{600}{400} \rfloor + \lfloor \frac{600}{400} \rfloor = 2$$

If you repeat the previous approach for your memory resource, you will calculate a separate calculation that defines the current spare capacity of the cluster in terms of memory. If we assume the worst-case ECS task for memory requires 500 MB of memory and both instances have 400 MB available, it's obvious that in terms of memory, the cluster currently has no spare capacity:

$$memoryCapacity_{cluster} = \sum_{i \in cluster} \lfloor \frac{currentFreeMemoryCapacity_i}{maxTaskMemoryCapacity} \rfloor = \lfloor \frac{400}{500} \rfloor + \lfloor \frac{400}{500} \rfloor = 0$$

If you now consider the two previous calculations for CPU (currently two free ECS tasks) and memory (currently zero ECS tasks), it's obvious that the worst case scenario is the memory capacity calculation of zero free ECS tasks, which can be formalized as follows:

$$capacity_{cluster} = \min\{cpuCapacity_{cluster}, memoryCapacity_{cluster}\} = \min\{2, 0\} = 0$$

Note that although we are not incorporating calculations for static network ports and network interfaces to help simplify our solution, the general approach is the same–calculate the current capacity for each instance and sum to obtain an overall cluster capacity value for the resource, and then incorporate the value into the overall cluster capacity calculation:

$$capacity_{cluster} = \min\{cpuCapacity_{cluster}, memoryCapacity_{cluster}, staticPortCapacity_{cluster}, networkInterfaceCapacity_{cluster}\}$$

Deciding when to scale out

At this point, we have established that you need to assess each of the current resource capacities in your cluster, express this in terms of the number of free or spare ECS tasks your cluster currently can support, and then use the worst-case calculation (minimum value) to determine your overall current cluster capacity. Once you have this calculation, you need to decide whether or not you should scale out the cluster, or leave the current cluster capacity unchanged. Of course, you also need to decide when to scale in the cluster, however we will discuss that topic separately soon.

For now, we will focus on whether or not we should scale *out* the cluster (that is, add capacity), as this is the simpler scenario to evaluate. The rule here is that at a minimum, you should scale out your cluster whenever your current cluster capacity is less than one:

$$capacity_{cluster} < 1$$

In other words, if you do not currently have sufficient capacity in your cluster to support one more *worst-case scenario* ECS task, you should add a new instance to the ECS cluster. This makes sense, in that you are attempting to ensure that your cluster always has sufficient capacity for new ECS tasks as they are started. Of course, you can increase this threshold higher if you want more free capacity, which might be applicable for more dynamic environments where containers are often spinning up and down.

Calculating the idle host capacity

If we now consider the scale-in scenario, this becomes a little bit harder to determine. The spare ECS task capacity calculation we have discussed is related and required, however you need to think in these terms: if you removed an ECS container instance from the cluster, would there be enough capacity for all of the current running ECS tasks plus spare capacity for at least one additional ECS task? Another way to express this is to calculate the *idle host capacity* of the cluster–if greater than 1.0 hosts are idle in the cluster, then you can safely scale in the cluster, as subtracting a host would result in a remaining positive non-zero capacity. Note that we are referring to idle host capacity across the cluster–so think of this as more of a virtual host calculation, as you probably won't have a completely idle host. This virtual host calculation is safe, because if we did remove a host from the cluster, the life cycle hooks and ECS container instance-draining features we introduced previously in Chapter 11 - *Managing the ECS Infrastructure Life Cycle* will ensure any containers that are running on the instance to be removed will be migrated to other instances in the cluster.

It's also important to understand that the idle host capacity must be greater than 1.0 and not equal to 1.0, as you must have enough spare capacity for one ECS task, otherwise you will trigger a scale-out action, resulting in an auto scaling scale-out/scale-in loop.

To determine the current idle host capacity, we need to understand the following:

- The maximum number of ECS tasks that each ECS container instance can run for each of the different types of ECS resources (expressed as $hostCapacity_{resource}$).
- The current free capacity for each type of ECS resource across the entire cluster (expressed as $currentFreeCapacity_{resource}$), which we already calculate when determining whether to scale out.

With these pieces of information, you can calculate the idle host capacity for a given resource as follows:

$$idleHostCapacity_{resource} = \frac{currentFreeCapacity_{resource}}{hostCapacity_{resource}}$$

Idle host capacity example

To make this more apparent, let's work through an example, as illustrated in the following diagram, which starts by assuming the following:

- Worst-case ECS task CPU requirement of 400 CPU units
- Worst-case ECS task memory required of 200 MB
- Each ECS container instance support has a maximum of 1,000 CPU units and 1,000 MB memory
- Two ECS container instances currently in the ECS cluster
- Each ECS container instance currently has 600 CPU units' spare capacity. Using the free capacity calculations discussed previously, this equates to a current free capacity across the cluster of two
- ECS tasks in terms of CPU resources, which we will refer to as $currentFreeCapacity_{cpu}$.

- Each ECS container instance currently has 800 MB of spare capacity. Using the free capacity calculations discussed previously, this equates to a current free capacity across the cluster of eight ECS tasks in terms of memory resources, which we will refer to as $currentFreeCapacity_{memory}$:

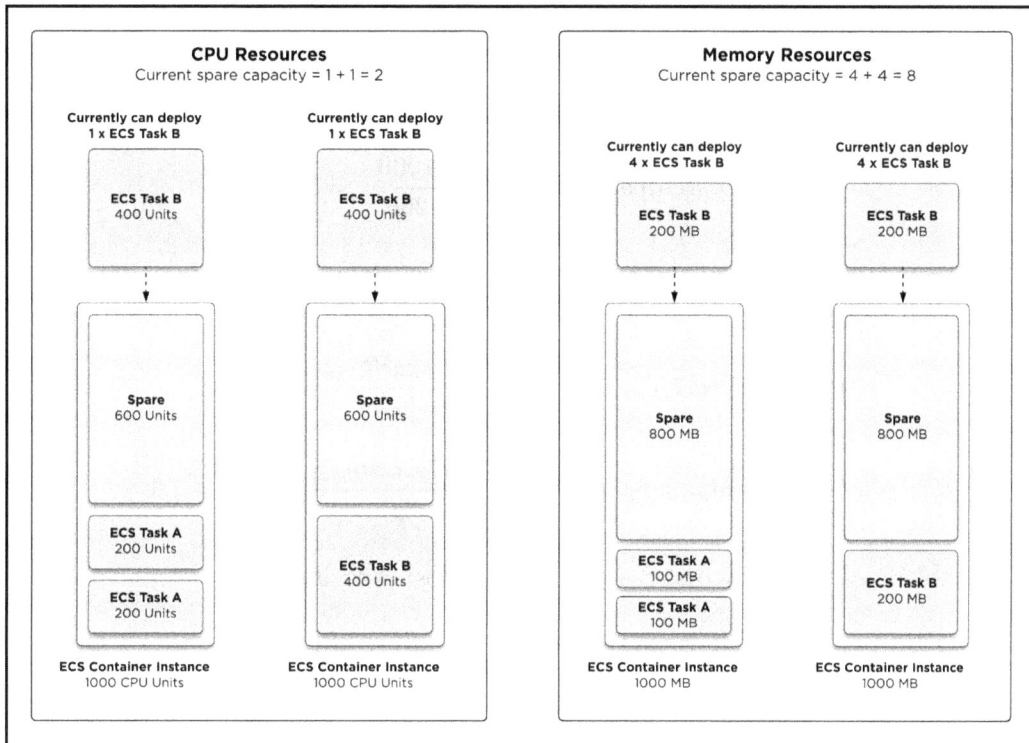

Idle host capacity

We can first calculate the $hostCapacity_{resource}$ value as follows:

$$hostCapacity_{resource} = \lfloor \frac{maxHostCapacity_{resource}}{maxTaskCapacity_{resource}} \rfloor$$

For CPU, it equates to a value of 2, and for memory equates to a value of 5:

$$hostCapacity_{cpu} = \lfloor \frac{1000}{400} \rfloor = 2$$

$$hostCapacity_{memory} = \lfloor \frac{1000}{200} \rfloor = 5$$

With these values calculated and knowledge of the current free capacity of the cluster, we can now calculate the idle host capacity for each resource:

$$idleHostCapacity_{cpu} = \frac{currentFreeCapacity_{cpu}}{hostCapacity_{cpu}} = \frac{2}{2} = 1.0$$

$$idleHostCapacity_{memory} = \frac{currentFreeCapacity_{memory}}{hostCapacity_{memory}} = \frac{8}{5} = 1.6$$

Here's how to calculate a worst-case overall idle host capacity:

$$idleHostCapacity_{cluster} = \min\{idleHostCapacity_{cpu}, idleHostCapacity_{memory}\} = \min\{1.0, 1.6\} = 1.0$$

At this point, given the idle host capacity is 1.0, we should *not* scale in the cluster as the capacity is not currently *greater* than 1. This may seem counterintuitive given you have exactly one idle host, but if you did remove an instance at this point, it would result in an available CPU capacity of 0 for the cluster, and the cluster would scale out given there is no free CPU capacity.

Implementing an ECS Auto Scaling solution

Now that you have a good understanding of how to calculate the ECS cluster capacity for the purposes of making scale-out and scale-in decisions, we are ready to implement an auto scaling solution, as illustrated in the following diagram:

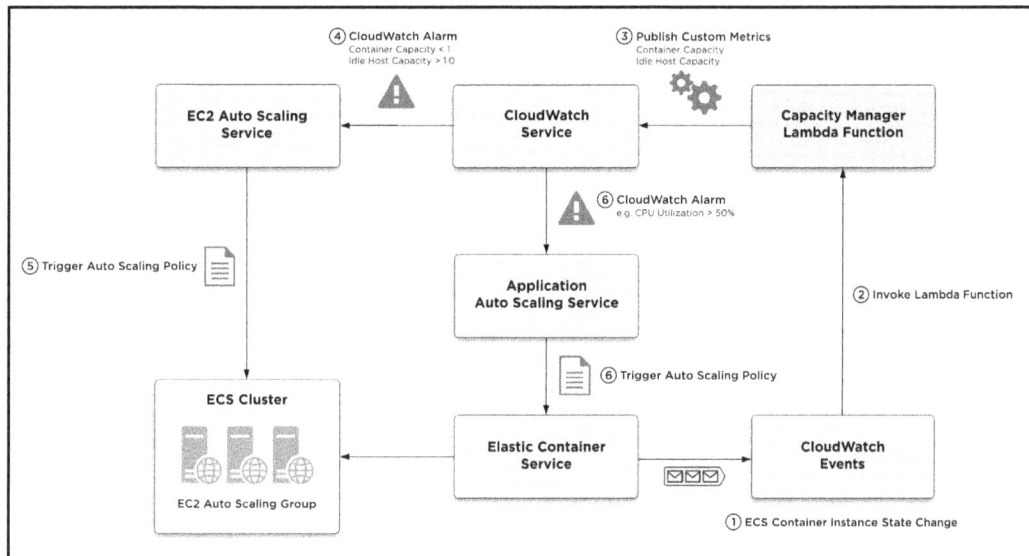

The following provides a walkthrough of the solution shown in the preceding diagram:

1. Before you calculate the ECS cluster capacity, you need a mechanism that will trigger calculations of capacity, ideally whenever the capacity of your ECS container instances changes. This can be achieved by leveraging the CloudWatch Events service, which publishes events for various AWS services including ECS, and allows you to create *event rules* that subscribe to specific events and process them using a variety of mechanisms, including a Lambda function. CloudWatch events support receiving information about ECS container-instance state changes, and this represents the ideal mechanism for triggering cluster capacity calculations, as any change to the available resources of an ECS container instance will trigger a state-change event.

2. A Lambda function responsible for calculating ECS cluster capacity is triggered for each ECS container-instance state-change event.

3. Rather than making a decision to auto scale the cluster, the Lambda function simply publishes the current capacity in the form of CloudWatch custom metrics, which report both the current free container capacity and the idle host capacity.

4. The CloudWatch service is configured with alarms that trigger EC2 auto scaling actions whenever the free container capacity or idle host capacity falls below or exceeds the threshold for scaling out or scaling in the cluster.

5. The EC2 auto scaling service is configured with EC2 auto scaling policies, which are invoked in response to alarms raised by CloudWatch.

6. In addition to the CloudWatch alarms configured to manage the ECS cluster capacity, you can configure appropriate CloudWatch alarms for each of your ECS services, which can then trigger the AWS application auto scaling service to scale out or scale in the number of ECS tasks that are running for your ECS services. For example, in the preceding diagram, the ECS service is configured with an application auto scaling policy that increases the number of ECS tasks should the CPU utilization for the ECS service exceed 50%.

Let's now implement the various components of the solution.

Configuring CloudWatch events for ECS

The first task we need to perform is to set up a CloudWatch event rule, which subscribes to ECS container-instance state-change events and is configured with a target of a Lambda function that will calculate the ECS cluster capacity.

The following example demonstrates adding a CloudWatch event rule to the todobackend-aws `stack.yml` CloudFormation template:

```
...
...
Resources:
  EcsCapacityPermission:
    Type: AWS::Lambda::Permission
    Properties:
      Action: lambda:InvokeFunction
      FunctionName: !Ref EcsCapacityFunction
      Principal: events.amazonaws.com
      SourceArn: !Sub ${EcsCapacityEvents.Arn}
  EcsCapacityEvents:
```

```
      Type: AWS::Events::Rule
      Properties:
        Description: !Sub ${AWS::StackName} ECS Events Rule
        EventPattern:
          source:
            - aws.ecs
          detail-type:
            - ECS Container Instance State Change
          detail:
            clusterArn:
              - !Sub ${ApplicationCluster.Arn}
        Targets:
          - Arn: !Sub ${EcsCapacityFunction.Arn}
            Id: !Sub ${AWS::StackName}-ecs-events
    LifecycleHook:
      Type: AWS::AutoScaling::LifecycleHook
  . . .
  . . .
```

The `EcsCapacityEvents` resource defines the event rule and includes two key properties:

- `EventPattern`: Defines the pattern that matches events to this rule. All CloudWatch events include `source`, `detail-type`, and `detail` properties, and the event pattern ensures only ECS events (as defined by the `source` pattern of `aws.ecs`) that relate to ECS container-instance state changes (as defined by the `detail-type` pattern) for the `ApplicationCluster` resource (as defined by the `detail` pattern) that will be matched to the rule.
- `Targets`: Defines the target resource that the event should be routed to. In the preceding example, you reference the ARN of a Lambda function called `EcsCapacityFunction`, which you will define shortly.

The `EcsCapacityPermission` resource ensures the CloudWatch events service has permission to invoke the `EcsCapacityFunction` Lambda function. This is a common approach for any service that invokes a Lambda function, where you add a Lambda permission that grants a given resource (as defined by the `SourceArn` property) for a given AWS service (as defined by the `Principal` property) the ability to invoke a Lambda function (`FunctionName` property).

Now, let's add the referenced Lambda function, along with an IAM role and CloudWatch logs group:

```
...
...
Resources:
  EcsCapacityRole:
    Type: AWS::IAM::Role
    Properties:
      AssumeRolePolicyDocument:
        Version: "2012-10-17"
        Statement:
          - Action:
              - sts:AssumeRole
            Effect: Allow
            Principal:
              Service: lambda.amazonaws.com
      Policies:
        - PolicyName: EcsCapacityPermissions
          PolicyDocument:
            Version: "2012-10-17"
            Statement:
              - Sid: ManageLambdaLogs
                Effect: Allow
                Action:
                - logs:CreateLogStream
                - logs:PutLogEvents
                Resource: !Sub ${EcsCapacityLogGroup.Arn}
  EcsCapacityFunction:
    Type: AWS::Lambda::Function
    DependsOn:
      - EcsCapacityLogGroup
    Properties:
      Role: !Sub ${EcsCapacityRole.Arn}
      FunctionName: !Sub ${AWS::StackName}-ecsCapacity
      Description: !Sub ${AWS::StackName} ECS Capacity Manager
      Code:
        ZipFile: |
          import json
          def handler(event, context):
            print("Received event %s" % json.dumps(event))
      Runtime: python3.6
      MemorySize: 128
      Timeout: 300
      Handler: index.handler
  EcsCapacityLogGroup:
    Type: AWS::Logs::LogGroup
    DeletionPolicy: Delete
```

```
    Properties:
      LogGroupName: !Sub /aws/lambda/${AWS::StackName}-ecsCapacity
      RetentionInDays: 7
  EcsCapacityPermission:
    Type: AWS::Lambda::Permission
...
...
```

By now, you should have a good understanding of how to define Lambda functions using CloudFormation, so I won't describe the preceding example in depth. Note, however, that for now, I have implemented a basic function that simply prints any received events–we will use to this to gain an initial understanding of how the ECS container instance state change events are structured.

At this point, you can now deploy your changes using the `aws cloudformation deploy` command:

```
> export AWS_PROFILE=docker-in-aws
> aws cloudformation deploy --template-file stack.yml \
    --stack-name todobackend --parameter-overrides $(cat dev.cfg) \
    --capabilities CAPABILITY_NAMED_IAM
Enter MFA code for arn:aws:iam::385605022855:mfa/justin.menga:

Waiting for changeset to be created..
Waiting for stack create/update to complete
Successfully created/updated stack - todobackend
```

Once deployment is complete, you can trigger an ECS container-instance state change by stopping an existing ECS task that is running on your ECS cluster:

```
> aws ecs list-tasks --cluster todobackend-cluster
{
    "taskArns": [
        "arn:aws:ecs:us-
east-1:385605022855:task/5754a076-6f5c-47f1-8e73-c7b229315e31"
    ]
}
> aws ecs stop-task --cluster todobackend-cluster --task
5754a076-6f5c-47f1-8e73-c7b229315e31
```

```
{
    "task": {
        ...
        ...
        "lastStatus": "RUNNING",
        "desiredStatus": "STOPPED",
        ...
        ...
    }
}
```

Because this ECS task is linked to an ECS service, ECS will automatically start a new ECS task, and if you head over to the CloudWatch console, select Logs, and then open the most recent log stream for the log group for the Lambda function that processes ECS container instance state change events (`/aws/lambda/todobackend-ecsCapacity`), you should see a couple of events have been logged:

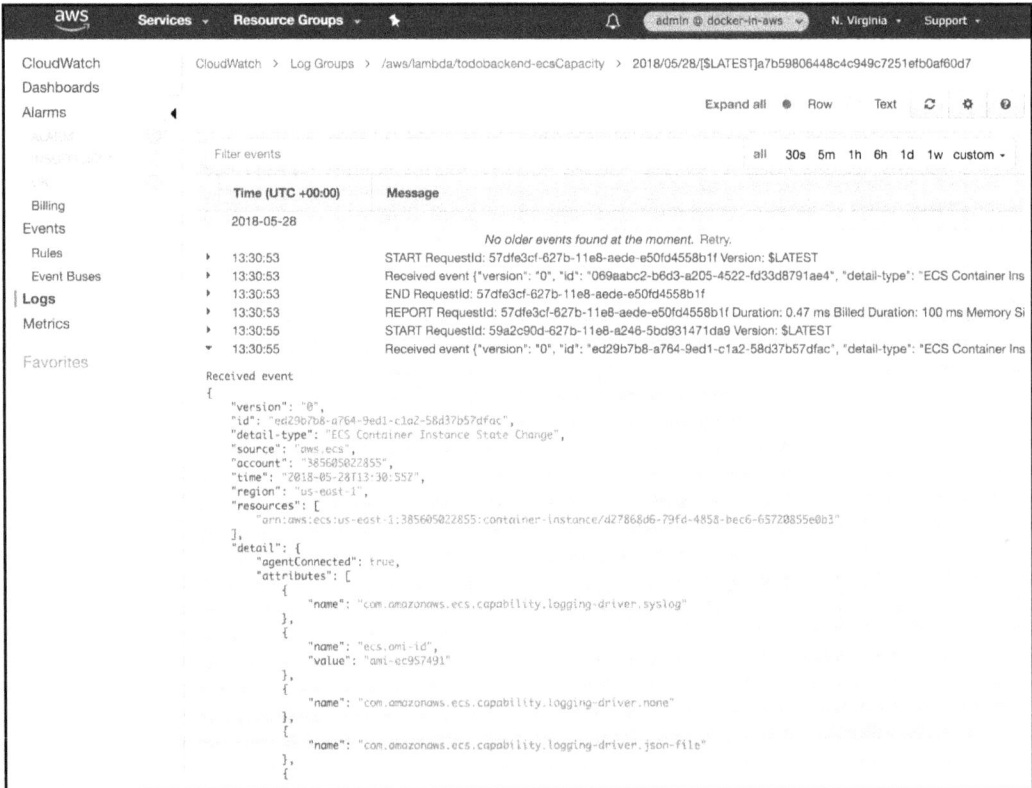

In the preceding screenshot, you can see that two events were logged within a couple of seconds, which represent you stopping the ECS task and ECS then automatically starting a new ECS task to ensure the linked ECS service meets its configured desired count.

You can see that the `source` and `detail-type` properties match the event pattern you configured earlier, and, if you scroll down further in the second event, you should find a property called `registeredResources` and `remainingResources`, as demonstrated in the following example:

```
{
  ...
  ...
  "clusterArn": "arn:aws:ecs:us-
east-1:385605022855:cluster/todobackend-cluster",
  "containerInstanceArn": "arn:aws:ecs:us-
east-1:385605022855:container-instance/d27868d6-79fd-4858-
bec6-65720855e0b3",
  "ec2InstanceId": "i-0d9bd79d19a843216",
  "registeredResources": [
    {
      "name": "CPU",
      "type": "INTEGER",
      "integerValue": 1024
    },
    {
      "name": "MEMORY",
      "type": "INTEGER",
      "integerValue": 993
    },
    {
      "name": "PORTS",
      "type": "STRINGSET",
      "stringSetValue": ["22","2376","2375","51678","51679"]
    }
  ],
  "remainingResources": [
    {
      "name": "CPU",
      "type": "INTEGER",
      "integerValue": 774
    },
    {
      "name": "MEMORY",
      "type": "INTEGER",
      "integerValue": 593
    },
```

```
    {
      "name": "PORTS",
      "type": "STRINGSET",
      "stringSetValue": ["22","2376","2375","51678","51679"]
    }
  ],
  ...
  ...
}
```

The `registeredResources` property defines the total resources allocated to the instance, while `remainingResources` indicates the current remaining quantity of each resource. Because the event in the preceding example is raised when ECS starts a new ECS task for the todobackend service, the total 250 CPU units and 400 MB of memory allocated to this task are deducted from `registeredResources`, which is then reflected in the `remainingResources` property. Notice also at the top of the output of Example 12-6 that the event includes other useful information, such as the ECS cluster ARN and ECS container instance ARN values (as specified by the `clusterArn` and `containerInstanceArn` properties).

Programming the Lambda function that calculates the cluster capacity

Now that you have set up a CloudWatch event and Lambda function that is invoked whenever ECS container-instance state changes are detected, you can now implement the required application code in the Lambda function that will perform the appropriate ECS cluster-capacity calculations:

```
  ...
  ...
Resources:
  ...
  ...
  EcsCapacityFunction:
    Type: AWS::Lambda::Function
    DependsOn:
      - EcsCapacityLogGroup
    Properties:
      Role: !Sub ${EcsCapacityRole.Arn}
      FunctionName: !Sub ${AWS::StackName}-ecsCapacity
      Description: !Sub ${AWS::StackName} ECS Capacity Manager
      Code:
        ZipFile: |
```

```python
import json
import boto3
ecs = boto3.client('ecs')
# Max memory and CPU - you would typically inject these as
environment variables
CONTAINER_MAX_MEMORY = 400
CONTAINER_MAX_CPU = 250

# Get current CPU
def check_cpu(instance):
  return sum(
    resource['integerValue']
    for resource in instance['remainingResources']
    if resource['name'] == 'CPU'
  )
# Get current memory
def check_memory(instance):
  return sum(
    resource['integerValue']
    for resource in instance['remainingResources']
    if resource['name'] == 'MEMORY'
  )
# Lambda entrypoint
def handler(event, context):
  print("Received event %s" % json.dumps(event))

  # STEP 1 - COLLECT RESOURCE DATA
  cluster = event['detail']['clusterArn']
  # The maximum CPU availble for an idle ECS instance
  instance_max_cpu = next(
    resource['integerValue']
    for resource in event['detail']['registeredResources']
    if resource['name'] == 'CPU')
  # The maximum memory availble for an idle ECS instance
  instance_max_memory = next(
    resource['integerValue']
    for resource in event['detail']['registeredResources']
    if resource['name'] == 'MEMORY')
  # Get current container capacity based upon CPU and memory
  instance_arns = ecs.list_container_instances(
    cluster=cluster
  )['containerInstanceArns']
  instances = [
    instance for instance in
ecs.describe_container_instances(
        cluster=cluster,
        containerInstances=instance_arns
      )['containerInstances']
```

```
            if instance['status'] == 'ACTIVE'
        ]
        cpu_capacity = 0
        memory_capacity = 0
        for instance in instances:
            cpu_capacity +=
int(check_cpu(instance)/CONTAINER_MAX_CPU)
            memory_capacity +=
int(check_memory(instance)/CONTAINER_MAX_MEMORY)
        print("Current container cpu capacity of %s" %
cpu_capacity)
        print("Current container memory capacity of %s" %
memory_capacity)

        # STEP 2 - CALCULATE OVERALL CONTAINER CAPACITY
        container_capacity = min(cpu_capacity, memory_capacity)
        print("Overall container capacity of %s" %
container_capacity)

        # STEP 3 - CALCULATE IDLE HOST COUNT
        idle_hosts = min(
            cpu_capacity / int(instance_max_cpu /
CONTAINER_MAX_CPU),
            memory_capacity / int(instance_max_memory /
CONTAINER_MAX_MEMORY)
        )
        print("Overall idle host capacity of %s" % idle_hosts)
Runtime: python3.6
MemorySize: 128
Timeout: 300
Handler: index.handler
...
...
```

In the preceding example, you first define the maximum CPU and maximum memory of the ECS tasks that your cluster will support, which is required to make the various cluster-capacity calculations, and we use the current configured CPU and memory settings for the todobackend service, given this is the only application we are supporting on our cluster. Within the handler function, the first step is to collect the current resource capacity data using the received CloudWatch event. The event includes details about the maximum capacity of your ECS container instance in the registeredResources property, and also includes the ECS cluster that the instance belongs to. The function first lists all of instances in the cluster, and then loads detailed information about each instance using the describe_container_instances call on the ECS client.

The information collected on each instance is limited to ACTIVE instances only, as you don't want to include resources for instances that may be in a DRAINING state or some other non-active state.

> The code in the preceding example, will only work correctly in a Python 3.x environment, so ensure your Lambda function is configured to use Python 3.6.

With the necessary information collected about each ECS container instance, you then iterate through each instance and calculate the CPU and memory capacity. This calls helper functions that query the `remainingResources` property for each instance, which return the current available capacity of each resource. Each calculation is expressed in terms of the maximum-sized containers you defined earlier, and is summed together to provide the CPU and memory capacity across the cluster, which is printed for informational purposes.

The next step is to calculate the overall container capacity, which is easily calculated by taking the minimum value of the previously calculated resource capacities, and this will be used to determine when your ECS cluster needs to scale out, at the very least when container capacity falls below zero. Finally, the idle host capacity calculation is made–this value will be used to determine when your ECS cluster should scale in, which should only happen if the idle host capacity is greater than 1.0, as discussed previously.

Adding IAM permissions for calculating the cluster capacity

One point to note about the code in the preceding example, is that it requires the ability to call the ECS service and execute the `ListContainerInstances` and `DescribeContainerInstances` API calls. This means you need to add the appropriate IAM permissions to the Lambda function IAM role, as demonstrated in the following example:

```
...
...
Resources:
  ...
  ...
  EcsCapacityRole:
    Type: AWS::IAM::Role
    Properties:
```

```
            AssumeRolePolicyDocument:
              Version: "2012-10-17"
              Statement:
                - Action:
                    - sts:AssumeRole
                  Effect: Allow
                  Principal:
                    Service: lambda.amazonaws.com
            Policies:
              - PolicyName: EcsCapacityPermissions
                PolicyDocument:
                  Version: "2012-10-17"
                  Statement:
                    - Sid: ListContainerInstances
                      Effect: Allow
                      Action:
                        - ecs:ListContainerInstances
                      Resource: !Sub ${ApplicationCluster.Arn}
                    - Sid: DescribeContainerInstances
                      Effect: Allow
                      Action:
                        - ecs:DescribeContainerInstances
                      Resource: "*"
                      Condition:
                        ArnEquals:
                          ecs:cluster: !Sub ${ApplicationCluster.Arn}
                    - Sid: ManageLambdaLogs
                      Effect: Allow
                      Action:
                      - logs:CreateLogStream
                      - logs:PutLogEvents
                      Resource: !Sub ${EcsCapacityLogGroup.Arn}
          ...
          ...
```

Testing cluster-capacity calculations

You have added the code required to calculate the cluster capacity, and ensured that your Lambda function has the appropriate permissions to query ECS to determine the current capacity of all ECS container instances in the cluster. You can now deploy your changes using the `aws cloudformation deploy` command, and, once deployment is complete, you can test your Lambda function again by stopping any ECS task that is running inside the todobackend ECS cluster.

If you review the CloudWatch logs for your Lambda function, you should see events similar to those shown here:

Notice that when you stopped the ECS task (as represented by the stop task event), the Lambda function reports a CPU capacity of **4**, memory capacity of 2, and an overall capacity of **2**, which is the minimum value of each of the calculated resource capacities.

If you sanity-check this, you should find that the calculations are accurate and correct. For the initial event, because you stopped the ECS tasks, there are no tasks running, so the available CPU and memory resources are 1,024 units and 993 MB, respectively (the capacity of a t2.micro instance). This equates to the following container capacities:

- CPU capacity = 1024 / 250 = 4
- Memory capacity = 993 / 400 = 2

When ECS automatically replaces the stopped ECS task, you can see that the cluster capacity drops, given a new ECS task (with 250 CPU units and 400 MB of memory) is now consuming resources:

- CPU capacity = 1024 - 250 / 250 = 774 / 250 = 3
- Memory capacity = 993 - 400 / 400 = 593 / 400 = 1

Finally, you can see that the overall idle host capacity is correctly calculated as 1.0 when you stop the ECS task, which is correct as no ECS tasks are running on your cluster at that time. When ECS replaces the stopped task, the overall idle host capacity reduces to 0.5, given the ECS container instance is now running one out of the maximum two ECS tasks that can be run on a single instance in terms of memory resources.

Publishing custom CloudWatch metrics

At this point, we are calculating the appropriate metrics that determine when you need to both scale out or scale in the cluster, and the final task that needs to be performed in the function is to publish custom CloudWatch event metrics, which we can use to trigger auto scaling policies:

```
...
...
Resources:
  ...
  ...
  EcsCapacityFunction:
    Type: AWS::Lambda::Function
    DependsOn:
      - EcsCapacityLogGroup
    Properties:
      Role: !Sub ${EcsCapacityRole.Arn}
      FunctionName: !Sub ${AWS::StackName}-ecsCapacity
      Description: !Sub ${AWS::StackName} ECS Capacity Manager
      Code:
        ZipFile: |
          import json
          import boto3
          import datetime
          ecs = boto3.client('ecs')
          cloudwatch = boto3.client('cloudwatch')
          # Max memory and CPU - you would typically inject these as
environment variables
          CONTAINER_MAX_MEMORY = 400
          CONTAINER_MAX_CPU = 250
          ...
          ...
          # Lambda entrypoint
          def handler(event, context):
            print("Received event %s" % json.dumps(event))
            ...
            ...
```

```
            # STEP 3 - CALCULATE IDLE HOST COUNT
            idle_hosts = min(
              cpu_capacity / int(instance_max_cpu /
CONTAINER_MAX_CPU),
              memory_capacity / int(instance_max_memory /
CONTAINER_MAX_MEMORY)
            )
            print("Overall idle host capacity of %s" % idle_hosts)
            # STEP 4 - PUBLISH CLOUDWATCH METRICS
            cloudwatch.put_metric_data(
              Namespace='AWS/ECS',
              MetricData=[
                {
                  'MetricName': 'ContainerCapacity',
                  'Dimensions': [{
                    'Name': 'ClusterName',
                    'Value': cluster.split('/')[-1]
                  }],
                  'Timestamp': datetime.datetime.utcnow(),
                  'Value': container_capacity
                },
                {
                  'MetricName': 'IdleHostCapacity',
                  'Dimensions': [{
                    'Name': 'ClusterName',
                    'Value': cluster.split('/')[-1]
                  }],
                  'Timestamp': datetime.datetime.utcnow(),
                  'Value': idle_hosts
                }
              ])
      Runtime: python3.6
      MemorySize: 128
      Timeout: 300
      Handler: index.handler
  ...
  ...
```

In the preceding example, you use the CloudWatch client `put_metric_data` function to publish the `ContainerCapacity` and `IdleHostCapacity` custom metrics within the AWS/ECS namespace. These metrics are dimensioned based upon the ECS cluster, as specified by the ClusterName dimension name, and are limited to the todobackend ECS cluster.

One final configuration task required to ensure the Lambda function operates correctly is to grant the function permissions to publish the CloudWatch metrics. This is achieved by adding the appropriate IAM permissions to the `EcsCapacityRole` you created earlier in the previous example:

```
...
...
Resources:
  ...
  ...
  EcsCapacityRole:
    Type: AWS::IAM::Role
    Properties:
      AssumeRolePolicyDocument:
        Version: "2012-10-17"
        Statement:
          - Action:
              - sts:AssumeRole
            Effect: Allow
            Principal:
              Service: lambda.amazonaws.com
      Policies:
        - PolicyName: EcsCapacityPermissions
          PolicyDocument:
            Version: "2012-10-17"
            Statement:
              - Sid: PublishCloudwatchMetrics
                Effect: Allow
                Action:
                  - cloudwatch:putMetricData
                Resource: "*"
              - Sid: ListContainerInstances
                Effect: Allow
                Action:
                  - ecs:ListContainerInstances
                Resource: !Sub ${ApplicationCluster.Arn}
              - Sid: DescribeContainerInstances
                Effect: Allow
                Action:
                  - ecs:DescribeContainerInstances
                Resource: "*"
                Condition:
                  ArnEquals:
                    ecs:cluster: !Sub ${ApplicationCluster.Arn}
              - Sid: ManageLambdaLogs
                Effect: Allow
                Action:
```

```
- logs:CreateLogStream
- logs:PutLogEvents
Resource: !Sub ${EcsCapacityLogGroup.Arn}
. . .
. . .
```

If you now deploy your changes using the `aws cloudformation deploy` command and then stop a running ECS task, after switching over to the CloudWatch console, you should be able to see new metrics being published in relation to your ECS cluster. If you select **Metrics** from the left-hand menu and then select **ECS > ClusterName** under **All metrics**, you should see your custom metrics (`ContainerCapacity` and `IdleHostCapacity`). The following screenshot shows these metrics graphed on the basis of the maximum value collected within a one-minute period. At 12:49 on the graph, you can see both the `ContainerCapacity` and `IdleHostCapacity` metrics increased when you stopped the ECS task, and then once ECS started a new ECS task, the values for both metrics decreased as the new ECS task was allocated resources from your cluster:

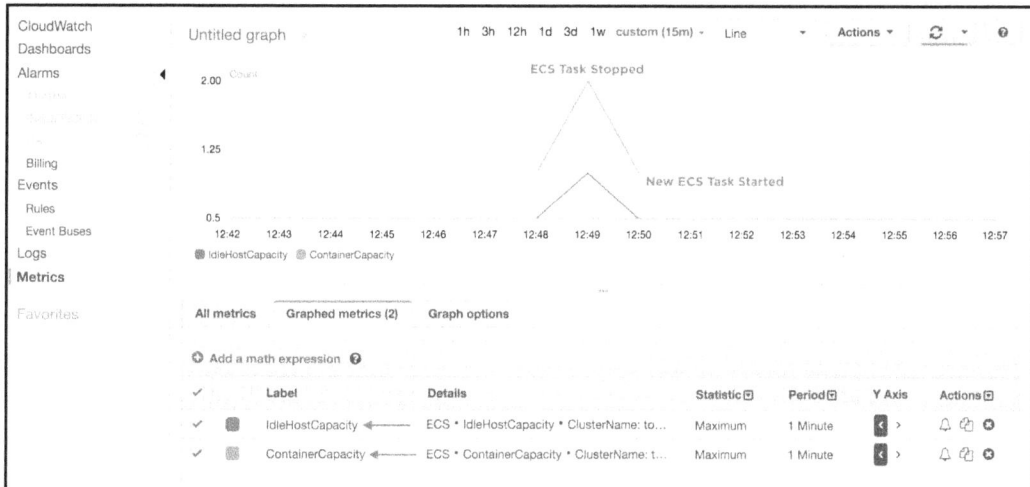

Creating CloudWatch alarms for cluster-capacity management

You now have the ability to calculate and publish ECS cluster capacity metrics whenever an ECS container-instance state change occurs in your ECS cluster. The next step in the overall solution is to implement CloudWatch alarms, which will trigger auto scaling actions whenever a metric exceeds or drops below a specified threshold that relates to cluster capacity.

The following code demonstrates adding two CloudWatch alarms to the todobackend stack:

```
...
...
Resources:
  ...
  ...
  ContainerCapacityAlarm:
    Type: AWS::CloudWatch::Alarm
    Properties:
      AlarmDescription: ECS Cluster Container Free Capacity
      AlarmActions:
        - !Ref ApplicationAutoscalingScaleOutPolicy
      Namespace: AWS/ECS
      Dimensions:
        - Name: ClusterName
          Value: !Ref ApplicationCluster
      MetricName: ContainerCapacity
      Statistic: Minimum
      Period: 60
      EvaluationPeriods: 1
      Threshold: 1
      ComparisonOperator: LessThanThreshold
      TreatMissingData: ignore
  IdleHostCapacityAlarm:
    Type: AWS::CloudWatch::Alarm
    Properties:
      AlarmDescription: ECS Cluster Container Free Capacity
      AlarmActions:
        - !Ref ApplicationAutoscalingScaleInPolicy
      Namespace: AWS/ECS
      Dimensions:
        - Name: ClusterName
          Value: !Ref ApplicationCluster
      MetricName: IdleHostCapacity
      Statistic: Maximum
```

```
    Period: 60
    EvaluationPeriods: 1
    Threshold: 1
    ComparisonOperator: GreaterThanThreshold
    TreatMissingData: ignore
  ...
  ...
```

In the preceding example, you add two CloudWatch alarms–a `ContainerCapacityAlarm` that will be used to trigger scale-out actions whenever the container capacity falls below 1, and an `IdleHostCapacityAlarm` that will be used to trigger scale-in actions whenever the idle host capacity is greater than 1. The various properties for each alarm are described in further detail here:

- `AlarmActions`: Defines the actions that should be taken should the alarm breach its configured criteria. Here we reference the EC2 auto scaling policy resources that we will define shortly, which trigger the appropriate auto scaling scale-out or scale-in action whenever an alarm is raised.
- `Namespace`: Defines the namespace of the metric the alarm relates to.
- `Dimensions`: Defines the context of how the metric relates to resources within the given namespace. In the preceding example, the context is configured as the ECS cluster within our stack.
- `MetricName`: Defines the name of the metric. Here, we specify the name of each custom metric we published in the previous section.
- `Statistic`: Defines the statistic of the metric that should be evaluated. This is actually quite an important parameter and, as an example in the case of the container capacity alarm, setting a value of maximum ensures transient metrics that fall below the configured threshold of 1 will not unnecessarily trigger the alarm, assuming that at least 1 value during each evaluation period exceeds the configured threshold. The same is applied for the idle host capacity alarm but in the opposite direction.
- `Period`, `EvaluationPeriods`, `Threshold`, and `ComparisonOperator`: These define the timeframe over which the metric must fall outside the bounds of the configured threshold and comparison operator. If these bounds are exceeded, an alarm will be raised.
- `TreatMissingData`: This setting defines how you should treat missing metric data. In our use case, missing metric data is a common occurrence given we only publish metrics whenever an ECS container instance state changes, so setting a value of `ignore` ensures we do not treat missing data as an indication that something is wrong.

Creating EC2 Auto Scaling policies

You now need to create the EC2 auto scaling policy resources that you referenced in each CloudWatch alarm resource.

The following example demonstrates adding a scale-out and scale-in policy to the todobackend stack:

```
...
...
Resources:
  ...
  ...
  ApplicationAutoscalingScaleOutPolicy:
    Type: AWS::AutoScaling::ScalingPolicy
    Properties:
      PolicyType: SimpleScaling
      AdjustmentType: ChangeInCapacity
      ScalingAdjustment: 1
      AutoScalingGroupName: !Ref ApplicationAutoscaling
      Cooldown: 600
  ApplicationAutoscalingScaleInPolicy:
    Type: AWS::AutoScaling::ScalingPolicy
    Properties:
      PolicyType: SimpleScaling
      AdjustmentType: ChangeInCapacity
      ScalingAdjustment: -1
      AutoScalingGroupName: !Ref ApplicationAutoscaling
      Cooldown: 600
  ...
  ...
  ApplicationAutoscaling:
    Type: AWS::AutoScaling::AutoScalingGroup
    DependsOn:
      - DmesgLogGroup
      - MessagesLogGroup
      - DockerLogGroup
      - EcsInitLogGroup
      - EcsAgentLogGroup
    CreationPolicy:
      ResourceSignal:
        Count: 1
        Timeout: PT15M
    UpdatePolicy:
      AutoScalingRollingUpdate:
        SuspendProcesses:
          - HealthCheck
```

```
            - ReplaceUnhealthy
            - AZRebalance
            - AlarmNotification
            - ScheduledActions
        MinInstancesInService: 1
        MinSuccessfulInstancesPercent: 100
        WaitOnResourceSignals: "true"
        PauseTime: PT15M
    Properties:
        LaunchConfigurationName: !Ref
  ApplicationAutoscalingLaunchConfiguration
        MinSize: 0
        MaxSize: 4
        DesiredCapacity: 1
        . . .
        . . .
```

In the preceding example, you define two auto scaling policies of the `SimpleScaling` type, which represents the simplest form of auto scaling that you can implement. A discussion of the various auto scaling types is outside the scope of this book, however if you are interested in learning more about the available options, you can refer to `https://docs.aws.amazon.com/autoscaling/ec2/userguide/as-scale-based-on-demand.html`. The `AdjustmentType` and `ScalingAdjustment` properties are configured to either increase or decrease the size of the auto scaling group by one instance, while the `Cooldown` property provides a mechanism to ensure further auto scaling actions are disabled for the specified duration, which can help avoiding auto scaling loops where your clusters keep on scaling out and scaling in frequently.

Notice that the `ApplicationAutoscaling UpdatePolicy` setting has been updated to include the `SuspendProcesses` parameter, which configures CloudFormation to disable certain operational processes whenever an auto scaling rolling update is taking place. This specifically disables auto scaling operations during a rolling update, which is important as you don't want auto scaling actions interfering with the rolling update that is orchestrated by CloudFormation. Finally, we also set the various count settings on the `ApplicationAutoscaling` resource to a fixed value of 1, as auto scaling will now manage the size of our ECS cluster.

Testing ECS cluster-capacity management

Now, that we have all of the components to calculate the ECS cluster capacity, publish metrics, and trigger alarms that will invoke auto scaling actions, let's deploy our changes and test the solution works as expected.

Testing scale out

To artificially trigger a scale-out action, we need to set the `ApplicationDesiredCount` input parameter to 2 in the `dev.cfg` configuration file, which will increase the ECS task count for our ECS service to 2 and will cause the single ECS container instance in the ECS cluster to no longer have enough resources to support any further additional containers:

```
ApplicationDesiredCount=2
ApplicationImageId=ami-ec957491
ApplicationImageTag=5fdbe62
ApplicationSubnets=subnet-a5d3ecee,subnet-324e246f
VpcId=vpc-f8233a80
```

This configuration change should result in the `ContainerCapacity` metric falling below the configured alarm threshold of `1`, which we can test by now deploying our changes to CloudFormation by running the `aws cloudformation deploy` command.

Once the deployment is complete, if you browse to the CloudWatch console and select Alarms from the left-hand menu, you should see your container capacity alarm go into an ALARM state (this may take a few minutes) as demonstrated earlier:

You can see in the **Actions** details that the CloudWatch alarm has triggered the application Auto Scaling scale-out policy, and notice in the graph on the left that this is because the container capacity has dropped to 0 due to the increase in ECS tasks running on the single ECS container instance.

If you now navigate to the EC2 console, select **Auto Scaling Group**s from the left-hand menu, and then select the **Activity History** tab for the todobackend auto scaling group, you can see that the current instance count in the auto scaling group is 2, and that a new EC2 instance was launched due to the container capacity alarm transitioning to an **ALARM** state:

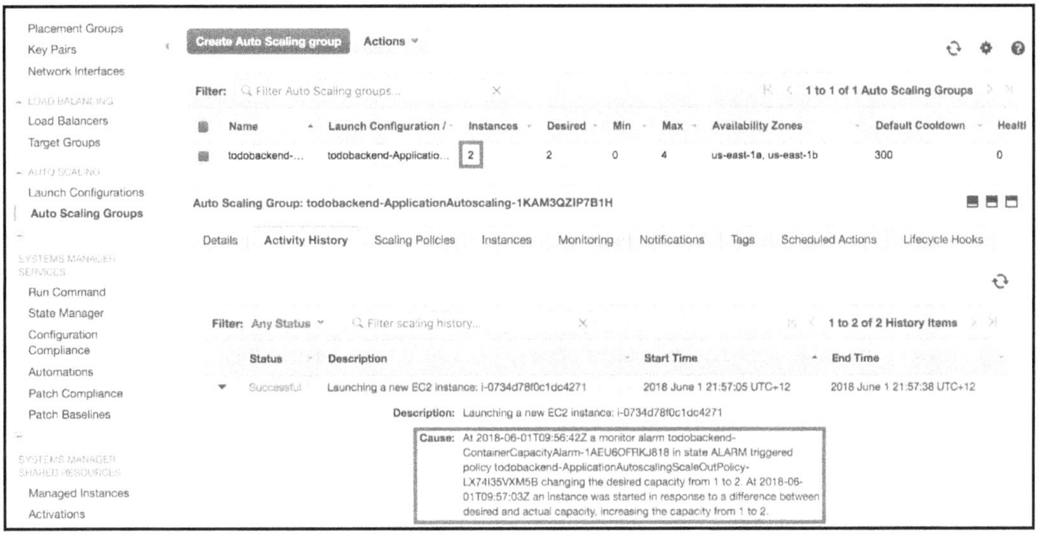

Once the new ECS container instance is added to the ECS cluster, a new capacity calculation will take place, and if you switch back to the CloudWatch console, you should see the **ContainerCapacity** alarm eventually transition to an OK state, as shown in the following screenshot:

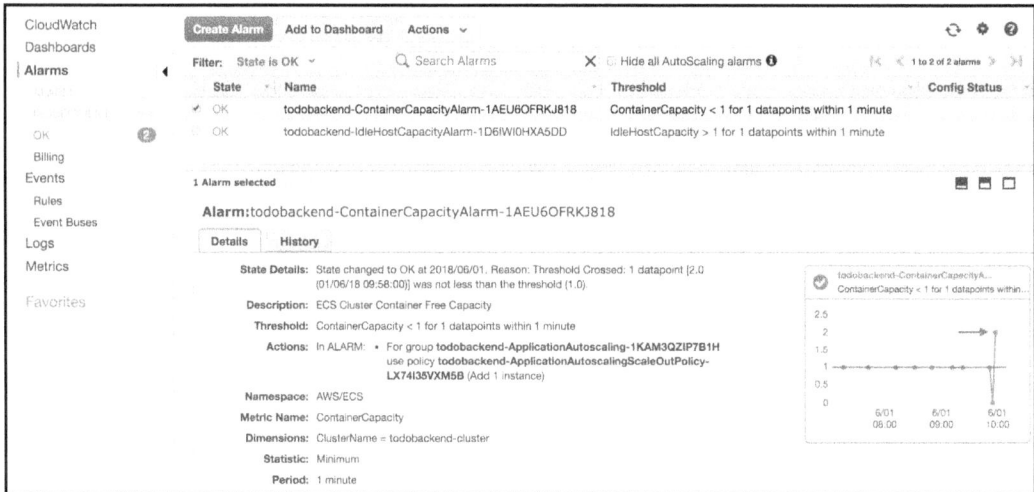

In the graph in the lower-right-hand corner, you can see the effect of adding a new ECS container instance, which increases the container capacity from 0 to 2, placing the container capacity alarm into an **OK** state.

Testing scale in

Now that you have successfully tested the scale-out behavior of your ECS cluster-capacity management solution, let's now artificially trigger scale-in behavior by reducing the `ApplicationDesiredCount` to 1 in the `dev.cfg` file and running the `aws cloudformation deploy` command to deploy the modified count:

```
ApplicationDesiredCount=1
ApplicationImageId=ami-ec957491
ApplicationImageTag=5fdbe62
ApplicationSubnets=subnet-a5d3ecee,subnet-324e246f
VpcId=vpc-f8233a80
```

Once this change has been deployed, in the CloudWatch console you should see the idle host capacity alarm change to an ALARM state after a few moments:

In the preceding screenshot, the idle host capacity has increased from 1.0 to 1.5, given we now only have one running ECS task and two ECS container instances in the cluster. This has triggered the configured application autoscaling scale in policy, which will reduce the ECS cluster capacity to a single ECS container instance, and eventually the idle host capacity alarm will transition to an OK state.

Configuring the AWS application Auto Scaling service

We now have an ECS cluster-capacity management solution in place that will automatically scale out and scale in your ECS cluster, as new ECS tasks come and go in your ECS cluster. To date, we artificially tested this by manually increasing the task count of the todobackend ECS service, however in your real world applications, you typically would use the AWS application auto scaling service to dynamically scale your ECS services up and down based upon whatever metrics make the most sense for your application.

Another scenario that impacts ECS cluster capacity is the deployment of new applications, in the form of ECS task definition changes to your ECS services. The rolling-update mechanism of ECS will often temporarily increase the ECS task count, which can result in your ECS cluster scaling out for a short period of time, and then scaling back in. You can tune this behavior by adjusting the period of time the container capacity can fall below your configured minimum threshold before raising an alarm, and also increasing the minimum container capacity threshold that must be available at all times. This approach builds more spare capacity in your cluster, which allows you to respond less aggressively to capacity changes and absorb the transient capacity fluctuations caused by rolling deployments.

AWS application auto scaling is more complex to configure than EC2 auto scaling, and requires, at a minimum, several components:

- **CloudWatch alarms**: This define the metrics that you are interested in and trigger when you should scale out or scale in.
- **Auto Scaling target**: This defines the target component that the application auto scaling will be applied to. For our scenario, this will be configured as the todobackend ECS service.
- **Auto Scaling IAM role**: You must create an IAM role that grants the AWS application auto scaling service permissions to manage your CloudWatch alarms, read your application auto scaling policies, and modify your ECS services to increase or decrease the ECS service task count.
- **Scale out and scale in policies**: These define the behavior associated with scaling your ECS services out and back in.

Configuring CloudWatch alarms

Let's get started by adding a CloudWatch alarm that will trigger application auto scaling in the todobackend `stack.yml` template:

```
...
...
Resources:
  ApplicationServiceLowCpuAlarm:
    Type: AWS::CloudWatch::Alarm
    Properties:
      AlarmActions:
        - !Ref ApplicationServiceAutoscalingScaleInPolicy
```

```
          AlarmDescription: Todobackend Service Low CPU
          Namespace: AWS/ECS
          Dimensions:
            - Name: ClusterName
              Value: !Ref ApplicationCluster
            - Name: ServiceName
              Value: !Sub ${ApplicationService.Name}
          MetricName: CPUUtilization
          Statistic: Average
          Period: 60
          EvaluationPeriods: 3
          Threshold: 20
          ComparisonOperator: LessThanThreshold
    ApplicationServiceHighCpuAlarm:
      Type: AWS::CloudWatch::Alarm
      Properties:
        AlarmActions:
          - !Ref ApplicationServiceAutoscalingScaleOutPolicy
        AlarmDescription: Todobackend Service High CPU
        Namespace: AWS/ECS
        Dimensions:
          - Name: ClusterName
            Value: !Ref ApplicationCluster
          - Name: ServiceName
            Value: !Sub ${ApplicationService.Name}
        MetricName: CPUUtilization
        Statistic: Average
        Period: 60
        EvaluationPeriods: 3
        Threshold: 40
        ComparisonOperator: GreaterThanThreshold
    . . .
    . . .
```

In the preceding example, alarms are created for low CPU and high CPU conditions, and are dimensioned to the todobackend ECS service running on the todobackend ECS cluster. A high CPU alarm will fire when the average CPU utilization for the ECS service is greater than 40% for a period of 3 minutes (3 x 60 seconds), and a low CPU alarm will fire when the average CPU utilization falls below 20%, again for a period of 3 minutes. In each case, an alarm action is configured, which references scale-out and scale-in policy resources that we will create shortly.

Defining an Auto Scaling target

The AWS application auto scaling requires you to define an auto scaling target, which is the resource that you need to scale up or scale down. For an ECS use case, this is defined as an ECS service, as demonstrated in the preceding example:

```
...
...
Resources:
  ApplicationServiceAutoscalingTarget:
    Type: AWS::ApplicationAutoScaling::ScalableTarget
    Properties:
      ServiceNamespace: ecs
      ResourceId: !Sub
service/${ApplicationCluster}/${ApplicationService.Name}
      ScalableDimension: ecs:service:DesiredCount
      MinCapacity: 1
      MaxCapacity: 4
      RoleARN: !Sub ${ApplicationServiceAutoscalingRole.Arn}
  ...
  ...
```

In the preceding example, you define the following properties for the auto scaling target:

- `ServiceNamespace`: Defines the namespace of the target AWS service. Set this to `ecs` when targeting an ECS service.
- `ResourceId`: The identifier of the resource associated with the target. For ECS, this is defined in the `service/<ecs-cluster-name>/<ecs-service-name>` format.
- `ScalableDimension`: Specifies the property of the target resource type that can be scaled. In the case of an ECS service, this is the `DesiredCount` property, which is defined as `ecs:service:DesiredCount`.
- `MinCapacity` and `MaxCapacity`: The minimum and maximum bounds to which the desired ECS service count can be scaled.
- `RoleARN`: The ARN of the IAM role that the application auto scaling service will use to scale out and scale in the target. In the preceding example, you references an IAM resource that you will create in the next section.

For more details on each of the preceding properties, you can refer to the `Application Auto Scaling API reference`.

Creating an Auto Scaling IAM role

In the resource definition for the application auto scaling target, you referenced an IAM role that the application auto scaling service will assume. The following example defines this IAM role and the permissions required by the application auto scaling service:

```
...
...
Resources:
  ApplicationServiceAutoscalingRole:
    Type: AWS::IAM::Role
    Properties:
      AssumeRolePolicyDocument:
        Version: "2012-10-17"
        Statement:
          - Action:
              - sts:AssumeRole
            Effect: Allow
            Principal:
              Service: application-autoscaling.amazonaws.com
      Policies:
        - PolicyName: AutoscalingPermissions
          PolicyDocument:
            Version: "2012-10-17"
            Statement:
              - Effect: Allow
                Action:
                  - application-autoscaling:DescribeScalableTargets
                  - application-autoscaling:DescribeScalingActivities
                  - application-autoscaling:DescribeScalingPolicies
                  - cloudwatch:DescribeAlarms
                  - cloudwatch:PutMetricAlarm
                  - ecs:DescribeServices
                  - ecs:UpdateService
                Resource: "*"
  ApplicationServiceAutoscalingTarget:
    Type: AWS::ApplicationAutoScaling::ScalableTarget
  ...
  ...
```

You can see that the application auto scaling service requires a number of read permissions associated with the application auto scaling service itself, an ability to manage CloudWatch alarms, and must be able to update the ECS services in order to manage the ECS service's desired count. Notice that you must specify the principal as `application-autoscaling.amazonaws.com` in the `AssumeRolePolicyDocument` section, which allows the application auto scaling service to assume the role.

Configuring scale-out and scale-in policies

The final task required when configuring application auto scaling is to add scale-out and scale-in policies:

```
...
...
Resources:
  ApplicationServiceAutoscalingScaleInPolicy:
    Type: AWS::ApplicationAutoScaling::ScalingPolicy
    Properties:
      PolicyName: ScaleIn
      PolicyType: StepScaling
      ScalingTargetId: !Ref ApplicationServiceAutoscalingTarget
      StepScalingPolicyConfiguration:
        AdjustmentType: ChangeInCapacity
        Cooldown: 360
        MetricAggregationType: Average
        StepAdjustments:
        - ScalingAdjustment: -1
          MetricIntervalUpperBound: 0
 ApplicationServiceAutoscalingScaleOutPolicy:
    Type: AWS::ApplicationAutoScaling::ScalingPolicy
Properties:
PolicyName: ScaleOut
PolicyType: StepScaling
ScalingTargetId: !Ref ApplicationServiceAutoscalingTarget
StepScalingPolicyConfiguration:
AdjustmentType: ChangeInCapacity
Cooldown: 360
MetricAggregationType: Average
StepAdjustments:
- ScalingAdjustment: 1
MetricIntervalLowerBound: 0
```

```
ApplicationServiceAutoscalingRole:
    Type: AWS::IAM::Role
  ...
  ...
```

Here you define scale-out and scale-in policies, ensuring the resource names match those you referenced earlier, when you configured the CloudWatch alarms used to trigger the policies. The `PolicyType` parameter specifies you are configuring Step-Scaling policies, which work in a similar manner to the EC2 auto scaling policies you defined earlier and allow you to scale up or down in incremental steps. The remaining properties are fairly self-explanatory, although the `StepAdjustments` property does warrant some further description.

The `ScalingAdjustment` indicates how much you will increase or decrease the ECS service count by each time you scale, while the `MetricIntervalLowerBound` and `MetricIntervalUpperBound` properties allow you to define additional bounds when your alarm thresholds are exceeded to which your auto scaling actions should apply.

The configuration shown in the preceding example is such that whenever the CPU utilization exceeds or falls below the configured CloudWatch alarm thresholds, the application auto scaling will always be invoked. This is because the unconfigured upper and lower bounds default to a value of infinity or negative infinity, respectively, so any metric value between the alarm threshold and infinity/negative infinity will trigger the alarm. To help further clarify the context of the metric interval bounds, if you instead configured a `MetricIntervalLowerBound` value of 10 and `MetricIntervalUpperBound` of 30, when the CloudWatch alarm threshold (currently configured as 40% CPU utilization) is exceeded, the auto scaling action would only apply between 50% utilization (threshold + `MetricIntervalLowerBound` or 40 + 10 = 50) and 70% utilization (`threshold +` `MetricIntervalUpperBound` or 40 + 30 = 70%).

Deploying application Auto Scaling

At this point, you are now ready to deploy your ECS application auto scaling solution. After running the `aws cloudformation deploy` command, if you browse to the ECS console, select the todobackend cluster and todobackend ECS service, on the **Auto Scaling** tab, you should see your new application auto scaling configuration in place:

Now whenever your ECS service is experiencing greater than 40% CPU utilization (averaged across all ECS tasks), the desired count of your ECS service will be increased by one. This will continue for as long as the CPU utilization exceeds 40%, up to a maximum of 4 tasks, and as per the configuration of the preceding example, a cool-down period of 360 seconds will apply between each auto scaling action.

At an ECS service level, you don't need to worry about the underlying ECS cluster resources, as your ECS cluster capacity management solution ensures there is always spare capacity for additional ECS tasks in the cluster. This means you now have the freedom to scale each ECS service independently according to its specific performance characteristics, and underscores the importance of understanding the optimal-per-ECS-task resource allocations for each of your applications.

Summary

In this chapter, you created a comprehensive auto scaling solution that allows you to auto scale your ECS services and applications in response to application load and customer demand, and at the same time ensures your underlying ECS cluster has sufficient resources to deploy new ECS tasks as required.

You first learned about key ECS resources including CPU, memory, network ports and network interfaces, and how ECS allocates these resources. When managing the ECS cluster capacity, these resources determine whether or not an ECS container instance can run a given ECS task, so it is critical that you understand how each resource is consumed.

You next implemented an ECS cluster-capacity management solution that calculates the ECS cluster capacity whenever an ECS container instance state change occurs. ECS publishes theses state changes via CloudWatch events, and you created a CloudWatch event rule that triggers a Lambda function that calculates the current cluster capacity. This function calculates two key metrics–container capacity, expressed as the number of additional containers or ECS tasks that the cluster can currently support, and idle host capacity, which defines how many "virtual" hosts are currently idle across the entire cluster. The container capacity is used to scale out your ECS clusters, adding additional ECS container instances whenever the container capacity falls below 1, meaning the cluster no longer has enough resources to deploy an additional ECS task. The idle host capacity is used to scale in your ECS clusters, removing ECS container instances whenever idle host capacity is greater than 1.0, meaning you can safely remove an ECS container instance and still have capacity to deploy new ECS tasks.

A key concept we discussed was the requirement to always make these calculations for the worst-case scenario collectively across all of your resources, which ensures you will never scale in when you have plenty of spare capacity of one type of resource, but may have low capacity for another type of resource.

Finally, you learned how to configure the AWS application auto scaling service to scale up and down your ECS services. Here you are scaling individual ECS services based on appropriate metrics specific to your applications, and because you are scaling in the context of a single ECS service, auto scaling at this level is simple to define and understand. Scaling your ECS services is ultimately what drives changes to your overall ECS cluster capacity, with the ECS cluster-capacity management solution you implemented taking care of this and allowing you to auto scale your ECS services without needing to worry about the impact to your underlying ECS cluster.

In the next chapter, you will learn how to continuously deliver your ECS applications to AWS, incorporating all of the features we have discussed in the previous chapters. This will allow you to deploy your latest application changes in a fully automated fashion, reducing operational overheads and providing fast feedback to your development teams.

Questions

1. True/false: When you use ECS and deploy your own ECS container instances, ECS automatically scales your clusters up and down for you.
2. Which AWS service do you use to scale your ECS clusters?
3. Which AWS service do you use to scale your ECS services?
4. Your application requires a minimum of 300 MB and maximum of 1 GB of memory to run. What parameters would you configure on your ECS task definition to support this configuration?
5. You deploy 3 different ECS tasks that each run a different application to a single instance ECS cluster, and configure each ECS task to reserve 10 CPU units. During busy periods, one of the ECS tasks hogs CPU, slowing down the other ECS tasks. Assuming the ECS container instance has 1,000 CPU units' capacity, what could you do to avoid one ECS task hogging CPU?
6. True/false: If you only use dynamic port mapping for your ECS tasks, you do not need to worry about network port resources.
7. You deploy an instance to AWS that supports four network interfaces in total. What is the capacity in terms of number of ECS tasks for the instance, assuming all ECS tasks use ECS task networking?
8. When should you disable auto scaling in an EC2 auto scaling group?How would you go about this?

9. Your ECS cluster currently has 2 ECS container instances each with 500 CPU units and 500 MB of memory of spare capacity. You are only deploying a single type of application to your cluster, and you currently have two ECS tasks running. Assuming the ECS task requires 500 CPU units, 500 MB of memory, and has a static port mapping to TCP port 80, what is the current overall spare capacity of the cluster in terms of number of ECS tasks?

10. Your ECS cluster needs to support 3 different ECS tasks that require 300, 400, and 500MB of memory, respectively. If each of your ECS container instances has 2 GB of memory, what would you calculate as the maximum number of containers per ECS container instance in terms of memory when performing ECS cluster-capacity calculations?

Further reading

You can check the following links for more information about the topics we covered in this chapter:

- ECS Service Auto Scaling: `https://docs.aws.amazon.com/AmazonECS/latest/developerguide/service-auto-scaling.html`
- EC2 Auto Scaling User Guide: `https://docs.aws.amazon.com/autoscaling/ec2/userguide/what-is-amazon-ec2-auto-scaling.html`
- EC2 Auto Scaling Policy Types: `https://docs.aws.amazon.com/autoscaling/ec2/userguide/as-scaling-simple-step.html`
- Recommended Best Practices for Auto Scaling Group Rolling Updates: `https://aws.amazon.com/premiumsupport/knowledge-center/auto-scaling-group-rolling-updates/`
- Application Auto Scaling User Guide: `https://docs.aws.amazon.com/autoscaling/application/userguide/what-is-application-auto-scaling.html`
- Task Definition Parameters Reference (See `cpu`, `memory`, and `memoryReservation` parameters): `https://docs.aws.amazon.com/AmazonECS/latest/developerguide/task_definition_parameters.html#container_definitions`
- CloudFormation CloudWatch Events Rule Resource Reference: `https://docs.aws.amazon.com/AWSCloudFormation/latest/UserGuide/aws-resource-events-rule.html`

- CloudFormation CloudWatch AlarmResource Reference: `https://docs.aws.amazon.com/AWSCloudFormation/latest/UserGuide/aws-properties-cw-alarm.html`

- CloudFormation EC2 Auto Scaling Policy Resource Reference: `https://docs.aws.amazon.com/AWSCloudFormation/latest/UserGuide/aws-properties-as-policy.html`

- CloudFormation Application Auto Scaling Scalable Target Resource Reference: `https://docs.aws.amazon.com/AWSCloudFormation/latest/UserGuide/aws-resource-applicationautoscaling-scalabletarget.html`

- CloudFormation Application Auto Scaling Policy Resource Reference: `https://docs.aws.amazon.com/AWSCloudFormation/latest/UserGuide/aws-resource-applicationautoscaling-scalingpolicy.html`

13
Continuously Delivering ECS Applications

Continuous delivery is the practice of creating a repeatable and reliable process for releasing software, so that you can deploy new features to production frequently and on demand, with a lower cost and risk. There are numerous benefits to adopting continuous delivery, and today, more and more organizations are adopting it, to get features to the market faster, increase customer satisfaction, and lower the cost of software delivery.

Implementing continuous delivery requires a high degree of automation across the end-to-end life cycle of software delivery. So far, in this course, you have worked with many technologies that support automation and continuous delivery, in general. For example, Docker inherently brings a high degree of automation and promotes repeatable and consistent build processes, all of which are critical components of continuous delivery. The make workflow in the `todobackend` repository takes this a step further, automating a full test, build, and publish workflow for your Docker images. We have also been using CloudFormation extensively throughout this course, which provides us with the ability to create, update, and destroy complete AWS environments in a completely automated fashion, and allows us to easily deploy new features (in the form of new Docker images) in a reliable and consistent manner. Continuous delivery brings all of these features and capabilities together to create an end-to-end process for the delivery of software changes, from the time they are developed and committed to source code, to the time they are regression-tested and deployed to production. To achieve this level of end-to-end orchestration and automation, we need to adopt new tools that are engineered for this purpose, and AWS offers a number of services that work together to deliver this, including AWS CodePipeline, CodeBuild, and CloudFormation.

In this chapter, you will learn how you can implement an end-to-end continuous delivery pipeline (using CodePipeline, CodeBuild, and CloudFormation) that will continuously test, build, and publish Docker images, and then continuously deploy your freshly built Docker images to a non-production environment. The pipeline will also support controlled releases into a production environment, by automatically creating change sets that must be reviewed and approved before deploying new changes into production.

The following topics will be covered in this chapter:

- Introducing CodePipeline and CodeBuild
- Creating a custom CodeBuild container
- Adding CodeBuild support to your application repository
- Creating a continuous integration pipeline using CodePipeline
- Creating a continuous deployment pipeline using CodePipeline
- Continuously delivering your applications to production

Technical requirements

The following lists the technical requirements for completing this chapter:

- Administrator access to an AWS account.
- A local AWS profile, configured as per the instructions in Chapter 3.
- The AWS CLI version 1.15.71 or higher
- This chapter continues on from Chapter 12, so it requires that you have successfully completed all configuration tasks defined in Chapter 12.
- This chapter requires you to have both the `todobackend` and `todobackend-aws` repositories published to a GitHub account that you have administrative access to.

The following GitHub URL contains the code samples used in this chapter: `https://github.com/docker-in-aws/docker-in-aws/tree/master/ch13`

Check out the following video to see the Code in Action:
`http://bit.ly/2BVGMYI`

Introducing CodePipeline and CodeBuild

CodePipeline and **CodeBuild** are two services from the developer tools portfolio of AWS that, along with the CloudFormation service that we have been working with extensively throughout this book, provide the building blocks for creating complete and comprehensive continuous delivery solutions to pave your application's path from development to production.

CodePipeline allows you to create complex pipelines that take your applications' source code, build, test, and publish application artifacts, and then deploy your applications into non-production and production environments. The top-level building blocks of these pipelines are stages, which must always start with a source stage that includes one or more source materials for your pipeline, such as the source code repository for your application. Each stage can then be comprised of one or more actions that produce an artifact that can be used later on in your pipeline, or achieve a desired outcome, such as deploying to an environment. You can define actions in sequence or in parallel, which allows you to orchestrate almost any scenario you want; for example, I have used CodePipeline to orchestrate the deployment of complete, complex, multi-application environments in a highly controlled fashion that can easily be visualized and managed.

Every CodePipeline pipeline must define at least two stages, and we will see an example of this initially, when we create a continuous integration pipeline including a source stage (which collects application source code from a source code repository) and a build stage (which tests, builds, and publishes application artifacts from the application source collected by the source stage).

An important concept to understand here is the concept of artifacts. Many actions in CodePipeline consume input artifacts and produce output artifacts, and the ability for one action to consume the output of an earlier action is the essence of how CodePipeline works.

As an example, the following diagram illustrates the initial continuous integration pipeline that we will create:

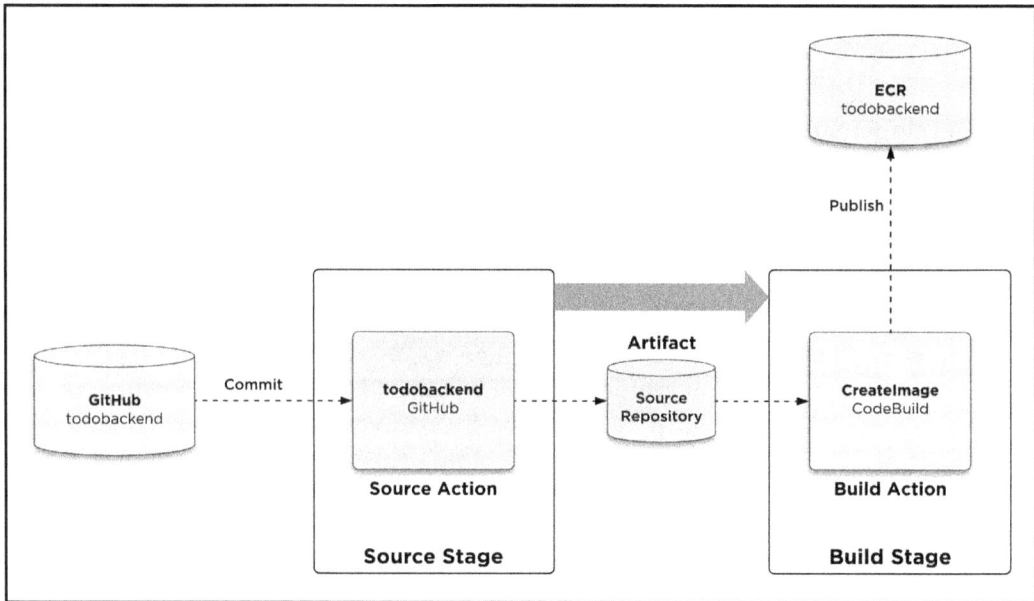

Continuous integration pipeline

In the preceding diagram, the **Source Stage** includes a single **Source Action** that is linked to your todobackend GitHub repository. This action will download the latest source code whenever changes are committed to your GitHub repository, and will produce an output artifact that zips up your source code and makes it available for the build stage that immediately follows. The **Build Stage** has a single **Build Action** that takes your source action output artifact as an input, and then tests, builds, and publishes a Docker image. The **Build Action** in the preceding diagram is executed by the AWS CodeBuild service, which is a fully managed build service that provides a container-based build agent for running build jobs on demand. CodePipeline ensures that the CodeBuild build job is supplied with an input artifact that includes your application source code, which allows CodeBuild to then run your local test, build, and publish the workflow.

So far, we have discussed the concept of the source and build stages in CodePipeline; the other common stage that you will use in your pipelines is a deploy stage, where you deploy your application artifacts into a target environment. The following diagram illustrates how you can extend the pipeline shown in the preceding diagram to continuously deploy your applications:

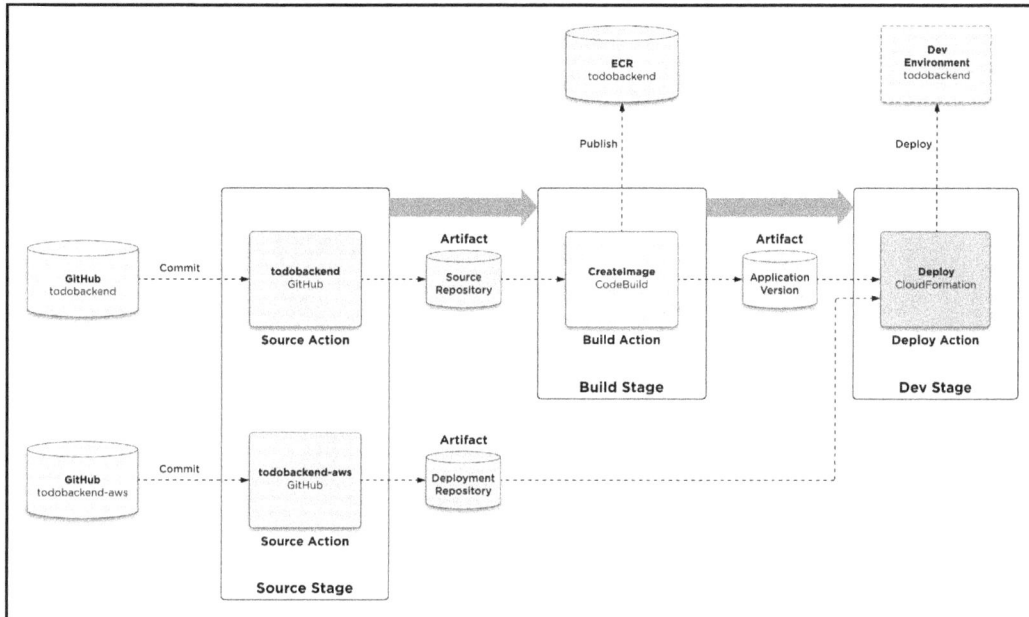

Continuous deployment pipeline

In the preceding diagram, a new stage (called **Dev Stage**) has been added; it leverages CodePipeline's integration with CloudFormation to deploy your applications into a non-production environment, which we refer to as dev (development). Because we are using CloudFormation for deployment, we need to provide a CloudFormation stack to deploy, and this is provided by adding the todobackend-aws repository as another source action in the source stage. The **Deploy Action** also requires another input artifact that defines the tag of the Docker image to deploy, and this is provided as an output artifact (called `ApplicationVersion`) of the CodeBuild build action in the build stage. Don't worry if this doesn't make too much sense right now; we will cover all of the details and set up these pipelines in this chapter, but it is important to at least understand the concepts of stages, actions, and how artifacts can be passed between them to achieved your desired outcomes.

Finally, CodePipeline can support deployments into multiple environments, and the final section of this chapter will extend our pipeline to perform a controlled release into a production environment, as illustrated in the following diagram:

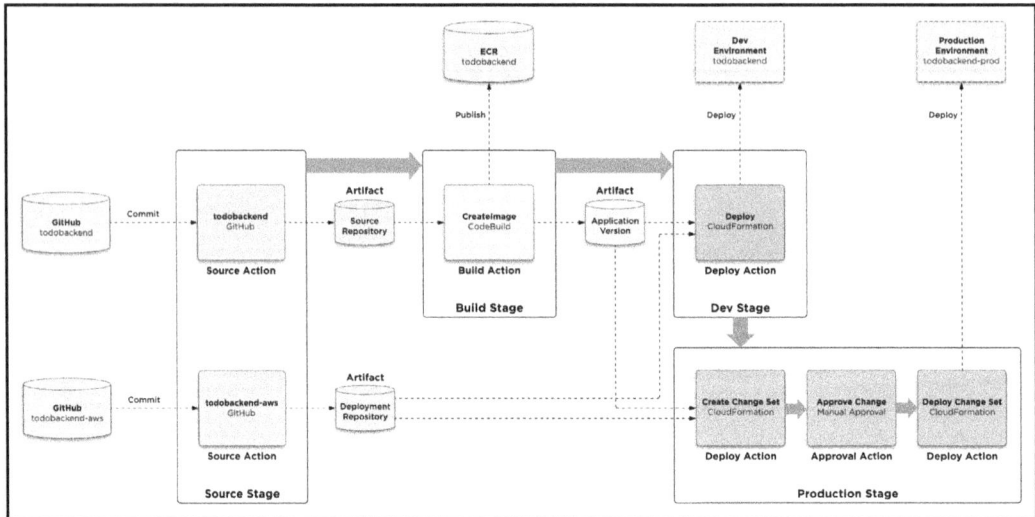

Continuous delivery pipeline

In the preceding diagram, a new stage (called **Production Stage**) is added to the pipeline, which can only be executed if your application has been successfully deployed in your dev environment. Unlike the continuous deployment approach of the dev stage, which immediately deploys into your dev environment, the production stage first creates a CloudFormation change set, which identifies all of the changes that will be made as part of the deployment, and then triggers a manual approval action that requires somebody to review the change set and approve or reject the changes. Assuming that the changes are approved, the production stage will then deploy the changes to the production environment, and these sets of actions will collectively combine to offer support for controlled releases into production (or other controlled) environments.

Now that you have had a high-level overview of CodePipeline, let's get started by creating the continuous integration pipeline that we discussed in the very first diagram. Before, we can build this pipeline, we need to build a custom build container to meet the requirements of the Docker workflow defined in the todobackend repository, and we also need to add support for CodeBuild, after which we can create our pipeline in CodePipeline.

Creating a custom CodeBuild container

AWS CodeBuild provides a build service that uses a container build agent to execute your builds. CodeBuild provides a number of AWS curated images that target specific application languages and/or platforms, such as `Python, Java, PHP and many more`. CodeBuild does provide an image that is designed for building Docker images; however, this image is somewhat limited, in that it does not include tools like the AWS CLI, GNU make, and Docker Compose, all of which we require for building the todobackend application.

Although you can run pre-build steps that install additional tools in CodeBuild, this approach slows down your builds, as the installation of the additional tools will happen on each and every build. CodeBuild does support using your own custom images, which allows you to pre-package all of the tools required for your application builds.

For our use case, the CodeBuild build environment must include the following:

- Access to a Docker daemon, given the build stands up a multi-container environment to run integration and acceptance tests
- Docker Compose
- GNU Make
- AWS CLI

You may be wondering how you can meet the first requirement, given that your CodeBuild runtime environment is located within an isolated container that has no direct access to the underlying infrastructure it is running on. Docker does support the concept of **Docker in Docker** (**DinD**), where the Docker daemon runs inside of your Docker container, allowing you to install a Docker client that can build Docker images and orchestrate multi-container environments, using tools like Docker Compose.

The practice of Docker in Docker is `somewhat controversial`, and is an example of using Docker more like a virtual machine than a container. However, for the purposes of running a build, this approach is completely acceptable.

Defining a custom CodeBuild container

First, we need to build our custom CodeBuild image, which we will define in a Dockerfile called `Dockerfile.codebuild`, located within the todobackend-aws repository.

The following example shows the Dockerfile:

```
FROM docker:dind

RUN apk add --no-cache bash make python3 && \
    pip3 install --no-cache-dir docker-compose awscli
```

Because Docker publishes a Docker in Docker image, we can simply base our customization from this image; we have the Docker in Docker functionality for free. The DinD image is based on Alpine Linux, and already includes the required Docker daemon and Docker client. Next, we will add the specific tools that we require for our build. This includes the bash shell, GNU make, and a Python 3 runtime, which is required to install Docker Compose and the AWS CLI.

You can now build this image locally by using the `docker build` command, demonstrated as follows:

```
> docker build -t codebuild -f Dockerfile.codebuild .
Sending build context to Docker daemon 405.5kB
Step 1/2 : FROM docker:dind
dind: Pulling from library/docker
ff3a5c916c92: Already exists
1a649ea86bca: Pull complete
ce35f4d5f86a: Pull complete
d0600fe571bc: Pull complete
e16e21051182: Pull complete
a3ea1dbce899: Pull complete
133d8f8629ec: Pull complete
71a0f0a757e5: Pull complete
0e081d1eb121: Pull complete
5a14be8d6d21: Pull complete
Digest:
sha256:2ca0d4ee63d8911cd72aa84ff2694d68882778a1c1f34b5a36b3f761290ee75
1
Status: Downloaded newer image for docker:dind
 ---> 1f44348b3ad5
Step 2/2 : RUN apk add --no-cache bash make python3 && pip3 install --
no-cache-dir docker-compose awscli
 ---> Running in d69027d58057
...
```

```
...
Successfully built 25079965c64c
Successfully tagged codebuild:latest
```

The command in the preceding example, creates the newly built Docker image with a name of `codebuild`. This is OK for now, but we will need to publish this CodeBuild to the **Elastic Container Registry** (**ECR**), so that it is available for CodeBuild.

Creating a repository for the custom CodeBuild container

Now, that you have built a custom CodeBuild image, you need to publish the image to a location that CodeBuild can pull the image from. If you are using the ECR, you will typically publish this image to a repository within ECR, and that is the approach we will take.

First, you need to add a new repository to the `ecr.yml` file, in the root of the `todobackend-aws` folder, which you created earlier in the chapter::

```
AWSTemplateFormatVersion: "2010-09-09"

Description: ECR Resources

Resources:
  CodebuildRepository:
    Type: AWS::ECR::Repository
    Properties:
      RepositoryName: docker-in-aws/codebuild
 RepositoryPolicyText:
 Version: '2008-10-17'
 Statement:
 - Sid: CodeBuildAccess
 Effect: Allow
 Principal:
 Service: codebuild.amazonaws.com
 Action:
 - ecr:GetDownloadUrlForLayer
 - ecr:BatchGetImage
 - ecr:BatchCheckLayerAvailability
  TodobackendRepository:
    Type: AWS::ECR::Repository
  ...
  ...
```

In the preceding example, you create a new repository with the name `docker-in-aws/codebuild`, which will result in a fully qualified repository by the name of `<account-id>.dkr.ecr.<region>.amazonaws.com/docker-in-aws/codebuild` (for example, `385605022855.dkr.ecr.us-east-1.amazonaws.com/docker-in-aws/codebuild`). Note that you must grant pull access to the CodeBuild service, as CodeBuild needs to pull the image to run as its build container.

You can now deploy the changes to the ECR stack by using the `aws cloudformation deploy` command, which you may recall from the chapter, Publishing Docker Images Using ECR is deployed to a stack called ecr-repositories:

```
> export AWS_PROFILE=docker-in-aws
> aws cloudformation deploy --template-file ecr.yml --stack-name ecr-
repositories
Enter MFA code for arn:aws:iam::385605022855:mfa/justin.menga:

Waiting for changeset to be created..
Waiting for stack create/update to complete
Successfully created/updated stack - ecr-repositories
```

Once the deployment is complete, you need to retag the image that you created earlier, with the fully qualified name of your new ECR repository, after which you can log in to ECR and publish the image:

```
> docker tag codebuild 385605022855.dkr.ecr.us-
east-1.amazonaws.com/docker-in-aws/codebuild
> eval $(aws ecr get-login --no-include-email)
WARNING! Using --password via the CLI is insecure. Use --password-
stdin.
Login Succeeded
> docker push 385605022855.dkr.ecr.us-east-1.amazonaws.com/docker-in-
aws/codebuild
The push refers to repository [385605022855.dkr.ecr.us-
east-1.amazonaws.com/docker-in-aws/codebuild]
770fb042ae3b: Pushed
0cdc6e0d843b: Pushed
395fced17f47: Pushed
3abf4e550e49: Pushed
0a6dfdbcc220: Pushed
27760475e1ac: Pushed
5270ef39cae0: Pushed
2c88066e123c: Pushed
b09386d6aa0f: Pushed
1ed7a5e2d1b3: Pushed
```

```
cd7100a72410: Pushed
latest: digest:
sha256:858becbf8c64b24e778e6997868f587b9056c1d1617e8d7aa495a3170761cf8
b size: 2618
```

Adding CodeBuild support to your application repository

Whenever you create a CodeBuild project, you must define how CodeBuild should test and build your application source code, and then publish application artifacts and/or Docker images. CodeBuild defines these tasks within a build specification, which provides the build instructions the CodeBuild agent should execute when running a build.

CodeBuild allows you to provide a build specification in several ways:

- **Self-defined**: CodeBuild looks for a file that is defined within the source repository of the project. By default, this is a file called `buildspec.yml`; however, you can also configure a custom file where your build specification is located.
- **Preconfigured**: When you create a CodeBuild project, you can define a build specification as part of your project setup.
- **On demand**: If you initiate a CodeBuild build job using the AWS CLI or SDK, you can override the preconfigured or self-defined build specification

In general, I recommend using the self-defined method, as it allows the repository owner (typically, your developers) to configure and maintain the specification independently of CodeBuild; this is the approach we will take.

The following example demonstrates adding a build specification to the todobackend repository, in a file called `buildspec.yml`:

```
version: 0.2

phases:
  pre_build:
    commands:
      - nohup /usr/local/bin/dockerd --
host=unix:///var/run/docker.sock --storage-driver=overlay&
      - timeout -t 15 sh -c "until docker info; do echo .; sleep 1;
done"
      - export BUILD_ID=$(echo $CODEBUILD_BUILD_ID | sed
```

```
's/^[^:]*:\/\/g')
      - export
APP_VERSION=$CODEBUILD_RESOLVED_SOURCE_VERSION.$BUILD_ID
      - make login
  build:
    commands:
      - make test
      - make release
      - make publish
  post_build:
    commands:
      - make clean
      - make logout
```

The build specification starts by specifying a version that must be included in every build specification, the most current version being 0.2, as of the writing of this book. Next, you define the phases sequence, which is required, defining the commands that CodeBuild will run during the various phases of the build. In the previous example, you define three phases:

- pre_build: Commands that CodeBuild will run before the build. Here, you can run commands such as logging into ECR, or any other commands that are required for your build to run successfully.
- build: These commands run your build steps.
- post_build: Commands that CodeBuild will run after your build. These typically involve clean up tasks, such as logging out of ECR and removing temporary files.

You can find more information about the CodeBuild build specifications at https://docs.aws.amazon.com/codebuild/latest/userguide/build-spec-ref.html.

During the pre_build stage, you perform the following actions:

- The first two commands are used to start the Docker daemon in your custom CodeBuild image; the nohup command starts the Docker daemon as a background task, while the timeout command is used to ensure the Docker daemon has started successfully, before attempting to continue.

- Export a `BUILD_ID` environment variable, which is used to add build information to the application version that will be generated for your build. This `BUILD_ID` value will be added to the application version tag that is attached to the Docker image that is built during the build phase, and therefore, it can only include characters that are compatible with Docker's tag format. The CodeBuild job ID is exposed to your build agent via the `CODEBUILD_BUILD_ID` environment variable, and has the format `<project-name>:<job-id>`, where `<job-id>` is a UUID value. The colon in the CodeBuild job ID is not supported in Docker tags; hence, you strip the `<project-name>:` portion of the job ID using a `sed` expression, leaving just the job ID value that will be included in the Docker tag.
- Export the `APP_VERSION` environment variable, which is used in the Makefile to define the application version that is tagged on the built Docker image. When you use CodeBuild with CodePipeline, it is important to understand that the source artifact presented to CodeBuild is actually a zipped version located in an S3 bucket that CodePipeline creates after cloning the source code from your source repository. CodePipeline does not include any Git metadata; therefore, the `APP_VERSION` directive in the todobackend Makefile - `export APP_VERSION ?= $(shell git rev-parse --short HEAD` - will fail, as the Git client will not have any Git metadata available. Luckily, the `?=` syntax in GNU Make means to use the value of the aforementioned environment variable, if it is already defined in the environment. So, we can export `APP_VERSION` in the CodeBuild environment, and Make will just use the configured value, rather than run the Git commands. In the previous example, you construct the `APP_VERSION` from a variable called `CODEBUILD_RESOLVED_SOURCE_VERSION`, which is the full commit hash of the source repository, and is set by CodePipeline. You also append the `BUILD_ID` variable calculated in the previous command, which allows you to trace a specific Docker image build to a CodeBuild build job.
- Log in to ECR using the `make login` command included in the source repository.

Once the `pre_build` stage has completed, the build stage is straightforward, and simply executes the various build steps that we have executed manually so far in this book. The final `post_build` stage runs the `make clean` task to tear down the Docker Compose environment, and then removes any local ECR credentials by running the `make logout` command.

One important point to note is that the `post_build` stage always runs, even if the build stage fails. This means you should only reserve `post_build` tasks for actions that you would run regardless of whether the build passes or fails. For example, you might be tempted to run the `make publish` task as a `post_build` step; however, if you do this, and the previous build stage fails, CodeBuild will still attempt to run the make publish task, given that it is defined as a `post_build` step. Placing the make publish task as the final action in the build stage ensures that if make test or make release fails, the build stage will immediately exit with an error, bypassing the make publish action and proceeding to execute the cleanup tasks in the `post_build` step.

You can find out more about all of the CodeBuild phases, and whether they execute on success/failure, at https://docs.aws.amazon.com/codebuild/latest/userguide/view-build-details.html#view-build-details-phases.

The final step that you need to perform is to commit and push your changes to your Git repository, so that the newly created `buildspec.yml` file will be available when you configure CodePipeline and CodeBuild:

```
> git add -A
> git commit -a -m "Add build specification"
[master ab7ac16] Add build specification
 1 file changed, 19 insertions(+)
 create mode 100644 buildspec.yml
> git push
Counting objects: 3, done.
Delta compression using up to 8 threads.
Compressing objects: 100% (3/3), done.
Writing objects: 100% (3/3), 584 bytes | 584.00 KiB/s, done.
Total 3 (delta 1), reused 0 (delta 0)
remote: Resolving deltas: 100% (1/1), completed with 1 local object.
To github.com:docker-in-aws/todobackend.git
   5fdbe62..ab7ac16 master -> master
```

Creating a continuous integration pipeline using CodePipeline

Now that you have established the prerequisites for supporting CodeBuild, you can create a continuous integration CodePipeline pipeline that will use CodeBuild to test, build, and publish your Docker image. Continuous integration focuses on continuously merging application source code changes into your master branch and validating the changes by creating a build and running automated tests against it.

As per the first diagram in this chapter, this generally involves two stages when you configure a CodePipeline pipeline for continuous integration:

- **Source Stage**: Downloads the source application repository and makes it available for subsequent stages. For our use case, you will connect CodePipeline to the master branch of your GitHub repository, and subsequent commits to this repository will automatically trigger a new pipeline execution.
- **Build Stage**: Runs the build, test, and publish workflow defined in the source application repository. For our use case, we will use CodeBuild to run this stage, which will execute the build tasks defined in the source repository `buildspec.yml` file that you created earlier in this chapter.

Creating a CodePipeline pipeline using the AWS console

To get started, first, select **Services** from the AWS console and choose **CodePipeline**. If this is the first time that you have used CodePipeline, you will be presented with an introduction page, and you can click the **Get started** button to start the CodePipeline wizard.

You are first asked to enter a name for your pipeline, and after clicking **Next step**, you are prompted to set up a source provider, which defines the provider of the source repository or files that will be used in your pipeline:

After selecting GitHub from the drop-down menu, click on the **Connect to GitHub** button, which will redirect you to GitHub, where you will be prompted to log in and grant CodePipeline access to your GitHub account:

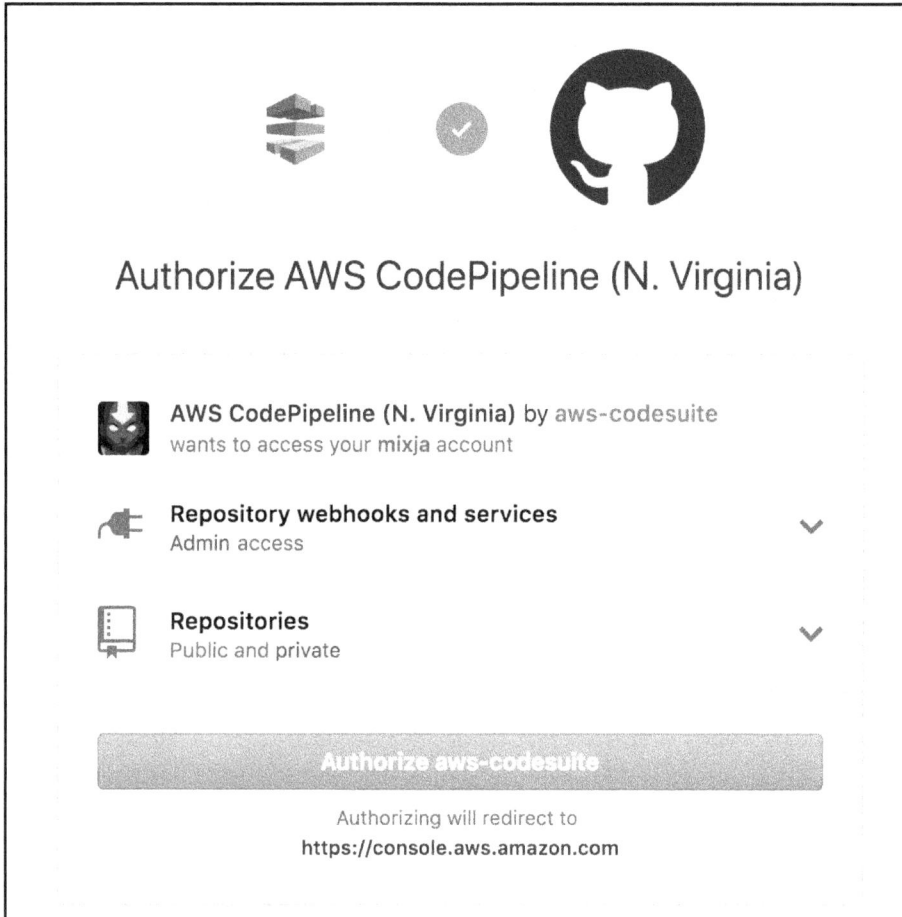

After clicking on the **Authorize aws-codesuite** button, you will be redirected back to the CodePipeline wizard, and you can select the todobackend repository and master branch:

If you click on **Next step**, you will be asked to select a build provider, which defines the provider of the build service that will perform build actions on your source repository:

Build   ❷

Choose the build provider that you want to use or that you are already using.

⟶ **Build provider***   AWS CodeBuild   ⬍

AWS CodeBuild

AWS CodeBuild is a fully managed build service that builds and tests code in the cloud. CodeBuild scales continuously. You only pay by the minute. Learn more

Configure your project

         Select an existing build project
    ●   Create a new build project

⟶ **Project name***   todobackend   ❶

Description   ⊕ Add description

Environment: How to build

Environment image*   Use an image managed by AWS CodeBuild
                     ●   Specify a Docker image

⟶ **Environment type***   Linux   ▼

⟶ **Custom image type***   Amazon ECR   ▼

⟶ **Amazon ECR repository***   docker-in-aws/codebuild   ▼

⟶ **Amazon ECR image***   latest   ▼

After selecting AWS CodeBuild and choosing the **Create a new build project** option, you need to configure the build project, as follows:

- **Environment image**: For **Environment image**, select the **Specify a Docker image** option, and then set the **Environment type** to **Linux**, **Custom image type** to **Amazon ECR**; then, choose the `docker-in-aws/codebuild repository/latest` image you published earlier in this chapter.
- **Advanced**: Ensure that the **Privileged** flag is set, as shown in the following screenshot. This is required whenever you run Docker in Docker images:

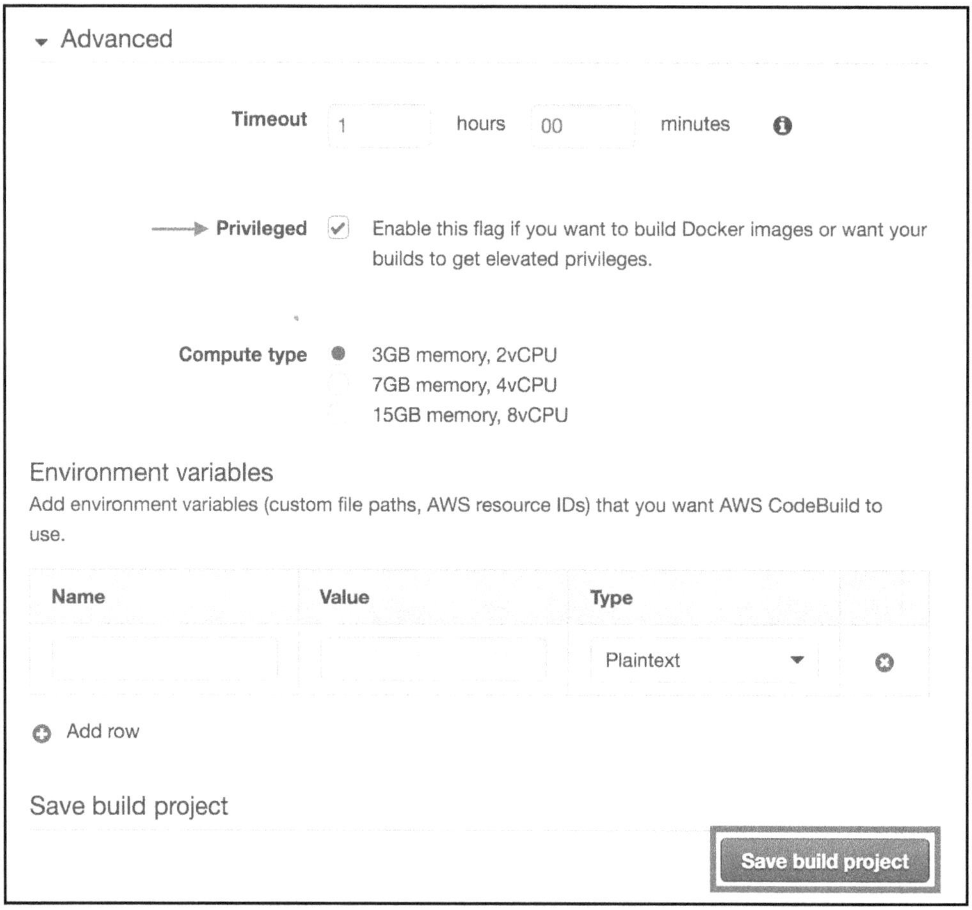

After completing the build project configuration, ensure that you click on **Save build project** before clicking **Next step** to continue.

In the next stage, you will be asked to define a **Deploy** stage. At this point, we only want to perform the continuous integration tasks of testing, building, and publishing our Docker application, so select the **No Deployment** option and click **Next step** to continue:

Deploy   ❓

Choose how you deploy to instances. Choose the provider, and then provide the configuration details for that provider.

Deployment provider*   No Deployment   ↕ ←——

No deployment

You are creating the pipeline without a deployment stage. You can edit your pipeline later to add one or more deployment stages.

* Required   Cancel   Previous   Next step

The final step is to configure an IAM role that CodePipeline can assume to perform the various build and deployment tasks in your pipeline. Click on the **Create role** button, which will open a new window that asks you to create a new IAM role, with the appropriate permissions, for CodePipeline:

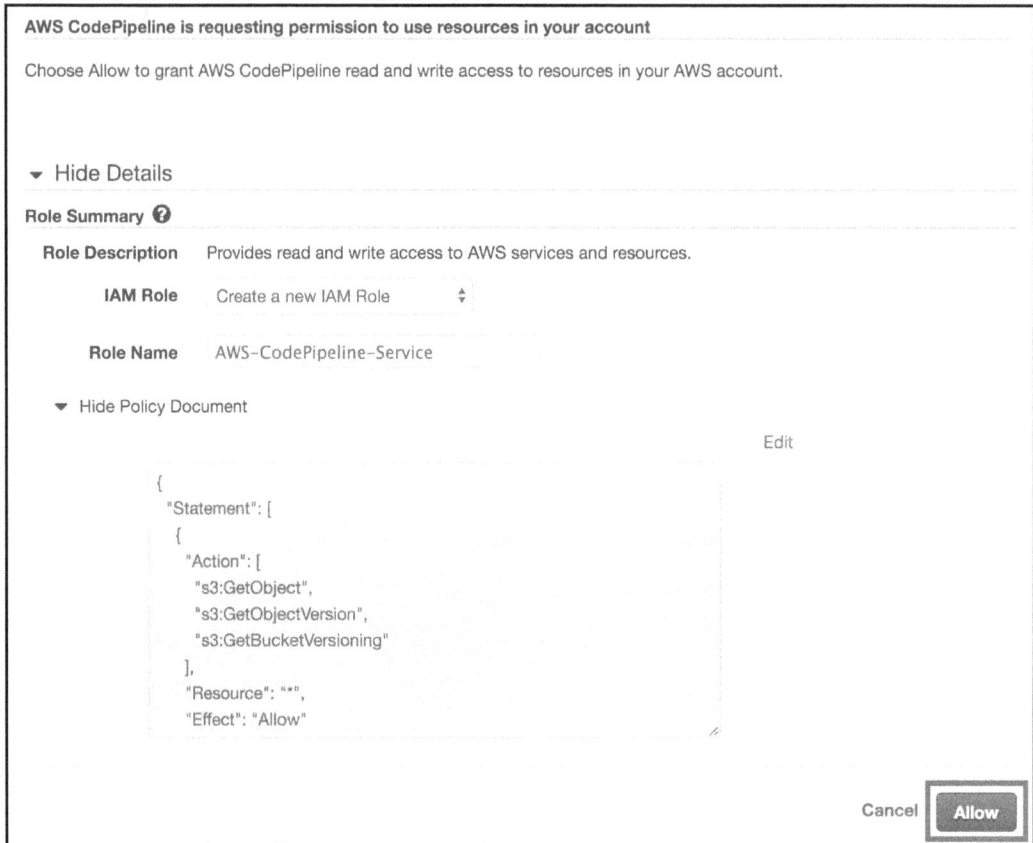

AWS CodePipeline is requesting permission to use resources in your account

Choose Allow to grant AWS CodePipeline read and write access to resources in your AWS account.

▼ Hide Details

Role Summary ❓

Role Description   Provides read and write access to AWS services and resources.

IAM Role   Create a new IAM Role   ⬍

Role Name   AWS-CodePipeline-Service

▼ Hide Policy Document

Edit

```
{
  "Statement": [
    {
      "Action": [
        "s3:GetObject",
        "s3:GetObjectVersion",
        "s3:GetBucketVersioning"
      ],
      "Resource": "*",
      "Effect": "Allow"
```

Cancel   **Allow**

After reviewing the **Policy Document**, click on **Allow**, which will select the new role in the CodePipeline wizard. Finally, click on **Next step**, review the pipeline configuration, and then click **Create pipeline** to create your new pipeline.

At this point, your pipeline will be created, and you will be taken to the pipeline configuration view for your pipeline. Whenever you create a pipeline for the first time, CodePipeline will automatically trigger the first execution of your pipeline, and after a few minutes, you should notice that the build stage for your pipeline has failed:

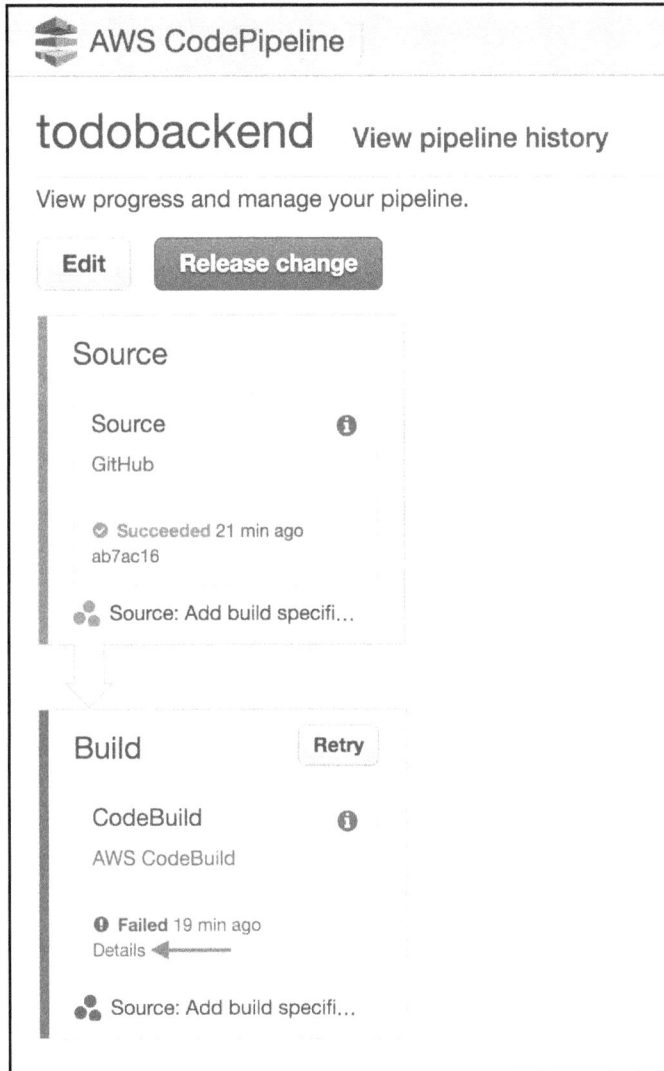

To find out more information about why the build failed, click on the **Details** link, which will pop up more details about the failure, and will also include a link to the CodeBuild job where the failure occurred. If you click on this link and scroll down, you can see that the failure occurred in the `pre_build` stage, and in the build logs that the issue is related to an IAM permission issue:

Phase details

	Name	Status	Duration	Completed
▶	SUBMITTED	Succeeded		26 minutes ago
▶	PROVISIONING	Succeeded	27 secs	26 minutes ago
▶	DOWNLOAD_SOURCE	Succeeded		26 minutes ago
▶	INSTALL	Succeeded		26 minutes ago
▶	PRE_BUILD	Failed	1 sec	26 minutes ago
▶	FINALIZING	Succeeded	2 secs	26 minutes ago
▶	COMPLETED	Succeeded		

Build logs

Showing the last 10000 lines of build log below. View entire log

```
104   Live Restore Enabled: false
105
106   WARNING: bridge-nf-call-iptables is disabled
107   WARNING: bridge-nf-call-ip6tables is disabled
108
109   [Container] 2018/06/03 07:53:10 Running command export BUILD_ID=$(echo $CODEBUILD_BUILD_ID | sed 's/^[^:]
          *://g')
110
111   [Container] 2018/06/03 07:53:10 Running command export APP_VERSION=$CODEBUILD_RESOLVED_SOURCE_VERSION
          .$BUILD_ID
112
113   [Container] 2018/06/03 07:53:10 Running command make login
114   $(aws ecr get-login --no-include-email)
115
116   An error occurred (AccessDeniedException) when calling the GetAuthorizationToken operation: User: arn:aws
          :sts::385605022855:assumed-role/code-build-todobackend-service-role/AWSCodeBuild-c7289fda-2257-4b3f-bbff
          -e7ac61944188 is not authorized to perform: ecr:GetAuthorizationToken on resource: *
117   make: *** [Makefile:7: login] Error 255
```

The problem is that the IAM role that was automatically created during the CodePipeline wizard does not include permissions to log in to ECR.

To resolve this, open the IAM console, select **Roles** from the left-hand menu, and locate the `code-build-todobackend-service-role` that was created by the wizard. In the **Permissions** tab, click on **Attach Policy**, locate the `AmazonEC2ContainerRegistryPowerUser` managed policy, and click on the **Attach Policy** button. The power user role grants login, pull, and push permissions, and because we will be publishing to ECR as a part of the build workflow, this level of access is required. Once you have completed the configuration, the **Permissions** tab for the role should look the same as what's shown in the following screenshot:

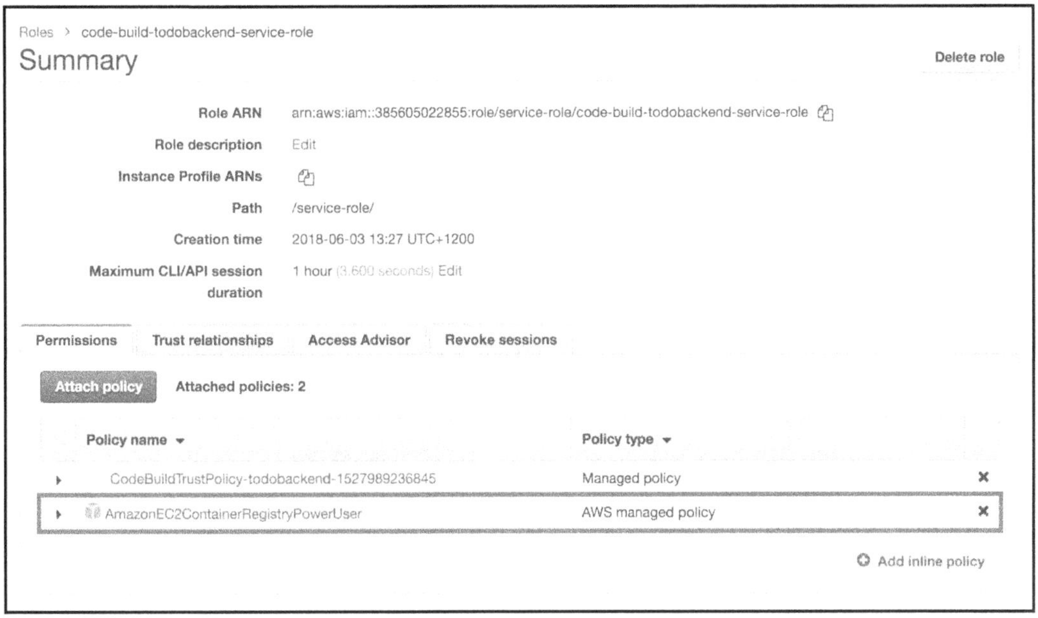

Now that you have resolved the permissions issue, navigate back to the CodePipeline details view for your pipeline, click on the **Retry** button in the build stage, and confirm retrying the failed build. This time, after a few minutes, the build should complete successfully, and you can use the `aws ecr list-images` command to verify that a new image has been published to ECR:

```
> aws ecr list-images --repository-name docker-in-aws/todobackend \
    --query imageIds[].imageTag --output table
-------------------------------------------------------------------
-------------
| ListImages
|
+-----------------------------------------------------------------
-----------+
```

```
| 5fdbe62
|
| latest
|
| ab7ac1649e8ef4d30178c7f68899628086155f1d.10f5ef52-
e3ff-455b-8ffb-8b760b7b9c55      |
+-----------------------------------------------------------------
-----------+
```

Notice that the last image published is in the format `<long commit hash>.<uuid>`, where `<uuid>` is the CodeBuild job ID, confirming that CodeBuild has successfully published a new image to ECR.

Creating a continuous delivery pipeline using CodePipeline

At this point, you have a continuous integration pipeline that will automatically publish new Docker images for your application whenever a commit is pushed on the master branch to your source repository. At some point, you will want to deploy your Docker images to an environment (perhaps a staging environment, where you may run some end-to-end tests to verify that your application works as expected), and then to a production environment that services your end users. Although you could deploy these changes manually by updating the `ApplicationImageTag` input to the todobackend stack, ideally, you want to be able to continuously deploy these changes automatically into at least one environment, which provides immediate access to developers, testers, and product managers, allowing for fast feedback from the key stakeholders involved in the development of your applications.

This concept is referred to as continuous deployment. In other words, whenever you are continuously integrating and building tested software artifacts, you then continuously deploy those artifacts. Continuous deployment is very common these days, especially if you are deploying into a non-production environment. What is far less common is continuous deployment all the way to production. To achieve this, you must have a high degree of automated post-deployment testing available, and, at least in my experience, this is something that is still difficult to achieve for most organizations. A far more common approach is what is referred to as continuous delivery, which you can think of as the ability to automatically deploy all the way to production once you are sure your release is ready for production.

Continuous delivery allows for the common scenario where you have a requirement to perform controlled releases into production, rather than continuously deploying into production as soon as a release is available. This is somewhat more achievable than continuous deployment all the way to production, as it allows for the manual testing of your non-production environments before you choose to deploy to production.

Now that you have some context around what continuous delivery is, let's extend our pipeline to support continuous delivery.

> CodePipeline includes support for ECS as a deployment target, where you can deploy new images published by your continuous integration pipeline to a target ECS cluster and ECS service. In this chapter, I will be using CloudFormation to deploy application changes; however, you can read more about the ECS deployment mechanism at `https://docs.aws.amazon.com/AmazonECS/latest/developerguide/ecs-cd-pipeline.html`.

The first stage of this is to configure the continuous deployment of your code changes into a non-production environment, requiring you to perform the following configuration actions, which will be discussed in further detail:

- Publish version information in your source repository
- Add CodePipeline support to your deployment repository
- Add your deployment repository to CodePipeline
- Add an output artifact for your build actions
- Create an IAM role for CloudFormation deployments
- Add a deployment stage to the pipeline

Publishing version information in your source repository

A key requirement of our pipeline is the ability to deploy a newly built Docker image into our AWS environments. At the moment, CodePipeline has no real awareness of the Docker image tag that is published. We know that the tag is configured within the CodeBuild environment, but CodePipeline has no understanding of this.

In order to use the Docker image tag that is generated in the CodeBuild build stage, you need to produce an output artifact that is first collected by CodeBuild, and then made available to future deployment stages in CodePipeline.

To do this, you must first define the artifact(s) that CodeBuild should collect, which you can do by adding an `artifacts` parameter to the `buildspec.yml` build specification in the todobackend repository:

```
version: 0.2

phases:
  pre_build:
    commands:
      - nohup /usr/local/bin/dockerd --
host=unix:///var/run/docker.sock --storage-driver=overlay&
      - timeout -t 15 sh -c "until docker info; do echo .; sleep 1;
done"
      - export BUILD_ID=$(echo $CODEBUILD_BUILD_ID | sed
's/^[^:]*://g')
      - export
APP_VERSION=$CODEBUILD_RESOLVED_SOURCE_VERSION.$BUILD_ID
      - make login
  build:
    commands:
      - make test
      - make release
      - make publish
      - make version > version.json
  post_build:
    commands:
      - make clean
      - make logout

artifacts:
  files:
    - version.json
```

In the preceding example, the `artifacts` parameter configures CodeBuild to look for an artifact at the location `version.json`. Notice that you also add an additional command to the build phase, which writes the output of the `make version` command to the `version.json` file where CodeBuild expects to find an artifact.

At this point, ensure that you commit and push your changes to the todobackend repository , so that the changes will be available for future builds.

Adding CodePipeline support to the deployment repository

When you use CodePipeline to deploy your environments using CloudFormation, you need to ensure that you can supply a configuration file that includes input stack parameters, stack tags, and stack policy configuration. This file must be implemented in a JSON format, as defined at `https://docs.aws.amazon.com/AWSCloudFormation/latest/UserGuide/continuous-delivery-codepipeline-cfn-artifacts.html#w2ab2c13c15c15`, so we need to modify the format of the input parameters file in the `todobackend-aws` repository, which is currently in a `<parameter>=<value>` format, located in a file called `dev.cfg`. As per the referenced document, all of your input parameters need to reside in a JSON file under a key called `Parameters`, which you can define in a new file called `dev.json`, located at the root of the `todobackend-aws` repository:

```
{
  "Parameters": {
    "ApplicationDesiredCount": "1",
    "ApplicationImageId": "ami-ec957491",
    "ApplicationImageTag": "latest",
    "ApplicationSubnets": "subnet-a5d3ecee,subnet-324e246f",
    "VpcId": "vpc-f8233a80"
  }
}
```

In the preceding example, notice that I have updated the `ApplicationImageTag` value to `latest`. This is because our pipeline will actually obtain the value for the `ApplicationImageTag` input dynamically, from the build stage of our pipeline, and the `latest` value is a safer default value, in the event that you want to deploy your stack manually, from the command line.

At this point, the `dev.cfg` file is redundant, and can be deleted from your repository; however, note that you will need to modify the way you run deployments manually, from the command line, given that the `aws cloudformation deploy` command expects input parameters to be provided in a `<parameter>=<value>` format.

One way that you can solve this is to use the `jq` utility to transform your new `dev.json` configuration file into the required `<parameter>=<value>` format:

```
> aws cloudformation deploy --template-file stack.yml --stack-name
todobackend \
    --parameter-overrides $(cat dev.json | jq -r
'.Parameters|to_entries[]|.key+"="+.value') \
    --capabilities CAPABILITY_NAMED_IAM
```

This command is now quite a mouthful, so, in order to simplify running this command, you could add a simple Makefile to the `todobackend-aws` repository:

```
.PHONY: deploy

deploy/%:
  aws cloudformation deploy --template-file stack.yml --stack-name
todobackend-$* \
    --parameter-overrides $$(cat $*.json | jq -r
'.Parameters|to_entries[]|.key+"="+.value') \
    --capabilities CAPABILITY_NAMED_IAM
```

In the preceding example, the `%` character in the task name captures a wildcard text value whenever you execute the `make deploy` command. For example, if you run `make deploy/dev`, then the `%` character would capture `dev`, and if you run `make deploy/prod`, then the captured value would be `prod`. You can then refer to the captured value by using the `$*` variable, which you can see that we have substituted in the stack name (`todobackend-$*`, which would expand to `todobackend-dev` and `todobackend-prod`, using the previous examples), and in the command to cat the `dev.json` or `prod.json` file. Note that because we have named our stack `todobackend` throughout this book, this command won't quite work for us, but if you rename your stack to `todobackend-dev`, this command will make it much easier to deploy to a given environment manually.

Before you continue, you need to add the new `dev.json` file, commit, and push your changes to the source Git repository, as we will soon add the `todobackend-aws` repository as another source in your CodePipeline pipeline.

Creating an IAM role for CloudFormation deployments

When you use CodePipeline to deploy your CloudFormation stacks, CodePipeline requires you to specify an IAM role that will be assumed by the CloudFormation service to deploy your stack. CloudFormation supports the ability to specify an IAM role that the CloudFormation service will assume, which is a powerful capability that allows for more advanced configuration scenarios, such as cross-account deployments from a central build account. This role must specify the CloudFormation service as a trusted entity that can assume the role; hence, you typically can't use administrative roles created for human access, such as the admin role that you have been using throughout this book.

To create the required role, navigate to the IAM console, select **Roles** from the left-hand menu, and click on the **Create role** button. In the **Choose the service** section, select **CloudFormation**, and then click **Next: Permissions** to continue. On the **Attach permissions policies** screen, you can create or select an appropriate policy with the various permissions required to create the resources in your stack. To keep things simple, I will just select the **AdministratorAccess** policy. However, in a real-world scenario, you should create or choose a policy that only grants the specific permissions required to create your CloudFormation stacks. After clicking the **Next: Review** button, specify the role name of `cloudformation-deploy`, and click on the **Create role** button to create the new role:

Adding a deployment repository to CodePipeline

Now that you have the appropriate stack configuration file and an IAM deployment role in place for CodePipeline, you can get started in modifying your pipeline to support the continuous delivery of application changes to your target AWS environments. The first modification that you need to perform is to add the todobackend-aws repository as another source action to the source stage of your pipeline. To do this, navigate to the details view for your pipeline, and click on the **Edit** button.

In the **Edit** screen, you can click on the pencil icon at the top right-hand corner of the source stage, which will change the view and allow you to add a new source action, either before, after, or at the same level as the current action for the **todobackend** repository:

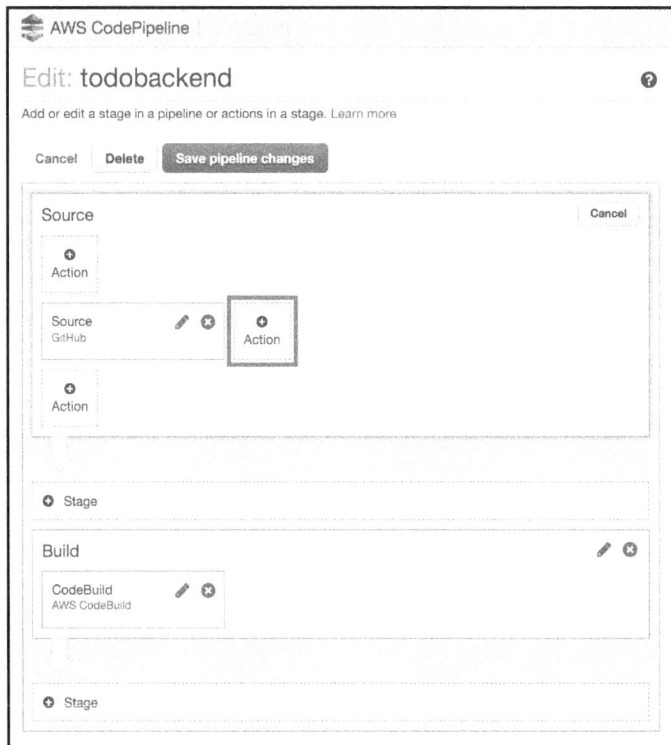

Editing a pipeline

For our scenario, we can download the deployment repository source in parallel; so, add a new action at the same level as the other source repository, which will open an **Add action** dialog. Select **Source** for the **Action category**, configure an **Action name** of `DeploymentRepository` or similar, and, after choosing **GitHub** as the **Source provider** and clicking on the **Connect to GitHub** button, select the master branch on the `docker-in-aws/todobackend-aws` repository:

Adding a deployment repository

Next, scroll to the bottom of the page, and configure a name for the output artifact of this source action. CodePipeline will make the infrastructure templates and configuration in the deployment repository available to other stages in your pipeline, which you can reference by the configured output artifact name:

Output artifacts

Choose a name for the output of this action. Learn more

Output artifact #1   DeploymentRepository

* **Required**   Cancel   **Add action**

Configuring an output artifact name

In the preceding screenshot, you also configure the output artifact name as `DeploymentRepository` (the same as the source action name), which helps, as the pipeline details view only shows stage and action names, and does not show artifact names.

Adding an output artifact to the build stage

After adding the **DeploymentRepository** action, the **Edit** pipeline screen should look as shown in the following screenshot:

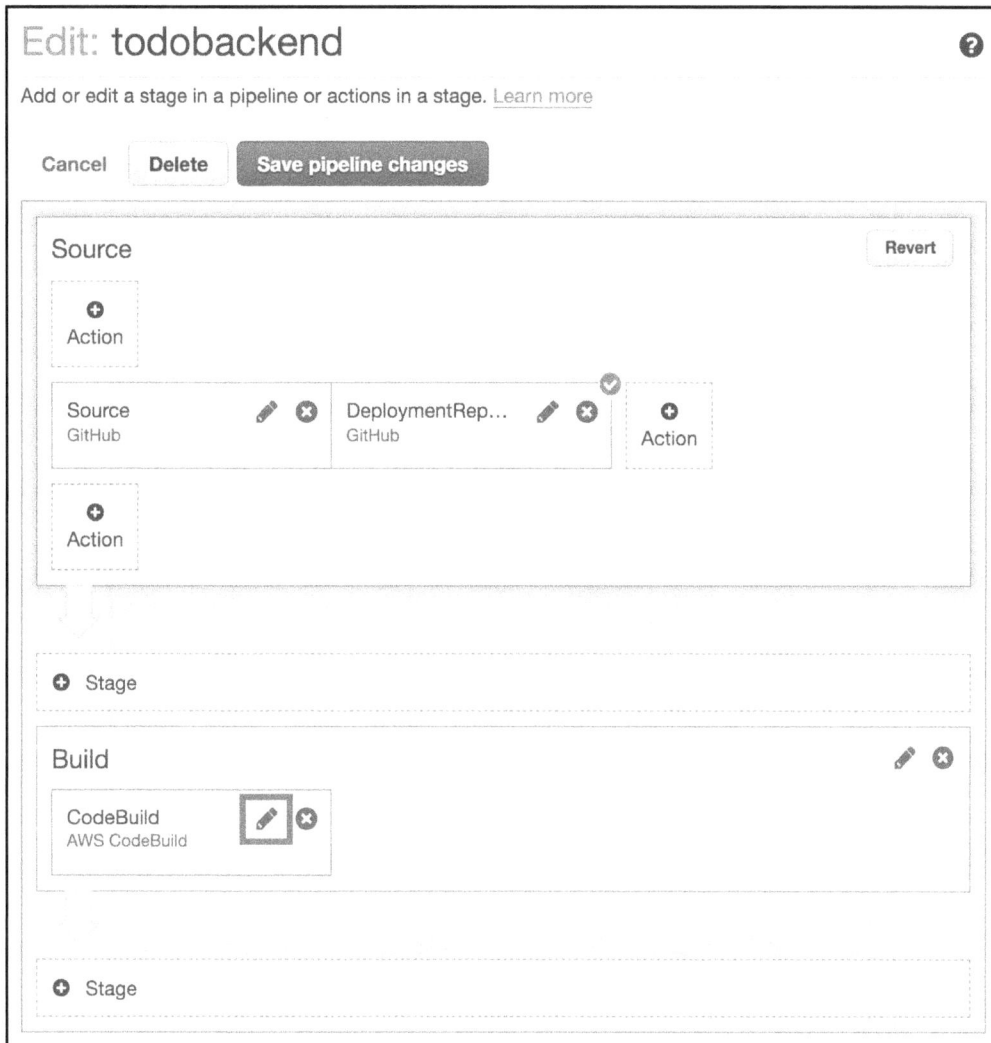

Edit pipeline screen

The next pipeline configuration task that you need to perform is to modify the CodeBuild build action within the build stage, which was created for you by the CodePipeline wizard, when you created the pipeline.

You can do this by clicking on the pencil icon in the right-hand corner of the CodeBuild action box as shown in the preceding screenshot, which opens the **Edit action** dialog:

Editing build action

In the preceding screenshot, notice that the CodePipeline wizard has already configured an input and output artifact:

- **Input artifacts**: The CodePipeline wizard names this `MyApp`, which refers to the output artifact associated with the source repository that you referenced when you created the pipeline (in this case, this is the GitHub todobackend repository). If you want to rename this artifact, you must ensure that you rename the output artifact name on the owning action (in this case, the source action in the source stage), and then update any action that uses the artifact as an input.
- **Output artifacts**: The CodePipeline wizard names this `MyAppBuild` by default, which can then be referenced in later stages of your pipeline. The output artifacts are determined by the artifacts property in the `buildspec.yml` file, and for our use case, this artifact is not the application build; instead, it is just a version artifact that captures version metadata (`version.json`), so we rename this artifact to `ApplicationVersion`.

Adding a deployment stage to the pipeline

After clicking on the **Update** button in the preceding screenshot, you can add a new stage by clicking the **Add Stage** box below the build stage. For the stage name, enter the name Dev, which will represent a deployment into an environment called Dev, and then click on the **Add Action** box to add a new action:

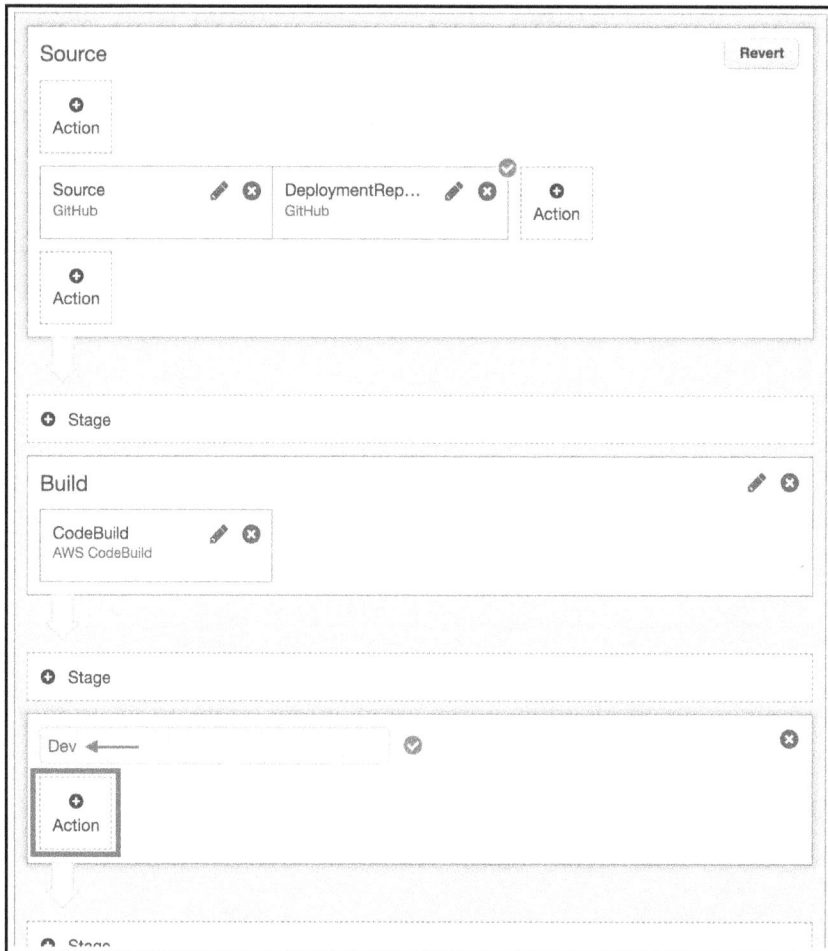

Adding a deploy action

Because this is a deployment stage, select **Deploy** from the **Action category** drop-down menu, configure an action name of **Deploy**, and select **AWS CloudFormation** as the **Deployment provider**:

Configuring a CloudFormation deploy action

This will expose a number of configuration parameters related to CloudFormation deployment, as shown in the preceding screenshot:

- **Action mode**: Select the **Create or update a stack** option, which will create a new stack if the stack does not exist, or update an existing stack.
- **Stack name**: References the existing **todobackend** stack that you have already deployed in previous chapters.
- **Template**: Refers to the CloudFormation template file that should be deployed. This is expressed in the format `InputArtifactName::TemplateFileName`, which, in our case, is `DeploymentRepository::stack.yml`, given that we configured an output artifact name of `DeploymentRepository` for the `DeploymentRepository` source action, and our stack is located in the file `stack.yml`, at the root of the repository.
- **Template configuration**: Refers to the configuration file that is used to provide stack parameters, tags, and a stack policy. This needs to reference the new `dev.json` file that you created earlier,, within the `todobackend-aws` deployment repository; it is configured in the same format as the template parameter, with a value of `DeploymentRepository::dev.json`.

Once you have configured the properties shown in the preceding screenshot, scroll down further and expand the **Advanced** section, as demonstrated in the following screenshot:

Add action

Capabilities	CAPABILITY_NAMED_IAM
Role name*	cloudformation-deploy

▾ Advanced

Output file name   File generated by this action

Parameter overrides

```
{
  "ApplicationImageTag": {
   "Fn::GetParam": [
     "ApplicationVersion",
     "version.json",
     "Version"
   ]
  }
}
```

Input artifacts

Choose one or more input artifacts for this action. The output of previous actions can be the input of this action. Learn more

Input artifacts #1	ApplicationVersion
Input artifacts #2	DeploymentRepository
Input artifacts #3	

* Required   Cancel   **Add action**

Configuring additional CloudFormation deploy action properties

The following describes each of the additional parameters that you need to configure:

- **Capabilities**: This grants permission to the CloudFormation deployment action to create IAM resources on your behalf, and is identical in meaning to the `--capabilities` flag that you pass to the `aws cloudformation deploy` command.

- **Role name**: This specifies the IAM role used by the CloudFormation deployment action to deploy your CloudFormation stack. Reference the `cloudformation-deploy` role that you created earlier.

- **Parameter overrides**: This parameter allows you to override input parameter values that are normally supplied by the template configuration file (`dev.json`), or default values within the CloudFormation template. For our use case, we need to override the `ApplicationImageTag` parameter, given that this needs to reflect the image tag that is created as part of the build stage. CodePipeline supports two types of parameter overrides (see `Using Parameter Override Functions`), and, for our use case, we are using the `Fn::GetParam` override, which can be used to extract property values from a JSON file in an artifact that is output by your pipeline. Recall that we added a `make version` task to the todobackend repository earlier in this chapter, which outputs the file `version.json` that is collected as an artifact as part of the CodeBuild build specification. We updated the build action to refer to this artifact as `ApplicationVersion`. In the preceding screenshot, the input list that is supplied to the `Fn::GetParam` call first references the artifact (`ApplicationVersion`), the path to the JSON file in the artifact (`version.json`), and finally, the key within the JSON file (`Version`) that holds the parameter override value.

- **Input artifacts**: This must specify any input artifacts that you reference in your deployment configuration. Here, we add `DeploymentRepository` (used for both the template and template configuration parameters) and `ApplicationVersion` (used in the parameter overrides configuration).

Once complete, click on the **Add action** button, and then you can click on **Save pipeline changes** to complete the configuration of your pipeline. At this point, you can test that your new deployment action is working by clicking on the **Release change** button, which manually triggers a new execution of your pipeline; within a few minutes, your pipeline should successfully build, test, and publish a new image as part of the build stage, and then successfully deploy your changes to your todobackend stack via the dev stage:

todobackend   View pipeline history

View progress and manage your pipeline.

Edit   **Release change**

Source

| Source | ℹ | DeploymentRepository ℹ |

GitHub   GitHub

⊘ Succeeded 16 min ago   ⊘ Succeeded 16 min ago
d89cbe5   f0e997b

⊙ Source: Add version artifact
  DeploymentRepository: Convert configuration file to JSON f...

Build

CodeBuild   ℹ

AWS CodeBuild

⊘ Succeeded 12 min ago
Details

⊙ Source: Add version artifact
  DeploymentRepository: C...

Dev

Deploy   ℹ

AWS CloudFormation

⊘ Succeeded 8 min ago
Details ◄────────

⊙ Source: Add version artifact
  DeploymentRepository: C...

Successful CloudFormation deployment via CodePipeline

In the preceding screenshot, you can click on the **Details** link, either during or after deployment, which takes you to the CloudFormation console and shows you details about the in-progress or completed deployment. If you expand the **Parameters** tab, you should see that **ApplicationImageTag** is referencing a tag in the format of `<long commit hash>.<codebuild job id>`, confirming that our pipeline has, in fact, deployed the Docker image that was built during the build stage:

Key	Value	Resolved Value
ApplicationDesiredCount	1	
ApplicationImageId	ami-ec957491	
ApplicationImageTag	d89cbe5828331ba737e4c6ae3ab4c55278... ◀———	
ApplicationSubnets	subnet-a5d3ecee,subnet-324e246f	
VpcId	vpc-f8233a80	

▼ Parameters

Confirming an overridden input parameter

Continuously delivering to production using CodePipeline

Now that we are continuously deploying into a non-production environment, the final step in our continuous delivery journey is to enable the ability to deploy application releases into production in a controlled fashion. CodePipeline supports this capability by leveraging a useful feature of CloudFormation, called change sets. A change set describes the various configuration changes that will be applied to a given CloudFormation stack, based on any changes that may have been applied to your stack template file and/or input parameters. For new application releases, you are typically only changing an input parameter that defines the version of your new application artifact(s). For example, the dev stage of our pipeline overrides the `ApplicationImageTag` input parameter. In some scenarios, you may make wider changes to your CloudFormation stack and input parameters. For example, you might need to add new environment variables for your container, or you might add new infrastructure components or supporting services to you stack. These changes are typically committed to your deployment repository, and, given that our deployment repository is a source in our pipeline, any changes to your deployment repository will be captured as a change.

CloudFormation change sets provide an opportunity for you to review any changes that are about to be applied to a target environment, and if the change set is deemed safe, you can then initiate a deployment from that change set. CodePipeline supports generating CloudFormation change sets as a deployment action, which can then be combined with a separate manual approval action, which allows for an appropriate person to review the change set and subsequently approve or reject the change. If the change is approved, you can then trigger a deployment from the change set, providing an effective means to provide controlled releases into your production environment, or any type of environment that requires some form of change control.

Let's now extend our pipeline to support the controlled deployment of application releases into a new production environment, which requires you to perform the following configuration changes:

- Add a new environment configuration file to your deployment repository
- Add a create change set action to the pipeline
- Add a manual approval action to the pipeline
- Add a deploy change set action to the pipeline
- Deploy to production

Adding a new environment configuration file to your deployment repository

Because we are creating a new production environment, we need to add an environment configuration file to the deployment repository, which will include input parameters specific to your production environment. As shown in the previous example, which demonstrates adding a new file called `prod.json` at the root of the `todobackend-aws` repository:

```
{
  "Parameters": {
    "ApplicationDesiredCount": "1",
    "ApplicationImageId": "ami-ec957491",
    "ApplicationImageTag": "latest",
    "ApplicationSubnets": "subnet-a5d3ecee,subnet-324e246f",
    "VpcId": "vpc-f8233a80"
  }
}
```

You can see that the format of the configuration file is identical to the dev.json file that we modified earlier. In a real-world scenario, of course, you would expect differences in the configuration file. For example, we are using the same application subnets and VPC ID; you would typically have a separate VPC, or even a separate account, for production, but to keep things simple, we will just deploy our production environment into the same VPC and subnets as our dev environment.

You will also need to make a few minor changes to our CloudFormation stack file, as there are some hardcoded names that will cause conflicts if you attempt to create a new stack in the same AWS account:

```
...
...
Resources:
  ...
  ...
  ApplicationCluster:
    Type: AWS::ECS::Cluster
    Properties:
      # ClusterName: todobackend-cluster
      ClusterName: !Sub: ${AWS::StackName}-cluster
  ...
  ...
  MigrateTaskDefinition:
    Type: AWS::ECS::TaskDefinition
    Properties:
      # Family: todobackend-migrate
      Family: !Sub ${AWS::StackName}-migrate
      ...
      ...
  ApplicationTaskDefinition:
    Type: AWS::ECS::TaskDefinition
    Properties:
      # Family: todobackend
      Family: !Ref AWS::StackName
  ...
  ...
```

In the preceding example, I have commented the previous configurations, and then highlighted the new configuration that is required. In all cases, we replace the hardcoded reference to todobackend with a reference to the stack name. Given that CloudFormation stack names must be unique within a given AWS account and region, this ensures that the modified resources will have unique names that do not conflict with other stacks in the same account and region.

To keep things simple, the CloudFormation stack for the production environment will use the same secret that we created back in the *Managing Secrets* chapter. In a real-world scenario, you would maintain separate secrets per environment.

With the new configuration file and template changes in place, make sure that you have committed and pushed your changes to GitHub before proceeding to the next section:

```
> git add -A
> git commit -a -m "Add prod environment support"
[master a42af8d] Add prod environment support
 2 files changed, 12 insertions(+), 3 deletions(-)
 create mode 100644 prod.json
> git push
...
...
```

Adding a create change set action to the pipeline

We are now ready to add a new stage to our pipeline that will deploy our application to production. We will create the first action in this stage, which creating a CloudFormation change set.

In the pipeline details view for your pipeline, click on the **Edit** button and add a new stage called **Production** after the dev stage, and then add an action to the new stage:

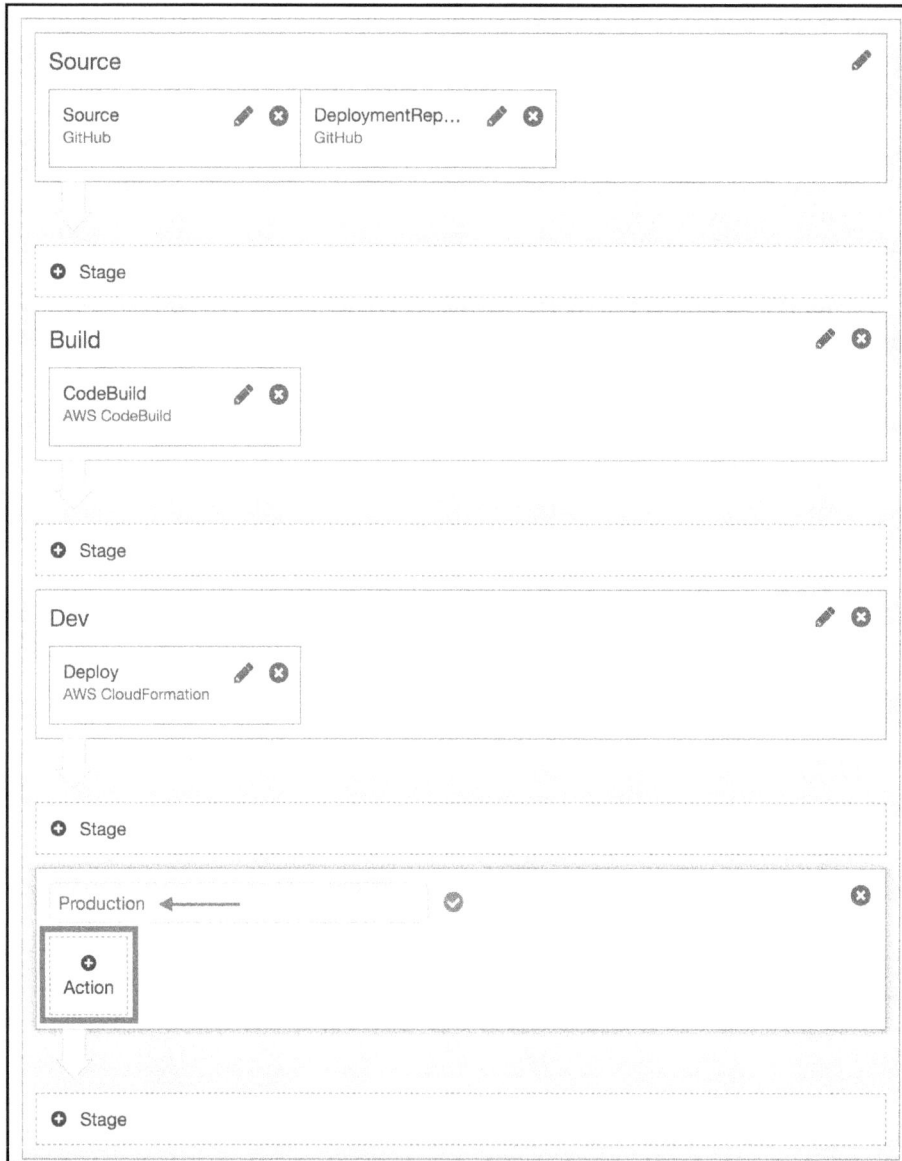

Adding a production stage to the pipeline

In the **Add action** dialog box, you need to create an action that is similar to the deploy action that you created for the dev stage, with a few variations:

Adding a create change set action to the pipeline

If you compare the deploy action configuration for the dev stage, with the new create change set action configuration as shown in the preceding screenshot, the configuration is very similar, except for the following key differences:

- **Action mode**: You configure this as `create` or `replace` a change set, which, instead of deploying the stack, will just create a new change set.
- **Stack name**: Because this action relates to our production environment, you need to configure a new stack name, which we will call `todobackend-prod`.
- **Change set name**: This defines a name for the change set. I typically just name this the same as the stack name, given that the action will create or replace the change set on each execution.
- **Template configuration**: Here, you need to reference the new `prod.json` file that you added to the `todobackend-aws` repository in the earlier example, as this holds the input parameters specific to your production environment. This file is made available via the `DeploymentRepository` artifact that is created from the `todobackend-aws` repository.

Next, you need to scroll down, expand the **Advanced** section, configure the **Parameter** overrides property using the `Fn::GetParam` syntax, and finally, configure both the `ApplicationVersion` and `DeploymentRepository` artifacts as input artifacts. This is identical to the configuration that you performed earlier, for the `dev/deploy` action.

Adding a manual approval action to the pipeline

After you have completed the configuration of the **ChangeSet action**, you will need to add a new action that comes after the **ChangeSet action**:

Add action

Choose a serial action from the action category list.

Action category*   Approval   ⬍   ⟵

Approval actions   ❓

Action name*   ApproveChangeSet   ⟵

Approval type*   Manual approval   ⬍   ⟵

Manual approval configuration ⓘ

Configure the approval request.

SNS topic ARN   [   ]   ↻

URL for review   Enter a URL for review. [Optional]

The URL you enter here will be provided to the
reviewer as part of the approval request. It should
begin with 'http://' or 'https://'.

Comments   Enter information for the reviewer. [Optional]

The information you provide will be displayed to the
approver in email notifications or the console.

* Required   Cancel   **Add action**

Adding an approval action to the pipeline

In the **Add action** dialog box, select **Approval** for the **Action** category, and then configure an **Action name** of **ApproveChangeSet**. After selecting an **Approval type** of **Manual approval**, notice that you can add an **SNS topic ARN** and other information to the manual approval request. This could then be used to send an email to the approver, or to trigger a lambda function that performs some custom action, such as posting a message into a messaging tool like Slack.

Adding a deploy change set action to the pipeline

The final action that you need to create is one that will deploy the change set created earlier in the **ChangeSet action**, once the **ApproveChangeSet action** has been approved:

Adding an execute change set action to the pipeline

In the preceding screenshot, we have selected an **Action mode** of **Execute a change set**, and then configured the **Stack name** and **Change set name**, which must match the same values that you configured earlier, in the **ChangeSet action**.

Deploying to production

After clicking on **Add action** in the preceding screenshot, your pipeline configuration for the new production stage should look as follows:

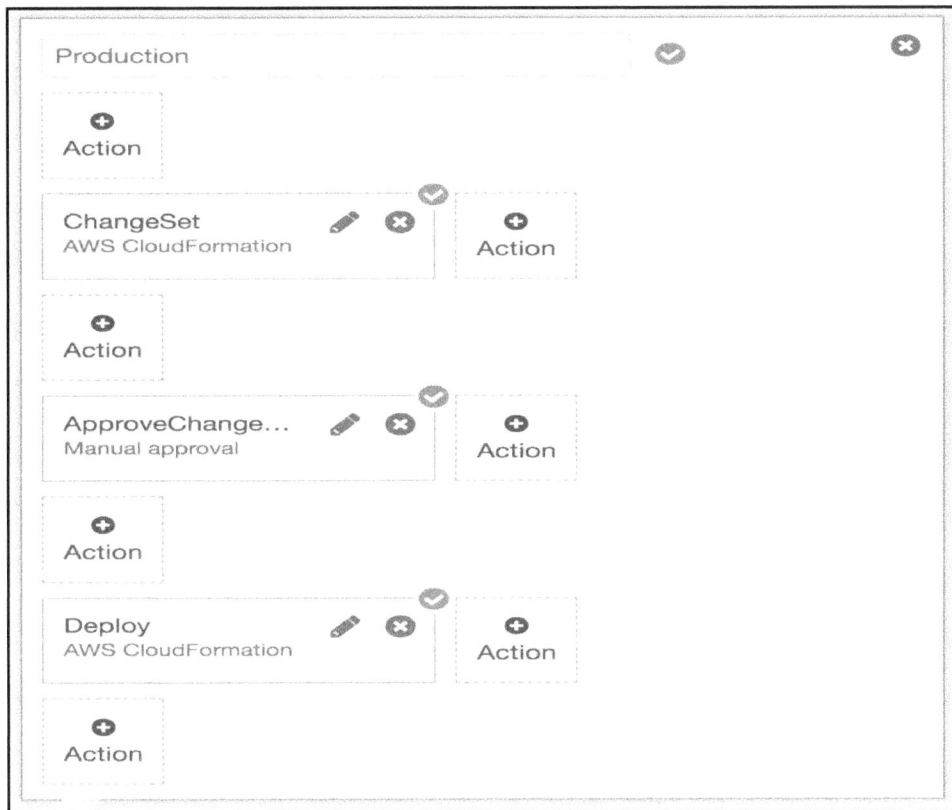

Adding a create change set action to the pipeline

At this point, you can save your pipeline changes by clicking the **Save pipeline changes** button, and test your new pipeline stage by clicking the **Release change** button, which will force a new pipeline execution. After the pipeline successfully executes the build and dev stages, the production stage will be invoked for the first time, with a CloudFormation change set created by the **ChangeSet action**, after which the approval action will be triggered:

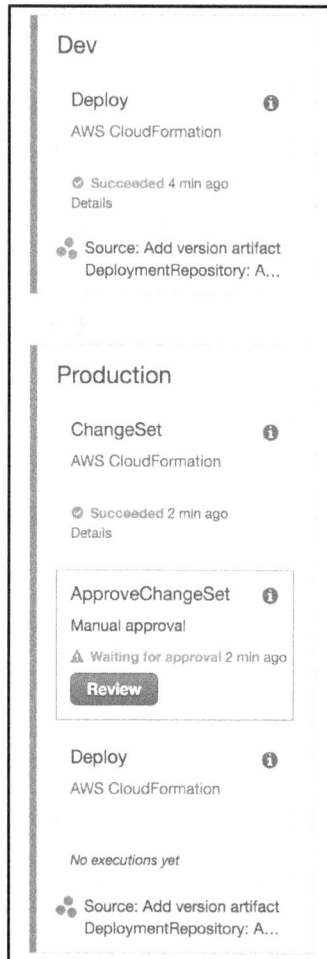

Adding a create change set action to the pipeline

The pipeline will now wait for approval, and this is where an approver would typically review the previously created change set by clicking on the **Details** link for the **ChangeSet action**:

CloudFormation change set

As you can see in the preceding screenshot, the change set indicates that all resources in the stack will be created, given that the production environment does not currently exist. Subsequent deployments should have very little changes, given that the stack will be in place, and the typical change is to deploy a new Docker image.

After reviewing the change set and returning to the CodePipeline details view, you can now approve (or reject) the change set by clicking on the **Review** button. This will present an **Approve or reject the revision** dialog box, where you can add a comment and either **Approve** or **Reject** the change:

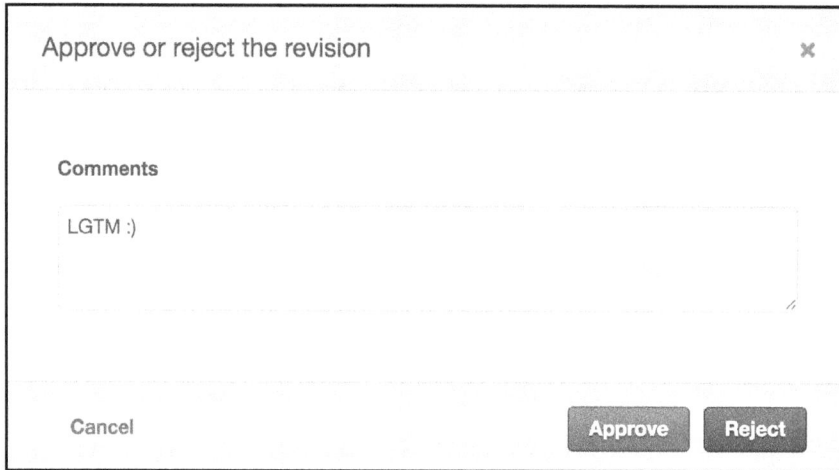

Approving or rejecting a manual approval action

If you click on **Approve**, the pipeline will proceed to the next action, which is to deploy the change set associated with the earlier **ChangeSet action**. For this first execution, a new stack called `todobackend-prod` will be deployed, and, once complete, you have successfully deployed a brand new production environment using CodePipeline!

At this point, you should test and verify that your new stack and application are working as expected, following the steps in the *Deploying an Application Load Balancer* section of the *Deploying Applications Using ECS* chapter to obtain the DNS name of the application load balancer endpoint that your production application endpoint will be served from. I also encourage you to trigger the pipeline, either manually or by making a test commit to either repository, and then reviewing the subsequent change set that is generated for an application deployment to an existing environment. Note that you can choose when you want to deploy to production. For example, your developers may commit application changes many times, with each change automatically deployed to your non-production environment, before you choose to deploy your next release to production. When you do choose to deploy to production, your production stage will take the most recent release that has been successfully deployed to your non-production environment.

Once you have completed testing your production deployments, if you are using a free tier account, bear in mind that you now have multiple EC2 instances and RDS instances running, so you should consider tearing down your production environment, in order to avoid incurring charges.

Summary

In this chapter, you created an end-to-end continuous delivery pipeline that automatically tests, builds, and publishes Docker images for your application, continuously deploys new application changes into a non-production environment, and allows you to perform controlled releases into production that generate change sets and require manual approval before deployment to production can commence.

You learned how to integrate your GitHub repositories with CodePipeline by defining them as source actions in a source stage, and then created a build stage that used CodeBuild to test, build, and publish Docker images for your application. You added a build specification to the todobackend repository, which CodeBuild uses to execute your builds, and you created a custom CodeBuild container that was able to run Docker in Docker, to allow you to build a Docker image and perform integration and acceptance tests in a Docker Compose environment.

Next, you created a deploy stage in CodePipeline, which automatically deploys application changes to the existing todobackend stack that we have worked with throughout this book. This required you to add a new source action in the source stage for the `todobackend-aws` repository, which makes the CloudFormation stack file and environment configuration file available as artifacts for later CloudFormation deployment actions. You also needed to create an output artifact for the todobackend repository, which, in this case, simply captures the Docker image tag built and published during the build stage, and makes it available for subsequent stages. You then referenced this artifact as a parameter override to your dev stage deployment action, overriding the `ApplicationImageTag` parameter with the Docker image tag output in the build action version artifact.

Finally, you extended the pipeline to support controlled releases in a production environment, which requires a create change set action that creates a CloudFormation change set, a manual approval action that allows somebody to review the change set and approve/reject it, and a deployment action that executes the previously generated change set.

In the next chapter, we will change tracks and introduce the AWS Fargate service, which allows you to deploy your Docker applications without a need to deploy and manage your own ECS clusters and ECS container instances. We will take this opportunity to add support for the AWS X-Ray service by deploying an X-Ray daemon using Fargate, and will publish the daemon endpoint by using ECS service discovery.

Questions

1. What file do you typically include at the root of your application repository to support AWS CodeBuild?
2. True/false: AWS CodeBuild is a build service that spins up virtual machines and runs build scripts using AWS CodeDeploy.
3. What is the Docker configuration that you need to run to support the building of Docker images and multi-container build environments?
4. You wish to review the changes made to your CloudFormation templates before they are deployed. What feature of CloudFormation would you use to achieve this?
5. When deploying CloudFormation stacks using the CodePipeline CloudFormation deploy action, which service must be the trusted for the service role that you specify for these actions?
6. You set up a new CodeBuild project that includes a build task that publishes to the Elastic Container Registry. Your first build fails when you attempt to publish the image. You confirm that the target ECR repository exists, and that you can manually publish images to the repository yourself. What is the likely cause of this problem?
7. You create a custom build container for CodeBuild that is published to ECR, and create a repository policy that allows ECR pull access from your AWS account. When executing a build, you get failures indicating that CodeBuild was unable to retry the custom image. How would you resolve this?
8. You create a custom build container that uses Docker in Docker to support Docker image builds. When the build container starts and you attempt to start the Docker daemon, a permissions error occurs. How would you resolve this?

Further reading

You can check the following links for more information about the topics covered in this chapter:

- CodePipeline User Guide: `https://docs.aws.amazon.com/codepipeline/latest/userguide/welcome.html`
- CodeBuild User Guide: `https://docs.aws.amazon.com/codebuild/latest/userguide/welcome.html`
- Build Specification Reference for CodeBuild: `https://docs.aws.amazon.com/codebuild/latest/userguide/build-spec-ref.html`
- Using AWS CodePipeline with CodeBuild: `https://docs.aws.amazon.com/codebuild/latest/userguide/how-to-create-pipeline.html`
- AWS CodePipeline Pipeline Structure Reference: `https://docs.aws.amazon.com/codepipeline/latest/userguide/reference-pipeline-structure.html`
- Using Parameter Override Functions with AWS CodePipeline Pipelines: `https://docs.aws.amazon.com/AWSCloudFormation/latest/UserGuide/continuous-delivery-codepipeline-parameter-override-functions.html`

14
Fargate and ECS Service Discovery

So far in this book, we have spent a considerable amount of time focused on building infrastructure that supports your ECS clusters, detailing how to build custom Amazon machine images for your ECS container instances and how to create EC2 Auto Scaling groups that can dynamically add or remove ECS container instances to your ECS cluster, with chapters dedicated to managing the life cycle and capacity of your clusters.

Imagine not having to worry about ECS clusters and ECS container instances. Imagine that somebody else managed them for you, to the extent that you didn't even really know they existed. For some use cases, having a strong level of control over hardware selection, storage configuration, security posture, and other infrastructure related concerns, is very important; by now, you should have a pretty strong understanding of exactly how ECS provides such capabilities. However, in many cases, having that level of control is not necessary, and being able to leverage a service that manages your ECS cluster patching, security configuration, capacity, and everything else, would be of significant benefit, lowering your operational overhead and allowing you to focus on delivering whatever it is your organization is striving to achieve.

The good news is that this is actually possible, thanks to a service called **AWS Fargate**, which was launched in December of 2017. Fargate is a completely managed service, wherein you simply define ECS task definitions and ECS services, and then let Fargate take care of the rest of the ECS cluster and container instance management that you have become accustomed to in this book. In this chapter, you will learn how to deploy container applications using AWS Fargate, using the **infrastructure as code (IaC)** approach of CloudFormation that we have been adopting throughout this book. To make this chapter a little bit more interesting, we will add support for an AWS service called X-Ray, which provides distributed tracing for your applications running in AWS.

When you want to use X-Ray with your container applications, you need to implement what is referred to as an X-Ray daemon, which is an application that collects tracing information from your container applications and publishes it to the X-Ray service. We will extend the todobackend application to capture tracing information for incoming requests, and will add an X-Ray daemon to your AWS environment by leveraging the AWS Fargate service, which will collect the tracing information and forward it to the X-Ray service.

As an added bonus, we will also implement a feature called ECS service discovery, which allows your container applications to be published and discovered automatically, using DNS. This feature is very useful for the X-Ray daemon, which is a UDP-based application that cannot be serviced by the various load balancing services that are available for frontending your TCP and HTTP-based applications. ECS includes built-in support for service discovery, taking care of service registration and de-registration as your ECS tasks start and stop, allowing you to creating highly available services that other applications can easily discover.

The following topics will be covered in this chapter:

- When to use Fargate
- Adding support for AWS X-Ray to applications
- Creating an X-Ray daemon Docker image
- Configuring ECS service discovery resources
- Configuring an ECS task definition for Fargate
- Configuring an ECS service for Fargate
- Deploying and testing the X-Ray daemon

Technical requirements

The following are the technical requirements for this chapter:

- Administrator access to an AWS account
- A local AWS profile, configured as per the instructions in Chapter 3
- AWS CLI version 1.15.71 or higher
- Docker 18.06 CE or higher
- Docker Compose 1.22 or higher
- GNU Make 3.82 or higher
- This chapter continues on from Chapter 13, so it requires that you have successfully completed all of the configuration tasks defined in Chapter 13

The following GitHub URL contains the code samples used in this chapter: `https://github.com/docker-in-aws/docker-in-aws/tree/master/ch14`

Check out the following video to see the Code in Action:
`http://bit.ly/2Lyd9ft`

When to use Fargate?

As discussed in the introduction to this chapter, AWS Fargate is a service that allows you to deploy your container-based applications, without requiring you to deploy any ECS container instances, auto-scaling groups, or any of the associated operational requirements that come with managing ECS cluster infrastructure. This positions AWS Fargate as a serverless technology that sits somewhere between running Functions as a Service using AWS Lambda and running your own infrastructure using traditional ECS clusters and ECS container instances.

Although Fargate is a great technology, it is important to understand that Fargate is very young (at least at the time of writing this book), and it does come with some limitations that may make it unsuitable for some use cases, outlined as follows:

- **No Persistent Storage**: Fargate does not currently support persistent storage, so if your applications need to use persistent Docker volumes, you should use an alternative service, such as the traditional ECS service.
- **Pricing**: Pricing is always subject to change; however, the initial pricing set for Fargate is viewed as expensive by many, as compared to the regular EC2 instance pricing that you get with ECS. For example, the smallest Fargate configuration that you can buy has 0.25v CPU and 512 MB of memory, and costs $14.25 USD per month. As a comparison, a t2.nano with 0.5v CPU and 512 MB of memory costs substantially less, at $4.75 USD (all prices are based upon `us-east-1 region`),
- **Deployment Times**: So far, in my experience, the ECS tasks running on Fargate typically take longer to provision and deploy, which may affect the length of time your application deployments take (this will also affect auto scaling actions).
- **Security and Control**: With Fargate, you don't get to control anything about the underlying hardware or instances that are running your containers. If you have strict security and/or compliance requirements, then Fargate may not offer you the assurances or necessary controls to meet your specific requirements. It is important to note, however, that Fargate is listed by AWS as both HIPAA and PCI Level 1 DSS compliant.

- **Network Isolation:** At the time of writing this book, Fargate does not support the use of an HTTP proxy for ECS agent and CloudWatch logs communication. This requires you to either place your Fargate tasks in a public subnet with internet connectivity, or in a private subnet with a NAT gateway, similar to the approach you learned about in the chapter *Isolating Network Access*. To allow access to the public AWS API endpoints, this does require you to open up outgoing web access, which may violate the security requirements of your organization.

- **Service Availability**: At the time of writing this book, Fargate is only available in the US East (Virginia), US East (Ohio), US West (Oregon), and EU (Ireland) regions; however, I would expect Fargate to become widely available across most regions reasonably quickly.

If you can live with the current limitations of Fargate, then Fargate will significantly reduce your operational overheads and make life simpler for you. For example, when it comes to auto-scaling, you can simply auto-scale your ECS services using the application auto-scaling approach that we discussed toward the end of the *ECS Auto-Scaling* chapter, and Fargate will take care of ensuring that there is sufficient cluster capacity. Similarly, you won't need to worry about the patching and life cycle management of your ECS clusters - Fargate takes care of all of the above for you.

In this chapter, we will be deploying an AWS X-Ray daemon service to support application tracing for the todobackend application. This type of service is well-suited to Fargate, given it is a background service that does not require persistent storage, does not affect the availability of the todobackend application (if it goes down), and does not process end user data.

Adding support for AWS X-Ray to applications

Before we can use the AWS X-Ray service, your applications need to support collecting and publishing tracing information to the X-Ray service. The X-Ray **software development kit (SDK)** includes support for a variety of programming languages and popular application frameworks, including Python and Django, which both power the todobackend application.

You can locate the appropriate SDK documentation for your language of choice at `https://aws.amazon.com/documentation/xray/`, but for our use case, `https://docs.aws.amazon.com/xray-sdk-for-python/latest/reference/frameworks.html` provides the relevant information on how to configure Django to automatically create traces for each incoming request to your application.

In the todobackend repository, you first need to add the X-Ray SDK package to the `src/requirements.txt` file, which will ensure that the SDK is installed alongside the other dependencies of the todobackend application:

```
Django==2.0
django-cors-headers==2.1.0
djangorestframework==3.7.3
mysql-connector-python==8.0.11
pytz==2017.3
uwsgi==2.0.17
aws-xray-sdk
```

Next, you need to add a Django X-Ray middleware component, which is included in the SDK, to the `MIDDLEWARE` configuration element in the release settings file for the Django project located in `src/todobackend/settings_release.py`:

```
from .settings import *
...
...
STATIC_ROOT = os.environ.get('STATIC_ROOT', '/public/static')
MEDIA_ROOT = os.environ.get('MEDIA_ROOT', '/public/media')

MIDDLEWARE.insert(0,'aws_xray_sdk.ext.django.middleware.XRayMiddleware')
```

This configuration does vary from the `X-Ray documentation for Django`, however in general you only want to run X-Ray in your AWS environments, and using the standard approach can cause X-Ray configuration issues in your local development environment. Because we have a separate release settings file that imports the base settings file, we can simply insert the X-Ray middleware component at the beginning of the base `MIDDLEWARE` list using the `insert()` function as shown. This approach ensures we will run X-Ray in our AWS environments that use the release settings, but not use X-Ray in a local development setting.

> It is important that the X-Ray middleware component is specified first in the `MIDDLEWARE` list, as this ensures that X-Ray can start tracing incoming requests before any other middleware components.

Finally, the Python X-Ray SDK includes tracing support for a number of popular packages, including the `mysql-connector-python` package, which is used by the todobackend application to connect to its MySQL database. In Python, X-Ray wraps calls made by supported packages using a technique referred to as patching, which allows X-Ray to intercept calls made by the package and capture tracing information. For our use case, patching the `mysql-connector-python` package will enable us to trace database calls made by the application, which can be very useful for troubleshooting performance issues. To patch this package, you need to add a few lines of code to your application entry point, which, for Django, is located in the file `src/todobackend.wsgi.py`:

```
"""
WSGI config for todobackend project.

It exposes the WSGI callable as a module-level variable named
``application``.

For more information on this file, see
https://docs.djangoproject.com/en/2.0/howto/deployment/wsgi/
"""

import os

from django.core.wsgi import get_wsgi_application

os.environ.setdefault("DJANGO_SETTINGS_MODULE",
"todobackend.settings")

from aws_xray_sdk.core import xray_recorder
from aws_xray_sdk.core import patch_all

# Required to avoid SegmentNameMissingException errors
xray_recorder.configure(service="todobackend")

patch_all()

application = get_wsgi_application()
```

The `xray_recorder` configuration will add a service name to each trace segment, which is required otherwise you will observe SegmentNameMissingException errors. At this point, you have added support at an application level to start tracing incoming requests, and you should be able to run the make workflow (running `make test` and `make release`) successfully before committing and pushing your changes to GitHub. Because you now have a continuous delivery pipeline in place, this will trigger that pipeline, which ensures that your application changes will be published to ECR once the pipeline build stage completes. If you haven't completed the previous chapter, or if you have removed your pipeline, then you will need to manually publish the new image by using the `make login` and `make publish` commands after running `make test` and `make release`.

Creating an X-Ray daemon Docker image

Before our application can publish X-Ray tracing information, you must deploy an X-Ray daemon that your application can send this information to. Our goal is to run the X-Ray daemon using AWS Fargate, but before we can do that, we need to create a Docker image that will run the daemon. AWS provides examples of how to build an X-Ray daemon image, and we will following a similar approach to what is documented by AWS by creating a file called `Dockerfile.xray` in the root of the `todobackend-aws` repository:

```
FROM amazonlinux
RUN yum install -y unzip
RUN curl -o daemon.zip
https://s3.dualstack.us-east-2.amazonaws.com/aws-xray-assets.us-east-2
/xray-daemon/aws-xray-daemon-linux-2.x.zip
RUN unzip daemon.zip && cp xray /usr/bin/xray

ENTRYPOINT ["/usr/bin/xray", "-b", "0.0.0.0:2000"]
EXPOSE 2000/udp
```

You can now build this image locally by using the `docker build` command, as demonstrated here:

```
> docker build -t xray -f Dockerfile.xray .
Sending build context to Docker daemon 474.1kB
Step 1/6 : FROM amazonlinux
 ---> 81bb3e78db3d
Step 2/6 : RUN yum install -y unzip
 ---> Running in 35aca63a625e
Loaded plugins: ovl, priorities
Resolving Dependencies
```

```
...
...
Step 6/6 : EXPOSE 2000/udp
 ---> Running in 042542d22644
Removing intermediate container 042542d22644
 ---> 63b422e40099
Successfully built 63b422e40099
Successfully tagged xray:latest
```

With our image now built, we need to publish it to ECR. Before you can do this, you need to create a new repository for the X-Ray image, which we can add to the existing `ecr.yml` file at the root of the `todobackend-aws` repository:

```
AWSTemplateFormatVersion: "2010-09-09"

Description: ECR Resources

Resources:
  XrayRepository:
    Type: AWS::ECR::Repository
    Properties:
      RepositoryName: docker-in-aws/xray
  CodebuildRepository:
    Type: AWS::ECR::Repository
  ...
  ...
```

In the preceding example, you created a new repository with the name `docker-in-aws/xray`, which will result in a fully qualified repository name of `<account-id>.dkr.ecr.<region>.amazonaws.com/docker-in-aws/xray` (for example, `385605022855.dkr.ecr.us-east-1.amazonaws.com/docker-in-aws/xray`).

You can now create the new repository by running the `aws cloudformation deploy` command:

```
> export AWS_PROFILE=docker-in-aws
> aws cloudformation deploy --template-file ecr.yml --stack-name ecr-repositories
Enter MFA code for arn:aws:iam::385605022855:mfa/justin.menga:

Waiting for changeset to be created..
Waiting for stack create/update to complete
Successfully created/updated stack - ecr-repositories
  ...
  ...
```

Once deployment has completed, you can log in to ECR, and then tag and publish the image that you created earlier with the fully qualified name of the new ECR repository:

```
> eval $(aws ecr get-login --no-include-email)
Login Succeeded
> docker tag xray 385605022855.dkr.ecr.us-east-1.amazonaws.com/docker-
in-aws/xray
> docker push 385605022855.dkr.ecr.us-east-1.amazonaws.com/docker-in-
aws/xray
The push refers to repository [385605022855.dkr.ecr.us-
east-1.amazonaws.com/docker-in-aws/xray]
c44926e8470e: Pushed
1c9da599a308: Pushed
9d486dac1b0b: Pushed
0c1715974ca1: Pushed
latest: digest:
sha256:01d9b6982ce3443009c7f07babb89b134c9d32ea6f1fc380cb89ce5639c3393
8 size: 1163
```

Configuring ECS service discovery resources

ECS service discovery is a feature that allows your client applications to discover ECS services in a dynamic environment, where container-based endpoints come and go. To date, we have used AWS application load balancers to perform this function, where you configure a stable service endpoint that your applications can connect to, with connections then load balanced across an ECS-managed target group that includes each of the ECS tasks associated with your ECS service. Although this is generally my recommended best practice approach, for applications that don't support load balancers (for example, UDP-based applications), or for very large microservice architectures where it is more efficient to have direct communication with a given ECS task, ECS service discovery may be a better approach than using load balancers.

> ECS service discovery also supports AWS load balancers, where ECS will publish the IP address of the load balancer listener if a load balancer is associated with a given ECS service.

ECS service discovery uses DNS as its discovery mechanism, which is useful, given that in its most basic form, DNS is universally supported by any application client. The DNS namespace that your ECS services are registered in is referred to as a **service discovery namespace**, which simply corresponds to a Route 53 DNS domain or zone, and each service that you register in the namespace is referred to as a **service discovery**. For example, you might configure `services.dockerinaws.org` as a service discovery namespace, and, if you have an ECS service called `todobackend`, then you will connect to that service using the DNS name `todobackend.services.dockerinaws.org`. ECS will automatically manage address (`A`) records registered against the DNS record for your service, dynamically adding the IP address associated with each active and healthy ECS task of your ECS service, as well as removing any ECS tasks that exit or become unhealthy. ECS service discovery supports both public and private namespaces, and for our example of running the X-Ray daemon, a private namespace is suitable, given that this service only needs to support internal application tracing communications from the todobackend application.

> ECS service discovery supports the provisioning of DNS service (SRV) records, which include both IP address and TCP/UDP port information about a given service endpoint. You typically use address (`A`) records when using static port mapping or **awsvpc** networking mode (as is the case with Fargate), and SRV records when using dynamic port mapping, given that SRV records can include the dynamic port information for the port mapping that is created. Note that application support for SRV records is somewhat limited, so I typically recommend using the tried and true approach of using `A` records for ECS service discovery.

Configuring a service discovery namespace

Like most AWS resources, you can configure service discovery resources using the AWS console, AWS CLI, any one of the various AWS SDKs, or CloudFormation. Given our infrastructure as code approach throughout this book, we will naturally adopt CloudFormation in this chapter; because the X-Ray daemon is a new service (and would typically be considered a shared service, which each of your applications publishes trace information to), we will create a new stack, in a file called `xray.yml`, at the root of the `todobackend-aws` repository.

The following example demonstrates creating the initial template and creating a service discovery namespace resource:

```
AWSTemplateFormatVersion: "2010-09-09"

Description: X-Ray Daemon

Resources:
  ApplicationServiceDiscoveryNamespace:
    Type: AWS::ServiceDiscovery::PrivateDnsNamespace
    Properties:
      Name: services.dockerinaws.org.
      Description: services.dockerinaws.org namespace
      Vpc: vpc-f8233a80
```

In the preceding example, we created a private service discovery namespace that simply requires the DNS name of the namespace, an optional description, and the VPC ID that the associated private Route 53 zone will be linked to. To keep things simple, I have also hardcoded an appropriate value for the VPC ID related to my AWS account, which you would typically inject via a stack parameter.

> Given that the intention of a service discovery namespace is to support multiple services, you would typically create the namespace in a separate CloudFormation stack, such as a dedicated network stack that creates shared network resources. However, in the interest of keeping things simple, we are creating the namespace in the X-Ray stack.

You can now deploy the initial stack to CloudFormation by using the `aws cloudformation deploy` command, which should create a service discovery namespace and the associated Route 53 private zone:

```
> aws cloudformation deploy --template-file xray.yml --stack-name
xray-daemon
Waiting for changeset to be created..
Waiting for stack create/update to complete
Successfully created/updated stack - xray-daemon
> aws servicediscovery list-namespaces
{
    "Namespaces": [
        {
            "Id": "ns-lgd774j6s2cmxwq3",
            "Arn": "arn:aws:servicediscovery:us-
east-1:385605022855:namespace/ns-lgd774j6s2cmxwq3",
            "Name": "services.dockerinaws.org",
            "Type": "DNS_PRIVATE"
```

```
        }
    ]
}
> aws route53 list-hosted-zones --query HostedZones[].Name --output
table
------------------------------
| ListHostedZones            |
+----------------------------+
| services.dockerinaws.org.  |
+----------------------------+
```

In the preceding example, once your stack successfully deploys, you will use the `aws servicediscovery list-namespaces` command to verify that a private namespace was created, while the `aws route53 list-hosted-zones` command shows that a Route 53 zone was also created, with a zone name of `services.dockerinaws.org`.

Configuring a service discovery service

Now that you have a service discovery namespace in place, the next step is to create a service discovery service, which has a one-to-one relationship with each ECS service, meaning that you need to create a service discovery service that represents the X-Ray ECS service that you will create later in this chapter:

```
AWSTemplateFormatVersion: "2010-09-09"

Description: X-Ray Daemon

Resources:
  ApplicationServiceDiscoveryService:
    Type: AWS::ServiceDiscovery::Service
    Properties:
      Name: xray
      Description: xray service
      DnsConfig:
        NamespaceId: !Ref ApplicationServiceDiscoveryNamespace
        DnsRecords:
          - Type: A
            TTL: 60
      HealthCheckCustomConfig:
        FailureThreshold: 1
  ApplicationServiceDiscoveryNamespace:
    Type: AWS::ServiceDiscovery::PrivateDnsNamespace
    Properties:
      Name: services.dockerinaws.org.
```

```
Description: services.dockerinaws.org namespace
Vpc: vpc-f8233a80
```

In the preceding example, you added a new resource, called
`ApplicationServiceDiscoveryService`, and configured the following properties:

- `Name`: Defines the name of the service. This name will be used to register
  the service in the associated namespace.

- `DnsConfig`: Specifies the namespace that the service is associated with (as
  defined by the `NamespaceId` property), and defines the DNS record type
  and time-to-live (TTL) that should be created. Here, you specify an address
  record (type `A`) and a TTL of 60 seconds, meaning that clients will only
  cache the record for a maximum of 60 seconds. Generally, you should set
  the TTL to a low value, to ensure that your clients pick up DNS changes
  when new ECS tasks are registered to the service or existing ECS tasks are
  removed from the service.

- `HealthCheckCustomConfig`: This configures ECS to manage health
  checks that determine whether or not an ECS task can be registered. You
  can also configure Route 53 health checks (see `https://docs.aws.amazon.`
  `com/AmazonECS/latest/developerguide/service-discovery.`
  `html#service-discovery-concepts`); however, for our use case, given that
  X-Ray is a UDP-based application and Route 53 health checks only support
  TCP-based services, you must use the `HealthCheckCustomConfig`
  configuration shown in the preceding example. The `FailureThreshold`
  specifies the number of `30` second intervals the service discovery will wait
  to change the health of a given service instance, after receiving a custom
  health check update (in this scenario, ECS provides custom health checks).

You can now deploy your updated stack to CloudFormation using the `aws`
`cloudformation deploy` command, which should create a service discovery
service:

```
> aws cloudformation deploy --template-file xray.yml --stack-name
xray-daemon
Waiting for changeset to be created..
Waiting for stack create/update to complete
Successfully created/updated stack - xray-daemon
> aws servicediscovery list-services
{
    "Services": [
        {
            "Id": "srv-wkdxwh4pzo7ea7w3",
            "Arn": "arn:aws:servicediscovery:us-
```

```
east-1:385605022855:service/srv-wkdxwh4pzo7ea7w3",
        "Name": "xray",
        "Description": "xray service"
    }
  ]
}
```

This will create a DNS record set for xray.services.dockerinaws.org, which won't have any address (A) records associated with it until we configure ECS service discovery support for the X-Ray ECS service that we will create later in this chapter.

Configuring an ECS task definition for Fargate

You are now ready to start defining your ECS resources, which you will configure to use the AWS Fargate service and leverage the service discovery resources that you created in the previous section.

When configuring ECS task definitions to support Fargate, there are some key considerations that you need to understand:

- **Launch type:** An ECS task definition includes a parameter called RequiresCompatibilities, which defines the compatible launch types for the definition. The current launch types include EC2, which refers to ECS tasks launched on traditional ECS clusters, and FARGATE, which refers to ECS tasks launched on Fargate. By default, the RequiresCompatibilities parameter is configured as EC2, meaning that you must explicitly configure this parameter if you want to use Fargate.
- **Network mode**: Fargate only supports the awsvpc network mode, which we discussed in Chapter 10 - *Isolating Network Access*.

- **Execution role**: Fargate requires you to configure an **execution role**, which is an IAM role assigned to the ECS agent and Fargate runtime that manages the life cycle of ECS tasks, based from your Fargate task definition. This is a separate role from the IAM roles for tasks feature that you configured back in Chapter 9 - *Managing Secrets*, which you use to grant IAM permissions to the application running in your ECS task. The execution role is typically configured with similar permissions to those that you would configure for an EC2 IAM instance role associated with a traditional ECS container instance, granting, at a minimum, permissions for the ECS agent and Fargate runtime, to pull images from ECR and write logs to CloudWatch logs.

- **CPU and Memory**: Fargate requires you to define CPU and memory requirements at the task definition level, as this determines the underlying target instance that ECS tasks based from your task definition will run on. Note that this is separate from the per-container definition CPU and memory settings that you configured in the ECS task definition for the todobackend application, back in Chapter 8 - *Deploying Applications using ECS*; you can still configure per-container definition CPU and memory settings, but you need to ensure that the total CPU/memory allocated to your container definitions does not exceed the overall CPU/memory allocated to the ECS task definition. Fargate currently supports only a limited set of CPU/memory allocations, which you can read more about in the *Task CPU and Memory* section at `https://docs.aws.amazon.com/AmazonECS/latest/developerguide/AWS_Fargate.html`.

- **Logging**: At the time of writing, Fargate only supports the `awslogs` logging driver, which forwards your container logs to CloudWatch logs.

With the preceding considerations in mind, let's now define a task definition for our X-Ray daemon service:

```
...
...
Resources:
  ApplicationTaskDefinition:
    Type: AWS::ECS::TaskDefinition
    Properties:
      Family: !Sub ${AWS::StackName}-task-definition
      NetworkMode: awsvpc
      ExecutionRoleArn: !Sub ${ApplicationTaskExecutionRole.Arn}
      TaskRoleArn: !Sub ${ApplicationTaskRole.Arn}
      Cpu: 256
      Memory: 512
      RequiresCompatibilities:
```

```
            - FARGATE
        ContainerDefinitions:
        - Name: xray
          Image: !Sub
${AWS::AccountId}.dkr.ecr.${AWS::Region}.amazonaws.com/docker-in-
aws/xray
          Command:
            - -o
          LogConfiguration:
            LogDriver: awslogs
            Options:
              awslogs-group: !Sub /${AWS::StackName}/ecs/xray
              awslogs-region: !Ref AWS::Region
              awslogs-stream-prefix: docker
          PortMappings:
            - ContainerPort: 2000
              Protocol: udp
          Environment:
            - Name: AWS_REGION
              Value: !Ref AWS::Region
    ApplicationLogGroup:
      Type: AWS::Logs::LogGroup
      DeletionPolicy: Delete
      Properties:
        LogGroupName: !Sub /${AWS::StackName}/ecs/xray
        RetentionInDays: 7
    ApplicationServiceDiscoveryService:
      Type: AWS::ServiceDiscovery::Service
    ...
    ...
```

In the preceding example, notice that the RequiresCompatibilities parameter specifies FARGATE as the supported launch type, and that the NetworkMode parameter is configured as the required awsvpc mode. The Cpu and Memory settings are configured as 256 CPU units (0.25 vCPUs) and 512 MB, respectively, which represents the smallest available Fargate CPU/memory configuration. For the ExecutionRoleArn parameter, you reference an IAM role called ApplicationTaskExecutionRole, which we will configure shortly, separate from the role configured for the TaskRoleArn parameter.

Next, you define a single container definition called `xray`, which references the ECR repository that you created earlier in this chapter; notice that you specify the `-o` flag for the `Command` parameter. This will append `-o` to the command specified in the `ENTRYPOINT` directive that you configured in the X-Ray daemon image back in the previous example, which stops the X-Ray daemon from attempting to query EC2 instance metadata, as this is not supported when you use Fargate.

The log configuration for the container definition is configured to use the `awslogs` driver, as required for Fargate, which references the `ApplicationLogGroup` CloudWatch logs group resource configured under the task definition. Finally, you specify the X-Ray daemon port (`UDP port 2000`) as a container port mapping, and you configure a single environment variable, called `AWS_REGION`, that references the region in which you deploy the stack, which is required for the X-Ray daemon to determine the regional X-Ray service endpoint that the daemon should publish trace data to.

Configuring IAM roles for Fargate

In the previous example, your ECS task definition refers to a task execution role (as defined by the `ExecutionRoleArn` parameter) and a task role (as defined by the `TaskRoleArn` parameter).

As discussed previously, the task execution role defines the IAM permissions that will be assigned to the ECS agent and Fargate runtime, and typically includes permissions to pull the require ECR images to run the containers defined in your task definition, as well as permissions to write to the CloudWatch log groups referenced in your container logging configuration:

```
...
...
Resources:
  ApplicationTaskExecutionRole:
    Type: AWS::IAM::Role
    Properties:
      AssumeRolePolicyDocument:
        Version: "2012-10-17"
        Statement:
          - Effect: Allow
            Principal:
              Service:
                - ecs-tasks.amazonaws.com
            Action:
              - sts:AssumeRole
```

```
        Policies:
          - PolicyName: EcsTaskExecutionRole
            PolicyDocument:
              Statement:
                - Sid: EcrPermissions
                  Effect: Allow
                  Action:
                    - ecr:BatchCheckLayerAvailability
                    - ecr:BatchGetImage
                    - ecr:GetDownloadUrlForLayer
                    - ecr:GetAuthorizationToken
                  Resource: "*"
                - Sid: CloudwatchLogsPermissions
                  Effect: Allow
                  Action:
                    - logs:CreateLogStream
                    - logs:PutLogEvents
                  Resource: !Sub ${ApplicationLogGroup.Arn}
ApplicationTaskDefinition:
  Type: AWS::ECS::TaskDefinition
...
...
```

The task role defines any IAM permissions that the applications running from your ECS task definition may require. For our use case, the X-Ray daemon requires permissions to publish traces to the X-Ray service, as demonstrated in the following example:

```
Resources:
  ApplicationTaskRole:
    Type: AWS::IAM::Role
    Properties:
      AssumeRolePolicyDocument:
        Version: "2012-10-17"
        Statement:
          - Effect: Allow
            Principal:
              Service:
                - ecs-tasks.amazonaws.com
            Action:
              - sts:AssumeRole
      Policies:
        - PolicyName: EcsTaskRole
          PolicyDocument:
            Statement:
              - Effect: Allow
                Action:
                  - xray:PutTraceSegments
```

```
            - xray:PutTelemetryRecords
            Resource: "*"
    ApplicationTaskExecutionRole:
    Type: AWS::IAM::Role
...
...
```

In the preceding example, you grant the `xray:PutTraceSegments` and `xray:PutTelemetryRecords` permission to the X-Ray daemon, which allows the daemon to publish application traces captured from your applications to the X-Ray service. Notice that for both the `ApplicationTaskExecutionRole` and `ApplicationTaskRole` resources, the trusted entity in the `AssumeRolePolicyDocument` section must be configured as the `ecs-tasks.amazonaws.com` service.

Configuring an ECS service for Fargate

Now that you have defined an ECS task definition for Fargate, you can create an ECS service that will reference your ECS task definition and deploy one or more instances (ECS tasks) for your service.

As you might expect, when configuring ECS services to support Fargate, there are some key considerations that you need to be aware of:

- **Launch type**: You must specify Fargate as the launch type for any ECS service that you want to run using Fargate.
- **Platform version**: AWS maintains different versions of the Fargate runtime or platform, which will evolve over time, and may at some point introduce breaking changes for your ECS services. You can optionally target a specific platform version for your ECS service, or simply omit configuring this property, to use the latest platform version available.
- **Network configuration**: Because Fargate requires the use of **awsvpc** networking mode, your ECS services must define a network configuration that defines the subnets your ECS service will run in, the security groups assigned to your ECS service, and also, whether or not your service is assigned a public IP address. At the time of writing this book, when using Fargate, you must either assign a public IP address or use a NAT gateway, as discussed in the chapter *Isolating Network Access*, to ensure that the ECS agent that manages your ECS service can communicate with ECS, pull images from ECR, and publish logs to the CloudWatch logs service.

> Although you can't interact with the ECS agent, it is important to understand that all ECS agent communications use the same network interface as your container applications running in Fargate. This means that you must consider the communication requirements of the ECS agent and Fargate runtime when attaching security groups and determining the network placement of your ECS service.

The following example demonstrates configuring an ECS service for Fargate and ECS service discovery:

```
...
...
Resources:
  ApplicationCluster:
    Type: AWS::ECS::Cluster
    Properties:
      ClusterName: !Sub ${AWS::StackName}-cluster
  ApplicationService:
    Type: AWS::ECS::Service
    DependsOn:
      - ApplicationLogGroup
    Properties:
      ServiceName: !Sub ${AWS::StackName}-application-service
      Cluster: !Ref ApplicationCluster
      TaskDefinition: !Ref ApplicationTaskDefinition
      DesiredCount: 2
      LaunchType: FARGATE
      NetworkConfiguration:
        AwsvpcConfiguration:
          AssignPublicIp: ENABLED
          SecurityGroups:
            - !Ref ApplicationSecurityGroup
          Subnets:
            - subnet-a5d3ecee
            - subnet-324e246f
      DeploymentConfiguration:
        MinimumHealthyPercent: 100
        MaximumPercent: 200
      ServiceRegistries:
        - RegistryArn: !Sub ${ApplicationServiceDiscoveryService.Arn}
  ApplicationTaskRole:
    Type: AWS::IAM::Role
...
...
```

In the preceding example, the first point to note is that although you don't run any ECS container instances or other infrastructures when using Fargate, you are still required to define an ECS cluster when configuring ECS services for Fargate, which you will then reference in your ECS service.

The ECS service configuration is similar to the configuration you defined when running the todobackend application using ECS task networking in the *Isolating Network Access* chapter, although there are a few key configuration properties to discuss:

- `LaunchType`: This must be specified as `FARGATE`. It is important to ensure that you place your ECS services in a public subnet and configure the `AssignPublicIp` property in the networking configuration as `ENABLED`, or, alternatively, place your services in a private subnet with a NAT gateway. In the preceding example, note that I have hardcoded the `Subnets` property to public subnets within my VPC; you need to change these to the appropriate values for your environment, and you would typically inject these values via a stack parameter.
- `ServiceRegistries`: This property configures your ECS service to use the ECS service discovery feature that we configured earlier in this chapter, and here, you reference the ARN of the service discovery service that you configured back in the previous example. With this configuration in place, ECS will automatically register/de-register the IP address of each of your ECS service instances (ECS tasks) in the DNS record set created for the linked service discovery service.

At this point, there is one final resource to configure—you need to define the `ApplicationSecurityGroup` resource referenced by your ECS service:

```
...
...
Resources:
  ApplicationSecurityGroup:
    Type: AWS::EC2::SecurityGroup
    Properties:
      VpcId: vpc-f8233a80
      GroupDescription: !Sub ${AWS::StackName} Application Security
Group
      SecurityGroupIngress:
        - IpProtocol: udp
          FromPort: 2000
          ToPort: 2000
          CidrIp: 172.31.0.0/16
      SecurityGroupEgress:
```

```
            - IpProtocol: tcp
              FromPort: 80
              ToPort: 80
              CidrIp: 0.0.0.0/0
            - IpProtocol: tcp
              FromPort: 443
              ToPort: 443
              CidrIp: 0.0.0.0/0
            - IpProtocol: udp
              FromPort: 53
              ToPort: 53
              CidrIp: 0.0.0.0/0
        Tags:
          - Key: Name
            Value: !Sub ${AWS::StackName}-ApplicationSecurityGroup
  ApplicationCluster:
    Type: AWS::ECS::Cluster
    Properties:
      ClusterName: !Sub ${AWS::StackName}-cluster
  ApplicationService:
    Type: AWS::ECS::Service
...
...
```

In the preceding example, again, note that I am using hardcoded values where I would typically use stack parameters, to keep things simple and to the point. The security group permits ingress access to UDP port 2000 from any host within the VPC, while the egress security rules allow access to DNS, HTTP, and HTTPS, which is required to ensure that the ECS agent can communicate with ECS, ECR, and CloudWatch logs, and that the X-Ray daemon can communicate with the X-Ray service.

Deploying and testing the X-Ray daemon

At this point, we have completed the configuration of our CloudFormation template that will deploy the X-Ray daemon to AWS using the Fargate service with ECS service discovery enabled; you can deploy the changes to your stack by using the `aws cloudformation deploy` command, including the `--capabilities` parameter, given that our stack is now creating IAM resources:

```
> aws cloudformation deploy --template-file xray.yml --stack-name
xray-daemon \
    --capabilities CAPABILITY_NAMED_IAM
Waiting for changeset to be created..
Waiting for stack create/update to complete
Successfully created/updated stack - xray-daemon
```

Once the deployment has completed, if you open the ECS dashboard in the AWS console and select **Clusters**, you should see a new cluster called **xray-daemon-cluster,** with a single service and two running tasks, in the **FARGATE** section:

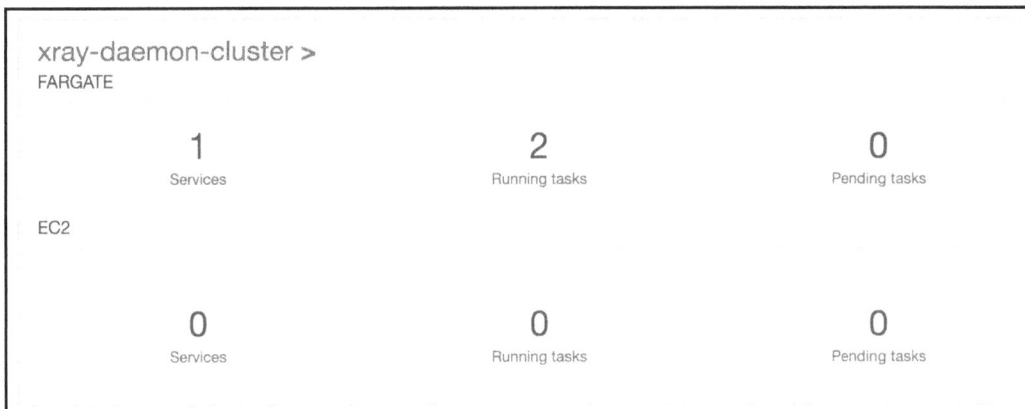

X-Ray daemon cluster

If you select the cluster and click on the **xray-daemon-application-service**, you should see the ECS service discovery configuration in place on the **Details** tab:

X-Ray daemon service details

Within the service discovery namespace, you should now find two address records attached to the `xray.services.dockerinaws.org` record set, which you can view by navigating to the Route 53 dashboard, selecting **Hosted zones** from the left-hand menu, and selecting the `services.dockerinaws.org` zone:

Service discovery DNS records

Notice that there are two A records present, one for each ECS task that supports our ECS service. If you were to stop one of these ECS tasks, ECS would automatically remove the record from DNS, and then add a new A record once ECS restored the ECS service count to its desired count and started a replacement ECS task. This ensures that your service is highly available, and that applications that rely on your service can dynamically resolve an appropriate instance of your service.

Configuring the todobackend stack for X-Ray support

With our X-Ray daemon service in place, we can now add support for X-Ray to the `todobackend-aws` stack. At the beginning of this chapter, you configured support for X-Ray in the todobackend application, and if you committed and pushed your changes, the continuous delivery pipeline you created in the last chapter should have already published an updated Docker image to ECR (if this is not the case, run the `make publish` command in the todobackend repository). The only other configuration that you need to perform is to update the security rules attached to your todobackend cluster instances to allow X-Ray communications, and to ensure that the Docker environment is configured with the appropriate environment variables that enable correct X-Ray operation.

The following example demonstrates adding a security rule to the `ApplicationAutoscalingSecurityGroup` resource in the `todobackend-aws` stack, which allows for X-Ray communications with the X-Ray daemon:

```
...
...
Resources:
  ...
  ...
  ApplicationAutoscalingSecurityGroup:
    Type: AWS::EC2::SecurityGroup
    Properties:
      GroupDescription: !Sub ${AWS::StackName} Application Autoscaling
Security Group
      VpcId: !Ref VpcId
      SecurityGroupIngress:
        - IpProtocol: tcp
          FromPort: 22
          ToPort: 22
          CidrIp: 0.0.0.0/0
      SecurityGroupEgress:
        - IpProtocol: udp
          FromPort: 2000
          ToPort: 2000
          CidrIp: 172.31.0.0/16
        - IpProtocol: udp
          FromPort: 53
          ToPort: 53
          CidrIp: 0.0.0.0/0
        - IpProtocol: tcp
          FromPort: 80
          ToPort: 80
          CidrIp: 0.0.0.0/0
        - IpProtocol: tcp
          FromPort: 443
          ToPort: 443
          CidrIp: 0.0.0.0/0
  ...
  ...
```

The following example demonstrates configuring the environment settings for the todobackend container definition, within the `ApplicationTaskDefinition` resource:

```
...
...
Resources:
```

```
    ...
    ...
  ApplicationAutoscalingSecurityGroup:
    Type: AWS::EC2::SecurityGroup
    Properties:
    ...
    ...
      ContainerDefinitions:
        - Name: todobackend
          Image: !Sub
${AWS::AccountId}.dkr.ecr.${AWS::Region}.amazonaws.com/docker-in-
aws/todobackend:${ApplicationImageTag}
          MemoryReservation: 395
          Cpu: 245
          MountPoints:
            - SourceVolume: public
              ContainerPath: /public
          Environment:
            - Name: DJANGO_SETTINGS_MODULE
              Value: todobackend.settings_release
            - Name: MYSQL_HOST
              Value: !Sub ${ApplicationDatabase.Endpoint.Address}
            - Name: MYSQL_USER
              Value: todobackend
            - Name: MYSQL_DATABASE
              Value: todobackend
            - Name: SECRETS
              Value: todobackend/credentials
            - Name: AWS_DEFAULT_REGION
              Value: !Ref AWS::Region
            - Name: AWS_XRAY_DAEMON_ADDRESS
              Value: xray.services.dockerinaws.org:2000
    ...
    ...
```

In the preceding example, you added a variable called `AWS_XRAY_DAEMON_ADDRESS`, which references the `xray.services.dockerinaws.org` service endpoint of our X-Ray daemon service and must be expressed in the format `<hostname>:<port>`.

> You can override the service name used in your X-Ray traces be setting the `AWS_XRAY_TRACE_NAME` environment variable. This would be important in our scenario where we have a dev and production instance of the todobackend application in the same account, and want to ensure each application environment has its own set of traces.

If you now commit and push all of your changes to the `todobackend-aws` repository, the continuous delivery pipeline from the previous chapter should detect the change and deploy your updated stack automatically, or alternatively you can run the `make deploy/dev` command to deploy your changes from the command line.

Testing the X-Ray service

After your changes have deployed successfully, browse to the todobackend URL for your environment and perform a few interactions with the application, such as adding a `todo` item.

If you next open the X-Ray dashboard from the AWS console (**Services** | **Developer Tools** | **X-Ray**) and select **Service map** from the left-hand menu, you should see a very simple map that includes the todobackend application:

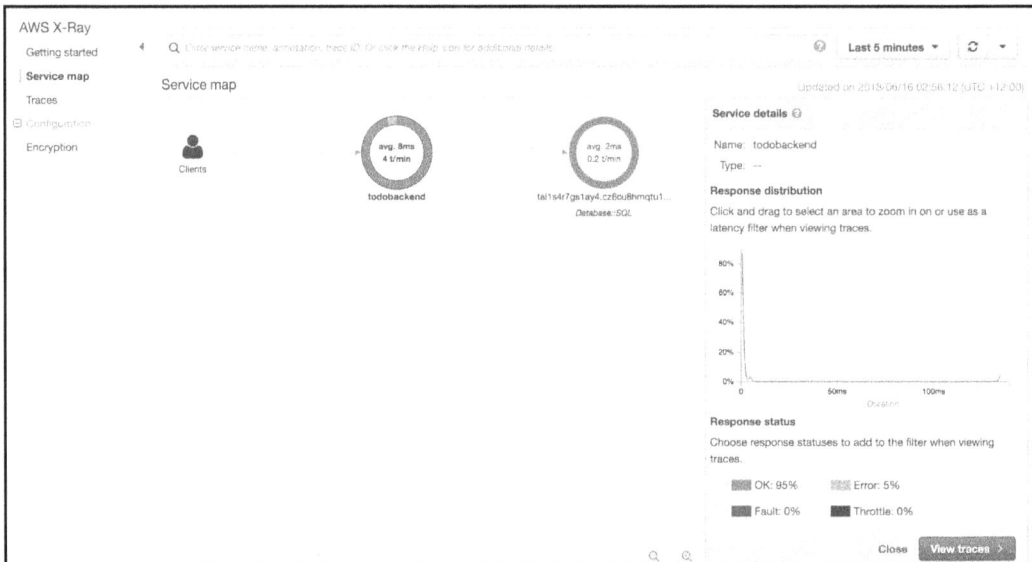

X-Ray service map

In the preceding screenshot, I have clicked on the todobackend service, which displays the **Service details** pane on the right, showing information such as the response time distribution and response status responses. Also, notice that the service map includes the todobackend RDS instance, given that we configured our application to patch the `mysql-connector-python` library back in the previous example in this chapter.

If you click on the **View traces** button, the traces for that service will be displayed; notice that the X-Ray middleware for Django includes URL information that allows your traces to be grouped by URL:

X-Ray traces

In the preceding screenshot, notice that 85% of traces are hitting an IP address URL, which corresponds to the ongoing application load balancer health checks. If you click on the **Age** column in the **Trace list** to sort traces from newest to oldest, you should be able to see the requests that you made to the todobackend application, which, in my case, was a `POST` request to create a new `todo` item.

You can view more details for the POST trace in the following screenshot, by clicking on the **ID** link:

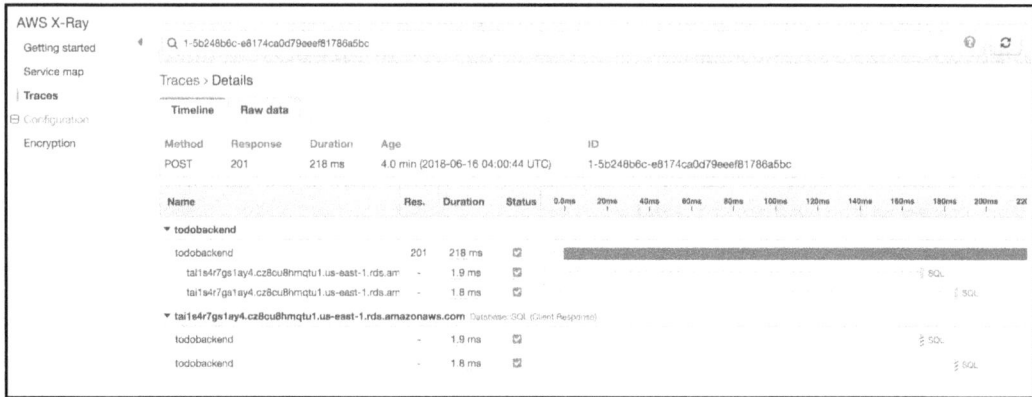

X-Ray trace details

In the preceding screenshot, you can see that the response took 218 ms to complete, in total, and that two database calls were made, which each took less than 2 ms. If you were using other libraries supported by the X-Ray SDK, you could also see trace information for calls made by those libraries; for example, any AWS service calls made via the boto3 library, such as copying a file to S3 or publishing a message to a Kinesis stream, would also be captured. Obviously, this type of information is very useful when troubleshooting performance issues for your application.

Summary

In this chapter, you learned how to deploy Docker applications using the AWS Fargate service. To make things more interesting, you also learned how you can leverage ECS service discovery to automatically publish service reachability information for your application endpoints, which is an alternative to the more traditional approach of publishing your application endpoints behind a load balancer. And, to cap off what I'm sure you found to be a fun and interesting chapter, you added support for the AWS X-Ray service to the todobackend application and deployed an X-Ray daemon service, using Fargate to capture application traces.

First, you learned how to add support for X-Ray to a Python Django application, which simply requires you to add an X-Ray middleware component that intercepts incoming requests, and to also patch support packages, such as the mysql-connector-python and boto3 libraries, which allows you to capture MySQL database calls and any AWS service calls that your application might make. You then created a Docker image for the X-Ray daemon, which you published to the Elastic Container Registry, to make it available for deployment in your AWS environment.

The, you learned how to configure the supporting elements required for ECS service discovery, adding a service discovery namespace that creates a public or private DNS zone where service discovery service endpoints are maintained, and then creating a service discovery service for the X-Ray daemon, allowing your todobackend application (and other applications) to discover all active and healthy X-Ray daemon instances via logical DNS names.

With these components in place, you proceeded to creating an X-Ray daemon service using Fargate, creating an ECS task definition and an ECS service. The ECS task definition had a few specific requirements for supporting Fargate, including defining a separate task execution role that grants privileges to the underlying ECS agent and Fargate runtime, specifying Fargate as a supported launch type and ensuring that the awsvpc networking mode was configured. The ECS service that you created required you to configure a network configuration to support the awsvpc networking mode of your ECS task definition. You also added support for ECS service discovery by referencing the service discovery service that you created earlier in the chapter.

Finally, you configured your existing ECS task definitions in the todobackend stack, to specify the service discovery service name as the AWS_XRAY_DAEMON_ADDRESS variable; after deploying your changes, you learned how to use X-Ray traces to analyze the performance of incoming requests to your application, with the ability to profile individual calls to the todobackend application database.

In the next chapter, you will learn about another AWS service that supports Docker applications, called Elastic Beanstalk. It provides a **platform-as-a-service (Paas)** approach to deploying and running your container-based applications in AWS.

Questions

1. True/false: Fargate requires you to create an ECS cluster.

2. When configuring Fargate, what networking modes are supported?

3. True/false: Fargate separates ECS agent **control plane** network communications from ECS task **data plane** network communications.

4. You deploy a new ECS service using Fargate, which fails, with an error indicating that the ECR image specified in the task definition cannot be pulled. You verify that the image name and tag are correct, and that the IAM role referenced on the `TaskRoleArn` property of the task definition permits access to the ECR repository. What is the most likely cause of this error?

5. You are determining the best technology to deploy your container-based applications in AWS. Your organization deploys Splunk to collect logs for all applications, and uses New Relic to collect performance metrics. Is Fargate a suitable technology, based on these requirements?

6. True/false: ECS service discovery uses Consul to publish service registration information.

7. Which service discovery resource creates a Route 53 zone?

8. You configure an ECS task definition to use Fargate, and specify that the task should be allocated 400 CPU units and 600 MB of memory. When you deploy an ECS service that uses the task definition, the deployment fails. How can you resolve this issue?

9. By default, which network protocol and port are used for AWS X-Ray communications?

10. True/false: When you add X-Ray support to your container-based applications, they will publish traces to the AWS X-Ray service.

Further reading

You can check the following links for more information about the topics covered in this chapter:

- AWS Fargate on Amazon ECS: `https://docs.aws.amazon.com/AmazonECS/latest/developerguide/AWS_Fargate.html`
- Amazon ECS Task Execution IAM Role: `https://docs.aws.amazon.com/AWSCloudFormation/latest/UserGuide/aws-resource-ecs-service.html`
- ECS Service Discovery: `https://docs.aws.amazon.com/AmazonECS/latest/developerguide/service-discovery.html`
- AWS X-Ray Developer Guide: `https://docs.aws.amazon.com/xray/latest/devguide/aws-xray.html`
- AWS X-Ray Python SDK: `https://docs.aws.amazon.com/xray/latest/devguide/xray-sdk-python.html`
- Running the X-Ray Daemon on Amazon ECS: `https://docs.aws.amazon.com/xray/latest/devguide/xray-daemon-ecs.html`
- CloudFormation Service Discovery Public Namespace Resource Reference: `https://docs.aws.amazon.com/AWSCloudFormation/latest/UserGuide/aws-resource-servicediscovery-publicdnsnamespace.html`
- CloudFormation Service Discovery Private Namespace Resource Reference: `https://docs.aws.amazon.com/AWSCloudFormation/latest/UserGuide/aws-resource-servicediscovery-privatednsnamespace.html`
- CloudFormation Service Discovery Service Resource Reference: `https://docs.aws.amazon.com/AWSCloudFormation/latest/UserGuide/aws-resource-servicediscovery-service.html`
- CloudFormation ECS Task Definition Resource Reference: `https://docs.aws.amazon.com/AWSCloudFormation/latest/UserGuide/aws-resource-ecs-taskdefinition.html`
- CloudFormation ECS Service Resource Reference: `https://docs.aws.amazon.com/AWSCloudFormation/latest/UserGuide/aws-resource-ecs-service.html`

15
Elastic Beanstalk

So far in this book, we have focused on the use of Elastic Container Service (ECS) and its variant, AWS Fargate, to manage and deploy Docker applications. The remainder of this book will focus on alternative technologies that you can use to run your Docker applications in AWS, and the first of these that we will cover is Elastic Beanstalk.

Elastic Beanstalk falls into a category that is commonly referred to by the industry as **Platform as a service** (**PaaS**), and is a service that is intended to provide a managed runtime environment for your applications that lets you focus on developing, deploying, and operating your application, rather than worry about the surrounding infrastructure. To reinforce this paradigm, Elastic Beanstalk is focused around supporting various popular programming languages and today includes support for Node.js, PHP, Python, Ruby, Java, .NET, and Go applications. When you create an Elastic Beanstalk application, you specify the target programming language, and Elastic Beanstalk will deploy an environment that supports your programming language and associated runtimes and application frameworks. Elastic Beanstalk will also deploy supporting infrastructure such as load balancers and databases, and more importantly will configure your environment so that you have easy access to logs, monitoring information, and alerts, ensuring you can not only deploy your applications, but also monitor them and ensure, they are up and running in an optimal state.

In addition to the aforementioned programming languages, Elastic Beanstalk also supports Docker environments, meaning it can support any application that can be run in a Docker container, regardless of programming language or application runtime, and in this chapter you will learn how you can use Elastic Beanstalk to manage and deploy your Docker applications. You will learn how to create an Elastic Beanstalk application using the AWS console and create an environment, which includes an application load balancer and RDS database instance that's required for our application. You will encounter some issues with the initial setup, and learn how to diagnose and troubleshoot these issues using the AWS console and Elastic Beanstalk command-line tools.

To resolve these issues, you will configure a feature known as **ebextensions**, which is an advanced configuration feature of Elastic Beanstalk that can be used to apply a number of custom configuration scenarios to your application. You will leverage ebextensions to address permissions issues with Docker volumes, transform default environment variables generated by Elastic Beanstalk to the format expected by your application, and finally ensure single shot deployment tasks such as executing database migrations are only run on a single instance for each application deployment.

> This chapter is not intended to provide exhaustive coverage of Elastic Beanstalk and will only focus on core scenarios related to deploying and managing Docker applications. For coverage of support for other programming languages and more advanced scenarios, refer to the `AWS Elastic Beanstalk Developer Guide`.

The following topics will be covered in this chapter:

- Introduction to Elastic Beanstalk
- Creating Elastic Beanstalk applications using the AWS console
- Managing Elastic Beanstalk applications using the Elastic Beanstalk CLI
- Customizing Elastic Beanstalk applications
- Deploying and testing Elastic Beanstalk applications

Technical requirements

The following are the technical requirements for this chapter:

- Administrator access to an AWS account
- Local environment configured as per the instructions in Chapter 1
- A local AWS profile, configured as per the instructions in Chapter 3
- Python 2.7 or 3.x
- PIP package manager
- AWS CLI version 1.15.71 or higher
- Docker 18.06 CE or higher
- Docker Compose 1.22 or higher
- GNU Make 3.82 or higher

This chapter assumes you have successfully completed all of the configuration tasks covered so far in this book

The following GitHub URL contains the code samples that are used in this chapter: `https://github.com/docker-in-aws/docker-in-aws/tree/master/ch14`.

Check out the following video to see the Code in Action: `http://bit.ly/2MDhtj2`

Introduction to Elastic Beanstalk

As discussed in the introduction to this chapter, Elastic Beanstalk is a PaaS offering from AWS that allows you to focus on application code and features rather than worry about the surrounding infrastructure required to support your application. To this end, Elastic Beanstalk is somewhat opinionated in its approach and generally works in a specific way. Elastic Beanstalk does leverage other AWS services as much as possible, and tries to take the effort and complexity out of integrating with these services, which works well if you follow the way Elastic Beanstalk expects you to use these services. If you are running a small team in a small to medium sized organization, Elastic Beanstalk can bring a lot of value to the table, providing lots of functionality out of the box. However, as soon as your organization grows and you look to optimize and standardize the way you deploy, monitor, and operate your applications, you may find that you outgrow the individual application-focused approach of Elastic Beanstalk.

For example, it is important to understand that Elastic Beanstalk operates on the concept of a single ECS task definition per EC2 instance, so if you are wanting to run multiple container workloads on a shared infrastructure, Elastic Beanstalk is not the right choice for you. The same applies for logging and operational tools—in general, Elastic Beanstalk provides its own toolchain that is very focused on individual applications, whereas your organization may want to adopt standard toolsets that operate across multiple applications. Personally, I prefer the more flexible and extensible approach that using ECS offers, but I must admit some of the out of the box operational and monitoring tools that you essentially get for free with Elastic Beanstalk are very attractive for getting an application up and running, and fully integrated with other AWS services.

Elastic Beanstalk concepts

This chapter is solely focused on running Docker applications using Elastic Beanstalk, so don't expect exhaustive coverage of Elastic Beanstalk and all of its supported programming languages. It is important to understand the basic concepts however, which I will cover off briefly now before we get started with creating an Elastic Beanstalk application.

When using Elastic Beanstalk, you create *applications* which can define one or more *environments*. Using the todobackend application as an example, you would define the todobackend application as an Elastic Beanstalk application, and create an environment called Dev and an environment called Prod to mirror the development and production environments we have deployed to date. Each environment references a specific version of your application, which contains the deployable code for your application. In the case of Docker applications, the source code includes a specification called `Dockerrun.aws.json` that defines the container environment for your application, which may reference an external Docker image or reference a local Dockerfile that is used to build your application.

Another important concept to understand is that behind the scenes, Elastic Beanstalk runs your application on regular EC2 instances, and follows a very strict paradigm of one instance of your application per EC2 instance. Each Elastic Beanstalk EC2 instance runs a specially curated environment based upon your target application—for example, in the case of a multi container Docker application, the EC2 instance includes the Docker Engine and ECS agent. Elastic Beanstalk also allows you to access and manage these EC2 instances via SSH in the case of Linux servers (which we will be using in this chapter), although you should generally reserve this access for troubleshooting purposes and never attempt to modify the configuration of these instances directly yourself.

Creating an Elastic Beanstalk application

Now that you understand the basic concepts of Elastic Beanstalk, let's turn our attention to creating a new Elastic Beanstalk application. You can create and configure Elastic Beanstalk applications using a variety of methods:

- AWS console
- AWS CLI and SDKs
- AWS CloudFormation
- Elastic Beanstalk CLI

In this chapter, we will first create an Elastic Beanstalk application in the AWS console, and then use the Elastic Beanstalk CLI to manage, update, and refine the application.

When you are creating a Docker application, it is important to understand that Elastic Beanstalk supports two kinds of Docker applications:

- Single-container applications: `https://docs.aws.amazon.com/elasticbeanstalk/latest/dg/docker-singlecontainer-deploy.html`
- Multi-container applications: `https://docs.aws.amazon.com/elasticbeanstalk/latest/dg/create_deploy_docker_ecs.html`

For our use case, we will be following a very similar approach to how we configured the todobackend application for the ECS in previous chapters, hence we will require a multi container application, given we previously defined a main application container definition called **todobackend** and a **collectstatic** container definition in our ECS task definition (see the *Defining an ECS task definition using CloudFormation* section from the chapter *Deploying Applications using ECS*). In general, I recommend the multi container approach, regardless of whether or not your application is a single container application, as the original single container application model goes against Docker best practices and forces you to run everything from a single container should your application requirements ever change or grow.

Creating a Dockerrun.aws.json file

Regardless of the type of Docker application you are creating, you must first create a file called `Dockerrun.aws.json`, which defines the various containers that comprise your application. This file is defined in a JSON format and is based upon the ECS task definition format that you configured in earlier chapters, which we will use as a basis for the settings in the `Dockerrun.aws.json` file.

Let's create a folder called `eb` in the `todobackend-aws` repository, and define a new file called `Dockerrun.aws.json` as follows:

```
{
  "AWSEBDockerrunVersion": 2,
  "volumes": [
    {
      "name": "public",
      "host": {"sourcePath": "/tmp/public"}
    }
  ],
  "containerDefinitions": [
```

```
    {
      "name": "todobackend",
      "image": "385605022855.dkr.ecr.us-east-1.amazonaws.com/docker-
in-aws/todobackend",
      "essential": true,
      "memoryReservation": 395,
      "mountPoints": [
        {
          "sourceVolume": "public",
          "containerPath": "/public"
        }
      ],
      "environment": [
{"name":"DJANGO_SETTINGS_MODULE","value":"todobackend.settings_release
"}
      ],
      "command": [
        "uwsgi",
        "--http=0.0.0.0:8000",
        "--module=todobackend.wsgi",
        "--master",
        "--die-on-term",
        "--processes=4",
        "--threads=2",
        "--check-static=/public"
      ],
      "portMappings": [
        {
          "hostPort": 80,
          "containerPort": 8000
        }
      ]
    },
    {
      "name": "collectstatic",
      "image": "385605022855.dkr.ecr.us-east-1.amazonaws.com/docker-
in-aws/todobackend",
      "essential": false,
      "memoryReservation": 5,
      "mountPoints": [
        {
          "sourceVolume": "public",
          "containerPath": "/public"
        }
      ],
      "environment": [
{"name":"DJANGO_SETTINGS_MODULE","value":"todobackend.settings_release
"}
```

```
    ],
    "command": [
      "python3",
      "manage.py",
      "collectstatic",
      "--no-input"
    ]
  }
 ]
}
```

When defining a multi container Docker application, you must specify and use version 2 of the specification format, which is configured via the `AWSEBDockerrunVersion` property. If you refer back to the *Defining an ECS task definition using CloudFormation* in the chapter *Deploying applications using ECS*, you can see that the version 2 specification of the `Dockerrun.aws.json` file is very similar, although the format is JSON as opposed to the YAML format we have been using in our CloudFormation templates. We use camel case naming to define each parameter.

The file includes two container definitions—one for the main todobackend application and one that generates static content—and we define a volume called `public` that is used to store static content. We also configure a static port mapping from the container port 8000 to port 80 on the host, as port 80 is where Elastic Beanstalk expects your web applications to be listening by default.

Note that there are some important differences from the approach we used for ECS:

- **Image**: We reference the same ECR image, however we do not specify an image tag, meaning the latest version of the Docker image will always be deployed. The `Dockerrun.aws.json` file does not support parameter or variable references, so if you wanted to reference an explicit image, you would need a continuous delivery workflow that automatically generates this file as part of the build process.
- **Environment**: Notice that we do not specify any environment variables related to database configuration, such as `MYSQL_HOST` or `MYSQL_USER`. We will discuss the reasons for this later on in this chapter, however for now understand that when you use the integrated support for RDS in Elastic Beanstalk, the environment variables that are automatically available to your applications follow a different format that we need to transform to meet the expectations of our application.

- **Logs**: I have removed the CloudWatch logging configuration to simplify this chapter, however there is no reason why you cannot include a CloudWatch logs configuration with your containers. Note that if you did use CloudWatch logs, you would need to modify the Elastic Beanstalk EC2 service role to include permissions for writing your logs to CloudWatch logs. We will see an example of this later in this chapter.

> I have also removed the XRAY_DAEMON_ADDRESS environment variable to keep things simple, as you may no longer have the X-Ray daemon running in your environment. Note that if you did want to support X-Ray, you would need to ensure the instance security group attached to your Elastic Beanstalk instances included security rules permitting network communications to the X-Ray daemon.

Now that we have defined a Dockerrun.aws.json file, we need to create a ZIP archive that includes this file. Elastic Beanstalk requires your application source to be uploaded in a ZIP or WAR archive format, hence this requirement. You can do this from the command line by using the zip utility as follows:

```
todobackend-aws/eb> zip -9 -r app.zip . -x .DS_Store
adding: Dockerrun.aws.json (deflated 69%)
```

This will create an archive called app.zip in the todobackend-aws/eb folder, with the -r flag specifying that zip should recursively add all files in any folders that may exist (this will be the case later on in this chapter). After specifying an archive name of app.zip, we reference the current working directory by specifying . rather than *, as using the . syntax will include any hidden directories or files (again, this will be the case later on in this chapter).

Also note that in a macOS environment, you can use the -x flag to exclude .DS_Store directory metadata files from being included in your archive.

Creating an Elastic Beanstalk application using the AWS console

We are now ready to create an Elastic Beanstalk application using the AWS console. To get started, select **Services** | **Elastic Beanstalk** and then click on the **Get started** button to create a new application. In the **Create a web app** screen, specify an application name of todobackend, configure a platform of **multicontainer Docker**, and finally upload the `app.zip` file you created previously using the **Upload your code** option for the **Application code** setting:

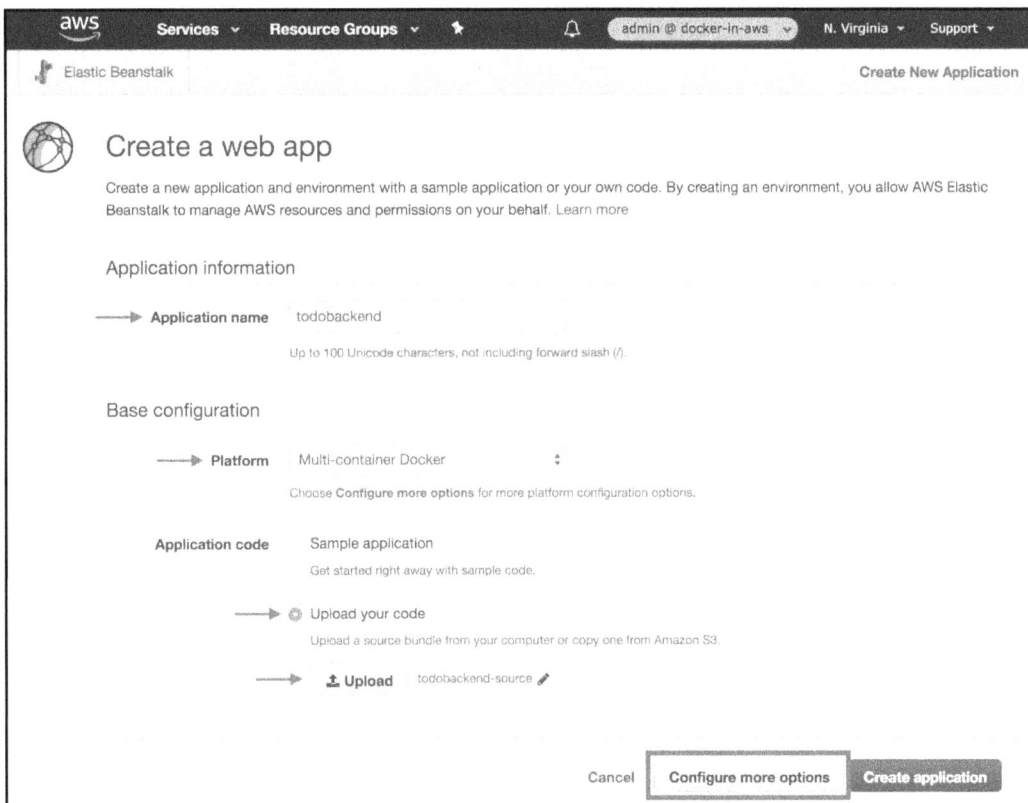

Creating an Elastic Beanstalk web application

Next, click on the **Configure more options** button, which will present a screen called **Configure Todobackend-Env** that allows you to customize your application. Note that by default, Elastic Beanstalk names your first application environment `<application-name>-Env`, hence the name **Todobackend-Env**.

In the **Configuration presets** section, select the **High availability** option, which will add a load balancer to your configuration:

Configuring an Elastic Beanstalk web application

If you review the current settings, you will notice that the **EC2 instance type** is **t1.micro** in the **Instances** section, the **Load balancer type** is **classic** in the **Load balancer** section, and that the **Database** section currently is not configured. Let's first modify the **EC2 instance type** to be the free tier **t2.micro** instance type by clicking the **Modify** link in the **Instances** section, changing the **Instance type** and then clicking **Save**:

Modifying EC2 instance type

Next, change the **Load balancer type** to **Application Load Balancer** by clicking the **Modify** link in the **Load Balancer**s section and then slicking **Save**. Note that the default settings expect to expose your application on **Port** - 80 to the outside world, as defined in the **Application Load Balancer** and **Rules** sections, and that your containers are exposed on Port 80 on your EC2 instances, as defined in the **Processes** section:

Modifying load balancer type

Finally, we need to define a database configuration for the application by clicking the **Modify** link in the **Database** section. Select **mysql** as the **Engine**, specify an appropriate **Username** and **Password**, and finally set the **Retention** to **Delete**, given that we are only using this environment for test purposes. The defaults for the other settings are sufficient, so you can click on the **Save** button after completing your configuration:

Modify database

Add an Amazon RDS SQL database to your environment for development and testing. AWS Elastic Beanstalk provides connection information to your instances by setting environment properties for the database hostname, username, password, table name, and port. When you add a database to your environment, its lifecycle is tied to your environment's.
For production environments, you can configure your instances to connect to a database. Learn more

Restore a snapshot

Restore an existing snapshot in your account, or create a new database.

Snapshot	None

Database settings

Choose an engine and instance type for your environment's database.

Engine	mysql
Engine version	5.6.39
Instance class	db.t2.micro
Storage	5 GB
	Choose a number between 5 GB and 1024 GB.
Username	todobackend
Password	···············
Retention	Delete
	When you terminate your environment, your database instance is also terminated. Choose **Create snapshot** to save a snapshot of the database prior to termination. Snapshots incur standard storage charges.
Availability	Low (one AZ)

Cancel **Save**

Configuring database settings

At this point, you have completed the configuration of your application and can click on the **Create app** button at the bottom of the **Configure Todobackend-env** screen. Elastic Beanstalk will now start creating you application and show you the progress of this in the console.

> The Elastic Beanstalk application wizard creates a CloudFormation stack behind the scenes that includes all of the resources and configuration you specified. It is also possible to create your own Elastic Beanstalk environments using CloudFormation without using the wizard.

After some time, the application's creation will complete, although you can see that there are problems with the application:

Initial application state

Configuring the EC2 instance profile

We have created a new Elastic Beanstalk application, however the current health of the application is logged as Severe due to several errors.

If you select the **Logs** option on the left hand menu and then select **Request Logs** | **Last 100 Lines**, you should be presented with a **Download** link that allows you to review the most recent log activity:

Initial application state

A separate tab should open in your browser, displaying various Elastic Beanstalk logs. At the top, you should see the ECS agent logs, and the most recent error should indicate that the ECS agent cannot pull the image into your `Dockerrun.aws.json` specification from ECR:

```
-------------------------------------
/var/log/ecs/ecs-init.log
-------------------------------------
2018-07-14T22:41:24Z [INFO] pre-start
2018-07-14T22:41:25Z [INFO] start
2018-07-14T22:41:25Z [INFO] No existing agent container to remove.
2018-07-14T22:41:25Z [INFO] Starting Amazon Elastic Container Service Agent



-------------------------------------
/var/log/eb-ecs-mgr.log
-------------------------------------




-------------------------------------
/var/log/ecs/ecs-agent.log.2018-07-14-22
-------------------------------------
        status code: 400, request id: 1ccbe760-87b7-11e8-a59f-bd89ff4fa4a1, Known Sent: NONE
2018-07-14T22:41:57Z [INFO] TaskHandler: Adding event: TaskChange: [arn:aws:ecs:us-east-1:385605022855:task/bcc51a2a-e356-
428f-906d-af560ec3f07a -> STOPPED, Known Sent: NONE, PullStartedAt: 2018-07-14 22:41:56.64095854 +0000 UTC
m=+30.428190609, PullStoppedAt: 2018-07-14 22:41:56.671509117 +0000 UTC m=+30.458741086, ExecutionStoppedAt: 2018-07-14
22:41:57.205437095 +0000 UTC m=+30.992669120, arn:aws:ecs:us-east-1:385605022855:task/bcc51a2a-e356-428f-906d-af560ec3f07a
collectstatic -> STOPPED, Reason CannotPullECRContainerError: AccessDeniedException: User: ◄───────
arn:aws:sts::385605022855:assumed-role/aws-elasticbeanstalk-ec2-role/i-0f636f261736facea is not authorized to perform:
ecr:GetAuthorizationToken on resource: *
```

Elastic Beanstalk ECS agent error

To resolve this, we need to configure the IAM role associated with the EC2 instance profile that is attached to our Elastic Beanstalk instances to include permissions to pull images from ECR. We can see which role Elastic Beanstalk is using by selecting **Configuration** from the left hand menu and reviewing the **Virtual machine instance profile** setting in the **Security** section:

Viewing security configuration

You can see that an IAM role called **aws-elasticbeanstalk-ec2-role** is being used, so if you select **Services** | **IAM** from the navigation bar, select **Roles**, and then locate the IAM role, you need to attach the `AmazonEC2ContainerRegistryReadOnly` policy to the role as follows:

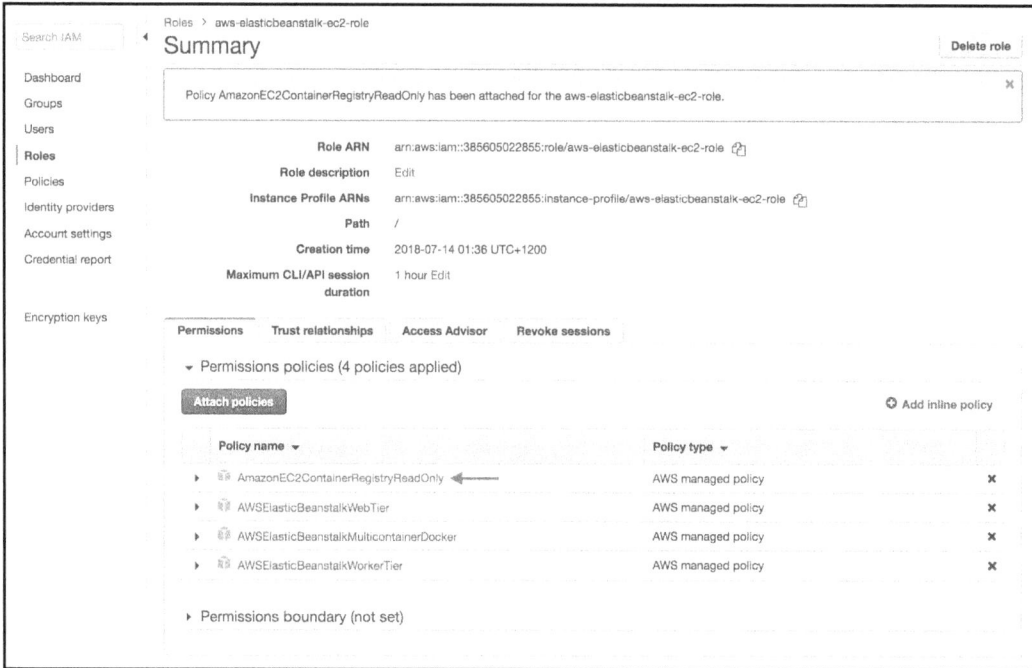

Attaching the AmazonEC2ContainerRegistryReadOnly policy to the Elastic Beanstack EC2 instance role

At this point, we should have resolved the permissions issue that caused our application to fail to start previously. You now need to configure Elastic Beanstalk to attempt to restart the application, which you can do using any one of the following techniques:

- Upload a new application source file—this will trigger a new application deployment.
- Restart app servers
- Rebuild the environment

Given our application source (which in the case of a Docker application is the `Dockerrun.aws.json` file) has not changed, the least destructive and fastest option is to restart the app servers, which you can do by selecting **Actions** | **Restart App Server(s)** in the top right hand corner of the **All Applications** | **todobackend** | **Todobackend-env** configuration screen.

After a few minutes, you will notice that your application still has problems, and if you repeat the process of obtaining the most recent logs, scanning these logs will show you that the **collectstatic** container is failing due to a permissions error:

```
-------------------------------------
/var/log/containers/collectstatic-20a43ad93d08-stdouterr.log ◄——
-------------------------------------
Processing secrets []...
Copying '/usr/lib/python3.6/site-packages/django/contrib/admin/static/admin/js/prepopulate.min.js'
Traceback (most recent call last):
  File "manage.py", line 15, in <module>
    execute_from_command_line(sys.argv)
  File "/usr/lib/python3.6/site-packages/django/core/management/__init__.py", line 371, in execute_from_command_line
    utility.execute()
  File "/usr/lib/python3.6/site-packages/django/core/management/__init__.py", line 365, in execute
    self.fetch_command(subcommand).run_from_argv(self.argv)
  File "/usr/lib/python3.6/site-packages/django/core/management/base.py", line 288, in run_from_argv
    self.execute(*args, **cmd_options)
  File "/usr/lib/python3.6/site-packages/django/core/management/base.py", line 335, in execute
    output = self.handle(*args, **options)
  File "/usr/lib/python3.6/site-packages/django/contrib/staticfiles/management/commands/collectstatic.py", line 189, in handle
    collected = self.collect()
  File "/usr/lib/python3.6/site-packages/django/contrib/staticfiles/management/commands/collectstatic.py", line 114, in collect
    handler(path, prefixed_path, storage)
  File "/usr/lib/python3.6/site-packages/django/contrib/staticfiles/management/commands/collectstatic.py", line 354, in copy_file
    self.storage.save(prefixed_path, source_file)
  File "/usr/lib/python3.6/site-packages/django/core/files/storage.py", line 49, in save
    return self._save(name, content)
  File "/usr/lib/python3.6/site-packages/django/core/files/storage.py", line 236, in _save
    os.makedirs(directory)
  File "/usr/lib/python3.6/os.py", line 210, in makedirs
    makedirs(head, mode, exist_ok)
  File "/usr/lib/python3.6/os.py", line 210, in makedirs
    makedirs(head, mode, exist_ok)
  File "/usr/lib/python3.6/os.py", line 220, in makedirs
    mkdir(name, mode)
PermissionError: [Errno 13] Permission denied: '/public/static' ◄——
```

collectstatic permissions error

Recall, earlier in this book, how we configured a folder with the correct permissions on our ECS container instances to host the public volume that the **collectstatic** container writes to? With Elastic Beanstalk, the default EC2 instance that is created for a Docker application is obviously not configured in such a fashion.

We will resolve this issue shortly, but for now it is important to understand there are also other problems. To understand these problems, you need to actually attempt to access the application, which you can do so by clicking the URL link at the top of the **All Applications** | **todobackend** | **Todobackend-env** configuration screen:

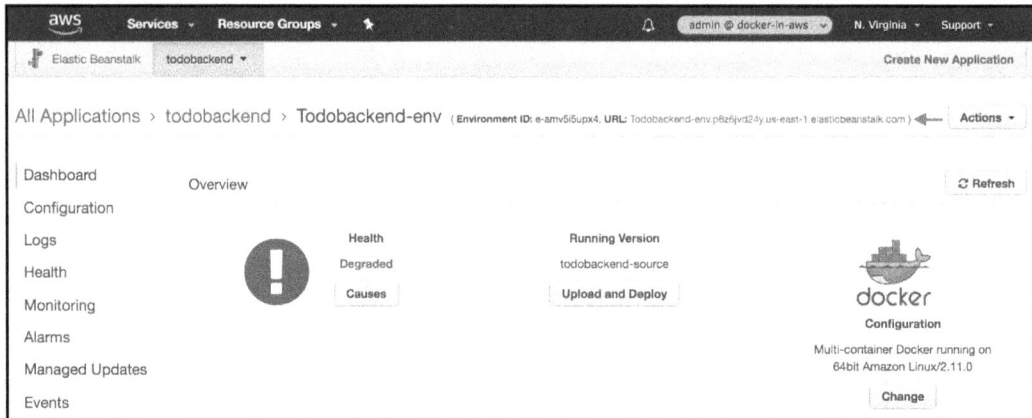

Obtaining the Elastic Beanstalk application URL

Browsing to this link should show you immediately that static content files are not being generated:

Django REST framework

- Api Root

GET

- json
- api

OPTIONS

Api Root

The default basic root view for DefaultRouter

GET /

HTTP 200 OK
Allow: GET, HEAD, OPTIONS
Content-Type: application/json
Vary: Accept

```
{
    "todos": "http://todobackend-env.p6z6jvd24y.us-east-1.elasticbeanstalk.com/todos"
}
```

Missing static content

And if you click on the **todos** link to view the current list of Todo items, you will receive an error indicating that the application cannot connect to the MySQL database:

InterfaceError at /todos

(2003, "2003: Can't connect to MySQL server on 'localhost:3306' (111 Connection refused)", None)

Request Method:	GET
Request URL:	http://todobackend-env.p6z6jvd24y.us-east-1.elasticbeanstalk.com/todos
Django Version:	2.0
Exception Type:	InterfaceError
Exception Value:	(2003, "2003: Can't connect to MySQL server on 'localhost:3306' (111 Connection refused)", None)
Exception Location:	/usr/lib/python3.6/site-packages/mysql/connector/network.py in open_connection, line 518
Python Executable:	/usr/bin/uwsgi
Python Version:	3.6.4
Python Path:	['.', '', '/usr/lib/python36.zip', '/usr/lib/python3.6', '/usr/lib/python3.6/lib-dynload', '/usr/lib/python3.6/site-packages']
Server time:	Sat, 14 Jul 2018 23:42:04 +0000

Database connectivity error

The problem is that we haven't added any database configuration to our `Dockerrun.aws.json` file, hence our application is defaulting to using localhost in an attempt to locate the database.

Configuring Elastic Beanstalk applications using the CLI

We will resolve the issues that still exist with our application shortly, but in order do so we are going to use the Elastic Beanstalk CLI to continue configuring our application and address these issues.

Before we start using the Elastic Beanstalk CLI, it is important to understand that the current version of this application does have some challenges when interacting with the multi-factor authentication (MFA) requirements we introduced for all console and API access in earlier chapters. If you continue to use MFA, you will notice that you are prompted each and every time you execute an Elastic Beanstalk CLI command.

To work around this, we can temporarily remove the MFA requirement by first removing your user from the `Users` group:

```
> aws iam remove-user-from-group --user-name justin.menga --group-name
Users
```

Next, comment out the `mfa_serial` line within the `docker-in-aws` profile inside your local `~/.aws/config` file:

```
[profile docker-in-aws]
source_profile = docker-in-aws
role_arn = arn:aws:iam::385605022855:role/admin
role_session_name=justin.menga
region = us-east-1
# mfa_serial = arn:aws:iam::385605022855:mfa/justin.menga
```

Note, this is not ideal, and in a real world scenario you probably would not have the ability to, nor want to, temporarily disable MFA for a given user. Bear this in mind when considering Elastic Beanstalk, as you will generally rely on the Elastic Beanstalk CLI for a number of operations.

With MFA now temporarily disabled, you can install the Elastic Beanstalk CLI, which you can do by using the Python `pip` package manager. Once it's been installed, it will be accessible via the `eb` command:

```
> pip3 install awsebcli --user
Collecting awsebcli
...
...
Installing collected packages: awsebcli
Successfully installed awsebcli-3.14.2
> eb --version
EB CLI 3.14.2 (Python 3.6.5)
```

The next step is to initialize the CLI in the `todobackend/eb` folder that you created earlier:

```
todobackend/eb> eb init --profile docker-in-aws

Select a default region
1) us-east-1 : US East (N. Virginia)
2) us-west-1 : US West (N. California)
3) us-west-2 : US West (Oregon)
4) eu-west-1 : EU (Ireland)
5) eu-central-1 : EU (Frankfurt)
6) ap-south-1 : Asia Pacific (Mumbai)
7) ap-southeast-1 : Asia Pacific (Singapore)
```

```
8) ap-southeast-2 : Asia Pacific (Sydney)
9) ap-northeast-1 : Asia Pacific (Tokyo)
10) ap-northeast-2 : Asia Pacific (Seoul)
11) sa-east-1 : South America (Sao Paulo)
12) cn-north-1 : China (Beijing)
13) cn-northwest-1 : China (Ningxia)
14) us-east-2 : US East (Ohio)
15) ca-central-1 : Canada (Central)
16) eu-west-2 : EU (London)
17) eu-west-3 : EU (Paris)
(default is 3): 1

Select an application to use
1) todobackend
2) [ Create new Application ]
(default is 2): 1
Cannot setup CodeCommit because there is no Source Control setup,
continuing with initialization
```

The `eb init` command uses the `--profile` flag to specify a local AWS profile, and then prompts for the region that you will be interacting with. The CLI then checks to see if there are any existing Elastic Beanstalk applications, and prompts you as to whether you want to manage an existing application or create a new application. Once you have made your selections, the CLI will add project information to the current folder under the a folder called `.elasticbeanstalk`, and will also create or append to a `.gitignore` file. Given our `eb` folder is a a subdirectory of the **todobackend** repository, it is a good idea to append the contents of the `.gitignore` file to the root of the **todobackend** repository:

```
todobackend-aws/eb> cat .gitignore >> ../.gitignore
todobackend-aws/eb> rm .gitignore
```

You can now use the CLI to view the current status of your application, list your application environments, and perform many other administrative tasks:

```
> eb status
Environment details for: Todobackend-env
  Application name: todobackend
  Region: us-east-1
  Deployed Version: todobackend-source
  Environment ID: e-amv5i5upx4
  Platform: arn:aws:elasticbeanstalk:us-
east-1::platform/multicontainer Docker running on 64bit Amazon
Linux/2.11.0
  Tier: WebServer-Standard-1.0
  CNAME: Todobackend-env.p6z6jvd24y.us-east-1.elasticbeanstalk.com
  Updated: 2018-07-14 23:23:28.931000+00:00
```

```
   Status: Ready
   Health: Red
> eb list
* Todobackend-env
> eb open
> eb logs
Retrieving logs...
============= i-0f636f261736facea =============
-------------------------------------
/var/log/ecs/ecs-init.log
-------------------------------------
2018-07-14T22:41:24Z [INFO] pre-start
2018-07-14T22:41:25Z [INFO] start
2018-07-14T22:41:25Z [INFO] No existing agent container to remove.
2018-07-14T22:41:25Z [INFO] Starting Amazon Elastic Container Service
Agent


-------------------------------------
/var/log/eb-ecs-mgr.log
-------------------------------------
2018-07-14T23:20:37Z "cpu": "0",
2018-07-14T23:20:37Z "containers": [
...
...
```

Notice that the eb status command lists the URL of your application in the CNAME property—take note of this URL as you will need it to test your application throughout this chapter. You can also use the eb open command to access your application, which will open the application URL in your default browser.

Managing Elastic Beanstalk EC2 instances

When using Elastic Beanstalk, it is useful to be able to have access to the Elastic Beanstalk EC2 instances, especially if you need to do some troubleshooting.

The CLI includes the ability to establish SSH connections to your Elastic Beanstalk EC2 instances, which you can set up by running the eb ssh --setup command:

```
> eb ssh --setup
WARNING: You are about to setup SSH for environment "Todobackend-env".
If you continue, your existing instances will have to be
**terminated** and new instances will be created. The environment will
be temporarily unavailable.
To confirm, type the environment name: Todobackend-env
```

```
Select a keypair.
1) admin
2) [ Create new KeyPair ]
(default is 1): 1
Printing Status:
Printing Status:
INFO: Environment update is starting.
INFO: Updating environment Todobackend-env's configuration settings.
INFO: Created Auto Scaling launch configuration named: awseb-e-
amv5i5upx4-stack-AWSEBAutoScalingLaunchConfiguration-8QN6BJJX43H
INFO: Deleted Auto Scaling launch configuration named: awseb-e-
amv5i5upx4-stack-AWSEBAutoScalingLaunchConfiguration-JR6N80L37H2G
INFO: Successfully deployed new configuration to environment.
```

Note that setting up SSH access requires you to terminate existing instances and create new instances, given you can only associate an SSH key pair with an EC2 instance upon creation. After selecting the existing `admin` key pair that you created earlier in this book, the CLI terminates the existing instances, creates a new auto scaling launch configuration that enables SSH access, and then launches new instances.

> You can avoid this step by configuring an EC2 key pair in the Security section of the configuration wizard when creating the Elastic Beanstalk application.

You can now SSH into your Elastic Beanstalk EC2 instance as follows:

```
> eb ssh -e "ssh -i ~/.ssh/admin.pem"
INFO: Attempting to open port 22.
INFO: SSH port 22 open.
INFO: Running ssh -i ~/.ssh/admin.pem ec2-user@34.239.245.78
The authenticity of host '34.239.245.78 (34.239.245.78)' can't be
established.
ECDSA key fingerprint is
SHA256:93m8hag/EtCPb5i7YrYHUXFPloaN0yUHMVFFnbMlcLE.
Are you sure you want to continue connecting (yes/no)? yes
Warning: Permanently added '34.239.245.78' (ECDSA) to the list of
known hosts.

 ____ _ _ _ ____ _ _ _
| ___| | | _ _ ___| |_(_) __| _ ) ___ __ _ _ __ __| | _ _ _| | | __
| _| | | |/ _` / __| __| |/ _| _ \ / _ \/ _` | '_ \/ __| __/ _` | | | |/
/
| |___| | (_| \__ \ |_| | (_| |_) | __/ (_| | | | | \__ \ || (_| | | <
|_____|_|\__,_|___/\__|_|\___|___/ \___|\__,_|_|
|_|___/\_\__,_|_|_|\_\
```

```
 Amazon Linux AMI

 This EC2 instance is managed by AWS Elastic Beanstalk. Changes made
 via SSH
 WILL BE LOST if the instance is replaced by auto-scaling. For more
 information
 on customizing your Elastic Beanstalk environment, see our
 documentation here:
 http://docs.aws.amazon.com/elasticbeanstalk/latest/dg/customize-contai
 ners-ec2.html
```

By default, the `eb ssh` command will attempt to use an SSH private key called `~/.ssh/<ec2-keypair-name>.pem`, which in this case is `~/.ssh/admin.pem`. If your SSH private key is in a different location, you can use the `-e` flag to override the file that is used, as demonstrated in the preceding example.

You can now take a look around at your Elastic Beanstalk EC2 instance. Given we are running a Docker application, you might be first inclined to run the `docker ps` command to see what containers are currently running:

```
[ec2-user@ip-172-31-20-192 ~]$ docker ps
Got permission denied while trying to connect to the Docker daemon
socket at unix:///var/run/docker.sock: Get
http://%2Fvar%2Frun%2Fdocker.sock/v1.37/containers/json: dial unix
/var/run/docker.sock: connect: permission denied
```

Somewhat surprisingly, the standard `ec2-user` does not have access to Docker—to resolve this, we need to add more advanced configuration referred to as **ebextensions**.

Customizing Elastic Beanstalk applications

As discussed in the previous section, we need to add an ebextension, which is simply a configuration file that can be used to customize your Elastic Beanstalk environment to our existing Elastic Beanstalk application. This is an important concept to understand, as we will ultimately use this same approach to resolve all of the issues that our application currently has.

To configure `ebextensions`, you first need to create a folder called `.ebextensions` in the `eb` folder where you are currently storing your `Dockerrun.aws.json` file (note that you will need to disconnect from the SSH session, go to your Elastic Beanstalk EC2 instance, and perform this in your local environment):

```
todobackend/eb> mkdir .ebextensions
todobackend/eb> touch .ebextensions/init.config
```

Each file with a `.config` extension in the `.ebextensions` folder will be treated as an ebextension and processed by Elastic Beanstalk during an application deployment. In the preceding example, we create a file called `init.config`, which we can now configure to allow the `ec2-user` access to the Docker Engine:

```
commands:
  01_add_ec2_user_to_docker_group:
    command: usermod -aG docker ec2-user
    ignoreErrors: true
```

We add a command directive called `01_add_ec2_user_to_docker_group` to the `commands` key, which is a top-level property that defines commands that should be run *before* the latest version of your application is set up and deployed to your instances. This command runs the `usermod` command to ensure that the `ec2-user` is a member of the `docker` group, which will grant `ec2-user` access to the Docker Engine. Notice that you can use the `ignoreErrors` property to ensure any command failures are ignored.

With this configuration in place, we can deploy a new version of our application by running the `eb deploy` command in the `eb` folder, which will automatically create a ZIP archive of our existing `Dockerrun.aws.json` and the new `.ebextensions/init.config` file:

```
todobackend-aws/eb> rm app.zip
todobackend-aws/eb> eb deploy
Uploading todobackend/app-180715_195517.zip to S3. This may take a
while.
Upload Complete.
INFO: Environment update is starting.
INFO: Deploying new version to instance(s).
INFO: Stopping ECS task arn:aws:ecs:us-
east-1:385605022855:task/dd2a2379-1b2c-4398-9f44-b7c25d338c67.
INFO: ECS task: arn:aws:ecs:us-
east-1:385605022855:task/dd2a2379-1b2c-4398-9f44-b7c25d338c67 is
STOPPED.
INFO: Starting new ECS task with awseb-Todobackend-env-amv5i5upx4:3.
INFO: ECS task: arn:aws:ecs:us-
```

```
east-1:385605022855:task/d9fa5a87-1329-401a-ba26-eb18957f5070 is
RUNNING.
INFO: New application version was deployed to running EC2 instances.
INFO: Environment update completed successfully.
```

We first remove the initial `app.zip` archive you created when you first created the Elastic Beanstalk application, as the `eb deploy` command automatically takes care of this. You can see that once the new configuration is uploaded, the deployment process involves stopping and starting the ECS task that is running our application.

Once the deployment is complete, if you establish a new SSH session to the Elastic Beanstalk EC2 instance, you should see that you are now able to run `docker` commands:

```
[ec2-user@ip-172-31-20-192 ~]$ docker ps --format "{{.ID}}:
{{.Image}}"
63183a7d3e67: 385605022855.dkr.ecr.us-east-1.amazonaws.com/docker-in-
aws/todobackend
45bf3329a686: amazon/amazon-ecs-agent:latest
```

You can see that the instance is currently running the todobackend container, and also runs the ECS agent. This demonstrates that the Docker support in Elastic Beanstalk uses ECS in the background to manage and deploy container-based applications.

Resolving Docker volume permissions issues

Earlier in this chapter, we ran into a problem where the collectstatic container was unable to write to the public volume. The issue here is that the ECS agent running on the Elastic Beanstalk EC2 instance creates a *bind* mount, which are always created with root permissions. This prevents the app user that our collectstatic container runs as from writing to the public volume, so we need some way to resolve this.

As we have already seen, the `ebextensions` feature can run commands on Elastic Beanstalk EC2 instances, and we will once again leverage this functionality to ensure that the public volume is configured to allow the `app` user in our containers to read and write in the `.ebextensions/init.config` file:

```
commands:
  01_add_ec2_user_to_docker_group:
    command: usermod -aG docker ec2-user
    ignoreErrors: true
  02_docker_volumes:
    command: |
```

```
mkdir -p /tmp/public
chown -R 1000:1000 /tmp/public
```

We add a new command directive called `02_docker_volumes`, which will be executed after the `01_add_ec2_user_to_docker_group` command. Notice that you can use the YAML pipe operator (`|`) to specify a multi-line command string, allowing you to specify multiple commands to run. We first create the `/tmp/public` folder that the public volume host `sourcePath` property refers to in the `Dockerrun.aws.json` file, and then ensure that the user ID/group ID values of `1000:1000` own this folder. Because the app user has a user ID of 1000 and a group ID of 1000, this will enable any process running as that user to write to and read from the public volume.

At this point, you can use the `eb deploy` command to upload a new application configuration to Elastic Beanstalk (see earlier examples). Once the deployment is complete, you can browse to the URL of your application by running the `eb open` command, and you should now see that the static content and formatting of the todobackend application is correct.

Configuring database settings

We have resolved the issue with accessing the public volume, however the application is still not working because we are not passing in any environment variables to configure database settings. The reason for this is that when you configure a database in Elastic Beanstalk, all database settings are made available via the following environment variables:

- `RDS_HOSTNAME`
- `RDS_USERNAME`
- `RDS_PASSWORD`
- `RDS_DB_NAME`
- `RDS_PORT`

The problem for the todobackend application is that it expects database-related settings that are prefixed with MYSQL—for example, `MYSQL_HOST` is used to configure the database hostname. Although we could update our application to use the RDS prefixed environment variables, we might want to deploy our application to other cloud providers, and RDS is an AWS specific technology.

An alternative, albeit more complicated approach, is to write the environment variable mappings to a file on the Elastic Beanstalk instance, configure this as a volume that the todobackend application containers can access, and then modify our Docker image to inject these mappings at container startup. This requires us to modify the entrypoint script for the todobackend application that is located in the `entrypoint.sh` file at the root of the `todobackend` repository:

```
#!/bin/bash
set -e -o pipefail

# Inject AWS Secrets Manager Secrets
# Read space delimited list of secret names from SECRETS environment
variable
echo "Processing secrets [${SECRETS}]..."
read -r -a secrets <<< "$SECRETS"
for secret in "${secrets[@]}"
do
  vars=$(aws secretsmanager get-secret-value --secret-id $secret \
    --query SecretString --output text \
    | jq -r 'to_entries[] | "export \(.key)='\''\(.value)'\''"')
  eval $vars
done

# Inject runtime environment variables
if [ -f /init/environment ]
then
  echo "Processing environment variables from /init/environment..."
  export $(cat /init/environment | xargs)
fi

# Run application
exec "$@"
```

In the preceding example, we added a new test expression that checks for the existence of a file called `/init/environment` using the syntax `[ -f /init/environment ]`. If this file is found, we assume that the file includes one or more environment variable settings in the format `<environment variable>=<value>`—for example:

```
MYSQL_HOST=abc.xyz.com
MYSQL_USERNAME=todobackend
...
...
```

With the preceding format, we then use the `export $(cat /init/environment | xargs)` command, which expands to `export MYSQL_HOST=abc.xyz.com MYSQL_USERNAME=todobackend ...` `...` using the preceding example, ensuring that each environment variable defined in the `/init/environment` file is exported into the environment.

If you now commit your changes to the `todobackend` repository and run the `make login`, `make test`, `make release`, and `make publish` commands, the latest `todobackend` Docker image will now include the updated entrypoint script. Now, we need to modify the `Dockerrun.aws.json` file in the `todobackend-aws/eb` folder to define a new volume and mount called `init`:

```
{
  "AWSEBDockerrunVersion": 2,
  "volumes": [
    {
      "name": "public",
      "host": {"sourcePath": "/tmp/public"}
    },
    {
      "name": "init",
      "host": {"sourcePath": "/tmp/init"}
    }
  ],
  "containerDefinitions": [
    {
      "name": "todobackend",
      "image": "385605022855.dkr.ecr.us-east-1.amazonaws.com/docker-in-aws/todobackend",
      "essential": true,
      "memoryReservation": 395,
      "mountPoints": [
        {
          "sourceVolume": "public",
          "containerPath": "/public"
        },
{
          "sourceVolume": "init",
          "containerPath": "/init"
        }
      ],
      "environment": [
```

```
{"name":"DJANGO_SETTINGS_MODULE","value":"todobackend.settings_release
"}
      ],
  ...
  ...
```

With this volume mapped to `/tmp/init` on the Elastic Beanstalk EC2 instance and `/init` in the `todobackend` container, all we need to do now is write environment variable settings to `/tmp/init/environment` on the EC2 instance, which will appear as `/init/environment` in the `todobackend` container, and trigger processing of the file using the modifications we made to the entrypoint script. The idea here is that we will write the Elastic Beanstalk RDS instance settings to the appropriate environment variable settings that the todobackend application expects.

Before we can do this, we need a mechanism to be able to obtain the RDS settings—fortunately, there is a file called `/opt/elasticbeanstalk/deploy/configuration/containerconfiguration` on each Elastic Beanstalk instance that includes the entire environment and application configuration in a JSON file format.

If you SSH into an instance, you can use the `jq` utility (which is already pre-installed on Elastic Beanstalk instances) to extract the RDS instance settings for your Elastic Beanstalk application:

```
> sudo jq '.plugins.rds.env' -r \
  /opt/elasticbeanstalk/deploy/configuration/containerconfiguration
{
  "RDS_PORT": "3306",
  "RDS_HOSTNAME": "aa2axvguqnh17c.cz8cu8hmqtu1.us-
east-1.rds.amazonaws.com",
  "RDS_USERNAME": "todobackend",
  "RDS_DB_NAME": "ebdb",
  "RDS_PASSWORD": "some-super-secret"
}
```

With this mechanism to extract RDS settings, we can now modify the `.ebextensions/init.config` file to write each of these settings to the `/tmp/init/environment` file that will be exposed to the `todobackend` container via the `init` volume at `/init/environment`:

```
commands:
  01_add_ec2_user_to_docker_group:
    command: usermod -aG docker ec2-user
    ignoreErrors: true
  02_docker_volumes:
```

```
command: |
  mkdir -p /tmp/public
  mkdir -p /tmp/init
  chown -R 1000:1000 /tmp/public
  chown -R 1000:1000 /tmp/init

container_commands:
  01_rds_settings:
    command: |
config=/opt/elasticbeanstalk/deploy/configuration/containerconfigurati
on
      environment=/tmp/init/environment
      echo "MYSQL_HOST=$(jq '.plugins.rds.env.RDS_HOSTNAME' -r
$config)" >> $environment
      echo "MYSQL_USER=$(jq '.plugins.rds.env.RDS_USERNAME' -r
$config)" >> $environment
      echo "MYSQL_PASSWORD=$(jq '.plugins.rds.env.RDS_PASSWORD' -r
$config)" >> $environment
      echo "MYSQL_DATABASE=$(jq '.plugins.rds.env.RDS_DB_NAME' -r
$config)" >> $environment
      chown -R 1000:1000 $environment
```

We first modify the `02_docker_volumes` directive to create the `/tmp/init` path that the init volume is mapped to, and ensure that the app user running in the todobackend application has read/write access to this folder. Next, we add the `container_commands` key, which specifies commands that should be executed *after* the application configuration has been applied but *before* the application is started. Note that is different from the `commands` key, which executes commands *before* the application configuration is applied.

> The naming of the `container_commands` key is somewhat confusing in that it implies commands will be run inside a Docker container. This is actually not the case and the `container_commands` key is completely unrelated to containers in the Docker sense.

The `01_rds_settings` command writes the various MYSQL prefixed environment variable settings the application requires, obtaining the appropriate value for each by executing the `jq` command, as we demonstrated earlier. Because this file is created by the root user, we finally ensure that the `app` user has read/write access to the `/tmp/init/environment` file, which will be present as `/init/environment` in the container via the init volume.

If you now deploy your changes using the `eb deploy` command, once deployment is complete and you navigate to the todobackend application URL, if you attempt to list Todos items (by accessing `/todos`), notice that a new error is now displayed:

Accessing todobackend Todos items error

Recall that when you previously accessed the same URL, the todobackend application was attempting to access MySQL using localhost, however now we get an error indicating that the `todo_todoitem` table cannot be found in the `ebdb` database. This confirms that the application is now communicating with the RDS instance, however because we have not run database migrations, the schema and tables to support the application are not in place.

Running database migrations

To fix the current issue with our application, we need to have a mechanism that allows us to run database migrations to create the required database schema and tables. This must also happen on each application update, however this should only occur *once* per application update. For example, if you had multiple Elastic Beanstalk instances, you do not want migrations to run on each instance. Instead, you want migrations to run only once for each deployment.

The container_commands key that you were introduced to in the previous section includes a useful property called leader_only, which configures Elastic Beanstalk to only run the specified command on the leader instance. This is the first instance that becomes available to deploy to. We can therefore add a new directive to the .ebextensions/init.config file in the todobackend-aws/eb folder that will run migrations only once per application deployment:

```
commands:
  01_add_ec2_user_to_docker_group:
    command: usermod -aG docker ec2-user
    ignoreErrors: true
  02_docker_volumes:
    command: |
      mkdir -p /tmp/public
      mkdir -p /tmp/init
      chown -R 1000:1000 /tmp/public
      chown -R 1000:1000 /tmp/init

container_commands:
  01_rds_settings:
    command: |
config=/opt/elasticbeanstalk/deploy/configuration/containerconfigurati
on
      environment=/tmp/init/environment
      echo "MYSQL_HOST=$(jq '.plugins.rds.env.RDS_HOSTNAME' -r
$config)" >> $environment
      echo "MYSQL_USER=$(jq '.plugins.rds.env.RDS_USERNAME' -r
$config)" >> $environment
      echo "MYSQL_PASSWORD=$(jq '.plugins.rds.env.RDS_PASSWORD' -r
$config)" >> $environment
      echo "MYSQL_DATABASE=$(jq '.plugins.rds.env.RDS_DB_NAME' -r
$config)" >> $environment
      chown -R 1000:1000 $environment
  02_migrate:
    command: |
      echo "python3 manage.py migrate --no-input" >>
/tmp/init/commands
      chown -R 1000:1000 /tmp/init/commands
    leader_only: true
```

Here, we write the `python3 manage.py migrate --no-input` command to
the `/tmp/init/commands` file, which will be exposed to the application container at
the location `/init/commands`. This, of course, requires us to now modify the
entrypoint script in the `todobackend` repository to look for such a file and execute
the commands contained within it, as follows:

```bash
#!/bin/bash
set -e -o pipefail

# Inject AWS Secrets Manager Secrets
# Read space delimited list of secret names from SECRETS environment
variable
echo "Processing secrets [${SECRETS}]..."
read -r -a secrets <<< "$SECRETS"
for secret in "${secrets[@]}"
do
  vars=$(aws secretsmanager get-secret-value --secret-id $secret \
    --query SecretString --output text \
    | jq -r 'to_entries[] | "export \(.key)='\''\(.value)'\''"')
  eval $vars
done

# Inject runtime environment variables
if [ -f /init/environment ]
then
  echo "Processing environment variables from /init/environment..."
  export $(cat /init/environment | xargs)
fi

# Inject runtime init commands
if [ -f /init/commands ]
then
  echo "Processing commands from /init/commands..."
  source /init/commands
fi

# Run application
exec "$@"
```

Here, we add a new test expression that checks for the existence of
the `/init/commands` file, and if this file exists we use the `source` command to
execute each command contained within the file. Because this file will only be
written on the leader Elastic Beanstalk instance, the entrypoint script will only invoke
these commands once per deployment.

At this point, you need to rebuild the todobackend Docker image by running the `make login`, `make test`, `make release`, and `make publish` commands, after which you can deploy your Elastic Beanstalk changes by running the `eb deploy` command from the `todobackend-aws/eb` directory. Once this has completed successfully, if you SSH to your Elastic Beanstalk instance and review the logs of the current active todobackend application container, you should see that the database migrations were executed when the container was started:

```
> docker ps --format "{{.ID}}: {{.Image}}"
45b8cdac0c92: 385605022855.dkr.ecr.us-east-1.amazonaws.com/docker-in-
aws/todobackend
45bf3329a686: amazon/amazon-ecs-agent:latest
> docker logs 45b8cdac0c92
Processing secrets []...
Processing environment variables from /init/environment...
Processing commands from /init/commands...
Operations to perform:
  Apply all migrations: admin, auth, contenttypes, sessions, todo
Running migrations:
  Applying contenttypes.0001_initial... OK
  Applying auth.0001_initial... OK
  Applying admin.0001_initial... OK
  Applying admin.0002_logentry_remove_auto_add... OK
  Applying contenttypes.0002_remove_content_type_name... OK
  Applying auth.0002_alter_permission_name_max_length... OK
  Applying auth.0003_alter_user_email_max_length... OK
  Applying auth.0004_alter_user_username_opts... OK
  Applying auth.0005_alter_user_last_login_null... OK
  Applying auth.0006_require_contenttypes_0002... OK
  Applying auth.0007_alter_validators_add_error_messages... OK
  Applying auth.0008_alter_user_username_max_length... OK
  Applying auth.0009_alter_user_last_name_max_length... OK
  Applying sessions.0001_initial... OK
  Applying todo.0001_initial... OK
[uwsgi-static] added check for /public
*** Starting uWSGI 2.0.17 (64bit) on [Sun Jul 15 11:18:06 2018] ***
```

If you now browse to the application URL, you should find that the application is fully functional, and you have successfully deployed a Docker application to Elastic Beanstalk.

Before we wrap up this chapter, you should restore the MFA configuration you temporarily disabled earlier in this chapter by adding your user account back to the `Users` group:

```
> aws iam add-user-to-group --user-name justin.menga --group-name
Users
```

And then re-enable the `mfa_serial` line within the `docker-in-aws` profile inside your local `~/.aws/config` file:

```
[profile docker-in-aws]
source_profile = docker-in-aws
role_arn = arn:aws:iam::385605022855:role/admin
role_session_name=justin.menga
region = us-east-1
mfa_serial = arn:aws:iam::385605022855:mfa/justin.menga
```

You can also delete your Elastic Beanstalk environment by browsing to the main Elastic Beanstalk dashboard and clicking the **Actions** | **Delete** application button next to the **todobackend** application. This will delete the CloudFormation stack that was created by the Elastic Beanstalk environment, which includes the application load balancer, RDS database instance, and EC2 instances.

Summary

In this chapter, you learned how to deploy multi-container Docker applications using Elastic Beanstalk. You learned why and when you would choose Elastic Beanstalk over other alternative container management services such as ECS, and the general conclusion here is that Elastic Beanstalk is great for smaller organizations with a small number of applications, but becomes less useful as your organization starts to grow and needs to start focusing on offering shared container platforms to reduce cost, complexity, and management overheads.

You created an Elastic Beanstalk application using the AWS console, which required you to define a single file called `Dockerrun.aws.json` that included the container definitions and volumes required to run your application, and then automatically deployed an application load balancer and RDS database instance with minimal configuration. Getting your application up and running into a fully function state was a bit more challenging, and required you to define advanced configuration files called `ebextensions` that allowed you to adapt Elastic Beanstalk to meet the specific needs of your application. You learned how to install and set up the Elastic Beanstalk CLI, connect to your Elastic Beanstalk instances using SSH, and deploy configuration changes to your `Dockerrun.aws.json` file and `ebextensions` files. This allowed you to set up volumes on the Elastic Beanstalk instances with correct permissions for container applications running as non-root users, and introduced a special init volume where you can inject environment variable settings and commands that should be executed as your container starts.

In the next chapter, we will take a look at Docker Swarm and how you can deploy Docker Swarm clusters on AWS to deploy and run your Docker applications.

Questions

1. True/false: Elastic Beanstalk only supports single container Docker applications.

2. What is the minimum required artifact to create a Docker application using Elastic Beanstalk?

3. True/false: The `.ebextensions` folder stores YAML files that allow you to customise your Elastic Beanstalk instances.

4. You create a new Elastic Beanstalk service that deploys a Docker application whose Docker image is stored in ECR. On initial creation. the application fails, with the Elastic Beanstalk logs showing an error including the words "CannotPullECRContainerError". How would you resolve this issue?

5. True/false: Out of the box without any additional configuration, Docker containers running as non-root users in an Elastic Beanstalk environment can read and write to Docker volumes.

6. True/false: You can set the `leader_only` property to true in the `commands` key to run a command on only one Elastic Beanstalk instance.

7. True/false: The `eb connect` command is used to establish SSH access to an Elastic Beanstalk instance.

8. True/false: Elastic Beanstalk supports application load balancer integration with your application.

Further reading

You can check the following links for more information about the topics covered in this chapter:

- Elastic Beanstalk Developer Guide: `https://docs.aws.amazon.com/elasticbeanstalk/latest/dg/Welcome.html`

- Multicontainer Docker Environments: `https://docs.aws.amazon.com/elasticbeanstalk/latest/dg/create_deploy_docker_ecs.html`

- Using Elastic Beanstalk with Other AWS Services: `https://docs.aws.amazon.com/elasticbeanstalk/latest/dg/AWSHowTo.html`

- Advanced Environment Configuration with Configuration Files: `https://docs.aws.amazon.com/elasticbeanstalk/latest/dg/ebextensions.html`

- The Elastic Beanstalk Command Line Interface: `https://docs.aws.amazon.com/elasticbeanstalk/latest/dg/eb-cli3.html`

Docker Swarm in AWS 16

Docker Swarm represents Docker's native container management platform that is built right into the Docker Engine, and for many people who are using Docker for the first time, Docker Swarm is the first container management platform that they read and learn about, given that it is an integrated feature of the Docker Engine. Docker Swarm is naturally a competitor to the ECS, Fargate, Elastic Beanstalk, and recent Elastic Kubernetes Service (EKS) offerings supported by AWS, so you might be wondering why a book on Docker in AWS would have a chapter dedicated to Docker Swarm. Many organizations prefer to use cloud-agnostic container management platforms that they can run on AWS, other cloud providers such as Google Cloud and Azure, as well as on premises, and if this is the case for you and your organization, then Docker Swarm is certainly an option worth considering.

In this chapter, you will learn how to deploy Docker Swarm to AWS using the Docker for AWS solution that makes it very easy to get a Docker Swarm cluster up and running in AWS. You will learn the basics of how to manage and access your Swarm cluster, how to create and deploy services to Docker Swarm, and how to leverage a number of AWS services that are integrated with Swarm in the Docker for AWS solution. This will include integrating Docker Swarm with the Elastic Container Registry (ECR), publishing your application to the outside world by integrating with AWS Elastic Load Balancing (ELB), creating shared volumes using the AWS Elastic File System (EFS), and creating persistent volumes using the AWS Elastic Block Store (EBS).

Finally, you will learn how to address key operational challenges, including running one-shot deployment tasks, performing secrets management using Docker secrets, and deploying your application using rolling updates. By the end of this chapter, you will know how to deploy a Docker Swarm cluster to AWS, how to integrate Docker Swarm with AWS services, and how to deploy your production applications to Docker Swarm.

The following topics will be covered in this chapter:

- Introduction to Docker Swarm
- Installing Docker for AWS
- Accessing Docker Swarm
- Deploying Docker services to Docker Swarm
- Deploying Docker stacks to Docker Swarm
- Integrating Docker Swarm with the ECR
- Creating shared Docker volumes using EFS
- Creating persistent Docker volumes using EBS
- Supporting one-shot deployment tasks
- Performing rolling updates

Technical requirements

The following are the technical requirements for this chapter:

- Administrative access to an AWS account
- Local environment configured as per the instructions in Chapter 1
- A local AWS profile, configured as per the instructions in Chapter 3
- AWS CLI version 1.15.71 or higher
- Docker 18.06 CE or higher
- Docker Compose 1.22 or higher
- GNU Make 3.82 or higher

This chapter assumes that you have completed all of the preceding chapters in this book

The following GitHub URL contains the code samples that are used in this chapter: `https://github.com/docker-in-aws/docker-in-aws/tree/master/ch16`.

Check out the following video to see the Code in Action:
`http://bit.ly/2ogdBpp`

Docker Swarm introduction

Docker Swarm is a native integrated feature of the Docker Engine, providing cluster management and container orchestration features that allow you to run Docker containers at scale in production. Every Docker Engine running version 1.13 or greater includes the ability to operate in swarm mode, which provides the following features:

- **Cluster management**: All nodes operating in swarm mode include native cluster features that allow you to quickly establish clusters that you can deploy your applications to.

- **Multi-host networking**: Docker supports overlay networking that allows you to create virtual networks over which all containers attached to the network can communicate privately. This networking layer is completely independent of the physical networking topology that connects your Docker Engines, meaning you typically don't have to worry about traditional networking constraints such as IP addressing and network segmentation—Docker takes care of all of this for you.

- **Service discovery and load balancing**: Docker Swarm supports a simple service discovery model based upon DNS that allows your applications to discover each other without requiring complex service discovery protocols or infrastructure. Docker Swarm also supports automatic load balancing of traffic to your applications using DNS round robin, and can integrate with an external load balancer such as the AWS Elastic Load Balancer service.

- **Service scaling and rolling updates**: You can easily scale your services up and down, and when it's time to update your services, Docker supports intelligent rolling update features with support for rollbacks in the event of a deployment failure.

- **Declarative service model**: Docker Swarm uses the popular Docker Compose specification to declaratively define application services, networks, volumes, and more in an easy to understand and maintained format.

- **Desired state**: Docker Swarm continuously monitors application and runtime state, ensuring that your services are operating in accordance with the desired state you have configured. For example, if you configure a service with an instance or replica count of 2, Docker Swarm will always try and maintain this count and automatically deploy new replicas to a new node when an existing node fails.

- **Production-grade operational features such as secrets and configuration management**: Some features such as Docker secrets and Docker configurations are exclusive to Docker Swarm, and provide solutions for real-world production issues such as the ability to securely distribute secrets and configuration data to your applications.

When it comes to running Docker Swarm on AWS, Docker provides a community edition offering referred to as Docker for AWS CE, which you can find further information about at `https://store.docker.com/editions/community/docker-ce-aws`. At present, Docker for AWS CE is deployed via a pre-defined CloudFormation template that integrates Docker Swarm with a number of AWS services, including EC2 Auto Scaling, Elastic Load Balancing, Elastic File System, and Elastic Block Store. As you will soon see, this makes it very easy to stand up a new Docker Swarm cluster in AWS.

Docker Swarm versus Kubernetes

First and foremost, as evidenced by the majority of the content of this book, I am an ECS guy, and if you are running your container workloads exclusively on AWS, my recommendation, at least at the time of the writing of this book, is almost always going to be ECS. However, many organizations don't want to be locked into AWS and want a cloud agnostic approach, and this is where Docker Swarm is one of the leading solutions available at present.

Right now, Docker Swarm competes head-on with Kubernetes, which we will discuss in the next chapter. It's fair to say that Kubernetes looks to have established itself as the leading cloud agnostic container management platform of choice, but that doesn't mean you should necessarily overlook Docker Swarm.

In general, I personally find Docker Swarm easier to set up and use, and a key benefit for me at least, is that it uses familiar tools such as Docker Compose, which means you can get up and running very quickly, especially if you have used these tools previously. For smaller organizations that just want to get up and running fast and ensure that things just work with minimal fuss, Docker Swarm is an attractive choice. The Docker for AWS solution makes it very easy to establish a Docker Swarm cluster in AWS, although AWS recently made Kubernetes a whole lot easier on AWS with the launch of the Elastic Kubernetes Service (EKS)—more on this in the next chapter.

Ultimately, I encourage you to try out both with an open mind and make your own decisions as to what container management platform works best for you and your organization's goals.

Installing Docker for AWS

The recommended and fastest way to get Docker Swarm up and running in AWS is to use Docker for AWS, which you can read more about at `https://docs.docker.com/docker-for-aws/`. If you browse to this page, in the **Setup & prerequisites** section, you will be presented with links that allow you to install both Docker Enterprise Edition (EE) and Docker Community Edition (CE) for AWS.

We will be using the free Docker CE for AWS (stable) variant, and notice that you can choose to deploy to a brand new VPC or to an existing VPC:

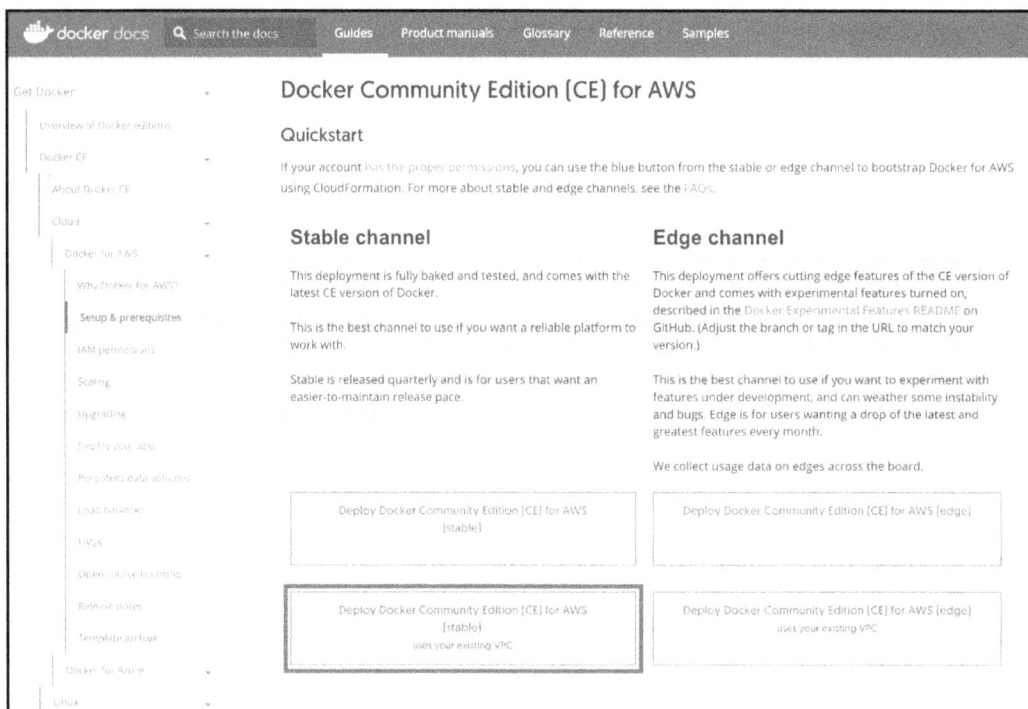

Selecting a Docker CE for AWS option

Given, we already have an existing VPC, if you click on the **Deploy Docker CE for AWS (stable) users your existing VPC** option, you will be redirected to the AWS CloudFormation console, where you are prompted to create a new stack from a template published by Docker:

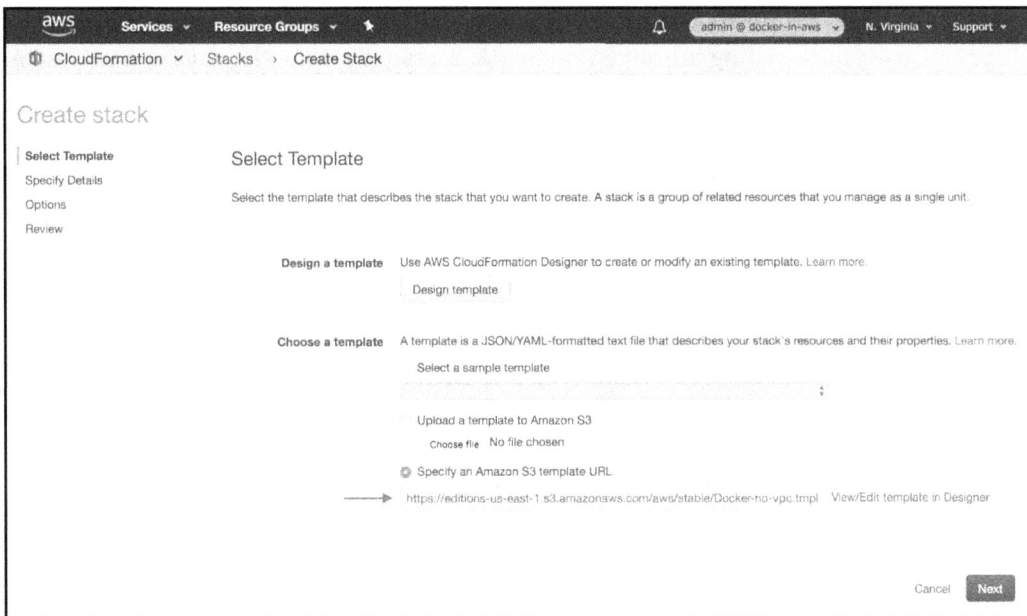

Creating a Docker for AWS stack

After clicking **Next**, you will be prompted to specify a number of parameters that control the configuration of your Docker Swarm Docker installation. I won't describe all of the options available, so assume that you should leave the default configuration for any parameters that I do not mention here:

- **Stack name**: Specify an appropriate name for your stack — for example docker-swarm.
- **Swarm Size**: Here, you can specify the number of Swarm managers and worker nodes. At a minimum, you can specify just one manager, however I recommend also configuring a worker node so that you can test deploying your applications to a multi-node Swarm cluster.

- **Swarm Properties**: Here, you should configure the Swarm EC2 instances to use your existing admin SSH key (EC2 key pair) and also enable the **Create EFS prerequisites for Store** property, as we will use EFS to provide a shared volume later on in this chapter.
- **Swarm Manager Properties**: Change the Manager ephemeral storage volume type to **gp2 (SSD)**.
- **Swarm Worker Properties**: Change the Worker ephemeral storage volume type to **gp2 (SSD)**.
- **VPC/Network**: Select your existing default VPC and then ensure that you specify the VPC CIDR Range that is displayed when you select the VPC (for example, `172.31.0.0/16`), and then select appropriate subnets from your default VPC for Public Subnets 1 through 3.

After completing the preceding configuration, click on the **Next** button twice, and finally on the **Review** screen, select the **I acknowledge that AWS CloudFormation might create IAM resources** option and then click on the **Create** button.

At this point, your new CloudFormation stack will be created, and should be complete within 10-15 minutes. Note that if you ever want to increase the number of managers and/or worker nodes in your cluster, the recommended way to do this is to perform a CloudFormation stack update, modifying the appropriate input parameters that define manager and worker count. Also, to upgrade Docker for AWS Swarm Cluster, you should apply the latest CloudFormation template that includes updates to Docker Swarm and various other resources.

Resources created by the Docker for AWS CloudFormation stack

If you review the **Resources** tab in the CloudFormation console for your new stack, you will notice a variety of resources are created, the most important of which are listed as follows:

- **CloudWatch Logs Group**: This stores all logs for the container's schedule via your Swarm cluster. This resource is only created if you enable the **Use Cloudwatch for container logging** parameter during stack creation (by default, this parameter is enabled).
- **External Load Balancer**: A classic Elastic Load Balancer is created, which is used to publish public access to your Docker applications.

- **Elastic Container Registry IAM Policy**: An IAM policy is created and attached to all Swarm manager and worker EC2 instance roles that permit read/pull access to ECR. This is required if you store your Docker images in ECR, which is applicable to our scenario.
- **Other resources**: A variety of resources are also created such as a DynamoDB table that is used for cluster management operations, and a Simple Queue Service (SQS) queue is used for EC2 auto-scaling life cycle hooks during Swarm manager upgrade scenarios.

If you click on the **Outputs** tab, you will notice an output property called **DefaultDNSTarget**, which references the public URL of the external load balancer. Take note of this URL, as this is where the sample application will be accessible from later on in this chapter:

Docker for AWS stack outputs

Accessing the Swarm cluster

In the CloudFormation stack outputs, there is also a property called **Managers**, which provides a link to the EC2 instance(s) for each of the Swarm managers:

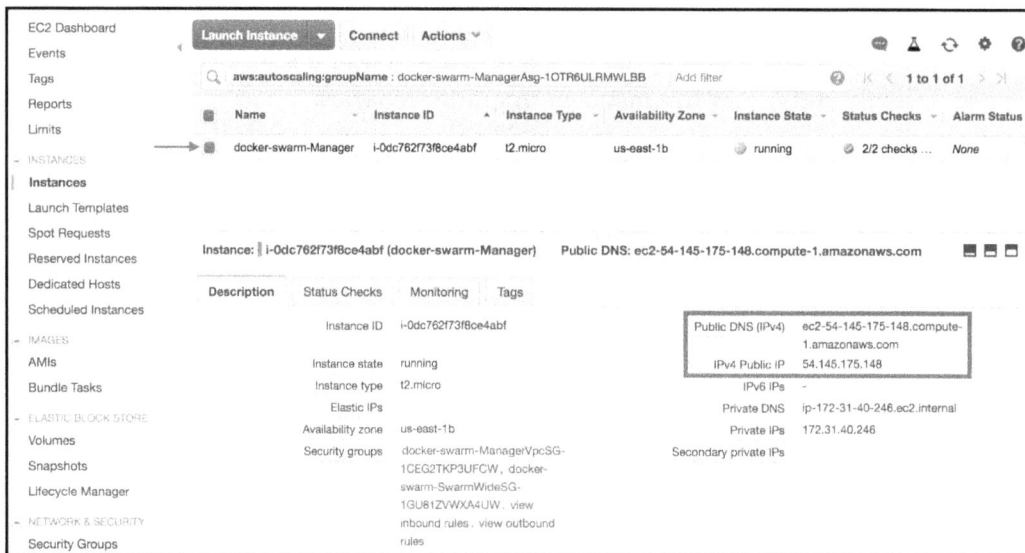

Swarm Manager Auto Scaling group

You can use this information to obtain the public IP address or DNS name of one of your Swarm managers. Once you have this IP address, you can establish an SSH connection to the manager:

```
> ssh -i ~/.ssh/admin.pem docker@54.145.175.148
The authenticity of host '54.145.175.148 (54.145.175.148)' can't be
established.
ECDSA key fingerprint is
SHA256:Br/8IMAuEzPOV29B8zdbT6H+DjK9sSEEPSbXdn+v0YM.
Are you sure you want to continue connecting (yes/no)? yes
Warning: Permanently added '54.145.175.148' (ECDSA) to the list of
known hosts.
Welcome to Docker!
~ $ docker ps --format "{{ .ID }}: {{ .Names }}"
a5a2dfe609e4: l4controller-aws
0d7f5d2ae4a0: meta-aws
d54308064314: guide-aws
58cb47dad3e1: shell-aws
```

Notice that you must specify a user name of `docker` when accessing the manager, and if you run the `docker ps` command, you can see that there are four system containers running on the manager by default:

- **shell-aws**: This provides SSH access to the manager, meaning the SSH session that you establish to the Swarm manager is actually running *inside* this container.
- **meta-aws**: Provides general metadata services, including providing tokens that allow new members to join the cluster.
- **guide-aws**: Performs cluster state management operations such as adding each manager to DynamoDB, and other housekeeping tasks such as cleaning up unused images and volumes and stopped containers.
- **l4controller-aws**: Manages integration with the external load balancer for the Swarm cluster. This component is responsible for publishing new ports and ensuring they are accessible on the elastic load balancer. Note that you should never modify the ELB for your cluster directly, and instead rely on the `l4controller-aws` component to manage the ELB.

To view and access the other nodes in your cluster, you can use the `docker node ls` command:

```
> docker node ls
ID                         HOSTNAME                    STATUS
MANAGER STATUS    ENGINE VERSION
qna4v46afttl007jq0ec712dk  ip-172-31-27-91.ec2.internal  Ready
18.03.0-ce
ym3jdy1ol17pfw7emwfen0b4e* ip-172-31-40-246.ec2.internal Ready
Leader            18.03.0-ce
> ssh docker@ip-172-31-27-91.ec2.internal
Permission denied (publickey,keyboard-interactive).
```

Note that worker nodes do not allow public SSH access, so you can only access worker nodes via SSH from a manager. There is a problem, however: you can't establish an SSH session to the worker node, given that the manager node does not have the private key of the admin EC2 key pair stored locally.

Setting up local access to Docker Swarm

Although you can run Docker commands remotely via an SSH session to a Swarm manager, it is much easier to be able to interact with the remote Swarm manager daemon using your local Docker client, where you have access to your local Docker service definitions and configurations. We also have the problem of not being able to access our worker nodes via SSH, and we can solve both of these problems by using a couple of techniques known as SSH agent forwarding and SSH tunneling.

Configuring SSH agent forwarding

To set up SSH agent forwarding, first add your admin SSH key to your local SSH agent using the `ssh-add` command:

```
> ssh-add -K ~/.ssh/admin.pem
Identity added: /Users/jmenga/.ssh/admin.pem
(/Users/jmenga/.ssh/admin.pem)
> ssh-add -L
ssh-rsa
AAAAB3NzaC1yc2EAAAADAQABAAABAQCkF7aAzIRayGHiiR81wcz/k9b+ZdmAEkdIBU0pOv
AaFYjrDPf4JL4I0rJjdpFBjFZIqKXM9dLWg0skENYSU19pfLT+CzValQat/XpBw/Hfwzbz
My8wqcKehN0pB4V1bpzfOYe7lTLmTYIQ/21wW63QVlZnNyV1VZiVgN5DcLqgiG5CHHAooM
IbiExAYvRrgo8XEXoqFRODLwIn4HZ7OAtojWzxElBx+EC4lmDekykgxnfGd30QgATIEF8/
+UzM17j91JJohfxU7tA3GhXkScMBXnxBhdOftVvtB8/bGc+DHjJlkYSxL20792eBEv/Zso
oMhNFxGLGhidrznmSeC8qL /Users/jmenga/.ssh/admin.pem
```

The `-K` flag is specific to macOS and adds the passphrase for your SSH key to your OS X keychain, meaning that this configuration will persist across reboots. If you are not using macOS, you can just omit the `-K` flag.

You can now access your Swarm manager using the `-A` flag, which configures the SSH client to use your SSH agent identities. Using the SSH agent also enables SSH agent forwarding, which means that the SSH key used to establish your SSH session with the Swarm manager can be automatically used or forwarded for other SSH connections you might establish from within your SSH session:

```
> ssh -A docker@54.145.175.148
Welcome to Docker!
~ $ ssh docker@ip-172-31-27-91.ec2.internal
Welcome to Docker!
```

As you can see, using SSH agent forwarding solves the issue of being able to access your worker nodes.

Configuring SSH tunneling

SSH tunneling is a powerful technique that allows you to tunnel network communications securely over an encrypted SSH session to a remote host. SSH tunneling works by exposing a local socket or port that is wired to a remote socket or port on the remote host. This can provide the illusion that you are communicating with a local service, which is particularly useful when working with Docker.

The following command demonstrates how you can make the Docker socket running on a Swarm manager appear as a port running on your local host:

```
> ssh -i ~/.ssh/admin.pem -NL localhost:2374:/var/run/docker.sock
docker@54.145.175.148 &
[1] 7482
> docker -H localhost:2374 ps --format "{{ .ID }}: {{ .Names }}"
a5a2dfe609e4: l4controller-aws
0d7f5d2ae4a0: meta-aws
d54308064314: guide-aws
58cb47dad3e1: shell-aws
> export DOCKER_HOST=localhost:2374
> docker node ls --format "{{ .ID }}: {{ .Hostname }}"
qna4v46afttl007jq0ec712dk: ip-172-31-27-91.ec2.internal
ym3jdy1ol17pfw7emwfen0b4e: ip-172-31-40-246.ec2.internal
```

The -N flag passed to the first SSH command instructs the client not to send a remote command, while the -L or local forwarding flag configures maps TCP port 2374 on the localhost to the /var/run/docker.sock Docker Engine socket on the remote Swarm manager. The ampersand (&) character at the end of the command causes the command to be run in the background, with the process ID published as the output of this command.

With this configuration in place, you can now run the Docker client, locally referencing localhost:2374 as a local endpoint that is wired to your remote Swarm manager. Notice that you can specify the host using the -H flag, or by exporting the environment variable DOCKER_HOST. This will allow you to execute remote Docker operations while referencing local files in your local environment, making it much easier to manage and deploy to your Swarm cluster.

Although Docker does include a client/server model that enables communications between a Docker client and remote Docker Engine, to do so securely requires mutual transport layer security (TLS) and public key infrastructure (PKI) technologies, which are complex to set up and maintain. Using SSH tunneling to expose the remote Docker socket is much easier to set up and maintain, and is considered as secure as any form of remote SSH access.

Deploying applications to Docker Swarm

Now that you have installed Docker Swarm using Docker for AWS and established management connectivity to the Swarm cluster, we are ready to start deploying applications. Deploying applications to Docker Swarm requires use of the `docker service` and `docker stack` commands, which we have not covered to date in this book, so we will get acquainted with these commands by deploying a few example applications before tackling the deployment of our todobackend application.

Docker services

Although you can technically deploy a single container to a Swarm cluster, you should avoid doing this and always work with Docker *services* as the standard unit of deployment to your Swarm clusters. We have actually worked with Docker services already using Docker Compose, however when used in conjunction with Docker Swarm, they are elevated to a new level.

To create a Docker service, you can use the `docker service create` command, and the following example demonstrates standing up a very simple web application using the popular Nginx web server:

```
> docker service create --name nginx --publish published=80,target=80
--replicas 2 nginx
ez24df69qb2yq1zhyxma38dzo
overall progress: 2 out of 2 tasks
1/2: running [==================================================>]
2/2: running [==================================================>]
verify: Service converged
> docker service ps --format "{{ .ID }} ({{ .Name }}): {{ .Node }} {{
.CurrentState }}" nginx
```

```
wcq6jfazrums   (nginx.1):  ip-172-31-27-91.ec2.internal   Running 2
minutes ago
i0vj5jftf6cb   (nginx.2):  ip-172-31-40-246.ec2.internal  Running 2
minutes ago
```

The `--name` flag provides a friendly name for the services, while the `--publish` flag allows you to publish an external port the service will be accessible from (in this case, port `80`). The `--replicas` flag defines now many containers should be deployed for the service, and finally you specify the name of the image (nginx, in this case) for the service that you want to run. Note that you can use the `docker service ps` command to list the individual containers and nodes that are running for the service.

If you now attempt to browse to the URL of the external load balancer, you should receive the default **Welcome to nginx!** web page:

Nginx welcome page

To remove a service, you can simply use the `docker service rm` command:

```
> docker service rm nginx
nginx
```

Docker stacks

A **Docker stack** is defined as a complex, self-contained environment that consists of multiple services, networks and/or volumes, and is defined in a Docker Compose file.

A good example of a Docker stack that will immediately add some value to our Swarm cluster is an open source Swarm management tool called **swarmpit**, which you can read more about at `https://swarmpit.io/`. To get started using swarmpit, clone the `https://github.com/swarmpit/swarmpit` repository to a local folder, and then open the `docker-compose.yml` file at the root of the repository.

```
version: '3.6'

services:

  app:
    image: swarmpit/swarmpit:latest
    environment:
      - SWARMPIT_DB=http://db:5984
    volumes:
      - /var/run/docker.sock:/var/run/docker.sock:ro
    ports:
      - target: 8080
        published: 8888
        mode: ingress
    networks:
      - net
    deploy:
      resources:
        limits:
          cpus: '0.50'
          memory: 1024M
        reservations:
          cpus: '0.25'
          memory: 512M
      placement:
        constraints:
          - node.role == manager

  db:
    image: klaemo/couchdb:2.0.0
    volumes:
      - db-data:/opt/couchdb/data
    networks:
      - net
    deploy:
      resources:
        limits:
          cpus: '0.30'
          memory: 512M
        reservations:
          cpus: '0.15'
```

```
        memory: 256M
    placement:
      constraints:
        - node.role == manager

  agent:
    ...
    ...

networks:
  net:
    driver: overlay

volumes:
  db-data:
    driver: local
```

I have highlighted my modifications to the file, which are to update the Docker Compose file specification version to 3.6, modify the ports property for the app service to publish the management UI externally on port 8888, and ensure that the database is only deployed to the Swarm manager in your cluster. The reason for pinning the database is to ensure that in the event the database container failed for any reason, Docker Swarm will attempt to re-deploy the database container to the same node where the local database volume is stored.

> In the event that you inadvertently wipe the swarmpit database, be warned that the admin password will be reset to the default value of admin, representing a significant security risk if you have published the swarmpit management interface to the public internet.

With these changes in place, you can now run the `docker stack deploy` command to deploy the swarmpit management application:

```
> docker stack deploy -c docker-compose.yml swarmpit
Creating network swarmpit_net
Creating service swarmpit_agent
Creating service swarmpit_app
Creating service swarmpit_db
> docker stack services swarmpit
ID             NAME           MODE         REPLICAS    IMAGE
PORTS
8g5smxmqfc6a   swarmpit_app     replicated   1/1
swarmpit/swarmpit:latest   *:8888->8080/tcp
omc7ewvqjecj   swarmpit_db      replicated   1/1
```

```
klaemo/couchdb:2.0.0
u88gzgeg8rym  swarmpit_agent  global       2/2
swarmpit/agent:latest
```

You can see that the `docker stack deploy` command is much simpler than the `docker service create` command, given that the Docker Compose file contains all of the service configuration details. Browse to your external URL on port 8888 and login with the default username and password of `admin/admin`, you should immediately change the admin password by selecting the admin drop-down in the top right-hand corner and selecting **Change Password**. Once you have changed the admin password, you can take a look around the swarmpit management UI, which provides a lot of information about your Swarm cluster. The following screenshot demonstrates the **Infrastructure** | **Nodes** page, which lists the nodes in your cluster and displays detailed information about each node:

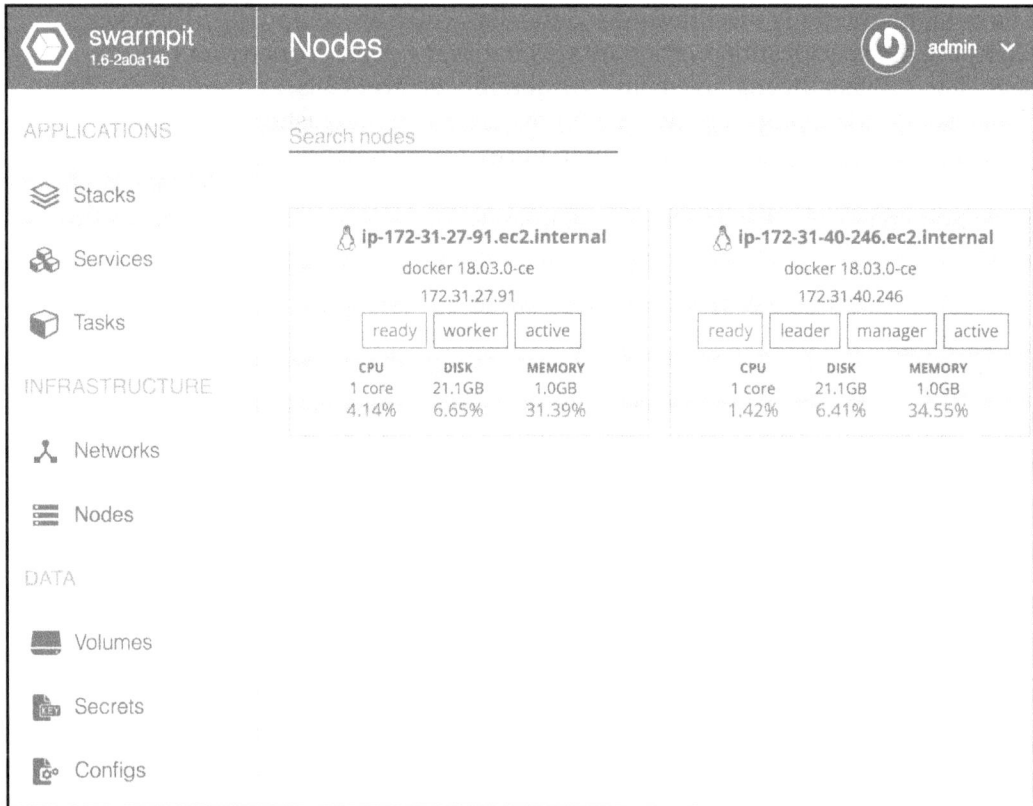

The swarmkit management interface

Deploying the sample application to Docker Swarm

We are now down to the business end of the chapter, which is to deploy our sample todobackend application to our newly created Docker swarm cluster. As you might expect, there are a few challenges we are going to encounter, which require the following configuration tasks to be performed:

- Integrating Docker Swarm with the Elastic Container Registry
- Defining a stack
- Creating shared storage for hosting static content
- Creating a collectstatic service
- Creating persistent storage for storing the todobackend database
- Secrets management using Docker Swarm
- Running database migrations

Integrating Docker Swarm with the Elastic Container Registry

The todobackend application is already published in an existing Elastic Container Registry (ECR) repository, and ideally we want to be able to integrate our Docker swarm cluster so that we can pull private images from ECR. As of the time of writing this book, ECR integration is supported in a somewhat limited fashion, in that you can pass registry credentials to your Docker swarm manager at the time of deployment, which will be shared across all nodes in the cluster. However, these credentials expire after 12 hours, and there is currently no native mechanism to automatically refresh these credentials.

In order to periodically refresh ECR credentials so that your Swarm cluster can always pull images from ECR, you need to perform the following:

- Ensure that your manager and worker instances have permissions to pull from ECR. The Docker for AWS CloudFormation template configures this access by default, so you shouldn't have to worry about configuring this.
- Deploy the `docker-swarm-aws-ecr-auth` auto-login system container as a service, which is published at `https://github.com/mRoca/docker-swarm-aws-ecr-auth`. When installed, this service automatically refreshes ECR credentials on all nodes in your cluster.

---

[677]

To deploy the `docker-swarm-aws-ecr-auth` service, you use the `docker service create` command as follows:

```
> docker service create \
    --name aws_ecr_auth \
    --mount
type=bind,source=/var/run/docker.sock,destination=/var/run/docker.sock
\
    --constraint 'node.role == manager' \
    --restart-condition 'none' \
    --detach=false \
    mroca/swarm-aws-ecr-auth
lmf37a9pbzc3nzhe88s1nzqto
overall progress: 1 out of 1 tasks
1/1: running [===================================================>]
verify: Service converged
```

Note that once this service is up and running, you must include the `--with-registry-auth` flag for any services that you deploy that use ECR images.

The following code demonstrates deploying the todobackend application using the `docker service create` command, along with the `--with-registry-auth` flag:

```
> export AWS_PROFILE=docker-in-aws
> $(aws ecr get-login --no-include-email)
WARNING! Using --password via the CLI is insecure. Use --password-
stdin.
Login Succeeded
> docker service create --name todobackend --with-registry-auth \
    --publish published=80,target=8000 --env
DJANGO_SETTINGS_MODULE=todobackend.settings_release\
    385605022855.dkr.ecr.us-east-1.amazonaws.com/docker-in-
aws/todobackend \
    uwsgi --http=0.0.0.0:8000 --module=todobackend.wsgi
p71rje93a6pqvipqf2a14v6cc
overall progress: 1 out of 1 tasks
1/1: running [===================================================>]
verify: Service converged
```

You can verify the todobackend service did indeed deploy by browsing to the external load balancer URL:

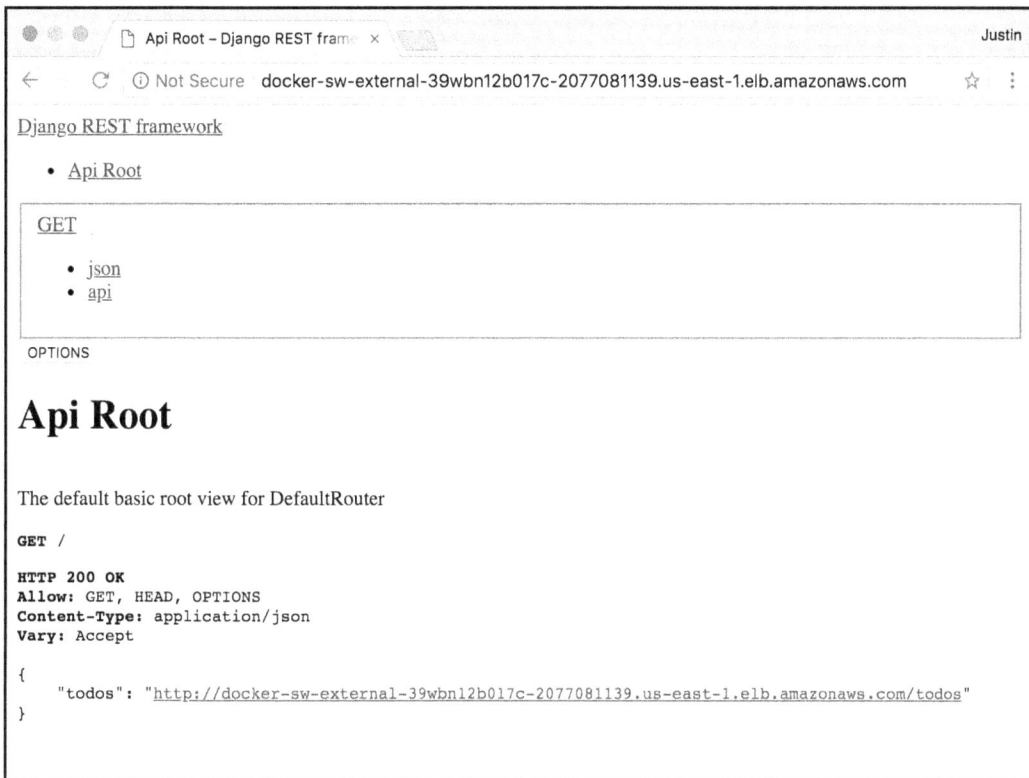

Deploying the todobackend service

Note that because we haven't generated any static files the todobackend service is missing static content. We will resolve this later on when we create a Docker Compose file and deploy a stack for the todobackend application.

Defining a stack

Although you can deploy services using commands like `docker service create`, you can very quickly deploy a complete multi-service environment as we saw earlier using the `docker stack deploy` command, referencing a Docker Compose file that captures the configuration of the various services, networks, and volumes that comprise your stack. Deploying stacks to Docker Swarm requires version 3 of the Docker Compose file specification, so we can't use the existing `docker-compose.yml` file at the root of the todobackend repository to define our Docker Swarm environments, and I recommend keeping your development and test workflow separate, as the Docker Compose version 2 specification exclusively supports features that work well for continuous delivery workflows.

Now, let's get started defining a stack for the todobackend application that we can deploy to our Docker Swarm cluster in AWS by creating a file called `stack.yml` at the root of the `todobackend` repository:

```
version: '3.6'

networks:
  net:
    driver: overlay

services:
  app:
    image: 385605022855.dkr.ecr.us-east-1.amazonaws.com/docker-in-aws/todobackend
    ports:
      - target: 8000
        published: 80
    networks:
      - net
    environment:
      DJANGO_SETTINGS_MODULE: todobackend.settings_release
    command:
      - uwsgi
      - --http=0.0.0.0:8000
      - --module=todobackend.wsgi
      - --master
      - --die-on-term
      - --processes=4
      - --threads=2
      - --check-static=/public
```

```
deploy:
  replicas: 2
  update_config:
    parallelism: 1
    delay: 30s
```

The first property we specify is the mandatory `version` property, which we define as version 3.6, which was the latest version supported at the time of writing this book. Next, we configure the top-level networks property, which specifies Docker networks that the stack will use. You will create a network called `net` that implements the `overlay` driver, which creates a virtual network segment across all nodes in the Swarm cluster over which the various services defined in the stack can communicate with each other. In general, each stack that you deploy should specify its own overlay network, which provides segmentation between each of your stacks and means that you don't need to worry about IP addressing or the physical network topology of your cluster.

Next, you must define a single service called `app`, which represents the main todobackend web application and via the `image` property specifies the fully qualified name of the ECR image for the todobackend application that you published in earlier chapters. Note that Docker stacks do not support the `build` property and must reference a published Docker image, which is a good reason why you should always have a separate Docker Compose specification for your development, test, and build workflow.

The `ports` property uses the long style configuration syntax (in previous chapters, you have use the short style syntax), which provides access to more configuration options, allowing you to specify that the container port 8000 (as specified by the `target` property) will be published externally on port 80 (as specified by the `published` property), while the `networks` property configures the `app` service to be attached to the `net` network you previously defined. Notice that the `environment` property does not specify any database configuration settings—the focus for now is to just get the application up and running, albeit in a somewhat broken state, but we will shall configure database access later on in this chapter.

Finally, the `deploy` property allows you to control how the service should be deployed, with the `replica` property specifying to deploy two instances of our service, and the `update_config` property configuring rolling updates to update one instance at a time (as specified by the `parallelism` property) with a delay of 30 seconds between deploying each updated instance.

With this configuration in place, you can now deploy your stack using the `docker stack deploy` command:

```
> $(aws ecr get-login --no-include-email)
WARNING! Using --password via the CLI is insecure. Use --password-
stdin.
Login Succeeded
> docker stack deploy --with-registry-auth -c stack.yml todobackend
Creating network todobackend_net
Creating service todobackend_app
> docker service ps todobackend_app --format "{{ .Name }} -> {{ .Node
}} ({{ .CurrentState }})"
todobackend_app.1 -> ip-172-31-27-91.ec2.internal (Running 6 seconds
ago)
todobackend_app.2 -> ip-172-31-40-246.ec2.internal (Running 6 seconds
ago)
```

Notice that I first login to ECR—this step is not absolutely required, however if are not logged into ECR, the Docker client is unable to determine the current image hash associated with the latest tag and you will be presented with this warning:

```
> docker stack deploy --with-registry-auth -c stack.yml todobackend
image 385605022855.dkr.ecr.us-east-1.amazonaws.com/docker-in-
aws/todobackend:latest could not be accessed on a registry to record
its digest. Each node will access 385605022855.dkr.ecr.us-
east-1.amazonaws.com/docker-in-aws/todobackend:latest independently,
possibly leading to different nodes running different
versions of the image.
...
...
```

If you now browse the external load balancer URL, the todobackend application should load, however you will notice that the application is missing static content and if you attempt to access `/todos`, a database configuration error will be presented, which is to be expected given we haven't configured any database settings or considered how to run the **collectstatic** process in Docker swarm.

Creating shared storage for hosting static content

The Docker for AWS solution includes the Cloudstor volume plugin, which is a storage plugin built by Docker and designed to support popular cloud storage mechanisms for persistent storage.

In the case of AWS, this plugin provides out of the box integration with the following types of persistent storage:

- **Elastic Block Store** (**EBS**): Provides block level storage intended for dedicated (non-shared) access. This provides a high level of performance with the ability to detach and attach volumes to different instances, and supports snapshot and restore operations. EBS storage is suitable for database storage or any applications that require high throughput and minimal latency for reading and writing local data.

- **Elastic File System** (**EFS**): Provides shared file system access using the **Network File System** (**NFS**) version 4 protocol. NFS allows for sharing storage at the same time across multiple hosts, however this is much less performant than EBS storage. NFS storage is suitable for applications that share common files and do not require high performance. Earlier, when you deployed the Docker for AWS solution, you selected to create the prerequisites for EFS, which sets up an EFS file system for the Swarm cluster that the Cloudstor volume plugin integrates with.

As you know from previous chapters, the todobackend application has a specific requirement for storing static content, and although I would typically not recommend EFS for such a use case, the static content requirement represents a good opportunity to demonstrate how to configure and use EFS as a shared volume in a Docker Swarm environment:

```
version: '3.6'

networks:
  net:
    driver: overlay

volumes:
  public:
    driver: cloudstor:aws
    driver_opts:
      backing: shared

services:
  app:
    image: 385605022855.dkr.ecr.us-east-1.amazonaws.com/docker-in-aws/todobackend
    ports:
      - target: 8000
        published: 80
    networks:
```

```
    - net
  volumes:
    - public:/public
  ...
  ...
```

You must first create a volume called `public` and specify a driver of `cloudstor:aws`, which ensures that the Cloudstor driver is loaded with AWS support. To create an EFS volume, you simply configure a driver option called `backing` with a value of `shared`, and then mount the volume at `/public` in the `app` service.

If you now deploy your changes using the `docker stack deploy` command, the `volume` will be created and the `app` service instances will be updated:

```
> docker stack deploy --with-registry-auth -c stack.yml todobackend
Updating service todobackend_app (id: 59gpr2x9n7buikeorpf0llfmc)
> docker volume ls
DRIVER          VOLUME NAME
local
bd3d2804c796064d6e7c4040040fd474d9adbe7aaf68b6e30b1d195b50cdefde
local           sshkey
cloudstor:aws   todobackend_public
>  docker service ps todobackend_app \
    --format "{{ .Name }} -> {{ .DesiredState }} ({{ .CurrentState }})"
todobackend_app.1 -> Running (Running 44 seconds ago)
todobackend_app.1 -> Shutdown (Shutdown 45 seconds ago)
todobackend_app.2 -> Running (Running 9 seconds ago)
todobackend_app.2 -> Shutdown (Shutdown 9 seconds ago)
```

You can use the `docker volume ls` command to view current volumes, and you will see that a new volume named according to the convention `<stack name>_<volume name>` (for example, `todobackend_public`) is created with a driver of `cloudstor:aws`. Notice that the `docker service ps` command output shows that `todobackend.app.1` was updated first, and then `todobackend.app.2` was updated 30 seconds later, which is based upon the earlier rolling update configuration you applied in the `deploy` settings for the `app` service.

To verify that the volume was successfully mounted, you can use the `docker ps` command to query the Swarm manager for any app service containers running locally, and then use `docker exec` to verify that the `/public` mount exists and is readable/writable by the `app` user that the todobackend container runs as:

```
> docker ps -f name=todobackend -q
60b33d8b0bb1
> docker exec -it 60b33d8b0bb1 touch /public/test
> docker exec -it 60b33d8b0bb1 ls -l /public
total 4
-rw-r--r-- 1 app app 0 Jul 19 13:45 test
```

One important point to note is that the `docker volume` and other `docker` commands shown in the preceding example are only executed in the context of the current Swarm node you are connected to, and won't display volumes or allow you to access containers running on other nodes in the cluster. To verify that the volume is indeed shared and accessible by the app service container running on the other Swarm node in our cluster, you need to first SSH to the Swarm manager and then SSH to the single worker node in the cluster:

```
> ssh -A docker@54.145.175.148
Welcome to Docker!
~ $ docker node ls
ID                          HOSTNAME                      STATUS
MANAGER   STATUS
qna4v46afttl007jq0ec712dk   ip-172-31-27-91.ec2.internal    Ready
Active
ym3jdy1ol17pfw7emwfen0b4e * ip-172-31-40-246.ec2.internal   Ready
Active    Leader
> ssh docker@ip-172-31-27-91.ec2.internal
Welcome to Docker!
> docker ps -f name=todobackend -q
71df5495080f
~ $ docker exec -it 71df5495080f ls -l /public
total 4
-rw-r--r-- 1 app app 0 Jul 19 13:58 test
~ $ docker exec -it 71df5495080f rm /public/test
```

As you can see, the volume is available on the worker node, who can see the `/public/test` file we created on the other instance, proving the volume is indeed shared and accessible to all `app` service instances, regardless of underlying nodes.

Creating a collectstatic service

Now that you have a shared volume in place, we need to consider how we will define and execute the collectstatic process to generate static content. To date, throughout this book, you have performed the collectstatic process as an imperative task that needs to happen at a specific point in time within a defined deployment sequence, however Docker Swarm promotes the concept of eventual consistency so you should be able to deploy your stack and have a collectstatic process running that may fail but will eventually succeed, at which point the desired state of your application is reached. This approach is quite different from the imperative approach we have taken previously, but is accepted as a best practice for well-architected modern cloud native applications.

To demonstrate how this works, we first need to tear down the todobackend stack so that you can observe failures that will occur in the collectstatic process while the Docker storage engine is creating and mounting the EFS backed volume:

```
> docker stack rm todobackend
Removing service todobackend_app
Removing network todobackend_net
> docker volume ls
DRIVER          VOLUME NAME
local           sshkey
cloudstor:aws   todobackend_public
> docker volume rm todobackend_public
```

One point to note is that Docker Swarm does not remove volumes when you destroy a stack, so you need to manually remove the volume to fully clean up the environment.

We can now add a collectstatic service to our stack:

```
version: '3.6'

networks:
  net:
    driver: overlay

volumes:
  public:
    driver: cloudstor:aws
    driver_opts:
      backing: shared

services:
  app:
```

```
    image: 385605022855.dkr.ecr.us-east-1.amazonaws.com/docker-in-
  aws/todobackend
    ports:
      - target: 8000
        published: 80
    networks:
      - net
    volumes:
      - public:/public
    ...
    ...
  collectstatic:
    image: 385605022855.dkr.ecr.us-east-1.amazonaws.com/docker-in-
  aws/todobackend
    volumes:
      - public:/public
    networks:
      - net
    environment:
      DJANGO_SETTINGS_MODULE: todobackend.settings_release
    command:
      - python3
      - manage.py
      - collectstatic
      - --no-input
    deploy:
      replicas: 1
      restart_policy:
        condition: on-failure
        delay: 30s
        max_attempts: 6
```

The collectstatic service mounts the public shared volume and runs the appropriate manage.py task to generate static content. In the deploy section, we configure a replica count of 1, given that the collectstatic service only needs be run once per deployment, and then configure a restart_policy that states Docker Swarm should attempt to restart the service on failure, with a delay of 30 seconds between each restart attempt up to a maximum of 6 attempts. This provides eventual consistency behavior as it allows collectstatic to fail initially while EFS volume mounting operations are taking place, and then eventually succeed once the volume is mounted and ready.

If you now deploy the stack and monitor the collectstatic service, you may notice some initial failures:

```
> docker stack deploy --with-registry-auth -c stack.yml todobackend
Creating network todobackend_default
Creating network todobackend_net
Creating service todobackend_collectstatic
Creating service todobackend_app
> docker service ps todobackend_collectstatic
NAME                            NODE                            DESIRED
STATE CURRENT STATE
todobackend_collectstatic.1 ip-172-31-40-246.ec2.internal Running
Running 2 seconds ago
\_ todobackend_collectstatic.1 ip-172-31-40-246.ec2.internal Shutdown
Rejected 32 seconds ago
```

The `docker service ps` command displays not only the current service state, but also service history (such as any previous attempts to run the service), and you can see that 32 seconds ago the first attempt to run `collectstatic` failed, after which Docker Swarm attempted to restart the service. This attempt succeeds, and although the `collectstatic` service will eventually complete and exit, because the restart policy is set to failure, Docker Swarm will not attempt to start the service again, given that the service exited with no error. This supports the concept of a "one-shot" service with retry capabilities in the event of a failure, and the only time Swarm will attempt to run the service again is in the event that a new configuration for the service is deployed to the cluster.

If you now browse to the external load balancer URL, you should find that the static content of the todobackend application is now presented correctly, however the database configuration error still exists.

Creating persistent storage for storing the application database

We can now shift our attention to the application database, which is an essential supporting component of the todobackend application. If you are running in AWS, my typical recommendation would be, regardless of container orchestration platform, to use the Relational Database Service (RDS) as we have done throughout this book, however the application database requirement for the todobackend application provides an opportunity to demonstrate how you can support persistent storage using the Docker for AWS solution.

In addition to EFS-backed volumes, the Cloudstor volume plugin also supports *relocatable* Elastic Block Store (EBS) volumes. Relocatable means that the plugin will automatically relocate the currently assigned EBS volume for a container to another node in the event Docker Swarm determines it has to relocate a container from one node to another. What actually happens during relocation of the EBS volume depends on the scenario:

- **New node is in the same availability zone**: The plugin simply detaches the volume from the EC2 instance of the existing node and reattaches the volume on the new node.

- **New node is in a different availability zone**: Here, the plugin takes a snapshot of the existing volume and then creates a new volume in the new availability zone from the snapshot. Once complete, the previous volume is destroyed.

It is important to note that Docker only supports singular access to a relocatable EBS-backed volume—that is, there should only ever be a single container that reads/writes to the volume at any given time. If you require shared access to a volume, then you must create an EFS-backed shared volume.

Now, let's define a volume called `data` to store the todobackend database, and create a `db` service that will run MySQL and attach to the `data` volume:

```
version: '3.6'

networks:
  net:
    driver: overlay

volumes:
  public:
    driver: cloudstor:aws
    driver_opts:
      backing: shared
  data:
    driver: cloudstor:aws
    driver_opts:
      backing: relocatable
      size: 10
      ebstype: gp2

services:
  app:
    image: 385605022855.dkr.ecr.us-east-1.amazonaws.com/docker-in-aws/todobackend
```

```
      ports:
        - target: 8000
          published: 80
      networks:
        - net
      volumes:
        - public:/public
      ...
      ...
  collectstatic:
      image: 385605022855.dkr.ecr.us-east-1.amazonaws.com/docker-in-
aws/todobackend
      volumes:
        - public:/public
      ...
      ...
  db:
    image: mysql:5.7
    environment:
      MYSQL_DATABASE: todobackend
      MYSQL_USER: todo
      MYSQL_PASSWORD: password
      MYSQL_ROOT_PASSWORD: password
    networks:
      - net
    volumes:
      - data:/var/lib/mysql
    command:
      - --ignore-db-dir=lost+found
    deploy:
      replicas: 1
      placement:
        constraints:
          - node.role == manager
```

First, we create a volume called `data` and configure the driver as `cloudstor:aws`. In the driver options, we specify a backing of relocatable to create an EBS volume, specifying a size of 10 GB and an EBS type of `gp2` (SSD) storage. We then define a new service called `db` that runs the official MySQL 5.7 image, attaching the `db` service to the previously defined net network and mounting the data volume at `/var/lib/mysql`, which is where MySQL stores its database. Note that because the Cloudstor plugin formats the mounted volume as `ext4`, a folder called `lost+found` is automatically created during the formatting process, which causes the `MySQL` `container to abort` as it thinks an existing database called `lost+found` is present.

To overcome this, we pass in a single flag called `--ignore-db-dir` that references the `lost+found` folder, which is passed to the MySQL image entrypoint and configures the MySQL daemon to ignore this folder.

Finally, we define a placement constraint that will force the db service to be deployed to the Swarm manager, which will allow us to test the relocatable features of the data volume by changing this placement constraint to a worker later on.

If you now deploy the stack and monitor the db service, you should observe that the service takes some time to come up while the data volume is initializing:

```
> docker stack deploy --with-registry-auth -c stack.yml todobackend
docker stack deploy --with-registry-auth -c stack.yml todobackend
Updating service todobackend_app (id: 28vrdqcsekdvoqcmxtum1eaoj)
Updating service todobackend_collectstatic (id:
sowciy4i0zuikf93lmhi624iw)
Creating service todobackend_db
> docker service ps todobackend_db --format "{{ .Name }} ({{ .ID }}):
{{ .CurrentState }}"
todobackend_db.1 (u4upsnirpucs): Preparing 35 seconds ago
> docker service ps todobackend_db --format "{{ .Name }} ({{ .ID }}):
{{ .CurrentState }}"
todobackend_db.1 (u4upsnirpucs): Running 2 seconds ago
```

To verify, an EBS volume has actually been created, you can use the AWS CLI as follows:

```
> aws ec2 describe-volumes --filters
Name=tag:CloudstorVolumeName,Values=* \
    --query
"Volumes[*].{ID:VolumeId,Zone:AvailabilityZone,Attachment:Attachments,
Tag:Tags}"
[
    {
        "ID": "vol-0db01995ba87433b3",
        "Zone": "us-east-1b",
        "Attachment": [
            {
                "AttachTime": "2018-07-20T09:58:16.000Z",
                "Device": "/dev/xvdf",
                "InstanceId": "i-0dc762f73f8ce4abf",
                "State": "attached",
                "VolumeId": "vol-0db01995ba87433b3",
                "DeleteOnTermination": false
            }
        ],
        "Tag": [
```

```
            {
                "Key": "CloudstorVolumeName",
                "Value": "todobackend_data"
            },
            {
                "Key": "StackID",
                "Value": "0825319e9d91a2fc0bf06d2139708b1a"
            }
        ]
    }
]
```

Note that EBS volumes created by the Cloudstor plugin are tagged with a key of CloudstorVolumeName and a value of the Docker Swarm volume name. In the preceding example, you can also see that the volume has been created in the us-east-1b availability zone.

Relocating an EBS volume

Now that you have successfully created and attached an EBS-backed data volume, let's test migrating the db service from the manager node to the worker node by changing its placement constraint:

```
version: '3.6'
...
...
services:
  ...
  ...
  db:
    image: mysql:5.7
    environment:
      MYSQL_DATABASE: todobackend
      MYSQL_USER: todo
      MYSQL_PASSWORD: password
      MYSQL_ROOT_PASSWORD: password
    networks:
      - net
    volumes:
      - data:/var/lib/mysql
    command:
      - --ignore-db-dir=lost+found
    deploy:
      replicas: 1
      placement:
        constraints:
          - node.role == worker
```

If you now deploy your changes, you should be able to observe the EBS relocation process:

```
> volumes='aws ec2 describe-volumes --filters
Name=tag:CloudstorVolumeName,Values=*
    --query
"Volumes[*].{ID:VolumeId,State:Attachments[0].State,Zone:AvailabilityZ
one}"
    --output text'
> snapshots='aws ec2 describe-snapshots --filters
Name=status,Values=pending
    --query "Snapshots[].{Id:VolumeId,Progress:Progress}" --output
text'
> docker stack deploy --with-registry-auth -c stack.yml todobackend
Updating service todobackend_app (id: 28vrdqcsekdvoqcmxtum1eaoj)
Updating service todobackend_collectstatic (id:
sowciy4i0zuikf93lmhi624iw)
Updating service todobackend_db (id: 4e3sc0dlot9lxlmt5kwfw3sis)
> eval $volumes
vol-0db01995ba87433b3 detaching us-east-1b
> eval $volumes
vol-0db01995ba87433b3 None us-east-1b
> eval $snapshots
vol-0db01995ba87433b3 76%
> eval $snapshots
vol-0db01995ba87433b3 99%
> eval $volumes
vol-0db01995ba87433b3 None us-east-1b
vol-07e328572e6223396 None us-east-1a
> eval $volume
vol-07e328572e6223396 None us-east-1a
> eval $volume
vol-07e328572e6223396 attached us-east-1a
> docker service ps todobackend_db --format "{{ .Name }} ({{ .ID }}):
{{ .CurrentState }}"
todobackend_db.1 (a3i84kwz45w9): Running 1 minute ago
todobackend_db.1 (u4upsnirpucs): Shutdown 2 minutes ago
```

We first define a `volumes` query that displays the current Cloudstor volume status, and a `snapshots` query that displays any EBS snapshots that are in progress. After deploying the placement constraint change, we run the volumes query several times and observe the current volume located in `us-east-1b`, transition to a state of `detaching`, and to a state of `None` (detached).

We then run the snapshot query where you can see that a snapshot is being created for the volume that was just detached, and once this snapshot is complete, we run the volumes query several times to observe that the old volume is removed and a new volume is created in `us-east-1a`, which is then attached. At this point, the `todobackend_data` volume has been relocated from the manager in `us-east-1b` to `us-east-1a`, and you can verify that the `db` service is now up and running again by executing the `docker service ps` command.

> Because the Docker for AWS CloudFormation template creates separate auto scaling groups for managers and workers, there is a possibility the manager and worker are running in the same subnet and availability zone, which will change the behavior of the example above.

Before we proceed to the next section, we actually need to tear down our stack as the current password management strategy of using cleartext passwords in our stack file is not ideal, and our database has already been initialized with these passwords:

```
> docker stack rm todobackend
Removing service todobackend_app
Removing service todobackend_collectstatic
Removing service todobackend_db
Removing network todobackend_net
> docker volume ls
DRIVER          VOLUME NAME
local           sshkey
cloudstor:aws   todobackend_data
cloudstor:aws   todobackend_public
> docker volume rm todobackend_public
todobackend_public
> docker volume rm todobackend_data
todobackend_data
```

Remember that, whenever you tear down a stack, you must remove any volumes you may have used in that stack manually.

Secrets management using Docker secrets

In the preceding examples when we created the `db` service, we didn't actually configure the application to integrate with the `db` service, as although we were focusing on how to create persistent storage, another reason I did not integrate the `app` service with the `db` service is because we are currently configuring passwords for the `db` service in plaintext, which is not ideal.

Docker Swarm includes a feature called Docker secrets, which provide a secure secrets management solution for providing secrets to applications running on your Docker Swarm clusters. Secrets are stored in an internal encrypted storage mechanism called the *raft log*, which is replicated to all nodes in your cluster, ensuring that any service and associated containers that are granted access to a secret can access the secret securely.

To create a Docker secret, you can use the `docker secret create` command:

```
> openssl rand -base64 32 | docker secret create
todobackend_mysql_password -
wk5fpokcz8wbwmuw587izl1in
> openssl rand -base64 32 | docker secret create
todobackend_mysql_root_password -
584ojwg31c0oidjydxkglv4qz
> openssl rand -base64 50 | docker secret create
todobackend_secret_key -
t5rb04xcqyrqiglmfwrfs122y
> docker secret ls
ID                         NAME                              CREATED
UPDATED
wk5fpokcz8wbwmuw587izl1in  todobackend_mysql_password        57
seconds ago    57 seconds ago
584ojwg31c0oidjydxkglv4qz  todobackend_mysql_root_password   50
seconds ago    50 seconds ago
t5rb04xcqyrqiglmfwrfs122y  todobackend_secret_key            33
seconds ago    33 seconds ago
```

In the preceding example, we use the `openssl rand` command to generate random secrets in Base64 format, which we then pass as standard input to the `docker secret create` command. We create 32 character secrets for the todobackend user's MySQL password and MySQL root password, and finally create a secret of 50 characters for the Django `SECRET_KEY` setting that is required for cryptographic operations performed by the todobackend application.

Now that we have created several secrets, we can configure our stack to consume these secrets:

```
version: '3.6'

networks:
  ...

volumes:
  ...
```

```
secrets:
  todobackend_mysql_password:
    external: true
  todobackend_mysql_root_password:
    external: true
  todobackend_secret_key:
    external: true

services:
  app:
    ...
    ...
    environment:
      DJANGO_SETTINGS_MODULE: todobackend.settings_release
      MYSQL_HOST: db
      MYSQL_USER: todo
    secrets:
      - source: todobackend_mysql_password
        target: MYSQL_PASSWORD
      - source: todobackend_secret_key
        target: SECRET_KEY
    command:
      ...
      ...
  db:
    image: mysql:5.7
    environment:
      MYSQL_DATABASE: todobackend
      MYSQL_USER: todo
      MYSQL_PASSWORD_FILE: /run/secrets/mysql_password
      MYSQL_ROOT_PASSWORD_FILE: /run/secrets/mysql_root_password
    secrets:
      - source: todobackend_mysql_password
        target: mysql_password
      - source: todobackend_mysql_root_password
        target: mysql_root_password
  ...
  ...
```

We first declare the top level `secrets` parameter, specifying the names of each of the secrets we previously created and configuring each secret as `external`, given we created the secrets outside of the stack. If you don't use external secrets, you must define your secrets in a file, which does not solve the issue of storing passwords securely outside of your stack definitions and configurations, so creating your secrets as separate entities independent of your stack is much more secure.

We then reconfigure the `app` service to consume each secret via the `secrets` property. Notice that we specify a target of `MYSQL_PASSWORD` and `SECRET_KEY`. Whenever you attach a secret to a service, an in-memory tmpfs-backed mount will be created at `/run/secrets`, with each secret stored at the location `/run/secrets/<target-name>`, so for the `app` service, the following secrets will be mounted:

- `/run/secrets/MYSQL_PASSWORD`
- `/run/secrets/SECRET_KEY`

We will learn how to configure our application to consume these secrets later on, but also note that we configure the `MYSQL_HOST` and `MYSQL_USER` environment variables so that our application knows how to connect to the `db` service and which user to authenticate as.

Next, we configure the `db` service to consume the MySQL password and root password secrets, and here we configure the targets for each secret so that the following secrets are mounted in the `db` service container:

- `/run/secrets/mysql_password`
- `/run/secrets/mysql_root_password`

Finally, we remove the `MYSQL_PASSWORD` and `MYSQL_ROOT_PASSWORD` environment variables from the `db` service and replace these with their file-based equivalents, referencing the path to each of the configured secrets.

At this point, if you deploy the newly updated stack (if you haven't previously removed the stack, you will need to do this prior to ensure that you can recreate the database with the new credentials), once your todobackend services have started successfully, you can determine the container ID of the `app` service instance running on the Swarm manager by running the `docker ps` command, after which you can examine the contents of the `/run/secrets` directory:

```
> docker stack deploy --with-registry-auth -c stack.yml todobackend
Creating network todobackend_net
Creating service todobackend_db
Creating service todobackend_app
Creating service todobackend_collectstatic
> docker ps -f name=todobackend -q
7804a7496fa2
> docker exec -it 7804a7496fa2 ls -l /run/secrets
total 8
-r--r--r-- 1 root root 45 Jul 20 23:49 MYSQL_PASSWORD
```

```
-r--r--r-- 1 root root 70 Jul 20 23:49 SECRET_KEY
> docker exec -it 7804a7496fa2 cat /run/secrets/MYSQL_PASSWORD
qvImrAEBDz9OWJS779uvs/EWuf/YlepTlwPkx4cLSHE=
```

As you can see, the secrets you created earlier are available in the /run/secrets folder, and if you now browse to the /todos path on the external load balancer URL where your application is published, unfortunately you will receive an access denied error:

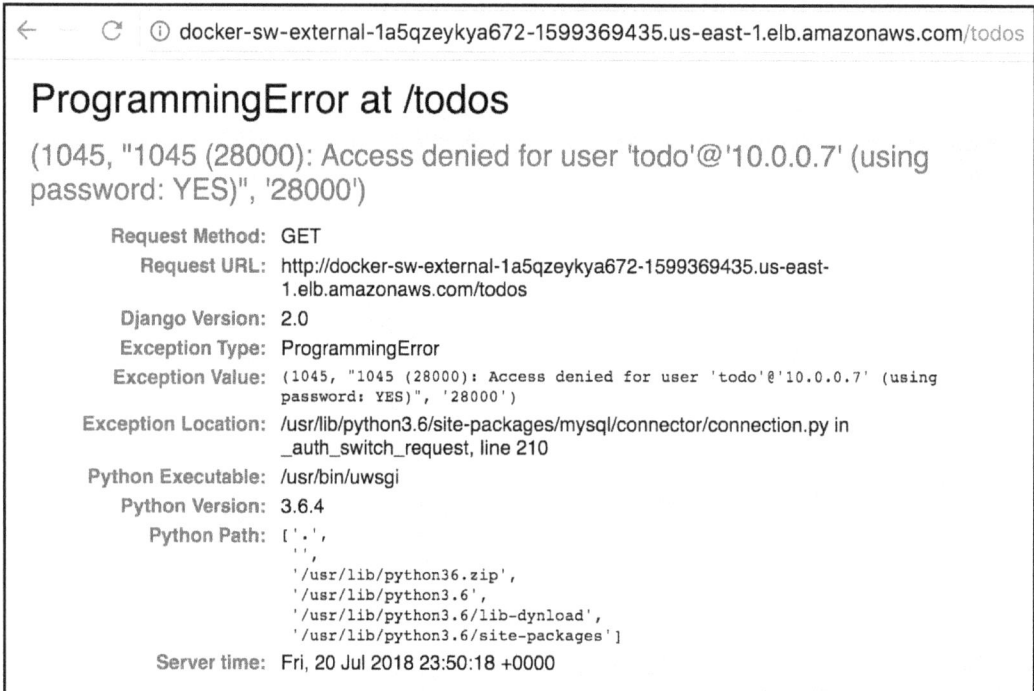

Database authentication error

The problem here is that although we have mounted the database secret in the app service, our todobackend application does not know how to consume these secrets, so we need to make some modifications to the todobackend application to be able to consume these secrets.

Configuring applications to consume secrets

In previous chapters, we have used an entrypoint script to add support for features such as injecting secrets at container startup, however an equally valid (and actually better and more secure) approach is to configure your application to natively support your secrets management strategy.

In the case of Docker secrets, this is very straightforward, given that the secrets are mounted at a well-known location (`/run/secrets`) in the local filesystem of the container. The following demonstrates modifying the `src/todobackend/settings_release.py` file in the `todobackend` repository to support Docker secrets, which, as you should recall, are the settings we pass to our `app` service, as specified by the environment variable configuration `DJANGO_SETTINGS_MODULE=todobackend.settings_release.`:

```
from .settings import *
import os

# Disable debug
DEBUG = True

# Looks up secret in following order:
# 1. /run/secret/<key>
# 2. Environment variable named <key>
# 3. Value of default or None if no default supplied
def secret(key, default=None):
    root = os.environ.get('SECRETS_ROOT','/run/secrets')
    path = os.path.join(root,key)
    if os.path.isfile(path):
        with open(path) as f:
            return f.read().rstrip()
    else:
        return os.environ.get(key,default)

# Set secret key
SECRET_KEY = secret('SECRET_KEY', SECRET_KEY)

# Must be explicitly specified when Debug is disabled
ALLOWED_HOSTS = os.environ.get('ALLOWED_HOSTS', '*').split(',')

# Database settings
DATABASES = {
    'default': {
        'ENGINE': 'mysql.connector.django',
        'NAME': os.environ.get('MYSQL_DATABASE','todobackend'),
        'USER': os.environ.get('MYSQL_USER','todo'),
```

```
        'PASSWORD': secret('MYSQL_PASSWORD','password'),
        'HOST': os.environ.get('MYSQL_HOST','localhost'),
        'PORT': os.environ.get('MYSQL_PORT','3306'),
    },
    'OPTIONS': {
      'init_command': "SET sql_mode='STRICT_TRANS_TABLES'"
    }
}

STATIC_ROOT = os.environ.get('STATIC_ROOT', '/public/static')
MEDIA_ROOT = os.environ.get('MEDIA_ROOT', '/public/media')

MIDDLEWARE.insert(0,'aws_xray_sdk.ext.django.middleware.XRayMiddleware
')
```

We first create a simple function called secret(), which takes as input the name of the setting or key, and an optional default value if the secret cannot be found. This function then attempts to look up the path /run/secrets (this can be overridden by setting the environment variable SECRETS_ROOT) and looks for a file with the same name as the requested key. If this file is found, the contents of the file is read using the f.read().rstrip() call, with the rstrip() function stripping the line break that is returned by the read() function. Otherwise, the function looks for an environment variable with the same name of key, and if all of these lookups fail, it returns the default value that was passed to the secret() function (which itself has a default value of None).

With this function in place, we can then simply call the secret function, as demonstrated for the SECRET_KEY and DATABASES['PASSWORD'] settings, and using the SECRET_KEY setting as an example, the function will return in the following order of preference:

1. Value of the contents of the /run/secrets/SECRET_KEY
2. Value of the environment variable SECRET_KEY
3. Value of the default value passed to the secrets() function (in this case, the SECRET_KEY setting imported from the base settings file)

Now that we have updated the todobackend application to support Docker secrets, you need to commit your changes and then test, build, and publish your changes. Note that will need to do this in a separate shell that is connected to your local Docker Engine (rather than your Docker Swarm cluster):

```
> git commit -a -m "Add support for Docker secrets"
[master 3db46c4] Add support for Docker secrets
> make login
```

```
...
...
> make test
...
...
> make release
...
...
> make publish
...
...
```

Once your image has been successfully published, switch back to your Terminal session that is connected to your Swarm cluster and redeploy your stack using the `docker stack deploy` command:

```
> docker stack deploy --with-registry-auth -c stack.yml todobackend
Updating service todobackend_app (id: xz0tl79iv75qvq3tw6yqzracm)
Updating service todobackend_collectstatic (id:
tkal4xxuejmf1jipsg24eq1bm)
Updating service todobackend_db (id: 9vj845j54nsz360q70lk1nrkr)
> docker service ps todobackend_app --format "{{ .Name }}: {{
.CurrentState }}"
todobackend_app.1: Running 20 minutes ago
todobackend_app.2: Running 20 minutes ago
```

If you run the `docker service ps` command as demonstrated in the preceding example, you may notice that your todobackend service is not redeployed (note in some cases the service may be redeployed). The reason for this is that we are using the latest image by default in our stack file. To ensure that we can continuously deliver and deploy our application, we need to reference a specific version or build tag, which is the best practice approach you should always take, as it will force an explicit version of your image to be deployed on each service update.

To do this with our local workflow, we can leverage the `Makefile` that already exists in the todobackend application repository and include an `APP_VERSION` environment variable that returns the current Git commit hash, which we can subsequently reference in our stack file:

```
version: '3.6'

services:
  app:
    image: 385605022855.dkr.ecr.us-east-1.amazonaws.com/docker-in-
aws/todobackend:${APP_VERSION}
    ...
```

```
    ...
  collectstatic:
    image: 385605022855.dkr.ecr.us-east-1.amazonaws.com/docker-in-
  aws/todobackend:${APP_VERSION}
    ...
    ...
```

With this configuration in place, we now need to add a deploy recipe to the
`Makefile` in the root of the `todobackend` repository, which will automatically make
the `APP_VERSION` environment variable available to the Docker client when it parses
the stack file:

```
.PHONY: test release clean version login logout publish deploy

export APP_VERSION ?= $(shell git rev-parse --short HEAD)

version:
  @ echo '{"Version": "$(APP_VERSION)"}'

deploy: login
  @ echo "Deploying version ${APP_VERSION}..."
  docker stack deploy --with-registry-auth -c stack.yml todobackend

login:
  $$(aws ecr get-login --no-include-email)
...
...
```

The `deploy` recipe references the `login` recipe, ensuring that we always run the
equivalent of `make login` first before running the tasks in the `deploy` recipe. This
recipe simply runs the `docker stack deploy` command so that we can now deploy
the updates to our stack by running `make deploy`:

```
> make deploy
Deploying version 3db46c4,,,
docker stack deploy --with-registry-auth -c stack.yml todobackend
Updating service todobackend_app (id: xz0tl79iv75qvq3tw6yqzracm)
Updating service todobackend_collectstatic (id:
tkal4xxuejmf1jipsg24eq1bm)
Updating service todobackend_db (id: 9vj845j54nsz360q701k1nrkr)
> docker service ps todobackend_app --format "{{ .Name }}: {{
.CurrentState }}"
todobackend_app.1: Running 5 seconds ago
todobackend_app.1: Shutdown 6 seconds ago
todobackend_app.2: Running 25 minutes ago
> docker service ps todobackend_app --format "{{ .Name }}: {{
.CurrentState }}"
```

```
todobackend_app.1: Running 45 seconds ago
todobackend_app.1: Shutdown 46 seconds ago
todobackend_app.2: Running 14 seconds ago
todobackend_app.2: Shutdown 15 seconds ago
```

Because our stack is now configured with a specific image tag, as defined by the `APP_VERSION` variable (`3db46c4` in the preceding example), a change is detected and the `app` service is updated. You can confirm this using the `docker service ps` command, as demonstrated previously, and recall that we have configured this service to update a single instance at a time with a 30 second delay between each update.

If you now browse to the `/todos` path on the external load balancer URL, the authentication error should now be replaced with a `table does not exist` error, which proves that we are now able to at least connect to the database, but haven't yet dealt with database migrations as part of our Docker Swarm solution:

Database error

Running database migrations

Now that we have established a mechanism to securely access the db service in our stack, the final configuration task we need to perform is to add a service that will run database migrations. This is similar to the collectstatic service we created earlier, in that it needs to be a "one-shot" task that only executes whenever we create the stack or whenever we deploy a new version of the application:

```
version: '3.6'

networks:
  ...

volumes:
  ...

secrets:
  ...

services:
  app:
    ...
  migrate:
    image: 385605022855.dkr.ecr.us-east-1.amazonaws.com/docker-in-aws/todobackend:${APP_VERSION}
    networks:
      - net
    environment:
      DJANGO_SETTINGS_MODULE: todobackend.settings_release
      MYSQL_HOST: db
      MYSQL_USER: todo
    secrets:
      - source: todobackend_mysql_password
        target: MYSQL_PASSWORD
```

```
command:
    - python3
    - manage.py
    - migrate
    - --no-input
  deploy:
    replicas: 1
    restart_policy:
      condition: on-failure
      delay: 30s
      max_attempts: 6
collectstatic:
  ...
db:
  ...
```

All of the settings for the new `migrate` service should be self-explanatory, as we've configured them previously for other services. The `deploy` configuration is especially important and is configured identically to the other one-shot collectstatic service, where Docker Swarm will attempt to ensure a single replica of the `migrate` service is able to start successfully up to six times with a delay of 30 seconds between each attempt.

If you now run `make deploy` to deploy your changes, the `migrate` service should be able to complete successfully:

```
> make deploy
Deploying version 3db46c4...
docker stack deploy --with-registry-auth -c stack.yml todobackend
Updating service todobackend_collectstatic (id:
tkal4xxuejmf1jipsg24eq1bm)
Updating service todobackend_db (id: 9vj845j54nsz360q70lk1nrkr)
Updating service todobackend_app (id: xz0tl79iv75qvq3tw6yqzracm)
Creating service todobackend_migrate
> docker service ps todobackend_migrate --format "{{ .Name }}: {{
.CurrentState }}"
todobackend_migrate.1: Complete 18 seconds ago
```

To verify that the migrations actually ran, because we enabled CloudWatch logs when we created the Docker Swarm cluster, you can review logs for the `migrate` service in the CloudWatch logs console. When using the Docker for AWS solution templates to deploy your cluster, a single log group called `<cloudformation-stack-name>-lg` is created, which in our case is `docker-swarm-lg`. If you open this log group in the CloudWatch logs console, you will see that log streams exist for every container that is running or has run in the Swarm cluster:

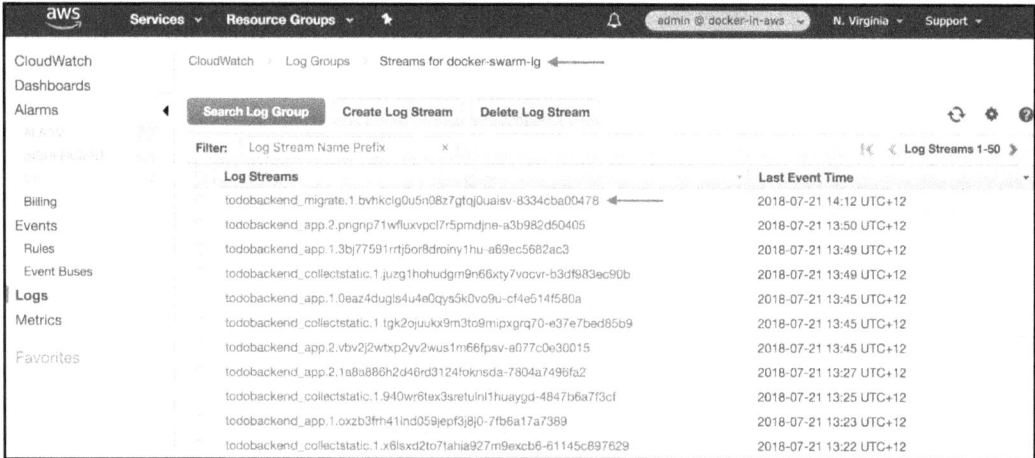

Deploying the migrate service

You can see that the most recent log stream relates to the `migrate` service, and if you open this log stream, you can confirm that database migrations ran successfully:

The migrate service log stream

At this point, your application should be running successfully, and you should be able to interact with the application to create, update, view, and delete Todo items. One good way to verify this, which could be used as a strategy for automated post-deployment testing, is to run the acceptance tests you created in earlier chapters that are included in the todobackend release image, ensuring that you pass in the external load balancer URL via the APP_URL environment variable:

```
> docker run -it --rm \
  -e
APP_URL=http://docker-sw-external-1a5qzeykya672-1599369435.us-east-1.e
lb.amazonaws.com \
  385605022855.dkr.ecr.us-east-1.amazonaws.com/docker-in-
aws/todobackend:3db46c4 \
  bats /app/src/acceptance.bats

Processing secrets []...
1..4
ok 1 todobackend root
```

```
ok 2 todo items returns empty list
ok 3 create todo item
ok 4 delete todo item
```

You have now successfully deployed the todobackend application to a Docker Swarm cluster running in AWS, and I encourage you to further test that your application is production ready by tearing down/recreating the stack, and running a few example deployments by making test commits and creating new application versions to deploy.

Once complete, you should commit the changes you have made, and don't forget to destroy your Docker Swarm cluster by deleting the `docker-swarm` stack in the CloudFormation console.

Summary

In this chapter, you learned how to deploy Docker applications using Docker Swarm and the Docker for AWS solution. Docker for AWS provides a CloudFormation template that allows you to set up a Docker Swarm cluster within minutes, and also provides integration with AWS services including the Elastic Load Balancer service, Elastic File System, and Elastic Block Store.

After creating a Docker Swarm cluster, you learned how to establish remote access to a Swarm manager for your local Docker clients by configuring an SSH tunnel, which links to the `/var/run/docker.sock` socket file on your Swarm manager and presents it as a local endpoint your Docker client can interact with. This makes the experience of managing your Swarm clusters similar to managing your local Docker Engine.

You learned how to create and deploy Docker services, which typically represent a long-running application, but may also represent one-shot tasks like running database migrations or generating static content files. Docker stacks represent complex multi-service environments, and are defined using the Docker Compose version 3 specification and deployed using the `docker stack deploy` command. One advantage of using Docker Swarm is access to the Docker secrets feature, which allows you to store secrets securely in the encrypted raft log that is automatically replicated and shared across all nodes in the cluster. Docker secrets can then be exposed to services as in-memory tmpfs mounts at `/run/secrets`. You have already learned how easy it is to configure your applications to integrate with the Docker secrets feature.

Finally, you learned how to address common operational challenges associated with running your containers in production, such as how to provide access to durable, persistent storage in the form of EBS volumes that can be automatically relocated with your containers, how to provide access to shared volumes using EFS, and how to orchestrate deployment of new application features , supporting the ability to run one-shot tasks and rolling upgrades of your application services.

In the next and final chapter of this book, you will be introduced to the AWS Elastic Kubernetes Service (EKS), which was launched mid 2018 and provides support for Kubernetes, the leading open source container management platform that competes with Docker Swarm.

Questions

1. True/false: Docker Swarm is a native feature of the Docker Engine.
2. What Docker client command do you use to create a service?
3. True/false: Docker Swarm includes three node types—manager, worker, and agent.
4. True/false: Docker for AWS provides integration with AWS application load balancers.
5. True/false: The Cloudstor AWS volume plugin creates an EFS-backed volume when the backing is set to relocatable.
6. True/false: You create a database service that uses the Cloudstor AWS volume plugin to provide an EBS-backed volume that is located in the availability zone us-west-1a. A failure occurs and a new database service container is created in the availability zone us-west-1b. In this scenario, the original EBS volume will be reattached to the new database service container.
7. What is the flag you need to append to Docker Stack deploy and Docker service create commands to integrate with private Docker registries?
8. You deploy a stack that downloads an image from ECR. The first deployment succeeds, however when you attempt to perform a new deployment the next day, you notice that your Docker swarm nodes cannot pull the ECR image. How can you fix this?
9. Which version of the Docker Compose specification should you use for defining Docker Swarm stacks?
10. True/false: When configuring a single shot service, you should configure a restart policy as always.

Further reading

You can check the following links for more information about the topics covered in this chapter:

- Docker Community Edition for AWS: `https://store.docker.com/editions/community/docker-ce-aws`
- Docker for AWS documentation: `https://docs.docker.com/docker-for-aws`
- Docker Compose file version 3 reference: `https://docs.docker.com/compose/compose-file/`
- Docker for AWS persistent data volumes: `https://docs.docker.com/docker-for-aws/persistent-data-volumes/`
- Docker for AWS template archive: `https://docs.docker.com/docker-for-aws/archive/`
- Managing sensitive data with Docker secrets: `https://docs.docker.com/engine/swarm/secrets/`
- Docker command-line reference: `https://docs.docker.com/engine/reference/commandline/cli/`
- Docker Get Started - Part 4: Swarms: `https://docs.docker.com/get-started/part4/`
- Docker Get Started - Part 5: Stacks: `https://docs.docker.com/get-started/part5`
- Docker for AWS Swarm ECR auto login: `https://github.com/mRoca/docker-swarm-aws-ecr-auth`
- SSH agent forwarding: `https://developer.github.com/v3/guides/using-ssh-agent-forwarding/`

17
Elastic Kubernetes Service

Kubernetes is a popular open source container management platform originally developed by Google, who based Kubernetes on Google's own internal **Borg** (`https:/ /kubernetes.io/blog/2015/04/borg-predecessor-to-kubernetes/`) container platform. Kubernetes draws on Google's extensive experience of running containers at scale, and is now supported by all of the major cloud platform providers with the release of the AWS Elastic Kubernetes Service (EKS). EKS provides a managed Kubernetes cluster to which you can deploy your container applications, without having to worry about day-to-day operational overheads and the complexities of cluster management. AWS has performed all the heavy lifting of establishing a robust and scalable platform, making it easier than ever to get up and running with Kubernetes.

In this chapter, you will be introduced to the world of Kubernetes, we will work through how we can configure Kubernetes to ensure we are able to successfully deploy and operate the sample application we have used through this book, and then establish an EKS cluster in AWS where you will deploy the application using the configuration you have developed locally. This will provide practical, real-world insights into how, as an application owner, you can deploy your container workloads to Kubernetes, and how you can quickly get up and running with EKS.

We will first learn how you can work with the platform locally, using the native support that Docker for Mac and Docker for Windows now include for Kubernetes. You can spin up a local single-node cluster straight out of the box, reducing much of the manual configuration you would typically require to get a local environment up and running. You will learn how to create the various types of resources required to run the sample application in Kubernetes, addressing key operational challenges such as providing persistent storage for your application database, secrets management, and running one-shot tasks such as database migrations.

Once you have established a working configuration to get the sample application up and running locally in Kubernetes, we will turn our attention to getting started with EKS, creating an EKS cluster, and establishing an EC2 auto scaling group where worker nodes that run your container workloads are managed. You will learn how to set up access to your cluster from your local environment and proceed to deploy the Kubernetes Dashboard, which provides a rich management user interface from which you can deploy and manage your applications. Finally, you will set up integrations with other AWS services including Elastic Block Store (EBS) and Elastic Load Balancing (ELB), and proceed to deploy the sample application to your EKS cluster.

The following topics will be covered in this chapter:

- Introduction to Kubernetes
- Kubernetes architecture
- Getting started with Kubernetes
- Installing Kubernetes using Docker Desktop
- Creating core Kubernetes resources including pods, deployments, and services
- Creating Persistent volumes
- Creating Kubernetes secrets
- Running Kubernetes jobs
- Creating an EKS cluster
- Establishing access to an EKS cluster
- Deploying applications to EKS

Technical requirements

The following are the technical requirements for this chapter:

- Administrator access to an AWS account
- A local AWS profile, configured as per the instructions in Chapter 3
- AWS CLI version 1.15.71 or higher
- Docker 18.06 or higher
- Docker Compose 1.22 or higher
- GNU Make 3.82 or higher
- This chapter assumes you have completed all of the preceding chapters in this book

The following GitHub URL contains the code samples used in this chapter: `https://github.com/docker-in-aws/docker-in-aws/tree/master/ch17`.

Check out the following video to see the Code in Action:
`http://bit.ly/2LyGtSY`

Introduction to Kubernetes

Kubernetes is an open source container management platform that was open sourced by Google in 2014, and achieved production readiness in 2015 with its 1.0 release. In the space of three years, it has established itself as the most popular container management platform, and is very popular for larger organizations that are looking to run their applications as container workloads. Kubernetes is one of the most popular open source projects (`https://github.com/cncf/velocity/blob/master/docs/top30_chart_creation.md`) on GitHub, and according to `Redmonk`, Kubernetes is used at 54% of Fortune 100 companies as of late 2017.

Key features of Kubernetes include the following:

- **Platform agnostic**: Kubernetes can run anywhere, from your local machine to your data centre and in cloud providers such as AWS, Azure, and Google Cloud, whom all now offer integrated managed Kubernetes offerings.
- **Open source**: Kubernetes' greatest strength is its community and open source nature, which has seen Kubernetes become one of the leading open source projects on the planet. Major organizations and vendors are investing significant time and resources contributing to the platform, ensuring that the entire community benefits from these ongoing enhancements.
- **Pedigree**: Kubernetes' roots are from Google's internal Borg platform, which has been running containers at scale since the early 2000s. Google is one of the pioneers of container technology and is without a doubt one of, if not the largest, adopters of containers – back in 2014, Google indicated that they were running 2 billion containers every week, at a time when most enterprises had only just heard about containers through a new project called Docker that was taking the tech industry by storm. This pedigree and heritage ensures many of the lessons Google has learned over its many years of running containers at scale are encapsulated in the Kubernetes platform.

- **Production grade container management features**: Kubernetes offers all of the container management features that you would expect to see and will come across with other competing platforms. This includes cluster management, multi-host networking, pluggable storage, health checks, service discovery and load balancing, service scaling and rolling updates, desired stage configuration, role-based access control, and secret management to name a few. All of these features are implemented in a modular building-block fashion that allows you to tune the system to meet the specific requirements of your organization, and is one of the reasons Kubernetes is now considered the gold standard for enterprise-grade container management.

Kubernetes versus Docker Swarm

In the previous chapter, I provided my own thoughts on Docker Swarm versus Kubernetes, and here I will continue, this time with more of a focus on why you would choose Kubernetes over Docker Swarm. As you work through this chapter, it should become apparent that Kubernetes has a more elaborate architecture that means there is a higher learning curve, and what I cover in this chapter only really scratches the surface of what is possible with Kubernetes. That said, once you get your head around these concepts, at least from my perspective, you should see that ultimately Kubernetes is more powerful with greater flexibility, and arguably it's probably fair to state that Kubernetes certainly feels more "enterprise-grade" than Docker Swarm, with many more knobs you can tune to tailor Kubernetes to your specific needs.

Probably the biggest advantage Kubernetes has over Docker Swarm and other competitors is its community, which is significant and means that information about almost any configuration scenario you can think of, can be readily found across the wider Kubernetes community and ecosystem. There has been a lot of momentum behind the Kubernetes movement, and this only seems to be growing as leading vendors and providers such as AWS embrace Kubernetes with their own offerings and solutions.

Kubernetes architecture

Architecturally, Kubernetes organizes itself in the form of a cluster, where master nodes form the cluster control plane, and worker nodes run your actual container workloads:

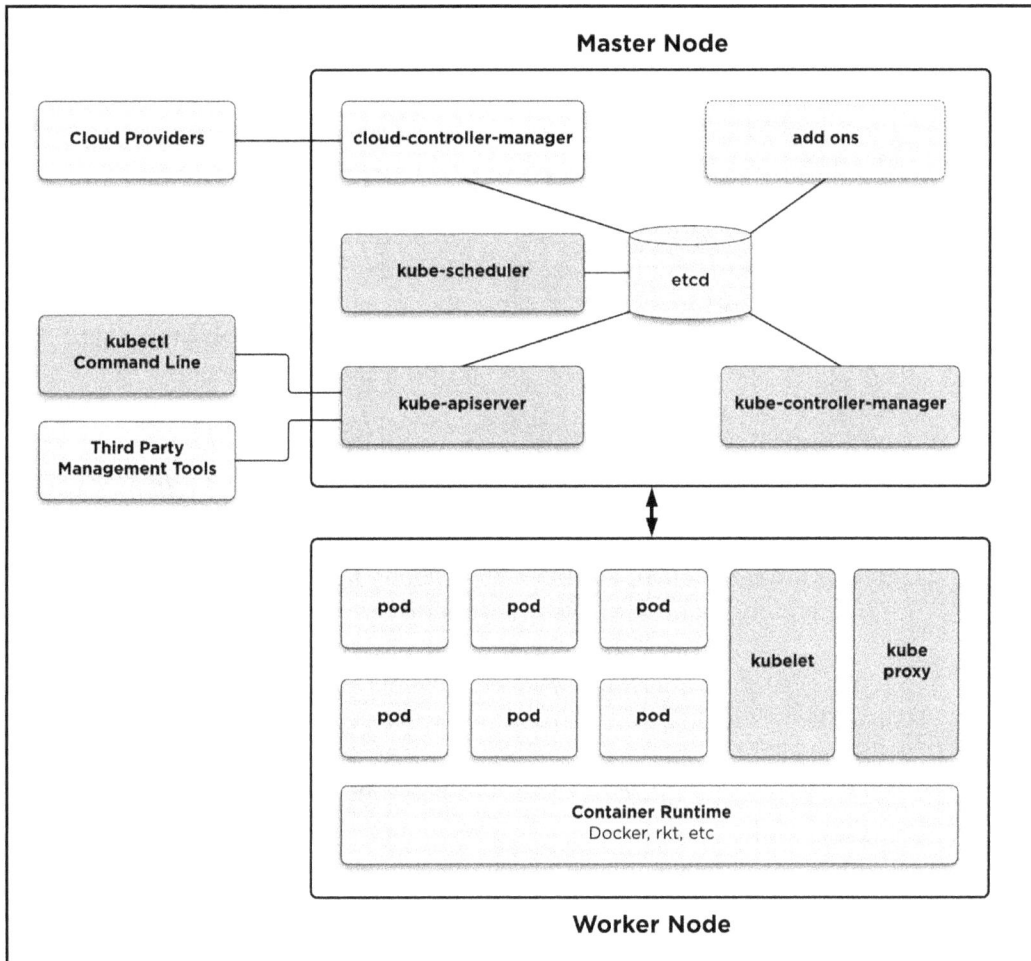

Kubernetes architecture

Within each master node, a number of components exist:

- **kube-apiserver**: This exposes the Kubernetes API and is the frontend component that you use to interact with the Kubernetes control plane.
- **etcd**: This provides a distributed and highly available key/value store across the cluster that is used to store Kubernetes configuration and operational data.
- **kube-scheduler**: This schedules pods onto worker nodes, taking into consideration resource requirements, constraints, data locality, and other factors. You will learn more about pods later on, but for now you can think of them as a collection of associated containers and volumes that collectively need to be create created, updated, and deployed together.
- **kube-controller-manager**: This is responsible for managing controllers, which consists of a number of components that detects when your nodes go down, ensures that the correct number of instances or replicas of your pods are running, publishes service endpoints for the applications running in your pods, and manages service accounts and API access tokens for the cluster.
- **cloud-controller-manager**: This provides controllers that interact with an underlying cloud provider, enabling cloud providers to support features specific to their platform. Examples of cloud controllers include service controllers, which create, update, and delete cloud provider load balancers, and volume controllers, which create, attach, detach, and delete the various storage volume technologies supported by the cloud provider.
- **Add-ons**: A number of add-ons are available that extend the functionality of your cluster. These run in the form of pods and services that provide cluster features. One add-on that is typically deployed on most installations is the cluster DNS add-on, which provides automatic DNS naming and resolution for services and pods running on the cluster.

On all nodes, the following components exist:

- **kubelet**: An agent that runs on each node in the cluster and ensures all containers in a pod are healthy and running. The kubelet can also collect container metrics that can be published to monitoring systems.
- **kube-proxy**: This manages network communications, port mappings, and routing rules required on each node to support the various service abstractions that Kubernetes supports.

- **Container runtime**: This provides the container engine that runs containers. The most popular container runtime that's supported is Docker, however under container runtimes such as rkt (Rocket) or any OCI runtime-spec implementation can be supported.
- **Pods**: A pod is the core unit of work for deploying your container applications. Each pod consists of one more containers and associated resources, and a single network interface, meaning each container in a given pod shares the same network stack.

Note that worker nodes only run the components previously listed directly, while master nodes run all of the components we have discussed to date, allowing master nodes to also run container workloads for scenarios such as a single-node cluster.

Kubernetes also provides a client component called **kubectl**, which provides the ability to manage your clusters via the Kubernetes API. **kubectl** is supported on Windows, macOS, and Linux, and allows you to easily manage and switch between multiple clusters, running both locally and remotely.

Getting started with Kubernetes

Now that you have been briefly introduced to Kubernetes, let's focus on getting up and running with Kubernetes in your local environment.

Earlier in this book when you set up your local development environment, if you are using macOS or Windows, you installed the community edition (CE) versions of Docker Desktop (Docker for Mac or Docker for Windows, which I may refer to collectively as Docker Desktop in this chapter), which includes native support for Kubernetes.

> If you are using a variant of Docker for Mac/Windows that does not support Kubernetes, or are using Linux, you can install minikube by following the instructions at `https://github.com/kubernetes/minikube`. Most of the examples included in this section should work with minikube, although features such as load balancing and dynamic host path provisioning may not be directly supported and require some additional configuration.

To enable Kubernetes, select **Kubernetes** in your local Docker Desktop settings, and check the **Enable Kubernetes** option. Once you click **Apply**, Kubernetes will be installed and will take a few minutes to get up and running:

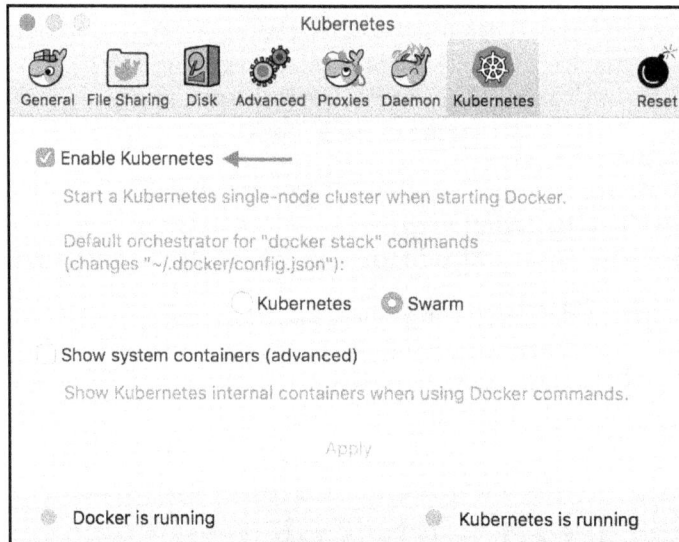

Enabling Kubernetes using Docker for Mac

Docker Desktop also installs and configures the Kubernetes command-line utility kubectl automatically for you, which can be used to verify your installation:

```
> kubectl get nodes
NAME                STATUS   ROLES    AGE   VERSION
docker-for-desktop  Ready    master   1m    v1.10.3
```

If you are using Docker for Windows in conjunction with the Linux subsystem for Windows, you will need to install kubectl into the subsystem by running the following commands (see https://kubernetes.io/docs/tasks/tools/install-kubectl/#install-kubectl-binary-via-native-package-management for more details):

```
sudo apt-get update && sudo apt-get install -y apt-transport-https
curl -s https://packages.cloud.google.com/apt/doc/apt-key.gpg | sudo
apt-key add -
sudo touch /etc/apt/sources.list.d/kubernetes.list
echo "deb http://apt.kubernetes.io/ kubernetes-xenial main" | sudo tee
-a /etc/apt/sources.list.d/kubernetes.list
sudo apt-get update
sudo apt-get install -y kubectl
```

After installing `kubectl`, if you previously changed your Linux subsystem home folder to your Windows home folder, you should be able now interact with your local Kubernetes cluster without further configuration.

If your home folder is different from the Windows home folder (this is the case by default), then you will need to set up a symbolic link that points to the `kubectl` config file in your Windows home folder, after which you should be able to use `kubectl` to interact with your local Kubernetes installation:

```
# Only required if Linux Subsystem home folder is different from
Windows home folder
$ mkdir -p ~/.kube
$ ln -s /mnt/c/Users/<username>/.kube/config ~/.kube/config
$ kubectl get nodes
NAME                STATUS  ROLES   AGE  VERSION
docker-for-desktop  Ready   master  1m   v1.10.3
```

> The Linux subsytem for Windows also allows you to run Windows command-line programs, so alternatively you can run `kubectl.exe` to invoke the Windows kubectl component.

Creating a pod

In Kubernetes, you deploy your applications as *pods*, which refer to one or more containers and other resources that are closely related to each other and collectively represent your application. A **pod** is the core unit of work in Kubernetes and is conceptually similar to an ECS task definition, although under the hood they work in a completely different way.

> A common shorthand code for Kubernetes is k8s, where the "ubernete" portion of the name Kubernetes is replaced with the digit 8, representing the number of characters in "ubernete".

Before we create our first pod, let's establish a folder called `k8s` in the todobackend repository that will hold all Kubernetes configuration for the todobackend application, and then create a folder called `app`, which will store all resource definitions that relate to the core todobackend applications:

```
todobackend> mkdir -p k8s/app
todobackend> touch k8s/app/deployment.yaml
```

The following code demonstrates a basic pod definition for the todobackend application, which we will save to the `k8s/app/deployment.yaml` file:

```
apiVersion: v1
kind: Pod
metadata:
  name: todobackend
  labels:
    app: todobackend
spec:
  containers:
  - name: todobackend
    image: 385605022855.dkr.ecr.us-east-1.amazonaws.com/docker-in-
aws/todobackend
    imagePullPolicy: IfNotPresent
    command:
    - uwsgi
    - --http=0.0.0.0:8000
    - --module=todobackend.wsgi
    - --master
    - --die-on-term
    - --processes=4
    - --threads=2
    - --check-static=/public
    env:
    - name: DJANGO_SETTINGS_MODULE
      value: todobackend.settings_release
```

The format of the pod configuration file is easy to follow, and in general most of the parameters that you see map to parameters of the same name if you are used to defining your containers using Docker Compose. One important difference that does tend to cause confusion is the `command` parameter – in Kubernetes, this parameter is the equivalent of the `ENTRYPOINT` Dockerfile directive and `entrypoint` parameter in a Docker Compose service specification, while the `args` parameter in Kubernetes is equivalent to the CMD directive (Dockerfile) and `command` service parameter (Docker Compose). This means that in the preceding configuration, the default entrypoint script in our container is bypassed, and instead the uwsgi web server will be run directly.

The `imagePullPolicy` property value of `IfNotPresent` configures Kubernetes to only pull an image if one is not available in the local Docker Engine registry, which means you must ensure the existing todobackend Docker Compose workflow has been run to build and tag the todobackend image locally, before attempting to create the pod. This is required as Kubernetes only includes native support for ECR when you are running Kubernetes on AWS EC2 instances, and does not natively support ECR when you are running Kubernetes outside of AWS.

> There are a number of third-party plugins available that allow you to manage AWS credentials and pull ECR images. A popular example can be found at `https://github.com/upmc-enterprises/registry-creds`

To create our pod and verify that it is running, you can run the `kubectl apply` command, with the `-f` flag referencing the deployment file you just created, followed by the `kubectl get pods` command:

```
> kubectl apply -f k8s/app/deployment.yaml
pod "todobackend" created
> kubectl get pods
NAME            READY    STATUS     RESTARTS    AGE
todobackend     1/1      Running    0           7s
> docker ps --format "{{ .Names }}"
k8s_todobackend_todobackend_default_1b436412-9001-11e8-
b7af-025000000001_0
> docker ps --format "{{ .ID }}: {{ .Command }} ({{ .Status }})"
fc0c8acdd438: "uwsgi --http=0.0.0...." (Up 16 seconds)
> docker ps --format "{{ .ID }} Ports: {{ .Ports }}"
fc0c8acdd438 Ports:
```

You can see that the status of the pod is `Running` and that a container has been deployed to the single-node Kubernetes cluster running in your local Docker Desktop environment. One important point to note is that the todobackend container that has been deployed has no means of communicating with the outside world, as there are no networks ports that have been published from the pod and its associated container.

An interesting aspect of Kubernetes is that you can use the Kubernetes API to interact with your pods. To demonstrate this, you first run the `kubectl proxy` command, which sets up a local HTTP proxy that exposes the API via a plain old HTTP interface:

```
> kubectl proxy
Starting to serve on 127.0.0.1:8001
```

You can now access the container port 8000 on your pod via the URL
`http://localhost:8001/api/v1/namespaces/default/pods/todobackend:8000/proxy/`:

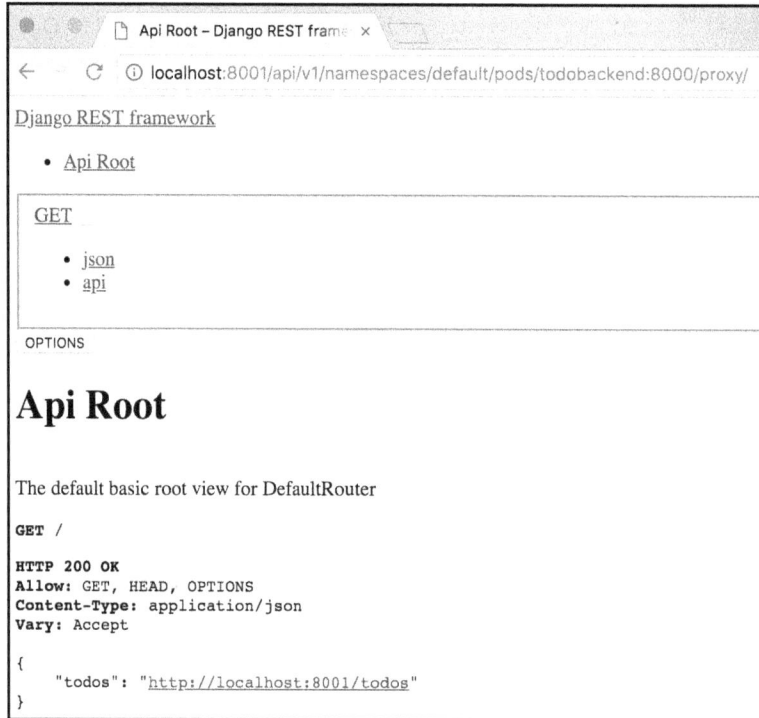

Running the kubectl proxy

As you can see, the todobackend application is running, although it is missing static content as we haven't generated this yet. Notice also that the todos link at the bottom of the page (`http://localhost:8001/todos`) is invalid, as the todobackend application has no knowledge of the API path that is called to access the application via the proxy.

Another interesting feature of Kubernetes is the ability to expose a port from your Kubernetes client to the application by running the `kubectl port-forward` command, which publishes a local port on the client and connects it to a specified pod using the Kubernetes API:

```
> kubectl proxy
Starting to serve on 127.0.0.1:8001
^C
```

```
> kubectl port-forward todobackend 8000:8000
Forwarding from 127.0.0.1:8000 -> 8000
Forwarding from [::1]:8000 -> 8000
Handling connection for 8000
```

If you now attempt to access `http://localhost:8000`, you should see the todobackend home page, and the todos link at the bottom of the page should now be accessible:

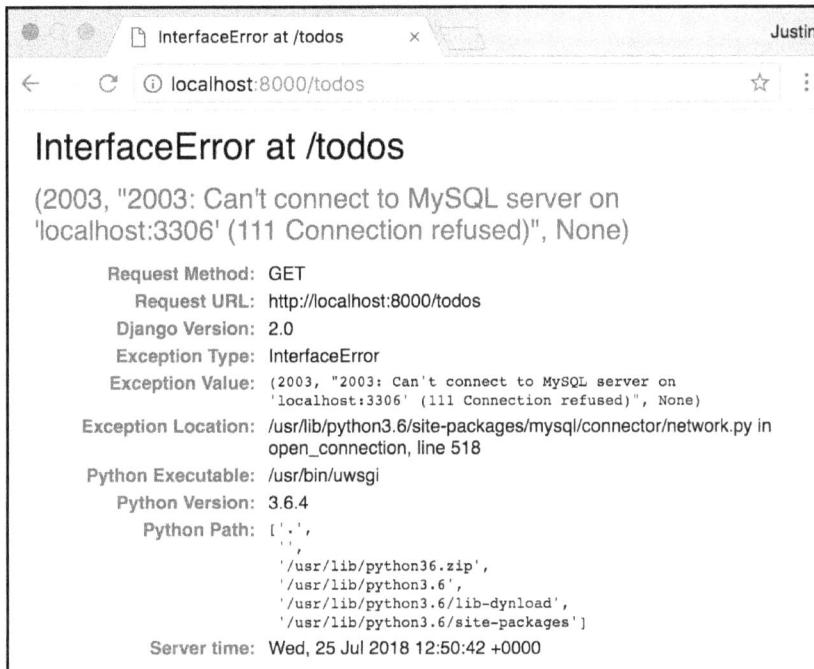

Accessing a port forwarded pod

You can see that, once again, our application is not in a fully functional state, given we haven't configured any database settings as yet.

Creating a deployment

Although we have been able to publish our todobackend application, the mechanism that we have used to do this is not suitable for real-world production use, and is only really useful for limited local development scenarios.

One key requirement for running our application in the real-world is the ability to scale up or down the number of instances or *replicas* of the application container. To achieve this, Kubernetes supports a class of resources referred to as *controllers*, which are responsible for coordinating, orchestrating, and managing multiple replicas of a given pod. One popular type of controller is the *deployment* resource, which as the name suggests includes support for creating and updating new versions of your pods along with features such as rolling upgrades and support for rollbacks should a deployment fail.

The following example demonstrates updating the `k8s/app/deployment.yaml` file in the `todobackend` repository to define a deployment resource:

```
apiVersion: apps/v1
kind: Deployment
metadata:
  name: todobackend
  labels:
    app: todobackend
spec:
  replicas: 2
  selector:
    matchLabels:
      app: todobackend
  template:
    metadata:
      labels:
        app: todobackend
    spec:
      containers:
      - name: todobackend
        image: 385605022855.dkr.ecr.us-east-1.amazonaws.com/docker-in-
aws/todobackend
        imagePullPolicy: IfNotPresent
        readinessProbe:
          httpGet:
            port: 8000
        livenessProbe:
          httpGet:
            port: 8000
        command:
        - uwsgi
        - --http=0.0.0.0:8000
        - --module=todobackend.wsgi
        - --master
        - --die-on-term
        - --processes=4
        - --threads=2
```

```
        - --check-static=/public
        env:
        - name: DJANGO_SETTINGS_MODULE
          value: todobackend.settings_release
```

We update the previous pod resource to now be a deployment resource, with the `template` property of the top-level `spec` property (i.e. `spec.template`) defining inline the pod that should be deployed. A key concept of deployments and Kubernetes in general is the use of set-based label selector matching (`https://kubernetes.io/docs/concepts/overview/working-with-objects/labels/#label-selectors`) to determine the resources or pods that the deployment applies to. In the preceding example, the deployment resource `spec` specifies two `replicas` and uses `selectors.matchLabels` to match the deployment to a pod that includes the label `app` with a value of `todobackend`. This is a simple yet powerful paradigm that allows you to create your own structures and relationships between resources in a flexible and loosely coupled manner. Notice that we also add the `readinessProbe` and `livenessProbe` properties to the container definition, which create a readiness probe and liveness probe, respectively. A readiness probe defines an action that should be performed by Kubernetes to determine if a container is ready, while a liveness probe is used to determine if a container is still healthy. In the preceding example, the readiness probe uses HTTP GET requests to port 8000 to determine when the deployment controller should permit connections to be forwarded to the container, while the liveness probe is used to restart the container in the event it no longer responds to the liveness probes. Refer to `https://kubernetes.io/docs/tasks/configure-pod-container/configure-liveness-readiness-probes/` for further information on the different types of probes and how they can be used.

To create the new deployment resource, we can first remove the existing pod and then apply the `k8s/app/deployment.yaml` file in the `todobackend` repository using `kubectl`:

```
> kubectl delete pods/todobackend
pod "todobackend" deleted
> kubectl apply -f k8s/app/deployment.yaml
deployment.apps "todobackend" created
> kubectl get deployments
NAME                      DESIRED   CURRENT   UP-TO-DATE   AVAILABLE   AGE
todobackend               2         2         2            2           12s
> kubectl get pods
NAME                                READY   STATUS    RESTARTS   AGE
todobackend-7869d9965f-1h944        1/1     Running   0          17s
todobackend-7869d9965f-v986s        1/1     Running   0          17s
```

After creating the deployment, you can see that the configured number of replicas are deployed in the form of two pods, each with a unique name. The state for each pod will transition to ready as soon as the readiness probe you configured is successful.

Creating a service

At this point, we have defined a pod for our application and deployed multiple replicas of our application using a deployment resource, and we now need to ensure external clients can connect to our application. Given that we have multiple replicas of our application running, we require a component that is able to provide a stable service endpoint, track the location of each replica, and load balance incoming connections across all replicas.

Services are the Kubernetes resources that provide such features, where each service is assigned a virtual IP address that can be used to access a given set of pods, and incoming connections to the virtual IP address are load balanced to each pod replica, based upon iptables rules that are managed and updated via a standard Kubernetes system resource called the kube-proxy:

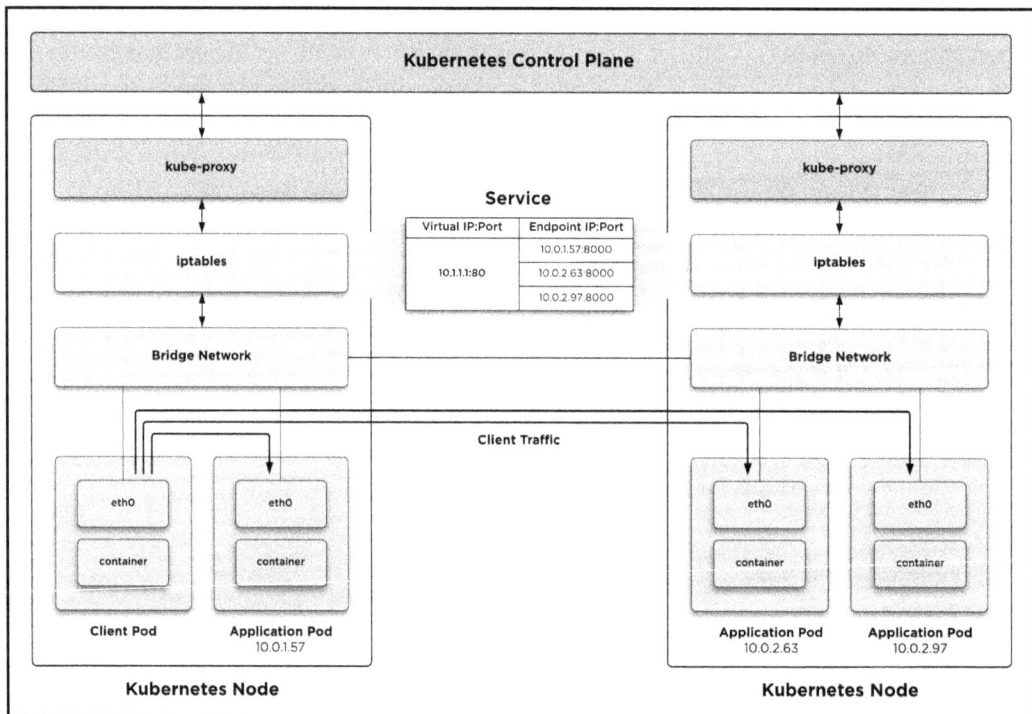

Services and endpoints in Kubernetes

In the preceding diagram, a client pod is attempting to communicate with the application pod using a virtual IP address of 10.1.1.1 on port 80 (10.1.1.1:80). Note that the service virtual IP address is published on every node in the cluster, with the **kube-proxy** component responsible for updating iptables rules that select an appropriate endpoint that client connections should be routed to in a round robin fashion. Because the virtual IP address is published on every node in the cluster, any client on any node can communicate with the service, and traffic is distributed across the cluster in an even manner.

Now that you have a high level understanding of how a service works, let's actually define a new service in the k8s/app/deployment.yaml file that's located within the todobackend repository:

```
apiVersion: v1
kind: Service
metadata:
  name: todobackend
spec:
  selector:
    app: todobackend
  ports:
  - protocol: TCP
    port: 80
    targetPort: 8000
---
apiVersion: apps/v1
kind: Deployment
metadata:
  name: todobackend
  labels:
    app: todobackend
...
...
```

Notice that you can define multiple resources in a single YAML file by using the --- separator to separate each resource, and that we can create a service called todobackend that uses label matching to bind the service to any pods with a label of app=todobackend. In the spec.ports section, we configure port 80 as the incoming or listener port on the service, which load balances connections to a targetPort of 8000 on each pod.

With the definition of our service in place, you can now deploy the service using the `kubectl apply` command:

```
> kubectl apply -f k8s/app/deployment.yaml
service "todobackend" created
deployment.apps "todobackend" unchanged
> kubectl get svc
NAME                TYPE        CLUSTER-IP      EXTERNAL-IP    PORT(S)
AGE
kubernetes          ClusterIP   10.96.0.1       <none>         443/TCP
8h
todobackend         ClusterIP   10.103.210.17   <none>         80/TCP
10s
> kubectl get endpoints
NAME            ENDPOINTS                       AGE
kubernetes      192.168.65.3:6443               1d
todobackend     10.1.0.27:8000,10.1.0.30:8000   16h
```

You can use the `kubectl get svc` command to view current services, and notice that each service includes a unique cluster IP address, which is the virtual IP address that other resources in the cluster can use to communicate with the pods associated with the service. The `kubectl get endpoints` command shows the actual endpoints associated with each service, and you can see that connections to the `todobackend` service virtual IP address of `10.103.210.17:80` will be load balanced to `10.1.0.27:8000` and `10.1.0.30:8000`.

Each service is also allocated a unique DNS name in the form of `<service-name>.<namespace>.svc.cluster.local`. The default namespace in Kubernetes is called `default`, so for our todobackend application, it will be assigned a name of `todobackend.default.svc.cluster.local`, which you can verify is reachable within the cluster by using the `kubectl run` command:

```
> kubectl run dig --image=googlecontainer/dnsutils --restart=Never --
rm=true --tty --stdin \
    --command -- dig todobackend a +search +noall +answer
; <<>> DiG 9.8.4-rpz2+rl005.12-P1 <<>> todobackend a +search +noall
+answer
;; global options: +cmd
todobackend.default.svc.cluster.local. 30 IN A    10.103.210.17
```

In the preceding example, you can simply query for todobackend, as Kubernetes sends the DNS search domain to
`<namespace>.svc.cluster.local` (`default.svc.cluster.local`, in our use case), and you can see that this resolves to the cluster IP address of the todobackend service.

It's important to note that the cluster IP address is only reachable within the Kubernetes cluster – we can't reach this service externally without further configuration.

Exposing a service

To allow external clients and systems to communicate with Kubernetes services, you must expose the service to the outside world. In true Kubernetes style, there are a variety of options available to achieve this, which are controlled by Kubernetes `ServiceTypes`:

- **Node ports**: This service type maps an external port on each Kubernetes node to the internal cluster IP and port configured for the service. This creates several external connection points for your service that may change as nodes come and go, making it difficult to create a stable external service endpoint.
- **Load balancer**: Represents an external dedicated Layer 4 (TCP or UDP) load balancer that is mapped exclusively to your service. The actual load balancer that is deployed depends on your target platform – for example, with AWS, a classic Elastic Load Balancer is created. This is a very popular option, however one significant limitation is that a load balancer is created per service, meaning that this option can become quite expensive if you have a lot of services.
- **Ingress**: This is a shared Layer 7 (HTTP) load balancer resource that works in a similar fashion to the AWS Application Load Balancer, where connections to a single HTTP/HTTPS endpoint can be routed to multiple services based upon host header or URL path patterns. This is considered the best option for HTTP-based services, given you can share one load balancer across multiple services.

The most popular method to publish your services externally is to use the load balancer method, which works as illustrated in the following diagram:

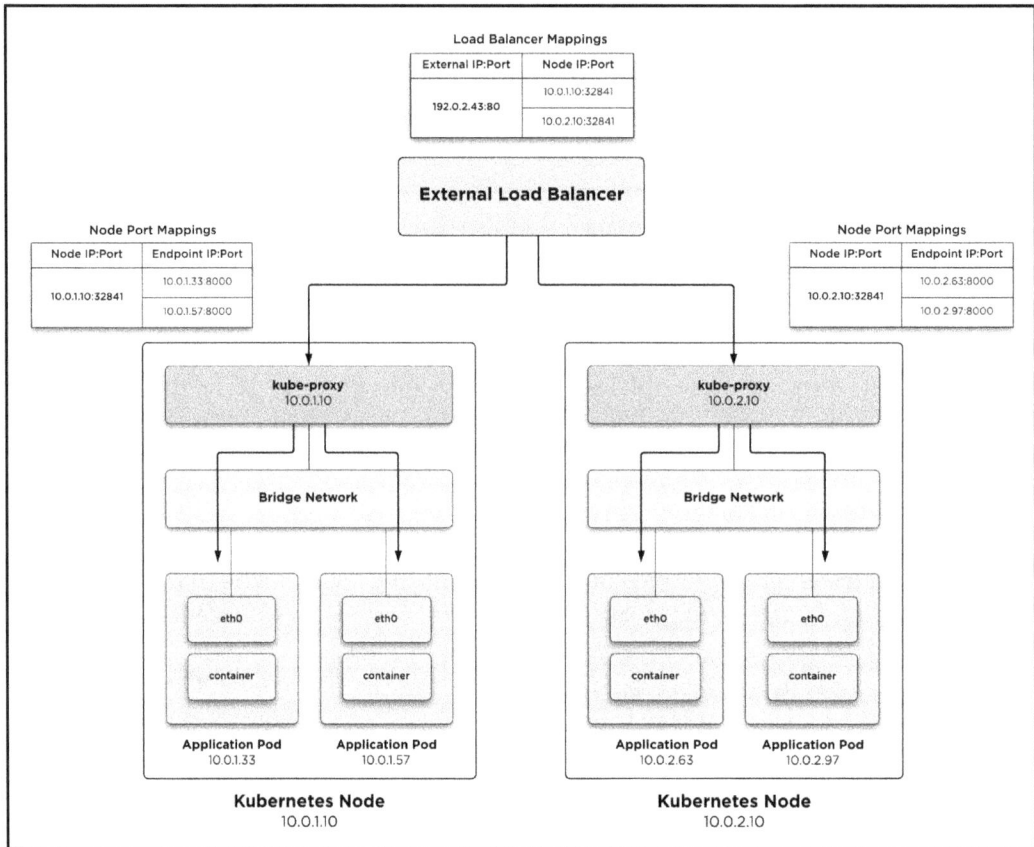

Load balancing in Kubernetes

The external load balancer publishes the external service endpoint that clients will connect to, which in the preceding example is `192.0.2.43:80`. The load balancer service endpoint will be associated with the nodes in your cluster that have active pods associated with the service, who each have a node port mapping set up via the **kube-proxy** component. The node port mapping is then mapped to each of the local endpoints on the node, allowing traffic to be load balanced efficiently and evenly across the cluster.

> For communications from internal clients within the cluster, communications still take place using the service cluster IP address, as described earlier in this chapter.

Later on in this chapter, we will see how to integrate AWS load balancers with EKS, however for now your local Docker Desktop environment includes support for its own load balancer resource, which publishes an external endpoint on your host for your service. Adding an external load balancer to a service is very simple, as demonstrated in the following example, where we modify the configuration of the k8s/app/deployments.yaml file in the todobackend repository:

```
apiVersion: v1
kind: Service
metadata:
  name: todobackend
spec:
  selector:
    app: todobackend
  ports:
  - protocol: TCP
    port: 80
    targetPort: 8000
  type: LoadBalancer
---
apiVersion: apps/v1
kind: Deployment
metadata:
  name: todobackend
  labels:
    app: todobackend
...
...
```

All that is required to deploy the appropriate load balancer for your environment is to set the spec.type property to LoadBalancer, and Kubernetes will automatically create an external load balancer. You can test this by applying your updated configuration and running the kubectl get svc command:

```
> kubectl apply -f k8s/app/deployment.yaml
service "todobackend" configured
deployment.apps "todobackend" unchanged
> kubectl get svc
NAME                    TYPE          CLUSTER-IP      EXTERNAL-IP
PORT(S)         AGE
kubernetes              ClusterIP     10.96.0.1       <none>
```

```
443/TCP         8h
todobackend              LoadBalancer    10.103.210.17    localhost
80:31417/TCP   10s
> curl localhost
{"todos":"http://localhost/todos"}
```

Notice that the `kubectl get svc` output now shows that the external IP address of the todobackend service is localhost (localhost is always the external interface that's reachable by your Docker client when using Docker Desktop) and that it is published externally on port 80, which you can verify is true by running the `curl localhost` command. The external port maps to port 31417 on a single node cluster, which is the port that the **kube-proxy** component listens on in order to support the load balancer architecture we described earlier.

Adding volumes to your pods

Now that we have an understanding of how to publish our application both internally within the Kubernetes cluster and externally to the outside world, we can focus on making the todobackend application fully functional by adding support for the various deployment activities and dependencies of the todobackend application.

We will first tackle the issue of serving static content for the todobackend application – as you know from previous chapters, we need to run a **collectstatic** task that ensures static content is available for the **todobackend** application, and this should be run any time the **todobackend** application is deployed. The **collectstatic** task needs to write static content to a volume that is then mounted by the main application container, so let's discuss how we can add volumes to Kubernetes pods.

Kubernetes has a powerful storage subsystem that supports a variety of volume types, which you can read more about at `https://kubernetes.io/docs/concepts/storage/volumes/#types-of-volumes`. For the **collectstatic** use case, the `emptyDir` volume type is suitable, which is a volume that follows the lifecycle of each pod – it is created and destroyed dynamically with the pod – hence it is suitable as an ephemeral storage type for use cases such as caching and serving static content that can be easily regenerated on pod creation.

The following example demonstrates adding a public `emptyDir` volume to the `k8s/app/deployment.yaml` file:

```
    ...
    ...
    ---
```

```
apiVersion: apps/v1
kind: Deployment
metadata:
  name: todobackend
  labels:
    app: todobackend
spec:
  replicas: 2
  selector:
    matchLabels:
      app: todobackend
  template:
    metadata:
      labels:
        app: todobackend
    spec:
      securityContext:
        fsGroup: 1000
      volumes:
      - name: public
        emptyDir: {}
      containers:
      - name: todobackend
        image: 385605022855.dkr.ecr.us-east-1.amazonaws.com/docker-in-
aws/todobackend
        imagePullPolicy: IfNotPresent
        readinessProbe:
          httpGet:
            port: 8000
        livenessProbe:
          httpGet:
            port: 8000
        volumeMounts:
        - name: public
          mountPath: /public
        command:
        - uwsgi
        - --http=0.0.0.0:8000
        - --module=todobackend.wsgi
        - --master
        - --die-on-term
        - --processes=4
        - --threads=2
        - --check-static=/public
        env:
        - name: DJANGO_SETTINGS_MODULE
          value: todobackend.settings_release
```

We define a volume called `public` in the `spec.Volumes` property of the pod template, and then use the `volumeMounts` property in the todobackend container definition to mount the `public` volume to `/public`. One important configuration requirement for our use case is setting the `spec.securityContext.fsGroup` property, which defines the group ID that will be configured as the group owner for any filesystem mounts in the pod. We set this value to `1000`; recall from earlier chapters that the todobackend image runs as the `app` user, which has a user/group ID of 1000. This configuration ensures that the todobackend container is able to read and write static content to the `public` volume.

If you now deploy your configuration changes, you should be able to use the `kubectl exec` command to inspect the todobackend container filesystem and verify that we can read and write to the `/public` mount:

```
> kubectl apply -f k8s/app/deployment.yaml
service "todobackend" unchanged
deployment.apps "todobackend" configured
> kubectl exec $(kubectl get pods -l app=todobackend -
o=jsonpath='{.items[0].metadata.name}') \
    -it bash
bash-4.4$ touch /public/foo
bash-4.4$ ls -l /public/foo
-rw-r--r-- 1 app app 0 Jul 26 11:28 /public/foo
bash-4.4$ rm /public/foo
```

The `kubectl exec` command is similar to the `docker exec` command, in that it allows you to execute a command within a currently running pod container. This command must reference the name of the pod, and we use the `kubectl get pods` command along with a JSON path query to extract this name. As you can see, the `app` user within the **todobackend** container is able to read and write to the `/public` mount.

Adding init containers to your pods

With an ephemeral volume in place for static content, we can now focus on scheduling the **collectstatic** task to generate static content for our application. Kubernetes has support for `init containers`, which are a special type of container within a pod that are executed before your main application container(s) are started. Kubernetes will ensure that your init containers run to completion and complete successfully before starting your application, and if you specify multiple init containers, Kubernetes will execute them in order, one by one, until all init containers have completed.

The following code demonstrates adding an init container to the `k8s/app/deployment.yaml` file:

```
...
...
---
apiVersion: apps/v1
kind: Deployment
metadata:
  name: todobackend
  labels:
    app: todobackend
spec:
  replicas: 2
  selector:
    matchLabels:
      app: todobackend
  template:
    metadata:
      labels:
        app: todobackend
    spec:
      securityContext:
        fsGroup: 1000
      volumes:
      - name: public
        emptyDir: {}
      initContainers:
      - name: collectstatic
        image: 385605022855.dkr.ecr.us-east-1.amazonaws.com/docker-in-aws/todobackend
        imagePullPolicy: IfNotPresent
        volumeMounts:
        - name: public
          mountPath: /public
        command: ["python3","manage.py","collectstatic","--no-input"]
        env:
        - name: DJANGO_SETTINGS_MODULE
          value: todobackend.settings_release
      containers:
      ...
      ...
```

You can now deploy your changes and use the `kubectl logs` command to verify that the collectstatic init container executed successfully:

```
> kubectl apply -f k8s/app/deployment.yaml
service "todobackend" unchanged
deployment.apps "todobackend" configured
> kubectl logs $(kubectl get pods -l app=todobackend -
o=jsonpath='{.items[0].metadata.name}') \
    -c collectstatic
Copying '/usr/lib/python3.6/site-
packages/django/contrib/admin/static/admin/fonts/README.txt'
...
...
159 static files copied to '/public/static'.
```

If you now browse to `http://localhost` in your browser, you should be able to verify that the static content is now rendering correctly:

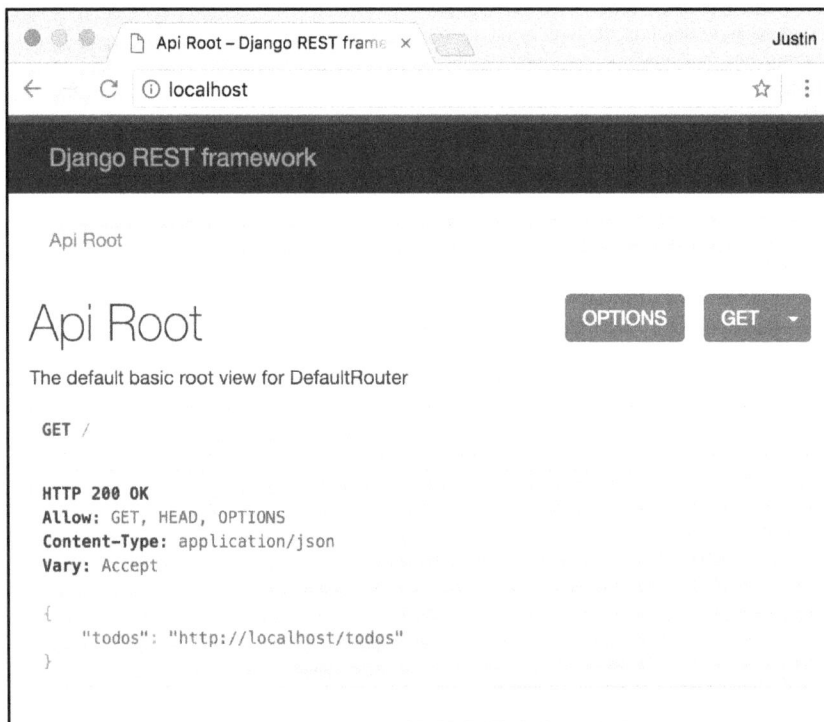

The todobackend application with correct static content

Adding a database service

The next step in getting the **todobackend** application fully functional is to add a database service that will host the **todobackend** application database. We will run this service within our Kubernetes cluster, however in a real-world production use case in AWS, I would typically recommend using the Relational Database Service (RDS).

Defining the database service requires two main configuration tasks:

- Creating persistent storage
- Creating a database service

Creating persistent storage

A key requirement of our database service is persistent storage, and for our single-node local Kubernetes development environment, the `hostPath` volume type represents the standard option for providing simple persistent storage requirements.

Although you can create a **hostPath** volume very easily by specifying a path directly in your volume definition (see the example pod definition at `https://kubernetes.io/docs/concepts/storage/volumes/#hostpath`), one problem with such an approach is that it creates a hard dependency on the underlying volume type, and also requires manual cleanup if you ever want to delete the pod and the data associated with the volumes.

A very useful feature of the Docker Desktop Kubernetes support is the inclusion of a dynamic volume provisioner called `docker.io/hostpath` that automatically creates volumes of type **hostPath** for you, which is available via the default *storage class* that you can view by running the `kubectl get sc` command:

```
> kubectl get sc
NAME                  PROVISIONER          AGE
hostpath (default)    docker.io/hostpath   2d
```

A storage class provides an abstraction over the underlying volume type, meaning your pods can request storage from a specific class. This includes generic requirements such as volume size, without needing to worry about the underlying volume type. In the case of Docker Desktop, a default storage class is included out of the box, which provisions storage requests using the **hostPath** volume type.

However, later on when we set up a Kubernetes cluster in AWS using EKS, we will configure a default storage class that uses the AWS Elastic Block Store (EBS) as the underlying volume type. Taking this approach means that we don't need to change our pod definitions, as we will be referring to the same storage class in each environment.

> If you are using minikube, a dynamic provisioner called `k8s.io/minikube-hostpath` provides similar functionality to the Docker hostpath provisioner, but mounts volumes under `/tmp/hostpath-provisioner`.

To use storage classes rather than specify your volume types directly with your pod definitions, you need to create a *persistent volume claim*, which provides a logical definition of storage requirements such as volume size and access mode. Let's define a persistent volume claim, but before we do this we need to establish a new folder called `k8s/db` in the todobackend repository that will store our database service configuration:

```
todobackend> mkdir -p k8s/db
todobackend> touch k8s/db/storage.yaml
```

Within this folder, we will create a file called `k8s/db/storage.yaml`, in which we will define a persistent volume claim:

```
kind: PersistentVolumeClaim
apiVersion: v1
metadata:
  name: todobackend-data
spec:
  accessModes:
    - ReadWriteOnce
  resources:
    requests:
      storage: 8Gi
```

We create the claim (called `todobackend-data`) in a dedicated file, as this will allow us to independently manage the life cycle of the claim. One property that is not included in the preceding example is the `spec.storageClassName` property – if this is omitted, the default storage class is used, however bear in mind that you can create and reference your own storage classes. The `spec.accessModes` property specifies how the storage should be mounted – in the case of both local storage and EBS storage in AWS, we only want a single container at a time to be able to read and write to the volume, which is encompassed by the `ReadWriteOnce` access mode.

The `spec.resources.requests.storage` property specifies the size of the persistent volume, which in this case we configure as 8 GB.

> If you are using Docker for Windows, you will be prompted to share your C:\ with Docker the first time you attempt to use the Docker hostPath provisioner.

If you now deploy the persistent volume claim using `kubectl`, you can use the `kubectl get pvc` command to view your newly created claim:

```
> kubectl apply -f k8s/db/storage.yaml
persistentvolumeclaim "todobackend-data" created
> kubectl get pvc
NAME                     STATUS   VOLUME
CAPACITY   ACCESS MODES STORAGECLASS   AGE
todobackend-data    Bound    pvc-afba5984-9223-11e8-bc1c-025000000001
8Gi         RWO          hostpath       5s
```

You can see that when you create a persistent volume claim, a persistent volume is dynamically created. When using Docker Desktop, this is actually created in the path `~/.docker/Volumes/<persistent-volume-claim>/<volume>`:

```
> ls -l ~/.docker/Volumes/todobackend-data
total 0
drwxr-xr-x 2 jmenga staff 64 28 Jul 17:04 pvc-afba5984-9223-11e8-
bc1c-025000000001
```

If you are using Docker for Windows and you are using the Windows Subsystem for Linux, you can create a symbolic link to the `.docker` folder on your Windows host:

```
> ln -s /mnt/c/Users/<user-name>/.docker ~/.docker
> ls -l ~/.docker/Volumes/todobackend-data
total 0
drwxrwxrwx 1 jmenga jmenga 4096 Jul 29 17:04 pvc-c02a8614-932d-11e8-
b8aa-00155d010401
```

Note that if you followed the instructions in `Chapter 1`, *Container and Docker Fundamentals*, for setting up the Windows Subsystem for Linux, you already configured `/mnt/c/Users/<user-name>/` as your home directory so you don't need to perform the configuration above.

Creating a database service

Now that we have created a persistent volume claim, we can define the database service. We will define the database service within a new file called k8s/db/deployment.yaml in the todobackend repository, where we create a service and deployment definition:

```
apiVersion: v1
kind: Service
metadata:
  name: todobackend-db
spec:
  selector:
    app: todobackend-db
  clusterIP: None
  ports:
  - protocol: TCP
    port: 3306
---
apiVersion: apps/v1
kind: Deployment
metadata:
  name: todobackend-db
  labels:
    app: todobackend-db
spec:
  selector:
    matchLabels:
      app: todobackend-db
  template:
    metadata:
      labels:
        app: todobackend-db
    spec:
      volumes:
      - name: data
        persistentVolumeClaim:
          claimName: todobackend-data
      containers:
      - name: db
        image: mysql:5.7
        livenessProbe:
          exec:
            command:
            - /bin/sh
            - -c
            - "mysqlshow -h 127.0.0.1 -u $(MYSQL_USER) -p$(cat
```

```
/tmp/secrets/MYSQL_PASSWORD)"
        volumeMounts:
        - name: data
          mountPath: /var/lib/mysql
        args:
        - --ignore-db-dir=lost+found
        env:
        - name: MYSQL_DATABASE
          value: todobackend
        - name: MYSQL_USER
          value: todo
        - name: MYSQL_ROOT_PASSWORD
          value: super-secret-password
        - name: MYSQL_PASSWORD
          value: super-secret-password
```

We first define a service called `todobackend-db`, which publishes the default MySQL TCP port `3306`. Notice that we specify a `spec.clusterIP` value of `None`, which creates a headless service. Headless services are useful for single instance services and allow the IP address of the pod to be used as the service endpoint, rather than using the **kube-proxy** component with a virtual IP address that would only ever load balance to a single endpoint. Defining a headless service will still publish a DNS record for the service but will associate the record with the pod IP address, ensuring that the **todobackend** application can connect to the `todobackend-db` service by name. We then create a deployment for the `todobackend-db` service, and define a volume called `data` which is mapped to the persistent volume claim we created earlier and mounted to the database data directory (`/var/lib/mysql`) in the MySQL container. Notice that we specify the `args` property (the equivalent of the CMD/command directive in Docker/Docker Compose), which configures MySQL to ignore the `lost+found` directory if it is present. Although this won't be a problem when using Docker Desktop, it will be a problem in AWS for the same reasons discussed in the previous Docker Swarm chapter. Finally, we create a liveness probe of type `exec` that executes the `mysqlshow` command to check that a connection to the MySQL database can be made locally within the MySQL container. Because the MySQL secret is located in a file, we wrap the MySQL command in a shell process (`/bin/sh`), which allows us to use the `$(cat /tmp/secrets/MYSQL_PASSWORD)` command substitution.

> Kubernetes allows you resolve environment variables at execution time by using the syntax `$(<environment variable>)`. For example, the `$(MYSQL_USER)` value included in the preceding liveness probe will be resolved to the environment variable `MYSQL_USER` when the probe is executed. See `https://kubernetes.io/docs/tasks/inject-data-application/define-command-argument-container/#use-environment-variables-to-define-arguments` for more details.

If you now deploy the database service and deployment resources, you can use the `kubectl get svc` and `kubectl get endpoints` commands to verify your headless service configuration:

```
> kubectl apply -f k8s/db/deployment.yaml
service "todobackend-db" created
deployment.apps "todobackend-db" created
> kubectl get svc
NAME                 TYPE           CLUSTER-IP      EXTERNAL-IP
PORT(S)         AGE
kubernetes           ClusterIP      10.96.0.1       <none>
443/TCP         8h
todobackend          LoadBalancer   10.103.210.17   localhost
80:31417/TCP    1d
todobackend-db       ClusterIP      None            <none>
3306/TCP        6s
> kubectl get endpoints
NAME             ENDPOINTS                         AGE
kubernetes       192.168.65.3:6443                 2d
todobackend      10.1.0.44:8000,10.1.0.46:8000     1d
todobackend-db   10.1.0.55:3306                    14s
```

Notice that the `todobackend-db` service is deployed with a cluster IP of none, which means that the published endpoint of the service is the IP address of the `todobackend-db` pod.

You can also verify that the data volume was created correctly by listing the contents of the physical volume directory in `~/.docker/Volumes/todobackend-data` on your local host:

```
> ls -l ~/.docker/Volumes/todobackend-data/pvc-afba5984-9223-11e8-bc1c-025000000001
total 387152
-rw-r----- 1 jmenga wheel 56 27 Jul 21:49 auto.cnf
-rw------- 1 jmenga wheel 1675 27 Jul 21:49 ca-key.pem
```

```
...
...
drwxr-x--- 3 jmenga wheel 96 27 Jul 21:49 todobackend
```

If you now delete just the database service and deployment, you should be able to verify that the persistent volume is not removed and persists, meaning that you can then recreate the database service and reattach to the data volume with no data loss:

```
> kubectl delete -f k8s/db/deployment.yaml
service "todobackend-db" deleted
deployment.apps "todobackend-db" deleted
> ls -l ~/.docker/Volumes/todobackend-data/pvc-afba5984-9223-11e8-
bc1c-025000000001
total 387152
-rw-r----- 1 jmenga wheel 56 27 Jul 21:49 auto.cnf
-rw------- 1 jmenga wheel 1675 27 Jul 21:49 ca-key.pem
...
...
drwxr-x--- 3 jmenga wheel 96 27 Jul 21:49 todobackend
> kubectl apply -f k8s/db/deployment.yaml
service "todobackend-db" created
deployment.apps "todobackend-db" created
```

The preceding code is a good example of why we separated out the persistent volume claim into its own file – doing this means that we can easily manage the life cycle of the database service without any data loss. In the event that you do want to destroy the database service and its data, you can choose to remove the persistent volume claim, in which case the Docker Desktop **hostPath** provisioner will automatically remove the persistent volume and any stored data.

> Kubernetes also supports a controller called a StatefulSet, which is specifically designed for stateful applications such as databases. You can read more about StatefulSets at `https://kubernetes.io/docs/concepts/workloads/controllers/statefulset/`.

Creating and consuming secrets

Kubernetes supports *secret* objects, which allow sensitive data such as a password or token to be stored securely in an encrypted format, and then exposed privately as required to your containers. Kubernetes secrets are stored in a key/value map or dictionary format, which is different from Docker secrets, which as you saw in the previous chapter typically just store the secret value.

You can create secrets manually using literal values, or by including your secret values in a file and applying the file. I recommend creating your secrets using literal values to avoid storing your secrets in your configuration files, which may be inadvertently committed and pushed to your source code repositories:

```
> kubectl create secret generic todobackend-secret \
 --from-literal=MYSQL_PASSWORD="$(openssl rand -base64 32)" \
 --from-literal=MYSQL_ROOT_PASSWORD="$(openssl rand -base64 32)" \
 --from-literal=SECRET_KEY="$(openssl rand -base64 50)"
secret "todobackend-secret" created
> kubectl describe secrets/todobackend-secret
Name: todobackend-secret
Namespace: default
Labels: <none>
Annotations: <none>

Type: Opaque

Data
====
MYSQL_PASSWORD: 44 bytes
MYSQL_ROOT_PASSWORD: 44 bytes
SECRET_KEY: 69 bytes
```

In the preceding example, you use the `kubectl create secret generic` command to create a secret called `todobackend-secret` that stores three secret values. Notice that each value is stored with a key that has the same name as the expected environment variable, which will make configuration of these values easy to consume.

With the secret now created, you can configure the `todobackend` and `db` deployments to consume the secret. Kubernetes includes a special volume type called secret that allows you to mount your secrets at a configurable location in your containers, which your applications can then read securely and privately.

Consuming secrets for the database service

Let's first update the database deployment resource that is defined in the `k8s/db/deployment.yaml` file to consume the `todobackend-secret`:

```
apiVersion: v1
kind: Service
metadata:
  name: todobackend-db
spec:
```

```
    selector:
      app: todobackend-db
    clusterIP: None
    ports:
    - protocol: TCP
      port: 3306
---
apiVersion: apps/v1
kind: Deployment
metadata:
  name: todobackend-db
  labels:
    app: todobackend-db
spec:
  selector:
    matchLabels:
      app: todobackend-db
  template:
    metadata:
      labels:
        app: todobackend-db
    spec:
      volumes:
      - name: data
        persistentVolumeClaim:
          claimName: todobackend-data
      - name: secrets
        secret:
          secretName: todobackend-secret
          items:
          - key: MYSQL_PASSWORD
            path: MYSQL_PASSWORD
          - key: MYSQL_ROOT_PASSWORD
            path: MYSQL_ROOT_PASSWORD
      containers:
      - name: db
        image: mysql:5.7
        livenessProbe:
          exec:
            command:
            - /bin/sh
            - -c
            - "mysqlshow -h 127.0.0.1 -u $(MYSQL_USER) -p$(cat
/tmp/secrets/MYSQL_PASSWORD)"
        volumeMounts:
        - name: data
          mountPath: /var/lib/mysql
        - name: secrets
```

```
        mountPath: /tmp/secrets
        readOnly: true
   env:
   - name: MYSQL_DATABASE
     value: todobackend
   - name: MYSQL_USER
     value: todo
   - name: MYSQL_ROOT_PASSWORD_FILE
     value: /tmp/secrets/MYSQL_ROOT_PASSWORD
   - name: MYSQL_PASSWORD_FILE
     value: /tmp/secrets/MYSQL_PASSWORD
```

You first create a volume called `secrets` that is of type `secret` which references the `todobackend-secret` we created earlier. By default, all secret items will be available, however you can control which items are published to the volume via the optional `items` property. Because the `todobackend-secret` includes the `SECRET_KEY` secret that is specific to the todobackend application, we configure the `items` list to exclude this item and only present the `MYSQL_PASSWORD` and `MYSQL_ROOT_PASSWORD` keys. Note that the specified `path` is required and is expressed as a relative path based from where the secret volume is mounted in each of your containers.

You then mount the `secrets` volume as read only to `/tmp/secrets` in the `db` container, and update the password-related environment variables to reference the secret files rather than using values directly from the environment. Notice that each secret value will be created in a file that is named based upon the key within the folder that the secret volume is mounted to.

To deploy our new configuration, you first need to delete the database service and its associated persistent volume as this includes the previous credentials, and then redeploy the database service. You can do this very easily by referencing the entire `k8s/db` directory when you execute the delete and apply actions, rather than specifying each file individually:

```
> kubectl delete -f k8s/db
service "todobackend-db" deleted
deployment.apps "todobackend-db" deleted
persistentvolumeclaim "todobackend-data" deleted
> kubectl apply -f k8s/db
service "todobackend-db" created
deployment.apps "todobackend-db" created
persistentvolumeclaim "todobackend-data" created
```

Once you have recreated the db service, you can use the kubectl exec command to verify that the MYSQL_PASSWORD and MYSQL_ROOT_PASSWORD secret items have been written to /tmp/secrets:

```
> kubectl exec $(kubectl get pods -l app=todobackend-db -
o=jsonpath='{.items[0].metadata.name}')\
 ls /tmp/secrets
MYSQL_PASSWORD
MYSQL_ROOT_PASSWORD
```

Consuming secrets for the application

We now need to update the todobackend service to consume our secrets by modifying the k8s/app/deployment.yaml file:

```
...
...
---
apiVersion: apps/v1
kind: Deployment
metadata:
  name: todobackend
  labels:
    app: todobackend
spec:
  replicas: 2
  selector:
    matchLabels:
      app: todobackend
  template:
    metadata:
      labels:
        app: todobackend
    spec:
      securityContext:
        fsGroup: 1000
      volumes:
      - name: public
        emptyDir: {}
      - name: secrets
        secret:
          secretName: todobackend-secret
          items:
          - key: MYSQL_PASSWORD
            path: MYSQL_PASSWORD
          - key: SECRET_KEY
```

```
            path: SECRET_KEY
      initContainers:
      - name: collectstatic
        image: 385605022855.dkr.ecr.us-east-1.amazonaws.com/docker-in-
aws/todobackend
        imagePullPolicy: IfNotPresent
        volumeMounts:
        - name: public
          mountPath: /public
        command: ["python3","manage.py","collectstatic","--no-input"]
        env:
        - name: DJANGO_SETTINGS_MODULE
          value: todobackend.settings_release
      containers:
      - name: todobackend
        image: 385605022855.dkr.ecr.us-east-1.amazonaws.com/docker-in-
aws/todobackend
        imagePullPolicy: IfNotPresent
        readinessProbe:
          httpGet:
            port: 8000
        livenessProbe:
          httpGet:
            port: 8000
        volumeMounts:
        - name: public
          mountPath: /public
        - name: secrets
          mountPath: /tmp/secrets
          readOnly: true
        command:
        - uwsgi
        - --http=0.0.0.0:8000
        - --module=todobackend.wsgi
        - --master
        - --die-on-term
        - --processes=4
        - --threads=2
        - --check-static=/public
        env:
        - name: DJANGO_SETTINGS_MODULE
          value: todobackend.settings_release
        - name: SECRETS_ROOT
          value: /tmp/secrets
        - name: MYSQL_HOST
          value: todobackend-db
        - name: MYSQL_USER
          value: todo
```

You must define the `secrets` volume and ensure that only the `MYSQL_PASSWORD` and `SECRET_KEY` items are exposed to the **todobackend** container. After mounting the volume as read only in the **todobackend** application container, you must then configure the `SECRETS_ROOT` environment variable with the path to the `secrets` mount. Recall in the last chapter that we added support to the **todobackend** application for consuming Docker secrets, which by default expects your secrets to be located at `/run/secrets`. However, because `/run` is a special tmpfs filesystem, you cannot mount your secrets using a regular file system mount at this location, hence we need to configure the `SECRETS_ROOT` environment variable, which reconfigure the secrets location the application will look in. We must also configure the `MYSQL_HOST` and `MYSQL_USER` environment variables, so that along with the `MYSQL_PASSWORD` secret, the **todobackend** application has the required information to connect to the database service.

If you now deploy the changes, you should be able to verify that the correct secret items are mounted in the **todobackend** container:

```
> kubectl apply -f k8s/app/
service "todobackend" unchanged
deployment.apps "todobackend" configured
> kubectl get pods
NAME                               READY   STATUS    RESTARTS   AGE
todobackend-74d47dd994-cpvl7       1/1     Running   0          35s
todobackend-74d47dd994-s2pp8       1/1     Running   0          35s
todobackend-db-574fb5746c-xcg9t    1/1     Running   0          12m
> kubectl exec todobackend-74d47dd994-cpvl7 ls /tmp/secrets
MYSQL_PASSWORD
SECRET_KEY
```

If you browse to `http://localhost/todos`, you should receive an error indicating that a database table does not exist, which means that the application is now successfully connecting and authenticating to the database, but is missing the required schema and tables that the application expects.

Running jobs

Our **todobackend** application is almost fully functional, however there is one key deployment task that we need to perform, which is to run database migrations to ensure that the correct schema and tables are present in the **todobackend** database. As you have seen throughout this book, database migrations should only be executed once per deployment, regardless of the number of instances running of our application. Kubernetes supports tasks of this nature via a special controller of type *job*, which as the name suggests, runs a task or process (in the form of a pod) until the job completes successfully.

To create a job for the required database migrations task, we will create a new file called `k8s/app/migrations.yaml` that's located in the `todobackend` repository, which allows you to run the job independently of the other application resources that are defined in the co-located `deployment.yaml` file:

```
apiVersion: batch/v1
kind: Job
metadata:
  name: todobackend-migrate
spec:
  backoffLimit: 4
  template:
    spec:
      restartPolicy: Never
      volumes:
      - name: secrets
        secret:
          secretName: todobackend-secret
          items:
          - key: MYSQL_PASSWORD
            path: MYSQL_PASSWORD
      containers:
      - name: migrate
        image: 385605022855.dkr.ecr.us-east-1.amazonaws.com/docker-in-aws/todobackend
        imagePullPolicy: IfNotPresent
        volumeMounts:
        - name: secrets
          mountPath: /tmp/secrets
          readOnly: true
        command: ["python3","manage.py","migrate","--no-input"]
        env:
        - name: DJANGO_SETTINGS_MODULE
          value: todobackend.settings_release
        - name: SECRETS_ROOT
```

```
        value: /tmp/secrets
    - name: MYSQL_HOST
        value: todobackend-db
    - name: MYSQL_USER
        value: todo
```

You must specify a kind of `Job` to configure this resource as a job, and for the most part, the configuration is very similar to the pod/deployment template we created earlier, except for the `spec.backoffLimit` property, which defines how many times Kubernetes should attempt to re-run the job should it fail, and the template `spec.restartPolicy` property, which should always be set to `Never` for a job.

If you now run the job, you should be to verify that database migrations ran successfully:

```
> kubectl apply -f k8s/app
service "todobackend" unchanged
deployment.apps "todobackend" unchanged
job.batch "todobackend-migrate" created
> kubectl get jobs
NAME                      DESIRED    SUCCESSFUL    AGE
todobackend-migrate    1          1             6s
> kubectl logs jobs/todobackend-migrate
Operations to perform:
  Apply all migrations: admin, auth, contenttypes, sessions, todo
Running migrations:
  Applying contenttypes.0001_initial... OK
  Applying auth.0001_initial... OK
  Applying admin.0001_initial... OK
  Applying admin.0002_logentry_remove_auto_add... OK
  Applying contenttypes.0002_remove_content_type_name... OK
  Applying auth.0002_alter_permission_name_max_length... OK
  Applying auth.0003_alter_user_email_max_length... OK
  Applying auth.0004_alter_user_username_opts... OK
  Applying auth.0005_alter_user_last_login_null... OK
  Applying auth.0006_require_contenttypes_0002... OK
  Applying auth.0007_alter_validators_add_error_messages... OK
  Applying auth.0008_alter_user_username_max_length... OK
  Applying auth.0009_alter_user_last_name_max_length... OK
  Applying sessions.0001_initial... OK
  Applying todo.0001_initial... OK
```

At this point, you have successfully deployed the todobackend application in a fully functional state, and you should be able to connect to the todobackend application and create, update, and delete todo items.

Creating an EKS cluster

Now that you have a solid understanding of Kubernetes and have defined the core resources required to deploy and run the todobackend application locally, it is time to shift our attention to the Elastic Kubernetes Service (EKS).

The core resource supported by EKS is the EKS cluster, which represents a fully managed, highly available cluster of Kubernetes managers that take care of the Kubernetes control plane for you. In this section, we will focus on creating an EKS cluster in AWS, establishing authentication and access to the cluster, and deploying the Kubernetes dashboard.

Creating an EKS cluster consists of the following primary tasks:

- **Install client components**: In order to manager your EKS cluster, you need to install various client components, including `kubectl` (which you have already installed) and the AWS IAM authenticator for Kubernetes tool.
- **Create cluster resources**: This establishes the control plane component of Kubernetes, which consists of Kubernetes masters. When using EKS, the masters are provided as a fully managed service.
- **Configure kubectl for EKS**: This allows you to manage EKS using your local kubectl client.
- **Create worker nodes**: This consists of Kubernetes nodes that are intended to run your container workloads. When using EKS, you are responsible for creating your own worker nodes, which you will typically deploy in the form of EC2 auto scaling groups. Just like for the ECS service, AWS provides an EKS-optimized AMI (`https://docs.aws.amazon.com/eks/latest/userguide/eks-optimized-ami.html`) that includes all of the necessary software components for a worker node to join your EKS clusters.
- **Deploy the Kubernetes dashboard**: The Kubernetes dashboard provides you with a web-based management interface to manage and monitor your cluster and container applications.

> At the time of writing, EKS clusters are not part of the AWS free tier and cost $0.20 USD per minute to run, so bear this in mind before you continue (see `https://aws.amazon.com/eks/pricing/` for latest pricing information). We will be using CloudFormation templates to deploy both the EKS cluster and EKS worker nodes, so you can easily tear down and recreate your EKS cluster and worker nodes as required to reduce costs.

Installing client components

To manage your EKS cluster, you must have `kubectl` installed, as well as the AWS IAM authenticator for Kubernetes components, which allows `kubectl` to authenticate to your EKS cluster using your IAM credentials.

You already have `kubectl` installed, so to install the AWS IAM authenticator for Kubernetes, you need to install a binary called `aws-iam-authenticator` that is published by AWS as follows:

```
> curl -fs -o /usr/local/bin/aws-iam-authenticator
https://amazon-eks.s3-us-west-2.amazonaws.com/1.10.3/2018-07-26/bin/da
rwin/amd64/aws-iam-authenticator
> chmod +x /usr/local/bin/aws-iam-authenticator
```

Creating cluster resources

Before creating your an EKS cluster, you need to ensure that your AWS account meets the following prerequisites:

- **VPC resources**: EKS resources must be deployed into a VPC with a minimum of three subnets. AWS recommends that you create your own dedicated VPC and subnets per EKS cluster, however in this chapter we will use the default VPC and subnets that are automatically created in your AWS account. Note that when you create a VPC and define the subnets that your cluster will use, you must specify *all* subnets where you expect your worker nodes *and* load balancers will be deployed. A recommended pattern is to deploy your worker nodes in private subnets, and ensure that you have also included public subnets so that EKS can create public facing load balancers as required.

- **EKS service role**: When creating an EKS cluster, you must specify an IAM role that grants access to the EKS service to manage your clusters.

- **Control plane security group**: You must provide a security group that is used for control plane communications between your EKS cluster managers and worker nodes. The security group rules will be modified by the EKS service, so you should create a new, empty security group for this requirement.

The AWS documentation includes a Getting Started (`https://docs.aws.amazon.com/eks/latest/userguide/getting-started.html`) section, which provides details on how to create EKS clusters using the AWS console. Given that EKS is supported by CloudFormation and the infrastructure as code approach we have used throughout this book, we need to create a folder called `eks` in the `todobackend-aws` repository and define our EKS cluster and the associated EKS service role in a new CloudFormation template file called `todobackend-aws/eks/stack.yml`:

```
AWSTemplateFormatVersion: "2010-09-09"

Description: EKS Cluster

Parameters:
  Subnets:
    Type: List<AWS::EC2::Subnet::Id>
    Description: Target subnets for EKS cluster
  VpcId:
    Type: AWS::EC2::VPC::Id
    Description: Target VPC

Resources:
  EksServiceRole:
    Type: AWS::IAM::Role
    Properties:
      RoleName: eks-service-role
      AssumeRolePolicyDocument:
        Version: "2012-10-17"
        Statement:
          - Effect: Allow
            Principal:
              Service:
                - eks.amazonaws.com
            Action:
              - sts:AssumeRole
      ManagedPolicyArns:
        - arn:aws:iam::aws:policy/AmazonEKSClusterPolicy
        - arn:aws:iam::aws:policy/AmazonEKSServicePolicy
  EksClusterSecurityGroup:
    Type: AWS::EC2::SecurityGroup
    Properties:
      GroupName: eks-cluster-control-plane-sg
      GroupDescription: EKS Cluster Control Plane Security Group
      VpcId: !Ref VpcId
      Tags:
        - Key: Name
          Value: eks-cluster-sg
  EksCluster:
```

```
Type: AWS::EKS::Cluster
Properties:
  Name: eks-cluster
  RoleArn: !Sub ${EksServiceRole.Arn}
  ResourcesVpcConfig:
    SubnetIds: !Ref Subnets
    SecurityGroupIds:
      - !Ref EksClusterSecurityGroup
```

The template requires two input parameters – the target VPC ID and target Subnet IDs. The `EksServiceRole` resource creates an IAM role that grants the `eks.awsamazon.com` service the ability to manage EKS clusters on your behalf, as specified by the managed policies referenced in the `ManagedPolicyArns` property. You must then define an empty security group for control plane communications, and finally define the EKS cluster resource, referencing the `EksServiceRole` resource for the `RoleArn` property, and defining a VPC configuration that targets the input `ApplicationSubnets` and uses the `EksClusterSecurityGroup` resource.

You can now deploy this template using the `aws cloudformation deploy` command, as follows:

```
> export AWS_PROFILE=docker-in-aws
> aws cloudformation deploy --template-file stack.yml --stack-name
eks-cluster \
--parameter-overrides VpcId=vpc-f8233a80 Subnets=subnet-
a5d3ecee,subnet-324e246f,subnet-d281a2b6\
--capabilities CAPABILITY_NAMED_IAM
Waiting for changeset to be created..
Waiting for stack create/update to complete
Successfully created/updated stack - eks-cluster
```

The cluster will take approximately 10 minutes to create and, once created, you can use the AWS CLI to obtain further information about the cluster:

```
> aws eks describe-cluster --name eks-cluster --query cluster.status
"ACTIVE"
> aws eks describe-cluster --name eks-cluster --query cluster.endpoint
"https://E7B5C85713AD5B11625D7A689F99383F.sk1.us-east-1.eks.amazonaws.
com"
> aws eks describe-cluster --name eks-cluster --query
cluster.certificateAuthority.data
"LS0tLS1CRUdJTiBDRVJUSUZJQ0FURS0tLS0tCk1JSUN5RENDQWJDZ0F3SUJBZ0lCQURBBT
kJna3Foa2lHOXcwQkFRc0ZBREFXTVJNd0VRWURWUVFERXdwcmRRSmwKY201bGRHVnNpNQjR
YRFRFNE1EY3l3Nak5V3TURRME9Gb1hEVEk0TURjeE9URXdNRFEwT0Zvd0ZURVRNQkVHQTFVR
QpBeE1LYTNWaVpYSnVaWFJsY3ppDQ0FTSXdEUVlKS29aSWh2Y05BUUVCQlRGBRGdnRVBBRREN
DQVFvQ2dnRUJBRUh5CkVskVsajhMMUQ4M1V3RDFmd2lhc1lp9TdGZZBK0tvWEtZ2NkVtZEhhdWdnNXhe
```

```
Wh1Snd2aGhkZDU2M0tVdGJnYW15Z0pxMVIKQkNCTWptWXVocG8rWm0ySEJrckZGakFFZDV
IN1lWUXVOSm15TXdrQVV5MnpFTUU5SjJid3hkVEpqZ3pZdmlwVgpJc05zd3pIL1lSa1NVS
ElDK0VSaCtURmZJODhsTTBiZlM1R1pueUx0VkZCS3RjNGxBREVxRE1BTkFoaEc5OVZ3Cm5
hL2w5THU2aW1jT1VOVGVCRFB0L1hxNGF3TFNUOEgwQlVvWGFwbEt0cFkvOFFdqR055RUhzU
HZHdXNXU3lkK3lkKNXB1Um8yR3Nxc0VqMGhsbHHpuV0RXWnlqQVU5Ni82QXVKRGZVSTB
ING1WNkpCZWxxVU0tTRTZBOU1GSjRjYgpHeVpkYmh0akg1d3Zzdit1akNjQ0F3RUFBYU1qT
UNFd0RnWURWUjBPQVFIL0JBUURBZ0trTUE4R0ExVWRFd0VCL0VVCVMCi93UUZNQU1CQWY4d0RRWUp
Lb1pJaHZjTkFRRUxCUUFFZ2dFQkFIRkRIRklODZnNkNoR2FFMejBQb21EK2tyc040SUMKRzhOb
0xSc2xxkTkJjQmlRczFFYK0hKemnNxTS9TN0svL1RhUndqVjRZZTE1hbnBqWGp4TzRRKUWh4Q0Z
HR1F2SHptUApST1FhQXRjdWRJUHYyJg5eUlOQW1rT0hDZGsyNm1Yazk1b2pekxxQRE1NT
lFVR2VmbFXUxK282T1ZRUldTKzBMClpta211KzVyQVVFMWtTK00yMDFPeFNGcUNnNLOVDd0F
4ZXd5YnFMNGw4elpPWCs3VzlyM1duMWh6a3NhSnIrRHhKKUVRyQ1p2MWJJ0ZENpSnhhmbFVxW
XN5UEs1UDh4NmhKOGN2RmRFUklfdmtYQm1VbjRkWFBWWU9IdUkwdwdElnU2h1RAp3K0IxVkV
OeUF3WXpXMWWxLaGRQQTV4R1BMN2I0ZmN4UXhCCS0VlVHpaUnUxQUhMM1R4THIxcVdkWbURUb
z0KLS0tLS1FTkQgQ0VSVElGSUNBVEUtLS0tLQo="
```

The cluster endpoint and certificate authority data are both required for later on in this chapter, so take note of these values.

Configuring kubectl for EKS

With your EKS cluster created, you now need to add the new cluster to your local `kubectl` configuration. All clusters that `kubectl` is aware of are defined in a file called `~/.kube/config` by default, which at the moment will include a single cluster called `docker-for-desktop-cluster` if you are using Docker for Mac or Docker for Windows.

The following code demonstrates adding your EKS cluster and associated configuration to the `~/.kube/config` file:

```
apiVersion: v1
clusters:
- cluster:
    insecure-skip-tls-verify: true
    server: https://localhost:6443
  name: docker-for-desktop-cluster
- cluster:
    certificate-authority-data: <Paste your EKS cluster certificate
data here>
    server:
https://E7B5C85713AD5B11625D7A689F99383F.sk1.us-east-1.eks.amazonaws.c
om
  name: eks-cluster
contexts:
- context:
```

```
      cluster: docker-for-desktop-cluster
      user: docker-for-desktop
    name: docker-for-desktop
- context:
    cluster: eks-cluster
    user: aws
  name: eks
current-context: docker-for-desktop-cluster
kind: Config
preferences: {}
users:
- name: aws
  user:
    exec:
      apiVersion: client.authentication.k8s.io/v1alpha1
      args:
      - token
      - -i
      - eks-cluster
      command: aws-iam-authenticator
      env:
      - name: AWS_PROFILE
        value: docker-in-aws
- name: docker-for-desktop
  user:
    client-certificate-data: ...
    client-key-data: ...
```

You must first add a new cluster called `eks-cluster` to the `clusters` property, specifying the certificate authority data and server endpoint you captured earlier after you created the EKS cluster. You must then add a context called `eks`, which will allow you to switch between your local Kubernetes server and your EKS cluster, and finally add a new user called `aws` to the users section which is used by the `eks` context to authenticate to your EKS cluster. The `aws` user configuration configures kubectl to execute the `aws-iam-authenticator` component you previously installed, passing the argument `token -i eks-cluster` and using your local `docker-in-aws` profile to authenticate access. Executing this command will automatically return an authentication token to `kubectl` that can then be used to authenticate to your EKS cluster.

With the preceding configuration in place, you should now be able to access a new context called `eks` and verify connectivity to your EKS cluster, as follows:

```
> kubectl config get-contexts
CURRENT   NAME                    CLUSTER                   AUTHINFO
NAMESPACE
*         docker-for-desktop   docker-for-desktop-cluster   docker-
for-desktop
          eks                     eks-cluster               aws
> kubectl config use-context eks
Switched to context "eks".
> kubectl get all
Assume Role MFA token code: ******
NAME                    TYPE       CLUSTER-IP    EXTERNAL-IP   PORT(S)
AGE
service/kubernetes   ClusterIP    10.100.0.1    <none>        443/TCP
1h
```

Note that if you are using the **multi-factor authentication** (**MFA**) configuration we set up in earlier chapters, you will be prompted to enter an MFA token every single time you run a `kubectl` command against your EKS cluster, which will quickly become tiresome.

To disable MFA temporarily, you can remove your user account from the Users group using the `aws iam remove-user-from-group` command:

```
# Removes user from Users group, removing MFA requirement
# To restore MFA run: aws iam add-user-to-group --user-name
justin.menga --group-name Users
> aws iam remove-user-from-group --user-name justin.menga --group-name
Users
```

And then comment the `mfa_serial` line for your local AWS profile in the `~/.aws/config` file:

```
[profile docker-in-aws]
source_profile = docker-in-aws
role_arn = arn:aws:iam::385605022855:role/admin
role_session_name=justin.menga
region = us-east-1
# mfa_serial = arn:aws:iam::385605022855:mfa/justin.menga
```

Creating worker nodes

The next step in setting up EKS is creating worker nodes that will join your EKS cluster. Unlike the Kubernetes master nodes that are fully managed by AWS, you are responsible for creating and managing your worker nodes. AWS provide an EKS-optimized AMI that includes all of the software required to join an EKS cluster and operate as an EKS worker. You can browse to `https://docs.aws.amazon.com/eks/latest/userguide/eks-optimized-ami.html` to obtain the latest AMI ID for your region:

Amazon EKS-Optimized AMI

At the time of writing this book, the EKS-Optimized AMI requires extensive configuration using the **cfn-init** framework that we learned about in earlier chapters. The recommended approach to create your worker nodes is to use a predefined CloudFormation template which is published by AWS that already includes the required configuration specified at `https://docs.aws.amazon.com/eks/latest/ userguide/launch-workers.html`:

Worker CloudFormation template URL

You can now create a new CloudFormation stack for your worker nodes by selecting **Services** | **CloudFormation** in the AWS console, clicking the **Create Stack** button, and pasting the worker template URL you obtained previously in the **Choose a template** section:

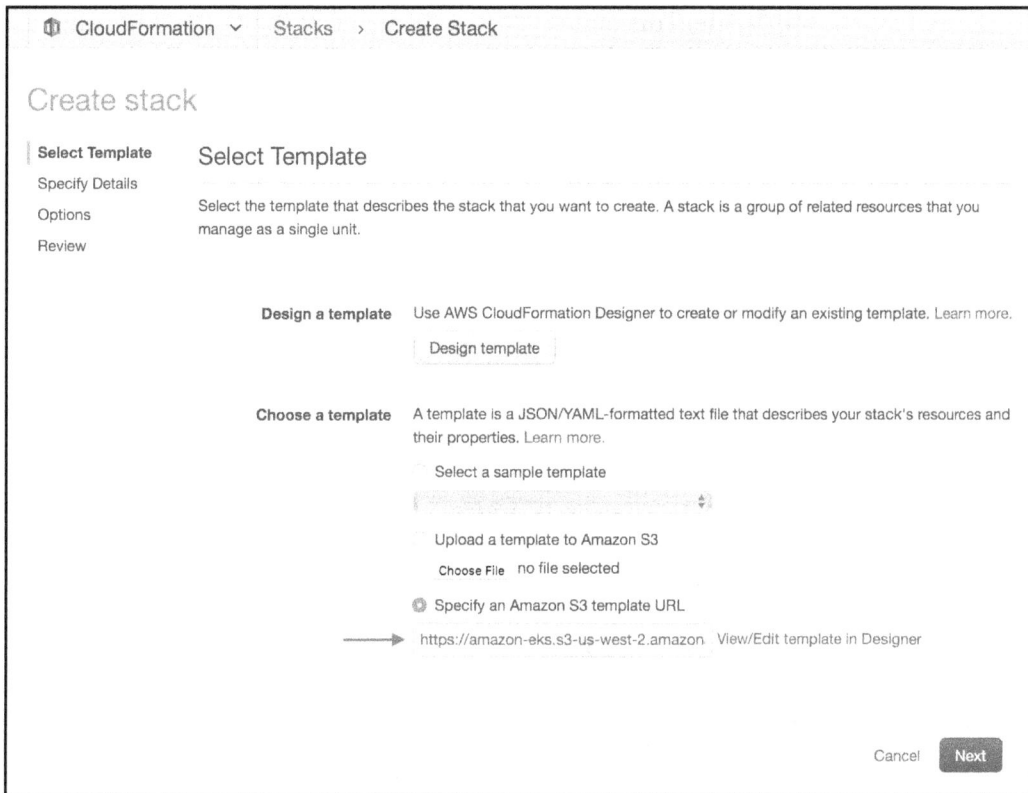

Creating a worker node CloudFormation stack

After clicking **Next**, you will be prompted to enter a stack name (you can specify a name of `eks-cluster-workers` or similar) and provide the following parameters:

- **ClusterName**: Specifies the name of your EKS cluster (`eks-cluster`, in our example).
- **ClusterControlPlaneSecurityGroup**: The name of the control plane security group. In our example, we previously created a security group called `eks-cluster-control-plane-sg` when we created our EKS cluster.

- **NodeGroupName**: This defines part of the name of the EC2 auto scaling group that will be created for your workers. For our scenario, you can specify a name of `eks-cluster-workers` or similar.

- **NodeAutoScalingGroupMinSize and NodeAutoScalingGroupMaxSize**: By, default these are set to 1 and 3, respectively. Note that the CloudFormation template sets the desired size of the auto scaling group to the value of the `NodeAutoScalingGroupMaxSize` parameter, so you may want to lower this value.

- **NodeInstanceType**: The smallest instance type you can specify using the predefined worker CloudFormation template is `t2.small`. For EKS, the node instance type is not just important in terms of CPU and memory resources, but also has implications on pod capacity in terms on networking requirements. The EKS networking model (`https://docs.aws.amazon.com/eks/latest/userguide/pod-networking.html`) exposes each pod in your EKS cluster as an IP address that's reachable within your VPC, using a combination of elastic network interfaces (ENI) and secondary IP addresses running on each ENI. You can refer to `https://docs.aws.amazon.com/AWSEC2/latest/UserGuide/using-eni.html#AvailableIpPerENI`, which describes the maximum number of ENIs and secondary IP addresses per interface for the various EC2 instance types and ultimately determines the maximum number of pods you can run per node.

- **NodeImageId**: Specifies the ID of the EKS-Optimized AMI for your region (see the previous screenshots).

- **KeyName**: Specifies an existing EC2 key pair in your account (for example, the admin keypair you created earlier in this book).

- **VpcId**: Specifies the VPC ID where your EKS cluster is located.

- **Subnets**: Specifies the subnets where you would like to place your workers.

Once you have configured the various parameters that are required, click on the **Next** button twice and finally acknowledge that CloudFormation may create IAM resources before clicking the **Create** button to deploy your worker nodes. When your stack has been created successfully, open the **Outputs** tab for the stack and take a note of the `NodeInstanceRole` output, which is required for the next configuration step:

Obtaining the NodeInstanceRole output

Joining worker nodes to your EKS cluster

After the CloudFormation stack has deployed successfully, your worker nodes will attempt to join your cluster, however before they can do this you need to grant access to the EC2 instance role of your worker nodes by applying an AWS authenticator `ConfigMap` resource called `aws-auth` to your cluster.

> A ConfigMap is simply a key/value data structure used to store configuration data that can be used by different resources in your cluster. The `aws-auth` ConfigMap is used by EKS to grant AWS users the ability to interact with your cluster, which you can read more about at `https://docs.aws.amazon.com/eks/latest/userguide/add-user-role.html`. You can also download a sample `aws-auth` ConfigMap from `https://amazon-eks.s3-us-west-2.amazonaws.com/1.10.3/2018-06-05/aws-auth-cm.yaml`.

To create the `aws-auth` ConfigMap, create a file called `aws-auth-cm.yaml` in the `todobackend-aws/eks` folder:

```
apiVersion: v1
kind: ConfigMap
metadata:
  name: aws-auth
  namespace: kube-system
data:
  mapRoles: |
    - rolearn: arn:aws:iam::847222289464:role/eks-cluster-workers-
  NodeInstanceRole-RYP3UYR8QBYA
      username: system:node:{{EC2PrivateDNSName}}
```

```
groups:
  - system:bootstrappers
  - system:nodes
```

In the preceding example, you need to paste the value of the `NodeInstanceRole` output you obtained when you created your workers CloudFormation stack. Once you have created this file, you can now apply it to your EKS cluster using the `kubectl apply` command, and then wait for your worker nodes to join the cluster by running `kubectl get nodes --watch`:

```
> kubectl apply -f aws-auth-cm.yaml
configmap "aws-auth" created
> kubectl get nodes --watch
NAME                                           STATUS     ROLES     AGE
VERSION
ip-172-31-15-111.us-west-2.compute.internal    NotReady   <none>    20s
v1.10.3
ip-172-31-28-179.us-west-2.compute.internal    NotReady   <none>    16s
v1.10.3
ip-172-31-38-41.us-west-2.compute.internal     NotReady   <none>    13s
v1.10.3
ip-172-31-15-111.us-west-2.compute.internal    NotReady   <none>    23s
v1.10.3
ip-172-31-28-179.us-west-2.compute.internal    NotReady   <none>    22s
v1.10.3
ip-172-31-38-41.us-west-2.compute.internal     NotReady   <none>    22s
v1.10.3
ip-172-31-15-111.us-west-2.compute.internal    Ready      <none>    33s
v1.10.3
ip-172-31-28-179.us-west-2.compute.internal    Ready      <none>    32s
v1.10.3
ip-172-31-38-41.us-west-2.compute.internal     Ready      <none>    32s
v1.10.3
```

Once all of your workers have a status of `Ready`, you have successfully joined your worker nodes to your EKS cluster.

Deploying the Kubernetes dashboard

The final step in setting up your EKS cluster is to deploy the Kubernetes dashboard to your cluster. The Kubernetes dashboard is a powerful and comprehensive web-based management interface for managing and monitoring your cluster and container applications, and is deployed as a container-based application within the `kube-system` namespace of your Kubernetes cluster. The dashboard consists of a number of components that I won't go into detail about here, but you can read more about the dashboard at `https://github.com/kubernetes/dashboard`.

To deploy the dashboard, we will first create a folder called `todobackend-aws/eks/dashboard` and proceed to download and apply the various components that comprise the dashboard to this folder:

```
> curl -fs -O
https://raw.githubusercontent.com/kubernetes/dashboard/master/src/depl
oy/recommended/kubernetes-dashboard.yaml
> curl -fs -O
https://raw.githubusercontent.com/kubernetes/heapster/master/deploy/ku
be-config/influxdb/heapster.yaml
> curl -fs -O
https://raw.githubusercontent.com/kubernetes/heapster/master/deploy/ku
be-config/influxdb/influxdb.yaml
> curl -fs -O
https://raw.githubusercontent.com/kubernetes/heapster/master/deploy/ku
be-config/rbac/heapster-rbac.yaml
> kubectl apply -f kubernetes-dashboard.yaml
secret "kubernetes-dashboard-certs" created
serviceaccount "kubernetes-dashboard" created
role.rbac.authorization.k8s.io "kubernetes-dashboard-minimal" created
rolebinding.rbac.authorization.k8s.io "kubernetes-dashboard-minimal"
created
deployment.apps "kubernetes-dashboard" created
service "kubernetes-dashboard" created
> kubectl apply -f heapster.yaml
serviceaccount "heapster" created
deployment.extensions "heapster" created
service "heapster" created
> kubectl apply -f influxdb.yaml
deployment.extensions "monitoring-influxdb" created
service "monitoring-influxdb" created
> kubectl apply -f heapster-rbac.yaml
clusterrolebinding.rbac.authorization.k8s.io "heapster" created
```

You then need to create a file called `eks-admin.yaml` that creates a service account and cluster role binding with full cluster-admin privileges:

```
apiVersion: v1
kind: ServiceAccount
metadata:
  name: eks-admin
  namespace: kube-system
---
apiVersion: rbac.authorization.k8s.io/v1beta1
kind: ClusterRoleBinding
metadata:
  name: eks-admin
roleRef:
  apiGroup: rbac.authorization.k8s.io
  kind: ClusterRole
  name: cluster-admin
subjects:
- kind: ServiceAccount
  name: eks-admin
  namespace: kube-system
```

After creating this file, you need to apply it to your EKS cluster:

```
> kubectl apply -f eks-admin.yaml
serviceaccount "eks-admin" created
clusterrolebinding.rbac.authorization.k8s.io "eks-admin" created
```

With the `eks-admin` service account in place, you can retrieve an authentication token for this account by running the following command:

```
> kubectl -n kube-system describe secret $(kubectl -n kube-system get secret | grep eks-admin | awk '{print $1}')
Name: eks-admin-token-24kh4
Namespace: kube-system
Labels: <none>
Annotations: kubernetes.io/service-account.name=eks-admin
             kubernetes.io/service-account.uid=6d8ba3f6-8dba-11e8-b132-02b2aa7ab028

Type: kubernetes.io/service-account-token

Data
====
namespace: 11 bytes
token:
eyJhbGciOiJSUzI1NiIsImtpZCI6IiJ9.eyJpc3MiOiJrdWJlcm51dGVzL3NlcnZpY2VhY2
2NvdW50Iiwia3ViZXJuZXRlcy5pby9zZXJ2aWN1YWNjb3VudC9uYW11c3BhY2UiOiJrdWJl
```

```
lLXN5c3RlbSIsImt1YmVybmV0ZXMuaW8vc2VydmljZWFjY291bnQvc2VjcmV0Lm5hbWUiO
iJla3MtYWRtaW4tdG9rZW4tMjRraDQiLCJrdWJlcm5ldGVzLmlvL3NlcnZpY2VhY2NvdW5
0L3NlcnZpY2UtYWNjb3VudC5uYW1lIjoiZWtzLWFkbWluIiwia3ViZXJuZXRlcy5pby9zZ
XJ2aWNlYWNjb3VudC9zZXJ2aWNlLWFjY291bnQudWlkIjoiNmQ4YmEzZjYtOGRiYS0xMWU
4LWIxMzItMDJiMmFhN2FiMDI4Iiwic3ViIjoic3lzdGVtOnNlcnZpY2VhY2NvdW50Omt1Y
mUtc3lzdGVtOnVrcy1hZG1pbiJ9.h7hchmhGUZKjdnZRk4U1RZVS7P1tvp3TAyo10TnYI_
3AOhA75gC6BlQz4yZSC72fq2rqvKzUvBqosqKmJcEKI_d6Wb8UTfFKZPFiC_US1DpnEp2e
8Q9jJYHPKPYEI19dkyd1Po6er5k6hAzY1O1Dx0RFdfTaxUhfb3zfvEN-
X56M34B_Gn3FPWHIVYEwHCGcSXVhplVMMXvjfpQ-0b_1La8fb31JcnD48Uo1kJ1Z_DH3zs
VjIR9BfcuPRoooHYQb4blgAJ4XtQYQans07bKD91mfnQvNpaCdXV_lGOx_I5vEbc8CQKTB
dJkCXaWEiwahsfwQrYtfoBlIdO5IvzZ5mg
```
```
ca.crt: 1025 bytes
```

The key piece of information in the preceding example is the token value, which you need to copy and paste when you connect to the dashboard. To connect to the dashboard, you need to start the kubectl proxy, which provides HTTP access to the Kubernetes API:

```
> kubectl proxy
Starting to serve on 127.0.0.1:8001
```

If you now browse to `http://localhost:8001/api/v1/namespaces/kube-system/services/https:kubernetes-dashboard:/proxy/`, you will be prompted to sign in to the dashboard, where you need to paste the token that you retrieved previously for the `eks-admin` service account:

Signing in to the Kubernetes dashboard

Once you have signed in, if you change the Namespace to **kube-system** and select **Workloads** | **Deployments**, it is possible that you may be shown an error indicating that the image for the **monitoring-influxdb** deployment could not be found:

Kubernetes dashboard deployment failure

If this is the case, you will need to update the `todobackend-aws/eks/dashboard/influxdb.yml` file that you downloaded earlier to reference `k8s.gcr.io/heapster-influxdb-amd64:v1.3.3` (this is a known issue (`https://github.com/kubernetes/heapster/issues/2059`)) that may or may not exist when you are reading this chapter):

```
apiVersion: extensions/v1beta1
kind: Deployment
metadata:
 name: monitoring-influxdb
 namespace: kube-system
```

```
spec:
 replicas: 1
 template:
 metadata:
 labels:
 task: monitoring
 k8s-app: influxdb
 spec:
 containers:
 - name: influxdb
 image: k8s.gcr.io/heapster-influxdb-amd64:v1.3.3
 ...
 ...
```

If you now re-apply the file by running `kubectl apply -f influxdb.yml`, the dashboard should now show all services running as expected.

Deploying the sample application to EKS

Now that our EKS cluster and worker nodes are in place and we have confirmed that we can deploy to the cluster, it's time to deploy the todobackend application to EKS. You have already performed the majority of the hard work earlier when you defined the various resources required to run your application locally in Kubernetes, and all that is required is to adapt some of the external resources such as the load balancer and persistent volume for the database service to use AWS native services.

You are now required to perform the following configuration tasks:

- Configuring support for persistent volumes using the AWS Elastic Block Store (EBS)
- Configuring support for AWS Elastic Load Balancers
- Deploying the sample application

Configuring support for persistent volumes using AWS EBS

Earlier in this chapter, we discussed the concepts of persistent volume claims and storage classes, which allow you to abstract the details of your storage infrastructure away from your applications. We learned that when using Docker Desktop, a default storage class is provided that will automatically create persistent volumes of type hostPath that are accessible from your local operating system at `~/.docker/Volumes`, which makes it easy to provision, manage, and maintain persistent volumes when using Docker Desktop with Kubernetes.

When using EKS, it is important to understand that unlike Docker Desktop, by default, no storage classes are created for you. This requires you to create at least one storage class if you want to support persistent volume claims, and in most use cases, you would typically define a default storage class that provides a standard default storage medium and volume type for your cluster. When using EKS, a good candidate for these storage classes is the Elastic Block Store (EBS), which provides a standard integrated mechanism to support block-based volume storage for the EC2 instances that run as worker nodes in your cluster. Kubernetes supports a volume type called `AWSElasticBlockStore`, which allows you to access and mount EBS volumes from your worker nodes, and also includes support for a storage provisioner called `aws-ebs`, which provides dynamic provisioning and management of EBS volumes.

With this native support for AWS EBS included out of the box, it is very easy to create a default storage class that will automatically provision EBS storage, which we will define in a file called `todobackend-aws/eks/gp2-storage-class.yaml`:

```
kind: StorageClass
apiVersion: storage.k8s.io/v1
metadata:
  name: gp2
provisioner: kubernetes.io/aws-ebs
parameters:
  type: gp2
reclaimPolicy: Delete
mountOptions:
  - debug
```

We will create a storage class called `gp2`, which, as the name suggests, will provision EBS storage of type `gp2`, or SSD, from AWS, using the `kubernetes.io/aws-ebs` storage provisioner. The `parameters` section controls this storage selection, and depending on the type of storage, there may be other configuration options available, which you can read more about at `https://kubernetes.io/docs/concepts/storage/ storage-classes/#aws`. The value for `reclaimPolicy` can be either `Retain` or `Delete`, which controls whether or not the storage provisioner should retain or delete the associated EBS volume whenever a persistent volume claim associated with the storage class is deleted from Kubernetes. For production use cases, you would typically set this to `Retain`, but for non-production environments, you may want to set this to the default reclaim policy of `Delete` to save you from having to manually clean up EBS volumes that are no longer used by your cluster.

Now, let's create this storage class in our EKS cluster, after which we can configure the new storage class to be the default storage class for the cluster:

```
> kubectl get sc
No resources found.
> kubectl apply -f eks/gp2-storage-class.yaml
storageclass.storage.k8s.io "gp2" created
> kubectl patch storageclass gp2 \
    -p '{"metadata": {"annotations":{"storageclass.kubernetes.io/is-
default-class":"true"}}}'
storageclass.storage.k8s.io "gp2" patched
> kubectl describe sc/gp2
Name: gp2
IsDefaultClass: Yes
Annotations: ...
Provisioner: kubernetes.io/aws-ebs
Parameters: type=gp2
AllowVolumeExpansion: <unset>
MountOptions:
  debug
ReclaimPolicy: Delete
VolumeBindingMode: Immediate
Events: <none>
```

After creating the storage class, you use the `kubectl patch` command to add an annotation to the storage class, which configures the class as the default class. You can see that when you run the `kubectl describe sc/gp2` command to view details about the storage class, the `IsDefaultClass` attribute is set to `Yes`, confirming that the newly created class is the default storage class for the cluster.

With this in place, the Kubernetes configuration for the **todobackend** application now has a default storage class that can be applied for the `todobackend-data` persistent volume claim, which will provision an EBS volume of type `gp2` based upon the storage class parameters.

> The `eksServiceRole` IAM role that you created earlier in this chapter includes the `AmazonEKSClusterPolicy` managed policy, which grants your EKS cluster the ability to manage EBS volumes. If you choose to implement your own custom IAM policies for the EKS service role, you must ensure that you include the various EC2 IAM permissions for managing volumes, such as `ec2:AttachVolume`, `ec2:DetachVolume`, `ec2:CreateVolumes`, `ec2:DeleteVolumes`, `ec2:DescribeVolumes`, and `ec2:ModifyVolumes` (this is not an exhaustive list). See `https://docs.aws.amazon.com/eks/latest/userguide/service_IAM_role.html` for details on the full list of IAM permissions that are granted by AWS-defined EKS service roles and managed policies.

Configuring support for AWS Elastic Load Balancers

Earlier in this chapter, when you defined your Kubernetes configuration for the todobackend application, you created a service for the todobackend application of type `LoadBalancer`. We discussed that the implementation details of the load balancer are specific to the platform that your Kubernetes cluster is deployed to, and in the case of Docker Desktop, Docker provides their own load balancer component that allows the service to be exposed to the local network interface on your development machine.

When using EKS, the good news is that you don't need to do anything to support services of type `LoadBalancer` – your EKS cluster will automatically create and associate an AWS Elastic Load Balancer with each service endpoint, with the `AmazonEKSClusterPolicy` managed policy granting the required IAM permissions for this.

Kubernetes does allow you configure vendor-specific features of the `LoadBalancer` type by configuring *annotations*, which are a metadata property that will be understood by a given vendor on their target platform and ignored if deploying on a different platform, such as your local Docker Desktop environment. You can read more about these annotations at `https://kubernetes.io/docs/concepts/services-networking/service/#publishing-services-service-types`, and the following example demonstrates adding several annotations that are specific to the AWS Elastic Load Balancer to the service definition within the `todobackend/k8s/app/deployment.yaml` file:

```
apiVersion: v1
kind: Service
metadata:
  name: todobackend
  annotations:
    service.beta.kubernetes.io/aws-load-balancer-backend-protocol:
"http"
    service.beta.kubernetes.io/aws-load-balancer-connection-draining-
enabled: "true"
    service.beta.kubernetes.io/aws-load-balancer-connection-draining-
timeout: "60"
spec:
  selector:
    app: todobackend
  ports:
  - protocol: TCP
    port: 80
    targetPort: 8000
  type: LoadBalancer
---
...
...
```

In the preceding example, we added the following annotations:

- `service.beta.kubernetes.io/aws-load-balancer-backend-protocol`: This configures the backend protocol. A value of `http` ensures that the `X-Forward-For` header is set on incoming requests so that your web applications can track client IP addresses.
- `service.beta.kubernetes.io/aws-load-balancer-connection-draining-enabled`: This enables connection draining.
- `service.beta.kubernetes.io/aws-load-balancer-connection-draining-timeout`: This specifies the connection draining timeout.

One important point to note is that the annotations expect every value to be a string value, so ensure that you quote boolean values such as "`true`" and "`false`", as well as any numeric values such as "`60`", as demonstrated in the preceding code.

Deploying the sample application

You are now ready to deploy the sample application to AWS, which you can do by first switching over to the todobackend repository and ensuring that use are using the `eks` context you created earlier in this chapter:

```
todobackend> kubectl config use-context eks
Switched to context "eks".
todobackend> kubectl config get-contexts
CURRENT   NAME                CLUSTER                   AUTHINFO
NAMESPACE
          docker-for-desktop  docker-for-desktop-cluster  docker-
for-desktop
*         eks                 eks-cluster               aws
```

Creating secrets

Recall that both the application and database services rely on secrets that we manually created in our local Docker Desktop context, so you first need to create these secrets in your EKS context:

```
> kubectl create secret generic todobackend-secret \
  --from-literal=MYSQL_PASSWORD="$(openssl rand -base64 32)" \
  --from-literal=MYSQL_ROOT_PASSWORD="$(openssl rand -base64 32)" \
  --from-literal=SECRET_KEY="$(openssl rand -base64 50)"
secret "todobackend-secret" created
```

Deploying the database service

You can now deploy the database service, which should create a new persistent volume backed by EBS as per the configuration of the default storage class you created earlier:

```
> kubectl apply -f k8s/db
service "todobackend-db" created
deployment.apps "todobackend-db" created
persistentvolumeclaim "todobackend-data" created
> kubectl get pv
NAME                                              CAPACITY STATUS  CLAIM
```

```
STORAGECLASS
pvc-18ac5d3f-925c-11e8-89e1-06186d140068   8Gi      Bound
default/todobackend-data  gp2
```

You can see that a persistent volume was created, and if you browse to **Services** | **EC2** in the AWS console and select **Volumes** from the left **ELASTIC BLOCK STORAGE** menu, you should be able to see a corresponding EBS volume for the persistent value:

Viewing EBS volumes

Notice that Kubernetes tags the EBS volume with a number of tags that allow easy identification of which persistent volume and persistent volume claim a given EBS volume it is associated with.

In the Kubernetes dashboard, you can verify that the `todobackend-db` deployment is running by selecting **Workloads | Deployments**:

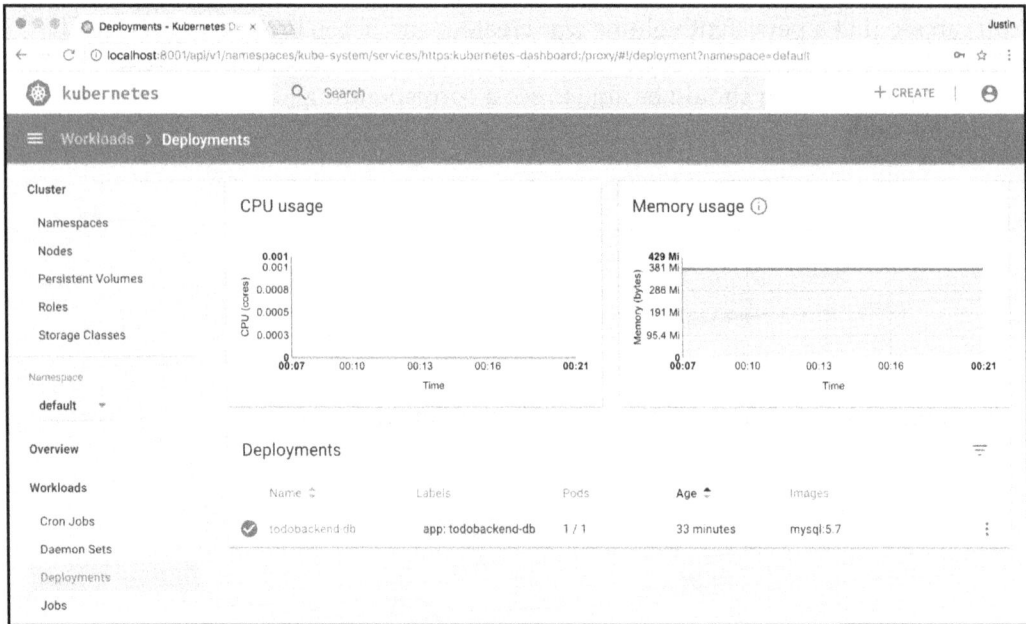

Viewing EBS volumes

Deploying the application service

With the database service in place, you can now proceed to deploy the application:

```
> kubectl apply -f k8s/app
service "todobackend" created
deployment.apps "todobackend" created
job.batch "todobackend-migrate" created
```

Deploying the application will perform the following tasks:

- Create the `todobackend-migrate` job, which runs database migrations
- Create the `todobackend` deployment, which runs a collectstatic initContainer and then runs the main todobackend application container
- Create the `todobackend` service, which will deploy a new service with an AWS ELB frontend

In the Kubernetes dashboard, if you select **Discovery and Load Balancing** | **Services** and select the **todobackend** service, you can view each of the internal endpoints for the service, as well as the external load balancer endpoint:

Viewing the todobackend service in the Kubernetes dashboard

> You can also obtain the external endpoint URL by running the
> `kubectl describe svc/todobackend` command.

If you click on the external endpoint URL, you should be able to verify that the todobackend application is fully functional, with all static content being displayed correctly and the ability to add, remove, and update Todo items in the application database:

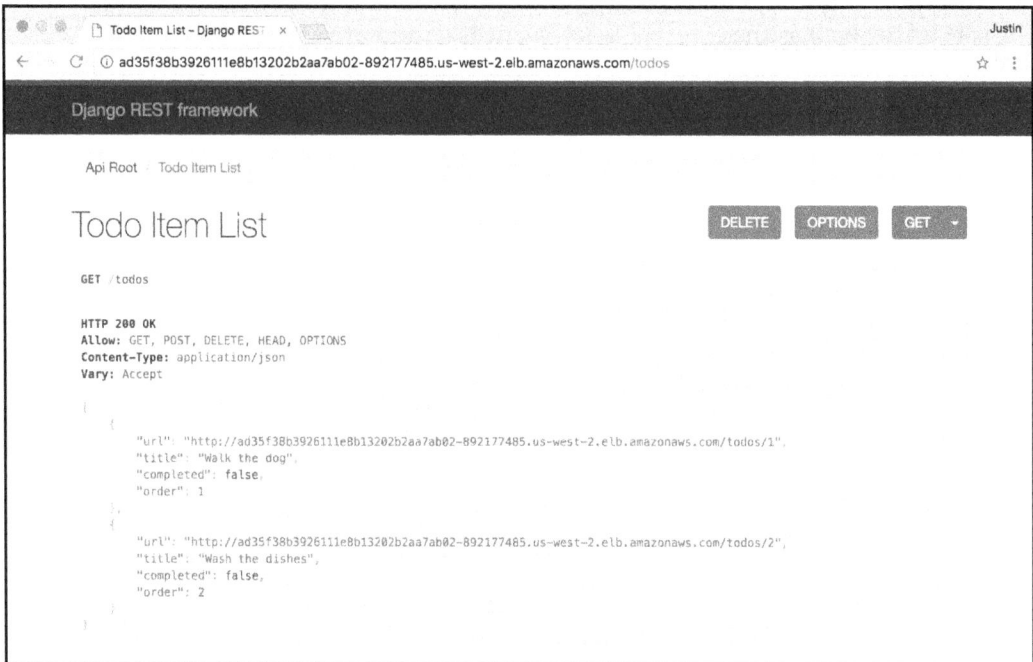

Verifying the todobackend application

Tearing down down the sample application

Tearing down the sample application is very simple, as follows:

```
> kubectl delete -f k8s/app
service "todobackend" deleted
deployment.apps "todobackend" deleted
job.batch "todobackend-migrate" deleted
> kubectl delete -f k8s/db
service "todobackend-db" deleted
deployment.apps "todobackend-db" deleted
persistentvolumeclaim "todobackend-data" deleted
```

Once this has been completed, you should be able to verify that the Elastic Load Balancer resource associated with the todobackend service has been deleted, along with the EBS volume for the todobackend database, given that you configured the reclaim policy for the default storage class as Delete. Of course you should also delete the worker node stack and EKS cluster stack you created earlier in this chapter, to avoid unnecessary charges.

Summary

In this chapter, you learned how to deploy Docker applications using Kubernetes and the AWS Elastic Kubernetes Service (EKS). Kubernetes has established itself as one of the leading container management platforms with a strong open source community, and with AWS now supporting Kubernetes customers with the EKS service, Kubernetes is certain to grow even more in popularity.

You first learned how to leverage the native support for Kubernetes in Docker Desktop, which makes it very easy to get up and running with Kubernetes locally. You learned how to create a variety of core Kubernetes resources including pods, deployments, services, secrets, and jobs, which provide the fundamental building blocks for running your applications in Kubernetes. You also learned how to configure support for persistent storage, leveraging persistent volume claims to abstract the application's storage requirements away from the underlying storage engine.

You were then introduced to EKS and learned how to create an EKS cluster and associated supporting resources, including an EC2 auto scaling group that runs your worker nodes. You established access to the EKS cluster, and tested that the cluster was working correctly by deploying the Kubernetes dashboard, which provides a rich and powerful management user interface for your cluster.

Finally, you proceeded to deploy the todobackend application to EKS, which included integration with the AWS Elastic Load Balancer (ELB) service for external connectivity and the Elastic Block Store (EBS) for providing persist storage. An important consideration here is that we did not need to modify the Kubernetes configuration we created earlier when deploying locally to our Docker Desktop environment, other than adding a few annotations to control the configuration of todobackend service load balancer (these annotations are ignored when using Docker Desktop, so are considered "safe" vendor-specific configuration elements). You should always strive for this goal, as it ensures that your applications will have maximum portability across different Kubernetes environments, and can be easily deployed independently of the underlying Kubernetes platform, whether it be a local development environment, AWS EKS, or the Google Kubernetes Engine (GKE).

Well, all good things must come to an end, and it's time for me to say congratulations and thank you for completing this book! It was a great pleasure to write this book and I hope that you have learned how to leverage the power of Docker and AWS to test, build, deploy and operate your own container applications.

Questions

1. True/false: Kubernetes is a native feature of Docker Desktop CE.
2. You define a custom command string to run in a pod definition using the commands property, and notice that the entrypoint script container is no longer executed. How can you resolve this?
3. True/false: Kubernetes includes three node types – manager, worker, and agent.
4. True/false: Kubernetes provides integration with AWS application load balancers.
5. True/false: Kubernetes supports relocating EBS volumes to other nodes in your cluster.
6. What component can you use to expose the Kubernetes API to web applications?

7. True/false: Kubernetes supports integration with the Elastic Container Registry.

8. What Kubernetes resource provides a virtual IP address that can be used to connect to multiple instances of a given application?

9. What Kubernetes resource is suitable for running database migrations?

10. True/false: EKS manages both Kubernetes manager nodes and worker nodes.

11. What type of EBS storage does the default storage class provision when using EKS?

12. You want to run a task every time you deploy a pod that needs to run before starting the main application in the pod. How would you achieve this?

Further reading

You can check the following links for more information about the topics covered in this chapter:

- **What is Kubernetes?:** `https://kubernetes.io/docs/concepts/overview/what-is-kubernetes/`
- **Kubernetes Tutorials:** `https://kubernetes.io/docs/tutorials/`
- **Kubernetes Pods:** `https://kubernetes.io/docs/concepts/workloads/pods/pod-overview/`
- **Kubernetes Deployments:** `https://kubernetes.io/docs/concepts/workloads/controllers/deployment/`
- **Kubernetes Jobs:** `https://kubernetes.io/docs/concepts/workloads/controllers/jobs-run-to-completion/`
- **Kubernetes Services:** `https://kubernetes.io/docs/concepts/services-networking/service/`
- **DNS for Services and Pods:** `https://kubernetes.io/docs/concepts/services-networking/dns-pod-service/`
- **Kubernetes Secrets:** `https://kubernetes.io/docs/concepts/configuration/secret/`
- **Kubernetes Volumes:** `https://kubernetes.io/docs/concepts/storage/volumes/`
- **Kubernetes Persistent Volumes:** `https://kubernetes.io/docs/concepts/storage/persistent-volumes/`

- Kubernetes Storage Classes: `https://kubernetes.io/docs/concepts/storage/storage-classes/`
- Dynamic Volume Provisioning: `https://kubernetes.io/docs/concepts/storage/dynamic-provisioning/`
- Kubectl Command Reference: `https://kubernetes.io/docs/reference/generated/kubectl/kubectl-commands`
- Amazon EKS User Guide: `https://docs.aws.amazon.com/eks/latest/userguide/what-is-eks.html`
- EKS Optimized AMI: `https://docs.aws.amazon.com/eks/latest/userguide/eks-optimized-ami.html`
- EKS Cluster CloudFormation Resource Reference: `https://docs.aws.amazon.com/AWSCloudFormation/latest/UserGuide/aws-resource-eks-cluster.html`

Assessments

Chapter 1, Container and Docker Fundamentals

1. False – the Docker client communicates via the Docker API.
2. False – the Docker Engine runs natively on Linux.
3. False – Docker images are published to Docker registries for download.
4. You need to enable the **Expose daemon on tcp://localhost:2375 without TLS** setting under **General** settings, and ensure the DOCKER_HOST environment variable is set to **localhost:2375** wherever you run the Docker client.
5. True.
6. You need to add the `USER_BASE/bin` path to your `PATH` environment variable. You can determine the `USER_BASE` portion by running the `python -m site --user-base` command.

Chapter 2, Building Applications Using Docker

1. False – you use the `FROM` and `AS` directives to define multi-stage Dockerfiles – for example, `FROM nginx AS build`.
2. True.
3. True.
4. True.
5. False – by default, the `docker-compose up` command does not fail with an error of any of the services started by the command fails. You can use the `--exit-code-from` flag to indicate whether a specific service failure should cause the `docker-compose up` command to fail.
6. True.

7. You must use the `docker-compose up` command if you want Docker Compose to wait until a service_healthy condition is met.

8. You should use a port-mapping of just `8000`. This will create a dynamic port mapping, where the Docker Engine will select an available port from the ephemeral port range on the Docker Engine operating system.

9. Makefile requires recipe commands to be intended with a single Tab character.

10. The `$(shell <command>)` function.

11. You should add the test recipe to the `.PHONY` target, for example, `.PHONY: test`.

12. The `build` and `image` properties.

Chapter 3, Getting Started with AWS

1. True.
2. False – you should set up an administrative IAM user to perform administrative actions on your account. The root account should only be used for billing or emergency access.
3. False – the AWS best practice is to create IAM roles that define a set of IAM permissions that apply to one or more resources. You should then grant IAM users/groups the ability to assume a given role or set of roles as applicable to your use cases.
4. AdministratorAccess.
5. `pip install awscli --user`
6. False – you must store an access key ID and a secret access key.
7. In the `~/.aws/credentials` file.
8. You need to add the `mfa_serial` parameter to the profile and specify the ARN of the MFA device for the user.
9. True.
10. True.
11. No – CloudFormation always attempts to create any new resources successfully before removing old resources. In this scenario, because you have defined a fixed Name value, CloudFormation will not be able to create a new resource with the same name.

Chapter 4, Introduction to ECS

1. ECS cluster, ECS task definition, and ECS service.
2. True.
3. YAML.
4. False – when using static port mappings, you can only have one instance of a given static port mapping per ECS container instance (assuming a single network interface).
5. False – the ECS CLI is recommended for sandbox/test environments only.
6. You would create an ECS task.
7. False – ECS task definitions are immutable and a given revision of a task definition cannot be modified. You can, however, create a new revision of a given ECS task definition that is based off the previous revision but includes changes.
8. False – you need to run `curl localhost:51678/v1/metadata`.

Chapter 5, Publishing Docker Images Using ECR

1. `aws ecr get-login`
2. False – at the time of writing, ECR only supports private registries
3. ECR life cycle policies – see `https://docs.aws.amazon.com/AmazonECR/latest/userguide/LifecyclePolicies.html`
4. True
5. False – you can use both ECR resource policies and/or IAM policies to configure access to ECR from the same account
6. True
7. True
8. False – it is possible (although not best practice) to use ECR resource policies to grant access to IAM principals, such as IAM roles in the same account
9. True – you must configure ECR resource policies in the source account, and IAM policies in the remote account

Chapter 6, Building Custom ECS Container Instances

1. The `variables` section.
2. True.
3. JSON.
4. False – you can (and should) reference environment variable values for your AWS credentials.
5. False – you can use the manifest post processor (`https://www.packer.io/docs/post-processors/manifest.html`) to capture the AMI ID.
6. By default, an 8 GB operating system partition and a 22 GB device-mapper logical volume is created.
7. File provisioner.
8. The cloud init startup script may be attempting to run package updates on the EC2 instance. This will fail after a lengthy timeout if there is no public internet connectivity.

Chapter 7, Creating ECS Clusters

1. False – EC2 autoscaling groups only support dynamic IP addressing.
2. The Base64 encoding.
3. Use the `AWS::Region` pseudo-parameter.
4. False – the `Ref` intrinsic function can refer to both resources and parameters in a CloudFormation template.
5. You need to first run `cfn-init` to download the CloudFormation Init metadata, and then `cfn-signal` to notify CloudFormation the result of running `cfn-init`.
6. You need to ensure that you are writing the name of the ECS cluster that each instance should join to `/etc/ecs/ecs.config` in the UserData script – for example, `echo "ECS_CLUSTER=<cluster-name>" > /etc/ecs/ecs.config`.

7. False – this command is only used to create stacks. You should use the `aws cloudformation deploy` command to create and update stacks as required.

8. The ECS agent on each instance cannot communicate with the ECS service API, which at the time of writing is only available as a public endpoint.

Chapter 8, Deploying Applications Using ECS

1. True.
2. A Listener.
3. False – a target group can only accept registrations once the associated application load-balancer listener has been created.
4. The `AWS::EC2::SecurityGroupIngress` and `AWS::EC2::SecurityGroupEgress` resources.
5. You should mark the `essential` property on the short-lived container definition as `false`.
6. The `DependsOn` parameter.
7. True.
8. `CREATE`, `UPDATE`, and `DELETE`.
9. The IAM role associated with the Lambda function does not have the permissions to create a log stream for the Lambda function log group.

Chapter 9, Managing Secrets

1. False – the KMS service allows you to use AWS-created keys as well as your own private keys
2. A KMS alias
3. CloudFormation Exports
4. False – you can recover the secret for a configurable period of time, up to a maximum of 30 days
5. The AWS CLI and `jq` utility
6. You must grant the `kms:Decrypt` permission for the KMS key that was used to encrypt the secret value

7. The `NoEcho` property
8. The `AWS_DEFAULT_REGION` environment variable

Chapter 10, Isolating Network Access

1. True.
2. You can use either the `awsvpc` (recommended) or `host` networking mode, which ensure your containers will obtain an IP address from the attached EC2 instance Elastic Network Interface (ENI).
3. False – the `awsvpc` network mode is required for ECS task networking.
4. You need to ensure the security groups configured for your ECS service permit access from the load-balancers.
5. You enable ECS task networking for an ECS task definition, however your containers fail on startup with an error that states they are unable to reach a location that is located on the internet. How can you resolve this issue?
6. Two – see `https://docs.aws.amazon.com/AWSEC2/latest/UserGuide/using-eni.html#AvailableIpPerENI`.
7. One – a t2.micro supports a maximum of two ENIs, however, one ENI must be reserved for operating-system and ECS-agent communications. Task-networking only allows a single task definition per ENI.
8. 10 – given you can have a maximum of 1 ECS task definition running in task-networking mode (see previous answer) and you can run up to 10 containers in a single ECS task definition (see `https://docs.aws.amazon.com/AmazonECS/latest/developerguide/service_limits.html`).
9. You must use the IP target type when using the awsvpc network mode.
10. You should remove the loadBalancers property from the ECS service definition.

Chapter 11, Managing the ECS Infrastructure Life Cycle

1. False – you are responsible for invoking and managing ECS container-instance draining.
2. `EC2_INSTANCE_LAUNCHING` and `EC2_INSTANCE_TERMINATING`.
3. `ABANDON` or `CONTINUE`.

4. False – you can publish life cycle hooks to SNS, SQS, or CloudWatch Events.

5. It is likely that your Lambda function is failing due to reaching the maximum function-execution timeout of 5 minutes, meaning the life cycle hook will never complete and eventually times out. You should ensure your Lambda function republishes the life cycle hook if the function execution-timeout is about to be reached, which will automatically re-invoke your function.

6. You should configure the `UpdatePolicy` attribute.

7. Set the `MinSuccessfulInstancesPercent` property to 100.

8. A Lambda permission.

Chapter 12, ECS Auto Scaling

1. False – you are responsible for autoscaling your ECS container instances.

2. EC2 autoscaling.

3. Application Auto Scaling.

4. Configure the `memoryReservation` parameter with a value of 300 and the `memory` parameter with a value of 1,024 .

5. Divide the ECS container-instance CPU-unit allocation evenly across each ECS task (that is, configure each task with a CPU allocation of 333 units).

6. True.

7. Three.

8. You should disable autoscaling during rolling updates. You can do this by configuring the `AutoScalingRollingUpdate.SuspendProcesses` property of the CloudFormation `UpdatePolicy` attribute.

9. Zero tasks – based upon the current state of the cluster, one ECS task is running on each instance. Given each task has a static port mapping to TCP port `80`, you cannot schedule another task as all ports are in use.

10. Four – you should use the worst-case scenario of 500 MB memory per container.

Chapter 13, Continuously Delivering ECS Applications

1. `buildspec.yml`
2. False – CodeBuild uses containers and includes its own agent to run build scripts
3. Docker in Docker
4. CloudFormation Change Sets
5. cloudformation.amazonaws.com
6. Ensure your build script logs into ECR before attempting to push the image
7. Allow the `codebuild.amazonaws.com` service principal to have pull access to the repository
8. Ensure the container is running with the privileged flag

Chapter 14, Fargate and ECS Service Discovery

1. True.
2. Only the `awsvpc` networking mode is supported.
3. False – you must ensure the ECS agent can communicate via the ENI allocated to your Fargate ECS task.
4. You need to ensure the IAM role referenced by the ExecutionRoleArn property of the task definition permits access to the ECR repository.
5. No – Fargate only supports CloudWatch logs.
6. False – ECS service discovery uses Route53 zones to publish service-registration information.
7. A service discovery namespace.
8. You must configure a supported CPU/memory configuration when configuring Fargate ECS task definitions. See `https://docs.aws.amazon.com/AmazonECS/latest/developerguide/task-cpu-memory-error.html` for supported configurations.
9. UDP Port `2000`.
10. False – traces must be published to an X-Ray daemon running in your environment.

Chapter 15, Elastic Beanstalk

1. False – Elastic Beanstalk supports single-container and multi-container Docker applications
2. The `Dockerrun.aws.json` file.
3. True.
4. Add IAM permissions to pull ECR images to the virtual machine instance role used by your Elastic Beanstalk EC2 instances.
5. False – Elastic Beanstalk uses bind mounts for volumes, which assign root:root permissions, causing non-root containers to fail when writing to the volume.
6. False – you can set the `leader_only` property to true in the `container_commands` key so it runs a command on only one Elastic Beanstalk instance.
7. False – the eb ssh command is used to establish SSH access to Elastic Beanstalk EC2 instances.
8. True.

Chapter 16, Docker Swarm in AWS

1. True.
2. `docker service create`
3. False – Docker Swarm includes two node types: master and slave.
4. False – Docker for AWS provides integration with classic AWS elastic load-balancers.
5. False – the Cloudstore AWS volume plugin creates an EBS-backed volume when the backing is set to relocatable.
6. False – because the EBS volumes are in different availability zones, a snapshot will first be created of the original volume, and then a new volume created from the snapshot will then be attached to the new database service container.
7. `--with-registry-auth`
8. You need to install a system component that will automatically refresh Docker credentials periodically, such as `https://github.com/mRoca/docker-swarm-aws-ecr-auth`.

9. Version 3.
10. False – you should configure the restart policy as either `never` or `on-failure`.

Chapter 17, Elastic Kubernetes Service

1. True – for Docker CE 18.06 and higher
2. Define the custom command string in the `args` property (this is the equivalent of the CMD directive in a Dockerfile)
3. False – Kubernetes includes two node types: manager and worker
4. False – at the time or writing, Kubernetes supported integration with classic Elastic Load Balancers
5. False
6. kube-proxy
7. True
8. A service
9. A job
10. False – EKS manages the Kubernetes manager nodes
11. None – there is no default storage class in EKS, you must create your own
12. Define the task as in initContainer in the pod

Other Books You May Enjoy

If you enjoyed this book, you may be interested in these other books by Packt:

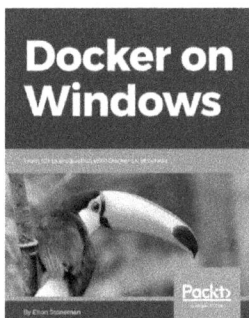

Docker on Windows

Elton Stoneman

ISBN: 978-1-78528-165-5

- Comprehend key Docker concepts: images, containers, registries, and swarms
- Run Docker on Windows 10, Windows Server 2016, and in the cloud
- Deploy and monitor distributed solutions across multiple Docker containers
- Run containers with high availability and fail-over with Docker Swarm
- Master security in-depth with the Docker platform, making your apps more secure
- Build a Continuous Deployment pipeline by running Jenkins in Docker
- Debug applications running in Docker containers using Visual Studio
- Plan the adoption of Docker in your own organization

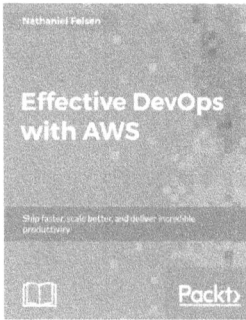

Effective DevOps with AWS
Nathaniel Felsen

ISBN: 978-1-78646-681-5

- Find out what it means to practice DevOps and what its principles are
- Build repeatable infrastructures using templates and configuration management
- Deploy multiple times a day by implementing continuous integration and continuous deployment pipelines
- Use the latest technologies, including containers and serverless computing, to scale your infrastructure
- Collect metrics and logs and implement an alerting strategy
- Make your system robust and secure

Leave a review - let other readers know what you think

Please share your thoughts on this book with others by leaving a review on the site that you bought it from. If you purchased the book from Amazon, please leave us an honest review on this book's Amazon page. This is vital so that other potential readers can see and use your unbiased opinion to make purchasing decisions, we can understand what our customers think about our products, and our authors can see your feedback on the title that they have worked with Packt to create. It will only take a few minutes of your time, but is valuable to other potential customers, our authors, and Packt. Thank you!

Index